LESSONS of LOVE

A Study Guide to The Daily Bible in Chronological Order

SHIRLEY BAKER LOGES

with contributions from Max L. Loges

Lessons of Love: A Study Guide to The Daily Bible in Chronological Order by Shirley Baker Loges, Ph.D., with contributions from Max L. Loges, Ph.D., M.Div.

REVISED EDITION

Copyright © 2014 by Shirley Baker Loges
ISBN: 978-1-59755-250-9

Published by: Advantage Books™
                www.advbookstore.com

All rights reserved. No part of this book may be reproduced, stored in a retrieval system, or transmitted in any form or by any means – electronic, mechanical, photocopy, recording, or any other – except for brief quotation in printed reviews, without the prior permission of the author. Requests for permission should be addressed to:

Dr. Shirley Loges
C/O Advantage Books
PO Box 160847
Altamonte Springs, FL 32716.

Unless otherwise indicated, Bible quotations are taken from the *New International Version* of the Bible. Copyright 1984 by International Bible Society.

Lessons of Love original copyright effective date 2003 by Shirley A. Loges.
Original ISBN: 1-59755-103-1

Graphics for Ezekiel's temple in the September 5th lesson are from *Ezekiel* by Ralph H. Alexander, Moody Press, Chicago, IL, 1976. Reprinted by permission of Moody Publishers.

Library of Congress Control Number: 2013956697

Cover Design by Pat Theriault

First Printing January 2014
14 15 16 17 18 19 20   10 9 8 7 6 5
Printed in the United States of America

ACKNOWLEDGMENTS

This book was written in response to a call from the Lord to develop a guide to assist lay people in reading through the Bible. Any errors are mine; they are totally mine. I pray you will read these lessons with an open heart to God's voice through the reading of His word.

Along the way, many people provided encouragement and guidance. About 100 people participated in the original Bible study conducted through the mail and Internet. Those participants greatly encouraged me during the process of the intense study and development of the written lessons. Many provided funds for the mailings and prayer for my strength to endure the rigorous one-year process. Above all, my parents, Garner and Jean Baker, provided the most support in love and dedication to my vision for the lessons. My son, Thomas Baker, assisted with some of the typing and drawings. My daughter, Letha Wallis, prayed for me and listened patiently to my complaints and words of exhaustion. I extend eternal thanks to my family and friends who stayed the course and made this book possible.

My husband wrote about 35 of the lessons so that I could attend to family emergencies and the lessons could proceed to the Bible study participants on time.

Hopefully, these lessons will be a blessing to you.

Shirley Ann Baker Loges, Ph.D.

To Those Who Seek the Truth:

Over the last few years, I have become increasingly aware of the large number of people who have never read the Bible in its entirety. Many of these people I consider to be great stalwarts of faith. Romans 10:17 says, "Faith comes from hearing the message, and the message is heard through the word of Christ." Obviously faith isn't dependent on reading the Bible but on hearing the word. For those who have faith, though, their lives are greatly enriched by reading God's word. We receive instruction on how to better serve God. Jeremiah 8:7 laments that "my people do not know the requirements of the LORD."

Since the advent of global terrorism, everyone in our world has become intensely cognizant of the brevity of life and the fulfillment of prophecy. We truly live in the last of the end times. How much longer we have to serve our Lord is known only to God. In Paul's second letter to Timothy (2 Timothy 2:15), he states, "Do your best to present yourself to God as one approved, a workman who does not need to be ashamed and who correctly handles the word of truth." God gives each of us 24 hours a day. Is it asking too much for us to spend 20-30 minutes a day reading His word? God has given me a burden for the many people who have never completely read the Bible. For the last few years, I have prayed and pondered about how I might lead or encourage people to develop a daily Bible reading habit, how I could get them to keep reading until the goal was accomplished.

In 2001 God gave me a vision of reaching as many people as possible through a weekly lesson or letter of encouragement. As I struggled with what version of the Bible to use, God placed in my path *The Daily Bible in Chronological Order* that is divided into 365 daily readings. It is in the popular New International Version (NIV). For those not familiar with chronological order, it simply means the Biblical text is arranged according to when the event occured not according to the usual books of the Bible. Therefore, it reads like an historical unfolding of the history, laws, prophecies, and literature of the will of God. *The Daily Bible* contains short sections of narrative throughout that explain the history or situations that influenced the Biblical verses. Each day's reading takes only 20-30 minutes. By December 31 you will have read all of God's word. It is my prayer and hope that you will prayerfully commit yourself to reading God's word with me. Give someone a copy of this book and a copy of *The Daily Bible* as a gift. If you don't want to use this Bible, I have posted the various Bible verses to read each day in the lesson. After the first month or so, these passages of scripture will be scattered throughout the Bible, though, requiring more time to locate and read. You will not have the advantage of the explanatory narrative.

As I see the prophecies of the end times unfold, I am reminded of the blessing proclaimed in the introduction to the Revelation of John (Revelation 1:3), "Blessed is the one who reads the words of this prophecy, and blessed are those who hear it and take to heart what is written in it, because the time is near."

Prayerfully consider becoming a part of this experience as lessons of love are revealed to us from God's word. I look forward to reading God's word with you this coming year!

May God bless the reading of His word,

Shirley Loges

Lessons of Love

GETTING STARTED

Start your study each day with a prayer asking God to open your heart to His word. Jeremiah 33:3 states, "Call to me and I will answer you and tell you great and unsearchable things you do not know." Just a few comments before we start.

1. If you are late getting your Bible, don't despair. Simply reading an extra day every day or so you will get caught up. On the other hand, you could choose to read on your own calendar timeframe.

2. The passages in the shaded gray areas in your accompanying *The Daily Bible* are narrative to assist your comprehension. They are not a part of the actual word of God.

3. Food for Thought is a section of thought-provoking questions or comments. I don't have the answers. Hopefully, they will encourage you to think on a different level.

4. Study for yourself. Pray for your own understanding of what the scriptures hold for you. Feel free to hold a different opinion or belief about the interpretation of scripture.

5. The lessons are dependent on your reading the Bible along with them.

Make this the best year of your life -- in God's word!

Shirley Ann Baker Loges, Ph.D.

Lessons of Love

A Study Guide to The Daily Bible in Chronological Order

> Verse of the Week: **Genesis 4:7** "If you do what is right, will you not be accepted? But if you do not do what is right, sin is crouching at your door; it desires to have you, but you must master it."

The first 11 chapters of Genesis tell of creation and early life. The rest of Genesis records background information on the Patriarchs (ancestral fathers of all human beings).

January 1
Bible Readings: Genesis 1-3

The first verse of the Bible makes it very clear that God created the heavens and the earth. Water covered the entire planet called earth. (Jewish people generally believe that creation began about 4000 B.C.) The Spirit of God, also called the Holy Spirit, hovered over the waters around the earth. John 1:1 tells us that "In the beginning was the Word, and the Word was with God, and the Word was God."[1] Then verse 14 of John 1 says, "The Word became flesh and lived for a while among us."[1] This last statement obviously refers to Jesus. (When Word is used in the Bible with a capital 'W,' it refers to Jesus.) Therefore, from the earliest reference to the creation of our world, we are told that God and His Spirit were present. Jesus' beloved apostle John makes sure we understand that Jesus was also with God from the beginning.

Every time (48 to be exact) that the Hebrew verb meaning 'to create' is used in the Old Testament, God is the subject for that verb.[2] All creation took place in 6 days. The following chart has impressed me with the organization of creation.

1st Day	**4th Day**
light [24 hour cycle] ---------------------->	sun, moon, stars
2nd Day	**5th Day**
firmament, separation of waters ------>	sea creatures, birds
3rd Day	**6th Day**
dry land, plants [vegetation] ----------->	land animals, human beings[2]
(Words in [ ] are mine.)	

The first 3 days were spent making the main foundation bodies (light, land, seas, heavens, etc.) and the last 3 days were spent putting the details on those bodies (sun, moon, and stars in the light and darkness, etc.). God simply **spoke** and all creation was formed. [I am reminded of Ezekiel 37 where God told the prophet to tell the valley of dry bones that the LORD said they were to reassemble, cover themselves with flesh, and come to life -- and they did! When God speaks, even through others, His creation responds.]

Before everything, God created light. Light is always a symbol of the presence of God. Jesus told us, "I am the light of the world" (John 8:12).[1] In Revelation, Heaven is seen as a place with no need for a sun or moon because God's glory provides all the light (Rev. 21:23 and 22:5). Thus the Bible begins and ends with God as the light.

On the 7th day, God rested. This day He set aside as a holy day. Josephus tells us this day was called the Sabbath, which in Hebrew means rest.[3] [Josephus' records of Jewish history are the second most widely read books on ancient Jewish history, the first being the Bible.]

God formed man in His image. That doesn't mean our body **looks** like His but rather that our spirit and abilities reflect God. Just as you see your image in a mirror, God should see His image in you. Can God see Himself in you? Can others see God in you? We learned above that God speaks, creates, organizes, plans, and thinks. We do these things, too. As we read on in Genesis, we see God has compassion, love, mercy, and patience. These, too, we should have.

Adam may mean man from the ground[2] or one that is red (as in red earth).[3] Regardless, we know that Adam was placed in the Garden of Eden to take care of it. The river that fed the Garden split into four rivers -- (1) Pishon, wound throughout the land of Havilah (thought to be in southern Saudi Arabia); (2) Gihon, wound throughout the land of Cush (believed to be Sudan, making this the modern day Nile River[3]); (3) Tigris, runs on the east side of Asshur (modern Iraq[4]); (4) Euphrates, runs from the northwest to the southeast through the middle of Iraq[4]. The Garden of Eden is often thought of in terms of a small acreage. From the above description, it could possibly have covered several countries. In the middle of the garden were the (1) tree of life and (2) the tree of knowledge of good and evil. The tree of life is also found in Rev. 22:2 where it bears fruit every month and its leaves are for the healing of the nations. Again it is mentioned in Rev. 22:14 where we are told that Christians are blessed with the right to eat of the tree of life and are allowed to enter the gates of Heaven.

The tree of the knowledge of good and evil was exactly as its name described. Whoever ate its fruit would know the consequences of evil through the experiences of guilt and shame. When Adam and Eve chose to sin by eating the fruit of this tree, God made sure they no longer had access to the tree of life so that they would not live eternally in their evil state. Thus, the process of aging and dying entered a heavenly place.

Back to the creation of woman, Eve (means mother of all living) was created as a helper and mate (helpmate) for Adam. Woman was the only creation God did not speak into existence. (My husband would say it is because He couldn't get a word in edgewise!) Instead, God took a portion of the man He had already created and formed a woman. Adam and Eve became the first married couple and the first family.

The serpent apparently could talk and walk at the beginning of creation. He twists God's words into a lie and appeals to Eve's curiosity, planting envy and selfishness in her mind. As with all evildoers, the serpent convinces Eve that she won't really have to undergo any negative consequences if she eats the fruit but will become better and equal to God! How many people have gotten into trouble because their friends convinced them that the forbidden was all right? They wouldn't suffer any negative results and, in the end, they would be better than before. God allowed us to be free to choose, but we are not free to choose the consequences of our choices! Is there any doubt why we refer to deceivers as speaking with a forked tongue (like a serpent)? (Notice in the last sentence of Genesis 3:6 that Adam was **with** Eve **during** the serpent's sales pitch. He ate because he believed the serpent's lie, too.)

Adam and Eve immediately experience guilt and shame and fear the moment they have to face God. When God comes to talk to them, Adam quickly blames God and then Eve before finally admitting "... and I ate it" (Genesis 3:12). The woman, in turn, blames the serpent before saying, "... and I ate" (Genesis 3:13). The moral of

Lessons of Love

this story is you can blame anyone and everyone but YOU made the choice to sin, therefore, YOU must suffer the consequences. Adam and Eve were banished from God's garden to a lifetime of pain and hardship. But, God is a just God; He pronounced judgment on the serpent, too. Forever the serpent and humans would fear and hate each other, the serpent would have to crawl in the dirt, and humans would try to smash the serpent's head. Josephus attributes this last curse, as well as losing the ability to talk, to God's wrath towards the serpent for **talking** deceit and lies.[3]

Eve is no longer a helpmate but is now doomed to be ruled-over by her husband. She must bear pain in childbirth and Adam must bear pain in working to provide for the family. God made coats of animal skins to clothe Adam and Eve. This is a picture of how God will cover our nakedness (guilt and shame) as the result of the death of His Lamb (Jesus) some 4000 years later.

Then God removed Adam and Eve and placed cherubim on the east side with a flaming sword to keep guard over the tree of life until God comes back to reign on earth forever in the New Jerusalem. "The basic direction for Hebrews was the east -- the direction of the rising sun" (p. 302).[5] All other directions were given in relation to the 'place of dawning.' Therefore, east is the direction they would face (the front). This leads you to understand that God placed a guard at the front gate to His garden. The only way mankind could ever enter 'The Gate' again would be through the shed blood of Jesus Christ washing away their sins. The Garden only has one gate because there is no back way into God's presence. You can't sneak into Heaven. Jesus said, "I am the way and the truth and the life. No one comes to the Father except through me" (John 14:6).[1]

Food for Thought: Where is the Garden of Eden now? Why can't we see this flaming sword? Why did God even make a serpent when He already knew what would happen? Why did God make the tree of knowledge of good and evil? Why are there fossils and rocks that are thousands and millions of years old when human existence is only 6000 years old? Read Ps. 102:25-27. Did God discard a worn out earthly surface in the past?

January 2
Bible Readings: Genesis 4-5

Adam and Eve begin to reproduce and have two sons. The eldest was named Cain (meaning a possession[3]) and the second was named Abel (meaning sorrow[3]). Josephus reports that they also have daughters.[3] This is quite likely since the Hebrews maintained their historical, census, legal, and family records based solely on the male children. It is a rare and important occasion when a female child is recorded in the genealogy.

The sons grow up and Cain becomes a farmer while Abel is a shepherd. Both boys brought a sacrifice to God. Abel brought the very **best** animals from the **firstborn** of his flock. Cain only brought **some** of his fruit (no grain or other produce is mentioned). In short, Abel gave a portion of his best to God, but Cain only gave part of his ordinary produce. Abel had a special love and a heart for God; Cain did not. God loves and accepts those who commit their hearts to Him. Lukewarm, apathetic, half-hearted efforts to worship God are not acceptable. Josephus tells us that Abel was righteous and virtuous from early childhood whereas Cain was wicked.[3] God accepts Abel's sacrifice and rejects Cain's. In a fit of rage and jealousy, Cain kills Abel. Most of us would believe this action warranted severe punishment, even death of the criminal. But, God spares Cain's life and places a mark on him forbidding others to kill him. God banished him from the family and took away his farming skills. Cain's punishment was worse than death. He was sentenced to wander the earth, cut off from family and God, alone in his wickedness.

Cain wanders in the land of Nod, traditionally believed to be in modern day Iran. Cain and his wife build a city and have children. One of his descendants, Tubal-Cain, is the first recorded vocational-technical instructor! He was a teacher of metalwork. Jubal becomes a musician and Jabal a shepherd. Note that Cain has a son named Enoch and a descendant named Lamech (who is also a murderer). These two wicked men should NOT be confused with two men by the same name from the lineage of Seth and are righteous!

Adam and Eve now have great, great, great, great, great-grandchildren who are old enough to be considered master craftsmen -- and they have another baby boy! (Can you imagine their thoughts?) The boy is named Seth, who will be ancestor of Jesus. God is going to once again put righteous people on earth. (Tradition says Adam and Eve had 33 sons and 23 daughters.[3]) Josephus reports that Adam was 230 years old at the time of Seth's birth[3] whereas our Bible states 130 years old. Therefore, it is safe to say that wickedness had about 100-200 years head start in populating the earth.

At the end of our reading today, we see the ancestral lineage of Jesus given. Note that this Enoch was so righteous that God took him to Heaven without experiencing death. Only two people are recorded in the Old Testament as being taken away by God: Enoch and Elijah (2 Kings 2:11).[1] Abraham walked **before** God (Genesis 17:1), Israel (Jacob) walked **after** God (Deut. 13:4), but Enoch and Noah walked **with** God (Genesis 5:23, 6:9).[2] After Noah is listed in the genealogy, all of his sons are listed. They will be responsible for repopulating the earth after the great flood, but it will be Shem who will continue the lineage of Jesus.

Food for Thought: Thinking about Cain and Lamech, how would the saying "Like father, like son" apply? Do you let sin enter your life by using Eve's process: I see, I want, I get?

January 3
Bible Readings: Genesis 6-9

There is a lot of controversy about who the "sons of God" are. Job uses this phrase in reference to angels (Job 1:6)[1], but the New Testament uses it as a description of Christians' relationship with God (Romans 8:14).[1] Josephus relates that the Hebrews traditionally believed these sons were fallen angels.[3] This belief is understandable when you remember that the early version of the Bible consisted of the Septuagint (the Greek translation of the Old Testament). As modern day Christians who also have a New Testament, we read in Matthew 22:30 that Jesus said angels (and people) in heaven do not marry. Therefore, "sons of God" may be human beings.

Genesis 6:1-2 makes it very clear that intermarriage between righteous believers and wicked non-believers only leads to the destruction of both. First Corinthians 15:33 is a verse all children should memorize from birth: "Do not be misled: 'Bad company corrupts good character.'" This brings us back to our lesson on January 1. You have the freedom of choice, but the consequences must be endured.

Next, God becomes impatient with man's selfish sins and decides to shorten his lifespan to 120 years. (Considering Methuselah lived 969 years, this was a huge decrease!) Ancient tradition is that 120 years was actually a judgment on the wicked living in that day. In other words, God gave Noah 120 lunar years to get the ark built before the flood wiped out the wicked.[2]

With possibly millions of people populating the earth at this point, it is a very sad comment indeed that only one found favor with the LORD. God told Noah to build an ark -- and a big one at that! Don't you think his neighbors thought he was crazy? After all, he was 400-500 miles away from any body of water that would support such a large boat. It was 1.5 football fields long, 2/3 of a football field wide, and 3 stories high. It was coated with pitch, which is a tar-like substance that was readily available in the Middle East even in ancient days. Can you imagine what Noah's neighbors thought of that eyesore? Not to mention the constant smell of tar!

God promised to preserve Noah and his family to repopulate the earth. Noah's instructions were to take 7 pairs of every kind of clean animal but only 1 pair of every kind of unclean animal. Clean animals were those God accepted as sacrifices and were the only animals allowed for consumption. Leviticus 11 describes in detail how clean animals were to be distinguished from unclean animals. Examples of clean animals are sheep, goat, dove, and cow. The reason for so many clean animals is so they would be available for sacrifice to God after the flood.[2] At 600 years old, Noah only had 7 days to move all this into the ark. Then God Himself sealed the ark.

For 40 days and nights, it rained during the months of October and November,[11] and water from inside the earth poured out as well. After one year, Noah can finally escape his rocking, smelly environment. (The location is believed to be the Ararat Mountains of eastern Turkey.[2]) All around him, the old is gone and new vegetation abounds. It is befitting that the first sign of this new life is an olive leaf. Olives provided fruit to eat, oil to heal, oil to provide light, and oil for anointing. The Garden of Gethsemane where Jesus prayed before His arrest was a grove of olive trees. During the flood the earth died to sin, was buried in water, and gave birth to new life. Of course, Jesus died for our sins, was buried, and rose to give us a new life in Christ. The olive symbolizes Jesus: Provider, Healer, Light, and Anointed.

Noah celebrates getting his land legs back by building an altar and sacrificing clean animals to God in praise and thanksgiving. God was so pleased that He promised to never destroy all living creatures again. His promise also includes a continuation of day and night, seasons of the year, planting and harvest until the end of time. (See Rev. 8.) He places a rainbow in the sky as a remembrance of His promise. (When the term remembrance is used in association with God, it means God intervened on behalf of that person(s).[2])

God blessed Noah and his sons commanding that they repopulate the earth. At the same time, He makes the animals fear man (this had not been the case before), He forbids the eating of blood, and He forbids the shedding of man's blood (murder). For the first time, man is given permission to **eat** animals.[2]

In Gen. 9, we see "fear and dread" instilled between mankind and animals. Prior to this, peace and harmony had reigned. Neither species maimed or killed. Today's definition of "wild animals" always brings fear or danger to mind. Whereas, in Noah's day (Gen. 8:1), wild animals simply meant they lived and roamed freely foraging for themselves. For the first time, mankind is told that "everything that lives and moves" is acceptable for food. (This will change as mankind learns to better produce and raise food and as evil rises to pose great danger to God's people through contaminated food and water. (See Lev. 11.)) Man would now rule over nature with violence and force.[11]

Genesis 9:5-7 records man's first endowment of governmental power. Mankind is given the authority to judge those who take lives and to sentence the perpetrators to death. By the end of the Book of Deuteronomy, the governmental system of mankind is well established. The Book of Judges implements a formal national system of self-government.[11]

Vineyards seem to get a lot of people in trouble. And so it was with Noah. He grew a vineyard, made wine, and got drunk, seemingly passed out drunk and naked. Ham goes in the tent and finds his father is naked. This accidental discovery is not his sin. His sin is staring at his father's nakedness and then gossiping about it to other family members, showing no respect for his father. Shem and Japheth do the honorable thing and discretely cover their father. When Noah wakens and discovers what has happened, he curses Ham's son Canaan and all his descendants. He then blesses Shem, elevating his status above both his brothers. Japheth is blessed with an increase in the land he will possess.

Food for Thought: Remember, when Noah was the only godly person left prior to the flood, God still saved him to carry forth His plan. If you were the only godly person left, God would still save you. Why do you think Canaan was cursed instead of Ham? Is this an example of where the sins of the father are visited upon the son (Exodus 20:5)?

January 4
Bible Readings: Genesis 10-11

Jump forward in time about 850 years and we find the regenerating population spreading out from Ararat. All mankind were descendants of Noah and spoke his language. They were building cities out of mud bricks and tar for there were no stones available in the delta land of Babylon. At the Plain of Shinar, later called Babylon, even later called Iraq, men decided to build a tower in their own honor that would reach to the heavens. God was displeased and decided to confuse them by making them speak various different languages -- appearing to babble -- thus, the Tower of Babel. Josephus states that Nimrod, the grandson of Ham who failed to receive a blessing from Noah, was the man who incited all the other men to commit such a sin as this idol to their own greatness.[3] (I wonder if God didn't have to chuckle at these great and mighty men running around like blind mice when they couldn't understand each other?)

Two points before we leave this story. One, Genesis 11:7 says, "Come let **us** go down...." Again we see God the Father, the Holy Spirit, and Jesus as Godhead in the plural pronoun "us." Two, if mankind had obeyed God's command to Noah and his sons to "fill the earth," then they wouldn't have had the concentrated numbers of men to dream up such a project as this tower. In Genesis 11:9 we are told that after their language was confused the LORD scattered them over the face of the earth. You can obey and be blessed or you can rebel and suffer the consequences. Either way, God's Will will be done.

Generally speaking, the descendants of Shem went eastward, the descendants of Ham went southward, and the descendants of Japheth went westward[6] and northward.[5] Ham's descendants become enemies of the Israelites, especially the Egyptians, Canaanites, and Arabs. Today these people are located in Egypt, Libya, Jordan, Ethiopia, Iraq, West Bank, Lebanon, and Asia, in other words many Arab, Palestinian, and African nations.

Japheth receives little attention but is believed to be a powerful player in the end times. His descendants populated Turkey, Greece, Italy, Russia, France, and Belgium -- basically Europe. Revelation 20:7-10 tells us that Gog and Magog will gather in battle against God's people, but God will intervene and destroy Gog and Magog. Notice that Magog was one of Japheth's sons. Gog is the prince or leader of Magog (Ezekiel 38:2-3).[1] Many modern scholars believe Magog is symbolic for Russia.

Shem's lineage will eventually include Jesus. Shem was the ancestral father of the Hebrews. Even though Shem had many descendants, only the Israelites have emerged as an identifiable nation. Shem's other descendants seem to have interspersed among peoples of Iran, India, and other Near Eastern countries. Modern day Arabs claim to be descendants of Ishmael, Abraham's son by the Egyptian maid, although Ishmaelites settled in northern Arabia (Saudi Arabia) and were nomadic merchants.[5]

Note, Abram and Sarai have the same father, Terah, making them half-brother and sister (Genesis 20:12). Abram's brother, Nahor, marries his niece. Though, marrying a close relative is now considered taboo and illegal, in ancient times it was the way God provided to preserve a righteous nation of followers. Remember the Israelites are all kin, descendants of Shem.

Also, notice that the lifespan is steadily decreasing. Before the flood, the average lifespan was about 930 years. After the flood, Noah's sons only lived about 600 years. Abram is born as the 10th generation from Noah. The lifespan is now down to 200 years. Three generations later, Joseph will live to be 110 years old. God's judgment that man's lifespan will be 120 years (Genesis 6:3) applies to all future generations, not just those living at the time of the flood.

Food for Thought: The descendants of Shem settled most of Iran, so why are Iranians not Christians? Why are Japheth and his descendants largely ignored?

January 5
Bible Readings: Genesis 12-14

Abram was called out by God to move to another land, be blessed of God, and become a great nation. God, knowing Abram's heart, called him because of Abram's great faith in the one and only true God. A God he had never seen or heard from before this time. This faith is itself amazing when we are told that Abram's father, Terah, served other gods (Joshua 24:2). Many of the names of Abram's family had their origin in pagan moon worship: Terah, Sarah, Laban, Milcah.[2]

Prior to Abram's call, Terah had moved his family from its ancestral home, Ur of the Chaldees, to Haran.[2] This trip covered a span of many months in order to make the approximate 600-mile journey. Most likely the group followed the northwest direction of the Euphrates River. Haran is located in ancient Padam-Aram, found today in the common border area of Turkey and Syria. Haran actually is in southeast Turkey.[4]

Abram's childhood was spent growing up in the Babylonian city of Ur. At that time, Ur was a seacoast city. (Silt deposited by the rivers emptying into the Persian Gulf ultimately turned Ur into an inland city. Today, the ancient city of Ur is located in southeastern Iraq.[4]) Ur was a thriving civilization boasting a complex system of government; large levees with an extensive irrigation system; a population around 250,000-300,000; huge state operated factories employing hundreds or even thousands of workers; and an education system that allowed upper class male members to study botany, geography, grammar, mathematics, geometry, theology, mineralogy, and zoology. The king was a monarch who was worshipped as a god. Homes were built of brick of varying sizes. Pottery, brick, wool and leather goods, grain, metalwork of copper and silver, jewelry, and sesame oil were their primary exports. Luxurious items such as fragrances, wood, and mineral ores were imported. Most trade was by overland merchant caravans. Businessmen kept detailed records of accounts, invoices, tax records, shipping bills, and credit letters, all on small clay tablets. Houses were furnished with rugs, cushions, oil lamps, wood and wicker chests, pottery, tables, bedrolls, and some folding stools. Because Ur was in rich delta river land, a bounty of various plants and animals was raised for food and clothing. Festivals, especially for the moon god Sin, were frequent. Haran, though some distance away, was under the same rule as Ur. Abram lived under the Third Dynasty of Ur that was considered its 'golden age.' As today, many women worked in the factories, particularly those whose product was associated with women, i.e., clothing, food, and pottery.[7]

Families negotiated marriages for their children, generally arranged by the father or patriarch of the clan. The contract usually consisted of the groom's family giving gifts to the bride's family. The bride's family then had a responsibility to provide a dowry for their daughter. The dowry was essentially the inheritance of a daughter. By custom and legal rights, only the sons inherited upon the father's death. This inheritance included the right of the eldest son to be chief of the clan, priest or religious leader, judge over family matters, and recipient of a double portion of the wealth. The main purpose for marriage was to produce male heirs. According to the laws of the Code of Hammurabi, if a wife was barren, then a slave girl could be substituted for the wife. Any resulting child would belong to the man. A surrogate slave mother may be given equal status with the wife or she may return to the slaves, depending largely on the wishes of the legal wife.[7] It was also permissible for a barren couple to adopt a child. This child would then become a legal heir.

To say the least, the empire of Ur, which included Haran, would be hard to leave to follow an unknown god to an unknown land filled with danger. Abram was a man of great faith. If God told you to leave all that you have and travel a great distance to a place you've never seen where strange languages are spoken, would you go? Every day God calls people to be missionaries.

This background information is important to understand the many parts of Abram's life. Abram's call from God consisted of a 7-part promise. Seven is significant throughout the Bible as a number indicating completion. God's promise was complete. It included everything Abram needed. As he starts his journey, he stops near Bethel to build an altar and praise God. Abram is 75 years old.

Twice Abram falls into the sin of passing Sarai off as his sister, not his wife: First in Egypt (Genesis 12:11-13) and again (20 years later) in Gerar (in southwestern Israel near the Gaza Strip today[4]). Now Sarai was his half-sister, but more importantly, she was his wife and the one who would be the source of Abram becoming a great nation through his son Isaac. Abram's real sin was not trusting God to protect them. When you are in danger, do you depend on God or do you look for ways to get yourself out? In both of Abram's deceptions, God protects Sarai and still keeps His promise to Abram.

Abram travels about a lot and usually along merchant caravan routes. He is becoming increasingly wealthier each year with more than a thousand people in his entourage. Many scholars believe he was a merchant as well as a shepherd. Generally, only merchants and noblemen had gold.

Lot was Abram's brother Haran's son. Haran died when Lot was young and Terah, his grandfather, took him in and reared him. Abram apparently was close to Lot, possibly viewing himself as Lot's substitute father. Lot also became a large group with many herds. An argument between Abram and Lot's herdsmen leads Lot to choose to take the lush Jordan valley land while leaving Abram with the hilly land. Lot goes to live in Sodom (southeast end of the Dead Sea). Abram settles in Hebron (the south end of today's West Bank[4]). Abram has now built altars to God at Bethel, Schechem, and Hebron. All three will play important roles in the lives of his offspring -- the Israelites.

When neighboring kings attack Sodom and surrounding cities and carry Lot off to slavery, Abram musters the fighting men of his clan and his allies and goes after them. He conquered the armies and recovered all the possessions and people. Melchizedek, king of Salem, comes to meet him bearing bread and wine. (In the New Testament, bread and wine are symbolic of the body and blood of Jesus.) Abram recognizes him as a priest of God and gives him a tenth of everything seized in the battle (tithe). Apparently, there were many others who served God besides Abram, at least enough to have a priest. Salem is now called Jerusalem. By Abram giving a tithe to Melchizedek, he was recognizing this priest as being spiritually greater than he.[5] Hebrews 7:1-10 tells us that another king and high priest came from Jerusalem -- Jesus. Jesus also offers us the gifts of bread and wine -- His body and blood -- so we may have eternal life.

Food for Thought: Why did Abram go to Egypt and Gerar if he thought there was danger? Why did he give away his wife for material gifts and safety?

January 6
Bible Readings: Genesis 15-17

God renews His promise to make Abram a great nation -- more numerous than the stars. Abram believed God and is forevermore considered a righteous man (Heb. 11:8-10). As a covenant or contract, God has Abram lay out a strange assortment of clean animals that have been split in half. Birds of prey attacking the carcasses are symbolic of the years the Hebrews will be enslaved and oppressed. The three-year old animals represent the three generations of Abram's descendants who will be captives. The sun sets on the age of God's grace on Abram and the darkness of the terror of bondage falls. Finally, God walks between the split halves of the animals in the form of a firepot and torch. A firepot was a portable bread oven. God appears as the Provider and Guide, showing His power and glory in fire and smoke. (See Ex. 19:18 and Ex. 24:17.) (Once again, God comes in the form of light.) This was a typical Near Eastern type of covenant. Usually both parties walked between the carcasses. It is significant that God holds only Himself responsible for the contract fulfillment. God knows man cannot fulfill a righteous contract. Near Eastern people held the violator of such a contract to the same fate as the animals.[2] (Jer. 34:18) The land of Canaan is definitely Abram's. Genesis 15:15 states God promises Abram will die in peace. This is the first time 'peace' is used in the Old Testament.

Sarai wants a child so much that she takes things into her own hands instead of waiting on God. Sarai gives her Egyptian maid, Hagar, to Abram for the purpose of bearing an heir. Abram, who makes daily decisions for more than a thousand people, can't seem to make any righteous decisions when it comes to his wife. Sarai becomes jealous of the pregnant Hagar and blames Abram for causing all her trouble. (Sin is rooted in our emotions.) In another bad decision, Abram allows Sarai to mistreat Hagar until she runs away. She headed home toward Egypt. God sent an angel to tell her to go back, be submissive, and then her son, too, would be a great nation. Abram and Hagar have a son named Ishmael. The Ishmaelites who are his descendants will be a nomadic tribe of merchants who claim the land of Arabia.

When Sarai is 89 and Abram is 99, God changes their names to Sarah (princess) and Abraham (father of many) to signify the great nation they are about to become. Abraham and Sarah both laughed (probably until they cried!) at the thought of a 90 year-old woman delivering a child to a 100 year-old father! Then God told them to call the child Isaac, meaning laughter -- a permanent witness that what you laugh at as impossible, God can do.

With this renewed promise, God tells Abraham he is to promise to circumcise every male child 8 days old or older as a physical reminder of his everlasting promise to follow God. Why circumcision rather than a more visible mark/scar elsewhere? Adam and Eve sinned in the Garden of Eden due to lust for the forbidden. After the expulsion from the garden, mankind's sinful lust became most prominent and evident in their sexual desires. But appropriate sexual union was necessary for the propagation of the species. Therefore, the same organ that could bring men to the depths of sin was also the one that could replenish the population of the earth in fulfillment of God's command in Gen. 1: 28. Ancient peoples believed the organ that produced life must be purified before the life it produces can be sanctified and holy. Thus, circumcision represented purification of the body and soul.[11] Circumcision was an ancient practice used by the Egyptians, Canaanites, Edomites, Ammonites, and Moabites, too.[2] (Jer. 9:25-26) The first 2 tribes are descendants of Ham (cursed lineage of Noah) while the last 3 are descendants of Shem (Edomites are from Esau, Abraham's grandson; Ammonites and Moabites are descendants of Lot's sons born out of incest).

Food for Thought: Think about being 115 and dealing with a teenager! (Sarah dies at 127. Compared to today's lifespan, Sarah was about 65 when she had Isaac!)

January 7
Bible Readings: Genesis 18-19

While Abraham is resting at the door of his tent one day around noon, he looks up and sees 3 men. As was the custom of the day, he bowed low to the men (an indicator of a non-aggressive stance) and offered them shade, food, and water. He also had water brought to wash their hot, dusty feet. All of this was the approved standard for hospitality of this time. After their rest and refreshments, Abraham learns that two of the men are messengers from God and the other is the LORD in the form of a man. The messengers have two messages: (1) In the spring, Sarah will give birth to a son, and (2) They are about to destroy Sodom and Gomorrah. Sarah overhears the first message and laughs only to find she is facing the LORD. He asks her, "Is anything too hard for the LORD?" (Genesis 18:14) Sarah's immediate response is to lie to God! This couple stands as constant reminders that regardless of the good Christians we are at some times, other times we are just dirty sinners. Abraham is the greatest man of faith in history, yet he has lied, acted outside God's Will, and allowed injustice toward Ishmael and Hagar.

We know the greatness of Abraham's faith because the LORD chooses to confide in him the approaching destruction of Sodom. Abraham is horrified to hear that an entire city will be wiped out. He immediately begins to plead on the behalf of any righteous ones in the city. (Can you imagine debating with God? Abraham would have been a good lawyer for the innocent. Alas, there were very few men in this category.) The LORD agrees not to destroy Sodom if 10 righteous people can be found.

At this point the LORD disappears and the 2 angels continue on to Sodom. Lot is sitting at the city gate, a place usually reserved for the esteemed elders of the city to form a type of city council. He sees the 2 men and immediately invites them to his house for the night. (It was commonplace for travelers to spend the night in the square.) During the night the men of the town demanded Lot send the visitors out to them so they could perform homosexual acts with them. Lot pleads with them and even offers his two daughters who are engaged instead. (During this time, to allow harm to come to any visitor staying with you would have meant complete shame and disgrace for the rest of the host's life.[2]) The men turn on Lot and the angels have to rescue him. Then the angels blind the men and tell Lot to hurry and get his family so they can escape the destruction. Lot's future sons-in-law refuse to come. Even Lot and his family dawdle until the angels have to take their hands and pull them out. They are told to flee and not look back, but Lot's wife does. She is turned into salt. (Lot is a whiner.) Lot now pleads not to go to the mountains but instead to the town of Zoar. (For a man who got rich as a herdsman, he sure liked the city life!) God destroys Sodom and Gomorrah with what appears to be a volcano eruption combined with an earthquake.[2] (Archaeology can't prove this, but Sodom is believed to currently be located underneath the Dead Sea.)

Josephus tells us that Lot's daughters participate in their incestuous scheme to have children because they believe that all mankind has been wiped out by the terrible destruction.[3] At the least we can assume there were no eligible bachelors available where they lived. They got their father drunk two nights in a row and each one lay with him. The result was a son born to the eldest daughter who would become the father of the Moabites and a son born to the younger daughter who would become the father of the Ammonites. Many years later Ruth (from the Moabite tribe) would marry Boaz (from the tribe of Judah) and they would become the great-grandparents of King David and ancestors of Jesus.

Food for Thought: Why do people still get drunk when it only brings about sin? Why did God choose a descendant of the son of willful incest to be a part of Jesus' lineage? Was it to show that all have sinned and fall short of God's Glory, but all can still be forgiven and turn to God?

Verse of the Week: **Genesis 31:49** "May the LORD keep watch between you and me when we are away from each other."

The Period of the Patriarchs (Abraham, Isaac, and Jacob)

January 8
Bible Readings: Genesis 20-21

Abimelech means 'my father is king.' According to many scholars, this may have been the title of the king rather than an actual name, i.e., Pharaoh was the title of Egypt's king. In Genesis 20:1-2, we are told that Abraham is in the region of the Negev. The Negev is a triangular piece of desert land in southern Israel that borders the Sinai Peninsula. The Negev covers a span of approximately 4,500 square miles, about the size of Connecticut.[7] Copper was its most important resource.[5]

Scholars believe Abraham may have gone to Gerar seeking food during a time of famine.[5] If so, that explains his willingness to face danger there, but his fear doesn't excuse him for passing his wife off as his sister. Once again, Abraham falters. But, once again, a loving God intervenes and prevents Abraham's lapse of faith from altering His covenant. Sarah is within weeks of conceiving Isaac, the key to fulfillment of God's promise to make Abraham a great nation. God is not going to let sin change His master plan for mankind. (I find it amazing that Sarah was so lovely and desirable at almost 90 years old that a king would want her, an oasis in the desert of life!)

God generally appears to people of ancient times through dreams. Later on in time, the prophets have visions. (I often think God communicates with us so much at night because we're too 'busy' to listen during the day.) God visits Abimelech and tells him Sarah is a married woman and his lust for her will result in his death. Abimelech immediately pleads innocent to any defilement of Sarah, wherein God informs Abimelech that he was kept from this sin because God, Himself, had prevented it. God pardons Abimelech provided Sarah is returned to Abraham. At this point, God reveals Abraham is a prophet, someone who communicated with and spoke for God. (This, too, I believe is revealing. Even those who speak for God have times of weakness and sin.)

Abimelech calls for Abraham demanding to know why he has brought this wrong on his kingdom. Again, Abraham shows his weak point, fear. Instead of just admitting his guilt, he makes excuses for it. Interestingly, these are the same excuses he used before. Neither time were these excuses any good, but both times God instills such fear into the kings that the excuses are accepted, Abraham is forgiven, and even great gifts of wealth are given to Abraham. Now this may seem as if God is rewarding lying and 'little white lie' excuses, but that is not the case. As I stated before, God does not let our sin alter His master plan. Abraham was to become a nation of many people and much blessed (in ancient times, the amount of wealth one had was believed to be equal to the amount of blessings he had). Pagan peoples called upon their gods to supply them with rain, sunshine, beauty, fertility, and all the things they needed to survive and prosper. Bounty (abundance of necessary items) indicated riches; bounty plus luxury indicated great wealth. Gold, in any amount, was great luxury. For these pagan people to understand that there was only one true God, His people would have to be wealthy -- the symbol of 'blessed' to pagans. Watch how the Patriarchs (Abraham, Isaac, and Jacob) are given enormous amounts of wealth through gifts, treaties, or plunder in our march through Genesis. Additionally, God blesses all their work and leads them through trials. I am reminded of the following:

> The LORD is my shepherd; I shall lack nothing.
> He makes me lie down in green pastures,
> He leads me beside quiet waters; he restores my soul.
> He guides me in paths of righteousness for his namesake.
> Even though I walk through the valley of the shadow of death, I will fear no evil, for you are with me;
> your rod and staff, they comfort me in the presence of my enemies.
> You anoint my head with oil; my cup overflows.
> Surely goodness and love will follow me all the days of my life, and I will dwell in the house of the LORD forever." (Psalm 23)[1]

Abimelech gives Abraham about 25 pounds of silver to be sure all people know that he acknowledges his mistake and is paying retribution. (In another show of God's power, all fertility among the women of Abimelech's household comes to a halt. God shows He is mightier than a pagan god of fertility.) Abraham, the prophet, intercedes for Abimelech through prayer -- and God answers. Proverbs 15:8 reminds us, "The LORD detests the sacrifice of the wicked, but the prayer of the upright pleases him."[1] God knew Abraham's heart, and loved him in spite of his faults.

(For some time now, I have asked God to make me a prophet, someone whose heart is attuned to His Will. Many times I have wondered if I could handle the 'bad news' as well as the 'good news' that God's prophets often announce. What I have discovered is that I get anxious (and, yes, impatient) waiting on God's action to follow upon His words to me.) After waiting 25 years for God's promise to be fulfilled, Abraham and Sarah, in their old age, have a son. Generally, women named the children[10] but, in this case, Abraham names his son Isaac, meaning laughter, or better translated as joy in Genesis 21:6. (Actually Abraham is obeying God's instructions (Genesis 17:19) to name the boy Isaac.) Isaac is circumcised on the eighth day, the sign of God's covenant with His people (Genesis 17:10).

Over the years, Abimelech recognizes that Abraham serves a mighty God and requests a permanent peace treaty between them. Abraham agrees. By now, Abraham's possessions are enormous in numbers of sheep, cattle, people, tents, silver, gold, etc. But on the edge of the desert, water is scarce and worth fighting over. Abraham complains when Abimelech's servants seize his water well. Abimelech stammers out the old 'ignorance of the situation' excuse, at which Abraham seizes the upper hand and offers him 7 lambs as complete payment for the well. (Remember the number 7 indicates completeness.) Abimelech has a dilemma: (1) if he refuses the money, he is openly opposing a powerful, wealthy man of God, or (2) if he accepts payment, he agrees that Abraham owns the well.[2] Abimelech chooses the high ground of virtue and accepts the offer. (Doesn't Abimelech remind you of one of those 'good' people that you hate to find out are unbelievers?) Abraham names his well Beersheba, the well of the oath (or the well of seven [complete]). In celebration, he plants a tamarisk tree.[1] These trees are hearty and very good for shade.[5] If you are hot and thirsty, the only thing more sought after than water is shade. Then Abraham called upon El Olam, Hebrew for 'God Everlasting.' This is the only place in the Old Testament where this name for God is used.[2]

We are reminded that Abraham is in the land of the Philistines. The Philistines are typically pictured in the Bible as a warrior tribe because of all the fighting they do with the Israelites for land. (Of course, you remember David and Goliath, a Philistine (1 Samuel 17)!) But, this occurs at a much later time, almost a thousand years later.[1] Abimelech is from an earlier settlement in Philistia that was a peaceful people.[5] (You will recall that the Philistines descended from Ham, the cursed lineage of Noah (Genesis 10:14).) Philistia runs along the coast of the southern half of modern day Israel, from Joppa (Tel Aviv today) in the north to Gaza in the south (which is in the Gaza Strip today).[4,5]

Meanwhile, Isaac is approaching a monumental point in his life -- weaning. Most people today (especially women!) are mortified to think of a child still nursing at 3 years old. In ancient days, there were very good reasons for this. Mother's milk contains a large supply of antibodies, from the mother's immune system, to help fight off infections. Until the recent Twentieth Century discoveries of antibiotics and vaccines, many babies died during their first year or two of life from infectious diseases. To make it to 3 years old was truly something to celebrate, thus, a weaning party! (I'd think Sarah would really be partying!) At the celebration, Sarah realizes that Ishmael is taunting Isaac (rather shameful thing for a 17 year old to do to a 3 year old). Sarah wants Hagar and Ishmael cast out of the clan. This is a sentence of death in the desert! Abraham is understandably upset. The family clan provided food, clothing, shelter, work, and security for its members. None of this would be available to Abraham's oldest son (referred to as his illegitimate son by Josephus[3]) if cast out. God talks to Abraham that night (maybe in a dream?) and tells him to do as Sarah says. (This is actually the first time Abraham is told by God to sacrifice a son. God promises that Ishmael will become a great nation, too. From this, Abraham knows Ishmael will live.) What a heavy heart Abraham must have had to send Hagar and Ishmael off into the desert with only the food and water she could carry. When the water is gone, Hagar lays a faint Ishmael under a bush to die then she goes a-ways off, unable to bear his moans and dying. God heard the boy's cries and responded to Hagar, telling her that Ishmael would become a great nation. (This is a renewal of the promise God made her before Ishmael was born (Genesis 16:10). Notice she was in the desert that time, also.) Suddenly, she sees a well of water and is able to revive the boy. (In the glare of the desert sun, dehydrated and weak, it is easy to imagine not initially seeing a well that was little more than a pit or hole in the ground. God, though, provides for His master plan, regardless.) Because God was with him, Ishmael manages to survive in the desert by learning to hunt wild game. He lived in the Desert of Paran or the central part of the Sinai Peninsula.[7]

Food for Thought: Was Abraham's experience with Ishmael God's way of preparing Abraham for the big test -- the sacrifice of Isaac? Can you think of times you were able to weather a hurricane because you had experience in weathering storms?

January 9
Bible Readings: Genesis 22-23

Our lesson opens with "God tested Abraham" (Genesis 22:1).[1] (The quickest way to strike fear in the heart of people today is to tell them there will be a test, meaning they have to meet some standard.[8]) And what a test it was! God tells Abraham to take his only son, Isaac, to the region of Moriah and sacrifice him as a burnt offering. Now, let's look at this. Isaac is not Abraham's only biological son, but he is the only one in God's master plan for the development of a special people set aside for Him. Genesis 22:4 states Abraham traveled three days to get to the region of Moriah. The Jews believe Moriah is in Jerusalem, located at the exact site where the temple's sacrificial altar was later built.[5] Sacrificing children was a common practice among the pagan cultures living around Abraham, but never had God asked one of His followers to do this. Abraham, though, doesn't even question the request! (I know I'd probably say, "God, I think our communication wires are crossed! I know you didn't say that!") Josephus states, "Now Abraham thought that it was not right to disobey God in anything, but that he was obliged to serve him in every circumstance of life..." (p. 43).[3] How much better off we'd all be if we had that attitude! Good ole Abraham doesn't even drag his feet. He sets out **early** in the morning. The Bible does not even hint that Abraham was sad or heart broken. Some might say he was in shock. I choose to believe he was just reacting in the characteristic way he had all his adult life to God's call -- in faith. God had obviously blessed him all his days, and God had never forsaken him. What a testimony! It's easy to see why Abraham is listed in God's Hall of Fame (Hebrews 11). Hebrews 11:17-19 reminds us that even though God promised Abraham that he would become a great nation **through Isaac**, Abraham prepared to sacrifice him anyway believing God could raise the dead! (Interesting to note that the Sadducees couldn't believe that when Jesus and the apostles preached it among them -- but that lesson comes later (Mark 12:18-27).)

Isaac obediently goes with his father, not knowing he is the sacrifice. How cruel it seems to have the sacrificial lamb (Isaac) carry his own wood! But wait -- didn't Jesus do that, too? (John 19:17) In Abraham's unwavering faith, he tells the two servants with him to wait. Then he says, "**We** [Abraham and Isaac] **will** worship and then **we will** come back to you" (Genesis 22:5).[1] When Isaac asks where the lamb is for the sacrifice, Abraham calmly states, "God himself will provide..." (Genesis 22:8).[1] After the altar is built, Abraham ties up Isaac, puts him on the altar, and takes out his knife. (Now, I would have started screaming and running long before this point.)

To understand Isaac's apparent cooperation and willingness, you must understand the role of the father or patriarch of the family. The patriarch ruled as judge, priest, and provider for everyone in the group. Life and security were possible if all worked together for the good of the family. Lack of cooperation in the team effort could result in banishment from the group and almost certain death (Remember Hagar's dilemma in Genesis 21:14?). Josephus gives an almost chilling account of Isaac. "Now Isaac was of such a generous disposition as became the son of such a father, and was pleased with this discourse; and said "That he was not worthy to be born at first, if he should reject the determination of God and of his father, and should not resign himself up readily to both their pleasures; since it would have been unjust if he had not obeyed, even if his father alone had so resolved" (p. 43).[3] This patriarchal command of obedience still exists in many areas of the Middle East today.

As Abraham draws his knife, God sends an angel to stop him. God sends His pardon for Isaac and His words of appreciation for Abraham. Yes, God loves and appreciates an obedient heart. 1 Samuel 15:22 states, "Does the LORD delight in burnt offerings and sacrifices as much as obeying the voice of the LORD? To obey is better than sacrifice, and to heed is better than the fat of rams." Abraham obeyed. Isaac obeyed. God provided a ram for the sacrifice and Abraham named the site 'The LORD Will Provide.' Likewise, God did not withhold His only son from being sacrificed for us. Likewise, Jesus went to the cross, obediently and willingly because it was the Will of His Father. But, unlike God, we (mankind) showed no mercy to God's sacrificial Lamb. God's plan for the salvation of all mankind is summed up in Romans 10:9 -- confess and believe.

At this point, we are updated on Abraham's brother, Nahor. Nahor's key role is as grandfather to Isaac's future wife, Rebekah. Abraham's only other brother, Lot's father, is dead. To maintain the religious purity of God's chosen people, Nahor's offspring would be Abraham's only source of suitable spouses for Isaac. (Remember Lot only had two daughters who both had sons before Isaac was born.) Now you may say, "Why doesn't he look in Sarah's family for a spouse?" Recall that Sarah was Abraham's half-sister. His family was her family, too.

Sarah dies at 127 years old. Isaac is now 37. She died at Hebron, the general area where she had lived most of her life. Because Abraham is a shepherd, he owns no land. He appeals to the Hittites for a place to bury his wife. Abraham is a wealthy, powerful man among a pagan people. They offer to give him a tomb, which would have placed Abraham beholding to them (and under their charge) for life. Even in his grief, Abraham is wise to this ploy. To repel this move, Abraham has to reveal he wants a particular tomb owned by Ephron, son of Zohar. (The Hittites were descendants of Canaan, cursed lineage of Ham.) The price is exorbitant -- 400 shekels (10 pounds) of silver. By comparison, Jeremiah paid 17 shekels for a field in Jeremiah 32:9[2] and King David paid 50 shekels for the threshing floor of Araunah where the Temple would later be built (2 Sam. 24:24). [Discrepancy: 1 Chron. 21:25 says David paid 600 shekels of gold.] Abraham agrees and finally owns a piece of the Promised Land. Sarah is the first member of Abraham's family to be buried, and the cave of Machpelah becomes the family tomb for all the Hebrew Patriarchs - Abraham, Isaac, and Jacob - and their wives who maintained the lineage of Jesus.

Food for Thought: Abraham was willing to give everything to God. How much are we willing to give? What if God asked for all your earthly possessions, would you respond obediently? Respond without question?

January 10
Bible Readings: Genesis 24

Before Abraham dies, he wants to be sure Isaac has a suitable wife. He chooses his oldest, most trusted servant to take charge of this search. Genesis 15:2 lists Eliezer of Damascus as the chief servant who was designated as the one to inherit Abraham's wealth had an heir not been born. Probably this is the same servant Abraham has selected now. Abraham gives specific instructions that a wife is not to be taken from the Canaanites but rather is to be sought from among his own relatives back in Haran.

The servant asks a very good question, "What if the woman is unwilling to come back with me to this land?" (Genesis 24:5) Put yourself in his place -- a servant traveling with a group of men about 500 miles to find a family who hasn't seen their relative, Abraham, in almost 60 years. The young, available women relatives would have never seen Abraham or his servant. In addition to that, he would be asking a young, virgin woman to make a long journey to an unknown land with an unknown servant and band of men to marry an unknown man! (Would you allow your daughter to do this?) His travel to Haran would include 10 camels heavily laden with gifts for the bride's family -- easy pickings for bandits. To his credit, the servant's concern seems only to carry out his assignment well. He inquires if he should take Isaac back to Haran if the selected woman will not come. Abraham emphatically states, "Make sure that you do not take my son back there" (Genesis 24:6). His faith still strong as ever, Abraham reminds his servant that God promised the Canaanite land, where he is now living, to Isaac. Abraham makes his servant promise not to take Isaac back to Haran. The servant is sent on his way with the reassurance that an angel of the LORD will go before him to show him the woman to choose. But, should she refuse, the servant will not be held responsible.

The journey takes him to Aram Naharaim, (Aram) generally known as Mesopotamia or Syria,[5] but (Naharaim) specifically referring to the northern land between the two rivers, Tigris and Euphrates.[5] Upon arriving at his destination, he has the camels kneel and then he prays. The hard part of his assignment is about to begin -- finding the right woman. So many years of living with Abraham have taught the servant to depend on God. He asks God to identify the right woman as the one who would not only provide water for his personal request but would also volunteer to water the camels. (This would be quite an undertaking for a young woman. I don't know how thirsty these camels were, but a camel can retain 15 gallons of water in his stomachs -- and there were 10 camels here! One young woman with a clay jar to haul water to 10 camels would seem like fighting a fire with a cup!) (Notice as we travel through the Old Testament that prayers do not end with 'Amen.' In fact, the model prayer Jesus taught his disciples (Matthew 6:9-13) does not end with 'Amen.' I, personally, like this open-ended, never-ending form of communicating with God. Continuing your conversation with God throughout the day and night is very comforting, calming, and reassuring. Try it.) God immediately answered the servant's prayer and sent Rebekah to him. Proverb 3:6 reminds us "in all your ways acknowledge him, and he will direct your paths." After she waters the camels, the servant gives Rebekah gold jewelry -- an extremely impressive gift from a wealthy man (even by today's standards!). (I would think a nose ring would be a big clue about the contract position she is about to be in!) He asks who her father is and rejoices to learn she is one of Abraham's relatives. God has blessed and the servant gives thanks.

Why Rebekah's brother Laban jumps into the marriage negotiations instead of the head of the family, Nahor or Bethuel, we do not know. Possibly, Nahor is dead. Considering Bethuel is Abraham's nephew, then it is reasonable that Bethuel is 100 years old. (Abraham's wife Sarah had just died at 127 years old. Most Hebrew men were betrothed around 40 years of age. We do not know how old Sarah was when she married, but Abraham would conservatively be around 140 years old at this time.) Also, Laban's true character may already be apparent even at this early date. His transactions with his nephew Jacob later in life are certainly proof that Laban is money oriented. Abraham's gifts to the bride's family would bring a handsome sum. Verse 50 states that Laban and Bethuel give Rebekah to be Isaac's wife. Apparently, Rebekah's brother Laban is as much responsible for her welfare as her father Bethuel. Regardless, Laban handles the marriage contract. It is important that he make good decisions because Rebekah's future is totally dependent on this arrangement. At this point, Rebekah's dowry, or inheritance, will be determined and the groom's gifts will be given to her family. All marriage arrangements are completed and Rebekah agrees to go immediately to her new home. Before she leaves, Rebekah receives her blessing -- to increase into a great nation and have control over her enemies. Part of Rebekah's inheritance (dowry) is the maids she takes with her.

Isaac has reached what apparently is the right age for an arranged marriage - 40. (Esau will also be 40 when he marries.) When Rebekah sees her fiancé, she veils herself. The typical marriage ceremony would involve a wedding feast where the veiled bride, wearing the groom's gift of jewelry, would participate with the groom in a simple, public pledging of marriage. The veil would be removed from her face and placed on the groom's shoulder.[9] This was symbolic of her revealing her intimate self to him -- of trusting him to care for her. (Not so very different from today's ceremonies.) The husband would then take his new wife to their new home. In Isaac's case, he was to soon inherit the entire family fortune. His mother and father's home tent was now his. So, he took Rebekah to the tent of his mother, Sarah. Now this was not a small camping tent. It was quite large with partitioned rooms. Remember this was the home of a wealthy man. The wife had a separate tent from servants and concubines. Abraham has such a large group that he didn't move the tent often, its furnishings were probably sparse and portable - rugs, bedrolls, mats, clay dishes, and chests.[7]

Food for Thought: By faith Rebekah left her family and country to marry a man she did not know. Hebrews 11:1 says, "Now faith is being sure of what we hope for and certain of what we do not see." Do you have faith? How much?

January 11
<u>Bible Readings: Genesis 25-26:33</u>

Isaac and Rebekah take over as the patriarchal family. Abraham retires and, at some point, marries Keturah. She bears 6 sons for him in his old age. (Abraham was more than 140 years old! This is comparable to today's retirement age of 65 years old.) The only one of these sons that has a distinctive tribal presence later in the Bible is Midian. Abraham gives gifts to all these other children and sends them away to the land of the east, i.e., Arabia, to separate them from Isaac. (Centuries later Moses will spend 40 years in Midian and marry a Midianite woman (Exodus 2:11-21).) (One author believes it is feasible that the three wise men from the east that came to visit Jesus, the baby, were descendants of Abraham.[10])

Abraham dies at 175 years old. His sons, Isaac and Ishmael, bury him in the cave of Machpelah where Sarah had been buried. Ishmael fades from the story. His descendants populate the central part of the Sinai Peninsula, considered the border of Egypt to the southern tip of Arabia. Genesis 25:18 tells us his tribe was hostile towards the rest of his relatives thereafter. His taunting of Isaac at the weaning party has developed into a nation of hostile people. (Next time a child is left alone to 'grow out of this phase,' remember the outcome of Ishmael.)

Isaac and Rebekah have moved to Beer Lahai Roi, Ishmael's home area. This was the well where the angel visited the pregnant Hagar when she ran away from Sarah (Genesis 16:14). It is located almost half way down the border of Israel and Egypt.[4] In answer to prayer, Rebekah becomes pregnant after 19 years of barrenness, but her womb seems to be in turmoil.

She seeks God's help and is told she is carrying twins. Each boy will be a nation, but the descendants of the older son will serve those of the younger son. (This is the opposite of the normal chain of command. In this time period, the eldest son should have been in control. Several times in the Old Testament, God purposefully shows that His Will is supreme, not man's way. For example, think of Isaac and Ishmael, Jacob and Esau, Ephraim and Manasseh (Joseph's sons - Genesis 48:14).) When the first boy was born, he was red and covered with hair. Named Esau, he was to become the father of the Edomites. (Esau, meaning hairy, is also known as Edom, meaning red. Red seems to play a key role in Esau's life. He is red, his descendants are called red, he is fond of red stew, he is a hunter (red meat), he settles in a land of red earth (Edom), and he sees red (much anger).) The second boy is born holding onto the heel of his brother. He is named Jacob, meaning the grasper or deceiver. Isaac was fond of the outdoors, wild game, and Esau. Jacob was more the quiet, stay-at-home type who was favored by Rebekah.

Our first glimpse into Jacob's and Esau's characters occurs when Esau comes home famished from a hunting trip. Jacob jumps at the opportunity to swap his red stew for Esau's birthright as the oldest son. Esau is more interested in his present needs than any future rewards. So, he agrees. (Those who focus only on the present and themselves will lose out on any stored up rewards in the future.)

As a result of a famine in the land, Isaac moves his family back to Gerar (following his father Abraham's footsteps in Genesis 20). God warns Isaac not to go to Egypt rather he is to maintain his stake in the land of Canaan. Isaac seems to have developed Abraham's weaknesses, too. (This is another example of how your children imitate you and mold their lives from your life. Your mistakes are magnified in them.) Isaac tells Abimelech, king of the Philistines, that Rebekah is his sister. (Abraham's story was at least partially true, but this one is totally false.) When the king discovers the truth and questions Isaac, he gives the same excuse his father did - fear. Abimelech then orders his subjects to stay away from Rebekah. God richly blesses Isaac with crops that year -- not because he lied, but because he obeyed God and stayed in Canaan - trusting God to provide for his family of thousands.

As if we are watching a rerun of the life of Abraham, Isaac and Abimelech's people quarrel over wells. (Allowing strangers to live in your town a while is one thing, but having thousands of them move in, take over the water wells, and get richer in the meantime is quite another!) Isaac still had claim to the wells Abraham dug. (Remember the lambs Abraham gave Abimelech for title to a well (Genesis 21:30)?) The Philistines are jealous and jealousy always breeds trouble. Abimelech asks Isaac to move. Isaac digs the third well, moving each time, before he can find peaceful living with the residents of the land. Some time later, he leaves the Philistines to travel southeast to Beersheba. God appears to Isaac that night and reassures him of His promise to his father, Abraham. Isaac settles down and digs a well. Meanwhile, Abimelech is concerned that this powerful, wealthy man so blessed of God has been asked to leave the country. What if he retaliated? What if his God retaliated? Abimelech rides out and asks Isaac to make a treaty between them never to engage in battle. This was done.

Food for Thought: Why is it our mistakes speak louder than our successes? Why would Isaac fear for his life enough to lie about Rebekah?

January 12
Bible Readings: Genesis 26:34-28

Esau and Jacob are at the marrying age - 40, but Esau is not content to wait for Isaac to arrange a marriage. Esau marries two Hittite women (Canaan's descendants). Their pagan background grieved Isaac and Rebekah. Isaac is now 100 years old (note Genesis 25:26). He is weak and blind (possibly cataracts from the desert sun). He wants to give his blessing (spiritual inheritance) to his eldest son, Esau. Isaac is tired and wants to pass the family leadership and responsibility on to a younger, stronger man. Isaac wants to retire. It appears he is unaware of Esau's sale of his birthright to Jacob (and Esau doesn't bother to tell him, either). Rebekah, though, overhears him tell Esau to hunt some game, make his favorite meal, and then receive his blessing. Rebekah tells Jacob to quickly slaughter two young goats and she will prepare Isaac's meal -- the meal **Jacob** will take to Isaac to receive his blessing. Jacob is afraid he will be discovered and then cursed by his father. After all, he doesn't resemble the red, hairy Esau at all. Rebekah says the curse will fall on her. Jacob puts on Esau's clothes, puts the goatskins on his arms and neck, and takes the food to Isaac. Isaac knows the voice is that of Jacob, but the odor and feel of his body are those of Esau. Jacob has announced himself as Esau, the firstborn. When Isaac asks if he **really** is Esau, Jacob lies again. Isaac obviously doesn't conceive of the possibility this man is lying. He eats the food and starts the blessing. (This is usually a private ritual transferring the head of the family to the son.) Isaac blesses him with an abundance of food and wine, power over nations and all his brothers, and the fulfillment of all his curses and blessings. Jacob leaves Isaac. (I'm sure he is relieved to have pulled off this great deception. I have learned that, in general, what goes around comes around. Jacob first took advantage of his brother's weakness and has now plotted to deceive, successful both times. Soon, he will be the victim of deception and get to spend many hard years learning a lesson in the evil of deception. Did I hear you say, "But it was God's Will for Jacob to become Isaac's successor!" Remember, God does not need our assistance, and He doesn't want our sinfulness, in order to carry out His master plan. God would have made Jacob the Patriarch without Rebekah and Jacob's deception. After all, that was His promise to Rebekah before the twins were born (Genesis 25:33). God is not in the business of **telling** futures; He is in the business of **making** futures. As with most of God's people, she wasn't willing to wait and trust God. Are you?)

Deception always carries the penalty of payback, sometimes sooner, sometimes later; but one thing is sure, it always comes. For Jacob, payback started when Esau arrived and discovered the deception. Not only is Esau angry and upset, but Isaac, we are told, "trembled violently" because he had been deceived. "Once the words of blessing had been spoken, they could not be revoked" (p. 33).[10] When Esau heard that Isaac had already blessed his brother, Jacob, Esau burst forth with a scream and begged his father to bless him, too. Isaac, sadly though, could think of little to bless him with that he had not already given totally to Jacob. Jacob had lied; he had stolen the blessing. At this point, Esau makes the comment, "Isn't he rightly named Jacob? He has deceived me these two times: He took my birthright, and now he's taken my blessing!" (Genesis 27:36) The distinction between a birthright and a blessing is made here, even though, in the past, it has been considered one and the same. In this distinction, Esau is saying, "Not only did he take my physical, earthly rights away as oldest son, but also he has taken my heavenly endowed rights to power and wisdom (given in the blessing from father to oldest son) away as well." The blessing is not just kind words but actually carries the power for those words to be enforced. Esau begs, "Do you have only one blessing, my father? Bless me, too, my father!" (Genesis 27:38) The Bible tells us Esau wept loudly. Isaac, obviously perplexed, thinks hard and comes up with the only words of blessing he has left. He tells him he will dwell away from the lush, farming area, he will live by the sword, he will serve his brother, but at some point in time, he will throw off the yoke of his brother's control. From that point forward, Esau holds a grudge against Jacob and makes the statement that he would like to kill him! (Holding grudges always leads to more serious sin. In Matthew 5:24, Jesus tells us that we are to first reconcile ourselves to our brothers and settle any strife among us before we come to the altar of God.)

Rebekah now feared for the life of her son, Jacob. Jacob, from all accounts, is a mild-mannered man, although deceptive. Esau, on the other hand, is a very violent man who devoted his life to hunting animals for food. Rebekah's first thought is to see that her beloved Jacob returns to her brother's home in Haran for safety. She fears now she may lose both her sons if Esau takes the life of Jacob. By ancient law, the life of Esau would have to be taken then for this sin. You will recall in Genesis 4:8 Cain killed Able, his brother, and later Cain expresses fear at being killed (Genesis 4:14). It is very obvious that murder is considered from the very beginning to be a terrible crime, punishable by taking the life of the murderer. We don't know how much time has passed between Jacob's deception and Rebekah approaching Isaac with her complaint about Esau's Hittite wives. Presumably, it would have been a short span of time due to the fear for Jacob's life. She tells Isaac that she does not want Jacob to take a Canaanite wife as Esau has done and bring even more grief to her. Isaac calls Jacob, commands that he not marry a

Canaanite woman, and that he go to Haran where Rebekah's brother, Laban, and his family live. Isaac tells Jacob to take a wife from among the daughters of Laban. He concludes by blessing him -- telling him to be fruitful and multiply, pass on the blessing of Abraham to his descendants, and take possession of the land where he is now living as an alien. Esau is so upset to learn that Isaac has sent Jacob to take a wife among legal relatives (his mother's people) that he immediately goes out and marries another wife in an effort to appease his father.[3] This wife is the daughter of Ishmael, son of Abraham and Hagar, Isaac's niece. (Another viewpoint is that this marriage was for spite. Genesis 25:18 tells us the Ishmaelites "lived in hostility toward all their brothers." [1]) (We're told in the Ten Commandments that we are to honor our mother and our father so that our days will be long upon the earth (Exodus 20:12).) It is obvious from the previous example that rebellion against parents has existed for thousands of years. Inevitably, though, every case of rebellion has an equal, or greater, set of consequences to pay. That is true whether the rebellion is against parental authority or any other type of authority. In last week's lessons, we learned that we are free to choose, but we are not free to choose the consequences of our choices. Esau is a case of someone who chose poorly and had a lifetime of consequences in hardships and violence.

Jacob has left Beersheba that is in the far southwestern area of Israel. He has an extremely long, hard trip ahead as he has to travel to the northern part of Mesopotamia. This is a distance of about 600-700 miles. Fifty-five miles into the journey, he sleeps by placing a stone under his head.[10] He has a dream in which he sees a stairway going from earth up to heaven with angels going up and down the stairs and the LORD standing above it. The LORD says to Jacob that He will give him the land he is now lying on, his descendants will be a great nation that spreads out in every direction and all peoples on earth will be blessed by him and his offspring (Genesis 28:13). (Of course, we know today that the blessing occurred through Jesus Christ.) The LORD promises to watch over him wherever he goes and to bring him back to that land. He concludes this promise with the assurance that He will not leave Jacob until this promise has been fulfilled. When Jacob woke up, he named the place Bethel because this was surely the house of God! (In Hebrew Beth means house and el means God.) Jacob sets up a large stone pillar for a monument marker and anoints the stone. [Counting backwards from Gen.47:28, Jacob may be 76 years old now.[112]]

Jacob vows that **if** God does carry out His promise, **then** Jacob will give Him back a tenth of everything God gives him. Notice Jacob still doesn't have the faith to trust in God's promise -- IF and THEN. Jacob wants to be sure he isn't out anything without something to show for it! Is this how God wants us to respond? Shouldn't we give freely to God rather than have to be PAID in blessings first? Jacob will eventually realize that his true birthright, passed down from his grandfather Abraham, was Abraham's great faith, not wealth and power.[10] (This is the second time we have seen a tenth given to the house of God. The first time was when we saw Abraham give a tenth to Melchizedek from the spoils of battle against the raiding kings who captured Lot (Genesis 14:18-20).)

Notice that Jacob lies throughout this lesson because of greed, but Abraham and Isaac had lied out of fear. One truth to be learned is that our weaknesses and sinful ways become accepted (and easy) ways in our children. What we may have considered good reasons (there are no good reasons for sin, though) to act as we did, our children and others who watch us see as the way they are to model their lives. After all, if our parents did it, then it must be right! Jacob will have to go down through all history as the deceiver, until he has an earth-shattering encounter with God. Doesn't this reflect our own lives? Don't we deceive others and ourselves until we have that earth-shattering encounter with God?

Food for Thought: Wonder how Jacob felt when Isaac called him in about going to Haran for a wife? Don't you think he probably was afraid (or at least ashamed) to face Isaac? Do we feel shame and guilt when we have selfishness, deceit, and greed in our lives and we go before the Lord? Though Esau claims Jacob has deceived him twice, that is not true. Esau's own desire for instant gratification and Jacob's greed resulted in the birthright exchange. This second time, Jacob progresses to lies and deceit. Clearly Rebecca's faith is weak and she encourages the obviously weak-willed Jacob to act sinfully. Jacob will soon have to pay dearly for his choices. Are you ready to face the consequences of your life choices? If not, have you repented and experienced God's forgiveness?

Lessons of Love

January 13
Bible Readings: Genesis 29-30

Jacob arrives in Haran and stops at the city well. This is a typical meeting place as shepherds arrive in the late evening to water their flocks. The stone is still over the well. Jacob asks the shepherds if they know Laban. They respond saying, "here comes his daughter Rachel with the sheep" (Genesis 29:6). Apparently, Jacob is smitten with the beautiful, young girl as he immediately wants the shepherds to water their flocks and head back to pasture because there is still plenty of daylight. The shepherds respond that they cannot do that because the stone is too heavy for the few of them to move. They are waiting for other shepherds to arrive. In Jacob's haste to be rid of onlookers, as well as to attract his young lady, he jumps up and quickly removes the stone over the mouth of the well by himself! He greets Rachel with a welcoming kiss and tells her he is her Aunt Rebekah's son. As soon as Laban hears of this, he rushes out and welcomes Jacob to his home. This is an interesting insight into Laban's life and his success. Typically, the owner of flocks moved from place to place with the flocks and lived in tents as Abraham and Isaac had done. But Laban was wealthy enough to have a home in the city, and the grass was good enough in that area that the flocks could graze within a small radius around the city. So Laban was able to visit his flocks daily, but he had hired shepherds that stayed with them. It is interesting to note that the Bible tells us Leah, Rachel's sister, had weak eyes (Genesis 29:17). Most likely that is the reason why Leah is not a shepherdess, too. Her eyes may be too weak to properly watch after a flock of sheep in the desert sun. Jacob stays with Laban for a month long celebration of his coming to live with Laban. It was the Hurrian custom of the time that if you lived with a clan then you and all your possessions became the property of the chieftain of the household. (This may also be an old Babylonian herding contract for labor.) Laban, from all accounts, was now head of the household with Leah being the older daughter and Rachel the younger daughter. We find out that Laban served the gods of the Haran area, which are pagan gods. You will recall that Terah, Abraham's father, lived in this area and he, too, worshipped other gods (Joshua 24:2). Jacob enters into an agreement with Laban. He agrees to work seven years for the hand of Rachel in marriage. Laban comments that it is better for him to give 'her' to Jacob than to someone else. You realize in this comment that Laban is already laying down the foundation for deception by saying 'her' instead of specifying 'Rachel.' So the contract in deception has been cut. Jacob says the seven years pass quickly because of his great love for Rachel. At the end of his contract time, he goes to Laban and asks for his wife. Apparently, the marriage ceremony in this particular case varied because it is in a pagan country rather than in the Hebrew custom. Instead of removing her veil during the ceremony, they allowed her to enter the marriage chamber heavily veiled. In fact, Leah was so heavily veiled that Jacob did not know it was Leah. After his wedding night, Jacob wakes up to discover he has been deceived! (What went around (Jacob, the deceiver), has now come around (Jacob, the victim).) (I am reminded of a verse that says, "Cast your bread upon the waters, for after many days you will find it again" (Ecclesiastes 11:1). We think of this as casting good works upon the waters and good will come back to us. It can also be casting evil upon the waters and evil will come back to us.) Jacob is angry. He has worked seven years for the hand of Rachel, and he has not received the wages he was promised. He demands to know why. Laban replies that it is not the custom of the land to marry the younger daughter before the older one. (If Jacob lived there 7 years, I wonder why he didn't know this? Maybe he trusted his relative too much!) Laban convinces Jacob to finish out his honeymoon week with Leah. Then he gives Rachel to him as a wife, but now Jacob must work another seven years for another wife! Now Laban manages to get 14 years of free work out of Jacob and get both daughters married to a wealthy relative. The marriage contract is of two types: (1) the bride goes to the groom's land to live, OR (2) the groom goes to the bride's land to live. The more common contract was the first one. In this case, since Jacob had escaped in fear of his life from Esau, he had lived with his wives' family for the 14 years. Laban, therefore, has every right, by custom, to believe that Jacob and all his possessions belong to the estate of Laban.[10] (Think about poor Leah. How would you feel if the morning after your wedding your husband jumped up and ran out in crazed anger over finding out he was married to you?) Genesis

29:30 tells us that Jacob loved Rachel more than Leah. But, God is good. He saw that Leah was not loved; He saw injustice. He rewarded her faithful perseverance in a bad situation. Leah quickly gives Jacob four sons, named Reuben, Simeon, Levi, and Judah. These are the first four tribes of Israelites. Each man will develop into his own nation. The tribe of Judah will be the lineage of Jesus. As we follow the sons of Jacob through history, remember that even though Rachel was loved more than Leah, God greatly rewarded Leah by making her an ancestor of His son.

By the time Leah had four children Rachel had become quite envious. (Jealousy is always a breeding ground for sin.) As was the practice of the Middle East, she decided to have her slave girl, Bilhah, produce a child for Jacob whom Rachel could call her own. This practice also required that Jacob provide separate tents for concubines, and he would not be allowed to sell the slave girls who mothered his children. From the Code of Hammurabi, slaves used for the production of heirs could be disciplined but not sold.[7] Bilhah gives birth to Dan and then later to Naphtali. Leah is not to be outdone and she gives Zilpah, her maid, to Jacob. Zilpah gives birth to a son named Gad and another one named Asher. (The children of the concubines will share equally with the children of Jacob's wives, Leah and Rachel.)

Leah's older son, Reuben, is working wheat harvest and comes across some mandrake plants. In the Bible, mandrakes are thought to have special power for fertility. Mandrakes produce small fruit and have bluish-purple flowers. As a relative of the potato family, the yellow fruit is small, sweet, and fragrant. It was sometimes referred to as the 'love apple' and was considered to be a love potion.[5] Rachel wants Leah's mandrakes. Seizing the opportunity, Leah makes a deal with Rachel to exchange her mandrakes for more time with Jacob. (Do you wonder how Jacob felt when one wife runs out to the field to tell him she has 'hired' him from the other wife?) Leah gets pregnant and has another son named Issachar. Shortly after that she has a sixth son named Zebulun. Even later, she gives birth to a daughter named Dinah. The Bible doesn't often record the birth of girls unless the girl plays an important role in the history of God's people. As we will see later, Dinah will alter the history of Leah's second and third sons, Simeon and Levi.

Then we are told that God remembered Rachel. We learned in the first week's lessons that any time God 'remembers' someone it means that God intervened on his/her behalf. God intervened for Rachel and she gave birth to a son, Joseph.

Jacob now has 11 sons and 1 daughter (all less than seven years old) and wants to go back to his homeland. He goes to Laban and requests that he give him his wives and his children for whom he had worked 14 years. Laban realizes that most of the wealth he has accumulated has been as a result of God blessing Jacob. Laban decides to strike a deal with Jacob and offers for Jacob to name his wages. Jacob is a wiser individual now after 14 years of heavy labor for Laban and is very familiar with Laban's character. Jacob offers to work just for the blemished lambs produced by the flock. Laban readily accepts. So, Laban immediately removes all speckled, streaked, or spotted lambs and goats from the flock and takes them 3 days journey from the rest of his flock. Jacob is still required to maintain Laban's flock. Jacob manipulates the mating animals so that the stronger animals had blemished lambs or goats and the weaker animals had white lambs and black goats.

Food for Thought: Wonder what Jacob's life would have been like if he and his mother had decided to trust God instead of trying to handle the situation themselves? What would your life be like if you trusted God in everything?

January 14
Bible Readings: Genesis 31-33

By this time Laban's sons were becoming very jealous by the wealth that Jacob had acquired. They also felt that Jacob was stealing their inheritance, flocks of lambs at a time. Jacob noticed that Laban's attitude toward him had changed. The LORD tells Jacob it is time for him to return to the land of his fathers. Next Jacob meets with his primary wives to discuss his plans for leaving. This meeting has to take place away from the household. The deception has begun again. Jacob reminds his wives about the many years he has worked for Laban and the many times Laban has cheated him by changing the terms of his contracted wages. Jacob remarks that God is responsible for taking Laban's livestock and giving them to Jacob. A fact that Jacob attributes to Laban's deceptions! (Is not the pot calling the kettle black?) Nevertheless, Jacob does have the assurance that God is with him, even though God does not approve of his tactics. Jacob recounts a dream he once had to his wives. The dream involved God revealing that He had seen the injustice, He had observed Jacob's faith, and He would judge the guilty. God reminds Jacob that, as the God of Bethel, He had promised not to leave Jacob until He had brought him back to his homeland and fulfilled His promise. Rachel and Leah agree with their husband's decision. They seem resentful at this stage because their father sold them for wages instead of allowing them to marry with a proper dowry. Therefore, their father got what was coming to him!

The end of contract period comes at shearing time. So at this season of shearing, Jacob would have been released from his contract and could have left honorably. Because he did not have the official approval of his father-in-law, Laban, and because legally everything did still belong to Laban, including his wives and children, Jacob chooses to leave stealthily and put as much distance between himself and Laban as possible before his absence is discovered. He leaves for the hill country of Gilead. Gilead is a strip of land that runs just to the east of the Jordan River, stretching the full length of the Jordan.[4] Jacob would have been coming from Haran which is now located in southeastern Turkey. He would have been carrying all of his possessions (children, flocks, tents, wives, food) all the way across the full length of Syria before he reached the land of Gilead. Just before reaching Gilead, the land of safety, he would have to cross into what is now modern day Jordan. Before leaving, Rachel steals her father's household gods. There may be more than one reason for this. First, these household gods often contained all or most of the precious metal that was owned by the head of the clan. Second, these gods were owned by the head patriarch of the family as an inherited symbol of the power and right to be patriarch of the family.[10] If Rachel may have stolen something of great wealth, we are not told, but she definitely has stolen Laban's graven images of his right to be head of the clan. Rachel has been Jacob's wife about 13 years, yet she still does not seem to be a true believer in the one and only God of Jacob. (Is this maybe one more reason Rachel is not selected to be a matriarch in Jesus' lineage?)

Three days later Laban finds out Jacob is gone. This goes back to a passage from the previous lesson where we are told that Jacob's flock is separated 3 days from Laban's flock (Genesis 30:36). Therefore, Jacob already has 3 days of advance start on the trip; it takes 3 days then for a messenger to bring Laban the news, resulting in Jacob being 6 days away. Laban gathers his relatives and pursues Jacob, overtaking him in 7 days. Before Laban reaches Jacob, God warns him in a dream not to do anything good or bad to Jacob. Laban's hands are really tied by God, yet his anger must have been very great. Think, also, of his anguish. His entire family who had lived with him for 20 years is now leaving and this will probably be the last time he will see any of them again. When Laban catches up with Jacob, his complaint is that Jacob has sneaked out of his household without even giving him a chance to say 'good-bye.' He reminds Jacob he has the power to harm him but was warned of God not to do so. He asks for the return of his household gods. Interestingly, Jacob angrily makes the comment, "But if you find anyone who has your gods, he shall not live" (Genesis 31:32). (This is interesting because Rachel dies early. Dying during childbirth was not unusual, but all of Jacob's other wives, as well as his possessions are blessed during their lives. Remember that as a part of his blessing, Isaac endows Jacob with the gift of making all of his curses on others be fulfilled.) Rachel has the stolen gods in the saddle of her camel, which she is sitting on. She pardons herself for not getting up because she claims to be on her monthly period. (She is good at deception, too. One liar breeds another.) In Leviticus 15:19-20 a woman having her monthly period is unclean and so is anything she lies on or sits on. Rachel and her saddle would have been unclean under this standard. (Levitical laws have not been written down at this time but may have been a part of this culture already.) Therefore, Laban was not inclined to look any further. Also, Laban would be unwilling to believe his gods were so weak and desecrated as to allow an unclean woman to sit on them, even greater proof that his gods were powerless. Jacob feels exonerated (found not guilty). Jacob, not knowing of the theft, 'tells Laban off,' unburdening himself of years of pent up anger.

In Genesis 31:42 we first see the phrase 'the Fear of Isaac.' The first mention of the fear of God is in Genesis 3:10 where Adam and Eve are afraid to meet God because of their sin. Here Jacob refers to "the God of my father, the God of Abraham, and the Fear of Isaac." Jacob tells Laban, in essence, that his God is one to be feared, thus the warning in a dream.

Laban finally comes to the realization that he is beaten. Laban suggests a treaty between them so he will not be permanently cut off from his children and grandchildren. Laban wants a covenant agreeing that Jacob will not take any other wives, he will take good care of Laban's daughters and grandchildren, and that neither party will ever try to harm the other. Jacob took the oath and they erected a pillar surrounded by stones as a permanent witness to the promise. Laban warns Jacob that God will be the witness of his honor of the oath. (Is it possible that Laban has come to believe in Jacob's God?) (Ironic situation, isn't it? One deceiver who doesn't trust another deceiver.) At least we see a true concern from a father and grandfather for the safety and security of his offspring. By making Jacob swear not to take any other wives, Laban has assured that all Jacob's possessions will be inherited by Laban's grandchildren. (After all, they would have gotten the wealth when Laban died if Jacob had stayed in Haran.) Laban sends Jacob and troop on their way with a blessing. (Remember that fathers always blessed their offspring before final separation.)

Jacob goes on his way and meets a band of angels of God. Now angels usually serve as messengers of God, but we are not told what these angels said to Jacob. He called the place Mahanaim, which is now believed to be southeast of Succoth, close to Mt. Gilead.[4] Jacob is in Esau's territory. He decides to take the offense and send messengers to Esau announcing his arrival. What a change for a man who just snuck out of town in Haran! In the message, Jacob refers to himself as "your servant Jacob" (Genesis 32:4). You will note that this is opposite to the blessing that Jacob received from Isaac (Esau would bow down to Jacob), but Jesus was fond of reminding his disciples that all things were in God's time. Such is true in this situation, too. Jacob receives word that Esau is coming with 400 men. He assumes the worst and plans his strategy in hopes that there will be survivors. Apparently, the group is divided into two groups; then Jacob prays. In his prayer he confesses his unworthiness of God's blessings, praises God for the blessings he received, reminds God of His promises, and asks for deliverance from the hand of Esau. This is a good way for us to pray, too --confess, praise, quote scripture (promises are in scripture), and ask for deliverance.

Jacob divides out a series of three sets of gifts for Esau to send ahead in hopes he will be appeased. Jacob takes his wives, children, and all his possessions across the Jabbok River at night (probably early dusk). Jacob returned to the camp alone. We are told a man came and wrestled with him until daylight. The man wrenches Jacob's hip out of socket by his touch. Jacob realizes he has hold of a heavenly being and he demands to be blessed. The man asks his name. By giving his name, Jacob has revealed his personality trait - the grasper or deceiver. The man tells him that he will no longer be Jacob but will be Israel, meaning he struggled with God and overcame. (Now Jacob is at least 60 years old!) Jacob named the site Peniel because he had come face-to-face with God and lived. (Don't we struggle to make our peace with God and with men? The goal is to overcome the struggles.) Jacob bears a limp for the rest of his life as witness of his struggle with God.

When Jacob sees Esau coming, he quickly divides his family according to the least loved first - the maidservants and their children, then Leah and her children, then Rachel and Joseph. He is obviously changed because instead of cowering behind his wives and children, Jacob runs ahead to meet Esau. Jacob bows low 7 times to show complete submission. Esau is thrilled to see his brother and runs to meet him, kiss and hug him, and weep.

Then Esau sees all the people and herds and inquires whose they are. (Remember Jacob left home with nothing to go to Haran.) To Jacob's credit he states they are the blessings he has received from God. Each group bows to Esau. Esau is gracious and forgiving. God has blessed him, too. Esau offers to escort Jacob to his homeland, but Jacob declines. (Maybe he is still not too sure of Esau's forgiveness.) Nevertheless, Jacob tells Esau he will join him in the land of Seir (Edom). (Edom is due south of Jacob's present location.) When Esau leaves, Jacob, however, turns due west to Succoth. (Some authorities believe he did this because to a wandering shepherd who has no real since of time[10], going to Edom may mean taking several years to get there. Others see this as another deceit. Still others believe it is simple distrust of Esau.)

Our lesson ends with Jacob buying a piece of ground in Shechem for 100 pieces of silver. He sets up an altar and names the place El Elohe Israel, the mighty God of Israel.

Food for Thought: How do you think Leah must have felt to have borne 6 sons and a daughter but still isn't loved as much as Rachel? Does someone change instantly and completely when they grapple with God? Or is it a slower maturing in the faith?

Verse of the Week: **Genesis 50:20** "You intended to harm me, but God intended it for good to accomplish what is now being done...."

The End of the Period of the Patriarchs (Abraham, Isaac, and Jacob)

January 15
Bible Readings: Genesis 34-35

The story of Dinah's rape is a dark tale that illustrates how several mistakes compounded with unchecked anger can lead to an atrocity. Jacob was wrong for not keeping a closer eye on Dinah. Shechem was wrong to take advantage of her. Jacob's sons were very wrong to deceitfully act under the guise of a religious practice to get the men within their power and then to slay them. After all, Shechem had attempted to make restitution by agreeing to marry Dinah and to become a Jew. Jacob was also wrong in that he did not accuse his sons with deception (like father, like sons) and murder but only with making his family unpopular with its neighbors. This act clearly illustrates the need for the Law of Moses that limits the punishment for a wrong. An eye for an eye is far more equitable than the mass murder that compensates for the brothers' wounded honor and Dinah's disgrace.

In spite of Jacob's inadequacies, we must admire him for realizing the sorry state of his family and for taking a lead in doing something about it. He keeps a commitment he made to God as a young man by returning to Bethel (the site of his encounter with God) and worshipping God. The laying aside of the idols, the change of clothes, and the removal of the earrings, which were amulets and most likely used to ward off evil, were all symbolic of repentance. Also, note that repentance (verses 2-4) comes before the worship (verses 5-8). God appears to Jacob and changes his name from Jacob to Israel with a promise of God's blessings.

Jacob's encounter with God will sustain him in the tragic death of Rachel at Bethlehem. Rachel calls her son Ben-Oni meaning son of my trouble, but Jacob, perhaps realizing that God can bring good out of every situation, calls him Benjamin meaning "son of my right hand." Rachel died and was buried on the way to Bethlehem.

The next significant event is simply told as "Reuben went in and slept with his father's concubine Bilhah, and Israel heard of it" (Genesis 35:22). Bilhah is the mother of some of Reuben's half brothers. She is about the equivalent of a stepmother today. Importantly, Bilhah is Reuben's father's wife. Note that we are only told that Jacob heard of it, not that he did anything about it. When it comes time to bless his children, though, Jacob doesn't forget this sin.

Isaac lived 80 years **after** his "I'm dying" blessing to his children (Genesis 27:4). (Compared to life spans today, Isaac would have been in a 'mid-life crisis' age of about 45 when the blessing was given.) But, he was already blind at that point. Isaac died at 180 years old and was buried by Jacob and Esau at Hebron. (Note the similarity of the situation to the estranged sons Isaac and Ishmael who bury Abraham, their father (Genesis 25:9).)

Food for Thought: Do we realize in times of failure our need for God? How often in our own lives have we felt God's nearness and grace just before an event that put our faith to the test? God knows our future and prepares us for it.

January 16
Bible Readings: Genesis 36

Your Bible's narrative for this session explains that God will punish Edom for its unbelief and hostile nature. Edom is located in modern day Jordan. This chapter looks at the descendants of the people of the land of Edom or the land of Seir. Esau moves his tribe into the land of Seir, which is occupied by the Horites who are identified later in the chapter. Edom becomes the name of the area because of the redness of the earth and the red hair of Esau, whose tribe soon possesses the land. The land of Seir or Edom is located south of the Dead Sea in a mountainous area that stretches to the Red Sea. Edom is not a land that is particularly lush in vegetation, but it is a land where a people can survive by hunting, Esau's special skill.

Before Jacob fled from Esau after the deception of Isaac's blessing, Esau had married two wives from the Canaanites (Genesis 26:34), a fact that sorely grieved Rebekah and Isaac (Genesis 27:46). God had told the Patriarchs several times that they were to keep themselves a pure and holy people, set aside for Him. Canaanites were a group of pagan peoples who worshipped idols. (Of course, Esau married without the customary pre-arrangement or blessing from Isaac.) After Jacob left to obtain a bride from Rebekah's relatives, Esau goes out and marries an Ishmaelite. Therefore, this chapter opens with the recounting of the wives and children of Esau. If you look back at the names of Esau's wives in Genesis 26:34, you will discover that they are not the same as the names given here, with one exception. Even Basemath is listed as a descendant of two different fathers in the two accounts. There are several theories as to why this difference may have occurred. One is that over the years of the books of the Bible being copied by hand, the spelling of the names was accidentally altered probably because of the difficulty of writing the Hebrew language. Another theory is that Esau actually had five wives, but the first ones were no longer alive or at least had no children. Third is the theory that the names shown on this account represent new names given to the wives of Esau that would better represent their characters. As you will recall a name meant a great deal to peoples of this day because a person's character was represented in the name he or she was given. Adah means the ornament (also called Basemath, the fragrant), Oholibamah (also spelled Aholibamah, may mean tent-height) was previously (Genesis 26) called Judith (also spelled Jehudith) meaning praiseworthy, and Basemath is later called Mahalath (mild) in chapter 28.[11] Regardless of the difference in spelling, I believe the important concept here is that Esau had two Canaanite wives (one definitely from the Hittites and one who was from one of the Canaanite tribes of Hittite, Hivite, or Horite) and one Ishmaelite wife. None of these was acceptable to the LORD for Israelite marriages.

Not many of Esau's descendants stand out in history. The ones that come to mind are, of course, Herod the Great who tried to kill the baby Jesus by ordering that all boys two years old and under in Bethlehem and the surrounding area be killed (Matthew 2:16), and Eliphaz the Temanite who was one of Job's unworthy friends (Job 2:11), and the Amalekites who were constantly fighting Israel (Exodus 17:14-16).

The people who Esau dispossessed of their land of Seir were known as Horites, meaning cave dwellers. In fact, the mountains of Edom are full of caves that made good year-round homes for the people of the land. It is significant to note the fame given to Anah simply because he discovered a hot springs in the desert. (I guess he was the first resort owner!) Water being a precious resource was always noteworthy, but hot water for bathing would truly have been a phenomenal discovery!

Food for Thought: Many ancestral people are named here. It is mind-boggling to think of the number of lives they would take throughout all history because of the attitude of rebellion passed down from their ancestor Esau.

Are you rebellious? Does God honor rebellion? Think how different history could have been if Esau had been an humble man. In our newscasts today, war in the Middle East is often referred as a 'rebellion.'

January 17
Bible Readings: Genesis 37-38

Joseph is now 17 years old and like most teenagers can be very trying to his family. As chapter 37 opens, we see that Joseph has an attitude of arrogance and is a tattletale. The root cause of this attitude is the special favor shown Joseph by his father Jacob. Joseph was the first-born son of Jacob's favorite beloved wife, Rachel, who is now dead. We are told the other brothers hated Joseph and never gave him a kind word. One of the problems with having hate in the heart and hate in the mind that produces unkind words is that this type of hate generally results in action (displayed sin). Hostility between Joseph and his brothers steadily increases as a result of two dreams Joseph has. In the first one, Joseph sees his brothers bow down to him. In the second, Joseph's mother, father, and brothers bow down to him (since Rachel is dead, this must refer to Leah). Now Jacob is himself upset with Joseph at this last dream. The idea that parents would bow down to a son is unthinkable in this period of time when parents held a place of high honor. (Ahhh--for the good ole days!) Jacob briefly questions such a pompous idea. Meanwhile, Jacob files away this event in his memory. (Later, we will see Jesus' mother, Mary, doing this same thing with the unusual events of her son.)

Josephus tells us that Jacob loved Joseph "above the rest of his sons, both because of the beauty of his body, and the virtues of his mind; for he excelled the rest in prudence." (p.53)[3] Jacob favored Joseph to the extent that he had even made a differentiation between Joseph and his brothers in terms of the type of clothing Joseph received. Joseph had a robe given to him by Jacob that the Bible refers to as 'richly ornamented.' We do not know exactly what that means, so there are several interpretations. One is that it was a coat of many different colored sections of cloth. Another is that it was a coat with long, flowing sleeves because most of the coats of this day were sleeveless. Third is the idea that the coat was highly embroidered with many rich colors. Nevertheless, this is obviously a coat that makes Joseph stand out to all those around. He could be seen for many miles away and be recognized because of his special attire. One day while his brothers are grazing their flocks about 50 miles due north in some mountainous terrain, Jacob decides to send Joseph to check on his brothers and report their safety. When Joseph arrives at Shechem, he discovers that his brothers have moved the flocks about 15-20 miles further north to Dothan.[10] The brothers can see Joseph coming from a great distance, probably because of his coat, and set about plotting a plan to kill him. Reuben, who is Jacob's eldest son, comes up with a plan to put Joseph in a dry well secretly hoping to rescue him after dark. He has to be careful not to turn the wrath of his brothers on himself. Obviously, the other sons seem to be in a murderous mood at this point. Reuben shows true love and compassion for his brother, Joseph, but not enough to risk his life. The brothers capture Joseph, strip off his robe, and immediately develop a lie they can tell their father. (Lying seems to be a basic building block of every sin.) By covering the robe with animal blood, they could convince their father that Joseph had met his death in the claws of a wild animal. About this time, they see an Ishmaelite caravan coming from Gilead (land on the east bank of the Jordan River) making their way to Egypt. There are some Midianite merchants included in this caravan. The brothers' greed overtakes their murderous hearts. (What a powerful statement about the love of money!) Judah convinces the brothers to sell Joseph for 20 pieces of silver (about 1/2 pound). Apparently, this is the wholesale price for a young slave.[10] It is interesting to note that Hagar was probably brought back from Egypt on Abraham's journey there for food (Genesis 12:16). Hagar was a young slave girl. Now, generations later, Joseph is carried back to Egypt under the same conditions, a slave.[2] Additionally, his passage is via an Ishmaelite caravan. In other words, the descendants of Hagar are returning to her homeland with a descendant of Abraham enslaved! (Interesting how what goes around, comes around -- eventually.)

We suddenly find Reuben upset because all of this has occurred without his knowledge. We do not know where Reuben was during the sale of Joseph but assume he was probably watching the flocks. Now he could not rescue his brother. He was destined to share in the great scheme of his brothers' deception. They take the bloody robe to Jacob and ask him to identify it. Jacob immediately leaps to the conclusion that an animal has killed Joseph. The brothers never confirm this outright but just 'imply' this by the way they have presented the coat. Although, to God -- a lie is a lie, is a lie -- implied or otherwise. We'll find later on that the brothers are allowed to wallow for many years in their guilt before Joseph's destiny is revealed. They also have to bear the intense grief and physical decline this assumption of Joseph's death brings to their father. Their consequences were heavy indeed!

Joseph is sold to Potiphar, who is in charge of Pharaoh's prisons and personal bodyguards. Life for a young Hebrew slave would be terrible among natives in Egypt. Earlier in time (about 1700 B.C.), the Nile valley inhabitants had been overcome militarily and were being ruled by a group of people ethnically related to the Hebrews called Hyksos. That meant that anyone who was related to or looked like the Hyksos received the wrath and spite of the native Egyptians.[7] To top all that, Joseph was the servant of a hated man, the one who executed and punished prisoners. The pharaohs, on the other hand, were Hyksoses who were distantly related to the Hebrews and, therefore, inclined to want a Hebrew slave among them. Thus, they were more receptive to a young Hebrew being in charge.[10] God had prepared the way.

The environment in which Joseph now found himself living was greatly different than any he had ever known. The pyramids had been in place over a thousand years at this point.[10] The royalty wore wigs and makeup. The men wore kilts of various lengths. These resembled a large piece of fabric slung over one hip and looped and secured low under the other hipbone. The kilt was little more than a large loincloth. Common Egyptian women wore straight dresses looped over one shoulder. Egyptians worshipped many gods. The huge assortment of vegetables, fruit, and fish must have seemed like a treasure in itself. Egyptians drank beer and made yeast breads. Their food was flavored with garlic, onions, coriander, dill, cinnamon, and mustard. Meats consisted of fish, veal, goat, beef, and pork.[7] The current of the Nile was so mild that barges and river traffic could easily make its way up and down the river. Trade was extensive with both overland caravans and river traffic. The pharaohs of the Old Kingdom who ruled with an iron fist (pharaohs of the pyramid building era) were gone and the Middle Kingdom was now in effect. Power was maintained by trying to convince the people that the royals had their best interest in mind.[7]

Meanwhile, life goes on for Joseph's brothers. Judah moves about 10 miles away from home and marries a Canaanite woman in Adullam. They have 3 sons. The oldest son marries Tamar, but God saw he was wicked and put him to death. By Jewish custom or law, the second son must marry the widow and have children to carry on the dead brother's name. Judah's second son, Onan, marries Tamar but refuses to complete the agreement to have children. God saw this as wickedness and Onan, too, died. Judah promised his youngest son to Tamar, when he grew up. Tamar's fate is to live as a poor widow in her father's house - waiting. But when the youngest son is grown, Judah doesn't marry him to Tamar for fear he will die, too.

Over time, Judah's wife dies. During sheep shearing time, he encounters a woman dressed as a prostitute. He gives her his seal, cord, and staff as a promise that he will return with payment in exchange for her favors. Judah sins. He does try to fulfill his contract by sending the payment by way of his friend. Note the friend is looking for a "shrine prostitute." Apparently, Judah's sin extends to the level of believing he was involved with a shrine prostitute who supposedly performed sexual acts as a form of worship to a pagan god. When the girl is not found, Judah hides his shame and goes about his business. Psalm 69:5 says, "You know my folly, O God; my guilt is not hidden from you." Three months later, Judah hears that Tamar is pregnant. Instantly he wants her killed for having sex outside of marriage. (Talking about a double standard!) When she sends him the cord, seal, and staff of the man who is responsible, he realizes his sin. He had not given his younger son to Tamar in marriage as the law required in order that the earth may be populated and God's people increased.

Tamar has twins. When the first arm appears, a scarlet thread is tied on it to remember which was born first. In this case, though, the arm is pulled back in and the second baby comes first. This baby is named Perez. You will find his name in the ancestors of Jesus. His brother is born last. Once again God gives the younger son preference over the older one (or the one expected to be the older one in this case).

Food for Thought: What happened to Shelah, Judah's youngest son? Why did God not choose Reuben (who showed a kind heart toward Joseph), or Simeon or Levi (who thought they were punishing the crime committed against their sister) for His son's lineage? How did Judah's lineage, through Tamar, provide what God wanted? What can ordinary people like you and me give God that He can use in a mighty way? Even in our sinfulness, we have a gift, too. What is your gift to God?

January 18
Bible Readings: Genesis 39-42:5

Most of what we know about the man Joseph is found in the last 11 chapters of Genesis. Joseph rises in the ranks because "the LORD was with Joseph and he prospered" (Genesis 39:2). Even the pagan peoples around Joseph could plainly see that his God was with him. Remember that Laban saw this same characteristic in Jacob, Joseph's father (Genesis 30:27), and Abimelech saw it in Abraham (Genesis 21:22). Later in time, we will see that God pours out an overflow of blessings on those who provide for the prophets (2 Kings 4:8-37) and the Ark of the Covenant (2 Samuel 7:11).

Joseph's first test under the Egyptians comes in the same way many young people experience their first major test in temptation, lust. The Bible tells us that Potiphar's wife "took notice" of Joseph. It's the ole "I see, I want, I get" philosophy at work. Joseph was at a disadvantage, too, because he was a servant. He could easily have reasoned "Who am I to refuse my owner's wishes?" but he didn't. Our story makes it clear that God owned Joseph and Joseph knew it. In fact, he didn't care who else knew it either! Joseph clearly states, "How then could I do such a wicked thing and sin against God?" (Verse 9) The sexual harassment continued daily over a long period of time. You will notice that Joseph's final test with the enticements of his master's wife came as a result of Joseph getting caught in the house with her alone. Why wasn't he more careful? Archaeologists have found that houses (from shortly after this time) of the wealthy in Egypt had apartments at the front of the house for the women of the family and the servants' quarters and storage areas were located in the back of the house. Generally, a long hall passed in front of the apartments and continued to the back section of the house. Not having fire codes to meet, they typically had only one door to a house -- the front door. That would mean that all of Joseph's duties as manager of the household would require that he walk the connecting hallway many times a day as he oversaw the cooking, cleaning, repairing, laundering, and general functions of the house. To do his duty, he had to be in the middle of temptation. He could not avoid it! (Have you ever been in a place you didn't want to be because you had no choice?) Apparently, she became obsessed with Joseph (that kind of thing happens when we allow ourselves to dwell on improper thoughts). Finally, she attempts to grab Joseph and manages to hold onto his cloak, but he wriggles out of it and runs! (Cloaks were coats or fringed wraps. Because Egypt is very hot, cloaks were usually only worn by aristocratic households at state functions or other formal type occasions. It is more likely that Joseph was wearing his daily long kilt (top garment) over his short kilt, which would be our equivalent to underwear.[7] Obviously, cloak is used here to inform the reader that Joseph was not left totally unclothed.) The master's wife is very angry now. She tells a lie (There it is again! A lie, it seems to me, is a part of every sin.) to her husband about Joseph. After all, evil's philosophy is don't get mad when you can get even! (But God tells us justice is His business not ours (Nahum 1:2-3).) Joseph finds himself in prison, which doesn't seem very just, but had he submitted to temptation, he would have been separated from God by his evil and probably lost his life over his sin. God has spared him. Josephus tells us that Joseph "silently underwent the bonds and the distress he was in, firmly believing that God, who knew the cause of his affliction and the truth of the fact, would be more powerful than those that inflicted the punishments upon him" (p. 57).[3]

While in prison for some time, Joseph meets the Pharaoh's cupbearer and baker. Both of these men have disturbing dreams in the same night. God gives Joseph the ability to interpret their dreams. In three days the cupbearer would be restored to his position serving the Pharaoh and the baker would be put to death. Joseph asked the cupbearer to remember his plight before Pharaoh. (Now this man's memory is even shorter than mine!) It was 2 years before he thought of Joseph again! Like many of us, his main concern had been his own hide.

Pharaoh is the next one who has a night of dreams, dreams no one in his kingdom could interpret. The cupbearer finally recovers from his self-centeredness and remembers Joseph. Joseph is cleaned up and brought before Pharaoh. Immediately, he testifies to Pharaoh that God will provide the interpretation of his dreams. (Wouldn't it be great to have such courage and conviction? To just be able to speak right up to a potential enemy and testify for the Lord?) Joseph tells Pharaoh that his dreams are the same. (Note: Cows were believed to be symbols of Egypt's fertility.[10]) There will be 7 years of plenty to eat followed by 7 years of extreme famine. He adds that Pharaoh was given this dream twice because "the matter has been firmly decided by God" (Genesis 41:32). Joseph advises Pharaoh to put a wise, discerning man in charge and to establish a commission to take (tax) 1/5 of all the harvest grown in Egypt during the next 7 years in preparation for the time of famine. (Just think, that's 20% federal taxes on all income, even back then!) Thinking Joseph to be the wisest man he knows, Pharaoh put him in charge. He instantly went from prisoner to royalty! (Joseph had persevered. God had rewarded.) Joseph was dressed in purple robes and the people bowed down to him. He wore gold jewelry and rode in chariots. Joseph was 30 years old. He had done a lot of living since he was 17! (Don't most of us do a lot of living in the decade of our 20s?) Another of Joseph's gifts from Pharaoh was a wife, the daughter of Potiphera, priest of On or Heliopolis, which was the center of sun worship. Joseph is given an Egyptian name, Zaphenath-Paneah. This seals his Egyptian citizenship. His new position will be similar to that of a Prime Minister, technically he is a vizier. Egyptologists believe that Sesostris II was probably the Pharaoh at the time of the 7 years of plenty and his son, Sesostris III, succeeded him during the years of famine.[7]

The irony of all Joseph's gifts is that he is now thoroughly immersed in a pagan world -- marrying a pagan priest's daughter, governing a pagan society, living in pagan surroundings. First Samuel 16:7 says, "The LORD does not look at the things man looks at. Man looks at the outward appearance, but the LORD looks at the heart." God knew Joseph's heart. Joseph's heart belonged to God, regardless of his circumstances. Joseph goes dutifully about the task of storing large amounts of food to be preserved at least 7 years, allowing rotation. The lives of many will depend on him. Joseph and Asenath have two sons, Manasseh and Ephraim. The seven years of plenty come to an end and famine strikes all the Middle East. Joseph's father, Israel, hears that food is available in Egypt and sends his sons to purchase grain for the family. He does not allow Benjamin to go. After Rachel's death and Joseph's disappearance, Israel has become very protective of the only son he has left by his beloved wife, Rachel. These last 20 years have really aged Israel.

Food for Thought: How would you have felt when you went from the favored son to a prisoner? from a prisoner to head of the house of middle aristocracy? from a favored, trusted manager to a prisoner -- again? from a prisoner to the second in command of a country? How would you feel if everyone in your world was dependent on your management for his or her life?

January 19
Bible Readings: Genesis 42:6-45:15

Imagine how Joseph must have felt to find his brothers who sold him into slavery bowing before him, needing his favor! Just think of all the things that went through his mind! We know he remembered the dreams he had about their bowing to him. He wonders if they have had any guilt or shame for what they did. Or, are they just mean-spirited people to the core? He decides to test them. Accused of being spies, they freely give him much information about themselves and their father in an effort to relieve the Vizier's concerns, for they do not recognize this Egyptian. (Remember the pharaohs of this time look like the Israelites because of the close ethnic origin between Hyksos and Israelites.) Joseph sets a trap to discover their true hearts. Have they changed? Joseph puts them in custody for 3 days. Then he tells them one must remain behind in prison while the others go home and return with the youngest son as evidence that they are telling the truth. Not knowing that the Vizier understood Hebrew, the brothers discuss among themselves, "Surely we are being punished because of our brother. We saw how distressed he was when he pleaded with us for his life, but we would not listen; that's why this distress has come upon us." (Genesis 42:21) For the first time, we have insight into how Joseph felt during the kidnapping ordeal. He was just like we would be, scared to death and begging for mercy. How sad to think that he had reached a point in his life where so many of his own family disliked him. Joseph had certainly been humbled. As you recall, Reuben was the brother that wanted to put Joseph in the dry well so he could rescue him later. Also, Reuben was away when the other brothers sold Joseph. Now Reuben, the eldest, gets to say 'I told you so!' At this point, though, he is so scared that he reaps no satisfaction from having been right all along. Joseph selects Simeon to stay behind in prison. Some scholars believe Simeon was selected because he was the primary instigator of Joseph's capture and sale, and that Joseph seized the opportunity to let him experience prison for a while. (Remember Simeon and Levi murdered all the men in a whole town before Joseph's kidnapping.) We have no way to know for sure. (With brothers like these, who needs enemies?) Maybe Simeon was selected because he was the second eldest and Reuben had already shown his compassion and remorse, maybe not. Nevertheless, the brothers go home without Simeon. On the way, they discover the money they paid for the grain is in their sacks. Imagine their horror just thinking of the trouble they were in with the Vizier! Poor Israel has to undergo grief again for the possible loss of another son. Again, Reuben volunteers to personally protect Benjamin if Israel will just let him go back to Egypt to get Simeon. Israel refuses.

With the passage of time, hunger wins out. Israel's enormous clan risks being wiped out completely if they don't get food. Israel relents and lets Benjamin go with his brothers to get more grain. This time they carry twice the amount of money and many gifts in hopes their honesty will win points with the Vizier. Joseph is unable to control his emotions at seeing his beloved brother Benjamin again. When they leave to return home, Joseph gives orders to not only return each man's silver to his sack but to also place his special silver cup in Benjamin's sack. After they have gone a ways, Joseph sends the equivalent of the Egyptian police after them. After a search for the cup, they arrest Benjamin. All the brothers return to plead with the Vizier on Benjamin's behalf. (Keep in mind that Joseph's practices of divination with this cup occur before the Law of Moses forbidding such practice. Also, over the years, it became associated with magic, future telling, fortune telling, etc., and was no longer practiced as a way of interpreting God's Will.) This time Judah pleads with the Vizier to release Benjamin. (Recall in Gen. 37:2, Judah was the one with the idea to sell Joseph for money. Judah obviously realizes his previous sin and is repentant. His new heart now tries to protect Rachel's other son by offering himself as a slave. What goes around comes around; enslave others and be enslaved. The money gained from Joseph's sale fades unimportantly from history, but the guilt of their sin haunts the men for life.) Judah offers to stay in Benjamin's place so that his father will not have to suffer the loss of Rachel's last son. Joseph is finally convinced of their change of hearts. When he revealed who he was, he wept so loudly that the whole household heard him. Joseph immediately relieves their fears by telling them he has forgiven them because his plight had really been God's Will. Joseph knows he was sent ahead to Egypt to make preparations to save the lives of the starving Israelites. God has preserved His special people.

Food for Thought: Would you have been as forgiving as Joseph? Would the power of your position make you seek revenge on your captors? There is a lot to be said for maturity, but the journey to get there is very painful. Many never complete the journey of maturing in God's love and will for their lives. Where are you on the journey? Are you still growing spiritually? Are you actively working at growing?

January 20
Bible Readings: Genesis 45:16-47:28

The Pharaoh is so pleased to hear that Joseph's family has come that he invites them to live in Egypt. Joseph sends food, clothing, silver, and carts with his brothers to get the Israelite clan and move to Egypt. Evidence that Joseph remembers his brothers well is found in the last statement Joseph makes to them, "Don't quarrel on the way!" (Genesis 45:24) Can you imagine Israel's joy to learn Joseph is alive! God comes to Israel in a night vision or dream telling him to go to Egypt without fear. God assures him that the Israelites will return to Canaan to possess the land. Finally, God tells him Joseph will be with him when he dies. Think of the anticipation Israel had with each passing mile on the journey to Egypt! How hard it would be to control the overwhelming joy! Our Savior feels the same joy when we come back to him. Hebrews 13:8 says, "Jesus Christ is the same yesterday and today and forever." Finding Jesus is easy - (1) Confess to Him you are a sinner, (2) Believe He is the Son of God, (3) Accept Him as your Savior. Staying close to Jesus throughout your journey in life is hard. Every time things go well, we seem to be too busy to remember our relationship with the Lord. We always seem to make the time when trouble arrives. Joseph knew God and stayed close to God in good times and bad. God made all the difference in his life.

All the clan of the Israelites settles in the land of Goshen. This was by God's design. Goshen was on the outskirts of the Nile valley. It was land plush with vegetation and plenty of water, but it was far enough away from the mainstream of Egyptian life to maintain the separation of religious practices and the separation of the people. Israel (Jacob) is now 130 years old.

When the Egyptians have used all their money, Joseph requires them to trade their land and possessions for food. When that, too, fails, they sell themselves into slavery to the pharaoh. So Pharaoh owned everything except the possessions of the priests. In fact, the priests were supported with a budgeted income from Pharaoh. At the end of the famine, Joseph gave the Egyptians seed to replant their fields. The only requirement placed on them was that a 20% portion of all the harvest belonged to Pharaoh. You will recall the pharaohs of the Middle Kingdom wanted to endear themselves to the people because they no longer had the military might to control the people otherwise. Joseph found a way to do this; he garnered the love of the reigning Pharaoh and the people.

Food for Thought: Is revenge more important to you than forgiveness? Humbling from a lofty position is a painful experience. Do you think more of yourself than you should? Can you pray "God break me until I'm humble?" God can use the humble in a mighty way. The rest of us have to be broken until we get to be humble. Read 2 Chronicles 7:14.

January 21
Bible Readings: Genesis 47:29-Genesis 50

The death of Jacob brings an end to the age of the Patriarchs. Between Genesis and Exodus, the Jews numerically progress from being the family of God to being the people of God. Notice that Jacob, as he nears death, requests that Joseph put his hand under Jacob's thigh and promise to bury him in the land of his fathers. Some especially solemn form of taking an oath is evidently intended. An explanation might be that since the Hebrews spoke of sons as coming out of their father's thigh or loin, the oath was meant as a symbolic invocation of a man's descendants to maintain the oath and to avenge any violations of it.[11] Thus, Joseph not only promises for himself but also promises on behalf of all his descendants.

Jacob also adopts Joseph's two sons, Ephraim and Manasseh. You will later note in Exodus, and still later in Joshua, that there is no tribe of Joseph, but there are tribes of Ephraim and Manasseh. In a sense, Joseph receives the birthright or double portion of his father's estate. In Genesis 48:14-49:27, Jacob speaks of his two new little boys and his older sons. Jacob prophesizes that Ephraim, the younger brother of Manasseh, will actually be greater. History bears out that Ephraim was one of the largest and the most influential of all the tribes that settled in the northern part of Palestine (Holy Land). (Joshua was an Ephraimite.)

Jacob then speaks of his elder sons; in some ways, his words are prophetic. He mourns for Reuben who foolishly committed adultery with one of his father's wives. Reuben will not excel. History bears this out, for the tribe of Reuben settled on the east bank of the Jordan River outside the area that God had promised to Abraham. Simeon and Levi are also chided for their murderous action in the incident regarding Dinah's violation. Jacob says they will be scattered and they were. Levi, the priestly tribe, was scattered throughout the other tribes. The tribe of Simeon settled next to Judah but was ultimately absorbed by its larger brother tribe. Judah, the fourth son, is given the blessing. The reference to the scepter and the ruler staff remaining with Judah until "he comes to whom it belongs" no doubt refers to Jesus, who was of the tribe of Judah. The tribe of Zebulun is the land of Nazareth, Jesus' home town. It is, however, warmly commended for its valor in Israel's great battle with Sisera in the book of Judges. The tribe of Issachar was given a very fertile area on which to settle. Jacob here speaks of the future complacency that grew out of their favored location. Dan is spoken of as a snake that bites the horse's heels. The tribe of Dan in the books of Kings is the center of pagan worship set up to rival God's temple in Jerusalem. Gad is also predicted a violent future. The tribe will settle on the east bank of the Jordan River, and its area will be contested by many nations. Asher, which means fortunate, will settle in a fertile area known for its wheat, wine, and olive oil. Naphtali will be blessed in his life. The tribe will later settle in a fertile area around the Sea of Galilee. Benjamin is referred to as a ravenous wolf. In the last few chapters of Judges, the tribe is almost destroyed by its brother tribes because of evil that takes place in Benjamin. The tribe will always be small yet influential. Two of its more important sons were King Saul and the Apostle Paul.

As Jacob dies at 147 years old, the Bible speaks of his being gathered to his people. Although Genesis does not elaborate on the doctrine of Heaven and the after-life, the Patriarch clearly believed that death was not the end.

Food for Thought: How does the image of being gathered to your people make death less mysterious and more inviting?

Verses of the Week: **Exodus 4:12** "Now go; I will help you speak and will teach you what to say." **Exodus 14:14** "The LORD will fight for you; you need only to be still."

Establishment of a Nation

January 22
Bible Readings: Exodus 1-4; 6:14-27

During the time the Hyksos ruled, the pharaohs were inclined to show favor towards the Hebrews, their ethnic relatives. The Hebrews were a minority group, but their numbers were increasing steadily, just as God had promised Abraham. Verse 8 is generally thought to mean a king from the native Egyptians came to power bringing about the end of the Hyksos' reign. The two pharaohs believed to be responsible for the slavery and exodus of the Hebrews are Thutmose III and his son, Amenhotep II. They feared the increasing number of the Hebrews would allow them to overthrow the government and create their own reign as the Hyksos had previously done. Most likely the pharaoh who issued the order to kill all Hebrew baby boys was Amenhotep I.[7] The Hebrew midwives 'feared God' and would not commit this terrible sin. Apparently, the elders of the Hebrew community had taught their people well about their God and His expectations of them. Fearing God refers to the fear of the wrath of God. This is similar to a child fearing his father's anger when he has done something he knows is wrong. God is a God of love and life, but He is also a holy and righteous God who cannot tolerate or look upon sin. When the pharaoh couldn't get the Hebrew midwives to kill the baby boys, he commanded the Egyptian people to do so. The Bible does not say how many Hebrew boys were killed. It seems likely that the number was very large.

Exodus 1:11 reveals the ruthlessness of the Egyptians' fear of the Hebrews. The Hebrews became slave labor used to build the enormous fortified cities of Pithom and Rameses. These cities were located between Egypt and the Sinai Peninsula area (Rameses in the north Nile delta area and Pithom about 30 miles south and slightly east).[4] [Delta land is the land around the low-lying flood plains. The Nile flows north and the delta of the Nile is the northernmost portion.] These cities were located to provide protection from invaders via the caravan routes along the upper portion of the land connecting Egypt and the Sinai. The lower portion of this land was harsh desert area and not considered a feasible route for travel. Without the Hebrews, these building projects could not be completed. Note in verse 11, the pharaoh fears the Hebrews may escape.

God does not allow sin to alter His master plan. God said His people would inherit Canaan and He would see that it happened. God chooses the son of a Levite couple to lead His people to the Promised Land. Moses was born during the time of the order to kill baby Hebrew males. God preserved him in the most unlikely way -- adoption into the pharaoh's own household! The pharaoh's best education, military training, and leadership development was given to Moses. In essence, the pharaoh provided all the necessary skills and education for Moses to lead the Hebrew children out of Egypt. On one hand, Pharaoh is trying to kill off all Hebrew baby boys to prevent their increase and might while, on the other hand, he is preparing one of their mightiest and most revered leaders!

We wonder at how Moses so easily stoops to kill an Egyptian. While the Bible does not hint at Moses' adult background in Pharaoh's court, Josephus tells us that Moses was a mighty general in Pharaoh's army who fought valiantly against the Ethiopians. Josephus also tells us the Egyptians hoped Moses would be slain during one of his battles. Moses is given credit for having surprised his enemies by choosing what was not considered a route feasible for travel. He marched not by the sea but through the desert where he had to contend with many poisonous snakes. Brilliantly, he devised a plan to carry along a particular type of bird (Ibis) in cages. These birds attacked and killed snakes but were friendly towards humans. Moses may have entered into a marriage contract with an Ethiopian princess upon victory.[3] When Moses leads the Hebrews out of Egypt, we will see how this military experience was helpful.

Moses is 40 years old when he kills the Egyptian and becomes a fugitive. He flees to Midian in northwestern Arabia. (The sons of Abraham's wife Keturah settled Midian.) Moses marries the daughter of a priest (who is not a believer in God but becomes one in Exodus 18: 9-12) and has children. For 40 more years, Moses lives in Midian serving as a shepherd for his father-in-law. At the age of 80, God calls Moses to the task of leading an estimated 2.5-3 million people out of bondage and into the Promised Land.[12]

I am impressed by the way God's great leaders have responded to His call to obedience. In Genesis 22:1 God called Abraham to sacrifice Isaac, in 31:11 God told Jacob to increase his possessions and then prepare to leave for Canaan, in Genesis 46:2 God told Israel (Jacob) to go down to Egypt to live with Joseph, in Exodus 3:4 God called Moses to lead His people, and later in 1 Samuel 3 God called Samuel to reveal the end of Eli's family as priests. Each and every time, these great men of faith answered, "Here I am." When God calls you, do you answer, "Here I am; use me" or "Here I am; send me" or "Here I am; what can I do for you?" Or do you hide like Adam did?

Moses sees a burning bush at the base of Mt. Sinai. This bush is unusual because it is not consumed. Burning bushes are often seen in this area due to the dry brush and the intense desert heat; but the fire didn't destroy this one! When Moses approaches, God speaks to him and tells him that he is standing on holy ground. There is a song I am fond of:

> *We are standing on Holy Ground, and I know that there are angels all around.*
> *Yes, we are praising Jesus now, standing in His Presence on Holy Ground!*

Moses has a great call and a great destiny. After his great first response of "Here I am," his second response is certainly a let down. Moses makes up every excuse possible for why he can't do the job! Do we ever do that? Can

God use us just as we are? Does God call us even in our weaknesses? Exodus 4:13 is the kind of answer I would expect out of myself, "O Lord, please send someone else to do it." Moses is human, just like you and me. Moses sees his weaknesses, but God sees his strengths. One of my favorite verses is Proverbs 17:17, "...a brother is born for adversity."[1] I believe God provided a brother for Moses for this adversity. Aaron has strengths that offset Moses' weaknesses. Together they make an awesome team. God calls us to form teams. Even the Apostle Paul maintained constant companions in his travels and ministry. The Bible teaches that two cords are better than one and three are not easily broken (Ecclesiastes 4:12). Developing companions in the faith are ties that sustain us when the road gets rough and the times are tough.

As with Moses, God always equips us for the work He has called us to do. Moses is given three signs he can show the Hebrews to assure them God sent him: (1) staff becomes a snake, (2) hand becomes leprous, and (3) Nile water becomes blood. Egyptians feared all three. Snakes were worn on Pharaoh's headpiece as a symbol of his power and might over the people. Desert snakes were fierce, poisonous vipers that killed many desert travelers. Leprosy was a debilitating disease that literally destroyed fingers and hands, toes and feet before ultimately killing its victims. There was no cure and the disease permanently separated its victim from all civilization as an outcast. Lepers even risked being murdered because of the fears surrounding the disease. The Nile River was the source of all life and wealth in the Egyptian way of thinking. It was revered and worshipped. Having the Nile water turn into blood would have been repulsive. Life and livelihood, as the Egyptians knew it, would have been endangered. In short, no Egyptian spy would have created these three signs to trick the Hebrews.

Because the Hebrews believed a person's character was depicted by his or her name, Moses asks God for His name. God's reply is "I AM WHO I AM." (3:14). God's name does not have boundaries. It is open-ended in that you can finish the name in any way to fit any situation: I AM Provider, I AM Healer, I AM Savior, I AM King, I AM Creator -- I think you get the picture. God is everything. He cannot be limited by a finite word; He is infinite.

Having come to live with his wife's family, Moses' wife, children, and all his possessions belong to his father-in-law by marriage contract custom (refer to the lessons on Jacob and Laban). Moses goes to his father-in-law, Jethro (also called Reuel), and receives permission to leave. Before leaving, the LORD gives Moses one last insight into what was to come. "Israel is my firstborn son. Let my son go, so he may worship me. But you [pharaoh] refused to let him go; so I will kill your firstborn son." (Exodus 4:22) Moses had lived among pagans too long. His own son did not have the circumcision of God's covenant. According to Ex. 12:48 only circumcised males could partake of the Passover. Moses is in route to Egypt where the first Passover will occur. God stopped him in anger because Moses' own household was not prepared to enter the battle with evil. Zipporah, who comes from a pagan background, recognizes what is needed when Moses does not. To do battle with the enemy, you must first prepare yourself and your family.

Food for Thought: Exodus 1:6 tells us Joseph and all his brothers died in Egypt. Wonder why the brothers didn't request that their bodies be brought out of Egypt when the Hebrew children left?

January 23
Bible Readings: Exodus 5-6:13; 6:28-Chapter 8

As in Exodus 2:24, we are told again that God remembered the Israelites (Ex. 6:5). God saw the abuse they were receiving at the hands of the Egyptians and Pharaoh. Making them maintain the same number of bricks per day with no straw provided was an impossible demand. (Straw was mixed with mud and shaped into bricks. After a few days, the straw turned to slime and became the 'glue' that strengthened the bricks. Bricks were dried in the desert sun for weeks to harden.[7] Having to scavenge the Nile delta for straw would really slow down the process. Josephus even reports that the straw gathering had to be done at night.[3])

Interestingly, Moses doesn't ask for his people to be freed, only that they be allowed to take some religious holidays to worship God. Pharaoh was not about to let the Hebrews travel 3 days into the desert. That would put them out of Egyptian jurisdiction and, essentially, allow them to escape. Pharaoh reveals his true heart in 5:2, "Who is the LORD, that I should obey him and let Israel go? I do not know the LORD, and I will not let Israel go."[1] Egyptians worshipped many gods as a sort of preventative measure to ward off generalized troubles, i.e., drought, storms, etc. They did not believe in a god being interested and actively involved in an individual's life.[12]

Moses is discouraged because even the Israelites turn against him. But the LORD tells him He will make Moses 'like God' to Pharaoh. In other words, what Moses says happens. Moses and Aaron go before Pharaoh, no longer asking to leave but now demanding he let the people go to worship. Yet, we are told repeatedly that Pharaoh's heart was hardened and he would not listen. Like us, God gave Pharaoh many opportunities to see His mighty works and hear His word spoken. The seed of biblical truths can only grow on fertile ground (receptive hearts). Rebellion and stubbornness hardens the heart. Each time we don't listen but instead shut God out, turning our lives around becomes harder.

The 10 plagues begin. It is important to realize that each plague strikes at an Egyptian god.[7]

- Plague 1 - Turning the Nile to blood was an attack on Egypt's Nile god, Hapi. Moses proved to Pharaoh that the God of the Hebrews was more powerful than Egypt's god of the Nile.[5] Notice we are not told that this plague is ever reversed. The Nile was used for bathing, drinking water, crop irrigation, fishing, and papyrus industries, transportation and trade, food preparation, recreation, and represented, in general, the 'good life.'
- Plague 2 - The Egyptian also worshipped a frog-goddess, Heket. Heket was believed to protect pregnant women and defend homes.[7] Having their homes totally invaded by frogs was overwhelming evidence that God was in control, not frogs. When Moses called off the frogs, the frog-gods were piled into rotting, stinking heaps.
- Plague 3 - Pharaoh was considered to be a god, himself, so a plague of biting gnats (Josephus calls them lice[3]) that he couldn't stop was proof that the God of Israel controlled even him.
- Plague 4 - We are told in this plague that God separates His people from the Egyptians to clearly show His favor on the Hebrews. We do not know if the Hebrews, as well as the Egyptians, were subjected to the previous plagues, but Josephus, at least, says they escaped the first one.[3] Pharaoh's magicians [Jannes and Jambres (2 Tim. 3:8)]were able to duplicate the first 3 plagues. I don't even understand how modern magicians make buildings, people, and animals disappear, but I can accept that it is an illusion, a trick to lead me into their power over my mind. The magic of Pharaoh's magicians was no different. God specifically wants to show His people are 'set aside' and holy unto Him. In the fourth plague, biting flies invade the homes of the Egyptians. This time Pharaoh is not only put down as a god but also God's people (the Hebrews the Egyptians detested) are lifted up as an example of God's protection and love. The Egyptian god Uatchit, who manifested himself in the form of a fly, was under the control of the God of the Hebrews.[111]
- Plague 5 - Now, Pharaoh wants to let the Hebrews sacrifice to their God there in Egypt. Moses tells Pharaoh that Hebrew sacrifices would be detestable to Egyptians, so much so that the Hebrews might be killed. The Egyptians worshipped bulls, cows, and calves. The Hebrews would be sacrificing bulls.

Before and after each decision, God allowed Pharaoh ample time to think about the display of power from the Hebrew's God and to meditate on his personal response to God's demands. Each time Pharaoh rebels.

Food for Thought: Do we rebel against God? How many plagues (troubles) do we encounter before we depend on God? When we call on God, do we relinquish our throne (control) to God?

January 24
Bible Readings: Exodus 9-11:10

- Plague 5 - (cont.) All Egypt's livestock are plagued and die, including the bulls (Mnevis god), cows (Hathor god), and calves (objects of their worship).[7] God created animals. None is greater than He.
- Plague 6 - Boils break out all over the Egyptians in direct defiance to the Egyptian gods of healing, i.e., Sekhmet. The Egyptian gods were powerless.[7]
- Plague 7 - In Exodus 9:12, God hardens Pharaoh's heart. Why would God do that? Verse 16 explains God allowed this particular man to become Pharaoh in order that the power and name of God could be proclaimed throughout the world. Exodus 10:1-2 further explains that God wanted to make a lasting impression on His people, miracles that would always be remembered. Hail pounds the whole land of Egypt, except where the Hebrews live. The sky goddess, Nut, could not help the Egyptians. Crops (flax and barley) and trees were severely damaged. Animals and people caught in the hailstorm were killed.[7] The mighty Pharaoh admitted he had sinned and Moses stopped the storm. Immediately, Pharaoh went back to his old ways. Do we promise God anything during troubled times but quickly return to our old ways when trouble has passed? Are we really different from Pharaoh?
- Plague 8 - Now, even Pharaoh's advisors have turned against him. The locust swarms come and destroy what little vegetation was left in the Egyptians' land. The gods of agriculture (Isis, Seth[111]) have been overpowered.[7]
- Plague 9 - The plague of darkness struck down one of Egypt's more revered gods, the sun god, Amon-Re. Other sun deities included Amon, Aton, and Re.[7] The moon god, Thoth, was powerless, as well as the god of the stars.[5] But the Israelites walked in light (light represents God). This time Pharaoh is really mad and threatens to kill Moses. The Egyptian people are so afraid of the Hebrews that they willingly give them all their gold, silver, and clothing. God provided the Hebrews with all the resources they would need to make the tabernacle later in the wilderness.
- Plague 10 - Moses warned all the Egyptian people that the LORD was going to kill their firstborn sons at midnight. All firstborn sons would die, from slaves to royalty and from birth to elderly. Osiris, pagan god worshipped as the giver of life, is defeated.[111]

Food for Thought: God had already provided Moses with Plague 10 before Moses ever appeared before Pharaoh after Plague 9. Notice 11:1 in the NIV says, "Now the LORD <u>had</u> said to Moses . . .." So Moses gave the 10th plague warning immediately after Pharaoh's command that Moses never come before him again, except on threat of death. Other versions do not use the word "had" but use "the LORD said to Moses" or "Then the LORD said." If you remove the chapter heading and break between chapters 10 and 11, you can read it smoothly and realize that Moses says this final Plague warning to Pharaoh as Moses is leaving Pharaoh's presence.

January 25
Bible Readings: Exodus 12:1-51; 13:1-16; 12:1-51

- Plague 10 (cont.) Killing of the firstborn sons represented the final 'death blow' to all Egyptian gods. None could protect the Egyptian people, not even Pharaoh.

The commemoration of God sparing the lives of Hebrew firstborn sons and freeing the Hebrew people occurs on the 14th of the first month (Nisan, later renamed Abib[5]) of the Hebrew calendar. This usually occurs in our month of April. Called Passover to recognize the night the death angel 'passed over' the Hebrews' houses, Passover occurs before our New Testament Easter celebration of a risen Savior. Going to Jerusalem for a Passover festival was the last event in the life of Jesus before His arrest and crucifixion.

Passover is celebrated the day before the Feast of Unleavened Bread because the LORD instructed the Israelites to eat unleavened bread. There would be no time to wait for yeast (leavening) to rise before baking. The bread eaten at the Eucharist, Lord's Supper, Passover, or Communion, as the different religions call their services, is always unleavened bread (usually wafer-type) to remember the hasty preparations the Israelite children made for the great exodus, or leaving, of Egypt. New Testament services also eat it as a reminder of Jesus' body that was given for us. For 7 days the Hebrew children would be on the move and eat unleavened bread.

God instructed Moses that each family or group of Israelites were to kill a year-old lamb or kid (goat) that was not blemished in any way. They were to kill and eat only what they needed for that meal. The animal was slaughtered and the blood drained into a basin. After skinning, the carcass was roasted on a pole over the fire. No bones were to be broken. (Most of the time the Hebrews boiled their meat using the stock for soups and stews. There was no time for that nor was any food to be left over.) They were to eat with their shoes on and their long coats tucked in their belts. In other words, they had to be well nourished and prepared to move quickly. The blood collected from the animal was to be brushed on the three sides of the doorframes. At midnight, the death angel passed over all houses with blood on the doorframes. In many of the pagan religions, the firstborn son was sacrificed to a pagan god. But the Israelite firstborn sons were set aside or redeemed for God. (Redeemed means something of value was given to God in place of the firstborn son.)

The lamb that is slain symbolizes God's plan of salvation for all people. Jesus, God's firstborn son, was slain and, by His blood covering us, the death angel passes over us so that we have eternal life with God. The doorframes represent the entry to the home, or heart. We are to consecrate our hearts, set them aside, for the Lord. This is done by covering them with the blood of Jesus, which we do when we accept Jesus as our Lord and Savior. Like the sacrificial lamb, none of Jesus' bones was broken, which was unusual. The Romans often broke the legs of those crucified so they would be unable to push themselves up to breathe, then death would be quicker. The two men crucified with Jesus had their legs broken.

God commanded that Passover be observed every year as a permanent reminder. The firstborn male of all families and animals was to be dedicated to God.

After the widespread death of firstborn Egyptians, the mass exodus of the Israelites begins. We are told there are 600,000 men on foot besides women and children. A good estimate is 2.5-3 million people marching out with their possessions.[7] What a sight! Can you imagine the news coverage that procession would have today? (This would be like the population of Chicago marching with their possessions into the desert.) After 430 years, God's people were going home to the Promised Land.

Food for Thought: How would you feel if you lived in one of the countries where this enormous group of people is traversing through your land? curious? scared? The plagues probably occurred over 8-9 months. The news of these events was surely carried throughout the land by merchants. Would the "fear of God" be more real to you? Would you have a healthier respect for God's power and might?

January 26
Bible Readings: Exodus 13:17-15:21

God leads the Israelites by the desert route, the unexpected route not often traveled. The caravan routes that followed close to the sea would have many fortifications along the way and would go through Philistine country. While the Israelites were spending centuries in bondage, the Philistines had become a feared, warlike people. Most assuredly the Israelites would have faced battles from the Egyptians and/or the Philistines. God didn't want His people disheartened so He chose the desert route. (This is similar to Josephus' story on Moses' background as an Egyptian general.)

The desert environment was brutal. God showed Himself in the form of a pillar of cloud by day, which provided shade and lowered the temperature, and a pillar of fire at night, which provided heat and light for His people. In this desert environment, a cloud in the sky would be as rare as fire in the sky.

God tells Moses to camp at Pi Hahiroth that is on the southwest side of the modern day Bitter Lakes, located between Sinai and Egypt. The Red Sea in Moses' day extended much further inland leaving only a small connecting strip of land between Egypt and Sinai. Bitter Lakes is believed to be part of the old Red Sea bed.[4]

Pharaoh has his own economic crisis! Suddenly, his labor force is gone, industry is at a near standstill, prices will have to increase due to increased labor costs, and many of the consumers are gone, too! His answer: I want it back the way it was! He pursues the Israelites with a huge mobile force. Moses tells the people to not be afraid. Stand firm. God will fight for them. The pillar of cloud moved to the rear of the Israelite group. God took a stand between the Israelites and Egyptians. The Israelites had light and the Egyptians had darkness. I often pray for my children that they will be planted squarely and firmly in God's light forever. As children of the light, we have nothing to fear. (Josephus goes so far as to record that Moses told the people they could fly out of there if God Willed it![3]) The Red Sea parted and the Israelites crossed to safety. God then proceeded to actively fight the Egyptians. They became stranded in the bed of the Red Sea; Moses stretched out his hand and the waters drown them -- every one. Note in Exodus 14:31, we are told "the people feared the LORD and put their trust in him...." This, at least, implies that with all the other signs and displays of God's power, they still didn't have the faith to be God's own holy people -- until now.

Food for Thought: Wonder what the Israelites thought the first time they saw the sky on fire?

January 27
Bible Readings: Exodus 15:22-18

The Israelites travel to Marah that is on the northeast shore of the Red Sea. Marah got its name from the bitter water. They moved on about 12 miles south to Elim (traditional site). Arriving one month after their march began in Egypt, the Hebrew children are blessed with a plentiful water supply, but now they are out of food. Their grumbling stomachs are soon manifested as grumbling attitudes. In only three weeks, they have gone from trusting God and His servant Moses to complaining because they don't have all the food that was available in Egypt. (By now my patience would be exhausted. If I were God, I would have already yelled at them from Heaven about their whiney, ungrateful attitudes and then I would have singed their tail feathers with a few good lightning bolts!)

God is a patient God, though. He loves us in spite of ourselves. Just like the Israelites, we quickly forget our numerous blessings and God's miracles in our lives when we experience the smallest bump in the road. God sent quail for the Hebrews to eat. Quail migrate north to Egypt from the Sudan usually along the coast of the Red Sea around March every year. Their migratory flight makes them tired so they are easily caught. Now, the Israelites are in the desert and there isn't any firewood. So how did they cook their food? Well, they saved the dried animal wastes from their livestock. We may not like the idea of that, but if we had spent our lives living in and around deserts, we would think firewood was a luxury.

God gave the Israelites their daily bread. Manna was tiny, only the size of coriander seed. It had a sweet taste and apparently supplied all the necessary nutrients, as it was their primary food for 40 years! In recent years, popular explanation for manna is that it is the secretion of a small insect that feeds on the tamarisk tree. These yellowish-white balls melt in the sun. On the surface, this appears to be the origin of manna. But this form of manna is only found 3-6 weeks out of the year. God provided manna six days a week for 40 years with twice as much produced on the sixth day. Clearly, whether God used these secretions or anything else, manna was a miracle. He fed millions daily, except on the Sabbath when everyone rested. (Today, many people disregard setting aside a day for rest. If they aren't at work, then they work at home.) A gold (Heb. 9:4) jar of manna was saved as a 'museum piece' for future Israelites. Later it will be placed in the Ark of the Covenant, only to disappear when the Philistines capture the Ark.

The next stop is Rephidim where God instructs Moses to strike the rock and water flows out. (Jesus is the rock that man will strike but from whom living water will flow.) Moses is steadily moving the people in the direction of Mt. Sinai where God told him to worship (Exodus 3:12). (Traditionally, Mt. Sinai is believed to be in the southern tip of the Sinai Peninsula. In 1998, Cornuke and Williams determined the likely location of Marah, Elim, and Mt. Sinai to be across the Gulf of Aqaba on the western edge of the land of Midian (Saudi Arabia).[4]) Either way, Mt. Sinai required a long trek through the desert.

At Rephidim, the Amalekites attack. Joshua is named commander of the Israelite army. As long as Moses lifts his staff up to God, Joshua wins. The Amalekites would continue to be the enemy of the Israelites until they are totally defeated by men from the tribe of Simeon over 700 years later. This should be a lesson to all of us; God fights for us when we lift our hearts to Him. When Joshua's troops prevail, Moses builds an altar and gives thanks. We need to remember to praise God and thank Him for all the great and small victories He gives us.

The last time we heard about Moses' family was when they were all headed to Egypt together. Apparently, Moses sent Zipporah and his two sons back to his father-in-law's house at some point, probably before reaching Egypt. Jethro and Moses' family go to meet the Israelites in the desert. By this time, Moses is spending all day settling disputes among the people. (Imagine Chicago having only one police officer/judge for the whole city!) Jethro outlined a hierarchical process for governing the people. This process is still essentially the same today. We would do well to choose our government leaders based on the same three characteristics Jethro specifies here: God-fearing, trustworthy, and honest.

Food for Thought: What do you think life would be like if all government leaders had the three qualities named?

January 28
Bible Readings: Exodus 19-20; 23:20-24:18

Exodus 20, like Hebrews 11 and 1 Corinthians 13, is a chapter of the Bible with which every Christian should be intimately familiar. The Ten Commandments, the core of God's law, is not only mentioned here but is also repeated in Deuteronomy 5. The first four commandments deal with our relationship to God, the fifth our relationship to our parents, and the sixth through the tenth our relationship to our fellow man.

1. The passage begins with prefatory remarks that remind the people of what God has recently done for them. Keep in mind that the plagues of Egypt were designed to discredit the false gods of Egypt that the Hebrews had been unfortunately exposed to for centuries.
2. You shall have no other gods before me. The indication here is not just worshipping God as the supreme God but worshipping Him as the only God. The words "before me" are best translated as "besides me."
3. You shall not make for yourself any graven image. The commandment is directed against attempts to capture the likeness of God. Cole speculates that the reason for this command is that no likeness could possibly be adequate, and any image would convey its own misunderstandings.[13] For example, the bull that the Israelites set up while Moses was on the mountain conveyed the idea of strength and power, but it also conveyed the idea of virility and sexual power that led Israel to sin after worshipping the image (Exodus 32:6).
4. You shall not take the name of the LORD your God in vain. Originally the commandment seems to have referred to swearing a lying oath in God's name. It has also come to be understood as a command against using God's name in any frivolous or unwholesome manner.
5. Remember the Sabbath day to keep it holy. This command was designed to require men to rest from their labors just as God had done in creation. We are also called upon to remember God's faithfulness to us, and our responsibility to obey Him. Jesus said that the Sabbath was made for man; it serves him as a day of rest.
6. Honor your father and mother. This is one of the few commandments that contain a promise for those that keep it. The idea is that any society that cares for and respects the elderly who no longer can be valued for their productivity will respect all others thus creating a stable society. A youth who has no regard for his parents and feels no obligation toward them will doubtless have no feelings of charity toward anyone else.

7. You shall not kill. The Hebrew word 'rasah' is translated here as kill. It implies a violent killing of a personal enemy and is perhaps best translated as murder.[13]
8. 7 & 8 & 9. These commandments are fairly forthright but Hebrew word for steal means embezzle or secret stealing.
9. The final commandment is an injunction against an attitude of mind. Dwelling on what is not rightfully ours is the first step on the road to outward acts (adultery, lies, murder, and larceny).

Food for Thought: How do the Ten Commandments influence the decisions you make each day? Can you think of a situation during this week in which the Ten Commandments guided your decision?

> Verses of the Week: **Exodus 34:6-7** "The LORD, the LORD, the compassionate and gracious God, slow to anger, abounding in love and faithfulness, maintaining love to thousands, and forgiving wickedness, rebellion and sin. Yet he does not leave the guilty unpunished...."

Instructions for the Tabernacle

January 29
Bible Readings: Exodus 25-28

The tabernacle is not to be confused with the temple that is built during Solomon's reign. The tabernacle is a portable, tent-type structure for God to 'meet' with representatives of His people. The tabernacle was the place where God dwelled among the people. You might think of it as God's house in the neighborhood. By contrast, the temple was a massive permanent building in Jerusalem where men and women, both Jews and Gentiles, came to worship. In some passages, tabernacle is used to refer to the entire portable compound area generically rather than specifying both tabernacle and tent of meeting.[7] The concept of the tabernacle is unique in religions of its time. Pagan religions believed their gods lived somewhere beyond their land, e.g., heavens, sun, moon, ocean depths. But the idea that **the** God lived **among** His followers was strictly Jewish. The tabernacle proper consisted of the ornate tent and its furnishings. The surrounding courtyard included the burnt offering altar (A), washbasin (laver) (B), and ash pit, known collectively as the tent of meeting[14] or tabernacle of the congregation (KJV).[5] The tent of meeting actually wasn't a tent at all but rather an open-air courtyard fenced off by walls of curtains. The tabernacle sat in the west end of the rectangular tent of meeting. Today we use the north as our reference point to determine direction; the Jews used the east, the 'place of dawning.'[5] Notice that the only entry or door from the outside is located on the east wall. (Matthew 24:27 tells us that Jesus will come again from the east. Often cemeteries are designed so that bodies will 'face the east' in preparation for the Second Coming when they will rise to meet Jesus.) Basically, the entire tent of meeting is the size of one-fourth of a football field (about 150 feet long by 75 feet wide or about 450 feet in perimeter, depending on how a cubit is defined[7]). [I find it very interesting that a desert environment needed such an extremely well waterproofed tent. But again, the Israelites weren't supposed to spend 40 years in the desert and Canaan had plenty of rain.]

The tabernacle tent was divided into 2 rooms (See Graphic): the Holy of Holies and the Holy Place. The Holy of Holies contained only the Ark of the Covenant (F). The Ark of the Covenant, also called the Ark of the Testimony, was covered in gold with a lid called the Mercy Seat. The Ark was a chest that contained the stone tablets of the Ten Commandments (Ex. 25:22) and a jar of manna (Ex. 16:32-34), with Aaron's budding staff next to the ark (Num. 17:10). The Mercy Seat, made of solid gold, was the place where God **met** with His people, or actually the representative of His people -- the High Priest. Many Jews falsely believed that God "dwelled" at the Mercy Seat causing them to worship the ark instead of God (1 Sam. 4:1-11). God dwelled among His people in Spirit but was not confined in a box or lid.

The Holy Place contained 3 pieces of furniture: the Golden Lampstand (D), the Table of Showbread (C), and the Altar of Incense (E). The Golden Lampstand was a decorative Menorah,[12] a seven-branched lampstand made of gold believed to be the height of the Table of Showbread.[11] The priests filled it with oil each evening.[7] The lampstand provided the only light for the tent.[9] Almond blossoms and buds decorated the lampstand. Almond nuts were valued for their oil and their medicinal power. The flowers were the first to bloom in the spring, resulting in the Hebrew name for almond meaning 'awakening.'[5] Clear olive oil served as the fuel for the lamp that was to burn nightly.

The Table of Showbread, or Shewbread, was made of acacia wood covered with gold. The 3-foot long table was made of an insect repellent wood, also known as shittim or shittah. It was an orange-brown hard-grained wood[5] that grew well in barren environments.[15] The table was about mid-thigh in height and held the 12 loaves of bread (1 for each tribe of Israel) that were placed there fresh each Sabbath. The bread symbolized the spiritual nourishment God provided His people.[15]

The Altar of Incense was about waist high (3 feet).[15] The incense was to be burned as a fragrant offering every morning and every night. "From ancient times, the smell of incense and the rising of its smoke upward symbolized the prayers of the people going up to God" (p, 132).[12] The Altar of Incense was located in front of the veil separating the Holy of Holies from the Holy Place.

The veil separated the two rooms of the tent or tabernacle. Only the High Priest could enter the Holy of Holies, and then only once a year on the Day of Atonement for the people (the day a blood sacrifice was made for the sins of the nation). Figures of Cherubim were woven into the linen. Three colors were selected for the decorations on the veil: blue, purple, and scarlet. Blue generally represented the sky (heaven) and was often used to clothe the rich. The dye came from a particular species of shellfish making it difficult to obtain. Purple is always a symbol of royalty. It took 250,000 mollusks (shellfish) found only in the Mediterranean Sea to make one ounce of purple dye.[5] It is easy to understand why only royalty could afford purple clothing. Scarlet is often used in conjunction with sin -- "though your sins are like scarlet, they shall be as white as snow" (Isaiah 1:18).[1] Scarlet also symbolizes blood or life. The colors of the veil represent a King (purple) coming from Heaven (blue) who gives His life (scarlet) for the people. Jesus Christ fulfilled the story of the veil. When Jesus died, God tore the veil apart from the top to the bottom (from Him to the people) so that all people could have access to the Holy of Holies -- to God, the great I AM (Matt. 27:51).[1] Jesus, our High Priest, provided a way for mankind to commune with God by replacing the barrier veil with the veil of His blood. In the death and resurrection of Jesus, all believers could be priests before God and enter into His presence.

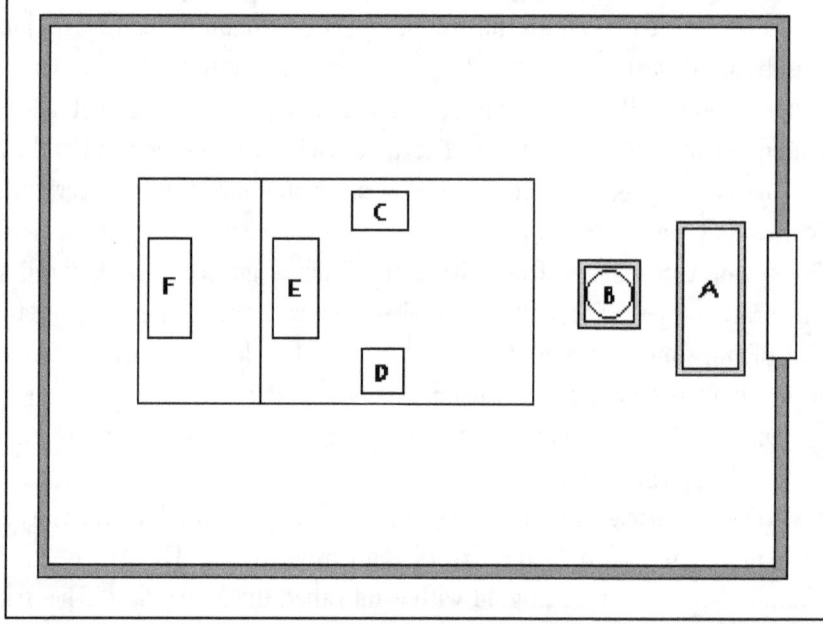

Food for Thought: Wonder what the Egyptians would have thought about the gold, silver, and clothing they gave the Hebrews being used for the tent of meeting and tabernacle of the <u>one</u> God of Israel? who lived among them?

January 30

Bible Readings: Exodus 29-31:11; 31:18 (continued from yesterday's lesson)

God leaves nothing to chance. He even gives detailed instructions on what the priests are to wear right down to their undergarments! First, the high priest put on a long white linen tunic that stopped about the ankles with matching short pants. These were his undergarments.[7] White linen symbolized the righteousness of God.[5] Over that layer, he put on the **robe** of the ephod. The robe of the ephod was made of blue (actually violet [13]) cloth that had tassels and bells around the bottom. The sound of the bells would keep the high priest from dying when he entered the Holy Place (first room of the tabernacle). It is believed that the bells allowed the people to hear the high priest performing his duties within the tabernacle and to know God had not struck him dead. In other words, their offerings had been accepted.[13] [Keep in mind, God knows everything and He knows what kind of problems Moses will find at the base of the mountain when he returns from just a 40-day absence (Jan. 31 lesson). The Israelites need continuous reinforcement that all is well. Does that sound like us?]

The ephod is placed over the **robe** of the ephod. The ephod contains the colors discussed earlier with all their symbolism and includes thin gold metal threads woven into the design. Gold symbolizes divinity.[5] Some scholars believe the ephod was a kilt-like skirt held on by two shoulder straps[12] (kind of like suspenders holding up a little boy's short pants). Other scholars believe the ephod was more of an apron-like vest that was open down the sides.[7] (Resembling the customer assistant vests in these large chain discount stores.) On top of the straps were the two stones, **each** containing the names of 6 tribes of Israel. Therefore, the high priest was always lifting up the 12 tribes of Israel before God. An ornate belt or sash was tied around this at the waist. A breastplate that contained twelve different stones hung by gold chains from the ephod's shoulder straps. Each stone had a different tribe's name engraved on it. The breastplate was really a highly decorated pouch or bag that hung over the high priest's heart and contained the national treasury -- the Urim (lights or revelation[3]) and the Thummim (perfections or truth[3]). Many scholars believe these stones had some type of symbols engraved on them to indicate yes or no, others believe one side was painted white and one side black. They were used to inquire God's response to questions posed. These questions were decisions that guided the nation's activity both in war and peace, contentment and strife.[5] (Wished I had a set of these!) Josephus gives an interesting viewpoint that the stones flashed bright lights or rays of light to determine God's response. But he also states they had quit shining 200 years before his written account due to "God having been displeased at the transgressions of his laws" (p. 93).[3] It's a shame we don't have them today.

The high priest wore a head covering or turban that is often referred to today as a miter. A gold plate was attached to the front that was engraved "Holy to the LORD." It was a constant reminder of the purity of God[7] and a foreshadowing of the Lamb of God (Jesus, our High Priest) who would bear the guilt of the people.

Ordination of the high priest and other lower priests was a sacred event to consecrate or set them aside as being dedicated to God. First, they went through a ritual washing as a symbol of cleansing themselves of the sinful world. Then they put on their priestly garments. Their sins were transferred symbolically to the bull by placing their hands on his head. Obviously, we have a picture of washing away the old way of life (basis of baptism), putting on the new way of life (following God's instructions), and having our sins forgiven (through the blood of Jesus who died for our sins).[12]

Offerings were of several kinds.

- Burnt offerings were totally burned on the altar (except for the skin [Lev. 7:8] or feathers and crop [Lev. 1:16]). These offerings were sacrificed twice a day for the sins of the nation. Individuals had to bring additional burnt offerings with their sin offerings for being unclean, i.e., touching a corpse. Burnt offerings signify the consecration of the people every day and night to the LORD.[11]

For most of us today, it seems rather strange to be ordained by putting blood on the right ear, thumb, and big toe. One scholar explained it as "the ear was touched with blood so it might hear the word of God, the hand was smeared with blood in order for it to perform priestly duties, and the foot was touched with blood so the priest would walk in the way of righteousness" (p. 130).[12]

- Grain offerings consisted of fine flour or cakes. (I've seen some cakes in my time that tasted like they had been sacrificed by fire!) Part of this offering was burned and the rest was used to feed the priests. Public grain offerings included the Showbread or bread of the Presence (God), the shock of barley used in Passover, and the wave loaves of bread at Pentecost.[7] These offerings were for the blessings from the earth.
- Peace offerings were in three forms: thank offerings, vow offerings, and free-will offerings. Thank offerings were given out of gratefulness for a special blessing[7] or for deliverance from a critical problem.[14] Vow offerings were made to seal a promise made to God, in other words, when entering a covenant or contract with God.[14] Free-will offerings were made out of a generous heart that just wanted to praise God. Peace offerings, as a whole, were very different from other offerings in that the person bringing the offering participated in eating the sacrifice.[14]
- Sin offerings were for careless or unintentional sins in general. They may be given for the sins of the whole nation or for an individual.[7]
- Guilt offerings, sometimes called trespass offerings, were given for specific crime sins.

Pretend you are an Israelite man for a year. Your family would have to donate one or more burnt offerings a year. Peace offerings would be donated for blessings and festivals (20-25/year or more). Sin offerings were made at most festivals, too. Guilt offerings had to be made for specific sins of family members. It seems to me you had to maintain a lot of animals in order to meet your obligations, especially since most had to be a year-old and unblemished. Now, that's per family! (Guess I know why they generally ate domesticated meat only at festivals.) Think of the herds required for sacrifices. Think of the acreage required to graze these animals in the desert!

An Israelite census could certainly get your attention. Bottom line was pay up or die! The ransom was half a shekel for anyone 20 years old or older. Talking about a cost of **living** tax! You'll, of course, recognize the need for this money to establish the tabernacle.

Food for Thought: Can you imagine what God's responses would be to our world's situations today? What would the Urim and Thummim say?

January 31
<u>Bible Readings: Exodus 32-34:16; 34:27-35</u>

Moses comes down from his third trip to the top of the mountain. (This is a steep, jagged rock mountain. I'm amazed an 80 year old man can climb this thing at all much less four times in quick succession.) [By now you have noticed the number 40 appears a lot in the Bible. It rained 40 days and nights, Moses was on the mountain 40 days and nights (twice), Israel wandered in the wilderness 40 years, and Jesus was tempted in the wilderness for 40 days. The number 40 may not be an exact number but rather a symbolic number to indicate a prolonged period of time.[13]] Moses knows what he will find. Indeed, God told him that these stiff-necked (stubborn and rebellious) people are eating, drinking, and playing (generally thought to be immoral activities[11]). In fact, Moses knows they have already broken their covenant with God (first and second commandments) because he had already been pleading with God not to kill them. Interestingly, God said to Moses, "Go down, because *your* people, whom *you* brought up out of Egypt have become corrupt...." (Ex. 32:7 - italics mine). I have a flashback to Adam saying to

God, "The woman *you* put here with me - she gave me some fruit from the tree, and I ate it." (Gen. 3:12 - italics mine) But on a closer comparison, I realize Adam was guilty of sin and trying to blame God. God, on the other hand, is pure and holy and makes His statement as an indication He has severed His ties with the Israelites. They weren't *His people* any more.

Moses' pleading for the people is a model for intercessory prayer that we can use. First, he reminds God of the negative impression God's wrath will have on the pagan nations watching the Israelites. Next, he reminds God of His promises (covenants) with Abraham, Isaac, and Jacob. Of course, God knows all of this, but He wants to hear that you are concerned about the example set before others. (How does your life appear to non-believers? Inconsistency between what you say and what you do?) And He wants to know that you remember His promises and treasure them enough to claim them in prayer -- to trust Him. God's promises are found in His word.

Aaron is like us; he just can't wait to excuse his part in this sin by telling a lie. Why that gold calf just jumped right out of the fire! Moses proves to the people that this god (idol) has no power. First, he burns it, then he grinds it to powder, next he scatters it over water, and finally, he makes the people drink it. The god they had worshipped was now nothing but a stomachache! Apparently, even this doesn't get everyone's attention because some are still "running wild." Moses' judgment was to put the violators to death by the sword. This is carried out by the Levites. (Remember Levi was one of Jacob's sons who killed the people of Shechem because of the sin committed against his sister Dinah.) The tribe of Levi becomes the religious judicial power for the Israelites. As with all sin, there were consequences to pay.

God repeats His promise from Exodus 23:23, but now He doesn't want a 'dwelling place' (tabernacle) among the people any more for concern He would destroy them because their sin was so great. Each time, God makes His promise to drive out six Canaanite tribes. These are called by name for a reason. Each tribe possessed a particular geographic region of Canaan. God was setting the boundaries of the Promised Land. God warns Moses to make no treaties with any of the people now living in Canaan. They and their gods are to be totally destroyed or the Israelites will become infiltrated and contaminated by paganism.

Because the Egyptians gave gold and silver jewelry to the Israelites at the exodus, it is probable that their ornaments were in the shapes or symbols of the Egyptians' various gods. These may have been a stumbling block to God's people, thus the golden calf. Regardless, all ornaments are now removed.

The very first tent of meeting is mentioned as a tent **outside** the camp where Moses met with God to seek His commands. (From this passage, we see that Joshua's relationship with God is growing stronger.) With Moses' pleadings, God relents and decides to dwell **inside** the camp, among the people. Because of God's great love for Moses, Moses is allowed to see God but not His face.

Notice that God, by His own hand, wrote out the first set of the Ten Commandments. The statement, "And he wrote on the tablets..." in Ex. 34:28 is referring to God per the *Complete Jewish Bible*. Other translations seem to indicate that Moses wrote out this second set of tablets based on verse 27 where God tells Moses to write. Either way, God wants our attention, obedience, and devotion. We are the ones who insist on doing it the hard way. —[Note: This is opposite to Deut. 10: 1-5.]

Food for Thought: See if you can identify Moses' 4 trips up the mountain. (HINT: The first one is in the Jan. 28th lesson.)

February 1
Bible Readings: Exodus 35:4 - 39:1

Today's reading focuses on the construction of the tabernacle complex. Keep in mind that there are two structures associated with this complex: an enclosure of linen curtains (portable wall) measuring 50 yards by 25 yards, and the inner tent. In many respects, this passage is a repetition of earlier material. So, instead of examining its literal message, let's try to understand what it is saying to us today. One obvious lesson is that to construct the facility many different types of material were needed. To build God's church today many types of gifts and talents are required. Examine the list of gifts in 1 Corinthians 12 and Ephesians 4 to determine in what ways you can contribute to God's tabernacle.

Another issue involves the gifts that God gives His people. Too often we think of ministers, missionaries, and others who have been called to full-time Christian service as the only ones possessing a special anointing of God. However, in 36:2 we find that God had called Bezalel, a construction foreman, and Oholiab, a craftsman, to serve Him. Not much is known about either man, but we do know that God gave them their abilities in their respective professions. Whether you are a housewife, truck driver, farmer, health care professional, teacher or any other profession in which you are called, God has given you abilities, and He expects you to develop them to their highest potential and to look for ways where you might serve Him and your fellow man through your unique gifts. We must realize that our lives and our abilities are God's gifts to us, and what we do with them is our gift to God. We must never be like the man in Jesus' parable in Matthew 25 who buried his talent, for when we do we lose these gifts of God. [Note: Jesus will come from the tribe of Judah, Bezalel's tribe. Golden calf worship (and possibly the anti-christ) will be associated with the tribe of Dan, Oholiab's tribe. Is this a picture of the spiritual battle of good versus evil? The Bible records "they made" everything in the tabernacle except one item: the Ark of the Covenant and Mercy Seat. Only Bezalel made the Ark. God knows the future and cannot be touched by sin.]

Another thought that emerges from the construction of the tabernacle is the need for separation. This facility was set apart from the rest of the camp. A six-foot high portable wall surrounded it and much of its function occurred inside a tent. Likewise, if we are to become the people of God, we must make time to get alone with our Father and pour out our heart to Him. We must be patient and wait silently before Him as he speaks to our heart and directs our mind. It is my prayer that these studies will not simply improve your knowledge of God's word, but that they will also inspire you to enter the inner sanctuary and to develop a meaningful relationship with God.

A final thought from today's passage is that there are great riches in the tabernacle of God. In Exodus 38:24-25, we are told that 2,195 pounds of gold and 7,550 pounds of silver were used in the construction. Today's value of just these two precious metals is well over ten million dollars. Likewise, there is great value in a relationship with God. We have comfort in sorrow, direction in times of confusion, strength in weakness, and hope in the midst of despair.

Food for Thought: John 1:14 says, "The Word became flesh and lived for a while among us."[1] God's plan of salvation for all people is still unfolding. What part does God want you to play?

February 2
Bible Readings: Exodus 39:2-40:35

Today's reading concerns the making of the high priest's garments, Moses' inspection of the tabernacle complex, the anointing of the implements and staff associated with the tabernacle, and the presence of God descending upon the tabernacle.

The high priest's garments were an impressive sight. Let yourself imagine the sight. His robe is of blue material covered by the ephod (vest or kilt-skirt resembling an overskirt with long shoulder straps) of blue, purple, and scarlet woven linen, glittering with pure strands of gold that have been woven into the fabric; onyx stones with the names of the tribes of Israel engraved into them were on top of the shoulder pieces; the breastplate with the twelve colorful stones representing the twelve tribes covered the chest; bells of pure gold softly jingled around the bottom of the robe; and a medallion of pure gold engraved with the words "Holy to the LORD" sparkled from the priest's turban. How breathtaking it must have been for these people who had few clothes that weren't off-white, brown, or black! How regal!

Verses 32-43 are basically the equivalent of a modern day building inspection. Moses compares what he sees to the blueprint design and material specifications that he had provided to the contractors. The third section,

40:1-33, concerns the dedication of the tabernacle. The main part of this ceremony is the anointing of the implements and staff of the tabernacle. In the Old Testament, to anoint something means that it was set apart for the service of the LORD. The oil is symbolic of the Holy Spirit. Just as the Holy Spirit's presence in a Christian's life causes him or her to be set apart from the world and to be looked upon with special favor by God, the anointing oil set apart these objects and people. They had a unique spiritual purpose in the religious life of the Jewish people.

In verses 34-38, we are provided with God's reaction to what the people had done. His approving presence is with them as a cloud (shade) by day and a fire (warmth) by night. I am reminded of Psalms 127:1, "Unless the LORD builds the house, its builders labor in vain."[1]

Food for Thought: Are you one of God's chosen workmen? One He has prepared with the skills to do the task? Myrrh was used in the anointing oil and frankincense in the incense. Think about how they are used here and compare this situation with the gifts the wise men brought the baby Jesus. What was the significance of the wise men's gifts?

February 3
Bible Readings: Lev. 8-10

Leviticus chapters 1-16 are a "How-to" guide on worship; most of its messages were given directly to Moses by God. The priests had to be set aside or consecrated for God. The consecration ceremony is completed in God's perfect time -- 7 days. Anointing oil is sprinkled 7 times on the altar to consecrate or set aside for God. Then the blood of the sacrifice is put on its base to purify it. The Israelite nation was consecrated for God in Exodus 19:10-15 and 24:5-8 by being washed with water and sprinkled with the blood of the sacrifice. The Israelites and God were in a binding contract. The priests and God were in an even more restricted contract, as Nadab and Abihu find out.

All of the ceremonies of the Old Testament's chosen people dramatize God's plan of salvation. In the New Testament, God's chosen people are those who repent of their sins and accept Jesus as their Savior. The shed blood of Jesus Christ atones for our sins. We can now meet God face-to-face and not die. Indeed, we have been adopted into God's family, co-heirs with Jesus, our Lord. As a result of belief in Jesus as Lord, Christians are anointed with the Holy Spirit who fills their hearts and minds with the love of God. In 1 John 2:20, John tells us that the Holy Spirit also allows us to know the truth, and John 8:32 says the truth will set us free of the bondage of sin. Jesus reminds us that if we are his disciples then we will follow His teachings (John 8:31) because we are now the temple of God who dwells <u>in</u> us. God fiercely protects His sanctuary from unauthorized fire. The Apostle Paul urges us to offer our "bodies as living sacrifices, holy and pleasing to God" (Romans 12:1). My pastor says the problem with those living sacrifices is they crawl off the altar! Is your body a living sacrifice to God? Or have you crawled off the altar? We can't crawl far enough to escape the love of God. Our God is a jealous God who wants to love and commune with us all the time. We don't escape His watchful eyes. He knows our secret sins, but He also knows our secret joys. The joys we share with God are mountaintop experiences. The radiance that shines forth should be a witness to those we meet. With the love of God, we need never fear death. We have eternal life in His presence.

We have seen the Israelites give willingly their time, money, and skills. What do we have to offer God? What sacrifices have we made to God? Have we given sacrificially? Is God pleased with our offerings? Or do we have a ready list of excuses?

Food for Thought: Where do you think they got all that wood to keep the altar fire burning? Surely, there isn't much wood in the desert. (Waste products can't be used on the altar for fuel. God's instructions, to wash the inner parts of the whole burnt offering, were to get rid of all fecal material.) Wasn't it like a dry sauna with all those priestly garments on in the enclosed Holy Place and a roaring fire outside, all in a desert? Ezekiel 44:18 states priests "...must not wear anything that makes them perspire."[1] This was the reason for linen garments.

February 4
Bible Readings: Numbers 3:1-13; 8:5-18, 19-26; 7-8:4

Moses, Aaron, and their sister Miriam were all from the tribe of Levi. Aaron has four sons, two of whom have now died without leaving any sons. God chooses the Levite tribe to do the work of the tabernacle and assist the priests and high priest. As New Testament Christians, this should be an emotion-packed picture of what we, God's people, are called to do. We have been set aside (consecrated) as the Lord's own. We have been anointed (filled) with the Lord's presence. God has chosen us to do the work of the tabernacle (God dwelling among [in] us). We are to assist the church spiritual leaders (priests, pastors, vicars, rectors, etc.) in carrying out the work of the Lord. The first century church selected deacons to be responsible for overseeing this work so that the preachers/teachers would be free to spread the gospel. In the twenty-first century, we recognize that time is growing very short and **all** are called to work. In God's perfect plan, those who had labored for 25 years at 'carrying the load' of the church work could now provide wisdom and assistance to those 25-50 year olds who should be 'carrying the load' and 'performing the services.' In our imperfect world, it seldom happens that way. In fact, most churches couldn't maintain many of the services if those workers over age 50 and those who were female were removed from their positions.

After the Levites were purified, God required the congregation to lay their hands on the Levites -- in essence, giving them a spiritual blessing. In ordination ceremonies today, we still practice the laying on of hands where a prayer of blessing is offered to God for the one(s) who has (have) received a special call from God to oversee His work and to lead His people.

The book of Numbers receives its title from the census that is ordered in chapter one. It records the major events of the Israelites' 40 years in the wilderness. When we get to Numbers 2 (February 6), we find that the order of presentation of offerings follows the order of encampment of the tribes around the tabernacle. God's tabernacle is always in the center of life. East being the primary direction in looking forward to God establishing His Kingdom (east also being the direction of the Promised Land), we start with the tribes camped on the east and continue clockwise around the tabernacle. In chapter 7 (second longest chapter in the Bible[12]), we see where each tribe brings their share of offerings to the Levites, one tribe per day for 12 days. Note the importance of the location of the tribe of Judah that is first (east). Judah received the blessing from Jacob (Israel) and will be the tribe of Jesus' lineage. Figuratively, Jesus leads the way in bringing His offering (His shed blood) to God. Next, we have the tribes from Leah's two youngest sons, Issachar and Zebulun. From the south, the tribe of Reuben (the compassionate son), Leah's eldest, is the leader. The last tribe descending from Leah is that of Simeon, last because of his violence at Shechem. (Of course, the tribe of Levi has been required to give their lives in service to God; therefore, no additional offering is needed here.) The tribe of Gad, known for their bravery, follows. The leader of the west encampment is the tribe of Ephraim followed by the tribe of Manasseh, both from the sons of Joseph. The tribe of Benjamin completes the west encampment. All the tribes descended from Rachel are located on the west. Then the tribe of Dan leads off for the northern encampment. Followed by the tribes of Asher then Naphtali. Dan and Naphtali were sons of Bilhah (Rachel's handmaid). Asher was Zilphah's youngest son (Leah's handmaid).

Food for Thought: God used ordinary people to dedicate offerings for the spiritual needs of His church. Churches today have offerings and pledges dedicated to the special needs of the church. Is God calling you to provide for a special need of the church?

Verse of the Week: **Numbers 11:29** "I wish that all the Lord's people were prophets and that the Lord would put his Spirit on them!"

Establishment of a Nation

February 5
Bible Readings: Numbers 1-2; 9:1-12

Today's reading concerns issues related to uncleanness during religious holidays and matters related to a military census and the distribution of troops during a march.

Keep in mind that the concept of being unclean relates to unholiness as well as hygiene and was a way for the ancients to guard against contagious diseases. A pus-type body emission could signal something relatively mild or very severe; medicine had not progressed to a state of making an accurate, immediate diagnosis. Likewise, a person who had become unclean through touching a dead body was kept in seclusion until it was evident that a contagious disease had not caused the death. In today's reading, God allows those who are unclean during Passover to observe it at an alternate date. These events were as important in the life of the Old Testament believer as church services are in the life of the New Testament believer.

Troop Designation	Troop Strength	% of Total	Commanding General
1st Division Judah	74600	12.3	Nahshon
2nd Division Issachar	54400	9	Nethanel
3rd Division Zebulun	57400	9.5	Eliab
Corps of Judah	186400	31	Nahshon
1st Division Reuben	46500	7.7	Elizur
2nd Division Simeon	59300	9.8	Shelumiel
3rd Division Gad	45650	7.5	Eliasaph
Corps of Reuben	151450	25	Elizur
1st Division Ephraim	40500	6.7	Elishama
2nd Division Manasseh	32200	5.3	Gamaliel
3rd Division Benjamin	35400	5.8	Abidan
Corps of Ephraim	108100	17.9	Elishama
1st Division Dan	62700	10.3	Ahiezer
2nd Division Asher	41500	6.8	Pagiel
3rd Division Naphtali	53400	8.8	Ahira
Corps of Dan	157600	26.1	Ahiezer
Army of Israel	603550	---	Joshua

The second part of our reading concerns a military census of the various tribes. Those counted are able-bodied men of military age. The above table organizes the number according to tribes. The various tribal divisions have been grouped according to the military corps to which they belong. You will note that the corps of Judah, which travels first in the order of march, and the corps of Dan, which brings up the rear, are the two largest corps. This order is consistent with military practice which guards against frontal and rear attacks by being strong in those areas.

Food for Thought: Make a note of Dan's strength and numbers. Before we leave the Old Testament, the tribe of Dan will be very small. Dan is thought to play a distinctive role in the end times. Because the tribe of Dan is not counted among the sealed 144,000 in Revelation 7, many believe the antichrist will come from this tribe. But for now, Dan uses his great strength to guard the back door of God's chosen people through the wilderness. Did Dan change from depending on God to depending on his own strength?

February 6
Bible Readings: Numbers 3:14-39; 4; 3:40-51

Just as the Levites are set aside to serve God, their census will be separated from the other Israelites, too. The Levites are the smallest clan with only 22,000 males one month old and older. All the other Israelite clans had counted males 20 years old and older for determination of available military draftees. The Levites are solely responsible for the care of the LORD'S house and furnishings, as well as the nation's religious teaching. Numbers 8:24 states that a Levite had to be 25 years old to work at the Tent of Meeting. So, why count males younger than 25? Remember, God declared the firstborn of every Israelite woman and animal belonged to Him as a result of being spared their lives at Passover. Numbers 3:12 says that God chose the Levite clan to serve him in place of the firstborn males of Israel. Numbers 18:16 states every firstborn male is to be redeemed at one month old. [Leviticus 12 states the laws for purification after childbirth. The new mother is 'ceremonially' unclean (can't participate in an activity of a holy nature) and anyone touching her is unclean (Lev. 15:20-23) for 7 days. After that, she must still wait 33 more days before purification rites can be performed. Purification ceremonies were designated for cleaning and purifying one before God and man.[5] Water in the desert is a scarce resource. Therefore, this was an opportunity to cleanse body and soul. The nursing baby would be 40 days old or approximately six weeks old and, therefore, purified mother and redeemed baby were accessible to the public.] Once counted, the Levites were short 273 males to equal the number of firstborn Israelite males. To redeem 273 sons, Moses had to collect five shekels for each one. This money was given to Aaron and his sons to support their families. Redemption is simply defined as one person exchanging something of value with another person in order to receive something they want or need. For instance, we redeem coupons at the grocery store. You give them the coupon and they give you a lower price on the food item. The redemption of the firstborn meant money was given to buy back the firstborn son from the LORD's service. In a way, we do that today. We donate money to the church to pay for the church services we want or need in place of ourselves having to perform it all.

Levi only had 3 sons: Gershon (or Gershom), Kohath, and Merari. The Gershonites were assigned to care for and transport the curtains and their ropes. They were to camp on the west side of the tent complex. The Kohathites were to transport the most holy things. They camped on the south side. Finally, the Merarites took care of the framework, crossbars, posts, bases, tent pegs, and ropes associated with erecting the structure. They camped on the north side. Aaron and his sons were responsible for packing all the holy items, including the anointing oil and incense. They camped on the east side near the entrance to the Tent of Meeting (See graphic.). The Levites camped around the tent complex not to protect the holy complex but rather to protect the people. Anyone getting too close to the holy tent and its furnishings would die.

The process for packing the holy items is interesting. The Ark is covered first by the Veil, then by a waterproof covering, and finally a blue cloth. The blue cloth clearly warned all those around it that it was holy or heavenly and was not to be touched. Jesus is represented by the Veil and stands between God and us (represented by the Mercy Seat of the Ark). The Table of Showbread is covered with a blue cloth signifying holiness; then after the dishes used for offerings were placed on it, a scarlet cloth was placed over everything, signifying Jesus' blood sacrifice. The other furnishings of the tabernacle were first covered with blue cloths and then covered with the weather protecting hides. The Altar of Burnt Offerings was covered in a purple cloth (royalty) that foretells of the time when Jesus, our King, would be sacrificed for our sins. On top of the purple cloth was placed the covering of hides. What a procession! Holy items covered and carried on poles, as well as an Ark displaying its blue covering and carried by poles, were all being moved along with God's people. One wrong move, one touch and the perpetrator would be dead. Second Samuel 6:6-7 tells of just such an incident. The Kohathites had received an awesome and stressful assignment. God even warns Aaron and Moses to oversee this group carefully to keep them all from being killed. The largest family of the tribe of Levi was the Kohathites.

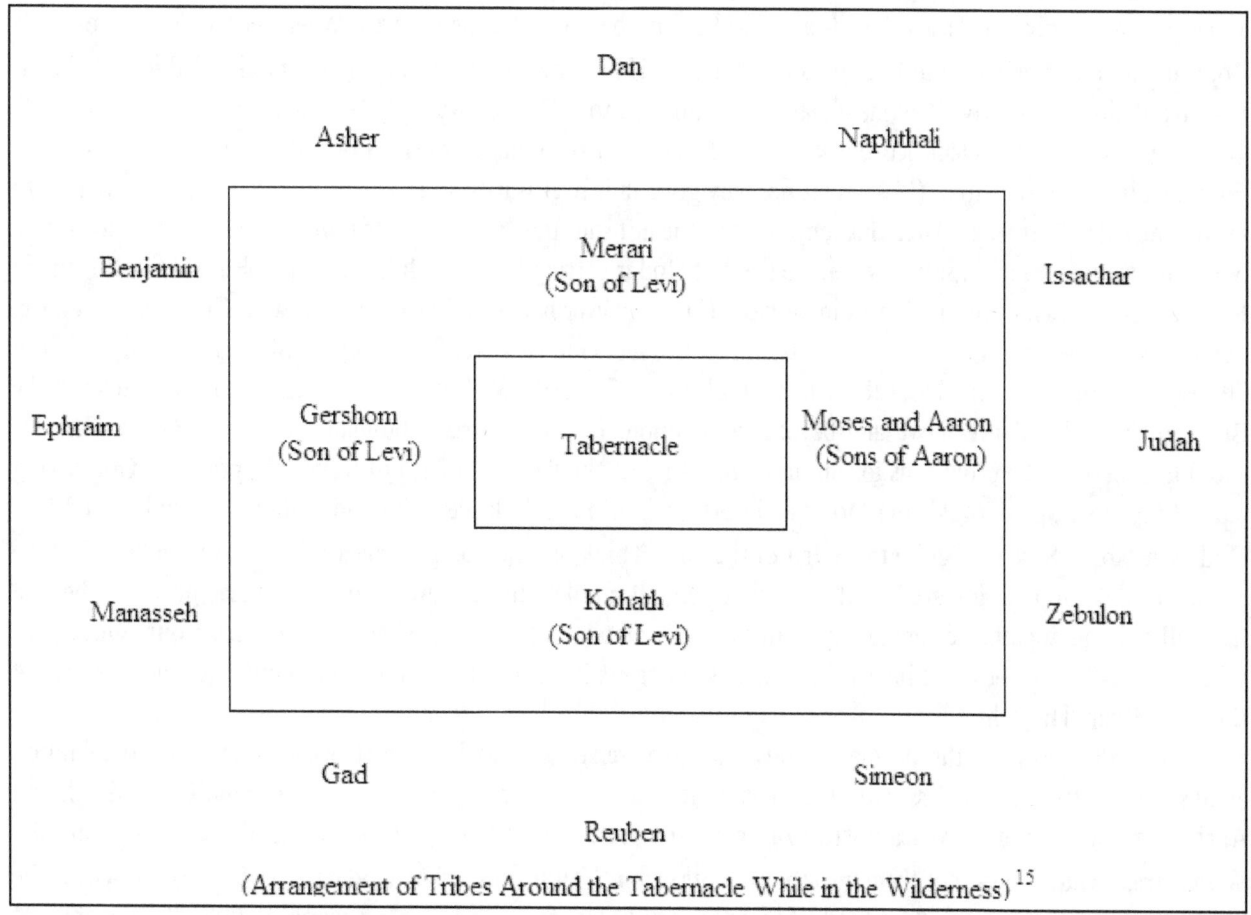
(Arrangement of Tribes Around the Tabernacle While in the Wilderness) [15]

Food for Thought: How would you feel if your first job was to carry a holy item? Do you wonder how many died as a result of touching the tabernacle items -- even accidentally?

February 7
<u>Bible Readings: Numbers 10:1-34; 9:15-23; 10:35-36; 11; Ex. 40:36-38</u>

God instructs Moses to develop a simple, but very effective, communication system. Two silver trumpets were made, which most likely produced two very different levels of sounds. A system of signals was developed. Many functions of our military and daily lives involve similar systems, e.g., flag signals to planes and telegraph signals. Millions of people were led through the wilderness by two silver trumpets!

Only the priests are allowed to blow the trumpets. In Revelation 8-11, we find the 7 trumpet judgments. Each angel sounds his trumpet and the judgment is announced. [All of these chapters in Revelation are fascinating, but I urge you to take the time to read Rev. 11:15-19 **after** reading Num. 10:1-10.] Angels are God's created servants; the Levites were God's chosen servants. Both have the authority to announce God's judgments. Rev. 11:19 reveals the role of God's trumpets being sounded - something important was happening. In our passage in Numbers, God commands that the trumpets are to be sounded to announce danger, joy, atonement and praise. We are also told that when God hears the sound, He remembers and He rescues His people from their enemies. Have you ever sent out a trumpet call to God when you were in danger from your enemies? Enemies are seldom of the flesh and blood type. More often they are spiritual. Second Corinthians 10:4 tells us our weapons have divine power to demolish these strongholds.

Moses prevails on his brother-in-law to stay with the Israelites to be a human guide. Many have speculated that

Moses' faith in God as their guide had weakened. On the contrary, Moses recognized the value of skills, knowledge, and experience. Hobab had spent his life as a shepherd in this particular desert area. Wherever God's pillar of cloud stopped, Hobab knew where to find grass and water.[11] Hobab was fulfilling the mission God called him to do. As Hobab did, do we often say, "Not me - I have something else to do," or do we say "Here I am, send me!"?

The Ark of the Covenant led the way with God's pillar of cloud overhead. For 3 days, the Israelites walked, carrying all their possessions. (It is easy to see why gold and silver is used so extensively for jewelry. It was easier to secure and carry that way.) After this long walk in the hot sun, the "rabble" or troublemakers began to complain. Now they wanted meat. (It seems evident to me that God is getting fed up with these people. He sent fire this time.) Even Moses was sick of them. He was in despair. Have you ever had a similar discussion with God? I know I have, and that's always when God lifts my spirits and carries me. God carried Moses, too, by placing the Holy Spirit in 70 of Israel's finest leaders. Note that 70 is a multiple of 7 (7x10). Multiples of seven are used many times in the Bible to show abundance above and beyond completion. In other words, abundance that only God's blessings could give beyond the provisions for an individual's need. Numbers 11:17 is **not** to be interpreted as God taking part of the Holy Spirit away from Moses and putting it into the 70 leaders. Instead it should be understood that God used Moses' Spirit to ignite the Spirit of the 70.[11] Think of a candlelight service. From one candle, all of the candles of the congregation are lit. At the conclusion, all candles burn brightly, none is dimmed or diminished. In fact, all shining together dramatically multiplies the amount of light provided. Do we share our Spirit with others? or, are we greedy and hoard the Spirit, keeping its light to a minimum? God multiplies the blessings of those who share His light.

Why did Moses tell the people to consecrate themselves? It was because they had sinned by complaining against the LORD. Nevertheless, God promises meat -- so much they'll be sick of it! Quail migrate in March and April from the interior of Africa north to Europe and are often seen along the coastline of the Sinai Peninsula. With a great wind, God swept them into the Israelite camp.[11] Think how many God had to provide in order for the least amount gathered to be 60 bushels! (If there were only 1.5 million **adults**, this would be 90 million **bushels** of quail.) Again God took a natural event and made it into a miraculous phenomenon. They had so many that they spread them out around camp to dry in the desert sun (for preservation of the meat). God was so upset with their greed and gluttony that He struck them with illness. The Bible doesn't tell us what kind of illness, but God usually makes the punishment fit the crime. My guess is it was gastrointestinal tract illness. A person would quickly die in the desert if rapid dehydration occurred from vomiting. (Read Psalm 78:26-31.)

Food for Thought: Do you depend on God to provide your daily bread or are you greedy? Greed is a stench unto God. Dead quail and dead people surrounded the Israelites. Both the object of the greed and the greedy decayed. The Bible tells us to store up treasures in Heaven. What do you spend most of your time doing? Talking about? Thinking about? Where does your heart lie -- with God or with the treasures of mankind?

February 8
<u>Bible Readings: Numbers 12-14</u>

Moses' brother and sister, Aaron and Miriam, are now jealous of Moses' special relationship with God. They start out complaining about Moses' Cushite wife. Cush was a land just south of Egypt composed of a portion of modern Sudan and a portion of modern Ethiopia. Most likely Cush, the son of Ham and grandson of Noah, settled this area. A review of the January 22nd lesson will point out a good possibility for Moses having a Cushite wife. Josephus tells us that Tharbis, daughter of the King of Ethiopia, fell deeply in love with Moses while watching him lead the Egyptian army against the Ethiopians. She sent her servant to Moses asking him to marry her. (Now this was a liberated woman!) Josephus states Moses agreed to this contract marriage provided she deliver the whole capital city into his hands. The story goes that she did, and he did. Thus, Moses acquired an Ethiopian wife.[3]

The Bible doesn't recount Moses' life during his years living in the king's palace. Therefore, the Josephus story is definitely a good explanation for Moses' Cushite wife. Assuming Josephus is right, Moses would have two wives: the first being Tharbis, and the second being Zipporah. Zipporah, as a daughter of the priest of Midian, may have been a contract wife herself. Exodus 2:21 says simply that "Moses agreed to stay with the man, who gave his daughter Zipporah to Moses in marriage."[1] This 'agreement' may simply have been a contract for Moses' labor in exchange for room and board and a wife. You recall this same type of contract was arranged between Jacob and Laban.

Why did God punish Miriam for complaining against Moses but not Aaron? This seems like a double standard! But, there are two possible answers. First, Aaron was the High Priest. He would have been unclean and unfit to serve God if he had been plagued with leprosy.[16] Additionally leprosy required banishment outside the camp. For Aaron to be publicly banished, even for a short period of time, would have permanently undermined his credibility as the one standing between God and the Israelites. The Israelites would have rejected his leadership. Second. Miriam was probably the leader or instigator in this family rebellion, as noted by her name coming first and the feminine form of the Hebrew verb that is used in verse one. We know Aaron was weak in the face of rebellion, based on the golden calf incident.[11] Nevertheless, Miriam becomes a leper. By God's command, she was sent outside the camp for 7 days. She had plenty of miserable time to think about her sin and its consequences.

After more than a year, the Israelites arrived at the edge of Canaan, their Promised Land. God commands Moses to send spies, one from each tribe, into the land. (God knows His people well. They had to be equally represented on this mission to avoid jealousy and distrust.) The spies are to scope out the land and the people. Moses needs to prepare for battle. The spies are gone a long time, as represented by the 40 days. They explored all along the Negev (southern part of modern Israel called the Desert Zin here), the west side of the Dead Sea (referred to as the Valley of Eshcol and Hebron), and as far north as Hamath (present day Syria). All this land is currently found in Israel, Gaza Strip, West Bank, Lebanon and Syria.[4]

Only Caleb (from the tribe of Judah) and Joshua (from the tribe of Ephraim) bring back positive reports. The other spies are too frightened by the size of the inhabitants. Instead of trusting God to deliver this land as He promised, the Israelites refuse to enter the land. God has had enough. He is ready to wipe out these people. This is the second time that God wants to make Moses into a great nation (first time is in Exodus 32:10). But, once again, Moses pleads for the people to be spared (Numbers 14:13-16). He uses the same intercessory prayer strategy that we saw in the January 31st lesson (Exodus 32:11-13). Then he concludes by quoting the LORD Himself! (Numbers 14:18 is quoted from Exodus 34:6-7.) (Don't you just hate it when your kids quote you at a time when you really want to punish them? It just takes the steam right out of your anger.) But sin has its consequences and God decides the present generation is condemned to the wilderness for 40 years, one year for each day spent in spying out the Promised Land. Only Caleb and Joshua were to be spared. This judgment also meant the innocent children, and even those who were not yet born, would suffer the consequences of their parents' sin -- wandering in the wilderness. This is what God meant when He said He punished the children for the sins of the father to the third and fourth generation. Being a parent is a major responsibility, not only in setting a righteous example for your children but also in leading a life as free from sin as possible to spare your children the impact of your consequences.

Food for Thought: Numbers 14:22 says the Israelites had tested God 10 times. Can you identify those 10? [HINT: The Talmud, a Jewish commentary on the law, says there were exactly 10 times. Only one has not been in our previous lessons, Psalm 106:7. Start back at Ex.14 on Jan. 26 lesson and identify each one.]

February 9
Bible Readings: Numbers 16-18

Immediately upon hearing God's judgment on the Israelites, the people start a series of rebellions. (Doesn't this sound like the reactions of today's people to judgment?) First, they decide to invade Canaan anyway. They are soundly defeated with many killed. Second, a Levite and some Reubenites instigate the 'City Council' to rebel. Moses puts them to the test -- everybody is to offer incense to God and God will sort them out. (Now you would think they would have learned something from Nadab's and Abihu's deaths in Leviticus 10:1-2.) God wants to kill the whole nation except Moses starts pleading again. (I know why the Bible says Moses was the most humble man on Earth; he spent all his time facedown on the ground begging for these people!) His pleas in Numbers 16:22 remind me of Abraham pleading for the people of Sodom and Gomorrah. God decides to show the people the consequences of sin. He uses a very unnatural event. The earth opens and swallows the rebels. There is no reason to believe that this is an earthquake. There is no quaking, pre- or post-shocks, no endangerment to anyone but the rebels, and fire came out to consume the council members. This was, beyond doubt, a holy judgment.

God's wrath on the people is in the form of a plague. At Moses' command, Aaron grabs his incense censer and runs into the middle of the crowd to atone for their sin. Numbers 16:48 says, "He stood between the living and the dead, and the plague stopped." This is a picture of Jesus, our High Priest, standing between the living (believers) and the dead (non-believers), and the judgment of our sin stopped with Him as He atones for us

God then instructs Moses to take a signed staff from each tribe plus Aaron's staff and place them in front of the ark. The next day Aaron's staff had buds, blossoms, and almonds! The people are so convinced, they fear for their lives. God tells Moses to keep Aaron's staff in **front** of **the** ark as a reminder to the rebellious. [The Holy of Holies now contains the Ark of the Covenant with the Mercy seat and Aaron's staff. Inside the Ark are the stone tablets of the Ten Commandments and a jar of manna.]

At this point, God gives directions to Aaron on how he is to manage offerings. First, all the **most holy offerings** go to **Aaron and his sons**, that is anything not consumed in the fire (burnt offering). These are to be eaten by the priests in the Tent of Meeting courtyard. The most holy offerings included the grain offerings, sin offerings, and guilt offerings. Second, **the holy gifts** or the wave offerings (another term for peace offerings) were to be eaten by all members of the priests' families, if they were ceremonially clean. In wave or peace offerings, the blood and fat belonged to God, the right thigh and breast belonged to the priests, and the rest of the meat belonged to the worshiper and his family. (Blood represented life and fat represented abundance. God was offered the life and abundance (wealth) of the worshipper.) (I have some 'abundance' in its natural state (fat) that I would love to offer.)

God was to be given 10% of the best of all the herds and crops. God allows the Levites to receive this 10% as an inheritance for their service to Him. But the Levites are to tithe also! A tenth of what God gives them is to be given to Aaron. The sequence goes thusly: the Israelites give the best tithe of their harvest to God, who gives all the tithes plus the best edible meat to the priests, who give the tithe of the best that they receive to Aaron. For grain and wine offerings, the best was tithed to Aaron and the rest was given to the priests and their families.

Food for Thought: God repeatedly relents from striking down millions of people because of the prayers of one righteous man. Do you practice intercessory prayer? Do you plead for the lives of your enemies before the Father?

February 10
Bible Readings: Numbers 20-21; 33:1-49

Our lesson opens with the death of Miriam. Apparently, she is one of the last to die of the condemned generation. The Israelites have returned to Kadesh (northeast part of the Sinai) 40 years later. But even this new generation is grumbling: they have no water. God tells Moses and Aaron to **speak** to the rock and the water will pour out. (The last time Moses brought water from a rock by striking it with his rod (Exodus 17:1-7). That was in the southwest section of the Sinai Peninsula.) Moses falls victim to temptation. His speech to the people includes "...must *we* bring you water...." (Numbers 20:10 - italics mine) He does not honor God before the people, a serious mistake for a spiritual leader. But like us, when the finish line is in site, we often let down our guard and sin is always waiting to take advantage of every opportunity. The closer you walk with God the harder evil tries to overcome you, and the greater diligence you have to maintain to prevent sin's opportunities. Moses and Aaron are finished as leaders. God is preparing their replacements.

Moses is denied passage through the land of Edom (south of the Dead Sea), a continuation of the struggle between Jacob (Israel) and Esau (Edom). Moses chooses not to fight his relatives but instead goes to Mt. Hor (southwestern border of modern Israel) where Aaron's position of High Priest is transferred to Eleazer, his son. Aaron dies at the age of 123 and all Israel mourns.

When Israel takes a different route to Canaan, the King of Arad attacks them. God is with His people. Arad and his towns are completely destroyed. On the heels of the victory, the people again grumble against God and Moses. Their grumblings in Numbers 21:5 don't seem so bad, even something we might say. After all, King David and Job repeatedly asked God, "Why?" but God knows the people's hearts, and it is in their hearts that we find their sin. Now they will deal with poisonous snakes. (Moses must have had a flashback to Ethiopia!) When the people repent of their sin, God instructs Moses to set up a bronze snake on a pole. Anyone who is bitten only has to look at the bronze snake to live. This 'brazen image' looked like the evil ones but was harmless itself. (Jesus looked like other people but was harmless or without sin.) The image was raised up on a pole for all to see. (Jesus was lifted up on a cross for all to see.) All who were bitten could look on the image in believing obedience and be saved. (All could look unto Jesus in believing obedience and be saved.)

We generally think of snakes as representing evil (from Genesis 3). This is **NOT** the case here. This is merely the image of the poisonous real snakes (representing sin). It was the faith of the Israelites that saved them, NOT some magic power of this image. God told them to do it, they believed and obeyed, and they were saved. The image was preserved and carried into Canaan.

The Israelites traveled to Oboth, about 30 miles south of the Dead Sea (called the Salt Sea in ancient times). From there they go up the east side of the Dead Sea to the Arnon River (half-way point on the Dead Sea on the east side). At this point Sihon, King of the Amorites, marches out against them; Israel triumphs capturing all the Amorite cities. The next group they battle is the Bashanites, defeating their king, Og.

A summary of the Israelites' journey out of Egypt reveals they started at the Mediterranean Sea and traveled in a big U-shape following the border of the Sinai Peninsula. After their desert wanderings of 40 years (around the border of the peninsula and current Israel), they finally traveled up the east side of the Dead Sea until they reached Jericho.

Food for Thought: How do you bury someone in a desert? Seems like the sand would keep filling up the hole. Besides, doesn't the sand shift with the winds? Documentaries indicate people were buried in small holes dug into the mountains. This is a rocky, mountainous desert rather than just an expanse of sand.

February 11
Bible Readings: Numbers 22-24

The story of Balaam is one of the most remembered stories from our early Sunday School classes. The lesson to be learned from Balaam's life is pointedly stressed in both 2 Peter 2 and Jude.

The victories Israel had gained over Arad, Sihon, and Og were not unnoticed by the other peoples of the area. Balak, apparently believing that military resistance was pointless, resorted to other means. There was a well-known diviner who had gained a reputation as a wonder worker. Balaam's hometown, Pethor, is usually identified with Pitru that was located near Carchemish approximately 400 miles from Moab.[16]

At first Balaam refuses to go, but persistent requests from Balak, and a vision from God received in the night, causes him to change his mind. (Just because Balaam receives a vision from God and is spoken to by the Angel of the LORD is not positive proof that he is a servant of God. The LORD can use even sinful men and women to do his work, e.g., 1 Samuel 28.) During Balaam's trip to Moab, God warns him that he is only to speak what the LORD tells him. This warning comes in a round-about manner and in a way that Balaam will never forget. Who can ever forget the much abused but faithful donkey that had the prudence to avoid danger? (Oh, if only all men and women were equally as wise.) In one of the most striking ways possible, God reveals Himself to Balaam, who should walk away from this experience realizing that he has indeed come in contact with the true God of the universe and who should make contact with Israel that he too might become one of God's people. (2 Pet. 2:15, Jude 11, Rev. 2:14)

In chapters 22, 23, and 24, Balaam pronounces blessings rather than curses upon Israel. In his first oracle he recognizes the greatness of Israel "Who can count . . . one fourth of Israel?" and expresses a desire to be like them "Let my end be like his!" In his second oracle Balaam declares that God "has not observed iniquity in Israel." (We must remember that when God forgives, God forgets.) He also recognizes that there is no sorcery that can stand against God's people. (If Balak is listening, he must now know that his plans have been frustrated.) In his third oracle, Balaam recognizes the beauty and strength of Israel. The reference to Agag in 24:7 probably means that Israel's kingdom will be greater than the Amalekite's kingdom. Agag may have been a title for an Amalekite king just as Pharaoh was the title for an Egyptian king.

In Balaam's fourth oracle, he prophesies of a "star" that will come out of Jacob that will subdue Moab and Edom and make them his possessions. This prophecy is fulfilled in one sense through the life of David, but in a far greater sense by the life of Jesus whose words have subdued all nations. Had Balaam's story ended here, his legacy would have been somewhat favorable. Balak, however, was not willing to accept his fate and apparently tempted Balaam with money to figure out a way to bring God's disfavor on Israel.

Food for Thought: How does God use unbelievers today to accomplish his purposes? Have you ever gained spiritual insight through an experience with a pet?

Verse of the Week: **Deuteronomy 4:39** "Acknowledge and take to heart this day that the LORD is God in heaven above and on the earth below. There is no other."

February 12
Bible Readings: Numbers 25; 31:1-54

Today's reading is like a Paul Harvey "the Rest of the Story" episode in so far as the life of Balaam is concerned. Realizing that God favored Israel and that God's power protected them from all the forces of hell, Balaam decided that the best way to defeat Israel was from within, that is to tempt them (Numbers 31:16). This temptation took the form of what we would call today a seductive woman.

While camped near Jericho, the men of Israel were enticed by the Moabite and Midianite women to engage in the worship of Baal. This worship took the form of religious ritual prostitution. One man from the tribe of Simeon was so bold as to bring a Midianite woman into the camp within sight of the tabernacle complex. There are indications that he may have intended to engage in Baal worship in the tabernacle. Notice the use of the definite article "**the**" tent" in vs. 8. Phinehas, the grandson of Aaron, is so incensed at the man's sinful boldness that he drives a spear through both the man and woman's bodies. Phinehas' action stops the plague that had come upon Israel because of their sin. This plague probably explains why the number of the tribe of Simeon in chapter 26 is so much smaller than in the census taken in chapter 1.

God rewarded Phinehas' zealous act: his descendants shall always constitute the priesthood. A descendant of Phinehas was still high priest when the Romans destroyed the temple in 70 A.D.[5] God also commands Israel to take action against the Midianites for this violation. The subsequent action is described in chapter 31. The fact that only 12,000 selected men made war on the Midianites, and that Phinehas and some of the holy articles were present with the army **may** indicate that this military action was taken in response to a violation of the tabernacle complex. The army exterminates the male population but spares the rest of the people. Moses, however, realizes that the problems originated with the female seductresses; he orders all but the female children killed. Just as the Jews were required to destroy all sources that might lead them astray, we as Christians should be equally vigilant in eradicating sin and **all** its sources from our lives.

Balaam was killed in this battle with the Midianites. His life is an example of a man who had seen the power of God, who had been used by God to achieve His purpose but who had allowed the temptation of riches to choke out the 'good seed' that God was trying to sow in his life. The irony of this entire story is that Balak's fears were totally unfounded. Had he met with Moses he would have learned that the Jews had no intention of conquering Moab. The land they wanted was on the other side of the river.

Food for Thought: Can you think of a time when you were your own worst enemy? Our biggest challenge is not in conquering others; it is in conquering ourselves.

February 13
<u>Bible Readings: Numbers 26</u>

After the plagues and battles, another census is needed (1st one is in Numbers 1). Again, the Levites are counted separately from the other tribes. Because the Levites did not participate in the military and because they were not part of the rebellious people who became victims of the plague, their numbers increased. The military force has only decreased slightly in the 40 years since the last census. They are camped across the river from Canaan. The Promised Land is in sight! Soon, it will be time to divide the land among the tribes. Only Caleb, Joshua, and Moses are left out of more than a million adults who first refused to take the Promised Land. You will recall that God's judgment was on all those 20 years old and older. Moses is 120 years old.

Tribe	1st Census	2nd Census	% Change	Change in Number
Reuben	46500	43730	-6.0	-2770
Simeon	59300	22200	-62.6	-37100
Gad	45650	40500	-11.3	-5150
Judah	74600	76500	2.5	1900
Issachar	54400	64300	18.2	9900
Zebulun	57400	60500	5.4	3100
Manasseh	32200	52700	63.7	20500
Ephraim	40500	32500	-19.8	-8000
Benjamin	35400	45600	28.8	10200
Dan	62700	64400	2.7	1700
Asher	41500	53400	28.7	11900
Naphtali	53400	45400	-15.0	-8000
Total	603550	601730	-0.3	-1820

Plagues that took their toll on the population included

- Golden calf plague (Ex. 32:35),
- Quail plague (Num. 11:33-34),
- Promised Land rebellion (Num. 14:37),
- Korah, Dothan, and Abiram rebellion (Num. 16:46-50), and
- Baal-Peor plague (Num. 25:9).[5]

An estimated 75,000-100,000 Israelites died of plagues alone. It is possible the numbers were double this because, by ancient custom, only men were counted.

The tribe of Simeon has a huge decrease possibly due to a large number of men being involved in Zimri's sin. The increases in Manasseh, Benjamin, and Asher are particularly striking. Manasseh's growth, while quite unusual, is not unbelievable. Between 1816-1855 the population of Prussia, which numbered in the millions, increased by more than 65%. In the years between 1815-1849, England's population increased by 47%.[11]

Food for Thought: Wonder what happened to Moses' wife and children? Even in the lineage given in Exodus 6:14-27, Moses' sons are left out. Why? 1 Chronicles 23:14-17 gives a little more information.

February 14
Bible Readings: Num. 27:15-23; 32; Deut. 4:41-43; Num. 33:50-56; 34-35:8; Deut. 25:17-19

God selected Joshua, from the tribe of Ephraim, to be Israel's new leader. But, there would never be another Moses. Moses' unique relationship with God is later emphasized in the transfiguration (Matt. 17:3) where the Apostles Peter, James, and John witnessed an appearance of Moses with Elijah and Jesus. Additionally, Moses and Elijah are generally thought to be the two witnesses foretold in Revelation 11.

In a public ceremony, Moses lays his hands on Joshua signifying the transfer of authority, clarified in verse 20 as "some authority." Moses was a man who talked directly to God. Joshua would have to go through Eleazer, the High Priest, who would seek decisions from God by using the Urim (abbreviated for Urim and Thummim[11]). As with most leaders, there is a period of transition.

The land of Gilead is on the east side of the Jordan. It is especially lush with grass and shade trees. The tribes of Reuben, Gad, and half of Manasseh settle there. The other tribes prepare to go across the Jordan. (Based on Deut. 1:3, the book of Numbers covers 39 years. In this case, 40 years is not only symbolic of a prolonged period of time but an exact number as well.) Their brothers settling on the east side agree to help them conquer Canaan. Meanwhile, the LORD gives strict orders that the Israelites are to demolish all idols or graven images and destroy all high places that are areas of religious worship. The warning is that any pagan worship not eliminated from the conquered land will continuously inflict pain and trouble for the Israelites.

God did not forget the way the Amalekites attacked those Israelites unable to keep up with the group and killed them. This occurred soon after they crossed the Red Sea. At the time, God instructed Moses to record the event and make sure Joshua knew of the record. For God declares, "I will completely erase the memory of the Amalekites from under heaven."[1] (Ex. 17:14) Throughout history, God has repeatedly avenged His people for wrongs done by other nations. God fiercely protects His people. He is a God of justice.

The borders of the Promised Land are clearly defined by God. The towns and mountains given for the northern border are no longer known for sure, but according to Deut. 1:7, the northern border was the Euphrates River. The southern border is exactly that given for the tribe of Judah in Joshua 15:2-3. It was not until the time of the intertestament period (about 400 years between the end of the Old Testament and the beginning of the New Testament[5]) that the Israelites were able to make the Great Sea (Mediterranean Sea) their western border. The eastern border ran along the east coast area of the Sea of Galilee down the Jordan River and along the east coast of the Dead Sea. It appears obvious that the tribes of Reuben, Gad, and the half tribe of Manasseh settled **outside** the Promised Land, thus Moses' great initial anger in Numbers 32. The *Life Application Bible* footnotes Numbers 35 stating, "The land of Gilead was also part of the Promised Land."[15] If this were true, then Moses entered the Promised Land. Because we know God prohibited Moses' entrance to the Promised Land, the above statement must be false. (This is a good example of why you need to read and study God's word for yourself. You must evaluate everything against God's word. People are fallible; God is not.) The Promised Land includes the current area of Israel, Gaza Strip, West Bank, Lebanon, Golan Heights, and much of Syria.[4]

One author believed the leaders named to participate with Caleb in dividing the land were significant based on the Hebrew meaning of their names (See table below). The names of these 9 men are mentioned nowhere else in the Bible. (Personally, I believe this is only interesting trivia because the Hebrew meaning for Caleb is 'dog.'[5] Possibly he got this name because his father was a Kenezzite that was absorbed into the Israelites. Dog is often a derogatory term used for pagan people. Kenezzites were initially part of Canaan (Matt. 15:26).)

NAME	HEBREW MEANING
Shemuel	Name of God
Elidad	My God Loves
Bukki	Proved
Hanniel	Grace of God
Kemuel	Raised by God
Elizaphan	My God Protects
Paltiel	God is My Deliverance[17]
Ahihud	Brother of Honor[5]
Pedahel	God Delivers[17]

By the way, Joshua means 'the LORD is Salvation.'[5] The Israelites put great emphasis on a name identifying one's character.

Our lesson now gets into the book of Deuteronomy. It primarily contains 3 messages on speeches Moses gave to the Israelites. He knows he will die soon. The Israelites have a history of being led astray by sin, rebellion, and faltering faith. Moses takes this last opportunity to provide instructions for righteous living to these people he loves so much.

Deuteronomy is the last of 5 books included in the Pentateuch (Greek) or Torah (Hebrew).[5] The Pentateuch or Torah is an ancient version of the laws of Moses, known simply as 'the law' or 'the books of the law' in our modern versions.[5] The word Deuteronomy means 'second copy.' In 622 B.C., King Josiah was informed that a Book of the Law had been found (2 Kings 22).[17] Many scholars believe this 'Book of the Law' was Deuteronomy. Having no official Hebrew title, it became known by the first few words of the book: 'These are the Words' or simply 'Words.'[18] It is Moses' legacy to the people. Its time period consists of a few days (anywhere from 7^{15} - 30^3) during which Moses reminds the people of their covenant with God, the many blessings they have received from God, the laws of God, and the dangers of not keeping God's laws. Jesus, often called rabbi (teacher) by the Hebrews, quoted scripture from Deuteronomy at each temptation during the 40 days He spent in the wilderness prior to beginning His public ministry.[17] In fact, the Hebrews were expected to commit to memory the laws of Moses. Therefore, we shouldn't be surprised to find that Deuteronomy is quoted more than 80 times in the New Testament.[17,19]

God is a God of justice. He designed cities of refuge for those who accidentally killed someone. During this period of time, the prevailing justice was an eye for an eye and a tooth for a tooth (Ex. 21:24). If someone caused a death, even accidentally, then the victim's relatives killed the perpetrator. God established 6 cities of refuge, where the Levites held court, to provide justice to the innocent or the guilty.

Food for Thought: Wonder what your character would have been named? God holds Caleb in high regard as evidenced in Numbers 14:24. Does giving him the name of 'dog' reflect his loyalty, obedience, and trustworthiness? Or was it meant to be degrading? Caleb is a shining example of someone who rose to the challenge and excelled beyond prediction.

February 15
Bible Readings: Deut. 1-4:40

The narrative for our lesson identifies today's lesson as the "first of two addresses." Most scholars identify this as the first of three addresses to the Israelites by Moses.[5,17,18,19] All agree that this address ends with chapter 4. The second address covers chapters 5-26, with a debate on whether chapters 27-28 belong in this address or the third. Moses' last speech to the people is short, chapters 29-30. The last 4 chapters of Deuteronomy report the historical account of the month involving the death of Moses and mourning of Israel.

Like all farewell addresses, Moses begins by reminding the Israelites of all the major events since they were at Mt. Sinai where they entered the covenant with God. Moses reviews the many blessings of God throughout their journey. But, he also reminds them of the penalty of sin. The Israelites are repeatedly warned to obey God's laws and be blessed or rebel and pay the consequences.

God did not reveal His form to the Israelites; they only heard His voice. The revelation of His magnificence would have struck them dead. Even Adam, Abraham, and Moses (Ex. 33) were not allowed to see God, only to talk with Him or walk with His Presence. You may recall that in Numbers 12:8, the LORD stated that with Moses He spoke face to face. The verse ends by saying Moses saw the form of God. The actual translation of the Hebrew text of Exodus 12:8 is "I speak to him mouth to mouth, and an appearance, and not in riddles; and he carefully looks upon the form of Jehovah."[20] The translation for Deut. 4:15 is "Therefore you shall carefully watch over your souls, for you have not seen any likeness in the day Jehovah spoke to you in Horeb out of the midst of the fire."[20] When you compare these two verses, you realize that form as used in Ex. 12:8 is defined as "the essence of something as distinguished from its matter."[8] No one has seen God's 'likeness' and lived. Only a few men of faith have seen God's 'form' or essence. Israel was to be very careful not to fall into the sin of worshipping a likeness or their 'image' of how they thought God looked, and for good reason. The Israelites' entire ancestry had lived among other nations who worshipped idols (Mesopotamia, Canaan, Egypt). It would be easy for them to drift back toward worshipping idols or graven images. Moses warns them of the severe consequences that will result from breaking the second commandment. Almost prophetically (Moses knows them all too well), he describes the destruction of the Israelites in the Promised Land, their dispersion among pagan people, and the deaths of all but a few. This warning becomes reality when the Assyrians and Babylonians take the Israelites captive. We all experience a time when we let material things become first in our lives. When that happens, we are exiled from the marvelous joy and delight of God's Presence. This Presence is the 'fuel' of the Holy Spirit's work in our lives. We are left to fight our earthly battles without the Spirit's power. We 'quenched' or put out the fire of the Spirit. But God is loving and merciful. From the place where we are exiled (by the consequences of our choices), we can still <u>seek</u> God. When we seek Him with all our heart and all our soul, **He will be found**. "For the LORD your God is a merciful God...." (Deut. 4:31)[1]

Food for Thought: I was once startled to hear a Jewish Christian preacher say that the pictures, statues, and stained glass windows of the man we have come to regard as Jesus were really graven images because we have no record of what Jesus looked like. He went on to say that he believed the antichrist (evil one) would come in this image and that is how he will fool the world! We will be led astray by our 'image' of God. Think about it and read Deut. 4:15-19, 24-31 again.

February 16
Bible Readings: Deut. 4:44-5:5; Deut. 5:22-8:20

At this time, only 3 men who participated in the great exodus out of Egypt are still alive: Moses, Caleb, and Joshua. Moses knows he has only days or, at best, a few weeks left to live. Moses is 120, Joshua is about 85, and Caleb is about 80 years old now. (They truly are the 'elders' of the congregation!) Joshua, at 85, is commander-in-chief of a huge army about to do battle in a foreign nation. The Israelites range in age from birth to 59 years old. This is the second address Moses makes to the 'young-uns.'

In this second address, Moses concentrates on the Israelites' covenant with God: to obey all God says (Ex. 19:8). He emphasizes teaching, studying, learning, and remembering God's laws. But above all else, they were to be obeyed from the heart (verse 6). Many non-believers know the Bible, but knowing is not the same as believing. The devil has all the scripture memorized and understands it well, as evidenced in the temptations of Jesus in the wilderness (Matt. 4). But the devil doesn't love God or recognize that God has dominion over him. As believers, we should not only know God's word and keep it in our hearts and minds but also love God and make Him Lord of our lives. We should strive to obey God and have a worshipful relationship with Him.

Many Jewish people observe a custom called Mezuzah where Deut. 6:4-9 and Deut. 11:13-20 are written on a piece of parchment which is placed in a container on all the doorframes. Every time they walk through a doorway, they touch the box with a finger that they then kiss.[11] Orthodox Jews still wear tephillin or phylacteries which are small leather boxes containing parchment rolls with Ex. 13:1-10; 13:11-16 and Deut. 6:8-9 written on them. One box is tied to the left wrist by a leather band and the other box is tied so it hangs on the forehead between the eyes. These are worn at the morning time of prayer every day except the Sabbath and special holy days.[21] The above rituals they do as literal responses to Deut. 6:8-9. In truth, the spirit of this command is to keep God's laws in your mind and heart to guide your thoughts and actions.

Moses lists seven nations as those God has chosen to be destroyed. These are completely pagan nations beyond redemption. To prevent the Israelites' minds and practices from being corrupted, every man, woman, and child of these 7 nations must be killed. **Nowhere** in the Bible will you find God advocating tolerance of evil. Our society that thinks we should tolerate all sorts of evil is in opposition to the word of God. We are to be like Caleb and Joshua who 'called it' as God saw it. God rewards those who take a stand for righteousness. When God first promised to give the land of Canaan to Abraham's descendants (Genesis 15:18-21), He named 9 tribes to be displaced. The Kenezzites were absorbed into the tribe of Judah and by the Edomites. Caleb's father was a Kennezzite.[5] The Kadmonites were a nomadic tribe that simply disappeared over time. The Rephaimites were a tribe of giants who lived in the land of Gilead, Bashan, and Argob (east of the Jordan River). Og was the last survivor of the Rephaimites. You will notice that the Hivites have been added to the Deut. 7:1 list. These were descendants of Canaan who were scattered in little pockets throughout the area north and west of the Jordan. Simeon and Levi killed many of them when they destroyed the men of Shechem. Even though Moses warns the people to make no treaties with these nations, Joshua is tricked into a peace treaty with the Hivites (Joshua 9). So the Hivites become slaves of the Israelites but are not completely wiped out.

Finally, Moses warns the people of the sin of pride. Proverbs 16:18 says, "Pride goes before destruction, a haughty spirit before a fall."[1] Pride is the sin of 'patting oneself on the back' or forgetting that God deserves all the credit for all good blessings. Moses didn't get to enter the Promised Land because of his pride over bringing forth water at Meribah. Where is pride causing you to self-destruct? Pride may knock us down to our knees, or even on our faces, but that is where we will find God waiting.

Food for Thought: Doesn't your heart just ache for Moses? This man was so successful in pleading for others but not for himself (Deut. 3:23-26).

February 17
Bible Readings: Deut. 9-11

Moses' second speech continues. Some of the summarization he gives does not exactly match earlier scripture. For example, Exodus 34:27 is a quote of God's instructions to Moses to write down the second set of the Ten Commandments and Deut. 10:4 states the LORD wrote on the tablets as He did before. Both of these passages are translated in accordance with the Hebrew text. After verifying this, you must then look outside the scripture words to the situational context. The Exodus account is an historical recording. You find Ex. 34:1 parallels Deut. 10:1-2. In Deuteronomy Moses presents an overview of all the history of the free nation. Only those in the congregation who were 49-59 years old would be able to remember any of these events. I believe these verses should be interpreted to mean the second set of tablets contained the same God-given laws as the first set. In other words, the people were to understand that God did not forget or change the Ten Commandments just because the original pair of tablets were broken -- His covenant with His people was not forgotten or broken either.

Another point that appears here for the first time is the statement that Moses spent 40 days and nights praying for God to spare Aaron and the Israelites. There are several possible interpretations. First, 40, in this case, may be symbolic of a prolonged period of time in prayer or, second, it could refer to his second trip to obtain the Ten Commandments in stone. Third, it could be an actual number of days he prayed that he is just now revealing. I tend to believe it is the second one with the understanding that you would be on your face when in the LORD's presence. I also believe the first interpretation to the extent that Moses must have pleaded long and hard to turn away God's wrath after this great sin of the people. Again, we need to remember that Moses is giving a speech which overviews key events.

Moses makes it very clear that they will be blessed only as long as they obey God's commands. They were to fear invoking God's wrath, walk in His ways, love Him, and serve Him with all their heart, soul, and strength. God's requirements of His people are the same today. Have you kept the covenant?

Food for Thought: It is not our sacrifices God wants but rather our obedience. Are you obedient?

The Laws of Moses

February 18

Bible Readings: Deut. 5:5-10; Ex. 22:20; 23:13; 34:17; Lev. 19:4; 26:1; Deut. 16:21-22; Lev. 20:1-5, 18:21; Deut. 14:1-2; Lev. 19:27-28; Deut. 12: 29-31; Deut. 13: 6-18, 17:2-7, 12:1-15, 12: 17-22, 12: 26-28

Today's reading is a variety of scriptures taken from Exodus, Leviticus and Deuteronomy. The common element in all these passages is idolatry. This concept is defined in terms of what one was not to do and how violators of the commandment were to be punished. Some may feel that the penalties were rather severe. We should remember, however, that back in Exodus at Mt. Sinai the Israelites willingly entered into a covenant with God and promised their obedience.

There is much that a contemporary Christian living in a secular society can learn from these passages. First, our authority, our sense of direction, our compass must be God's word. We cannot allow even our dearest family members to entice us to do those things that God's word and our spirit-directed conscience tells us is wrong (Deut. 13:6-11). The Apostle John said (1 John 2:15) "Do not love the world or anything in the world. If anyone loves the world, the love of the Father is not in him." Yes, Christ has called us to influence others and to bring them into his kingdom, but we must be ever vigilant of the dire effects the world's influence can have on us.

Food for Thought: My mother bought me a pin for the lapel of my suit coat. It was a lighthouse with its rays shining forth. A card came with it bearing the verse John 8:12, "I am the light of the world. Whoever follows me will never walk in darkness, but will have the light of life." The pin reminds me that I am to influence others with the light of God's word. How can each of us influence others for good?

Verse of the Week: **Leviticus 5:1** "If a person sins because he does not speak up when he hears a public charge to testify regarding something he has seen or learned about, he will be held responsible."

Lessons of Love

February 19

Bible Readings: Lev. 19:26, 19:31, 20:6-8; Deut. 18:9-14; Ex. 22:18; Lev. 20:27; Deut. 13:1-5; 18:15-22; Deut. 5:11; Ex. 22:28; Lev. 24:10-16, 24:23; Ex. 22:29-30; Ex. 34:19-20; 23:19, 34:26; Deut. 15:19-23; Deut. 18:1-8; Deut. 14:22-29; Deut. 26:1-15; Lev. 19:23-25; Ex. 23:12, 35:1-2; Lev. 19:3; Deut. 5:12-15; Ex. 31:16-17; Lev. 19:30, 26:2, 23:1-3; Ex. 35:3, 34:21, 31:12-15; Num. 15:32-36

Moses makes it perfectly clear that God's people are not to tolerate those practicing magic, séances, palm reading, and psychic revelations. Within ten minutes drive of my house, there are palm readers and witches coven meetings. My television carries advertisements nightly for psychics and full-length programs on black magic. The movies are full of spell casters, evil spirits of the dead, poltergeists, and other forms of evil divination. We have become a world of people enticed and entranced by evil. Deut. 18:14-15 pointedly states that God's people are not to listen to anyone who practices sorcery or divination. In fact Exodus, Leviticus, and Deuteronomy all state that those who practice such things are to be put to death. Of course, it is just as wrong to become so zealous that you have the witch-hunts of Salem, Massachusetts, in America's colonial days. A few years ago, my husband and I went to Salem to see the famous 'House of the Seven Gables' from Hawthorne's book. We were both in shock at the open, rampant witchcraft being practiced and encouraged throughout the town. Neither of us could wait to get out of that place. It literally made our flesh crawl being in the middle of such evil. The Bible plainly tells us that anyone who practices black magic, witchcraft, psychic readings, palm readings, etc., is detestable to the LORD. The Israelites were being given land from nations who listened to such evil. God kicked evildoers out of their land and instructed the Israelites to kill every one of them. Why are we surprised by the September 11 disaster in America? We have earned our destruction. As the old saying goes, "He who does not stand for anything falls for everything." For too many years we have tolerated everything; our nation has been led astray. It is detestable to God.

A liberal church in our area is proud to stand as a symbol of tolerance of everything -- including witchcraft. God condemns this type of liberalism. Christians need to take a stand for God. God not only said we should not listen to or follow evil practitioners, He also said we should not allow such evil to live in our midst. Look around your community. Will you be dispossessed from your land because you were tolerant of evil practices?

Deut. 18:15-19 foretells of the coming of Jesus Christ. We are told that Jesus will be sent as one from among the Israelites as God's response to the fear expressed by the people at Mt. Horeb (Mt. Sinai) at hearing the voice of God. If we do not listen to the words of Jesus, God states we will have to account to Him personally. Have you listened? Do you read your Bible and attend a Christian church regularly? Do you know what the words of Jesus are?

Tithing and offerings, as commanded in the Old Testament, was to be a tenth of all grain, herds, wine, fruit, and vegetables. This was taken to the LORD's house to be used by the Levites. The Levites were given no inheritance of land in the Promised Land except for 48 towns where they could settle. The duties of the ministry were assigned on a rotational basis. Food given in the form of tithes and offerings supported them and their families so their lives could be dedicated to the LORD's work. Notice in Deut. 14:33, the worshipper was to eat the food during his sojourn at the LORD's house. It is interesting to note that out of this whole land, God would choose to have only one place to dwell. It would mean very long trips for many of the Israelites to reach the LORD's house.

Tithing is mentioned several times in the Old Testament but is only mentioned in the New Testament in reference to Old Testament practices or Jewish practices. "Nowhere does the New Testament expressly command Christians to tithe. However, as believers we are to be generous in sharing our material possessions with the poor and for the support of Christian ministry. Christ Himself is our model in giving. Giving is to be voluntary, willing, cheerful, and given in the light of our accountability to God. Giving should be systematic and by no means limited to a tithe of our incomes. We recognize that all we have is from God." (p. 1057)[5]

Food for Thought: There is an old saying, "Put your money where your mouth is." It is meant as a challenge. Are you confident enough in what you say to support it with your money? How many of us confess faith in Christ with our mouths but are miserly in supporting the work of His church?

February 20

Bible Readings: Ex. 23:14-17, 34:23; Deut. 16:16-17; Ex. 34:24 & 18; Deut. 16:1-7; Num. 9:13-14; Lev. 23:4-8; Num. 28:16-17; Deut. 16:8; Num. 28:18-25; Deut. 16:9-12; Lev. 23:9-14; Ex. 34:22; Lev. 23:15-21; Num. 28:26-31; Lev. 23:23-25; Num. 29:1-6; Lev. 16; Lev. 23: 26-32; Num. 29:7-11; Lev. 23:33-36, 39-43; Num. 29:12-38; Deut. 16:13-15; Lev. 23:37-38, 44; Num. 29:39-40

The rather disperse set of scriptures making up today's reading are all concerned with the major religious holidays of the Jewish people. The following table summarizes vital information about them.

Name	When Celebrated	Length	Purpose	How Celebrated
Passover and Feast of Unleavened Bread	Nisan 14th (Abib) 15th-21st (Mar.-Apr.)	1 day 7 days	To commemorate the deliverance from Egypt	Passover Meal 1st and 7th days sacred assemblies. Special offering of animals and grain. Sin offering (1 male goat)
Feast of Weeks (Feast of Harvests, First Fruits, or Pentecost)	50 days after Feast of Unleavened Bread (3rd month 6th day) (May-June)	1 day	Thanksgiving for harvest	Special offerings of animals and grain. Sin offering
Feast of Trumpets (Rosh Hashanah)	Tishri 1st (Sept.-Oct.)	1 day	As a preparation for the Day of Atonement	Sacred assembly, sounded trumpets, animal and grain offerings, sin offering
Day of Atonement (Yom Kippur)	Tishri 10th day	1 day	Confession of sin	Day of fasting, High Priest offers bull as sin offering for himself and male goat as a sin offering for the people, blood of animals sprinkled on the mercy seat of the ark, HP lays hands on a 2nd goat and sins are transferred to this animal who is led into desert and released (source of the term 'scapegoat'), ceremony ends with offering of 2 rams as burnt offerings.
Feast of Tabernacles, Booths, or Ingathering	Tishri 15th-22nd	7 days	To commemorate the time spent in the wilderness	1st and 8th days sacred assemblies, people live in tents made of tree branches, animal and grain offerings, sin offering.

Food for Thought: Keep in mind these animals were the main source of domesticated meat the Israelites had during the year. It would take a lot of animals for all members of the tribes to get even a little meat to eat. More importantly, these festivals were a time to remember the blessings of God. Take time to think about all the trials and troubles the Lord has brought you through. You thought you couldn't make it, and YOU couldn't. We can do all things through Christ who strengthens us (Philippians 4:13).

A long-term friend shared this with me. I thought you might reflect on it. Have you made time to read God's word?

THE POEM

I knelt to pray but not for long,
I had too much to do.
I had to hurry and get to work
For bills would soon be due.
So I knelt and said a hurried prayer,
Then jumped up off my knees.
My Christian duty was now done
My soul could rest at ease.
All day long I had no time
For to spread a word of cheer.
No time to speak of Christ to friends,
They'd laugh at me I'd fear.
No time, no time, too much to do,
That was my constant cry,
No time to give to souls in need
But at last the time, the time to die.
I went before the Lord,
I came; I stood with downcast eyes.
For in His hands God held a book;
It was the Book of Life.
God looked into His book and said
"Your name I cannot find.
I once was going to write it down...
But never found the time."

February 21
Bible Readings: Lev. 1:1-17; Lev. 6:8-13; Num. 28:1-8; Lev. 17:8-9; Lev. 2:1-16; Lev. 6:14-23; Num. 15:1-21

There is much in the sacrificial system that confuses the mind of modern man. Some concepts of the ancient Israelites seem so foreign to our way of thinking as Christians that to understand them requires an entirely different way of looking at things. The purpose of my comments in the next three days' readings is to help readers categorize the sacrifices and perhaps to gain some appreciation for what is happening. I will not attempt to address all the "whys" and "wherefors" of the sacrificial system, for even after much study, I have more questions than answers.

The Burnt Offering as described in Leviticus was the most common of all sacrifices. Its purpose was varied. Some verses seem to suggest that the person sacrificing is making atonement (Lev. 1:4). Some commentators suggest, however, that the sacrifice is a ritual in which the person sacrificing is dedicating himself to God.[11]

Bulls, lambs, doves, goats or pigeons could be offered. For the larger animals, a male without blemish is demanded. The variety of choices in terms of the animal sacrificed provides some leeway in terms of what type of farmer was sacrificing and his financial circumstances. (Bulls cost more than doves.)

Unlike the passive worship of contemporary Christians, the Old Testament worshipper was actively involved. He brought his sacrifice before the priest who asked him why he brought it. It is likely the worshipper may have recited one of the Psalms such as 40, 51, or 6. The priest may have possibly replied by reciting Psalms 20 or 50. The worshipper then placed his hand on the sacrifice's head and confessed his sin. After this, he killed the sacrifice in a way that allowed him to capture a maximum amount of blood that was gathered in some type of container. Most likely, he cut its throat. He then skinned the carcass and washed out the intestines and all other excrement from the body, for nothing unclean can ever be offered to God. The blood was sprinkled about the altar and the carcass of the animal was totally burned in the fire.

The sacrifice of a choice animal along with the part that the worshipper was required to play in the ceremony, to me, represents a strong deterrent to sin. Witnessing an animal that I had tended on a daily basis die in such a way for something that I had done would cause me to be more careful about what I said and did.

The Cereal Offering followed a Burnt Offering, but it could also be offered on its own. It was a way of thanking God for His blessings. Only a small portion of the cereal offering was consumed in the flame. Most of the sacrifice was given to the priests. It could be presented in uncooked or cooked forms. When it was cooked, the worshipper could bake it or cook it on a griddle or in a pan. Oil and salt were always added. Salt is represented in the Bible as that which prevents decay. Leaven and honey were prohibited because both contributed to fermentation.

Food for Thought: Did you know that the word salt is where our word salary comes from? It developed as a result of people being paid with salt. It was a necessary component of life. You used it mostly as a preservative or for preventing infection in wounds. You rarely cooked with it because it was too scarce and valued to waste for ordinary cooking. Do you take salt for granted? Are you the salt of the earth (Matt. 5:13)?

February 22
Bible Readings: Lev. 3:1-17; Lev. 7:11-21, 28-36; Lev. 17:1-7; Lev. 19:5-8; Lev. 4:1-35; Lev. 5:1-13; Lev. 6:24-30; Num. 15:2

Today's reading focuses on two of the sacrifices performed in the Old Testament. The Peace Offering could be offered as a type of confession. Here the emphasis seems to be on seeking God's mercy. Peace offerings also were offered as a result of a vow, i.e., "If God helps me to get through this difficult situation, I will offer a sacrifice." In addition, Peace offerings were offered as a spontaneous act of generosity on the part of a worshipper for God's blessings.

The ceremony was similar to the other sacrifices except that only part of the body was burned. The priest was given the breast and the right thigh, and the rest of the body the worshipper might enjoy as a meal at the tabernacle complex. This meal had a religious significance, perhaps like the communion meal that Christians partake.

Those items burned on the altar, the fat, the kidneys, and various entrails, had a special significance. The fat was considered the best part of the animal (See Gen. 45:18, Psalm 81:17). This suggests that when we do the LORD's work, we must always do our best. The kidneys and entrails as used in the Old Testament are always thought of as the seat of the emotions (See Job 19:27; Psalm 9:7; Jer. 4:14, 12:2). Thus, the offering of these parts symbolizes the dedication of the worshippers best and deepest emotions to God.

The Sin (purification) Offering deals with unintentional sin. Here, however, the emphasis is on cleansing from the effects of unintentional sin rather than seeking forgiveness of sin. In the Old Testament, the idea of purification and what constituted the need for it, was more broadly defined than it is today. For example, people sought purification after experiencing childbirth and after suffering from various types of physical afflictions. The occurrences of these situations today would not necessarily suggest that a spiritual problem existed and that there was a need for cleansing. The types of offerings and the rites of the ceremony differed depending on who was seeking purification.

Food for Thought: Read Psalm 40:6-8.

February 23
Bible Readings: Lev. 5:14-19; Lev. 6:1-7; Lev. 7:1-10, 37-38; Num. 28:9-15; Deut. 21:1-9; Lev. 22:17-25; Deut. 17:1; Lev. 22:26-30; Ex. 23:18; 34:25; Lev. 24:1-9; Num. 6:22-27

The last major offering is the Guilt or Reparation Offering. Only one type of sacrifice was allowed, a ram. The ram was apparently appraised by the priest and one-fifth of its worth was offered in money along with the ram. This reparation offering appears to have been offered when a worshipper felt he may have trespassed against holy things or have trespassed against God's name by taking false oaths in court or committed a serious crime. The idea appears to be that if a person realized or suspected he had committed a sin of this nature, which could lead to a penalty of death, he could bring this sacrifice that was put to death in his place.

These chapters in Leviticus dealing with the various sacrifices give me a greater appreciation for the ideas expressed in Hebrews 10. Read this chapter to get an appreciation for what Christ has done.

Food for Thought: Could you have lived under these laws? Would you be poor from having offered every animal you had for all your sins? We are blessed to be New Testament Christians with a risen Savior who has borne our sins and intercedes for us. We have a Savior, advocate, friend, protector, confidant, King, ...

February 24
Bible Readings: Lev. 21:1-24; Lev. 22:1-16; Lev. 25:1-10; Ex. 23:10-11; Lev. 25:8-34, 39-43, 47-55

The Levites were chosen by God to be set aside to serve Him as priests. Of these, only those without physical defect could serve in the functions with the Tent of Meeting. Wholeness (physically) is symbolic of holiness (perfection). The job of priest was not something a young Levite sought to do but rather he was selected by God to serve. He was a priest by birth, not necessarily by choice. But choice is often 'groomed' into us by our parents' training and the environment or culture we experience. God commanded priests to be dutiful in training their children. They were to set an example for all God's people by living righteous and holy lives. They were to marry only virgins or widows of irreproachable character. The High Priest could marry only a virgin Israelite woman to ensure that all successors to the position were of the pure lineage of Aaron. Their children were to be honorable.

Initially, it seems harsh not to allow priests to grieve for someone outside their immediate family. After further thought, you realize that if all relatives mourned there wouldn't be anyone left clean and holy to serve God because all the Levites were kin to each other; they were of the same tribe. To be a good head of the family unit, though, each priest would necessarily be impacted by a death in his immediate family, usually in the tent. Anything a corpse touched is considered unclean, after all the soul had left the sinful body behind. Contacting sin (the body) or anything contaminated by it would make a priest or worshipper unclean. God cannot look upon the filth of sin. Sin is incompatible with a holy God. The list of those for whom the priest can mourn does not include his wife because it is understood that they are of one flesh after marriage[11] (Gen. 2:24). As a result, the death of a wife would automatically defile his flesh, even if separated by distance. Cutting the body as a sign of mourning was prohibited in Lev. 19:28, as well as tattoos. Both of these acts were performed in pagan funeral rituals as a sign of deep mourning for the deceased. Therefore, disfiguring scars and tattoos were outward, permanent signs of paganism.

The Sabbatical Year was a year of rest for the land. Today we rotate crops, apply various chemicals, or strip farm in order to accomplish this goal -- allowing the ground to remain fallow to replenish its nutrients. The Israelites grew basically the same grain crops repeatedly. Without the Sabbatical Year, the land would soon be depleted and worthless.

The Year of Jubilee was a time of rejoicing. We still celebrate Fiftieth Anniversaries, 50-year reunions, 50 years in business. It is a time to rejoice and praise God for the ultimate completion (7x7) by managing to survive the pitfalls to reach that point. Men had their inherited family property returned, debts erased, their freedom returned, and a year of rest. (Now, I could really celebrate having a Jubilee Year!) God provided your food and you just rested. (Talking about a dream vacation! These days you have to be at death's door to get to spend an extra hour in bed!)

Food for Thought: Look around you. How many signs of paganism can you count that we tolerate today but would not be tolerated by Mosaic Laws?

February 25
<u>Bible Readings: Lev. 12:1-8; Lev. 14:1-32; Lev. 15:13-15, 28-30; Num. 19:1-22</u>

Purification regulations were not only to cleanse the body of all uncleanness but also the heart and the mind. After being separated from the other Israelites and from the worship of God, the unclean needed to literally wash their bodies of all secretions that could contribute to the spread of disease and symbolically cleanse their minds and hearts of all ungodliness. The purification ritual was a way to prepare oneself to enter the worship of God after a prolonged absence, a time when one's faith has been tested and strengthened by God's miraculous power.[11]

We have already discussed that the number 40 is often symbolic rather than an exact number. It symbolizes a prolonged period of time, but even more than that, this period of time is a time for reflection, testing of one's faith, and strengthening of one's faith.[11] There are those who fail the testing of their faith and their lives are given over to sin. A well-known fact is the 40s are a difficult time for most people. Our bodies and minds start showing physical, mental, and emotional signs of decline. It is a time when our faith grows stronger from the trials and temptations or a time when we grow weak and fall into the perils of sin. The importance of a strong relationship with God early in life is never more apparent or appreciated than the decade of one's 40s. Job experienced a long, painful period of trials. But, Job's faith sustained him and grew stronger. Job 42:12 tells us, "The LORD blessed the latter part of Job's life more than the first."[1] Job 23:10-12 are verses that encourage me to stay the course and remain faithful to the end so that I, too, can "come forth as gold."

As we look at the purification after childbirth, it seems inequitable that the birth of female babies required a confinement of the mother for twice as long as the birth of male babies. Baby girls were often born with physiologic leukorrhea, a vaginal discharge that lasted up to 2 months due to high maternal hormone levels. Additionally, God's law required circumcision on the 8th day for sons and redemption of the firstborn male. The baby, itself, was not unclean, only the mother. The only satisfactory explanation is that the life was in the blood and the discharge after birth contained much blood. Being in the company of one who was bleeding could result in contracting any type of blood disease. Without modern methods for sanitation and personal cleanliness, anything the woman touched or sat on could be contaminated by the discharge. Being labeled unclean, and thereby untouchable, prevented the husband from demanding any marriage rights to intimacy. This protected the woman from infection and possible death.

The fear associated with bodily emissions may have had its origins in the decay process of the dead. Dead bodies would lose large quantities of body fluids during the breakdown of the tissue. Without the Egyptian embalming techniques, the Israelites had to bury the dead quickly to avoid the resultant putrefying of the body. Many scholars believe the 'discharges' of the dead also led to the unclean label on the discharges of normal life functions. The bottom line, though, is that all discharges were seen as a lack of wholeness and perfection. Wholeness symbolizes holiness (perfect, without blemish, not maimed or deformed).[17] Only when the person's body had returned to a state of wholeness, and any imperfections had been cleansed from it, could she or he present a sin offering and burnt offering. These offerings reconciled the people to God by the forgiveness of both unintentional and intentional sin and renewed their consecration and dedication to God.

Personally, I believe the main basis for these skin infection laws was to prevent the Israelites from becoming infected with the endemic (continually occurring) disease of leprosy. This disease is largely found in Asia, Africa, the Pacific Islands, and Latin America. There are more than 7,600 cases registered in the United States with it being endemic in Texas, Louisiana, and Hawaii. Leprosy is caused by *Mycobacterium leprae* that is highly infectious but only results in 5% of the victims becoming lepers. It takes 1-30 years, depending on the individual, for the disease to manifest itself. Then the disease progresses very slowly over years, but the resulting deformities are striking. Often found in nasal and other body secretions, the bacteria attack the peripheral nerves causing paralysis, skin lesions, death (and decay) of the tissues, blindness, and deformity. Smaller appendages are often lost to decay, i.e., ears, nose, fingers, toes. The testicles of men may waste away or swell painfully. Given these symptoms, it is easy to understand why God would want the people to refrain from contacting any body fluids. (Today, the federal government requires blood and body fluid precautions for all workers. If we had abided by God's Laws all along, the world would have been spared many of its epidemics.) In some cases spontaneous recovery occurs. Medical science believes it is due to the body's immune system kicking itself into high gear. The Israelites believed it was the blessing of God. Antibiotics have allowed lepers to arrest or cure the disease today.[22]

Food for Thought: Wonder how long you were confined if you had a set of twins - one boy and one girl?

Verse of the Week: **Deuteronomy 23:21** "If you make a vow to the LORD your God, do not be slow to pay it, for the LORD your God will certainly demand it of you and you will be guilty of sin."

February 26

Bible Readings: Deut. 23:1-8; Num. 6:1-21; Lev. 27:1-34; Deut. 23:21-23; Lev. 19:1-2; Deut. 22:9-11; Lev. 19:19

The focus of today's lesson is on vows of separation and dedication made to God. A vow is to dedicate or give something to God above and beyond that required by God. Vows are voluntary dedications of persons, possessions, or behavior to God. Vows in any form are to be taken seriously. Many people make promises or vows to God if He will only deliver them from trouble. Shortly after the trouble passes, the vows are forgotten -- but God doesn't forget. Those who fail to keep their vows will be held accountable. Malachi 1:14 tells us that anything less than what we promised is breaking our vow and brings down God's curse. Vows are so commonplace today that they frequently are not seen as binding, i.e., swearing to tell the truth, marriage vows, donation vows, oath of office. Instead of being made out of spontaneous emotion or ritual, vows should be carefully considered and prayerfully made. Vows are not easy to fulfill, but the fulfillment brings its own rewards.

In Matthew 5:33-37, Jesus gave instructions on oaths.

"Again, you have heard that it was said to the people long ago, 'Do not break your oath, but keep the oaths you have made to the LORD.' But I tell you, do not swear at all; either by heaven, for it is God's throne; or by the earth, for it is his footstool; or by Jerusalem, for it is the city of the Great King. And do not swear by your head, for you cannot make even one hair white or black. Simply let your 'Yes' be 'Yes,' and your 'No,' 'No'; anything beyond this comes from the evil one."[1]

This is the season of Lent. Millions of people have vowed to give up something during Lent. The problem is that the idea of Lent is to give up something that is sinful -- permanently, not just for 6 weeks or so. A large portion of the participants in Lent spend the entire time bemoaning and dwelling on the sin they have given up! This is not the intent. The intent is to self-evaluate, see how squarely you stand in the light of God's word and to change your life for the better - permanently. Lent is about making a vow to God. Review the Verse of the Week.

Food for Thought: Two of the best-known Nazirites are Samson and John the Baptist. Are you called to dedicate part or all of your life to God? [For most of us, God calls us to serve Him right where we are.] Is your word your bond?

February 27
Bible Readings: Deut. 17:14-20; Ex. 22:28; Deut. 16:18; Deut. 17:8-13; Ex. 23:3, 6, 8; Lev. 19:15; Deut. 24:17-18; Deut. 16:19-20; Deut. 5:20; Ex. 23:1-2, 7; Deut. 19:16-21; Deut. 19:15; Deut. 24:16; Deut. 25:1-3; Deut. 21:22-23

This lesson is best summarized in the following lists. You will recognize the basis for our own government and judicial system.

Laws of Government

1. Requirements for a King
   - Israelite
   - Moderate income
   - Not polygamous
   - Not allied with Egyptians
   - Not greedy
   - Not covetous
   - Lifelong student of the law
   - Law-abider
   - Reveres God

Said to be the wisest man to ever live, Solomon failed to keep all of the above requirements God laid down for the kings of Israel. Briefly scan 1 Kings 9-11. Chapter 11 is especially revealing. (If you haven't discovered it yet, there is a great cross-reference guide in the back of this Bible that will allow you to find the page number of the reference instantly.) Solomon ultimately fails all the requirements that are within his control (he can't undo his Israelite heritage).

2. Requirements for the Court System
   - Judges and officials in every town
   - Right to Appeal
   - Contempt of court = death
   - No bribes accepted
   - Fair and impartial justice
   - Truthful testimony
   - Two or more witnesses
   - Perjury = punishment of the accused
   - Sin = personal consequences
   - Flogging limited to <40 lashes
   - Executed must be buried same day

Deuteronomy 21:23 talks of the curse of anyone who is hung on a tree. Jesus will be hung on a tree (Gal. 3:12-14) and take God's curse on the sinful upon Himself. Praise God we have a Savior!

Food for Thought: If we had more flogging today, there would be fewer criminals. Think of the outrage Americans had when a young male American found guilty for a crime committed in a foreign country was publicly switched (caned). What are your sentiments on floggings? Spankings? Are your beliefs Biblical or emotional?

February 28
Bible Readings: Deut. 5:17; Ex. 21:12-14, 16, 22-25; Lev. 24:17,21; Num. 35:9-15, 20-28, 16-19, 29-34; Ex. 22:2-3; Deut. 19:1-13; Deut. 24:7; Lev. 24:19-20; Ex. 21:26-27; Deut. 22:25-29; Ex. 21:15, 18-21; Deut. 25:11-12; Deut. 5:19; Ex. 22:1-4; Deut. 19:14

When you review this chart, you will realize God was serious about crime. He didn't have a 'three strikes before you are out' plan. The laws were laid down; it was your responsibility to know them (and your parents' responsibility to teach them to you). Punishments were harsh and public.

CRIMES AGAINST PEOPLE				
CRIME	**INTENT**	**VICTIM**	**VERDICT**	**PUNISHMENT**
Murder	Murder	Anyone	Guilty	Death
Manslaughter	Unintentional	Anyone	Not Guilty	City of Refuge
Homicide	Unintentional	Anyone	Not Guilty	City of Refuge
Murder	Assault	Anyone	Guilty	Death
Premature Delivery	Unintentional	Pregnant Woman	Guilty	Fine
Personal Injury	Unintentional	Pregnant Woman	Guilty	Penalty = to injury
Kidnapping	Willful	Citizens	Guilty	Death
Assault	Willful	Slaves	Guilty	Forfeit of slave
Assault	Willful	Parents	Guilty	Death
Assault - disabling	Willful	Anyone	Guilty	Fine
Homicide	Willful	Slaves	Guilty	Punishment
Personal Injury	Willful	Slaves	Not Guilty	Fine
Rape	Willful	Virgin	Guilty	Fine - marry girl
Rape	Willful	Married Woman	Guilty	Death
Personal Injury	Willful	Man (testicles)	Guilty	Loss of female's hand
Theft - personal	Willful	Anyone	Guilty	Fine
Theft - property	Willful	Neighbors	Guilty	Cursed by God

There is much controversy as to the interpretation of Exodus 21:22. The primary concern of this verse, as well as verse 23, is the possible injury to the woman.[13] My Hebrew Bible reference translates this verse to mean premature delivery of a baby.[20]

Food for Thought: This is obviously a male dominated culture, but God designed life to be that way. He never intended for men to reach the point where women had to take over as head of the family to survive. He certainly didn't intend for women to have to perform most of the religious teaching. Why do you think men have moved to the background instead of the forefront in our church leadership? It is increasingly more difficult to get men to serve as deacons and teachers. Why are today's men not putting as much emphasis on their spiritual duties as they do on their trucks, football teams, guns, and big-screen TVs?

March 1

Bible Readings: Num. 5:5-10, Ex. 22:5-17, Ex. 21:28-36, Lev. 24:18, 21, Deut. 22:8, Lev. 19:13, Deut. 24:14-15, Lev. 25:44-46, Deut. 23:15-16, Deut. 15:12-18, Ex. 21:1-11, 26-27, Deut. 23:19-20, Ex. 22:25-27, Deut. 24:12-13, 17, Deut. 24:6-7, 10-11, Deut. 15:1-11, Lev. 19:12, Num. 30:1-16, Lev. 19:11, 35-37, Deut. 25:13-16, Deut. 21:15-17, Deut. 25:5-10, Num. 27:1-11, Num. 36:1-13

This lesson can be summed up in the Golden Rule (Matt. 7:12): "In everything, do to others what you would have them do to you, for this sums up the Law and the Prophets."[1] The following summarizes sections A-G of the reading.

    a. Do not cheat anyone. Be responsible.
    b. Men are responsible for seduction.
    c. Pay for damages incurred to another's property through negligence. Animals who kill are treated

the same as men who kill -- death sentence. Err on the side of caution and safety.
- d. Be compassionate.
- e. Do not take advantage of others. Maintain their dignity.
- f. Do not lie. Oaths and vows are to be taken seriously and fulfilled.
- g. Be honest.

Inheritance plays a role in preserving and building a nation, holy unto God. The firstborn represents the excellence of his father. Jesus is repeatedly referred to as the firstborn.

1. Firstborn over all creation (Col. 1:15)
2. Firstborn son of Mary (Luke 2:7)
3. Firstborn from the dead (Col. 1:18; Rev. 1:5)
4. Firstborn among many brothers (Rom. 8:29)

Those of us who have accepted Jesus as our Savior and have become the children of God also share in the inheritance of the firstborn (Heb. 12:23). God commanded the Israelites to set aside the firstborn of every animal and human (Ex. 13:11-13) consecrated and dedicated to God. The firstborn could be redeemed for a price. We are redeemed through the blood of Jesus. He paid the price so that we could share Heaven with Him.[5]

Levirate marriage (marriage to the childless widow of one's brother) provided a home and security for childless widows, who were the poorest of the poor. Two well-known examples of Levirate marriage laws involve Judah and Tamar (Genesis 38) and Ruth and Boaz (Ruth). It was important that the family lineage be continued. God's people were to be a race that was not contaminated by pagans and it was to multiply. A man who refused to perform his duty to build up the family lineage was disgraced forever, including all his ancestors.

Zelophehad had five daughters but no sons. By tradition, the daughters could not inherit the land. Instead, it would be given to the nearest next of kin. This effectively meant the end of a family lineage leaving the daughters with no inheritance. (At the time of a contracted marriage, the groom paid a bride price to his future father-in-law to cover the loss of a family worker. The future bride, though, would bring a dowry with her that would, in essence, be her portion of the family inheritance.) Moses wisely ruled that the order of inheritance of a man's property was (1) sons, (2) daughters, (3) brothers, (4) uncles, or (5) nearest relatives in the clan. To prevent the land from transferring to another tribe, inheriting daughters must marry members of their tribal clan.

Food for Thought: Judah and Tamar was an example of how the Levirate law was not always kept; yet eternal disgrace did not fall on Judah. In fact, he was blessed by having Jesus come from the lineage maintained by the child he and Tamar had. Why do you think that was the case? How did Judah actually keep the law? What kept Judah from completing his responsibility to Tamar with the marriage of his youngest son? (Review Jan. 17, if you have forgotten the story.)

March 2

Bible Readings: Deut. 21:10-14, Deut. 24:1-5, Deut. 22:13-21, Lev. 18:1-5, Deut. 5:18, Lev. 18:20; 20:10, Deut. 22:22-24, Lev. 19:20-22, Num. 5:11-31, Lev. 19:29, Deut. 23:17-18, Lev. 18:6-8, Deut. 22:30, Lev. 20:11-14, 17, 21-Lev. 18:9-30, Lev. 20:15-24, Ex. 22:19, Deut. 22:5

Deuteronomy 22 emphasizes virginity until marriage. As proof, the blood stained cloth or sheet from the honeymoon night must be kept. This cloth maintained the innocence of the bride in the face of any accusations presented by the husband. If a man maliciously made such derogatory claims of promiscuity against his bride, and the cloth of proof was presented, then he was fined 100 shekels of silver and 39 lashes. Additionally, he was never allowed to divorce her. (Who exactly was punished here?) If the wife could not produce a cloth of evidence, she was stoned to death.

I have found two rather different explanations for this passage. The most widely accepted one is that young girls were contracted for marriage (betrothed) shortly after puberty onset. During their long years of engagement, they were to remain true to their betrothed. (You will remember that Isaac and Esau were 40 years old when they married. The girl would be only half their age or younger at the time of marriage.) At the time of the honeymoon, the bride's hymen was ruptured causing blood-tinged secretions on the sheets of the marriage bed. If there was no blood, then the woman's virginity could be questioned. Keil and Delitzsch comment that she was sentenced to death not because she was not a virgin at marriage but rather because she lied, misrepresenting herself as a virgin although she had not been faithful during the betrothal.[11]

The second explanation comes from J.A. Thompson. He contends that virgin should be translated as female adolescent and the cloth of proof was presented as the last token of menstruation of the young girl prior to marriage. Thus, parents would have easy access to this cloth that proved the girl was not pregnant prior to marriage.[19]

Malachi 2:15 states, "Has not the LORD made them one? In flesh and spirit they are his. Why one? Because he is seeking godly offspring."[1] Here we find our reason for the importance of faithfulness to the betrothed, later becoming the spouse.

Divorce is final. Reconciliation and remarriage after a divorce is forbidden. This law is designed to prevent frivolous divorces out of momentary anger or frustration. All long-term relationships suffer times of conflict, discontent, and disappointment. "'I hate divorce,' says the LORD God of Israel, 'and I hate a man's covering himself with violence as well as with his garment,' says the LORD Almighty."[1](Malachi 2:16) Divorce is a serious decision, not one to be taken lightly. In Matthew 19:6, Jesus said, "Therefore, what God has joined together, let man not separate."[1] So why was divorce allowed at all? Most likely letters of divorce was a practice adopted from the Egyptians.[11] But also, an official divorce allowed the woman to marry again rather than being without the necessities of life: food, shelter, clothing, safety, and family.

Sexual Violations

Violation	Other Party Involved	Penalty
Adultery	Anyone other than spouse	Death for both
Fornication	Unmarried person	Disgrace
Prostitution	Anyone with the money	Separated from God
Incest	Relative by blood or marriage	Separated from God
Sex with Unclean	Menstruating female	Separation
Homosexuality	Person of same gender	Death for both
Bestiality	Animal	Death for both
Transvestite	[Wearing clothing of opposite gender so that one's true gender is not apparent.]	Separation from God

Lev. 18:27-28 provides a fitting conclusion for today's lesson. "...for all these things were done by the people who lived in the land before you, and the land became defiled. And if you defile the land, it will vomit you out as it

vomited out the nations that were before you."[1] Is your nation defiled? Will you be vomited out?

Food for Thought: What would it take to reverse our very liberal views toward sexual violations? Read Proverbs 6:20-35.

March 3
<u>Bible Readings:</u> Lev. 13, Lev. 14:33-57, Deut. 24:8-9, Lev. 15:1-12, 16-27, 32-33, Num. 5:1-4, Lev. 15:31

The Levites were responsible for pronouncing judgment upon buildings having 'leprosy,' in other words buildings having mold and mildew. In the last couple of years, Americans have experienced enormous damages to buildings due to mold in the wood structural components. This problem has become known as 'sick building syndrome' in reference to the illnesses the occupants have developed. The Levites had rules for determining the actions needed for such problems.

Leprosy of Buildings

Problem	Article	Color	Spreading	Isolate	Clean/Unclean	Treatment
Mildew	Cloth/leather	green/red	yes	7 days	Unclean	Burn it
Mildew	Cloth/leather	green/red	no	wash & 7 days: if spot faded	Clean	Tear out contamination & burn piece
Mildew	Houses	green/red	yes penetrates surface to under layers	7 days: if spread	Remove stains then Clean	Renovate
Mildew	Renovated House	green/red	yes penetrates surface to under layers	-------	Unclean	Torn down

The Hebrew word translated as leprosy actually refers to any infectious skin disease. The following chart is designed to be helpful. The diseases listed are examples, not all inclusive of every skin disease.

Classification of Skin Disorders

Lesion	Appearance	White Hair	More than Skin Deep	Treatment	Diagnosis
Leprosy, contagious	Swelling, rash, bright spot	X	X	Ceremonially unclean	Infectious skin disease
Skin Diseases	White spot	----	----	Isolate 7 days, if not spread, repeat (a) if spreads – unclean	Infectious disease
				(b) if faded – clean	Rash
				(c) if returns & spreads - unclean	Infectious disease
Psoriasis, eczema, seborrhea, etc.	raw flesh & white	X	X	Unclean	Chronic
	white swelling only	----	----	Clean	Skin disease
Boil	white swelling or reddish-white spot	X	X	Unclean	Infectious skin disease
		----	----	Isolate 7 days: (a) if spreads = Unclean	Infectious skin disease
				(b) not spread = Clean	Scar
Burn	reddish-white or white spot in raw flesh	X	X	Unclean	Infectious skin disease
	reddish-white or white spot in raw flesh	----	----	Isolate 7 days: (a) if spreads = unclean	Infectious skin disease
				(b) not spread = clean	Scar
Lice, etc.	sore	yellow hair	X	Unclean	Itch
		no black hair	----	Isolate 7 days: no change = shave all body except sore then isolate 7 more days: (a) no change = wash & be clean (b) spread = unclean	
Spots	dull white	----	----	Clean	Rash
Baldness		no hair		Clean	Bald
		receding hairline	----	Clean	Bald
	reddish/ white sore	----		Unclean	Infectious disease

Those who are pronounced unclean must:

1. tear clothing,
2. not groom hair,
3. cover lower half of face,
4. cry out "Unclean! Unclean!",
5. live alone, and
6. live outside the camp.

Jesus had His clothing removed; His hair was matted with blood and thorns. Probably His lower face was missing much of its skin and flesh from having His beard pulled out in chunks. When the sins of the world fell upon Him, His Heavenly Father could no longer commune with Him. He was unclean because of our sins. He fought the final battle alone. Jesus was crucified outside the camp or city of Jerusalem. Hebrews 13:12-13 tells us, "Jesus also suffered outside the city gate to make the people holy through his own blood. Let us, then, go to him outside the camp, bearing the disgrace he bore."[1]

"In Christ, there is redemption, even for those 'outside the camp.' No uncleanness can be so vile, no sin so horrendous, no estrangement so severe, that it is beyond the reach of Christ's redemptive love 'outside the camp.' That is the great Good News of the gospel!" (p. 78)[17]

The uncleanness attached to bodily discharges is not only necessary for hygiene purposes but also for the prevention of disease transmission via body fluids. You will recall that Rachel was able to hide the household gods she had stolen by claiming to be experiencing her monthly period (Gen. 31:35). Laban did not risk touching her or her seating area or he would be unclean. The interesting note here is that Laban did not worship the God of Jacob but rather he worshipped idols. Therefore, this law may have its roots in Mesopotamian law.

It seems rather burdensome for women to have to go through the 7-day unclean period with its final cleansing ritual on a monthly basis for decades. Remember, though, that many women do not experience any monthly discharge during the period of nursing a baby. We learned in an earlier Lessons week that babies nursed until age three. Including nine months of pregnancy, the woman had only three monthly weeks of uncleanness, plus the month or two after childbirth (based on the gender of the baby) in a time span of four years. (It is the discharge that makes the childbirth experience unclean.) Given that women married young and produced many children, their periods of uncleanness were infrequent, unless they had a health problem. Thus, unmarried women had the lack of security and the social disgrace of frequent uncleanness to bear. But, the periods of being unclean played a role in sexual restraint among young men and women.[14]

Pagan cultures incorporated temple prostitutes (both men and women) into their worship practices. In contrast, Israelite worship strictly forbade sexual contact just prior to or during worship ceremonies. Both sexual partners were considered unclean for a full day and could not participate in worship rites. This law ensured that prostitution would be detestable before God. [Sexual relations were also prohibited during war. Thus, the law protected captured slave women from sexual assault by the soldiers.][14]

Food for Thought: For Jesus' view on the unclean, read Matt. 8:1-4 and Mark 5:24-34.

March 4

Bible Readings: Lev. 11:46-47; Lev. 11: 1-40; Deut. 14:3-21; Lev. 20:25-26; Lev. 17:10-16; Ex. 22:31; Lev. 7:22-27; Lev. 19:26; Deut. 12:16, 23-25; Ex. 23:19, 34:26

The Israelites were to sacrifice and eat only clean animals. Guidelines were designated so that animals could be easily classified as clean or unclean.

Clean Animals

Distinguishing Characteristics	Animals
Chew cud AND have split hoofs	ox, sheep, goat, deer, gazelle, roe deer, wild goat, ibex(type of goat), antelope, mountain sheep, beef
Fins and scales	fish that swim in schools
Winged insects/walk on 4 jointed legs	locust, katydid, cricket, grasshopper
Birds	sparrow, pigeon, partridge, dove, quail

Unclean Animals

Distinguishing Characteristics	Animals
Only chew the cud OR only have split hoof	camel, rock badger, rabbit, pig
Scavenger/walk close to ground	rat, chameleon, gecko, skink (sand lizard), snake, weasels, lizards
Scavenger birds (birds of prey)	vultures, kites, ravens, owls, cormorant, osprey, stork, heron, hoopoe, bats, gulls, hawks, eagles, falcons
No fins and scales (water scavengers)	oysters, lobster, shrimp, eels, turtles, mussels, catfish, clams
Walks on paws	bears, cats, dogs, lions
Swarming	flies, gnats
Died of natural causes or disease or roadkill	any animal dying other than by butchering

Blood and fat may not be eaten. Both are reserved for God from the clean animals. Fat from unclean animals could be used for lubricant or soap or water repellent. Young are nurtured by their mother and, therefore, are not to be boiled in their mother's milk. Orthodox Jews do not eat meat dishes and milk dishes at the same meal.

According to Wenham, there are 4 possible explanations for classifying animals as clean or unclean: arbitrary, cultic, hygienic, or symbolic.

1. Arbitrary - The dietary laws provide a test of our obedience and only God knows the reasons behind such classifications.
2. Cultic - Unclean animals were those that had been worshipped or used in pagan worship rituals by other cultures.

3. Hygienic - Clean animals were safe to eat, but unclean animals harbored pathogenic bacteria or parasites.
4. Symbolic - The behaviors and habits of clean animals illustrated the way Israelites should live. Likewise, the behaviors and habits of unclean animals represented sinful men.[14]

If the classifications were for cultic or hygiene reasons why does the New Testament teach that Christians are freed from these dietary laws? If for arbitrary reasons, why did God change His mind in the New Testament? Symbolically, the classification may represent the righteous Jew as opposed to the sinful Gentile. All clean animals were used as a sacrifice. As a result, every meat meal was a reminder that the Israelites were a chosen nation, holy and consecrated to God.[14]

Food for Thought: What would the ancient Israelites think of our dietary habits? Why were only animals classified as clean and unclean and not plants, too?

Verse of the Week: **Joshua 3:5** "Joshua told the people, 'Consecrate yourselves, for tomorrow the LORD will do amazing things among you.' "

March 5
Bible Readings: Lev. 19:9-10, 23:22; Deut. 24:19-22; Deut. 23: 24-25; Lev. 25:35-38; Deut. 5:16; Lev. 19:3; Ex. 21:17; Lev. 20:9; Deut. 21:10-14, 18-21; Lev. 19:32; Ex. 22:21-24, 23:9; Lev. 19:33-34; Lev. 24:22; Lev. 19:14, 16-18; Ex. 23:4-5; Deut. 22:1-4; Deut. 5:21; Deut. 25:4; Deut. 22:6-7; Deut. 20:1-20; Deut. 23:9-14; Deut. 24:5

Today's reading covers a variety of related passages from the books of Moses. These passages focus on various practices that the Jews are commanded to observe after they possess the land that God has promised them.

The first group outlines a basic welfare system. There was, of course, no elaborate bureaucracy to care for the poor. These restrictions against reaping the corners of the field and not passing a second time over trees and vines to pick fruit which had been left untouched the first time, etc., were a way of allowing the poor to survive. The poor were still able, however, to maintain their dignity. They had to do something. The fruit or grain was not just set on their doorstep. For an example of how this system actually functioned, read the short book of Ruth.

The second group of laws, duties of respect and support, presents a logical plan for developing a civilized society. The witness of history testifies that any society that ignores the aged, the unfortunate, and the handicapped and that discriminates against those from outside who honestly want to become part of that society is bound to fail. Likewise, the children were called upon to be good neighbors by doing all the good they could, to all the people they could, in all the ways they could.

The remaining passages are in some respects the origins of certain practices we have in our society. Certainly Deuteronomy 22:6-7 is saying something about protecting the environment. Do not ravage the land or the creatures of the land; otherwise, there may be nothing left. A perfect example of why this law was needed was the wholesale slaughter of the buffalo during the nineteenth century. An entire species, which once literally numbered in the millions, was almost wiped out by hunters only interested in making a personal fortune.

Deuteronomy 20:5-9 probably is saying something about military deferment.

Some readers may be disturbed by Deuteronomy 20:16-18. The peoples named here had drifted deep into sin and had rejected the light that God had given them. After contending with them for centuries, God has given them up and has given their land to others who will keep His law. This is a determination that only God can make. It serves as a warning to our modern society, which often refuses to acknowledge that there is a price to be paid for turning a blind eye to sin. Any society that persists in its sins, that refuses to repent, can expect a similar fate.

Food for Thought: For a good example of how God wants us to address the needs of the poor, read Ruth. It becomes very obvious that we are to make food available to the poor provided they work for it. Ruth worked long and hard to feed herself and her mother-in-law. How would our nation fare today if the poor all had to work to eat? This seems to be the way we are trying to go, but has it worked? Children are the largest population of poor people. How can we make their parents responsible for their care and support?

March 6
Bible Readings: Lev. 22:31-33; Deut. 12:32; Num. 15:37-41; Deut. 22:12; Deut. 31:9-13; Lev. 26:3-46

The readings for today largely relate to the blessings that come from following the law and the punishments for disobedience. For faithful obedience the Jews are promised abundant harvests and peaceful conditions. If, however, they decide to set aside God's law, they can expect problems.

God's judgments begin with wasting diseases (Lev. 26:14-17) and disastrous harvests. These judgments are meant to bring the people back to God. You will note that there is a progression of sterner and sterner judgments if the people continue in their sins. The ultimate punishment for the nation is exile from the land. Biblical history testifies to the accuracy of these judgments. In 585 B.C. the Jews were removed from their land and forced to live in Babylon for seventy years. This period in biblical history is known as the Babylonian Captivity.

We should consider these judgments today. Is there a connection between contemporary society's acceptance of all types of sinful behaviors and the new fatal diseases that are sweeping some segments of our population and threatening other segments? Is there a connection between the nation's belief that character is not an important criterion in selecting a leader and the terrorists' attacks?

Food for Thought: The prediction of eating their own children will come true when Samaria is under siege (2 Kings 6:25 – 31). What kind of horror and sin turns people to commit barbaric acts? Hebrews 12 gives us guidance on discipline and functioning under hardship.

March 7
Bible Readings: Deut. 26:16-19; Deut. 28:1-68; Deut. 29:1-29; Deut. 30:1-20; Deut. 27:1-26

Today's reading, like yesterday's reading, focuses on the blessings and curses. The list in Deuteronomy is far more complete than the one mentioned in Leviticus. We must remember that Moses is giving his last speech to the people and really wants to impress upon them the need to be faithful in their commitment to God. He reminds them how God has cared for them: sending manna each day and bringing water forth from rocks in places where there were no wells. He makes an important point to which we all can relate: our past and what God has done for us and meant to us in that time.

Since I was a teenager at least one and often both of my parents have suffered several life threatening medical conditions. For the vast majority of my life thus far, I have lived under the shadow that one or possibly both of my parents could be dead in a number of hours or months. This situation had an impact on my life. As a young person, I often worried that the people I trusted more than anyone else would suddenly be taken from me. I had an older brother, but I did not feel close to him, and my sister was 13 years younger and handicapped in such a way that I doubted that she could ever be a source of emotional support. These circumstances caused me to look upon God as my Father, as the one thing in my life that could never be taken from me.

As the years have gone by, I have faced many challenges. I have worked at several jobs requiring different kinds of talents to be successful. I have also lived in several places ranging from small towns to large cities. There have been a lot of changes, but God and my relationship to Him has always stayed the same. He has always been my Father.

That is what Moses is encouraging in the lives of the people. They will be going into a new country and facing new challenges, but their devotion to God must remain constant.

Food for Thought: There are times when we all feel like we are under a curse. Make yourself stop and count the blessings you have experienced in spite of the problems. Think of how much worse things could have been had you not had the Father's love and guidance. Maybe you are going through some trying times now. Stop and think of the 'coincidences' that have occurred that kept you from total despair. God is good.

March 8
Bible Readings: Deut. 31:1-8, 14-30, Deut. 32:1-47

In chapters 31 and 32 of Deuteronomy, Moses transfers his authority to Joshua and sings Israel a song God has given him about their future unfaithfulness.

In Moses' charge to Joshua, note the two warnings he gives him: do not be afraid and do not get discouraged. Fear and discouragement are, perhaps, the two biggest enemies of any great project. Most people desire safety and tend to be overcautious in accepting life's challenge. We are content with the 'pretty good' situation we think we have and we are unwilling to try for the 'much better' situation we dream about.

A recent television commercial has young children talking about their future plans. Instead of talking about the great dreams they have, they mouth the sentiments of the middle-aged people they will become. One little boy says he wants to grow up to be a 'yes-man.' One little girl says she wants to be 'paid less for doing the same work.' The commercial's purpose is to shame the adults watching it by reminding them of their youthful dreams and comparing them to their present apathetic lives.

God calls us to be brave, not to hide behind a tree. We're only going to pass this way once, so let's make it count for Him.

Discouragement is another enemy with which we all contend. What many do not realize is that all people feel it. The chief way to defeat discouragement is to believe in what you're doing and to persist at it.

Milton Hershey, the great candy maker and philanthropist, failed in the candy making business three times. His aunt took out a mortgage on her property so he could try again. His efforts were unsuccessful and the bank initiated a foreclosure. Hershey asked for one additional week. On Friday of that week, he got a large order from England for the caramels he had been making. He sold this business, paid off the mortgage, and had a good-sized profit. Hershey took this money and started to work on an idea he had to develop an optimum recipe for milk chocolate. The rest is history.

Moses organizes his song of unfaithfulness similar to a literary form used in diplomatic circles of his day. It begins with an appeal to the accused to pay attention. Heaven and earth are then summoned as witnesses to the declaration. A series of rhetorical questions are then asked. Their obvious answers are meant to establish the guilt of the accused. Next comes a declaration of past benefits, which is meant to establish that the accused is without excuse. Finally, the charge is leveled against the accused and a proclamation of coming judgment is announced.

Food for Thought: With such an elaborate warning of their impending unfaithfulness, why do you think they didn't keep watch for signs of disobedience? Do we continue in our stubborn way even when we are warned about danger?

March 9
Bible Readings: Num. 27:12-14; Deut. 32:48-52; Deut. 33:1-29; Deut. 34:1-12

God calls Moses to climb Mt. Nebo for his view of the Promised Land. Moses knows he is to die on this mountain, as his brother Aaron had died on Mt. Horeb. Moses takes this last opportunity to address the people and gives his blessings, as any father would do. He truly loves the Israelites.

Deuteronomy 33:1-5 are verses generally believed to be poorly preserved and possibly not ordered correctly. God is depicted as having shone like the sun rising in the east with rays bursting forth from all directions. He both loves and protects His holy people.[19]

Many of the fulfillments of the blessings given can be traced to a time period of the eleventh century. For example, Reuben suffers many casualties from Ammonite attacks during the 11th century. Benjamin is said to be the one the LORD loves. Joseph (Ephraim and Mannaseh) receives the greatest blessing. The descendants of Joseph will inherit a large portion of the Promised Land. The sun and moon refers to the bounty of seasonal harvests. (Moon refers to changes of the months.) Zebulun and Issachar, after settlement, will offer unauthorized worship on Mt. Tabor (Hosea 5:1). Genesis 49:13 indicates Zebulun was a commercial seafaring tribe, but Joshua 19:10-16 does not have this tribal land encompassing any seacoast. Possibly, Moses was repeating the blessing of Jacob for this tribe. Dan does not originally occupy any land even close to Bashan, but about the 11th century, Dan moved to the north to establish the city of Dan (Judges 18). Naphtali will inherit the Sea of Galilee. Asher will inherit land that becomes famous for its olives but also its fortifications against invaders arriving via the coastal highway. You will notice that Simeon is not mentioned at all. Because of the sinful transgressions of this tribe, its numbers are so reduced that Judah absorbs it. Some distinct Simeonites will survive but in small units.[19]

Moses died at 120 years old. His eyesight and strength were still strong. The Israelites mourned for 30 days for the man whom the LORD knew face to face.

Food for Thought: Wonder what Moses thought when he saw the land of his dreams? Imagine the sense of relief and thankfulness that he had for finally getting this stiff-necked people to the land of milk and honey!

Conquering a Land

March 10
Bible Readings: Joshua 1:1-18, 3:1-17, 2:1-24, 4:1-24, 5:1-15

God's promise to Joshua is the same promise He makes to us. "As I was with Moses, so I will be with you; I will never leave you nor forsake you." (Joshua 1:5)[1] Now read that promise again but substitute your name for the "you." Claim God's promise. He's always there for you; just depend on it!

God promised the Israelites a great deal of land. All they had to do was obey Him. Look at a map. Find the Euphrates River that runs through Iraq. God promised Israel all the land from the Euphrates to the Arabian Desert to the Mediterranean Sea. Now look at Israel. It is very small compared to God's vision. Israel never reached its potential because its people became tolerant and complacent. These two adjectives are of the devil. God's people must never be tolerant and complacent. Toleration means to accept the beliefs, practices, and traits of others.[8] We must always be striving to be better Christians, setting examples and encouraging others to do the same.

After 400 years of bondage and 40 years wandering in the wilderness, Joshua is now ready to take possession of his new homeland. First, he sends spies to 'scope out the lay of the land' around Jericho. Contrary to our conception, Jericho is not a very large city. It covered only about 8.5 acres in 1400 B.C. Jericho was built on a mound and encompassed by two city walls. The outside one was little more than a stone retaining wall to hold the ground in place. (Wonder if they were worried about mudslides?) The inside wall was built of mud-brick. Houses were built between the two walls to provide further reinforcement.[7] Rahab, the harlot, lived in one of these houses. (Some commentaries prefer to call Rahab an innkeeper, but my Hebrew Bible translates the word as 'harlot.'[20] I, personally, think the real problem is that people can't accept that Jesus' lineage had a harlot in it. I believe this is another way God tells us that <u>all</u> who come to Him can be forgiven, saved into eternal life, and used in mighty ways for His Kingdom.) Rahab hides the spies, sends the king's men on a wild goose-chase, and then lowers the spies down from the window on the outside wall. In return, she is promised safety for those family members in her house at the time of the siege.

During the time of Joshua, the Jordan River was a hundred feet or more wide and at least 10-12 feet deep.[7] (Wonder if Joshua had any doubts about getting these millions of people across before they could be attacked?) Your verse for this week clearly states Joshua's bold confidence in God. He put God's presence in front of all the people -- the priests bore the Ark of the LORD well ahead of the people. It was harvest time and the Jordan River was at flood stage and very dangerous. Yet when the priests' feet touched the water, the Jordan stopped flowing. It backed up to a town called Adam (modern Damieh) some 16 miles north of Jericho and it dried up all the way to the Dead Sea -- over 20 miles![7] Many researchers believe this phenomenon was due to an earthquake. Similar occurrences have taken place in 1267, 1906, and 1927. Psalm 114:4 talks of the mountains and hills skipping. Regardless of how the Jordan dried up, God's timing was perfect -- as soon as the priests' feet touched the water. Once again God uses what may have been a natural event in a supernatural timeframe to achieve His Will.[7] Why not? After all, He is ruler of all things.

Joshua psyched out the inhabitants of Jericho. He took long enough to allow word of all the miracles God performed for the Israelites to reach the people of Jericho. Rahab had already told the spies that everyone in town was scared to death of the Israelites. Without fear, Joshua goes about erecting a 12-stone memorial to the Israelites, one stone for each tribe of Israel, all carried out of the Jordan River bed. Even more cool-headed, he has all the males 8 days and older circumcised! Had they not been the people of God, they would have been vulnerable. A few days later, the Israelites celebrate the Passover and the day after they start eating off the land of milk and honey. That very day the manna stopped. Joshua marshals his forces and marches toward Jericho. In front of him appears a heavenly messenger (the commander of God's army) who tells Joshua to remove his shoes for he is standing on holy ground!

Food for Thought: Joshua was surely singled out by God as Moses was in the burning bush experience. Imagine being an Israelite during this time. What would you think and how would you feel seeing all these miracles and signs? Would you feel joy, confidence, and fear?

March 11
Bible Readings: Joshua 6:1-27, 7:1-26, 8:1-35

Joshua uses the fear of Jericho's citizens to his advantage. Every day for six days, he marched the Israelite army around Jericho. Only the lone sounds of the trumpets (rams' horns) could be heard. God had commanded one division of armed men to head the column (possibly the army of the eastern tribes of Reuben, Gad, and half tribe of Manasseh.[23] It may be that the eastern tribes inherited the booty, including arms, from Sihon and Og when they conquered the towns and countryside.) Then would follow 7 priests blowing 7 rams' horns. Priests bearing the Ark of the LORD would be next with the rest of the fighting men (other 9 1/2 tribes) bringing up the rear. The Ark is repeatedly called the 'Ark of the LORD' to emphasize the presence of the LORD on the Mercy Seat.[23]

On the 7th (Sabbath) day the procession marched 7 times around the city upon which the 7 priests sounded the 7 horns (trumpets). Then all the people shouted and the walls fell down. Basically, the retaining wall gave way allowing the mud-brick wall to be thrown forward down the mound along with all the houses between the walls. Whether this was an after effect of the earthquake thought to have stopped the Jordan's flow or of the intense vibration of marching and horn blowing is debatable. But the final result is that God's timing was perfect. Only the supernatural intervention of God can explain the flawless timing.

After Rahab and her family were rescued, all other living things were killed, both people and animals devoted to God. In Genesis 15:16, God tells Abraham that his descendants will inherit the land when the sin of the Amorites has reached its 'full measure.' In Deuteronomy 20:17, God commands it is time to exterminate them. (God knows our hearts and our future.) All the silver, gold, and bronze went into the LORD's treasury and the town was burned.

Archaeological digs have born out these facts. Everything was to be consecrated to the LORD; nothing was to be taken by the people. Joshua placed a curse on anyone who ever tried to rebuild the fortified walls of Jericho. (We find that the Benjamites inherit Jericho, calling it the city of palms, and inhabit it. But the curse is invoked when Hiel the Bethelite undertakes to build it into a fortified city again (1 Kings 16:34).[23])

At the advice of his spies, Joshua sends only 3,000 men to take Ai. This time they met failure and 36 men were killed. Joshua prostrates himself before the Ark of the LORD. Joshua's prayer is one of a faithful man wrestling with God. (Remember Jacob wrestling with the angel?) Joshua is so devastated that he says, "Oh LORD, what can I say...?"[1] (Joshua 7:8) (Have you ever been so hurt, frightened, bewildered, or defeated that you didn't know what to even say to God? Romans 8:26 tells us "the Spirit helps us in our weakness. We do not know what we ought to pray, but the Spirit himself intercedes for us with groans that words cannot express."[1]) Joshua finishes his prayer with the tact of Moses -- reminding God that the heathen nations would view Israel's destruction as being due to a god who was weak. God reveals to Joshua that there is sin in the camp. Joshua methodically reviews the tribes until the sin is narrowed down to Achan. Why did Achan take some of the loot from Jericho? Was it greed for riches? Was it lust for beauty, i.e., the ornate robe? The answer lies in the evil nature that rationalizes "I see, I want, I take." Achan and all his family and belongings are taken to the Valley of Achor (or Valley of Achar) and stoned to death. [Josephus states the man's name was Achar,[3] meaning trouble.] The evil has been eliminated.

Joshua sends 5,000 men to ambush from the west of Ai and camped 25,000 men in the valley north of Ai. (The exact location of Ai is unknown.) Joshua sent a frontal attack that then fell back in mock retreat. When all the men chased them out into the fields, the ambush on the defenseless town is sprung -- Ai and all her people are totally destroyed.[7] Joshua built an altar and sacrificed burnt offerings and peace offerings to God. He concludes by reading the Book of the Law (Deut. 26-34) to the people.

Food for Thought: Have you ever thought that God gave us many senses and emotions, i.e., sight, smell, hearing, taste, love, anger, which can bring us great joy or great sorrow, depending on whether we allow our evil human nature or the Holy Spirit to rule our lives?

> Verse of the Week: **Joshua 22:5** "Be very careful to keep the commandment and the law that Moses the servant of the LORD gave to you: to love the LORD your God, to walk in all his ways, to obey his commands, to hold fast to him and to serve him with all your heart and all your soul."

March 12
Bible Readings: Joshua 9:1-27, 10:1-43, 11:1-23, 12:1-24

The Gibeonites trick Joshua into making a peace treaty with them by pretending to be from a distant land outside the Promised Land territory. Recall in Exodus 23:32 God specifically states the Israelites are to make no treaties with the pagan people of Canaan? Joshua's big mistake was acting without asking God first. How many times have we done the same thing? When Joshua discovers the deception, he places a curse on the Gibeonites. They will always be slaves. (Of course, their attitude is better a slave than a dead man. But then, they don't know the Lord.)

In fear and anger at the actions of the Gibeonites in allying with Israel, five Amorite kings ban together and attack Gibeon. Their new ally, Israel, comes to their defense. To do this was not an easy feat. Joshua led his men (remember he's over 90 years old now) on a night march fifteen miles uphill from Gilgal to Gibeon over wooded terrain![7] After that workout, they then have to fight the combined army of five kings! Then God intervenes. Huge hailstones started pelting down (God's throwing rocks at them!) and killed more than the sword killed. Joshua prays that God will make the sun and moon stand still until he has killed the enemy. Commentators disagree as to whether the daylight hours lengthened[23] or the moonlit hours lengthened.[7] Either way, space-age technology has been able to measure the exact amount of time that elapsed during this extended period plus the other time when the shadows moved backward on the steps (2 Kings 20:9-11) by simply measuring the exact time the earth has not been in perfect rotational timing since its creation! Joshua's men chase the survivors for 11 miles![7] (Whew, I'm exhausted just thinking about it all!) He captures and kills all five kings, then destroys the town of Mekkedah. (This 90 year old can get pretty riled up!) I guess he finally got tired because it was the next day before he finished taking the town of Lachish. In short order, all five towns associated with the executed kings were completely destroyed leaving no survivors. These victories brought almost all of southern Canaan under Israelite control. Only the coastal towns remained. (Hebron, you will remember, was the burial site of Sarah, Abraham's wife.)

Upon news of Israel's victory in the south, the northern kings join forces to fight Israel. God delivered the northern kings into Israel's hands. Their chariots were burned, their horses hamstrung, and all their people were destroyed. Hazor was the only town burned. The tribes of Israel inherited the other towns.

In summary, Moses had led the Israelites to defeat two kings (Sihon and Og) east of the Jordan River. Joshua led them to defeat 31 kings west of the river. Today, the towns captured by Joshua are located in Israel, West Bank, and Golan Heights. Those taken by Moses are located in western Jordan. Is it easier to understand why Israel is constantly at war in these areas? They are trying to regain control of the land they inherited from Moses and Joshua's campaigns, their homeland.

Food for Thought: Gilgal, meaning liberty, was Joshua's home base. He always went back to Gilgal to refresh and prepare for his next campaign. Where is your Gilgal? How do people function without a Gilgal? Or when their Gilgal is in constant turmoil?

March 13 & 14

Bible Readings: March 13: Joshua 13:1-12,14-33, 14:1-15, 15:1-12, 15:20-62, 16:1-9, 17:1-10,14-18; Jdgs 1:20a
<u>Bible Readings: March 14</u>: Joshua 18:1-28, 19:1-51, 20:1-9, 21:1-45

Joshua had led the Israelites to many victories over the hill country inhabitants. Cities and peoples of the plains were still unconquered. The most probable reason is that chariots of iron (a plentiful ore of the plains) were very fast and effective on flat plains but were useless on the slopes and rocks of the hill country. The land of Canaan that was promised to the Israelites encompassed territory that was bound on the:

South by the Brook (or River) of Egypt and extended to the southern end of the Dead Sea,
West by the Mediterranean Sea,
North to include Lebanon and the Golan Heights, and
East by the Jordan River and the east side of the Dead Sea.[7]

According to Caleb's testimony in Joshua 14:10, the Israelites have been fighting the inhabitants of the Promised Land for 5 years. Joshua decides it is time to divide the land among the tribes and let each tribe settle their land and dispossess its remaining Canaanites. The tribes of Reuben, Gad, and half tribe of Manasseh had settled for land east of the Jordan River. So, Joshua divided land west of the river among the remaining 9 1/2 tribes. Altogether, the land was dispersed according to the following table.

Lessons of Love

Promised Land Allotments

Mother	Son	Location of Land Area	Cities
Leah	Reuben	East of Dead Sea and north of Arnon River	Arnon, Medeba, Heshbon, Dibon, Bamoth Baal, Jahaz, Beth Baal Meon, Kedemoth, Mephaath, Kiriathaim, Sibmah, Zereth Shahar, Beth Peor, Beth Jeshimoth, *plus others*
	Levi	None	See next chart
	Simeon	Triangular piece carved out of Judah's territory in the Negev	Beersheba (Sheba), Moladah, Hazar Shual, Balah, Ezem, Eltolad, Bethul, Hormah, Ziklag, Beth Marcaboth, Hazar Susah, Beth Lebaoth, Sharuhen, Ain, Rimmon, Ether, Ashan
	Judah	All land west and southwest of Dead Sea (except for Simeon's land around Beersheba)	Kabzeel, Eder, Jagur, Kinah, Dimonah, Adadah, Kedesh, Hazor, Ithnan, Ziph, Telem, Bealoth, Hazor Hadattah, Kerioth, Hezron, Amam, Shema, Moladah, Hazar Gaddah, Heshmon, Beth Pelet, Hazar Shual, Beersheba, Biziothiah, Baalah, Iim, Ezem, Eltolad, Kesil, Hormah, Ziklag, Madmannah, Sansannah, Lebaoth, Shilhim, Ain, Rimmon, Eshtaol, Zorah, Ashnah, Zanoah, En Gannim, Tappuah, Enam, Jarmuth, Adullam, Socoh, Azekah, Shaaraim, Adithaim, Gederah, Zenan, Hadashah, Migdal Gad, Dilean, Mizpah, Joktheel, Lachish, Bozkath, Eglon, Cabbon, Lahmas, Kitlish, Gederoth, Beth Dagon, Naamath, Makkedah, Libnah, Ether, Ashan, Iphtah, Ashnah, Nezib, Keilah, Aczib, Mareshah, Ekron, Ashdod, Gaza, Shamir, Jattir, Socoh, Dannah, Kiriath Sannah, Anab, Eshtemoh, Anim, Goshen, Holon, Giloh, Arab, Dumah, Eshan, Janim, Beth Tappuah, Aphekah, Humtah, Kiriath Arba, Zior, Maon, Carmel, Ziph, Juttah, Jezreel, Jokdeam, Zanoah, Kain, Gibeah, Timnah, Halhul, Beth Zur, Gedor, Maarath, Beth Anoth, Eltekon, Kiriath Baal, Rabbah, Beth Arabah, Middin, Secacah, Nibshan, the City of Salt, En Gedi, *plus others*

	Issachar	Small portion of land south of Naphtali with Jordan River on its east side and Manasseh to the south	Jezreel, Kesulloth, Shunem, Hapharaim, Shion, Anaharath, Rabbith, Kishion, Ebez, Remeth, En Hannim, En Haddah, Beth Pazzez, Tabor, Shahazumah, Beth Shemesh
	Zebulum	Small portion of land wedged between Issachar, Naphtali, Asher, and Manasseh	Kattath, Nahalal, Shimron, Idalah, Bethelem, Chisloth-tabor, Neah, Gath Hepher, Eth Kazin, Rimmon, Daberath, Japhia, Hannathon,
Rachel	Manasseh	Full width of land from Mediterranean Sea across Jordan to the Syrian Desert. Most of west side of Jordan Valley – all of eastern side of Sea of Galilee down to Jabbok River	All of Bashan + 60 cities of Jair, half of Gilead, including Edrei, Ashtaroth (royal cities), Beth Shan, Ibleam, Dor, Endor, Taanach, Megiddo
	Benjamin	Land between Judah and Joseph-From Jordan River north to Jericho, west through hill country and wilderness, south over Mt. Ephron to Jerusalem to north bay of Dead Sea	Jericho, Beth Hoglah, Emek Keziz, Beth Arabah, Zemaraim, Bethel, Avvim, Parah, Ophrah, Kephar Ammoni, Ophni, Geba, Gibeon, Ramah, Beeroth, Mizpah, Kephirah, Mozah, Rekem, Irpeel, Taralah, Zelah, Haeleph, **Jerusalem**, Gibeah, Kiriath
	Ephraim	Centrally located between Benjamin and Manasseh – no sea or river coast	Some cities of the territory of Manasseh, Taanath Shiloh, Janoah, Ataroth Addar, Upper Beth Horon, Michmethath, Naarah, Tappuah, Gezer, Ataroth
Bilhah	Dan	Seacoast land west of Ephraim	Zorah, Eshtaol, Ir Shemesh, Shaalabbin, Aijalon, Ithlah, Elon, Timnah, Ekron, Eltekeh, Gibbethon, Baalath, Jehud, Bene Berak, Gath Rimmon, Me Jarkon, Rakkon, Leshem (Dan), territory near Joppa
	Naphtali	Hill country west of Sea of Galilee extending to northern border	Ziddim, Zer, Hammath, Rakkath, Kinnereth, Adamah, Ramah, Hazor, Kedesh, Edrei, En Hazor, Iron, Migdal El, Horem, Beth Anath, Beth Shemesh, Adami Nekeb, Jabneel, Lakkum
Zilpah	Gad	East of Jordan River between Jabbok River and north end of Dead Sea	Ramath Mizpah, Betonim, Mahanaim, Beth Haram, Succoth, Beth Nimrah, Zaphon

	Asher	All seacoast land west of Naphtali	Helkath, Hali, Beten, Achshaph, Allammelech, Amad, Mishal, Mahalab, Aczib, Ummah, Aphek, Rehob, Carmel, Shihor Libnath, Kabul, Ebron, Hammon, Kanah, Tyre, Hosah, Beth Emek, Neiel

Above list is not all-inclusive. Many towns are not stated but simply listed as 'the territory of.' Judah had more than it needed so some of its towns were given to Simeon and Benjamin.

Caleb received his own town from Judah's land. Six cities of refuge were named. They were located in different areas of the land so that all Israelites would have equal access to refuge, if needed. Joshua, also, received a town of his own in his tribe of Ephraim.

The Levites were allotted no land of their own but were given towns, with the pastureland around them. The Levites' inheritance was to be called to serve the LORD. They shared in the sacrifices brought to the LORD.

Towns of Levi

Location	Descendant of	Cities (Cities of Refuge in bold)
Southwest	Aaron	From Judah – **Hebron**, Libnah, Jattir, Eshtemoa, Holon, Debir, Beth Shemesh, Juttah From Simeon – Ain From Benjamin – Gibeon, Geba, Anathoth, Almon
West	Kohath	From Dan – Eltekeh, Gath Rimmon, Gibbethon, Aijalon From Manasseh West – Taanach, Gath Rimmon From Ephraim – **Shechem**, Gezer, Kibzaim, Beth Horon
North	Gershon	From Manasseh East – **Golan**, Be Eshtarah From Issachar – Kishion, Daberath, Jarmuth, En Gannim From Asher – Mishal, Abdon, Helkath, Rehob From Naphtali – **Kedesh**, Hammoth Dor, Kartan
East & Northwest	Merari	From Zebulun – Jokneam, Nahalal, Kartah, Dimnah From Reuben – **Bezer**, Jahaz, Kedemoth, Mephaath From Gad – **Ramoth**, Mahanaim, Jazer, Heshbon

Despite the doubts and fears and rebellions, the children of Israel had inherited the Promised Land.
Food for Thought: Wonder how long it took them to take their blessings for granted?

March 15
Bible Readings: Joshua 22:1-34, 23:1-16, 24:1-28; Judges 2:6

After Joshua's farewell speech to the troops from east of the Jordan, he dismisses them to return home. It's interesting to note how suspicious the Israelites were of each other. Although massive in number, they are still typical family siblings. They get angry and lash out at each other, but they stick together when an outside threat appears. On the way home, the 'easterners' get worried that their children might someday be denied access to the LORD's dwelling place in the west. They decided to erect a monument to remind the 'westerners' that they had helped them claim their land and they, too, worshipped God. Their monument is a replica of the LORD's altar, now located in Shiloh. Immediately, their western relatives become suspicious of their actions and assume their motives are evil. A delegation is sent to the easterners to determine the facts and plead for voluntary obedience to God. (How many delegations of Christians have pled with you to obey God's call or His commandments?) They are pleased to find out their assumptions about their siblings were wrong. Have you assumed the worst about friends or family without finding out the facts? Or, maybe you assumed the best just because they were friends or family and you couldn't see the truth for your blinders? Either way, we have to see people for who and what they are before we can understand their actions. Many times understanding is the key to reaching someone for the LORD.

Once when I worked the geriatric floor, I had a patient who was famous for her acid tongue and hatefulness. These are not good characteristics in anyone. Since I worked the desk, I got to spend several days listening to the staff complain about her. One day we were short-handed so I took lunch to her. The nastier she got, the more I tried to meet her demands and ask about her problems. Then tears rolled down her face. She had spent her adult life in her cherished home on the Gulf Coast -- that is, until Hurricane Camille came. It took her house, her pictures, her furniture, her clothing, and her relics -- monuments of her past. She walled her true self up so she would never have to experience the full extent of that loss. She lashed out at those around her to be sure no one got close enough to make her 'feel' again. Without even knowing it, she had let monuments to her past become her god. Now in her 70s, she needed an understanding person to show her the way to find real meaning to life. She needed the love and comfort of a heavenly Father.

Food for Thought: At first glance, the monuments the Israelites erect seem strange and almost bizarre (often only piles of rocks). But, if you are a Civil War buff, like we are, you realize that people erect monuments to remind future generations of their ties to the great events and/or people of the past. The Israelites, also, erected reminders of their ties to each other. What monuments mark your past? A monument can be anything that we frequently revisit in our hearts and minds that remind us of the past -- both good and painful reminders. How will others remember you? During your time on earth, what monuments or markers are you leaving behind to remind your descendants of how to find their way through life?

March 16
Bible Readings: Judges 2:8-9; Joshua 24:29-30, 24:32-33; Judges 1:1-10, 1:16-20; Joshua 15:13-14; Judges 1:11-15, 1:22-29; Joshua 13:13, 16:10, 17:11-13, 15:63; Judges 1:21, 1:30-36, 2:1-5

With the deaths of Joshua and Eleazer, the High Priest, the regime of Moses has ended. The Israelites have a new generation of leaders. But, will they do as well? Now the tribes must run out the remaining Canaanites from their allotted land. Judges 1:32-33 reports that the people of Asher and Naphtali "lived among the Canaanite inhabitants of the land."[1] Manasseh, unable to drive the Canaanites out, forced them into slave labor. Ephraim, Zebulun, and Dan did the same. In fact, all tribes except Judah, Benjamin, and Simeon are well infiltrated with Canaanites. The Simeonites are slowly absorbed into Judah. Jerusalem is on the border between Benjamin and Judah. The Jebusites continue to maintain their hold on Jerusalem. Judah is not able to seize the coastal plains from the Canaanites. The coastal plains provided the main highways and most of the trade traffic between Egypt and Europe and Asia. The inhabitants and their trade allies would heavily protect this area. Centuries later, the Israelites will be divided into the Northern Kingdom (9 tribes north and east of Judah) and the Southern Kingdom (Judah, Benjamin, and the remaining pockets of Simeonites). The people become contaminated, morally and spiritually. Ultimately, the Northern Kingdom will be taken captive first and years later the Southern Kingdom is enslaved, too. This should be a warning to all of us, little sins of disobedience or negligence grow into big sins. I saw a sign on a church marquee recently that said "From little acorns, grow mighty oaks." From the smallest of pinecones grows the giant Sequoias. Disobeying God, even in ways we believe are insignificant, produces huge results later.

Food for Thought: Little works for God can also grow mighty witnesses in a community. What small kindness can you do today that will make someone else's day wonderful? If you couldn't speak, would strangers recognize you as a Christian from your works?

March 17
Bible Readings: Judges 2:7, 10, 11-23; Judges 3:1-31; Joshua 24:31

As long as Joshua and those leaders of his generation were alive, Israel followed God. Once that generation had passed away, the new generation 'knew not God.' The realization that every nation is only one generation away from paganism should frighten all people to rise up and preach the gospel. There are primarily two reasons the Israelites fell away from God. First, they did not obey God and completely destroy all pagans and pagan worship from their midst. Not only did they tolerate pagans, they intermarried, worked, and traded with them. (Doesn't this sound like the so-called 'civilized' nations of today?) They were thoroughly integrated. Second, the Israelites did not teach their children about God and the mighty miracles He had performed.[23] All of us, both as parents and/or citizens, are commanded to "train a child in the way he should go, and when he is old he will not turn from it."[1] (Proverbs 22:6) We are also told, "the fear of the LORD is the beginning of knowledge . . . ."[1] (Proverbs 1:7) In the late 1990s, a popular athletic apparel company had the slogan 'No Fear.' It always made me shudder. Invariably, it was worn on the shirts of most young people. The words of Jesus, as He suffered on the cross, come to mind, "Father, forgive them, for they do not know what they are doing."[1] (Luke 23:43) They are "like sheep going astray."[1] (1 Peter 2:25) We are all only one generation away . . . .

Food for Thought: How have you influenced the younger generation to serve the Lord? Have they watched you pray, study the word, attend worship, and remain faithful? Every day you touch lives. It's not too late to serve God.

Period of the Twelve Judges			
Judge	Years Israel Oppressed	Enemy Killed	Years of Peace
Othniel	8	?	40
Ehud	18	10,000	80
Shamgar	?	600	?
Deborah	20	?	40
Gideon	7	135,000	40
Tola	3	Abimelech	23
Jair	--	--	22
Jephthah	18	20 towns (42,000 brethren in civil war)	6
Ibzan	--	--	7
Elon	--	--	10
Abdon	--	--	8
Samson	40	4,000	20

Cushan-Rishathaim is probably a nickname meaning 'double-wickedness' -- a terrible legacy. For 8 years the Israelites were his subjects. Caleb's nephew, Othniel, is called by God to deliver the people from oppression. (Caleb's parents must have been very proud of their family.) For 40 years there is peace. Then the Moabites overpower them and rule 18 years. God uses a trait as simple as being left-handed to empower Ehud to kill the evil king. Israel was in a cycle of freedom to oppression to freedom. Over and over the cycle replayed for about 350 years, almost as long as they were slaves in Egypt. (Some commentators say it was 400 - 450 years.) God had removed His hand from them, but even then, He didn't abandon them. Periodically, He raised up judges (leaders would be a better translation) to save the Israelites.

March 18
Bible Readings: Judges 4:1-24; Judges 5:1-31

The only female leader Israel ever has is Deborah. Keeping in mind the dominance of the Israelite male in religious, political, family, and social life, it is truly remarkable that the people seem to readily accept that God has called Deborah to a leadership position. Not only a political leader but also a military commander, she seems to be Israel's version of Joan of Arc. Maybe the reason for Barak's insecurity is the oppression had been heavily inflicted on the males. Women may have escaped much of this due to the perception they were the 'weaker sex.' In other words, they were underestimated to be of no danger or threat! This would explain Deborah's ease at rising to a leadership role and the military leader Barak's weakness.

We are not told the size of Sisera's army, only that it had 900 iron chariots. Historically, the Israelites never chose to use captured chariots for fighting, preferring simpler weapons, i.e., slings, bow and arrows, swords, clubs, axes. (You don't need much when God is on your side!) Israel defeats Sisera's army, sending survivors in retreat.

Again a woman is underestimated. Sisera sought refuge with a Kenite woman named Jael. (Recall Moses' father-in-law was a Kenite who moved into the Israelite nation and became one of them in practice.) Jael calmly goes about luring her prey into a deep sleep (milk induces sleep) and then with a steady hand and a powerful blow, she drives a tent spike through his temple into the ground! (I bet her husband slept with one eye open after that!)

Deborah and Barak composed a victory song that gives more insight into the battle between the armies. God had intervened with a powerful assault -- the earth shook and the heavens poured. Josephus says the mighty storm was at the Israelites' backs, blinding the enemy. He further states there was "a vast quantity of rain and hail" (p. 140).[3] The song recounts how the flooded river Kishon swept many of the enemy away. Deborah credited the fighting men of Naphtali and Zebulun (the battle was on their border with Issachar) with saving Israel while the tribes of Reuben, Dan, and Asher are openly disgraced for lack of participation. Supporting troops from Ephraim and Benjamin are praised, but it is unknown as to whom the "princes of Issachar" refers.

Food for Thought: God has again used earthquakes, hail, and a swollen river to defeat those who are evil. We are told such disasters will increase in the end times. How many thousands have been killed by such events the last 20 years?

> Verses of the Week: Ruth 1: 16-17 "Where you go I will go, and where you stay I will stay. Your people will be my people and your God my God. Where you die I will die, and there I will be buried."

March 19
Bible Readings: Judges 6:1-40; Judges 7: 1-25; Judges 8: 1-3

The Midianites were distant relatives of Israel, having arisen from the son of Abraham and Keturah. The Israelites and Midianites were initially on good terms with each other. When Moses fled from the Egyptians to Midian, he married Zipporah who was a daughter of a Midianite priest, from the subgroup called Kenites. The

Kenites were skilled metal craftsmen, possibly descended from Tubal-Cain.[5] Moses' in-laws joined up with the Israelites in the Sinai Peninsula. In Genesis 25:6, Abraham gives gifts to his son Midian and sends him eastward to live. Midian is not allowed to share in Isaac's inheritance. This sets the stage for rivalry and bitterness between Israel and the Midianites. As long as Israel was a small nation enslaved by Egypt, there was no reason for the Midianites to despise them. After all, the Israelites were slaves and the Midianites were free. But when Israel exited Egypt as a large nation of people out to conquer the people of Canaan, Midian became a lifelong foe. In Numbers 22, the Midianites team up with the Moabites to hire Baalam to curse the Israelites. Later the Midianites use their women to try to entice Israel to sin. By the time of Numbers 25, God had singled out the Midianites for destruction.[7]

The Amalekites descended from Esau -- a bad lot. By the time of Gideon, the Midianites had made another ill-fated alliance. The Midianites, Amalekites, and other eastern people (almost surely included Moabites) join in raiding parties on the fertile agricultural ground of the Gilead region where the eastern 2 1/2 tribes of Israel lived.[7] These raids were most likely so they and their herds could reap the benefits of plenty of food they didn't have to grow. They were nomads whose numbers were large enough to take whatever food and grass they wanted and leave nothing behind. The Israelites had worked hard to build up their land and now they were reduced to poverty and hiding in caves.

Normally wheat was threshed on the top of a hill or mound. The sheaves of wheat were initially beaten or trampled to dislodge the grains from the head. Then a winnowing fork was used to toss the grain in the air where the wind blew the chaff away. Thus, an elevated area made better use of the wind. These threshing floors were always located well outside the city, near the fields where there would be no protection from raiders. So, Gideon is found threshing wheat inside the city of Ophrah in the city winepress (a pit dug out of solid rock). He was trying to hide his activities from the raiders. Ironically, the angel of the LORD addresses Gideon as the "mighty warrior!" (Keep in mind he's cowered in a rock pit inside the city.) Gideon's response to God's call for him to save the people is almost identical to Saul's years later (1 Samuel 9:21). Gideon says his clan is the weakest of his tribe and he is the least in his family. (God frequently calls the weakest, so His great might is able to be revealed. The weakest must be wholly dependent on God for deliverance.) Gideon is very insecure and doubtful. First, God has to convince Gideon He really is God by consuming in fire a sacrifice Gideon offers. Second, God has to convince Gideon that he really has been called by God to save Israel. This last testing of God's Will is frequently referred to as 'putting out the fleece.' Those who doubt their abilities to hear and understand God's Will symbolically put out the fleece by praying for God to do something unusual (give a sign) and then waiting to see if it happens. Gideon was a very cautious doubter; he put out the fleece twice. At this point, note that God is being very patient. A man who admits to being the weakest of the weak is interrogating God. In fact he is such a coward, his first action to God's command that he tear down his father's pagan altar and idols is to sneak out at night and do it like a delinquent boy. Although, his father saves him from the mad townspeople!

Finally, Gideon is confident enough to raise an army. But then God tells him to send the frightened ones home and 22,000 left! (The amazing thing about this is that Gideon wasn't the first one out of there!) Out of the 10,000 remaining, God says to let them all drink and keep only those men who kneel and drink out of a cupped hand. (Conjecture is they used their left hands to drink while keeping their right hands on their swords.[7]) Gideon is really scared now. He has only 300 men left to attack 135,000 Midianites! God allows Gideon to overhear an enemy soldier describe his dream of being overrun by the Israelites.

Gideon separates the men into groups of 100 and places them on 3 opposing sides of the Midianite camp. His strategy is simple: attack at night and trick the enemy into believing the Israelite army is enormous. In Gideon's time, night fighting wasn't done because of the inability to hold a torch while fighting hand-to-hand. Any night maneuvers required the leader to carry a torch for each group (platoon) of men. All the way back to the exodus, a combination of trumpet sounds were used as signals to the marching crowd, an effective means of relaying orders.

Each group would have a trumpet to sound orders to the men. Gideon had all 300 men carry hidden torches and trumpets so that at the signal the enemy would believe they were being attacked by 300 platoons of men! Additionally, he chose 10 p.m. to attack when the watch guards were in the process of changing shifts.[7] He was so successful in surprising and frightening the enemy that they killed each other in their confusion! It just goes to show, God can use us all even those of us who are just scared chickens!

Food for Thought: Have you ever spoken up for what was right even though you were frightened to do so? Did you seek God's help and presence? Our Father hears even a brief plea. God loves His children and never leaves them, even during times of fear and weakness. To paraphrase Paul, "When I am weak, He is strong."

March 20
Bible Readings: Judges 8:4-35; Judges 9:1-57

As with most weak people, a major success goes to their heads. Their confidence is bolstered into a huge ego that now looks down on those who portray the same weaknesses our heros left behind. Gideon is now truly considered a mighty warrior among his men. When he entered the cities of Succoth and Peniel, the frightened elders of the towns took one look at the small band of men and were sure they hadn't been able to eliminate so many Midianites. So they refused food to Gideon's army for fear of Midianite retaliation. When Gideon finally manages to kill the escaped Midianite kings, he returns to retaliate. Proverbs 16:18 says, "Pride goes before destruction, a haughty spirit before a fall."[1] I believe pride was working in Gideon's life. Although, he refuses to be king and states his son won't be king either, this turns out to be a false statement. Gideon's son Abimelech becomes ruler of Israel in a most ruthless way; he murders 70 of his brothers, only one (Jotham) escapes. But this happens after Gideon's death. Gideon declared God would rule Israel, but at the same time he collects 43 pounds of gold from the plunder and makes it into an ephod (a holy object). The Israelite people of the area start worshipping the object. Regardless of what Gideon's reasons might have been for making the ephod, the outcome was still idol worship.

Josephus describes Abimelech as the illegitimate son of Gideon's concubine.[3] (Remember that the consequences of sin always catch up with you.) Gideon started out as a coward and doubter, became egotistical and domineering, made an idol that, as a leader of Israel, he allowed the people to worship, and committed adultery. This last act brought judgment on all his sons so that even Jotham must have been scarred by Abimelech's violence. But worshipping the idol brought judgment on the people. The enemy from without killed Gideon's brothers and the enemy from within killed his sons.

Jotham makes use of Shechem's natural amphitheater to announce his condemnation of its citizens for making Abimelech king. His vantage point is atop Mt. Gerizim that is opposite Mt. Ebal with the city of Shechem in the valley. The two mountaintops are about 2 miles apart. The acoustics are so good a speaker could be heard on both hillsides.[7] This was the same site where Moses commanded the Israelites to read the blessings on one mountaintop and the curses on the other, after they crossed the Jordan (Deut. 27:11-13). From his distant mountain perch, Jotham easily escapes capture.

Abimelech reigned for 3 years before there was an insurrection. Abimelech puts down the move by killing all Shechem's people and burning the town. (Review Gen. 34 for more history.) Jotham's curse of fire on the city has come true.

In need of a new city to reign over, Abimelech attacks Thebez. The people locked themselves in a guard tower. When Abimelech got close to the tower, a woman dropped the upper millstone on his head. Abimelech commanded his armor-bearer to run him through with his sword so no one could say a woman killed him. (Too late, old boy!)

[Today, we think of an upper millstone as an enormous, extremely heavy stone that turns on top of one equal to it in size to grind the grain. My grandfather Baker and great-grandfather Burns had mills like this. But in the time of the judges, a saddle-quern millstone was used. The bottom stone was 20-30 inches long by 10-15 inches wide. It was higher at the back and lower at the front (like a saddle). The upper stone was flat on the grinding surface and rounded on the topside. An Israelite would kneel behind the high back of the stone, put some grain on the surface, and rub the upper stone back and forth to grind the grain.[7] This was very similar to the position and motions used by people of the 1800s to wash clothes on a washboard.]

Food for Thought: We must always be on alert not to allow any object or person to become an idol in our lives. Look around you and do a self-evaluation. If there is any thing (or person) that you truly believe would stop your life and service to God if it were removed, then you have an idol. God commands that we serve and worship Him. He is to be first and foremost in our lives. How do you get rid of an idol? Through prayer and the strength of God you make a concentrated effort to refocus your life solely on the Lord. Objects that are idols can be eliminated, but you will find it hurts. God can overcome.

March 21
<u>Bible Readings: Judges 10:1-18; Judges 11:1-40; Judges 12:1-15</u>

The Israelites seem to never learn. Again they have turned to pagan worship. God delivered them from 7 pagan nations, but they have in turn come to serve 7 pagan gods. Their iniquity was complete. The measure of their sin equaled the measure of God's delivering grace. God allowed the Philistines and Ammonites to rule over the Israelites and oppress them for 18 years because they had forsaken the one, true God.[23]

<u>Pagan gods Served</u>

Nation	god	Traits
Canaan	Baal	Male sexual love and fertility god
	Ashtoreth	Female sexual love and fertility god (Baal's wife)
Moab	Chemosh	Human sacrifice
Ammon	Moloch or Milcom	Child sacrifice
Sidon	Astarte	Unknown
Philistines	Dagon	Chief god
Aram	?	Unknown

God loves His people so much that he again raises up a leader to save them when they cry out for help. Jephthah first finds out what the Ammonites want from Israel. The answer is simple -- they want their land back. Jephthah tries to reason with them, reminding them that they would take whatever their god provided for them, so why shouldn't the Israelites? Ultimately, he destroys the Ammonites. But before he does, he makes a foolish vow that on the surface seems to hark back to pagan worship. He vows to sacrifice whatever comes out of the door of his house to meet him when he returns. Now, unless he has a very unusual household, the "whatever" is going to be a person. Any prudent individual would know at the time of the vow that human sacrifice would be the result. Therefore, it is possible this vow is about dedicating a person of the household to the service of God. Jephthah's only child, a daughter, turns out to be the "whatever." First, let's analyze the situation. God has made it clear throughout His word that human sacrifice is an abomination. Second, Jephthah was soliciting God's help to be victorious. God would not have answered his prayer if human sacrifice had been intended. Third, the concept of burnt offering was a continual sacrifice of the whole offering showing complete obedience and submission, such as the spiritual sacrifice of one whose life is dedicated to the service of God. Fourth, the girl was mourning that she would never marry, not that she was about to die. Fifth, it becomes an annual custom for the young Israelite women to honor the daughter of Jephthah. They honor her for her complete unselfish obedience to submit to her father's vow as a spiritual burnt offering (whole) to the LORD's service.[23] Today, we think of nuns and missionaries who never marry but instead serve God all their lives.

Food for Thought: Israel can't even enjoy their freedom from oppression without fighting each other. Why does every nation have to experience a civil war? Why can we not love our neighbors as ourselves? Civil war starts out like a cancer cell -- it eats a nation alive from the inside out. Civil war cannot be stopped until it has self-destructed. Are you part of a family headed on a course of civil war and self-destruction? is your town? is your church? is your workplace?

March 22
Bible Readings: Ruth

The story of Ruth is often hailed as the greatest love story of all time. Many mistake this to mean a great love between Ruth and Boaz, the kinsman-redeemer who enters a levirate marriage with her. The great love displayed by Ruth is the love and dedication to her mother-in-law Naomi.

Ruth was from a nation that frequently antagonized and attacked the Israelites during their history. She was a Moabite. Naomi, along with her husband and two sons, sought relief from a famine by fleeing to Moab. The sons married Moabite women, Ruth's husband was Mahlon, of the tribe of Judah from the city of Bethlehem. During Naomi's ten-year sojourn in Moab, her husband and both sons die. When she packs up and leaves to go home to Judah, she tells her widowed daughters-in-law to return to their fathers' homes where they will have security and a chance to remarry. Ruth then utters the famous words, "Don't urge me to leave you or to turn back from you. Where you go I will go, and where you stay I will stay. Your people will be my people and your God my God. Where you die I will die, and there I will be buried. May the LORD deal with me, be it ever so severely, if anything but death separates you and me."[1] (Ruth 1:16-17) (These words have been used in many marriage ceremonies since, but few people realize they were originally meant as a vow of allegiance to one's mother-in-law!)

Upon reaching Judah, Ruth proceeds to perform the lowly, dangerous task of gleaning in order to feed Naomi and herself. By Devine Will she chooses Boaz's field and works hard all day. She is noticed by Boaz and treated kindly. Boaz makes arrangements for her safety, water, and food. (Sounds like he's making overtures to me!) When Naomi hears of all this, she proceeds to become a matchmaker. (Can't you just imagine her ole eyes and ears all perked up for this juicy bit of intervening? Why, she's forgotten all about being a sad, old, impoverished widow woman!) Next thing you know Naomi has cooked up an elaborate plan for Ruth to get the ole nose ring in Boaz (not literally). Boaz is much older than Ruth so he is flattered beyond belief that Ruth wants to marry him. (Now don't you just know Ruth must have asked herself several times if she was crazy following her mother-in-law's advice?) Boaz immediately starts making the legal arrangements to marry Ruth.

By levirate marriage contract law, there is someone ahead of Boaz with the right to marry Ruth. Boaz tracks the ole boy down and presents the case that it is time for the levirate contract to be fulfilled. Now the ole boy jumps at the chance to redeem the family land until he finds out Ruth comes with it as a bride. He doesn't want to take any chances that the property of his estate might become controlled by any children he would have with Ruth. (By levirate law, their first son would carry Ruth's dead husband Mahlon's name, but all other children would belong to Ruth's current kinsman-redeemer husband. Thus, they would share in his estate.) Boaz has played his cards right! He jumps up and says, "SOLD!" As they say, the rest is history. Boaz and Ruth have a son, Obed, who is destined to be the grandfather of king David and a predecessor of Jesus. (Just goes to show that sometimes your mother-in-law is right! The Bible is just full of miracles!) [Note: Be sure you read the literal version of Ruth out of your Bible, so you can get more details than my hillbilly version provides.]

Food for Thought: Wonder how many fewer marriages there would be if both people had to vow to live and die with their mothers-in-law? Many times life turns out that way, but that is seldom one's course from the beginning.

March 23
Bible Readings: Judges 13:1-25; Judges 14:1-20; Judges 15:1-20; Judges 16:1-31

In contrast to the beautiful story of Ruth, we come to Samson, considered a judge or leader of Israel during this period. (If Ruth is a 'woman's story,' then Samson is definitely a 'man's story.') In my opinion, Samson is a rather crude, arrogant, bad-tempered spoiled brat! Not at all the kind of man you want for a husband or a son. (Samson is from the tribe of Dan who are always known as ferocious warriors. Dan's blessing from Jacob was that he would be the judge who provided justice for Israel (Genesis 49:16-18). Because of their bravery, Dan's tribe provided the rear guard for Israel when they marched from Sinai through the wilderness to the Promised Land in Numbers 10:25. But by the time of the Revelation, Messianic Jews are convinced the antichrist will come from the tribe of Dan.)

The conception of Samson resembles that of Isaac. In both cases, an angel visits their mothers, heralding the blessed event about to occur. Through Isaac a great nation was to be born; whereas, through Samson a great nation was to be saved. Centuries later an angel would announce the coming birth of another baby, Jesus, who would provide eternal salvation for all who believe in Him.

The angel tells Samson's parents that he is to be raised a Nazirite. His mother is not to eat grapes of any kind nor eat anything unclean. (Yeast is found on the outside of grapes and is responsible for the fermentation process to make wine. The high sugar and water content of grapes and their growth in the sun provide the three requirements for yeast growth: sugar, moisture, and warmth.) The angel specifies the boy's hair is never to be cut. This is a rule for life because he is to be a Nazirite until his death. Nazirite vows were often made by many people but generally lasted for 30, 60, 90, or 100 days. The only Nazirites for life recorded in the Bible are Samson, Samuel, and John the Baptist. Although not specifically called a Nazirite, Samuel's life indicates he was one. The long hair was to be a visible sign to the world that they were consecrated to the LORD.[5]

There is no indication of what Samson's childhood was like, only that he was born and grew to be a man. But when God's timing was right, the Spirit stirred within Samson. Samson chose a Philistine woman for his wife, over the protests of his parents. From the very beginning of adult life, Samson is a rebel. He knows it is a violation of law to marry a pagan woman and he would disgrace his parents by marrying one from Israel's most fierce enemy. The disrespectful way he talks to his parents in Judges 14:2 gives some insight into his character -- selfishness. But God does not allow sin to alter His master plan. Samson was to start the deliverance of Israel from the Philistines. (I wonder how God would have used Samson's skills if he had been an obedient, kind person?) God knew Samson's heart and used his selfishness to accomplish the task God had predetermined. Samson is an example of a man who had great potential but wasted it away, even though in the end he trusts God and receives His promise. In Hebrews 11:32-34 Samson is listed with other leaders, such as Gideon and Barak, whose weakness was turned to strength.

On one of Samson's trips to visit his fiancée, he tears an attacking lion apart with his bare hands. By the Will of God, he doesn't tell anyone. When he returned for the wedding, he found a swarm of bees had produced honeycomb in the lion's carcass. Always the prankster and bad boy, Samson makes a bet with his wedding guests that they can't solve his riddle. Whoever loses has to provide the other with 30 linen garments and 30 sets of clothes. His riddle was "Out of the eater, something to eat; out of the strong, something sweet."[1] (Judges 14:14) Not to be outdone, his guests convince the bride to sweet talk Samson out of the answer. Samson is furious when he loses the bet. He crudely comments, "If you had not plowed with my heifer, you would not have solved my riddle."[1] (Judges14: 18) God gives Samson the strength to go out and kill 30 Philistines, remove their clothes, and, thus, pay off his bet. Then Samson's fiancée marries his best man.

Samson is really mad at being jilted. He captures 300 foxes, ties their tails together in pairs, attaches a lit torch to each pair, and sets them free in the Philistine farms. His action causes the murders of his 'almost' wife and father-in-law. Samson is now hated and hunted by the Philistines. He is captured in a cave in the land of Judah and bound with rope. On the way back, the Spirit of the LORD comes over him. He frees himself and kills 1,000 Philistines with the jawbone of a donkey that had not yet gotten brittle. Almost incidentally, the Bible includes a short sentence that Samson led Israel for 20 years.

The end of Samson's life is for what he is most famous. Samson meets Delilah. Upon a large bribe, she agrees to try to learn the source of Samson's great strength. In the beginning, Samson is as deceptive as she. He tells her he could be subdued by

- 7 fresh bowstrings,
- New ropes,
- Weaving 7 braids of his hair into the fabric of the loom and tightening the pin.

She tried to weaken him with each of these but to no avail. (Now this man was already blind not to suspect a problem with this woman!) Judges 16:16 states, "With such nagging she prodded him day after day until he was tired to death."[1] (I can relate to that.) Finally, he just doesn't care anymore and tells her his secret is in never having a haircut. Of course, she cuts his hair as soon as he is asleep. (You almost want to punch this guy yourself for being so dumb!)

All of a sudden, Samson gets a painful wake-up call. He is captured, blinded, and used as an ox to tread out grain. In a sacrifice celebration to the Philistine god Dagon, Samson is brought out to entertain the crowd. He placed his outstretched arms against the pillars of the grandstands and prayed God would give him one last mighty show of strength. But even this last request is for God to let him get revenge on the Philistines for blinding him. Samson is selfish to the end. God can still use him, though. With a mighty push, he brings down the grandstands and kills 3,000 Philistines and himself.

The story of Samson proves that God can use all of us regardless of our weaknesses. Our joy and fulfillment is much greater, though, when we obey His commands and seek His Will for our lives. Samson made poor choices for his companions. God tells us we are not to be unequally yoked and Samson is an excellent example why. At times he seems to take for granted the mighty strength with which God has blessed him. To his credit, in the final tally, he is found to be a man of faith. I have a plaque on my wall that serves as a reminder:

> Throughout the years of your life,
> Many sad words cross your path,
> But the saddest of all are these:
> "What might have been?"

Food for Thought: Have you achieved your God-given potential? It's never too late to change. Ask God for His strength and direction.

March 24
Bible Readings: Judges 17:1-13; Judges 18:1-31

The tribe of Dan was known throughout Israel for its bravery, yet they could not drive the Canaanites and Philistines from their land. When God commands you to do something, He will provide for your needs. Apparently, the Danites had not followed God's Will wholeheartedly. The story of Samson indicated they had become somewhat integrated and tolerant of the Philistines. If this had not been the case, neither the Danites nor

Israelites would have consented to being led for 20 years by a man with Samson's personal history. By way of our vote or lack of voting, we give consent to leaders who are morally and ethically unfit to lead a nation dedicated to God. [NOTE: Do not confuse the Micah of this lesson with the prophet Micah we'll study later on.]

Micah starts out on a bad foot by being a thief. He confesses having stolen 1100 shekels of silver from his mother. Instead of being mortified and chastising her son for his sin, Micah's mother praises him for confessing. (This sounds like our child psychology theories that are designed to avoid all negative comments to our children. Then they aren't equipped to handle the negative world in which they live.) Micah's mother through one act of idolatry led not only her son astray but also ultimately a whole tribe of people. She gives Micah 200 shekels of silver to obtain a carved (wooden) idol and a silver cast idol. Micah then proceeds to set up a shrine and install one of his sons as the priest. Throughout this part of the story this family claims that their idols are consecrated to the LORD. They don't seem to be able to conceive of God without some form to see. They are compelled to limit God to an image confined to the parameters of the human mind. Micah goes so overboard that he hires a Levite to be the private family priest. This is a sad commentary to how low the Levites have become. The sinful state of the Israelite nation, though, is a testimony to the lack of religious leadership.

Instead of following God's command to seize their allotted land from the pagans, the tribe of Dan just decides to move. In essence, they give up their inheritance to the Philistines! The spies go to a remote city called Laish (sometimes spelled Leshem) located in the far northeast corner of modern day Israel. In a rest stop at Micah's house, they are impressed with the Levite priest. Laish is vulnerable. Six hundred Danite soldiers set out to attack the city seizing Micah's idols and priest while in route. The people of Laish were all killed and the city was burned. The tribe of Dan relocates and builds the city back, renaming it Dan. For the rest of their existence as a tribe, they worship the idols of Micah. One misguided mother has contributed to the paganism of an entire nation. Had it not been the idols of Micah, though, it would have been someone else's. The tribe of Dan had abandoned the one and only true God.

Food for Thought: What "little" sins do we let go unchecked because we don't see how they will ever matter? After all, just declaring you are doing it for the Lord makes it acceptable or does it?

March 25
Bible Readings: Judges 19:1-30; Judges 20:1-48; Judges 21:1-25

The moral decline of the Israelites is no more evident than at Gibeah in the land of Benjamin. The scene that unfolds is more debase than Sodom and Gomorrah. Never in the history of Israel has such evil pervaded a tribe. The other Israelites rise up in anger and form a huge army that first seeks God's instructions on how to handle the Benjamites. God tells the tribe of Judah to lead the way to battle. Judah, being the tribe blessed by Jacob as the family head, is also the tribe of Jesus. Jesus, Himself, will be foremost in the battle against evil.

The Benjamites are allowed to do what is right by turning over the guilty men to be killed. But they refuse to obey God's laws. The Benjamites form an army of 26,700 and go up against their brethren. For two days the Benjamites are victorious, but each day the Israelites prostrate themselves before the LORD, seeking guidance. On the third day, the Israelites kill more than 25,000 Benjamites. Only 600 escape into the desert. All their women and children are dead and their towns are burned. Before the battle, all the men of Israel swore to never let their daughters marry a Benjamite.

In a flood of remorse, the Israelites realize they have created a situation that will lead to the total demise of an entire tribe of their nation. They offer sacrifices before God, as is the norm after a victory. It was mandatory for all the tribes to assemble for this worship service. The people of Jabesh Gilead weren't present. The Israelite army attacks their brethren's town and kills everything but 400 virgin girls that they capture. They make peace with the Benjamites and give them the girls from Jabesh Gilead as wives. They are still short 200 girls. Because of their vow, the Israelites cannot **give** their daughters to the Benjamites. So, they decide that if the Benjamites **kidnap** some of the girls participating in a local celebration at Shiloh, then everything would be okay because they had not actually **given** the girls to them. Even though they took the moral high ground initially with the Benjamites, they now stoop to endorse ways to circumvent their vow to God. Benjamin's original sin involved kidnapping and sexual perversion. Now after fighting a bloody war, the Israelites encourage the Benjamites to kidnap women for reproduction purposes. Even the good actions they take to make peace among them are stained by the evil contained in their plan of reparation. The last sentence of this section says it all. "In those days Israel had no king; everyone did as he saw fit."[1] (Judges 21:25)

Food for Thought: Good intentions can have evil within. All actions must be God inspired to be within God's Will for our lives. Wonder if God really wanted this tribe annihilated? After all, we are not told that God responded to the Israelites wailing about the loss of a tribe. The Bible tells us it is better to lose a member of the body than for the whole body to go down in sin.

Verse of the Week: **1 Samuel 16:7** "The LORD does not look at the things man looks at. Man looks at the outward appearance, but the LORD looks at the heart."

Israel as a Monarchy

March 26
Bible Readings: 1 Samuel 1-2

One could well argue that Samuel is one of the most important men in the Old Testament. Moses and Samuel are alike in that from their infancy their lives seem to have a special significance. Both men left their families when they were very young and were reared by others. Both men were transitional in that they took the nation of Israel from one situation to another much different situation. Moses led Israel from a land of bondage to the edge of the Promised Land. During Samuel's ministry, Israel moved from a loose tribal confederation to a centralized state governed by a king. In another way Samuel is a transitional figure in that he is the last of the judges and the first of the prophets.

Samuel was from a deeply religious family. Elkanah was diligent in making the annual pilgrimage to Shiloh where the tabernacle had been permanently located. Samuel's mother was one of those many women found in the Bible who had difficulty getting pregnant. She asks God to take away her shame and vows that the child will be dedicated to the LORD.

In chapter two the Family of Eli is described. Its fall is almost parallel to the rise of Hannah and her son Samuel. Although Eli seems to be a faithful servant of God, his sons have no respect for the priestly regulations. They take the best parts of the sacrifice, including the fat (1 Sam. 2:16), even though the law had commanded that these were to be burned on the altar. Eli's sons become even bolder and engage in sexual acts with some of the women serving in the tabernacle complex. During this time when the priests are losing the respect of the people, the young Samuel grows in stature and favor with God and men.

Food for Thought: Think about the devotion to God Hannah had to feel to leave her young son with strangers forever! Can you image her heart as she left the city that first year? Then how she must have felt in subsequent years to see him reared among people breaking the laws. I believe Hannah was a woman of prayer. Are you a prayer warrior?

March 27
Bible Readings: 1 Samuel 3-7

First Samuel 3-7 basically deals with the fall of the priestly family of Eli and the rise of Samuel to the position of judge of Israel. Chapter three is about one of our best-remembered childhood Sunday school lessons: the call of Samuel. Josephus tells us that Samuel was twelve at the time.[3] God's voice called Samuel in the early hours of the morning as the light from the golden candlestick began to grow dim. The message that God gave Samuel was so severe that it made Samuel's ears tingle. Remember that God had previously warned the family of Eli about its sin, but they had not listened.

Chapter four describes how God's judgment came upon Israel and the priesthood. The people suffer a defeat in battle, but instead of seeking God's counsel as to why they were unsuccessful, they decide unwisely to carry the ark into battle, as though its presence there will magically bring them victory. These people are like some folks today whose religion is purely external. They attend the services, sing the songs, and light the candles, but their conduct on Monday does not match their confession on Sunday. I remember an old preacher from long ago who always said, "It's not how high you jump; it's how straight you walk that really matters."

The Israelites are again defeated and the ark is captured. This event had a very sobering effect on the religious life of the people. Just imagine your own feelings if suddenly the national government closed all of the churches and confiscated all of the Bibles. People began to wander if God was powerless. In chapter five and six God reveals His power to the Philistines. First, he destroys the idol, Dagon. This idol had the hands and head of a man but the body of a fish. Next, God brings a plague upon the Philistines. The references to tumors and rats would seem to suggest that the malady was the bubonic plague. The judgment traveled to the various cities of the Philistines as the ark was moved from place to place. They finally decided to send it back to Israel, but when they do, they offer the golden images of the rats and tumors hoping that the plague will end. This experience has really made the Philistines believe in the power of Israel's God.

The events in chapter seven take place twenty years later. Samuel is now an adult. He leads the people in a great revival. The Philistines hear of it and try to break it up, but God demonstrates His mighty power, which allows Israel to throw off the yoke of bondage. The lesson for us is that revival comes before deliverance. We must decide to seek God's kingdom. Then, as Jesus said, all of those other things will be added unto you (Matt. 6:33).

Food for Thought: Have you experienced a revival? Or, have you been in automatic for so long you don't even remember the extreme joy of revival? How can you find revival? Old time preachers used to talk about praying down a revival. It can be done. Sincere prayer for revival in your life will result in just that.

March 28
Bible Readings: 1 Samuel 8-12

Today's reading details the biblical opposition to the office of king and the selection of Saul as the first King of Israel. Both God and Samuel are angered by the people's request for a king. God is unhappy with them because they are willing to throw away one of the greatest gifts that He has given us: the gift of freedom. Instead of working together to develop an orderly society with loyal citizens who will defend the group against Philistine opposition, the people desire a king who will make all of the decisions for them. The request for a king runs counter to the Old Testament faith that stressed the dignity of man and the value of the individual.

Because the Israelites were not willing to work to realize God's perfect will for them as a nation, God reluctantly gives them His acceptable will, a king. Saul, the man selected to be king, possessed a number of characteristics that indicated that he was an ideal candidate. First, he was of the tribe of Benjamin. In Israel's history under the judges, the various tribes did not always work together. Over time there became two Israels: the northern tribes largely dominated by Ephraim and the southern tribes largely dominated by Judah. Geographically, Benjamin was located between these two groups and had ties with each of them. Benjamin was also one of the smallest tribes, so none of the other tribes would feel that Benjamin was forcing its man on the rest of the nation. Second, Saul was of a well-respected family in the tribe of Benjamin. Third, being much taller and stronger than anyone else, Saul looked like a king.

Saul's progress to the throne comes in three steps. First, Samuel anoints him privately in chapter ten. Then in chapter eleven, Saul is publicly selected at Mizpah to be king. The mean of selection on this occasion was likely the Urim and Thummin. In chapter eleven Saul demonstrates that he is worthy to be king by rallying all Israel behind him in rescuing the town of Jabesh-Gilead, hometown of 400 Benjamite wives, from the Ammonites.

Food for Thought: Can you imagine what our own nation would be like if we collectively worshipped God and sought His Will rather than have leaders stuffing their pockets? Think of the millions, even billions, we spend each year trying to prosecute our evil leaders. But then, our nation hasn't been united 'under God' in many decades. Pray for our nation to return to God. If terrorism doesn't do it, it probably won't ever happen.

March 29
Bible Readings: 1 Samuel 13-14:45, 49-51; 1 Chronicles 9:35-44

Chapters 13 & 14 describe the beginnings of the Jewish war of independence against the Philistines. Apparently after the incident at Jabesh-Gilead, Saul established a small standing army of 3,000 troops. Jonathan begins the struggle by destroying the garrison of Philistines at Gibeah. This action causes the Philistines to marshal a vast army. In turn, Saul must appeal to the people to reinforce his ranks. These citizen soldiers are not yet psychologically prepared for what lies ahead. Upon arriving they take one look at the Philistines and their state-of-the-art weapons and the Jews decide to skedaddle. Saul, too, is apparently being tested. Will he be controlled by his circumstances or his faith? He offers the burnt offering, which was his way of asking for God's favor in the coming battle. Samuel, who shows up one second longer than Saul was willing to wait, denounces Saul's conduct. Most commentators are unsure just exactly what Samuel is upset about. To me it seems he is angry that Saul, the political leader, is now trying to usurp the religious function reserved for the priests. In 2 Chronicles 26 a later king Uzziah, who is described as being for the most part good, attempted to usurp the priestly function of burning incense on the Altar of Incense. For his prideful act, Uzziah is stricken with leprosy. Saul's punishment is that his house will not be established as a dynasty in Israel. In addition, Samuel leaves without giving his blessing to Saul's initiative.

By now, not only have all the citizen soldiers left but also four-fifths of Saul's standing army is no longer with him. Jonathan and his armor bearer personally begin the fight; God honors Jonathan's courage by causing the earth to shake, which panics the Philistines. The Israelites see the advantage that has developed and attack. Saul, wanting to be "macho" now that the enemy is on the run, takes an oath that he will kill any man who stops even for a moment to eat. Saul's command limits the destruction the Israelites are able to inflict upon their enemy.

Later, when Saul realizes that Jonathan has unknowingly disobeyed him, he's more than willing to prove just how much value he places on his word. He prepares to kill Jonathan, but the people rescue him.

In this incident, an unattractive characteristic of Saul is revealed: an eagerness to prove, when others are at his mercy, that he is a big, mean man you better avoid.

Food for Thought: Saul was a man who could never repent when he was wrong. How many problems have occurred in this world because no one would take responsibility and repent for being wrong? Nations have gone to war, states have gone to war, and families have broken up -- all over pride. You read my Proverb March 20 about pride. The follow-up to that is Proverb 13:10, "Pride only breeds quarrels..." and Proverb 11:2, "When pride comes, then comes disgrace...." Is pride keeping you from peace and joy? Is pride a barrier between you and the Lord?

March 30
Bible Readings: 1 Samuel 14:46-48, 52; 1 Chronicles 5:10, 18-22; 1 Samuel 15

After Saul's victory over the Philistines, he began to make war on the various neighboring countries that have been persecuting Israel. In fact, almost all of Saul's reign consisted of wars against neighboring states. One of

Israel's bitterest enemies was the Amalekites (descended from Esau). Besides worshipping pagan idols, they had preyed on the Jews since the time of the wilderness wanderings. The Amalekites are placed under the ban; that is they, along with all their property, were to be destroyed. You will remember that the city of Jericho suffered the same fate.

The Kenites, who were allies of Israel but who lived in the same area as the Amalekites, are given warning to desert the area until the war is over. Saul then makes war on the Amalekites. Although he brings great destruction on the nation, he does not carry out the requirements of the ban. When Samuel confronts him about this failure, Saul tries to blame the people. Samuel tells him that God has rejected him as king because he can't be depended upon to carry out God's command.

Food for Thought: Are you willing to carry out God's command but only to a point? Do you follow God completely or just as far as you want to go? God wants our obedience, not our sacrifices.

March 31
Bible Readings: 1 Samuel 16-17

Chapters 16 & 17 deal with the anointing of David, in addition to the two versions of how he became acquainted with the house of Saul. From the action of Samuel in going to Bethlehem and the reaction to his visit by the town's elder, there is every indication that there was a major breach between the king and prophet and that this fact was well known. Samuel goes to sacrifice. The elders greet him fearfully. Perhaps they wonder what Saul will think of Samuel's visit there. Will he conclude that they are plotting with the prophet against him? Saul's action against the priestly city of Nob in chapter 22 describes the depth of sin to which Saul's paranoid behavior had led him. Perhaps these men suspect the level of sin that he is yet capable of reaching.

In Samuel's selection of Jesse's son (David is about 12 years old[112]), God reminds the prophet not to let physical appearances sway his judgment. God looks upon our heart, not our face or shoulder. Perhaps Samuel, in anointing Saul, had been a little too eager to select a king that looked the part. His subsequent experiences with Saul taught the prophet a king needs more than broad shoulders.

In the latter part of chapter 16, we are told that Saul suffered from a tormenting spirit. In examining the biblical records, modern psychologists have determined that Saul's behavior is characteristic of a paranoid-schizophrenic. Chapter 16 tells us that David's first connection with the king grew out of the illness. David was known for his ability with the lyre. This music apparently was helpful to Saul in the earlier stages of his disease. David ultimately became Saul's armor bearer, an honored position.

Chapter 17 seems to present an alternate version of how Saul and David first met. The event described here is David's victory over Goliath. The two accounts are not necessarily mutually exclusive. Keep in mind that Saul is suffering from mental illness and may not recall their former relationship. As for David's part, remember that at this time in history, it was always best to humor a king.

David's victory over Goliath is a demonstration of why God selected him to be king. David had faith; he didn't look at external circumstances; instead, he looked to a mighty God. There are some indications that David's original name was Elhanan (2 Samuel 21:19) and that when he became king he changed it to David. [We know that this occurred when Solomon became king (2 Sam. 12:25). Although, 1 Chr. 20:5 states, "the son of Jair killed Lahmi the brother of Goliath."[1]] David's victory over Goliath gave him a permanent place in Saul's court.

Food for Thought: Have you ever had to perform what seemed like an impossible task? Something too big for you to do alone? God is always there to support and guide us. He is also there to cheer us on. Just listen.

April 1
Bible Readings: 1 Samuel 18-20; Psalm 59

[Note: Jonathan and David are thought to have a father-son type of relationship because Jonathan is about 30 years older than David.[112]] Today's reading concerns Saul's persecution of David. The incident that prompts Saul's action is the rather innocent words of the young women who are perhaps just a little infatuated by David, this brave, young newcomer. Saul, however, has a rather fragile sense of self-esteem that can tolerate no rival to his people's affections. Saul imagines that David is plotting against him and intends to overthrow him.

Saul's unfounded fear causes him to take more and more desperate measures to rid himself of David. First, in one of his maniacal seizures, Saul attempts to kill David with a spear. Later, he offers David his daughter Michal as a wife and requests a rather sordid dowry. No doubt, he hopes a Philistine will do his dirty work for him. Having failed again to kill David, Saul hires men to kidnap David and arranges for him to be killed. Saul's own daughter comes to David's aid and assists in his escape.

Saul persists in his persecution of David in spite of everything. His much trusted and honored son, Jonathan, assures him that David has done nothing wrong. On multiple occasions when Saul is in his right mind he realizes that David is a faithful servant and that he (Saul) has done wrong by persecuting David.

Psalm 59 has been included in this day's reading because the incident that inspired it is mentioned in 1 Samuel 19:11-17. Note David's trust in God. There are indications in the Psalm that there may have been some officials in Saul's court who were jealous of David and attempted to encourage Saul in his unfounded fears. In verse 11, David as king, expands his personal experience to fit the need of his people when they, as a nation, encounter similar hostilities. David's attitude towards his enemies is different than the position Jesus took, but it is certainly understandable.

Food for Thought: Have you ever gone out of your way to make people like you, but they became more and more derogatory the harder you tried? Only God can change their hearts, and only then when they allow Him. Preconceived ideas about people hurt all involved and result in missed blessings. Pray for those who dislike you and for your own feelings toward them. Sometimes changing your reaction, changes theirs.

Verses of the Week: **Psalm 34:17-18** "The righteous cry out, and the LORD hears them; he delivers them from all their troubles. The LORD is close to the brokenhearted and saves those who are crushed in spirit."

April 2
Bible Readings: 1 Samuel 21-22:5; 1 Chronicles 12:8-18; Psalm 56, 34, 142

First Samuel 21 records David's visit to the priestly city of Nob. He had left in such haste from Saul's court that he had failed to take either a sword or provisions. David is not totally forthright in his request to the priest. Perhaps he felt that the less the priest actually knew about the state of affairs, the better.

David is forced to flee to the Philistine city of Gath. There he pretends to be mad, hoping that they might leave him alone. The king, however, suspects that it is all an act and sends David away.

David then hides in the wilderness. Gradually, great men of valor are drawn to David. Note that David cares for his aged parents by taking them to Moab where they will be safe from Saul. (Ruth, the Moabitess, was David's great-grandmother.)

Psalms 56, 34, and 142 are included in today's reading because these incidents in Samuel and Chronicles inspired David to write them. In 56 and 34, David praises God in the midst of his trouble. Here we can see David's finest attribute: he is not controlled by his circumstances, rather he rejoices in God who can change his desperate situation. Note that he asks to be released from his captivity that others may be gathered to him; that is exactly what happened.

Food for Thought: Have you ever tried praising God in the midst of your trouble? Just think how much worse it could be. God may already have intervened for you to keep the trouble from being devastating. What you are experiencing could only have been a small portion of what evil had planned for you. Next time there is trouble, praise God for being with you through all situations. I once heard a story of a lady who prayed fervently that her husband would not die from his cancer. He lived seven years as an invalid in great pain. By the end of that time, she was praying fervently that God's Will would be done and he would be spared the pain. Our view of a situation is always contaminated with human emotions; God sees it like it really is.

April 3
Bible Readings: 1 Samuel 22:6-23; 23-24; 25:1; Psalm 52, 63, 54, 57

First Samuel 22-24 concerns Saul's attempt to capture David. Chapter 22 records the tragic story of Saul's mass murder of the priests at Nob. Clearly, this incident reveals his unstable mental condition. Seeing conspiracy behind every bush and encouraged in these delusions by men like Doeg, Saul's action erodes what little support he has. David stands in stark contrast to Saul. Instead of quarreling with Saul, in chapter 23 David fights the Philistines, the real enemies of Israel. Even when David holds Saul's life in his hands, as in the cave near En Gedi, he refuses to harm him. David recognizes Saul as the LORD's Anointed and realizes that God, in His own good time, will deal with Saul. In his more lucent moments, even Saul knows he is wrong and asks David to be merciful to his family.

David wrote Psalms 52, 63, 54, 57 during this time in his life. In all of them, we see David's confidence in God and his firm conviction that God will bring judgment on his enemies in the end. These psalms also suggest that there were a number of men who were jealous of David and encouraged Saul in his pursuit of him.

Food for Thought: Do you do things in your time or in God's? When we try to rush ahead of God, we circumvent His glorious Will for our lives and His complete fulfillment of our joy. Pray for patience and acceptance of God's Will and His timing.

April 4
Bible Readings: 1 Samuel 25-28:2; 29-30; 1 Chronicles 12:1-7; 12:19-22

Sheep-shearing time was a time of feasting and celebrating for the shepherd just like harvest time was for the farmer. As with all of us, Caleb (Judah), too, had some black sheep in the family. Nabal was a Calebite who was very rich. Shepherds and their flocks were vulnerable to raiding parties. They were isolated from reinforcements and few in number when compared to the raiders. For unknown reasons, David and his men had served as protective forces around Nabal's shepherds and flocks. Probably just the presence of David's men made bandits steer clear for fear of an encounter. Feeding 600 men is a huge task for any exiled leader on the move. David knew Nabal was very rich and his profits would definitely be increased as a result of David's protection. Therefore, David asks for a reasonable share of the bounty. Sharing in the loot or bounty they received was the pay afforded soldiers of the time.

Nabal, whose name means fool, hatefully and insultingly refuses to share his bounty. When his wife Abigail hears of all this, she quickly acts to save her family. Abigail is an interesting woman. For a time when women were to serve almost as slaves, Abigail secretly defies her husband by sending a large amount of food to David to appease his anger. Abigail evens rides out to meet this band of men. We are told she was intelligent and beautiful. She was also courageous and righteous in her actions. (What amazes me is that she actually had 200 loaves of bread to send to David! Remember they had to be made by hand!) Her actions save her household, but God takes Nabal's life. He suffers either a stroke or a heart attack, ultimately dying. This story is a forerunner to the parable Jesus tells in Luke 12:16-21. In both cases, the men were rich, referred to as fools, hoarded earthly treasures, feasted, and died in their sinfulness.

This story is important in David's life because Abigail prevents David from killing Nabal and his household out of vengeance. Nabal was an Israelite of the tribe of Judah. God had commanded the Israelites to kill the evil pagan people of the area, but taking the life of another Israelite was forbidden. Furthermore, Lev. 19:18 forbade anyone to take vengeance other than God, more specifically Israelites were forbidden to take vengeance on their own people. If David had killed Nabal, it would have been a violation of law and a sin before God. At Nabal's death, David takes Abigail as his wife and becomes her protector. Prompt remarriage, whether through levirate marriage or contract, was the norm; otherwise, the women couldn't support themselves.

On several occasions David seems to tantalize Saul by sneaking up on him and taking something (corner of robe, jug and spear) and then taunting Saul from a safe distance. In many respects, this seems to be a cat-and-mouse game. The interpretation of David's actions is that he was trying to show Saul that he (David) had no intention of harming God's anointed king. The sparing of Saul's life always brought remorse from Saul as his guilty conscience convicted him. David was upheld in his righteousness. He knew he was to become king, but he was willing to wait for God's timing, in contrast to Saul who was always too impatient to wait on God.

The Wilderness of Ziph was west and central of the Dead Sea. The Ziphites, as its people were known, have now plotted with Saul twice to capture David and his men. David's back is to the wall. Both Saul and the Ziphites are his enemies. He takes a bold step in faith by moving into the land of Israel's greatest enemy, the Philistines. Not only was David a hated Israelite but he also was the Israelite who had killed the hero of Gath, Goliath, and the same one who had pretended to be insane at his previous meeting with Achish. So what does David do? He moves all his men and their entourage of families to Gath, marches up to king Achish, and pretends to be a defector! David establishes himself in Ziklag, a city 30 miles south of Gath, given to him by Achish. During David's time in Ziklag, he totally annihilates many southern Philistine towns but reports to the king that he is raiding Hebrew towns. God had to have been with David for him to have pulled-off such a huge ruse for so long.

While David is away at war, the hated Amalekites seize the opportunity to capture the people and loot and burn Ziklag. When David returns, his grief and that of his men is overwhelming. When his strength is gone, he turns to God for advice. The psalmist reminds us that God is an ever-present help in time of trouble (Psalm 46:1). When David catches up with the Amalekites, he kills all but a few that escape. Saul had lost favor with God because he did not obey God and kill the Amalekites and all their animals (1 Sam. 15: 2-10).

Food for Thought: Do you remember a time when someone intervened to prevent you from committing a sin? Did you thank God for the intervention?

April 5
Bible Readings: 1 Samuel 28:3-25; 31; 1 Chronicles 10:1-14; 2 Samuel 4:4; 2 Samuel 1

God had left Saul. His confidence was gone; indecision reigned. Judgment calls he so easily and impatiently made years earlier now eluded him altogether. Out of desperation he seeks a medium (spiritist). Deut. 18:10-11 condemns witchcraft, mediums, and spiritists. Again Saul disobeys God. He asks for Samuel's spirit to be brought before them. The witch is so used to trickery and illusions that she cried out when Samuel appeared and her eyes were opened to who Saul was (for he had disguised himself). God doesn't communicate to His people through witches. That would be abominable. But He can and does use our acts of disobedience to convict our hearts and condemn our actions. God used Samuel to repeat Saul's condemnation for his disobedience.

As predicted, Saul and his sons die in battle with the Philistines. The enemy fastened their bodies to a wall. The Israelites believed that bodies should be buried before sundown. But it was the third day before the valiant men of Jabesh-Gilead (east of the Jordan) reached Beth Shan to recover the bodies. In the beginning of Saul's reign, he had saved Jabesh-Gilead from the Ammonites. Now the citizens showed their respect for Saul.

Ironically, it is one of the few surviving Amalekites who comes to tell David about the deaths of Saul and his sons. The messenger admits to having finished off the dying king and stolen his crown and armband. Apparently, he didn't see anything wrong with his actions. Maybe he even believed it would bring him the favor of the new king, or possibly it was viewed as a chance for an Amalekite to survive. Regardless of the reason for the confession, the messenger of bad news is killed for having struck down the LORD's Anointed. David mourns for the loss of Saul and Jonathan. After all, much of David's life, whether positive or negative experiences, had involved Saul and Jonathan.

Food for Thought: Unfortunately, we frequently hear of persons who grew up in families with an abusive parent or family member. They naturally desire to love their family, but they fear the abuse. David both loved and feared Saul. Have you known anyone you loved but feared? David depended on seeking God's guidance and obeying God's Will even when his instinct was to do the opposite. Are you seeking and obeying God's Will for your life?

April 6
Bible Readings: 2 Samuel 2-5:5; 1 Chronicles 11:1-3; 3:1-4; 29:26-27; 12:23-40; 1 Kings 2:11

David is crowned king of Judah while Ishbosheth, Saul's son, becomes king of Israel. As is often the case, they go to war with each other. Joab, David's commander of the army and his nephew, encamps the army on one side of the pool of Gibeon. Abner, commander of Saul's army, encamps his forces on the other side of the pool. The pool of Gibeon was about 36 feet wide and 33 feet deep. It was dug out of solid rock and had a spiral rock stairwell that descended into the pit. In fact, the stairwell continues for another 36 feet below the pit to a water chamber room. It was the water in this chamber that was used for the city's water and later for their winemaking industry. Gibeon was an appropriate location for a civil war. This was neutral ground for fighting. You recall that the Gibeonites tricked Joshua into a treaty. They were a protected group as a result of that treaty and were used as slave labor.[5]

In an effort to avoid a major conflict between the armies, Abner proposes that a dozen men from each side fight hand-to-hand. Presumably, the last man standing would be the winner of the war. Unfortunately, there were no survivors, so the battle was on. During the fighting, Abner kills Asahel, one of Joab's brothers. The men of Benjamin rally behind Abner. (If you have been paying close attention the last few weeks, you have noticed that the men of Benjamin are always on the wrong side. Saul was a Benjamite. We tend to rally around our own and close ranks when threatened -- even when our own members are wrong. So was the case of the Benjamites.) Abner becomes the voice of reason, negotiating peace between the related tribes but not before 360 Benjamites were dead and 19 of David's army. David had a well-trained army of men who had fought with him for years, but Abner's army was made up of stragglers, new recruits, and the remnants of Saul's army that had been overrun at Mt. Gilboa (when Saul was killed).[23]

By this time we see that David had six sons by six different wives. This list doesn't include David's first wife, Michal, because she was given to another man when David was hiding out from Saul. Some of David's wives appear to have been due to political treaties or contracts. For example, Geshur was a small kingdom northeast from the Sea of Galilee.[23] When Abner wants to strike a deal for deliverance of Israel to David, David's first demand was the return of Michal, his wife. Second Samuel 3:14-16 is a very sad passage. Michal was forcibly taken from her husband, Paltiel, to be returned to David. Poor Paltiel followed behind her for miles weeping. Finally, at the border of David's kingdom of Judah, Abner made him go home. Politically speaking, Michal's return to David showed there was no animosity between the houses of David and Saul.

When David's commander and nephew, Joab, returns from a raid, he seizes the opportunity to avenge his brother's death by killing Abner. David places a curse on the house of Joab (his sister's family!) -- politically separating himself from Joab's murderous deed. David then enters a public mourning period and positions himself as chief mourner at the funeral. All of these actions were politically correct for winning over the affections of the northern tribes. In his address to Judah's armed forces, David claims to be weak in comparison to his nephew, even though he is the anointed king. In other words, David has made a number of political moves: (1) reuniting his family with Saul's through Michal's return, (2) mourning Abner, a prince of the northern tribes, publicly as foremost of the mourners, (3) denying his own family for the deed done, and (4) humbling himself before the troops as being too weak to overcome his nephews, therefore vengeance is left to God. David has won the allegiance of the people of Israel.

Two of Ishbosheth's own men assassinate him, bringing his head to David. It is evident they expected to be rewarded by the new king. (Boy, were they in for a surprise!) Instead, David had them executed for murder.

At 30 years old, David had certainly lived in the fast lane. He was king over Judah for the next 7 1/2 years and then king over the combined country (Israel and Judah) for 33 years. The house of David grew stronger and stronger, for God was with him. But, there were still battles to be fought.

Food for Thought: God promised to be with us but not to pave the road in front of us. His plan is for us to walk in faith and dependence on Him. Are you depending on God? for everything?

Israel as a Monarchy

April 7
Bible Readings: 2 Samuel 5:6-12; 6:1-11; 5:17-25; 22:1-51; 1 Chron.11:4-9; 14:1-2; 13:1-14; 14:8-17; Psa. 18

Today's reading is concerned with early events in David's reign as king. Most scholars feel that the events described here are not necessarily in chronological order. Second Samuel 5:5 states that David ruled over Judah from Hebron 7 1/2 years; 2 Samuel 2:10 states that Ishbosheth ruled over the north part of Israel two years. If we assume that David became king over all Israel shortly after Ishbosheth's death, it is logical to assume that Jerusalem was captured five years into David's reign over all Israel.

David had many reasons for locating his capital there. First, Jerusalem's geographical situation made it very difficult to conquer. Both the Babylonians and later the Romans were held off for years before the city actually fell. Second, the city was centrally located. Third, because the palace had not been previously conquered it was not associated with any tribe. Fourth, because David's mighty men took the city, it was primarily loyal to him; for instance, note how often later in the Bible, Jerusalem is referred to as "the city of David."

The first actual crisis in David's reign was the Philistine war, which likely occurred before his conquest of Jerusalem. David had previously been a friend of the Philistines when he sought refuge there during the time he was fleeing from Saul. Now, that he is king of a united Israel, they march against him.

In chapter six, David arranges for the Ark to be permanently located in Jerusalem. David's concern for the Ark's welfare illustrates one of his grand characteristics and shows how he is different from Saul. During his reign of 40 years (Acts 13) or 32 years (1 Sam. 13) or 12 years based on history, Saul, had chosen to spend much of his energies chasing his baseless fear, not once does the Bible record any attempt on Saul's part to re-establish a centralized place of worship. David, however, makes it one of his first objectives. Although he made many mistakes and did some very bad things, David sincerely loved God.

Food for Thought: What is the motive for your faith? Is it based on fear and uncertainty or is it based on a real love for God? Call upon God today as your Father. After all, as the songwriter says, "Christ receiveth sinful men."

April 8
Bible Readings: 2 Samuel 6:12-19; 1 Chron. 15:1-29; 16:1-36; Psa. 105, 96

The passages for today begin with David's attempt to move the Ark of the Covenant into Jerusalem. Much of the problem that foiled David's previous attempt was that the Ark was being transported in a bouncing cart over (likely) a rough road. The law had dictated that the Ark was to be carried by the Levites. Apparently, David consulted the Law of Moses and discovered the cause of his failure. This situation is an example for us all. When things go wrong in our lives, we need to go to God's word and find out what we are doing wrong.

The passage of the Ark into Jerusalem was a joyous event. A band made up of brass and stringed instruments along with choristers taken from among the priests and Levites were also part of the procession. Apparently, after the Ark was located in the tent that had previously been prepared for it, refreshments were provided for everyone attending the event.

Not everyone was happy. Michal, David's wife and Saul's daughter, chastises David for dancing in the streets in a linen ephod. Perhaps she felt that wearing a priestly garment and associating with the common people in their celebration was conduct unbecoming in a king (or at least her idea of one). David, however, chose the right way and one that we should follow. He had more regard for his honest, spontaneous desire to worship God than for any sort of false code of formality that dictated what he should or should not do.

Psalms 105 and 96 have been included in today's reading because it is likely that these were the songs the choristers sang as they marched into Jerusalem.

Food for Thought: Is your faith just a Sunday ideal? How often do you take the Bible with you and use its wisdom in the practical affairs of life?

> Verses of the Week: **Psalm 51:10,12,17** "Create in me a pure heart, O God, and renew a steadfast spirit within me.... Restore to me the joy of your salvation and grant me a willing spirit, to sustain me.... The sacrifices of God are a broken spirit; a broken and contrite heart, O God, you will not despise."

April 9

Bible Readings: 1 Chron. 16:37-43; 18:14-17; 17:1-27; 2 Sam. 6:20-23; 8:15-18; 9:1-13; 7:1-29

After establishing the Ark in Jerusalem, David appointed men to set up a plan of worship and sacrifice. One of the more important of these men, Asaph, was responsible for the music and songs in the tabernacle/temple. His family is credited with having written Psalms 50, 73-83. Another question readers may have relates to the Kerethites and Pelethites mentioned in 2 Samuel 8:18. These two groups were a select company of soldiers who formed David's bodyguard and who may have been responsible for executing criminals.[5]

Second Samuel 9 largely concerns David's kindness towards Jonathan's lame son, Mephibosheth. In a way David's relationship with Mephibosheth is a picture of our relationship with God. First, because Mephibosheth was related to the former king, he was David's enemy. We, by walking in sin, are God's enemy. Second, like all of us, Mephibosheth was lame through a fall. Third, when David found Mephibosheth, the young man was in a distant and desolate country. Lo-debar literally means 'the place of no bread.' Fourth, the king searched for him; likewise, God searches for us. Fifth, Mephibosheth was received in his deformity. If we could compare ourselves as we are to what God intended for us to be when He made us, we would be shocked by how sin has twisted, torn, and deformed us. Sixth, Mephibosheth was received for another's sake. It was David's remembrance of his covenant with Jonathan that caused him to seek out Mephibosheth. Likewise, it is due to what Christ did on our behalf that opens the gates of Heaven before us.[24]

In reading 2 Sam. 9:1-13, you realize that Ziba and his sons must have felt enormous resentment about suddenly becoming servants again, making the former master's grandson wealthy at the expense of their work and sweat. In the upcoming lessons, we find Ziba attempting subterfuge to even the score.

Food for Thought: Can you recall a time when someone trusted you or gave you an advantage because of the favorable reputation of your parents? Remember, just as Jonathan's kindness towards David provoked David's kindness towards Mephibosheth, our reputations as honest and decent people make the path easier for our children in the future.

April 10

Bible Readings: 2 Sam. 21:15-22; 8:1; 10:1-19; 11:1-27; 12:1-17; 1 Chron. 20:1,4-8; 19:1-19; Psa. 60, 51

Unfortunately, David's greatest failure is the event most often associated with his name. David spent his lifetime devoted to God, yet his yielding to temptation brought him public disgrace. Even pagan people know the sinful part of the story of David and Bathsheba, while often being unaware that they held prominent places in the lineage of Jesus. All people have an Achilles' heel, a weak spot that can cause them to falter and fall. It can even lead to destruction for those who don't fight to overcome it. David's weak spot was lust. He liked beautiful women and married many of them. Deuteronomy 17:14-20 states God's requirements for a king. Verse 17 specifically declares that the king must not take many wives. David's inability to control his lust was a powerful example to his son Solomon. There is an old saying, "What you do in moderation, your children will do in excess." David had a dozen or so wives (an exact number is not known); Solomon had 700 wives. David had many concubines (we know at least 10); Solomon had 300 concubines (1 Kings 11:3). David set a bad example for Solomon. Solomon let his many wives lead him into idolatry, and the Israelites became slaves exiled in a foreign land. One sinful weakness given a little free reign eventually brought down the land of Israel.

After David's secret affair with Bathsheba, she became pregnant, an event that would be hard to explain to a husband who had been away at war for many months. (I might add that her husband had been a loyal, faithful friend and defender of David's.) [Levitical law stated, "If a man commits adultery with another man's wife -- with the wife of his neighbor -- both the adulterer and the adulteress must be put to death."[1] (Lev. 20:10)] David and Bathsheba's secret sin would now be found out. So David devises a plan to get Uriah to come home to spend some time with his wife and, thus, be convinced the child was his when the pregnancy was discovered. David failed to calculate Uriah's devotion to be a good soldier. Deut. 23:9 warned that soldiers were to abstain from anything impure while encamped with the enemy. As we have studied in the past, any emission of semen made a man unclean until evening. Touching someone unclean was forbidden, thus exclusion from the troops. Uriah was not about to enjoy the pleasures of the home front with his comrades still at war. David's next plan is to arrange Uriah's death on the battlefront. To do this, he has to include Joab, his commander, in his scheme. Joab later uses this knowledge to his advantage (engaging in implied blackmail to get his way). David married the widow Bathsheba and for almost a year, his sin was concealed -- but not from God. God called David 'on the carpet' through Nathan, the prophet. Sin always has its consequences. David's consequences included (1) death of Bathsheba's baby, (2) rape of a daughter by one of his sons, (3) fighting among his descendants, (4) public sexual violation of ten of his concubines (at this point the Bible calls them wives), (5) murder of one son by another, and (6) a plot by one son to murder him and overthrow his government.

David was a man after God's own heart, though. When he was confronted with his sins, he instantly confessed and repented. He gave no excuses; he knew he was wrong. He knew God was just and begged His mercy. God knows we aren't capable of being perfect, that's why He sent Jesus to wash away our sins. God only asks that we be obedient; but when we do sin, we must repent and come back into His Will. Are you a person of God's own heart?

Food for Thought: What 'little' weakness or sin in your life have you tolerated instead of attacked? What example is it setting for others? A weak spot in our lives can have all the trappings of being something good, i.e., eating, saving money, reading, working. When we let it dominate our lives, though, it becomes our Achilles' heel. It's never too late to change. Pray that God will strengthen you so you can overcome your desire or 'lust' for your weakness.

April 11

<u>Bible Readings:</u> 2 Samuel 12:18-23, 26-31; 8:2-14; 23:8-39; 1 Chron. 20:1-3; 18:2-13; 11:10-47

In Deut. 20:17, God commands that the Israelites are to completely destroy the Hittites, Amorites, Canaanites, Perizzites, Hivites, and Jebusites. Because this did not happen, these people lived among the Israelites, often as slaves. Interestingly, Uriah was a Hittite. Uriah had defected to join David during David's pursuit by Saul. In today's lesson you'll find Uriah the Hittite listed as one of David's mighty men. David had spent many years fighting side-by-side with a man in whom he had complete confidence and trust. When David confessed his sin, it must have deeply grieved him to realize his own betrayal.

Three of David's men were especially brave and mighty: Jashobeam, Eleazer, Shammah. Each had conquered enemy warriors in unbelievable numbers. Only with the blessings of God could three men accomplish such feats. So famous were they that even the Bible refers to them as the "Three" and everyone knows who they are. A monument of their devotion to David is depicted in the story of the mighty three sneaking through enemy lines just to get David a drink of water. In David's humble fashion, he refused to drink the water, realizing it represented the very lifeblood these three men risked to serve him. David poured it out as a drink offering to God who had brought them back safely. (I'll admit my first thought was how mad I'd be at him for pouring out the water I had risked so much to get for him! How ungrateful! Or was he? He thought so much of the gift that he used it as a sacrifice to God. How much greater could his gratitude have been?) The well at Bethlehem (David's hometown) is actually believed to be a water cistern (cave) dug out of rock. It was located about a 15 minute walk (that's a lot shorter distance for some of us than others!) northeast of Bethlehem and is often referred to as David's well. As an underground cavern, the water was clear and cool. There were three openings to the cave on the surface. It is thought to have been 17-21 feet deep.[23]

Throughout David's reign, he fought cities and states adjacent to Israel, continually expanding the borders. By the time Solomon takes the throne, Israel is the largest in size it will ever be through conquest. Jerusalem, at only 15 acres[7], was a relatively small capital for such a large nation.

Food for Thought: Have you ever been totally overwhelmed by someone's sacrificial gift to you? As a young person, I read the story of the "Gift of the Magi." It involves a young couple at Christmas. Each one sells their most valued possession to give the other a special gift. Ironically, the gifts are to complement the valued possessions that they no longer had! But that didn't diminish the magnitude of the gift. A sacrificial gift to someone you love is never out-of-date, out-of-style, or out-of-place. God wants and deserves our sacrificial gifts in the form of our obedience to Him. Is your gift sacrificial? David didn't pour out some of the water to God and drink the rest of it. He gave it all to God.

April 12
Bible Readings: 2 Samuel 12:24-25; 5:13-16; 13:1-39; 14:1-24; 1 Chron. 3:4-9; 14:3-7

God is pleased with David's repentance and obedience to Him. He blesses David and Bathsheba with four sons. One son, Nathan, will be the ancestor of Jesus' mother, Mary. Another son, Solomon, will be the ancestor of Mary's husband, Joseph. God's promise that David's house would always retain the throne of Israel is realized through Jesus.

The consequences of David's sins are about to befall his household. David's son Amnon rapes his half-sister, Tamar (David's daughter by another wife). Totally devastated by this experience, Tamar turns to her full brother Absalom for support. He is obliged to take her into his house permanently as she is no longer eligible to marry. I can understand the bitterness and hate Absalom must have felt toward Amnon. God tells us that vengeance is His, but Absalom allows his hatred to fester into a full-blown plan of murder. After the deed is done, Absalom becomes a fugitive and flees to Geshur, his mother Maacah's hometown. David was furious with Amnon over his assault on Tamar, according to the scripture. After Amnon's death, David goes into mourning over the loss of Absalom through exile. For three years, both David and Absalom are grieved over their separation. Joab is David's relative and friend. He devises a plan to reveal to David the errancy of not seeking to bring Absalom back to Jerusalem. Second Samuel 14:14 tells us David is reminded that God has a plan for banished ones (sinners) to be brought into God's fold. David sends for his son but refuses to see him. For two years the two men live in the same town without seeing each other. This self-imposed exile is hard on both of them. This time it is Absalom who chooses to make the first move toward reconciliation. He realizes he could be killed. Remember, murder was against the law, punishable by death (Ex. 21:12). Not only had he murdered his brother, but his victim had been a prince of the kingdom!

From what we know of Absalom, he was very headstrong, arrogant, and vain. We are told he was without blemish and handsome with a thick, full head of hair. His sister Tamar is also attractive. In reading about his actions, one can surmise the young man is very charming but self-centered. Absalom began to acquire state chariots, followers, and the aspirations of a politician. By winning the hearts of the people, Absalom is sure he can overthrow his father's government. What a terrible way to repay the mercy he had received from David! Doesn't this remind you of mankind's relationship to God? When we are in trouble, we run to God for mercy, but when all is well, we arrogantly go our own way, too busy for God. We also know Absalom adored his sister Tamar, even naming one of his daughter's after her. But Absalom's heart was evil.

Food for Thought: The best way I can describe Absalom is as a 'con artist.' Think of people you know who charmed their way into your life with the sole purpose of improving their lives at your expense. Remember how easy it was to love them and go along with their requests? David is about to discover that too much love and trust for a 'charmer' is a dangerous thing. God gives us talents and skills. It's up to us to use them wisely.

April 13
Bible Readings: 2 Samuel 14:25-33; 15:1-37; 16:1-14; Psa. 3

From the April 10th lesson, we know that David's sin with Bathsheba had many consequences; one, of which, we now study. Four years after returning to Jerusalem, Absalom's conspiracy to overthrow his father's rule reached its maturity. Absalom went to Hebron with 200 of the men of Jerusalem and Ahithophel, one of David's advisors but also Bathsheba's grandfather[69]. Secret messengers carried the news throughout Israel, "Absalom is king in Hebron." [Hebron was the burial site of Abraham and Sarah (Gen. 23), a city of refuge (Josh. 20:7), and the capital of David's original kingdom of Judah (2 Sam. 2:1-4).] His plan was complete. King David and his household fled for their lives. But he left behind 10 concubines to take care of the palace. He sent the priests Zadok and Abiathar back into the city with the Ark. David's complete faith and dependence on God is evidenced by his statement in 2 Samuel 15:25-26. It is the theme of David's prayer for his life. David places his faith in a just God who will choose to restore him to the throne or seal his fate. Either way, David will depend on God. Is it any wonder he was a man after God's own heart? All of Israel mourns over the exile of David. But Mephibosheth, Saul's grandson, sees this as an opportunity to take Saul's kingdom back! Now there are two traitors who had previously eaten at David's table. (Keep in mind we only have Ziba's testimony about Mephibosheth's intent.)

Food for Thought: With friends and family like these, who needs enemies!? David must have been totally discouraged with so much bad news at one time. But it could be worse. Job's one day of bad news is unparalleled (Job 1:13-19). And Job's days went downhill from there! From both of these men, we can learn to keep the faith, realize that all that we have is God's to do with as He sees fit, and to praise God regardless of the situation. We also must remember that God loves us and is a merciful, just God. He only wants our obedience.

April 14
Bible Readings: 2 Samuel 16:15-23; 17:1-29; 18:1-33; 19:1-4

Possibly this is the lowest point of David's life. He is exiled in the desert, once again fleeing for his life. How often he must have remembered his days of fleeing Saul. Back then he could not have imagined his next evacuation would be provoked by his own son's evil heart. Absalom sends 12,000 soldiers to hunt down and kill one man -- his father. In the meantime, he defiles his father's bed by lying with his father's concubines in a tent on the roof of the palace for all to see. (An act so perverted, Levitical law called for the death sentence.) Absalom may be a charmer, but David has his loyalists and spies. David and his entourage were aided and assisted in evading Absalom's ambush. David then organizes his troops and he chose the battleground -- the forest of Ephraim. On that day, David prevailed. Twenty thousand of Absalom's men lay dead. David's last words to his commanders Joab, Abishai, and Ittai were for them to be gentle with Absalom for David's sake! Even in this harshest of rebellions, David's paternal instinct is overwhelming. Can't you feel his pain? Any parent who has survived rearing children from 15-25 years of age knows the extreme anguish mixed with extreme love experienced during those years. The source of Absalom's pride becomes the source of his downfall -- his handsome face and luxurious mane of hair. Caught in a tree by his head, Absalom is killed by Joab while dangling. (This is Joab's second murder; the first was Abner.)

During Absalom's life he set up a monument to himself in the King's Valley. This was done to preserve his name. Apparently his three sons died young.[23] The monument stood as a lasting example of Absalom's misappropriated loyalty and affection -- to himself instead of God.

When David was told of Absalom's death, he wept saying, "O my son Absalom! My son, my son Absalom! If only I had died instead of you -- O Absalom, my son, my son!"[1] (2 Sam. 18:33) What Christian parent wouldn't feel the same way over a child condemned to hell? David knew God. David had eternal life with God. But there was no reconciliation for Absalom anymore. The time for third chances was over. Good looks, good family name, wealth, and charm were of no use to him now.

Food for Thought: All people have eternal life. The question is "Where will you spend it? Heaven or hell?" If you do not know Jesus as your Savior, bow your head now and pray the following:

C - confess your sins and ask for God's forgiveness,

B - believe that Jesus died for your sins and rose again,

A - accept Jesus as Lord and Savior of your life.

Dear God: I confess I am a sinner and am in need of your cleansing. Forgive me and wash my sins away with the blood of the risen Savior. I declare Jesus as Lord and Savior of my life, to live in my heart forever. Amen

April 15
Bible Readings: 2 Samuel 19:5-43; 20:1-26

Joab chastised David for mourning over the death of his enemy -- his son, Absalom. Joab is only concerned about the morale of his army. One has to wonder if David put up with Joab's ruthlessness, murder, and disrespectful demands because of the knowledge Joab had of David's order to abandon Uriah at the battlefront to bring about his death. But Abner's murder occurs before Uriah died. So the question remains, "Why does David put up with this man?" Even though Joab had been a successful army commander, David attempted to replace him earlier with Abner. Now David promises Amasa, Joab's cousin and David's nephew, the commander position as a political move to win back his fellow Judeans' loyalty. Surely Amasa knew how Abner died. But nonetheless, Amasa allows himself to get in the same situation. Again Joab stabs his replacement to death.

If you think about Jesus and Judas in the Garden of Gethsemane, you can see a similar picture with Joab and Amasa. In each situation the betrayers seek to greet their 'brother' with a kiss while harboring malice and evil in their hearts. Each time innocent men lost their lives. Both died with public onlookers. Is Judas any less guilty of the murder of Jesus just because he wasn't the one who actually committed the act? Certainly not! Both Judas and Joab are murderers. In Matthew 5:21-22, Jesus said, "You have heard it said to the people long ago, 'Do not murder, and anyone who murders will be subject to judgment.' But I tell you that anyone who is angry with his brother will be subject to judgment."[1] Murder does not call love its mother and peace its father. The origins of murder are hate and anger. Jesus tells us not to allow anger to abide in our hearts. Anger leads to hate which leads to murder; whether it is literal or through slander, it is still sin.

An interesting irony occurs with David in reference to Shimei, the Benjamite who cursed him and threw rocks at him while David was fleeing from Jerusalem to avoid Absalom's death squad. Shimei is rightly scared witless because David is now restored to power. Abishai, Joab's brother, wants to kill Shimei. You get a powerful impression of David's disgust with the two brothers in verse 22 when David responds, "What do you and I have in common, you sons of Zeruiah? This day you have become my adversaries!"[1] David goes on to say that this day of his restoration to the throne was a day of celebration not death. An interesting observation is that Joab and Abishai are nephews of David, as well as Amasa. (Zeruiah is a sister or half-sister of David.[5]) Therefore, David physically had much in common with his nephews. But David's question is referring to the hearts and characters of the men. David had a heart for God; his nephews had hearts that were earthly-oriented. David spares Shimei's life on oath of his promise. David's acceptance of Shimei's apology seems admirable, but the irony is that in 1 Kings 2:1-9, David's last words to his son King Solomon are to be sure Shimei is executed. How this is to be accomplished is left to Solomon. In 1 Kings 2:36-38, Solomon confines Shimei to the area of Jerusalem, instructing that he must never go beyond the Kidron Valley (eastern border of Jerusalem) or he will be killed. But three years later Shimei goes to Gath to retrieve two run-away slaves. Solomon hears of his violation of confinement and has him executed. The final verses on this topic are 1 Kings 2:44-46. The point of insight into this story is that the house of David, as the royal lineage, is now secure. So how does Shimei's death make Solomon's throne and David's lineage secure? Shimei was a relative of Saul's. He had committed treason in his cursing of David (2 Samuel 16:5-14) for reigning in Saul's place and falsely accused him of bloodshed in order to get the throne. Keil and Delitzsch call the cursing "malicious blasphemy."[23] Shimei deserved execution for the crime committed against King David, but he received mercy. We deserve eternal death for the sins committed against God, but we receive mercy. David's son, Solomon, bound Shimei by regulation and oath, executing him at the first violation. God's son, Jesus, freed us from the confining restrictions of the law that required death to all violators. Jesus brought the gift of eternal mercy to all those who choose to follow Him.

Upon David's return to Jerusalem, Mephibosheth also has some explaining to do. Mephibosheth claims his servant Ziba betrayed him. Realizing Mephibosheth and Ziba's stories are complete opposites, David shows some of the type of wisdom that would make Solomon famous. David divides the land equally between the two men. Mephibosheth then states that having the king home safely is more important and Ziba can have all the land. (This reminds me of Solomon wanting to divide the baby in half for the two women, each claiming to be its mother. The real mother gave up her half to spare the life of the child.) Mephibosheth appears to be exonerated.

Today's lesson ends with yet another Benjamite making trouble. (To be the smallest tribe, it sure was a problem. I have to wonder if Benjamin was a spoiled brat.) Sheba, son of Bicri, manages to get the men of Israel (counting Joseph as two tribes, the total includes the 10 tribes other than Judah, Levi, and Simeon) to abandon David in an insurrection. Sheba sought refuge in the town of Abel Beth Maacah, for now he was a condemned man. To avoid being totally destroyed by the king's army, the town's citizens executed Sheba themselves. Thus ends this rebellion.

Food for Thought: When Shimei was cursing King David, David would not allow Shimei to be punished. David believed he deserved this treatment for his sins, otherwise God would not allow it. Remember that all of these 'consequences' in David's life were a result of his sin with Bathsheba followed by the murder of Uriah. Have you ever felt like David, that you had been your own worst enemy? God loves a humble, repentant sinner and issues out mercy to the broken and contrite spirit. Pray today for God's mercy.

Verse of the Week: **Psalm 17:3** "I have resolved that my mouth will not sin."

April 16
Bible Readings: 2 Samuel 21:1-14; 24:1-25; 1 Chron. 21:1-30; 22:1-19; Psa. 30

Second Samuel 21 is a very difficult chapter for us to understand. The final outcome of David's decision to avenge the wrong Saul inflicted on the Gibeonites was the execution of seven of Saul's descendants. Because of his oath to Jonathan, David spared Mephibosheth. The Gibeonites were the only Canaanite tribe to deceive Joshua into a peace treaty, but they had to serve as slaves. Saul apparently had killed many of them. After three years of famine, David came to realize that it was judgment rather than a natural weather occurrence. It was the Gibeonites who decided on the sentence against Saul's house. According to Numbers 35:33, only the blood of the criminal could satisfy the guilt of bloodshed on the land. Of course, you recognize the number seven as one of completion. Rizpah, mother of two of the slain, took mourning cloth (sackcloth) and made herself a bed by their bodies to keep away birds and wild animals. She stayed there until the rain came, ending the famine. David had compassion on her and Saul's family. He had the bones of Saul, Jonathan, and the slain seven transported to the family tomb in the land of Benjamin.

The second major sinful event in David's life lies in his decision to count <u>his</u> troops. This angers God because numbers do not equal power or success. Dependence on and obedience to God determine success. To Joab's credit, he tries diligently to make the king see that he would bring God's wrath on the nation. Unfortunately, David doesn't abandon this evil plan until the counting is reported more than 9 months later. Through the prophet, Gad, God gives David three options for the consequences of his sin. All these meant death and destruction for the people. Now this seems unfair and unjust for 'innocent' people to suffer for David's sin. But remember, these 'innocent' people had demanded a king to lead them rather than depending on God. God warned them in 1 Samuel 8:6-20 that an earthly king would bring about their oppression. David's choice was to be placed in God's hands rather than mankind's, for God was merciful. So a plague hits.

As pertaining to the above account, Josephus states the sin committed for counting the troops was not the counting but rather the failure of the people to redeem themselves in accordance with Exodus 30:12-13. The ransom for each person was a half shekel to be donated to the LORD. These verses specifically state this is done to prevent a plague from coming upon the people. Josephus further explains that David reasoned if he chose famine as his consequence, he wouldn't incur any hardship himself because of his vast stores of grain. His second option was to choose military defeat for three months. David, of course, was protected by mighty, valiant men and was unlikely to be in danger himself. According to Josephus, David chose plague because he would be as equally likely to suffer as the people would. The plague came on the people so quickly that they dropped dead with little or no warning. Between morning light and evening sacrifice (about 10 hours), 70,000 men died; some choked, some were blinded, others died instantly.[3] We do not know how many women and children died. The Bible does tell us this happened by way of the drawn sword of the angel of the LORD. The plague was to last three days. But God could no longer bare such destruction of His people. He halted the angel at the threshing floor of Araunah. Second Chronicles 3:1 calls this site Mount Moriah. Genesis 22:2 gives Mount Moriah as the location where Abraham offered Isaac. God commands David to go build an altar there. David purchased the land, oxen, and wood from its owner. The altar was built and the sacrifice made. God accepted David's offering. Mount Moriah became the site of the Temple Mount. Solomon would build the temple of the Jews on the north side of Jerusalem.[7]

David is the only recorded person allowed to choose the consequences of his sin. All three choices were designed to reduce the manpower and resources of the kingdom. All three would humble the people[7] -- pride before destruction. A footnote in Josephus is especially appropriate. "Nor do I think that negligence peculiar to the Jews: those nations which are called *Christians*, are sometimes indeed very solicitous to restrain their kings and governor from breaking the human laws of their several kingdoms, but without the like care for restraining them from breaking the laws of God."[3]

Food for Thought: In 2002, I had jury duty during this week in a civil case. Of twelve jurors, seven jurors wanted automatic negligence declared based on the testimony of one witness, the plaintiff's grandson. The other two witnesses to the alleged event refused to testify for the plaintiff. After many hours, the vote became 9 to 3. After several days, the three of us that stood firm were battle weary. (Jesus tells us in Matt. 18:16 that two or more witnesses are required to declare guilt.) Finally, a mistrial was declared. God allowed me to view a microscopic portion of America: 58% stand ready to automatically condemn, 17 % give in when the pressure starts, 25% are prepared to fight for right. The judge stated only a 10-2 vote was needed for a verdict. One person made all the difference! But a triple cord is not easily broken. What do you stand for? What are you willing to invest or sacrifice to defend your beliefs?

April 17
Bible Readings: 1 Chron. 23:1-32; 24:1-30; 25:1-31; 26:1-11

David displayed the same concern for his son and the people that any good father and king would. He was concerned his young son Solomon would be too inexperienced to handle such a large kingdom with the enormous temple building project. Either one alone could be overwhelming. David works feverishly all the later years of his reign collecting materials for the temple and organizing the administrative structure of the government.

David was king for more than 40 years. He died at the age of 71.[5] In his last years, the kingdom was very prosperous, but David did not store up riches for himself (in accordance with the requirements for kings given in Deut. 17:14-20). Instead, David donated vast amounts of gold, silver, metal, semi-precious stones, and wood to the LORD, stockpiling supplies needed for the temple construction.

During David's time, much of the social, cultural, and political life of the people revolved around worship and religious functions. Thus the Levites played a significant role in maintaining the infrastructure of the kingdom. David now turned his attention to organizing the Levites into the various group assignments needed to carry out the administrative work of the temple. You will note that 1 Chron. 23:3 differs from verse 24 in the ages of the Levites counted for service. Numbers 4 records a census of all Levite males 30-50 years old to be used for the service of the Tent of Meeting, as required by God. The age range is modified in Numbers 8:24 to 25-50 years. The younger Levites served in apprentice-type positions to the older ones. The ages given in 1 Chron. 23:24 are confirmed in 2 Chronicles 31:17 and Ezra 3:8. From reading 1 Chron. 23:3, we can conclude that it reflects more of a formal head of state record using the original Mosaic Law reference to service age to appoint supervisors (whether intentional or unintentional). Verse 24 reads more informally, introducing the census records for workers.[25] Those Levites eligible for service by age and lack of physical defects were divided into 24 groups by lot, each group serving on a rotating basis.

In the original Hebrew, 1 and 2 Chronicles, Ezra, and Nehemiah were written as one continuous book, believed by many scholars to have been written by Ezra. You will notice the last two verses of 2 Chronicles are exactly the same as the first 2 1/2 verses of Ezra.[5] First and second Chronicles record several centuries of history. The author used many sources for the books, including court histories, prophetic writings, and religious records.[5]

Food for Thought: It is hard to imagine the enormity of responsibility young Solomon was about to receive. One can better understand why Solomon asked for wisdom. He would soon be 'on his own' (David dies) "to work out his salvation with fear and trembling" (Philippians 2:12) before the Lord. Have you accepted God's free gift of salvation? Have you worked it out through confession and repentance? God gives wisdom to those who ask, but be prepared to use it wisely.

April 18
Bible Readings: 1 Chron. 26:12-32; 27:1-34; 28:1-21; 29:1-22

David gave his farewell address to the assembly of the nation's officials. David gave the new king sage advice, even as outgoing leaders do today. He warned young Solomon to always seek and serve God, that God would know his heart and motives, and if he forsook God he would forever be rejected. David finished by giving Solomon the 'blueprints' for the temple and its surrounding complex. David had planned well. As a final gesture, David donated his personal fortune to the LORD's temple. (Reckon Solomon was surprised to hear his inheritance was gone? One could say he went from riches to rags, except that he was king!) David would have made a good preacher. Before letting all those people out of the assembly, he passed the offering plate! The leaders of Israel donated generously. David closes out his last official state function with prayer that God bless the people and his son Solomon.

Food for Thought: David loved the LORD so much that his last duties were dedicated to the temple. Do we love the Lord so much that we become single-minded in building His kingdom? Do we openly talk about God and His love everyday?

April 19
Bible Readings: Psalms 5, 6, 7, 10, 11

Having reviewed the life of David, we next look at the psalms or songs he wrote. Although he was a great

Lessons of Love

king, David is primarily known for these songs of praise and devotion.

Psalm 5 is a prayer for help against evil forces. It is also a morning song. David **began** his day by asking for the LORD's help. Very likely the psalm was written during his flight from Absalom. The reference to the temple probably refers to the tent David set up in Jerusalem when the Ark was located there.

Psalm 6 is one of the seven penitential songs found in the book. David is obviously in deep anguish. He weeps over his failures and problems. There are numerous references that David is beginning to feel old (vs. 2, 5, 7). The source of David's problems appears to be enemies who seek his harm. It would seem that the psalm was written during his problems with Absalom. Verse one suggests that David is partly to blame for his circumstances. Perhaps he mourns over his folly with Bathsheba and the chain of sordid events in his own family that has led to this rebellion.

Psalm 7 was written most likely in connection with events that occurred during and immediately after the rebellion of Absalom. Although the Bible says nothing about a Benjamite named Cush, we do know that there were some lingering resentments against David in the tribe of Benjamin probably due to his problems with Saul. Shimei curses David when he flees from Absalom. After Absalom's rebellion a Benjamite named Sheba led a short-lived rebellion. In the psalm, David asks God to judge him. If David is guilty he will accept the blame.

Psalm 10 is a prayer for action. The psalmist questions why God does not immediately judge and condemn those who have no regard for Him. What the psalmist learns is what we all must learn. God has His own timetable. His patience and mercy are enduring, but once it has been exceeded, His judgment is swift, awesome, and final.

Psalm 11 is written during a time of crisis. David rejoices that God is a source of strength and stability during these times.

Food for Thought: It is so nice to discover that a man after God's own heart had so many questions of God, too. David was a musician. When times were happy, he sang a song. When times were bad, he sang a song. When he was confused, sad, tired, he sang a song. Next time you feel any of these ways, purposely start singing a song of praise. You will be surprised how impossible it is not to feel enlightened and joyful!

April 20
Bible Readings: Psalms 13, 17, 23, 26, 28, 31

Today's Psalms involve a variety of issues. In Psalms 13, David wonders if the LORD has forgotten him, but remembrances of God's past blessings convince David that God will remember him again.

In Psalm 17, David prays for God to silence the mouth of his enemies. David is convinced of his own virtue. He is weary of those who seek his life like a lion his prey.

Psalm 23 is perhaps the most familiar and quoted passage from the Old Testament. For those of us who live in urban areas, it is hard to understand the relationship that forms between a man and the animals he tends. The good farmer doesn't let the elements prevent him from making sure that the hay is scattered and the ice is broken on the water tank. He realizes the animals depend on him and look to him to care for them. David realized that God is looking out for us. We may feel that we have everything under control and every need provided, but along comes trouble and we realize how much we need God's love and protection.

Psalm 26 is somewhat unusual. David is calling upon God to bear witness to David's dedication and virtue. David very likely would have written such a psalm, for he spent years of his life living in some secluded cave because some crazy king he had served faithfully suspected him of treason. David's troubles did not cause him to become bitter or angry at life. These psalms testify to the fact that life's calamities could not take from David the thing he valued most: his relationship with God.

Chapters 28 and 31 echo a similar concern. David prays for protection against slanderers. Many people like to categorize sin. Murder and adultery are among the worst. Then comes stealing and outright lying. We hardly think of gossip as anything above a simple annoyance, but when we attack a man or woman's character, aren't we really destroying that person? What innate benefit do we receive by verbally crucifying others? The prayers of

David remind us to only speak what we know for sure and to have a more noble purpose in our speaking than putting down others.

Food for Thought: If you have never read the book *A Shepherd Looks at Psalm 23* by Phillip Keller, I highly recommend it. You will have a whole different view of Psalm 23. When life gets too hectic, I ask the shepherd to lead me beside still waters and comfort me. Ask God to prepare a table of blessings for you in the presence of the enemies surrounding you. May your cup overflow. This week look for God's presence in everything and every situation. Ask for his calm reassurance through his guidance and protection.

April 21
Bible Readings: Psalms 35, 41, 43, 46, 55

Psalm 35 and Psalm 34 form a pair. These psalms are an outpouring of David's dismay at Saul's constant persecution. Psalm 35 is divided into three distinct parts: (1) verses 1-10, (2) verses 11-18, and (3) verses 19-28.[26] Each part begins with a plea for deliverance from one's enemies and closes with the assumption that the LORD will provide that deliverance.[25] David asks God to take up His armor and fight against David's enemies. Part 1 addresses the scheming of enemies, part 2 mourns witnesses who were once friends, and part 3 confronts the gloating of the enemies.[27]

Psalm 41 is a prayer for those who aid the weak or down and out. David mourns the loss of friends turned betrayers. This psalm ends with a double amen. This double amen is found at the end of Books I-III of Psalms. Just as we have our modern hymns grouped into songbooks, so did the early worshippers. Psalms is comprised of five 'books.' The following books contain the psalms shown: I, 1-41; II, 42-72; III, 73-89; IV, 90-106; V, 107-150.[27]

Although short, Psalm 43 paints a decidedly dark picture of one deeply distressed over the oppression from the enemy. But it ends with bright hope. David takes a look at himself as an outsider would and makes the observation that a child of God has no reason to despair, for God is always with him.

The directions for the 46th psalm state it is to be sung "According to *alamoth*."[1] The exact meaning of this term is not known, but it is believed to mean soprano voice.[5] The first two lines are often quoted and provide comfort for those in trouble. The song then evolves into a reminder that all our earthly struggles pale in comparison to God's power. The psalm ends with God speaking to us saying, "Be still, and know that I am God; I will be exalted among nations, I will be exalted in the earth."[1] Notice the emphatic phrase "I **will** be."

Much of David's life was plagued by the betrayals of friends and family. In Psalm 55, David expresses his deep distress and sadness over these disappointments. According to the directions, it is a *maskil*, a form of the word *maschil*, probably indicating an annual festival song that has special musical accompany.[5] In reading this psalm, you are immediately drawn to verses 12-14. Most of us can relate to the distress of betrayal by a close friend. Verses 22-23 provide a finale that cannot be overstated. The power packed into those few lines is awesome. Any underdog will be enlightened and feel uplifted by meditating on the message of verse 22.

Food for Thought: Have you cast your cares on the Lord? Remember, "he will never let the righteous fall."[1]

April 22
Bible Readings: Psalms 61, 62, 64, 69

Psalm 61 first offers a prayer for security and then switches after "Selah" to thanking God for His answer.[27] Selah occurs 71 times in Psalms, but scholars disagree as to its meaning. It is most likely a musical direction that may mean (1) pause, (2) repeat, or (3) instrumentation.[5]

Psalm 62 is for Jeduthun, who was one of the chief musicians appointed by King David to lead the musical portion of worship.[27] David declares that God, and God alone, is the source of his strength and power. Earthly treasures come and go, but God is forever.

David tells us God will turn the tables on those who conspire to do evil. Psalm 64 is a condemnation of evildoers.

In Psalm 69, we see mankind floundering and crying out for help as the undercurrents of evil in this world are pulling them under. In verse 7 we clearly see a picture of the one true Savior, Jesus, emerging. By verse 17, David is asking God not to hide His face, just as Jesus felt forsaken on the cross. There can be no mistake of the parallel with Jesus by verse 21 when both gall and vinegar are mentioned. Suddenly, in verse 22 when you are expecting to hear a "Father, forgive them" type of prayer, you get instead a curse declared on the enemies. David prays for every possible type of punishment to be cast upon the enemies. Jerking us back into the reality of our human qualities, David's words have been very effective. God the Son is eternally kind, forgiving, and merciful. Mankind is filled with vengeance, anger, and cruelty. Thanksgiving and praise for the one and only living God commands the final verses.

Food for Thought: When life is dishing out troubles and enemies seem to be everywhere, pour your heart out in prayer as David did. Tell God how you truly feel about what is happening to you. After all, God already knows and pouring your fears and worries out to Him purges the anger from your heart. Make an effort to pray for forgiveness of an enemy.

Verses of the Week: **Psalm 121:7-8** "The LORD will keep you from all harm -- he will watch over your life; the LORD will watch over your coming and going both now and forevermore."

April 23
Bible Readings: Psalms 70, 71, 77, 83, 86

In each of the Psalms for today, David cries out to God for help. On most of the occasions, David is either being lied about or persecuted by others. In Psalm 83, a group of nations is allied together against Israel. David is perceptive enough to recognize God as his ultimate source and trusts in Him to provide not only for his personal needs but also the needs of the nation.

David also realizes that God is the ultimate therapist. He doesn't divulge confidential information; He is constantly available; and because He is David's maker, God can diagnose what is wrong in David's life. Unlike human counselors whose advice is often little more than a shot in the dark, God's guidance is always appropriate and fulfills all our needs.

Food for Thought: In the still of the night, God waits for you to call out to Him. Question is, "Do you wait expectantly for God to call out to you?" Every day God calls to us, but most of the time we are not listening. Spend time in God's word today, then pray, then wait in the silence for God's voice. Remember, everything takes practice, even silence and listening.

April 24
Bible Readings: Psalms 88, 91, 95, 108, 109

Most of the Psalms for today are expressions of praise rather than requests for help. Certainly the most inspirational of this group is Psalm 91. In this psalm David describes the believer's relationship with God in very personal terms. God is depicted as a fortress and refuge. He protects us from pestilence, the danger of war (arrows). The passage also suggests that we have guardian angels to protect us. David rejoices in God's love that is directed not only at David but all who choose to put their faith in God.

Food for Thought: Sometimes when I'm depressed I open my Bible to one of these psalms. It just lifts my spirits to pour out my praise to God. Just think of God sending an angel to care for you. Are you making your guardian angel proud? Or does your secret behavior or thoughts shame even your angel?

April 25
Bible Readings: Psalms 120, 121, 140, 143, 144

This group of psalms expresses prayer and supplication for God's protection and deliverance from persecution. Psalms 120 and 121 are listed as 'songs of ascents.' These were probably songs sung when one went up to Jerusalem to ascend the mount to the temple. All psalms from 120 to 134 are ascent songs, sometimes referred to as "Pilgrim" songs, or songs of those on a pilgrimage.[5]

Psalm 121 offers complete security and peace-of-mind for those who trust in the LORD. David thirsts after the LORD and seeks His protection in Psalm 143. The psalmist pleads, "Let the morning bring me word of your unfailing love."[1]

Food for Thought: Pray Psalm 143:10, "Teach me to do your will, for you are my God."[1]

April 26
Bible Readings: Psalms 1, 14, 15, 36, 37, & 39

Beginning today, we look at a group of psalms that focus on the difference between the righteous and the wicked. Psalms 1, 14, and 15 are three of the better-known psalms of this group. Let's look at them in greater detail.

Psalm 1 outlines the characteristics of a godly man in terms of what he isn't and in terms of what he is. First, he doesn't get his advice from wicked people. He doesn't walk, stand, or sit with them. They have no influence on him. He may have contact with them, for that can't be avoided, but in all cases he seeks to influence them. The righteous man has many positive traits; he is joyful (his delight is in the LORD), he is serious and thoughtful (on His law he meditates), and he is fruitful. In addition, his work endures (his leaf does not wither), which is in stark contrast to the wicked that are compared to chaff.

Psalm 14 is rather unique in that it appears twice in the book of Psalms (compare to 53). Its theme is the utter failure of man when viewed from God's perspective. The word "fool" in verse 1 comes from a Hebrew term meaning the act of withering. Only one with a withered heart and mind denies a creator. God looks down from heaven and sees that all men have turned from Him. The Apostle Paul quotes this passage in Romans 3 where he demonstrates that all men have fallen and are in need of God's forgiveness. The psalm ends with a hope for future salvation, which was fulfilled in Jesus Christ.

Psalm 15 asks a question that all of us have wondered about. This question demonstrates a typical feature of Hebrew poetry. The poet makes a statement or asks a question and then repeats himself by making the same statement or asking the same question but using different wording the second time. This trait is known as synonymous parallelism. The remaining verses answer the question raised in verse one. If one wants to go to Heaven, he/she must be blameless in his walk, truthful in his heart, charitable to his neighbor, careful of his company, faithful to his promises, and merciful in his dealings. I don't measure up, and I doubt if you do either. So you and I can forget about ever going to Heaven!

But wait, God sent his Son Jesus Christ to earth, and He did measure up! The Apostle Paul says in 2 Corinthians 5:21 "For He [God] made Him [Jesus] who knew no sin to be sin for us, that we might become the righteousness of God in Him."[29] In other words Jesus Christ changed places with us and that is why Good Friday is good. What must we do to be saved? First, we must recognize that by our own actions we have made ourselves ineligible to live in God's kingdom! Second, we must trust in the person of Jesus Christ to redeem us! John 14:6 says "I [Jesus] am the way, and the truth, and the life; no one comes to the Father [God], but through Me." Third, we must confess before others our faith in Jesus Christ![29] Jesus said in Matthew 10:32 "Everyone therefore who shall confess Me before men, I will also confess him before My Father who is in heaven."[29]

Why not accept God's salvation through Jesus Christ? It can make an eternity of difference!

Food for Thought: What is keeping you from coming to Christ?

April 27
Bible Readings: Psalms 40, 49, 50, & 73

The value of the righteous life is the focus of today's psalms. In chapter forty we share the experience of someone passing from darkness into light. The psalm speaks to us because all of us have had a similar experience at one time or another. We have become immersed in what seemed like a horrible pit of miry clay. When we cried to God, he heard us for there is no place, in this life, that can absolutely separate us from Him. Often in my life I have felt like Ishmael at the end of Moby Dick. I am floating on a casket in the middle of the sea, but then my salvation comes "Like a boat out of the blue, faith steps in and sees me through." Once saved from my predicament, I am placed on the solid rock and given a new song to sing.

Chapter 73 also is about a universal theme. Who among us has never envied the super-rich? We would like to have the financial security, the power, and the pleasures their riches can buy. Many of the super-rich have lied, cheated, and stolen to get where they are. Things like ethics and their responsibilities to God and man have not been their concern. At times we wonder, "Isn't it unfair that they should have so much and we so little?" Notice Ps. 73:23 says God will hold you by your right hand. That means you are holding God's left hand – not the hand of judgment.

When I read this psalm, I am reminded of the story of the old missionary who returned to his home in New York City after a life of faithful service preaching the gospel and teaching children in a far country to read and write. When the boat arrived at the dock, he saw a large crowd and brass band gathered. A famous singer/movie star was also on the boat. The star got a big reception. The mayor gave him a key to the city, and the band played songs from the actor's famous movies. As the old missionary helped his aged wife down the gangplank, he felt bitter. No one was there to welcome him home; nobody cared how he had sacrificed for others. He thought, "Lord this just isn't fair!" The Lord responded, "Be patient my child, you aren't home yet!"

Food for Thought: Can you recall a time when the Lord delivered you from a serious problem?

April 28
Bible Readings: Psalms 76, 82, 84, 90, 92, 112, & 115

One of the best known of all the psalms is part of today's reading. Chapter 90 deals with the brevity of man's life. The author of the psalm is Moses whose life was long compared to ours, but not as long as Moses would have liked. The first paragraph begins with God, who has always been and always will be. In paragraph two, time as measured by man is compared to time as viewed by God. From God's view, William the Conqueror won the Battle of Hastings shortly after midnight, Columbus discovered the new world around noon, Lincoln was killed around 8:30 this evening, and now it is a tick after midnight. The third paragraph again focuses upon man. We must remember that the indignation referred to is a result of man's fall in the Garden of Eden and our support of our ancestor's decision by our own personal actions. Our plight is not what God intended. We are here for a moment, we struggle continually, and then we fly away.

In the last four paragraphs, Moses prays for seven things.
1. Instruction (teach us to number our days)
2. Restoration (have compassion on your servants)
3. Satisfaction (satisfy us in the morning with your unfailing love)
4. Compensation (make us glad for as many days as you have afflicted us)
5. Manifestation (may your deeds be shown to your servants)
6. Sanctification (may the favor of the LORD rest upon us)
7. Confirmation (establish the works of our hands)

Food for Thought: Your life in this world is short. Are you prepared for the next one?

April 29
Bible Readings: Psalms 8, 9, 16, 19, 21, & 24

Beginning today we look at psalms praising God for His glory and creation. Psalm 8 is often quoted. It begins and ends in the same way: recognition of God's grandeur. Much of the excellence of His name is revealed in His dealing with man. God has made us a little lower than the heavenly beings. We have the ability to reason, to plan. We have tamed other creatures like horses and dogs to serve us. We have built skyscrapers, tamed mighty rivers, and traveled to another planet. All of these abilities are God-given.

Psalm 19 is of particular interest. The opening verse declares that the heavens testify to the existence of God and that there is no place where their testimony fails to be heard. This chapter goes hand in hand with Paul's observation in Romans 1. The natural order, without doubt, suggests the existence of a creator. Have you ever considered that all things have the same organizational structure? The largest thing most people understand is the structure of the solar system. It consists of a central object (sun) surrounded by smaller objects (planets) rotating in orbits around the central object. The smallest thing is the atom. It consists of a central core that is surrounded by various numbers of electrons rotating around the central core in orbits. They both have the same structure.

Food for Thought: Where do you see God's glory in the natural world?

> Verses of the Week: **Psalm 119:143, 147** "Trouble and distress have come upon me, but your commands are my delight. . . . I rise before dawn and cry for help; I have put my hope in your word."

April 30
Bible Readings: Psalms 29, 33, 65, 66, 67, 68

Previous psalms have focused on nature's proclaiming God's eternal glory; Psalm 29 is more specific in that we are given an example of God's power manifested in the natural world. The psalm begins with the angels being called upon to praise God. The rest of the psalm examines the power in God's voice. The psalm acknowledges the universal power of God (it is over many waters). The idea is that it is not limited to one land or people. The voice of the LORD is majestic; it breaks the cedars and makes its branches skip like a calf. His voice also divides the flame. The idea is that He divides the lightning causing it to be forked. God's voice also shakes the wilderness and causes the wild animals to give birth in their panic.

As anyone from the Sooner state can testify, the psalm was inspired by a fierce thunderstorm. I have seen many of these myself. One knows the moment they arrive; the air grows cold, the winds grow strong. Frequently, one is both amazed and terrified at the sheer force of the wind, rain, lightning, and thunder. After the storm has passed, there is always a special cleanness in the air and an unusual calm. These storms without fail bring life to a dry and parched earth just as God's presence brings peace and hope to our hearts.

Food for Thought: Have you heard God's voice lately? Have you been listening? God speaks to our hearts in many ways. We must be ready to hear and accept His voice and acknowledge His presence.

May 1
Bible Readings: Psalms 75, 93, 94, 97, 98, 99, & 100

These psalms continue with the theme of praise to God. Chapters 96, 97, and 98 all seem to go together. The last verse of 96 (not in today's reading) declares, "He cometh to judge the earth." Psalm 97 begins with "The LORD reigns, let the earth be glad; let the distant seas rejoice." Psalm 98 begins with "Sing to the LORD a new song, for He has done marvelous things." Thus, taken as a whole we see the LORD's (1) coming, (2) reigning, and creation's (3) rejoicing. In this new song there is the note of:

Wonder: "He has done marvelous things." The Bible speaks of the great acts of God. The dividing of the Red Sea,

David's victory over Goliath, and the resurrection of Jesus are all examples of these marvels, but the most marvelous thing of all is that God should love us. My most heartfelt song of praise is "I am so glad that Jesus loves me."

Faithfulness: "He has remembered His love and His faithfulness to the House of Israel." Always remember that what God's mercy has promised, His faithfulness will perform.

Praise: "Shout for joy to the LORD!" When we realize all that God has done for us, can we do anything but shout praises to His name?

Hope: "He comes to judge the world." All creation seems joyful at the thought of His coming. The idea here is similar to Paul's teaching in Romans 8:21, "The creation itself will also be delivered from the bondage of corruption into the glorious liberty of the children of God."

Food for Thought: Spend some time pondering the marvelous events that have occurred in your life as a result of God's intervention. Questions have to arise. What if God had not been with you? Would you still be alive? Would you have a place to live? food? a career? What would your attitude be like?

May 2
Bible Readings: Psalms 103, 104, 113, 114, 117

This selection of psalms centers on praising God's characteristics of love, faithfulness, sensitivity, and compassion. They also review, in awe, the wonders of God's creation.

Psalm 103 calls on us to praise God for all His many blessings poured out on us, blessings we often take for granted. First, God provides all our needs. Nothing that we need in this life has been withheld from us, not even God's own son. Second, God forgives our sin and gives us His mercy. God's mercy is infinite. Just think of the millions He forgives daily, but then think of the billions of people He is ready to forgive if they would just turn to Him and repent. Third, God is the Great Physician, the healer of all illness. This doesn't just refer to literal physical ailments but also the diseases of the heart and mind that give root to sin. Sin is the identifiable act of hate, adultery, greed, murder, lust, etc. The disease, though, is the flaw in our character that allows sin to breed and grow in our lives. God heals those flaws. He seals them with His love. Fourth, God saves us from condemnation to hell. He reaches out to us, draws us into His loving arms, and holds us securely for eternity. The blood of God's only son has redeemed our lives. How much He loves us! Fifth, God not only saves us, He also makes us Princes and Princesses of His kingdom. We are co-heirs with Jesus. We share in Jesus' inheritance -- the kingdom of God. Sixth, those who are saved and have been healed by God receive the good and pure pleasures given only by God. These good gifts of God satisfy all the desires of our hearts. Finally, those who have been saved find that they have a new life, a renewed joy that makes their steps light and their youth renewed.[24] I am reminded of my favorite Bible verse, Isaiah 40:31, "but those who hope in the LORD will renew their strength. They will soar on wings like eagles; they will run and not grow weary, they will walk and not be faint."[1]

Psalm 103:12 is often quoted. We are separated from our sins as far as the east is from the west, in other words, an infinite distance. The two shall never meet again. God cleanses us, heals us, forgives us, and saves us. We are His redeemed children.

Psalm 104 praises God by revisiting the creation story of Genesis 1. Each day or stage of creation brings praises to God for all His created wonders. The parallel passages are outlined below.

Genesis 1	Created	Psalm 104
Day 1 (3-5)	light	2a
Day 2 (6-8)	firmament divides waters	2b-4
Day 3 (9-10)	land and water separated	5-10
(11-13)	vegetation and trees	14-17
Day 4 (14-19)	sun/moon and seasons	19-23
Day 5 (20-23)	creatures of the sea and air	25-26, 17
Day 6 (24-28)	animals and man	21-24, 18, 11
(29-31)	food for all creatures	27-28, 14

That glorious old hymn 'O Worship the King' was inspired by this psalm.[28]

Psalm 113 is part of a group of psalms (113-118) used at the annual Passover celebration. These are often called the Egyptian Hallel (praise). Verses 2-3 are later reflected in Malachi 1:11 as a prediction of the Messianic Age. Verses 7-8 are almost a direct quote from Hannah's prayer in 1 Samuel 2:8. Therefore, you can understand the sudden reference to a barren woman in verse 9 becoming a happy mother.[28]

Psalm 114 addresses the exodus of the children of Israel from Egypt. The reaction of God's creation to His presence on earth is simply awe-inspiring. Psalm 117, the shortest chapter of the Bible, is a chorus of praise. All should praise God because His love and faithfulness endure forever. Paul quotes Psalm 117:1 in his letter to the Romans (15:11). Paul is making a plea for the Jews to accept the Gentile Christians as children of the same God of Jacob. May all nations praise God.[28]

Food for Thought: Spend some time listing all God's blessings that you take for granted -- nourishing sunshine, quenching rain, shading clouds, relaxing nightfall, invigorating morning. Think of the many joys you have just because you can see, hear, taste, and smell. There is much for which we should praise God. Offer up a prayer of pure praise as your sacrifice to an everlasting God who loves you.

May 3
Bible Readings: Psalm 119

The longest chapter of the Bible (Psalm 119) follows the middle chapter of the Bible (118). Thus, you have the middle chapter sandwiched between the shortest (117) and the longest (119) chapters. Also, Psalm 119 is an acrostic. Each section of 8 verses is headed by one of the Hebrew alphabet: from aleph to taw or A to Z, we might say. The Hebrew alphabet has 22 letters; each is presented in order here. In the original Hebrew, each verse begins with the alphabet letter of its section.[28]

This psalm may also be dissected into the "I Am's," "I Will's," and "I Have's" verses.

I Am . . .
1. A stranger on this earth; Heaven is my home. (19)
2. A friend of other Christians. (63)
3. Tested in the smoke of the devil's fire while on earth. (83)
4. Thine, O LORD. (94)
5. Your suffering servant. (125)
6. Fearful of judgment. (120)
7. Your willing servant. (125)
8. Lowly and despised. (141)[24]

Lessons of Love

<u>I Will . . .</u>
1. Praise God. (7)
2. Obey God's laws. (8)
3. Meditate on God's word. (15)
4. Delight in God's statutes. (16)
5. Observe God's commandments. (32)
6. Be free from the world's bindings. (45)
7. Testify for God. (46)
8. Be thankful always. (62)
9. Never forget God's word. (93)[24]

<u>I Have . . .</u>
1. Gone astray. (176)
2. Sought after God whole-heartedly. (10)
3. Rejoiced in the ways of God. (14)
4. Declared my path. (26)
5. Chosen to be faithful. (30)
6. Remembered the name of the Lord. (55)
7. Believed God's commandments. (66)
8. Refrained from evil. (101)
9. Longed for the Lord's salvation. (174)[24]

This psalm has so many jewels in its crown that they simply can't all be covered in the course of this lesson. I encourage you to meditate on some empowering, encouraging, and enlightening passages (verses 1-2, 5, 9, 11, 18, 36, 50, 67, 73, 84, 103, 105, 107, 133, 147, 165, 176).

Food for Thought: Actor Leonard Nimoy is Jewish. As Spock, his hand sign for 'live long and prosper' is actually the sign for the Hebrew letter 'shin.' (It looks much like a W.) I wonder if he built that into Star Trek as a witness to other Jews? Is he a Christian Jew? I don't know. But I do know that people can and do witness with what they have, wherever they are. Are you witnessing with what God has blessed you? How many people worldwide recognize and daily use Spock's hand signal? You have a witness, too.

May 4
<u>Bible Readings: Psalms 122, 124, 133, 134, 135, 136, 138</u>

These psalms lend themselves well to brief summaries or key components.
1. Psalm 122 praises Jerusalem for the house of the Lord is there. From Jerusalem (Zion) God issues His judgment. Jesus, from the house of David, ascended His throne at Jerusalem.
2. Israel survived serious threats to the nation and the house of David at the hands of the Philistines. This psalm (124) reveals the depth of dependence David had in God.[28]
3. David's rejoicing in the unity of brotherhood took place prior to his curse of never having the sword depart from his house (2 Samuel 12:10). Both the high as well as the low in life receive the same gift of salvation. Hermon is the highest mountain in Israel while Mt. Zion is one of the lowest.[28] (Psalm 133)
4. Verses 1 and 2 of Psalm 134 appear to be a salutation or address to the Levites by the Jewish pilgrims ascending to worship. Verse 3, then, would be the response of the Levites.[28]

5. Every verse of Psalm 135 is echoed from another verse in the Bible or is quoted elsewhere or quotes scripture from other Bible passages. Examples of the verses are below.[28]
    a. 1-4 = Psa. 134:1; 52:9; 147:1; Heb. 11
    b. 5-7 = Ex. 18:11; Jer. 10:13; Psa. 115:3
    c. 8-14 = Num. 21:21, 33; Deut. 3:11; Ex. 3:15; Deut. 32:36; Psa. 136:10, 18-22
    d. 15-18 = Psa. 115:4-6, 8
    e. 19-21 = Psa. 115:9-11; 134:3
6. Psalm 136 is a responsive reading designed to show God as: (a) God of gods, (b) Creator, (c) Rescuer, (d) Victor, (e) Friend, (f) God of Heaven. This psalm is known as the Great Hallel (the Great Psalm of Praise).[28]
7. Psalm 138 praises God because He answers, encourages, reviews, protects, and perfects.[24]

Food for Thought: It is hard to have a heavy heart while singing God's praises. The next time you are depressed, sing a hymn or chorus of praise, or pop in a tape of upbeat gospel music. Believe me, it works better and faster than all the medicine in the world.

May 5
Bible Readings: Psalms 139, 145, 148, 150

God knows us inside and out. He even knew every detail of our bodies, personalities, characters, and thoughts centuries before we ever lived. God knows our actions before we even do them! I can't imagine the disappointment He has had to bear for so long because of me. Just think of some disappointment you have had with a child, friend, or other loved one. Now imagine having known for years prior to the event that it would happen. Most of us wouldn't be able to bear the strain and anxiety. Multiply that by the billions of people on earth! God is good. We are blessed that He doesn't just wipe us all off the face of the earth from disgust. Psalm 139 offers thanksgiving and praise to a loving God who loves us in spite of knowing us. Preachers and Sunday School teachers frequently quote verse 16. God truly does know the day we will be born and the day we will die and all that will happen to us in the interim -- and He knows it long before we are born. In verses 23 and 24, David asks God to (1) search him, (2) know him, (3) try him, (4) see him, and (5) lead him.[24] We would do well to pray these same verses regularly.

Psalm 145 is another acrostic poem. Each verse begins with a letter of the Hebrew alphabet. You will recognize the line "Great is the LORD and most worthy of praise" (vs. 3)[1] as one that has been prominent in modern gospel songs. (This line is identical to Psa. 48:1a.) The last two stanzas of this psalm (vs. 14-20) praise God's works to (1) uphold, (2) raise, (3) provide, (4) satisfy, (5) fulfill, (6) save, and (7) preserve His children.

Psalm 148 is a Hallelujah chorus designed to elicit praise, first from the heavens and next from the earth. All creation is to praise God. The horn raised up in verse 14 is the horn of salvation -- Jesus Christ. All the saints will praise Him. Horn is a word we do not readily relate to as a symbol of deity. But in David's day, the blood of the sacrificial animal was put on the horns of the altar. Therefore, mercy was sought at the horns of the altar; one sought to be cleansed from sin by the sacrificial blood. Jesus is our sacrificial lamb. He was raised up to become our horn of salvation. In Psalm 18:2, David refers to God as his rock, fortress, deliverer, refuge, shield, horn of salvation, and stronghold. Jesus, as the Son of God, is all these to us, too.

Psalm 150 is the last song in the book of Psalms. This short psalm answers the famous questions that form the backbone of news journalism: What? Where? Why? How? Who?[24] The only question not explicitly answered is "When?" Of course, the implied answer is "continually."

Food for Thought: Read Psalm 150 and answer the above questions. I'll get you started. (1) What is happening? Praise. (2) Where is it happening? In God's sanctuary and His heavens. -- Now you answer. (3) Why is praise happening? (4) How are they praising Him? (5) Who is being praised? Who is giving the praise?

May 6
Bible Readings: Psalms 4, 12, 20, 25, 32, 38

Psalm 4 was to be accompanied by stringed instruments, frequently denoted by the Hebrew word *'neginah.'* These would be the asor, kinnor, and nebel. The asor had 10 strings and was probably similar to a zither. Kinnor is usually translated as harp but would better be translated as lyre. The lyre is much smaller and more portable than the massive harp. Nebel is often referred to as psaltery or violin. This, though, was a true harp, often as big as the adult playing it.[7]

Often when night approaches, evils, fears, worries, and troubles seize our minds, throwing us relentlessly into the blackness of despair. Never is there a time when counting one's blessings and praising the LORD is more important. Night is a time when evil tries to gain a foothold in our mind. The devil builds his strongholds on our doubts and fears. What we allow in our minds forms the basis for our future. The adage "garbage in, garbage out" is very appropriate here. Psalm 3 was written during Absalom's revolt against his father, David. Psalm 4 was probably written in the aftermath of that revolt. David has been humiliated. He was surrounded by lies, exasperated, and depressed.[27] David calls us to be confident in our God and to trust Him with our safety. We are to offer "right sacrifices" or obedience to God. Then we can sleep in peace.

Sheminith is believed to refer to tenor or bass voices as opposed to *alamoth* (1 Chr. 15:19-21 *Tanakh*) that is thought to mean soprano voices.[5] Psalm 12 reminds us that the ability to talk is a gift from God that is not to be used for evil. This is the first psalm to provide an answer from God (vs. 5).[27] We are told that God's words are pure and complete (7 times).

Psalm 20 is written like a blessing. We would do well to pray this psalm for our children and loved ones. Remember, as Christians, we are God's anointed.

Psalm 25 is another acrostic poem. The major theme of this song is God's guidance. David was a man of war. His life was spent fighting personal and national enemies. Thus, it is not surprising that this musician would write songs that usually included a plea for victory over his enemies. We, like David, have enemies, some physical but many spiritual. Also, like David, we need to be men and women of war but likewise men and women of prayer. Pray for God's strength and power to overthrow our enemies. The last chapter of Ephesians reminds us to put on the whole armor of God so that we might stand against the forces of evil (Eph. 6:11). David's guilt for past sins and rebellion are briefly reflected on with sorrow. Trusting in God is a natural outcome or finale of David's works. One is always to trust God and wait patiently on His hand to guide your life, regardless of the circumstances.[27]

Psalm 32 is the second of the penitential psalms that include Psalms 6, 32, 38, 51, 102, 130, and 143. The penitential psalms are comprised of two main parts. The first part of the psalm involves expression of penitence or remorse. The last part of the psalm is a declaration of God's faithfulness. Sometimes this declaration is a single sentence or two, e.g., Psa. 38, and other times it is many verses, as in this psalm. Psalm 32:1 tells us we are blessed, indeed, if our sins are forgiven and covered by the blood of the sacrifice (washed away by the blood of the lamb -- Jesus). This foundation sets the tone for the entire psalm.[27] This song expresses the complete joy found in walking close to God and experiencing His matchless love and faithfulness to forgive. The psalmist pleads with the listener to seek God while He can be found, before the last trumpet sounds (Rev. 11:15).

I can fully relate to the psalmist's cry when he says, "there is no health in my body."[1] "My back is filled with searing pain" (Psa. 38:7)[1] seems to have been the theme song of my life. Anyone who has lived beyond the childhood years can relate to the feelings expressed in Psalm 38. So many times we feel we cannot go on, that we are "about to fall." But confident trust in God allows the psalmist to declare, "I wait for you, O LORD; you will answer, O LORD my God." (vs. 15)[1]

Food for Thought: I had a MRI of my back this week. The day started off badly. For the first time in years, my 30-year-old clock radio didn't wake me. It was my fault. It has a short in the volume knob and has to be set just right to make any sound. Of course, I had decided to 'adjust' the sound the night before. Waking up 1.5 hours later than normal resulted in no private time for Bible study and prayer. As I waited for the MRI, I found myself looking forward to the 'down time' to talk with God. The time just flew. An hour later, I wasn't finished talking with God, but the technologist was finished with the MRI. God provided makeup time for me. Do we provide makeup time for God? Regardless of how our day starts or ends, it belongs to God. Be sure a portion of it is dedicated solely to Him.

> Verse of the Week: **Psalm 27:1** "The LORD is my light and my salvation – whom shall I fear? The LORD is the stronghold of my life – of whom shall I be afraid?"

May 7
Bible Readings: Psalms 42, 53, 58, 81, 101

Psalm 42 begins Book II of Psalms. The Sons of Korah were the temple musicians. Psalm 42 is the first half of a single poem composed of Psalms 42 and 43. It is a sorrowful lament of a temple singer (choir member) who is exiled from God's holy temple. We are not told if this is a temporary or permanent situation for this psalmist far from home. This is possibly the lament of a traveler on a journey or of a captured Israelite (2 Kings 14:14). The Jordan River begins in the mountains to the north where Mt. Hermon is located. As the water cascades down the mountain, waterfalls are formed. Mount Mizar is only mentioned this one time in the Bible. It is apparently a hill east of the northern Jordan River area.[5]

'Mahalath' is only used in the directions for Psalms 53 and 88. It probably refers to the choreographic direction of the music. Coupled with *'Leannoth'* in Psalm 88, it is interpreted to mean antiphonal singing.[27] Antiphonal singing was the favorite style of the Israelites and could be accomplished in three ways: (1) with a leader and a choir, (2) with a choir and the congregation, or (3) with two choirs.[7] Antiphonal singing involves one person or group singing a part with the other group responding.[8] The same idea as responsive readings, only set to music. Stanzas 2 and 4 of this psalm are responsive to stanzas 1 and 3. When read like a responsive reading, the psalm is easier to understand. First there is the declaration, then followed by the response that fills out or expounds the declaration.

Miktam may also be spelled *michtam*. It appears in the directions of six psalms (16, 56-60). It is believed to be a musical term about how the song is to be sung. Its exact meaning is unknown.[5] Possibly, it means 'a silent prayer' as all the psalms where it appears have titles indicating the danger of speaking aloud.[27] There have been many nations throughout history that could have used Psalm 58 as their theme song. It is a condemnation of unjust leaders. The righteous plead for God to avenge them.

Psalm 81 is the trumpet call song for the Feast of Tabernacles. This song was written by one of the choir directors, Asaph. *Gittith* has three possible meanings. First, it is the feminine form of Gath that means winepress but is also the name of a Philistine city that was prominent in Jewish history. It may refer to a particular vintage of wine associated with this festival.[27] Second, it may be a musical instrument used or made in Gath. Third, it could have been a marching song for the Gittite army.[5] A fourth possibility has been suggested, that it was written for the processional march when the Ark was carried from the Gittite's house to Jerusalem (2 Sam. 6:11). Gittith is found in the directions of Psalms 8, 81, 84.[27] Verses 6 and 7 refer to the wilderness experience. If Israel wants to defeat its enemies, it would do well to heed verses 13-14.

Psalm 101 is an admirable declaration by a king determined to rule his nation under God. How very much we need more leaders who truly strive to lead like this!

Food for Thought: Many church denominations today do not allow any instruments, except pianos and organs, to be used in worship. A few allow no instruments at all. I believe King David would be appalled at any musical instrument being excluded. The psalms testify to the many various instruments used by the Hebrews in worship. Some of the fastest growing churches in America are non-denominational. Wonder why? Many of the denominations have become too rigid, too political, too legalistic, and too pharisaical. Be sure you worship God and not the denomination.

May 8
Bible Readings: Psalms 111, 130, 131, 141, 146

I believe the most profound statement in all of the psalms is found in Psalm 111:10, "The fear of the LORD is the beginning of wisdom."[1] Anyone who does not fear the judgment of God is truly a fool. Psalms 53:1 defines fool as an atheist. I can only remember meeting one person in my life who openly attested to being atheist. I distinctly remember the fear I felt at even being near him. His jeers and snarls at "those who celebrate the little Jewish boy's birthday" were overwhelmingly evil. This person was deemed successful and prosperous by the standards of men, yet he had not wisdom.

This set of psalms addresses one's personal relationship to God. The central theme of each is outlined as follows.

Psalm 111 - Recognize God's works around you
　　　　130 - Rescued out of the depths
　　　　131 - Display a childlike spirit
　　　　141 - Have no compromises
　　　　146 - Praise your Maker

Food for Thought: A chorus I like begins, "We bring the sacrifice of praise into the house of the LORD." God owns all that we have and He has made us all that we are. Praise should not be the only sacrifice we bring, but it is the first that must be brought. Do you praise God daily? Have you developed a personal relationship with the Lord? All that you must do is accept Jesus as Lord and Savior of your life. God's gift is free to you. Jesus paid the price of your sins. Don't delay.

May 9
Bible Readings: Psalms 2, 22, 27

We begin a collection of songs that reflect the coming of the Messiah, Jesus Christ. Psalm 2 clearly declares the King will be installed on Zion (Jerusalem). The next stanza is a proclamation from God. His Son will rule with an iron scepter over all the nations. This psalm is often referred to in the New Testament, e.g., Acts 4:25-26; 13:33. Psalm 22 is the crucifixion prophecy. David had no known experience that would have prompted him to write this song. This truly was prophecy from Divine inspiration. The very words Jesus would say from the cross begin this song. The verses that follow explicitly predict the scene of the cross. The mocking of the crowd is in verse 8. His enemies are described as "strong bulls of Bashan" (v. 12). You will recall Bashan extended north of the Jabbok River (east of the Jordan) to Mt. Hermon. It had rich pasturelands and thick oak forests. The terrible physical pain of the crucifixion is foretold in verses 14-17. Even the soldiers casting lots for Jesus' clothes is depicted in verse 18. Hebrews 2:11-12 tells us that Jesus is not ashamed to call us brethren. In 27-28 the psalmist says all will remember and all will bow down, which we know will happen at the second coming of Christ. This psalm ends declaring that all "future generations will be told about the Lord" (vs. 30).[1]

Psalm 27 inspires even the meek and mild to boldly proclaim confidence in the LORD. I frequently claim this psalm or portions of it as one of God's promises. I claim it for myself and for others. The LORD is my light, my salvation, my stronghold, my protector, my teacher, and my guide. In times of trouble, I repeatedly recall the last verse, "Wait for the LORD; be strong and take heart and wait for the LORD." (14)[1]

Food for Thought: Sometimes we become so engulfed by our problems that we can't see the forest for the trees. In other words, we can't see God for the situations in life that are looming over us. Commit verses 27: 1 and 14 to memory. Say them daily. Remember them in all situations of life.

May 10
<u>Bible Readings: Psalms 45, 47, 48, 87, 110, 72:20</u>

Psalm 45 is the benediction for a royal wedding. The description is that of a majestic regal affair. The prince is victorious and righteous. The bride is beautiful and glorious. They are wed in joy and gladness. Their future sons will rule the earth.[28] This is a Messianic song foretelling the marriage of the Son of God to the bride of Christ -- the church. (Of course, the Bible only refers to Christians as the 'church'.) The marriage feast of the lamb will take place with great celebration in Heaven as Jesus claims His bride. The last verse of this psalm declares that the memory of Jesus will always be perpetuated; it will never end.

God is seated on His throne and is declared King over all the earth in Psalm 47. Psalm 48 continues that line of thought by describing the City of God, Zion. The dwelling place of God is so magnificent that it will be talked about for generations. This psalm describes the glory of ancient Jerusalem, ending with a forward look to a New Jerusalem (Rev. 21).

In Psalm 87, Christ establishes His kingdom on Zion. It is so glorious that even His enemies to the south (Rahab or Egypt) and to the north (Babylon) are forced to recognize Him. Other nations, too, will follow suit.

Jesus refers to verses from Psalm 110 in His discourse with the Pharisees in Matthew 22:41-46 (also recorded in Mark 12:35-40 and Luke 20:41-47). Notice the lettering of the word Lord in the first line. The first one is all capital letters while the second Lord only has the first letter capitalized. LORD is the translation for the Hebrew name for God, YHWH, commonly written as Yahweh. <u>Lord</u> is translated from the Hebrew word Adonai. God revealed Himself to Moses in Exodus 3:14 as Yahweh. Yahweh is also translated as Jehovah. In Old Testament Judaism, Adonai (My Lord) was an acceptable substitute word that could be written and spoken for Yahweh. Yahweh means "I Am Who I Am." This psalm is thus interpreted, "Yahweh says to Adonai" or "God says to Jesus." (I actually penciled in 'God' everywhere LORD appeared in the psalm and 'Jesus' everywhere Lord appeared. It makes it easier to understand.)

In the first stanza of Psalm 110, we see God placing Jesus in a position of power and authority -- the right hand of God. Jesus' enemies (the lost) would be beneath His feet. He would rule over them. In the second stanza, God exalts Jesus as King. (See Acts 5:30.) Then Jesus is declared a priest forever in the order of Melchizedek. Jesus must first be exalted as King in our lives before He can become our eternal High Priest. Melchizedek was both king of Salem and a priest of God (Heb. 7:1). He blessed Abraham and received a tithe from Abraham. We are told (Heb. 7:3) Melchizedek had no father or mother, no beginning or end, and remained a priest forever (like Jesus). In Abraham's act of giving tithes to Melchizedek, Abraham was, in essence, tithing for the whole Israelite nation that was to descend from Abraham. Melchizedek was priest over Abraham and thus over his descendant Levi. Therefore, as a priest in the order of Melchizedek, Jesus was over the Levite priests. (The original story of Abraham and Melchizedek is in Genesis 14:18-20).

Food for Thought: There is a lot of prophecy packed into a few short verses in Psalm 110. It reminds me that great things often come in small packages. Some of the greatest presents of all include a single sense: the touch of a baby's skin, the smile of a loved one, the joy of a child, the sight of a wildflower, the sound of music, the warmth of the spring sunshine, the cool of the shade, the smell of fresh baked cookies, the smell of spring blossoms, the warmth of "I love you" or "Thank you very much." To avoid loneliness or depression, do for others. The gift you will receive will make all the difference.

May 11

Bible Readings: 1 Kings 1; 2 Sam. 23:1-7; 1 Kings 2:1-10, 12; 1 Chron. 29:23-25, 28-30; 2 Chron. 1:1

At this point, David had become rather feeble, not even able to stay warm at night. Abishag was brought in to nurse David and to provide body heat for him during the night. Even though there was no consummated union, they were considered married because of the intimate duties she performed for the king.

By this time, David had lost his eldest three sons: Ammon (killed by Absalom), Absalom (killed by Joab), Chileab (son of Abigail, most likely died as a child[25]). Adonijah was the fourth son, now the eldest. Realizing David's infirmity, Adonijah elevates himself to king and throws a celebration to announce his kingship. He invites his supporters Joab, commander of David's army, and Abiathar, the priest, and all the royal officials. Adonijah tried to appear to be God's anointed by sacrificing many animals. Nathan, the prophet, reports the event to Bathsheba, Solomon's mother. In 1 Kings 1:17, we are told that David had vowed (in accordance with God's blessing in 2 Sam. 12:24-25) to Bathsheba that her son would be king. David was a man of his word. He immediately called three trusted officials: Zadok the priest, Nathan the prophet, and Benaiah a loyal supporter. David has Solomon placed on the king's own mule. This was a significant endorsement because, in Israel, only royalty rode on mules. Horses weren't even available in the Israelite culture.[30] In other nations, the position of king may have been automatically granted to the eldest son or eldest child but not in Israel. God had always chosen Israel's king (first Saul, then David, now Solomon). Nathan's presence testified that Solomon was divinely chosen. Then David instructed his core group of advisors to take Solomon down to Gihon. Gihon was a spring located outside the east wall of Jerusalem in the Kidron Valley.[7] This spring was Jerusalem's primary source of water -- the most precious resource in an arid environment. The last verse of Psalm 110 indicated Jesus would drink from a brook beside the way when He becomes the ruler. Many scholars believe that drinking from Gihon spring became a coronation tradition based on David's prophecy of the coming King.[5] I believe this particular ceremony symbolizes the new king divinely anointed in the east (remember the importance of east to the Hebrews), on the royal but humble mule (servant to his followers), at the source for all life on earth (water). Additionally, there was to be an official proclamation that Solomon was king along with blowing the trumpet (read Num. 10:4-5, 8-9 to recall the significance of a priest blowing a single trumpet). After all this, Solomon and his royal advisors were to ascend the hill into Jerusalem where Solomon would officially be placed on his father's throne.[7] There is no way to read this without seeing a picture of Jesus in every step. When Jesus comes to take over the rule of the earth, a trumpet will sound (Isaiah 27:13; Matt. 24:30-31); He will come from the east (Ezekiel 43:2) and be the source of all life (Rev. 21:6). He will ascend to the throne of His Father (Rev. 4:1-2; 5:6); He will come riding the offspring of a donkey (Zech. 9:9). Proclaimed King thousands of years ago (Zech. 9:9), Jesus first came as a servant-King (Zech. 3:8).

As with all things, David gave thanks to God for giving him a successor to the throne. Solomon is about 21 years old. He warns his half-brother Adonijah that no evil must be found in him thereafter or he will die. David's last charge to Solomon warns him to be true to God, keeping all God's decrees and commands, and walking in His way. In spiritual matters, David was a wise man.

Food for Thought: Do you think Jesus ever had a pity party? You know, one of those times when you wallow face down in the mud feeling sorry for yourself before you finally give up, turn over, and look up. I had one of those today. It seemed like the whole day was a string of bad news. Reading God's word is a surefire way to be a party-pooper. You can't stay down when you're looking up!

May 12
<u>Bible Readings: 1 Kings 2:13-46; 3:1-28; 9: 16; 2 Chron. 1:2-13</u>

In our last lesson, Solomon warned Adonijah to do no evil. Today we find Adonijah asking Bathsheba to request of the king Abishag's hand in marriage. Abishag was considered one of David's wives, thus a widow. Solomon reacted explosively to his mother's request. He knew Near Eastern customs well. The man who is successful in claiming the widows or harem of the dead king becomes the new ruler.[7] This coupled with Adonijah being older posed a clear threat to Solomon's rule and his life. Generally kings killed all opposition. Adonijah had apparently been very clever in deceiving the queen mother into requesting this for him. He underestimated the youthful Solomon's knowledge. Solomon acted swiftly to eliminate his adversary Adonijah. Then Abiathar was permanently removed from serving in the tabernacle. Because he was a priest, Solomon didn't have him killed, even though treason warranted the death penalty. Nevertheless, Abiathar paid a high price. As a Levite, he had only a small amount of land allotted to him because priests received a portion of the people's offerings. At approximately 80 years old, Abiathar was probably not able to do much farming anyway. Solomon's respect for Abiathar's past service as High Priest has already resulted in a lesser sentence for Abiathar. Most likely, Solomon also allowed Abiathar to continue receiving a Levite allotment of food, even though he would no longer receive the best portions given the high priest. Therefore, he wouldn't need to raise large quantities of food. Additionally, his disbarment from service put him in a status position lower than the deformed or blemished priests, who could not be held responsible for their elimination from service. Abiathar had been able to escape Saul's slaughter of the priests at Nob (1 Sam. 2:22-25, 30-33) only to finish his life in shame.

The last remaining turncoat was Joab. The fearsome commander who had murdered innocent people so easily was now quivering in his shoes! He raced to the Tent of Meeting and grabbed the horns of the altar (the place where one's sins were atoned and mercy was bestowed). But Joab didn't count on being sacrificed -- his shed blood removed the guilt of his criminal acts from the house of David. Solomon's reign was now secure. (See April 15th lesson for story of Shimei.)

Solomon now enters into the first of many mistakes in affairs of the heart. He agrees to a contract marriage to the daughter of the Pharaoh, king of Egypt. The Pharaoh's wedding gift to his daughter is the city of Gezer! Solomon's problem begins first with marrying an alien. Israelites were not to marry pagans (Ex. 34:15-16). Second, Deuteronomy 17:16-17 states the king is not to return to Egypt. Third, the requirements God set down for a king forbid having many wives. As we all know, this will be the first of many marriages for Solomon.

First Kings 3:3 gives us great insight into how the road to one's downfall begins. Solomon obeyed God "except" when he sacrificed on the high places. One little 'except,' one little variance from walking with God that doesn't seem to merit much attention becomes the beginning of destruction. At this point in time, the tabernacle had lost much of its stature among the people. This occurred as a result of the Ark of the Covenant being captured and returned but not having made it back to the tabernacle yet. The Tent of Meeting was now located in Gibeon while the Ark was in a temporary tent in Jerusalem.

Solomon went to Gibeon and offered a thousand burnt offerings. That night the LORD appeared to him in a dream. (This should remind you of the many times in Genesis that God's message came in the form of a dream, e.g., Genesis 40; 41:32; 46:2). God allowed Solomon to ask for one gift. (Now I have thought about this numerous times over the years and wondered what I would 'wish' for. Seems to me the best response is "that all people everywhere would be Christians." I believe God could fulfill my request, but I don't think He would. He still wants people to turn to Him of their own free will. Therefore, my request would be displeasing to God.) Solomon's youthful innocence is revealed when he confesses to being a little child. (Remember in Genesis 21:15-18 Ishmael was referred to as a boy at 17 years old and the early patriarchs didn't marry until age 40.) Mark 10:15 reveals that only those with the heart of a little child can enter Heaven. Solomon's one request was to be given "a discerning heart to govern your people and to distinguish between right and wrong" (1 Kings 3:9).[1] God was so pleased that Solomon's request had not been a selfish one, but rather one that benefited the Israelite people that He also promised to give Solomon riches and honor. But was Solomon wise in all areas of his life? No, he wasn't. He asked for and God provided judicial wisdom, in other words, wisdom needed to govern the people. Solomon was very unwise in his affairs of the heart and also in financial matters. By the end of his reign, Israel is almost bankrupt.[7] When you read about the vast tonnage of gold and silver he was given, it is hard to believe all of that could be gone. But Solomon used a lot of it for building materials, serving dishes, and decorations. Much more was used in buying exotic animals and construction materials for building His fortified cities.

After his inaugural ceremony in Gibeon, Solomon returned to Jerusalem and presented offerings before the Ark of the Covenant. With the celebration over, he went to work. In an early judicial hearing, Solomon was presented with the case of two prostitutes arguing over one baby. Each claimed the baby to be hers. Both had given birth, but one baby had been smothered when its mother rolled over on him in the night. Solomon announced the living baby would be cut into and half given to each woman. One woman immediately forfeited her rights to the child. Obviously this was the baby's real mother, the one who loved him so much she would give him up entirely rather than see him killed. Solomon recognized this and awarded the baby to the real mother. This case thrust Solomon's wisdom into the forefront of daily conversation throughout the kingdom.

Food for Thought: If God agreed to grant you 3 requests, what would they be? If you could only have two, which ones would you choose? Now, what if it was only one request? Most of us don't get the opportunity to exercise judicial wisdom much, so this may not be our request. Solomon asked for something he lacked or at least believed was a weak area for him. Carefully evaluate your own characteristics. Write the good points on one side of a page and the bad ones on the other side. Be honest! Praise God for the good characteristics, pray He will help you change the bad ones, and ask Him to grant you one request (purely a gift from Him), something that would enhance your ability to serve Him.

May 13
Bible Readings: 1 Kings 5:1; 6; 7:13-51; 9:25, 2 Chron. 2; 3; 4; 5:1; 8:12-16

Now it is time to build God's Temple. David had made many of the arrangements prior to his death: purchased the land; obtained the wood, metals, and precious stones; developed the floor plans; organized the Levites. Solomon secured the cedar from King Hiram of Tyre. Tyre (currently known as Sur, Lebanon) was a principal seacoast town that was a leader in shipping and commerce. It had large numbers of craftsmen who manufactured glass and metal products for sale. As you recall from our study of the tabernacle articles, Tyre produced a purple dye from the shells of mollusks. Tyre's wealthy economy was made possible by its enormous shipping commerce.[5]

Solomon declares the Temple he will build will be great because his God is greater than all others. He contracts with King Hiram for craftsmen and wood in exchange for wheat, barley, wine, and olive oil. The craftsman, Huram-Abi, turns out to be half Hebrew. His mother had lived in Dan. One can assume, Huram-Abi brought most, if not all, of the craftsmen he employed to work with him on the Jerusalem Temple project. Even though 2 Chron, 2:9 records Solomon as declaring this Temple would be large and magnificent, it really isn't very large, but it was magnificent. The Temple was twice the size of the tabernacle with the primary layout the same. At 90 feet long, 30 feet wide, and 45 feet high, it was a small temple compared to the massive pagan temples of its day. (Think of it like this, you could put 3 temples lengthwise on a football field and still have lots of room on all sides.)

Pagan Temple	Location	Size (L-W-H)
Parthenon	Athens, Greece	238/111/65 feet
Jupiter	Athens, Greece	354/135/90 feet
Baalbek	Lebanon	290/160/120 feet
Bacchus	Lebanon	87/75/57 feet
Ishtar	Babylon	111/102/?? feet
Ninmah	Babylon	175/115/?? feet
Marduk	Babylon	281/262/?? feet

Of all these enormous structures, the Parthenon is the only one still known by most people. But it pales in comparison to the number of people who still discuss and study the Temple of the one and only God. It just goes to show it is not the size that counts but what dwells within.

The front of the Temple (east side) had a 15-foot deep porch across the building. Two large bronze pillars whose tops or capitals were shaped like lilies flanked the entrance to the building. Both the east and west sides had a series of narrow windows, with fixed lattice grillwork, placed high on the wall. These allowed air circulation while keeping out birds.[7] A south side entrance provided easy access to the rooms found on every side except the east (front). The Temple was three stories high made out of stone dressed at the quarry site. The foundation stones were massive. According to Vos, "Palestinian limestone is quite soft when first quarried and hardens with exposure." (p. 172)[7] The stones of the second story were not as wide, leaving a ledge to place the wood posts for supporting the beams. The third story stones were narrower still to accommodate more structural posts. Because the stones were thinner as the wall went higher, the size of the rooms increased with the height. The walls were of cedar with carved cherubim, palm trees, and open flowers. The wood served effectively as a sound barrier. The wood walls and beams were covered in thin sheets of hammered gold and decorated with gemstones. The doors of the Most Holy Place were of carved olive wood covered in gold and the doors of the Holy Place were made of cypress covered in gold with the floor made of pine covered in gold.

The Most Holy Place (or Holy of Holies) was a 30-foot cube made of cedar overlaid with gold with a new veil in front of the Ark. The Ark would make this its new home. All of the furnishings and utensils for the Temple were made. The Sea is much larger than a regular home swimming pool, holding about 5,000 more gallons of water. Solomon made ten stands and basins rather than only one. (I'm sure the priests appreciated the increased elbowroom at the washbasins, but can you imagine hauling that water up Mount Moriah into the Temple!) Two cherubim fifteen feet high and with a wingspan of 15 feet were made of olive wood, covered in gold, and placed inside the Most Holy Place with their wings touching opposite walls and each other in the center.

The final construction was the courtyard walls. Because Israel is on a fault line, earthquakes are frequent. The courtyard wall was designed to absorb the shock of earthquakes. It was made "of three courses of dressed stone and one course of trimmed cedar beams."[1] (1 Kings 7:12). The Temple took 7 1/2 years to build, 30,000 slaves, 153,600 alien helpers and foremen, and craftsmen from Tyre. At last, it was finished!

Food for Thought: Have you ever started a project that seemed doable at first but as you went along it became more and more massive? Wonder if Solomon didn't feel that way often. There is an old joke that goes, "How do you eat an elephant? One bite at a time!" When your projects and commitments seem overwhelming, tackle them one piece at a time. Pray for strength and guidance.

> **Verse of the Week: 2 Chronicles 7:14** "if my people, who are called by my name, will humble themselves and pray and seek my face and turn from their wicked ways, then will I hear from heaven and will forgive their sin and will heal their land."

May 14
Bible Readings: 1 Kings 8; 6:40-42; 2 Chron. 5:2-14; 6; 7:1-10

It was time to dedicate the Temple to God. The Ark of the Covenant must be transported from the city of Jerusalem at the bottom of Mt. Moriah to the Temple at the top. It was the Hebrew month of Ethanim (earlier called Tishri) that corresponds to our late September and early October.[7] Like any great celebration, there was music and food and a speech by the king. Then the Temple filled with a cloud and the glory of the LORD dwelt among them. The sacrifices consisted of 22,000 cattle and 120,000 sheep and goats. The celebration lasted two weeks. The first week was the dedication of the Temple and the second week was the Feast of Tabernacles. It seems most appropriate to celebrate the new while remembering the old. It took the large number of sacrifices for the fellowship meals that fed the crowds. People from all parts of Israel were present at the celebration.[7]

First, Solomon blessed the crowd and then he prayed. Solomon humbled himself before God, kneeling and spreading his hands out toward Heaven. Solomon asks God to keep the promises He made to David: (1) to always have a descendant on the throne, (2) to always be present in the Temple to hear their prayers, (3) to judge between the righteous and the guilty, (4) to forgive the sins of Israel when they confess, (5) to send rain in times of drought, (6) to hear their prayers and forgive in accordance with their hearts in times of disaster and disease, (7) to hear and answer the prayers of foreigners, (8) to hear Israel's prayers for victory in battle, (9) to hear their pleas and forgive their sins if they are ever taken captive so their captors will be merciful, (10) to hear the prayers of the people and respond favorably to them.[30] Solomon closes his prayer by asking God to always be near them, never forsaking them. Further, Solomon asks God to turn the hearts of the people to Him so that they would keep His commands and walk in His ways so that all the people of the world would know that He is the one and only God. At this close, fire came down from Heaven and consumed the burnt offerings and sacrifices. Just as in the wilderness, God was seen as a cloud and a fire, leading His people.

Solomon's prayer was especially unique in two areas. First, the pagans of that time believed their gods would literally dwell in a particular place or building. Solomon acknowledged that God lived in Heaven but asked Him to watch over the people and hear their prayers as they came to the Temple to worship. In other words, God is omnipresent. Second, in asking that God hear and answer the prayers of foreigners, Solomon was acknowledging that God was the God of all people, not just the Hebrews. Pagan people believed gods protected certain nations in designated geographical areas while dwelling in a temple built by the worshippers. In short, their god or gods had limits. Solomon's God was unlimited.[7]

Food for Thought: Wonder what they did with the old Tent of Meeting and its furnishings when they got it to the Temple? Josephus says they arranged the furnishings in the same places in the Temple that they had occupied in the tabernacle.[3] Reckon they stored the tent?

May 15
Bible Readings: 1 Kings 4; 8; 7:1-12; 9:1-15, 17-28; 10; 2 Chr 1:14-17; 8:1-11, 17-18; 9:1-28; 7:11-22; Ps 72

The buildings making up Solomon's private dwelling, as well as Israel's administrative buildings, are known collectively as the palace complex. It included (1) the Palace (or House) of the Forest of Lebanon, (2) the hall of pillars, (3) the throne hall, (4) the palace of Pharaoh's daughter, and (5) Solomon's palace. A stone wall, like the one used for the Temple courtyard, encompassed the complex.[7] The Palace of the Forest of Lebanon was the size of half a football field. It functioned as a storehouse and armory (1 Kings 10:17). Its exterior was white stone. Inside, four rows of cedar posts with cedar beams supported the upper chambers. The 45 beams are interpreted to be 45 chambers (each supported by beams) with 15 on each story of the building. This would allow each room to be about 10 feet wide. Built much like the Temple, the center portion of the building was a large assembly hall with the chambers around the sides. It had the same narrow windows with lattice grillwork. There were three rows of windows at each end of the assembly hall above three doors in each end.[7]

The hall of pillars was an open portico that was probably attached to the Palace of the Forest of Lebanon. Those desiring a judicial decision by the king waited in the hall of pillars until their turn.[7] The king's official judgment room was called the throne hall or the Hall of Justice. It may have been a separate building or attached to the hall of pillars. The throne hall was lined with cedar. The throne itself was made of wood, inlaid with ivory, and covered with gold so the ivory was exposed. There were 6 steps up to it with lions on each side of each step. The number of lions (12) represents the tribes of Israel. The tribe of Judah used the lion as its symbol. The throne had a rounded back with armrests.[7]

According to Josephus, it took Solomon 13 years to complete his own palace because the materials were not already available nor was he so anxious to complete the palace as he was the temple.[3] Both palaces were built of white stone lined with cedar. The foundation stones were often 12-15 feet each.[7]

After Solomon finished the palace complex, God came to him at night in answer to Solomon's dedication of the Temple prayer. (This prayer was about 6 years earlier!) God promises to always hear the people's prayers, provide for the needs of the people, and maintain a king from the house of David on the throne, but God also issues a warning. The people must humble themselves and seek forgiveness when they sin, and then turn from their wicked ways. The king must walk in the ways of the LORD, keeping His commands and decrees. God warns that if the people forsake Him to worship other gods, He will reject them and remove His Presence from the Temple. If that happens, the magnificent Temple will be destroyed.

Second Chronicles 8:3 gives the appearance that Solomon attacked and captured Hamath Zobah. Solomon was a king of peace, not war. So how did this happen? Actually, David had captured Hamath and Zobah years before and combined the two towns that bordered each other (1 Chron. 18:3, 9). (It is located in the north-central portion of Syria.[4]) Apparently, this kingdom had rebelled against Solomon who was then obliged to suppress the rebellion and maintain order. Hamath is more than 200 miles from Jerusalem, north of the two mountain ranges containing Mt. Hermon and Mt. Lebanon. Transporting an army and weapons that far wasn't easy. Additionally, the three main highways for north-south commerce between Asia and Africa were in Israel's territory. Solomon decided to establish fortified cities where he would keep chariots, horses, grain, and arms in preparation for defending against invaders. Solomon divided the nation into 12 districts and appointed a governor for each one. These governors would be responsible for the administration, defense, and government of their districts, reporting directly to Solomon.[7] (The Hebrews had little need for chariots outside of state functions. Most of the nation was too hilly, mountainous, or rocky to make chariots useful.)

Solomon and Hiram become close friends. Josephus records that they would send riddles to each other with a bet on whether or not the answer could be determined. Scholars believe large amounts of gold were passed back and forth between the two kings to pay off bets.[3] (More reason why Solomon may not have been too wise in financial matters.)

Sheba was located in modern day Yemen. It controlled the trade route between India and East Africa, as well as water routes to countries along the Red Sea and the Gulf of Aden.[4] A visit from the Queen of Sheba out of admiration of Solomon was obviously a good political alliance.

Food for Thought: Solomon was already letting his heart get away from the ways of God. Look at your own life. Are you getting away from God? Our churches wished they could have as many worshippers as our nation's casinos have patrons. It is a sad time in our country, a time when preachers and priests are having their sins expose them and negatively impact the church, a time when denominations have major political battles within the organizations make headlines and weaken the church, a time when one's rights overrule God's commands. America is on the fast track to destruction. Any nation that turns from the commands and decrees of God will be destroyed when God removes His Presence. Solomon built an amazing complex, but sin brought it down. Start by getting the sin out of your own life and then reach out to others and help them turn their lives around!

NOTE: Depending on whether you are reading Chronicles or Kings and depending on which translation of the Bible you are reading, the woods and sometimes dimensions of various buildings in the palace complex are not the same. Some of these differences can be attributed to copyist error in the many handmade copies of the early centuries. Others are attributed to translators' disagreements on the translation of the Hebrew words for the construction material. One example is the floors of the buildings are sometimes given as pine, sometimes cypress, and other times cedar.

May 16
Bible Readings: Proverbs 8; 9:1-6; 2; 3:13-24; 1:20-33; 4; 9:13-18

Most of the proverbs are little couplets, only 2 lines of poetry. Even though the proverbs are generally attributed to Solomon, they may have been written, in part, by any number of wise men. Several nations boast of collections of wise sayings by their esteemed citizens. In America, Ben Franklin is well known for his wit and wisdom, as seen in *Poor Richard's Almanac*.

The wisdom literature of Proverb 8 describes wisdom as a virtuous woman who is prudent and righteous. Verses 10-11 beckon us to choose wisdom over silver, gold, or precious gems. Solomon could very appropriately write these lines, having chosen wisdom over riches himself. The last line (vs. 11) states, "nothing you desire can compare with her."[1] Wisdom is in knowing God, and knowing God brings wisdom. In verse 12, wisdom is now talking directly to us, describing all the blessings bestowed on one possessing her. This passage goes on to tell us wisdom was present with God before the creation of the world, before the heavenly bodies were put in place. Where God is, wisdom is also. Wisdom is described as a characteristic of God. I am reminded of Jesus' words in Matthew 7:7, "Ask and it will be given to you; seek and you will find; knock and the door will be opened to you. For everyone who asks receives; he who seeks finds; and to him who knocks, the door will be opened."[1] Proverb 8 continues by stating we will be blessed to keep the ways of wisdom (God); whoever finds wisdom, finds life.

We now shift from wisdom talking to a loving father pleading with his son to walk in the way of wisdom to preserve for himself a righteous life protected from evil men. (The intriguing characteristic of couplets is that you can read only the first line of each pair and fully understand the writer's message. Beginning with Proverb 2:1, read line 1 and every odd numbered line thereafter, e.g., 1, 3, 5, 7 . . ..) Those who reject wisdom can expect to suffer the consequences. Folly is fun and enjoyable at the time, but like sheep to the slaughter, it leads its victims to the depths of the grave.

We finish this lesson with Solomon's personal appeal to his sons to heed the words of an experienced father and follow wisdom. He appeals that they (1) keep his words in their hearts, (2) guard their hearts from sin, (3) keep their mouths from corrupt language, (4) look straight ahead to the goal, and (5) walk in the way of the LORD.

Food for Thought: It is never too early or too late to pray for the children. At every stage of life they need to be uplifted in prayer. Young people today have an enormous number of evil temptations that people of my generation didn't have. In the 60s, hippies had drugs and pot, but I didn't know any hippies and didn't care to know any. Today, drugs and pot are on every sidewalk whether you are aware of it or not. There are literally some sidewalks that have crack cocaine in the cracks of the sidewalk because of the heavy drug traffic. Children of all ages need prayer. They are our future and the future of the church. They are the ones God depends on for the spread of His gospel. As friends, parents, church leaders, grandparents, or great-grandparents, you have an obligation to pray for the children and train them in the ways of the Lord. Spend some time praying for the young people you know and the parents who have such a difficult job in rearing children in our secular world.

May 17

Bible Readings: Proverbs 22:17-21; 1:1-7; 25:1; 9:10-12; 10:23,27,13,14; 14:2, 26, 27, 12, 18, 6, 24, 8, 15,33; 15:33, 21, 24, 3, 14; 19:2, 8, 3, 21, 23; 29:14; 3:5-8; 16:25,3,20,16,22,1,4,9,33; 18:2,4,15,10; 20:24,5,12,15; 21:22,11,30,31; 26:12; 28:14,26; 29:25,9; 22:12; 27:1, 22; 13:14-16; 17:12, 24; 24: 3,4,7,13,14; 26: 4-11;23:12

Proverb 1:7 gives us the key to wisdom -- fear of the LORD. The fear talked about here is reverence of the LORD's awesome power. Fear of His judgment motivates us to discipline our lives to walk within His commands and decrees. Wisdom, knowledge, and discipline all develop as a result of walking in the ways of the LORD. Proverbs 3:5-6 tells us to trust totally on the LORD, always acknowledging His hand in your life, and He will guide you on the paths of righteousness. In 16:3 we are told to commit everything we do to God, then we will be successful.

The proverbs addressing the divine providence of God reminds us that God is everywhere. He sees all and knows all. Those who are wicked will certainly come to a day of disaster. God controls every day. To lose sight of that principle causes one to lose sight of God's controlling power in life.

At first glance, Proverbs 26:4 & 5 appear to be exactly opposite to each other. But in the first one, the wise man recognizes the fool by the foolish questions he asks concerning worldly matters. The wise man chooses not to even give the fool the satisfaction of an acknowledgment of his questions because the simple act of responding to a foolish question would lend it some credence, thus diminishing the stature of the wise. Verse 5 refers to questions about religious matters. Any question pertaining to religion should never be considered folly but should be answered as wisely as possible. If the question goes unanswered, the fool may suppose his own answer is as good as any wise or knowledgeable man's answer.[31]

Again we are told in several verses that wisdom is better than gold, silver, or gemstones. Knowledge, discernment, and understanding come with wisdom. A wise man has peace.

Food for Thought: I always think a smart aleck is a fool, trying to act like he knows something when he doesn't or is something he isn't. Have you ever been foolish? Do we do foolish things at every age? I know I have trouble deciding when the 'show is over' so to speak, when that time of my life is past. This week I had to make some decisions to drop several of my certifications because they were no longer profitable (in fact they were costly to maintain) and I would no longer be able to use them anyway. It is tough getting older and having to wind down your life. Young people have no comprehension of that exercise. But through it all, every stage of life, God is with us. We need to always remember Him. But we are never too old or infirmed to tell others about Jesus, not as long as we have our mental capabilities. God is good at every age!

May 18

Bible Readings: Proverbs 3:1-2,11-12,33-35; 9:7-9; 10:3,6-9,16,17,22,24-25, 28-30; 12:1-3,5-8,12,15,21,28; 13:1,6,9,18,21,24-25, 13; 14:9,11,14,19,22,34; 15:5,6,9,10,12,22,26,32,31; 17:10; 19:16,18, 20,25,27,29; 23:9,13,14; 25:12; 27:5-6,17; 29:1,2,10,15-19,21,27; 11:5-10,14,18-21,27,23,30-31; 20:18,30,7; 24:5-6, 8-9,15-16; 16:7; 22:6,8,15; 28:4,7,9,12,13,18,28; 21:8,12,16,18,21; 29:2,16,27; 17:13; 18:3; 26:1,3,27

Starting with Proverb 22:17, there are six collections of proverbs that are attached much in the same way as appendices to the main body of proverbs attributed to Solomon. These collections usually have subtitles that we don't even notice. In the following list I have given the NIV subtitles and a comment on the collection.

A word that always stands out to me is "hope." For the righteous, our hope for eternal life is in salvation through Jesus Christ. For the wicked, hope is limited to worldly possessions. If those are lost, everything is lost; no hope or anticipation of a future exists. Evil men live lives of despair, desperately trying to capture that which

Proverbs	NIV Subtitle	Comments
22:17 - 24:22	Sayings of the Wise	Wisdom writing teaching respect and discipline
24:23-34	Further Sayings of the Wise	Urges one to be industrious and humble
25 - 29	More Proverbs of Solomon	Hezekiah king of Judah's collection of Solomon's Proverbs
30	Sayings of Agur	No idea who Agur, son of Jakeh, is--not Hebrew
31:1-9	Sayings of King Lemuel	Instructions to an unknown king by his mother
31:10-31	Epilogue: The Wife of Noble Character	Acrostic poem[30]

eludes them--the peace that comes with hope. But wise men heed the instructions of their Christian fathers and elders; they seek the ways of the righteous. Obtaining wisdom requires discipline. He who has not discipline has not wisdom. Proverb 19:18 tells parents to discipline their children so that the children may find eternal hope, too. Parents are warned, "Do not be a willing party to [their] death."[1] In other words, don't be an accomplice to a child's eternal condemnation by not disciplining and shaping a child's life for the Lord. When parents have done their best to rear a child in the ways of the Lord, then they can prayerfully claim the promise, "Train a child in the way he should go, and when he is old he will not turn from it."[1] (Prov. 22:6) As I have said before, the proverb says, "when he is <u>old</u>." That is never our definition of old but generally is defined by the number and degree of troubles he experiences. A child trained to know the Lord will always know where to turn when trouble strikes, even if parents are gone. High school graduates are often given a book of the Proverbs for graduation. Unfortunately, by then it is way too late to train the adult on how to live. If the foundation is made of rotted mulch, then whitewashing with the proverbs won't make any difference. The first rain in life will destroy it. On the other hand, a solid foundation is made more appealing by wearing the wisdom of the Bible.

As Christians, we often moan about how we struggle while the wicked prosper. Proverbs condemn the wicked to misfortune, temporary prosperity, disgrace, calamity, and eternal death. Proverb 10:16 says, "The income of the wicked brings them punishment."[1] (Now, I haven't noticed them looking very pitiful!) If you think about it, the wicked always want more; they "are trapped by their evil desires."[1] (Prov. 11:6) They are never satisfied even when their 'cup overflows.' Knowing God is about being joyful in whatever situation you are in because "even though I walk through the valley of the shadow of death, I will fear no evil, for you are with me."[1] (Psalm 23:4)

Proverb 24:16 reminds us that a righteous man can fall seven times (completely broken), but he will rise again (to eternal life); the wicked have no hope. The righteous are promised they will see the downfall of the wicked (29:16) whether now or later, on earth or in Heaven. "Be sure of this: The wicked will not go unpunished" (11:21).[1] "The faithless will be fully repaid for their ways, and the good man rewarded for his" (14:14).[1]

Food for Thought: Our definition of wicked has dramatically changed over the centuries. In the Bible, wicked represents anyone who does not know the Lord as God. Even if a man appears to be a 'good' person, he is wicked if he knows not God. Jesus came to lead all people to know His Father. We only have to accept His free gift of salvation -- believing He is the risen Son of God whose blood washes away the sins of the penitent. When God sorts the wheat from the chaff, are you going to be the redeemed or the wicked? Do you have friends or relatives who will be among the wicked? Pray for them. Ask God to lead you to be a witness to them. Yes, even to the ones who hate you.

May 19

Bible Readings: Proverbs 3:3-4; 15:8, 11, 17, 29; 6:12-15; 10:10-12; 11:2-3, 16-17; 12:9-10, 25; 13:7, 10; 14:30; 15:25; 16:2, 5, 6, 18-19, 30; 17:3, 5; 18:1, 12; 19:10; 20:6, 9, 11,14, 27; 21:2-4, 10, 24, 27; 22:4; 23:6-8; 24:17-20; 25:16-17, 19, 21-22,27; 26:16, 23-26; 27:2,4, 19,21; 28:25; 29:23

Proverbs 16:2 and 21:2 are slightly different versions of the same principle. No matter how we rationalize or defend our thoughts or actions, God will judge us based on the motives of our hearts. God's searchlight leaves nothing hidden. *The Living Bible* states, "We can always 'prove' that we are right, but is the LORD convinced."[15] In 20:11 we are humbled by the knowledge that even children are known (or labeled) by their actions (mean, hateful, selfish, sweet, loving). Heating in a crucible purifies silver by separating out the waste elements. Gold is purified similarly in a furnace. Just as precious metals are purified by fire, our walk before the Lord is purified by trials. Job 23:10 declares, "But he knows the way that I take; when he has tested me, I will come forth as gold."[1] The painful tribulations of our lives separate the dross from the gold. Those who collapse under trials to become bitter, evil, and vengeful are but dross to God -- waste products of impure hearts. Those who persevere, becoming even more resolute in their faith, are the gold of God's creation. The purest, most valuable, most beautiful of gold is highly sought after by people all over the world, but are they prepared to walk through fire to obtain it? He who isn't tested by fire has no confident assurance that his faith will sustain him.

First Samuel 15:22 tells us, "Obedience is far better than sacrifice."[15] The psalmist continues that line of thinking with, "You don't want penance; if you did, how gladly I would do it! You aren't interested in offerings burned before you on the altar. It is a broken spirit you want -- remorse and penitence. A broken and a contrite heart, O God, you will not ignore."[15] (Psalm 51:16-17) Proverbs 15:29 and 21:3 summarize this by stating the LORD hears the prayers of the righteous (but not those of the wicked) and is pleased with those who are right and just. The words of the righteous are truthful and the righteous walk uprightly, but the wicked bring curses and shame on themselves in the community.

If our enemy is in need we should show Christian love and charity towards him. Interestingly, the outcome of our efforts is to "heap burning coals on his head."[1] (Prov. 25:22) In other words, your enemy's guilty conscience will sentence him to torment over his actions toward you. The LORD will reward your efforts, but those who are evil have no hope. Pride becomes their disgrace. Before one can become honorable and wise, he must first be humble.

Food for Thought: Are you obedient? even in the fire? I'm sure you've heard the old saying, "God helps those who help themselves." Its real meaning is that those who do the Will of the LORD, even when they don't comprehend the significance of their actions, will be blessed for their obedience. God never leads us down the wrong path.

May 20

Bible Readings: Proverbs 25:8,28; 29:3,11,20; 20:25; 12:16; 14:16-17,29; 15:18; 16:32; 19:11,19; 22:14,25; 29:8,22; 20:1; 23:19-21,26-35; 5:1-14, 21-23; 6:20-35; 7:1-27; 21:5

Self-control is probably the hardest attribute to attain and the hardest to maintain out of all aspects of our lives. We can display great control in those arenas of life that interest us little, but our passions overrule our control in activities that captivate our minds and emotions. In the proverbs collected here, we are admonished to control our (1) temper, (2) impetuousness, (3) eating, (4) drinking, and (5) sexual desires. Every person reading today's lesson can identify their weakness and lack of control in one or more of these categories. All of you have known people who "shot off their mouth" to gain attention or popularity, but primarily in an effort to increase their own self-worth. But the "proof is in the pudding" as my Momma would say. A limousine declaration with a bicycle follow-through shows the speaker to be a fool and ultimately decreases his self-esteem even more; failure begets more failure.

My friend, Mary, tells me, "As losers we are winners!" Of course, I know she is talking about weight loss, but I also realize the greater depth of that comment. Because we have given ourselves to the Lord, we have chosen to yield our exercise of (believed) control over our destiny to putting God in control. Even though we are losers to the evil world, we are winners in God's kingdom. As children of the King, we are secure in our future. But even princes and princesses must learn to control their thoughts and actions. Everything they do or say impacts the public's view of the King.

More warnings are issued in Proverbs about illicit sex than any other sin. No one who reads popular books, listens to the radio, goes to the movies, or watches TV can avoid the daily continuous bombardment by the pagan world that sexual desires should be given free reign. The Bible teaches that sex outside of marriage brings ruin and destruction. Unfortunately, not only the perpetrator is destroyed but also all of his/her loved ones as well. Sex is one of the few areas where decisions are black or white -- no gray or ambiguous areas. God blesses the sexual union of married couples. Sex with anyone other than your heterosexual marriage partner is condemned. As I said, it is black or white, acceptable or unacceptable, blessed or condemned. Yet, we allow our emotions to be given over to the devil. All actions or reactions are rationalized and kneaded by some form of pagan logic until we no longer can distinguish black and white. At that point, everything is gray. The joy of an exclusive relationship with one's committed partner is no longer a pleasure. God removes His blessing -- contentment. Contentment eludes its would be captor and the search for the perfect relationship that fulfills all our needs leaves a trail of victims. All is gray: gray skies, gray moods, gray relationships, gray morals, gray hopes, gray futures. Then the consequences of sin begin -- loneliness, unhappiness, fear, desperation, guilt, blame, shame, disease, and despair. Proverb 23:32 states its outcome concisely, "In the end it bites like a snake and poisons like a viper."[1]

Food for Thought: Regardless of the sins in your life, God is greater than they are. He can forgive AND forget! You must simply accept His free gift of salvation through His Son, Jesus Christ. Admit your sins to God and express your sorrow for your deeds or thoughts. God is always ready to forgive, love, and bless a broken and remorseful heart. Self-control can only be attained when walking with God. Happiness and contentment are only found in God's plan for life, not in our own. Again a Proverb says it best. "In his heart a man plans his course but the LORD determines his steps."[1] (16:9) Are you in-step with God?

Verse of the Week: **Proverb 15:1** "A gentle answer turns away wrath, but a harsh word stirs up anger."

May 21

Bible Readings: Proverbs 14:3; 15:2,4,7,23,28; 16:21,23-24,27-28; 17:4,9,14,19-20,27-28; 18:6-8,13,20-21; 19:1,5,22; 20:3,19; 21:6,23; 22:10; 23:15-16; 10:18-21,31-32; 11:11-13; 12:13-14,18-19,22-23; 13:2-3; 25:11,15,23; 26:2,20-22,28; 27:14; 28:23; 29:5; 15:1; 23:26-28

James 3:1-12 gives us a lecture on the damage that can be done by the tongue. Both blessings and curses come from the same mouth. No human can tame the mouth, only God living in us can do that. The tongue is the rudder of your ship. If your ship comes in, it is because the rudder was controlled.

Many pearls of wisdom can be found in today's lesson. Read more than one Bible translation for added insight into the verses. I recommend *The Living Bible* version for your comparison. An example is Proverb 25:11. "A word aptly spoken is like apples of gold in settings of silver"[1] can be compared to "Timely advice is as lovely as gold apples in a silver basket."[15]

One's words should not only be appropriate to the situation but also truthful and constructive. Gossip and slander have only one underlying theme: to tarnish or destroy something or someone else. Why do we allow the devil to make us feel powerful and in control because we 'know' something others don't? There is a difference between gossip and slander. Slander is the powerful destruction of another through the spoken word. Slanderers have a designated person they target. They then stage an all-out effort to destroy the person's reputation. Gossipers, on the other hand, tell everything they hear, good or bad. Some famous phrases gossipers use are "This is not to leave this room," "I'm only telling you so you can be in prayer for them," "Have you heard . . .?" Slander is the result of an envious, jealous heart. Gossip develops out of loneliness or low self-esteem. Slander comes out of wickedness; gossip comes out of a lack of discipline. Both are very damaging to their victims.

An old adage is "It's better to be silent and thought a fool, than to open your mouth and remove all doubt!" This is the basis of Proverb 17:28. A person's speech labels his/her character: evil/loving, kind/hateful, constructive/destructive, blasphemous/blessed. God created us with the ability to speak; designed to communicate with Him. From the beginning of time, God walked and talked with mankind (Gen. 3:8-19). After the fall of man, speech became a tool of the devil. After all, he had been extremely successful with deceiving words in the Garden of Eden. We are often on guard for the large, obvious sins of life but allow the small tongue to topple friendships, families, governments, and nations.

Proverbs also remind us of the usefulness of gentle, kind words. They soothe and comfort in times of physical or emotional pain. They give guidance to the lost, support to the uncertain, encouragement to the downtrodden. The person who speaks the truth finds peace through integrity. "Truth stands the test of time; lies are soon exposed."[15] (Prov. 12:19)

Food for Thought: Make your words sweet for you never know when you may have to eat them! Though a popular saying, the principle is often disregarded. For the next 24 hours, say nothing but kind, constructive words to others. Then see if you can continue that for a week. Observe the different responses you get from others, the change in their attitudes (or is it the change in your attitude?).

May 22
Bible Readings: Proverbs 1:10-19; 16:11,29; 25:18; 27:3; 28:10,17; 3:29-32; 21:7,14-15,28,29; 20:10,22-23; 24:11-12,23-26,28-29; 6:16-19; 17:1,8,15,23,26; 18:5,17-19; 26:17-19; 12:20; 13:5; 11:1; 22:28; 23:10-11; 10:2; 13:11; 20:17,21; 15:27; 12:17; 14:5,25; 19:9,28; 28:5; 29:26; 25:26

First Corinthians 15:33 announces, "Do not be misled: 'Bad company corrupts good character.'"[1] The Apostle Paul did not mince words. He told it like it is. Today's people have more avenues to be influenced by corruption than at any other time in history. The Internet opened up a world of knowledge to all people with a few strokes of the keyboard. But it also opened a Pandora's box of evil as well: violent games, recipes for bombs, pornography, fortune telling, gambling, prostitution, swindling, and adultery. I distinctly remember the overwhelming confusion I felt the first time I saw an Internet 'home page.' I had never seen so much 'stuff' in such a small space. It was so crowded I couldn't even determine where to enter my key words to do a search! I am still perturbed when I have to close a half dozen advertisement boxes before I can get the results of my search. Most of them are intent on theft by deceit or depravity. The wisdom writer of Proverbs warns us not to lead the upright down an evil path. Those who do will fall into their own trap. It is no mystery that those who keep company with evil are soon devoured by its vices.

God abhors violence, revenge, assault and battery, and murder. There are 7 things listed as detestable to God: (1) haughtiness, (2) lying, (3) murder, (4) wickedness, (5) eagerness to do evil, (6) slander, and (7) trouble making. God, and only God, should seek vengeance. We must wait and watch Him work in His time. He will right the wrongs we have received. Honesty and justice should be our beacons, guiding us through the perils of the deep and the darkness. We are reminded that ultimately the LORD is the judge who issues justice to all mankind.

Food for Thought: Every life is touched by violence, a sad commentary on our twenty-first century. The Bible predicts that it will only get worse. Too often I find I know the criminal or the victim. May God have mercy on our nation and our world! The time is growing short for Christians to win others to Christ. Jesus clearly showed the way as He tirelessly walked from town to town seeking the lost, caring for His sheep. When the Rapture comes, will you be part of it? Will you be left behind? What about your family and friends? Today, God has given you another chance to make an eternal difference in someone's life. Who will it be?

May 23

Bible Readings: Proverbs 3:9-10,27-28; 10:15; 11:4,15,24-26,28; 13:4,8,22-23; 14:4,20-21,23,31; 15:15-16,19; 16:8,26; 17:16,18; 18:9,16,11,23; 19:4,6-7,15,17,24; 22:2,7,9,16,22-23,26-27,29; 23:4-5; 25:14; 27:7,13,18,23-27; 28:6,8,11,19-22,27; 21:13; 29:7,13,17,25-26; 6:1-11; 10:4-5,26; 12:11,24,27; 26:14-15; 20:4,13,16; 24:27,30-34; 21:17,20,25-26; 28:27

The astounding truth of a simple proverb humbles us all. "Rich and poor have this in common: The LORD is the Maker of them all."[1] (Prov. 22:2) I seem to have spent my life treading water -- fighting to stay afloat in a sea of bills and more bills. Sometimes I feel I am desperately treading and still I am in danger of being washed out by the tide. For every dollar I make, there seems to be two dollars in bills. Just when I think I can see the shore, a major repair or illness washes me out again. Proverbs 23:4-5 remind me, "Do not wear yourself out to get rich; have the wisdom to show restraint. Cast but a glance at riches, and they are gone. . . ."[1] As I evaluate my too busy life, I realize that most of my work is something I love. Additionally, it has provided me with many venues to witness for the Lord at times and in ways I would not have been afforded otherwise.

The proverbs are many which charge us to give to the needy. "A generous man will prosper . . ."[1] (11:25), "He who is kind to the poor lends to the LORD . . ."[1] (19:17), "He who gives to the poor will lack nothing . . ."[1] (28:27), "If a man shuts his ears to the cry of the poor, he too will cry out and not be answered"[1] (21:13). Anyone who exploits the poor will come to poverty. Those who are righteous will seek justice and fairness for all people. No one is above God's law. Praise God that justice comes to all in the final judgment!

Solace can be found in the numerous proverbs addressing blessings for those who are industrious and work hard so much of the week. The rewards of the worker are contrasted to the bleak outcomes of the idle. Country people know that "idleness is the devil's workshop." Those who stay busy can see God at every turn while those who are lazy turn their thoughts to pleasures soon forgotten. "All hard work brings a profit, but mere talk leads only to poverty."[1] (Prov. 14:23)

Finally, proverbs are presented that address co-signing or backing another's debt. I believe *The Living Bible* translation is better, especially for Proverbs 6:1-5. In this passage, we are warned to get out of any situation where we have placed our very survival as collateral for someone we hardly know. We should escape such an agreement as quickly as possible. Committing to such a pledge is witness to our own poor judgment.

Food for Thought: The city of Jerusalem had even more poor and needy than our modern cities today. The lame, widowed, and poverty-stricken were dependent on the generosity of others to survive. There was no welfare system, no free lunch, no private charities, no public housing, no charity healthcare or national health system. The churches of the first century were continuously sending money to help the poor of Jerusalem. But we, like the citizens of Jerusalem, often turn our heads and look the other way. Jesus told us the poor would always be with us, but He also taught us to show compassion and justice. In the book of Ruth, we saw the poor work for their food, and God blessed all involved. "Give a man a fish and you feed him for a day; teach him to fish and you feed him for a lifetime." Have you helped someone learn the skills to work this week? Have you provided them with the key to survival? Jesus is the way, the truth, and the life. Teach others to be fishers today.

May 24
Bible Readings: Proverbs 1:8-9; 10:1; 11:22,29; 12:4,26; 13:12,19-20; 14:1,7,28,32,35; 15:20; 17:2,6,7,11,17,21,25; 18:22,24; 19:12-14, 26; 20:2,8,20,26,28,29; 21:1,9,19; 22:1,3,5,11,13; 23:1-3,17-18,22-25; 24:1-2,10,21-22; 25:2-7,9-10,13,24; 26:13; 27:8-10,12,15-16; 28:1-3,15-16,24; 16:10,12-15,17,31; 29:4,12,14,24; 13:17; 3:25-26

Proverb 17:6 hails grandchildren as the glory of the old and parents as the pride of their children. This bit of wisdom looks through the generational lineage both to the future and to the past. Parents who have reared their children by setting a good example produce children who are proud of them. They are honored and blessed with grandchildren in whom they can take pride. Furthermore, their crown of white hair evidences the wisdom of the righteous.

For those of us living in countries without kings, we need to view the proverbs addressing kings and their subjects as leaders and their people. Read these verses and determine how the leaders of your town, county, state, and country measure up. Proverb 20:28 states, "If a king [leader] is kind, honest and fair, his kingdom stands secure."[15] Leaders should surround themselves by righteous advisors and not allow the wicked in their presence. Leaders must live by the truth and shun lies and bribes. All of the people they represent should be treated fairly and with justice. Good leaders protect their people and value their trust.

One of my favorite verses is Proverb 17:17. "A true friend is always loyal, and a brother is born to help in time of need."[15] I have both and praise God for them. God does provide Christian friends and relatives to comfort, support, and advise us in good times and bad. People who believe they don't need a church affiliation, because they aren't able to attend or have to work on Sundays or have other restrictions, are missing a lot of God's blessings. God's church does the work of Jesus by ministering to the needs of its members and the community. Some churches have telephone Sunday School classes which provide a chance for shut-ins to visit with each other, study God's word, and pray together. If you don't have a church family, seek one that meets your needs. You can simply make a list of your needs and then call or visit each church, asking about their services. Most of all, pray for God's leadership to find the church He has chosen for you.

As Christians, we are to be prudent (use good judgment) and guard our souls from the wicked. We must also value and protect our good names, meaning our reputation should be sterling. Our Christian values, principles, and morals should sustain us in bad times as well as good. "If you falter in times of trouble, how small is your strength!"[1] (Prov. 24:10) Our strength is in Jesus. "I can do all things through Christ who strengtheneth me."[32] (Phil. 4:13) Our hope is in Him. "Hope deferred makes the heart sick, but a longing fulfilled is a tree of life."[1] (Prov. 13:12) As we wait and long for our heavenly home, there are times when we are actually heartsick. When we at last have completed our journey and are welcomed to our reward, we get to see and eat from the tree of life (Rev. 22:14) as we praise the one and only Lord God Almighty!

Food for Thought: Some of my best memories from places I have lived are of good friendships and fellowships with my church family. Everywhere I go, I can find family. Jesus was about His Father's business when He visited the temple. We, too, need to be about our Father's business. We get the hope and encouragement we need from other Christians. This week, be sure to attend a church of your choice. If you are unable, call and find out what services are available in which you could participate. Maybe you could have a note-writing ministry or be a prayer warrior. God calls all of us right where we are to do His work. Pray to be used.

May 25
Bible Readings: Proverbs 14:10,13; 15:13,30; 17:22; 18:14; 25:20,25; 27:11,20; 29:6; 30:1-33; 31:1-31

The readings for today are from two unknown writers. The names Agur and Jakeh are not found elsewhere in the Old Testament and nothing is known elsewhere of a King Lemuel. The term "Massa" used in each chapter may be translated "oracle" or "burden."

Lessons of Love

Chapter 30 might well be referred to as the chapter of lists. This chapter, of astute observations, begins with a rather ironic statement, "I am too stupid to be a man." Agur is far advanced in wisdom if he realizes his own inabilities to understand all that exists. Harm usually comes when men claim to understand everything. Agur further reveals his insights by recognizing the truth of God's word and by requesting neither riches nor poverty, both conditions have undone many a man: in the case of poverty, by destroying his confidence and self-worth; in the case of riches, by depriving him of the necessary struggles of life that allow all his talents and noble characteristics to be revealed. I have often told my classes that their job is one of the best friends they will ever have. It keeps them busy and out of trouble and gives them a sense of self-worth.

The remainder of the chapter focuses on lists. They include:

1. Four insatiable things (15-16)
2. Four incomprehensible wonders (18-20)
3. Four unbearable kinds of people (21-23)
4. Four small but wise creatures (24-28)
5. Four beings with stately strides (9-31).

Chapter 31 is the words of King Lemuel that he received from his mother. The passage begins with a warning against women and wine but ends with a familiar passage praising a good wife. The good wife has five positive characteristics:

1. Rare (10)
2. Precious (10)
3. Not afraid of work (13-19)
4. Has a generous spirit (20)
5. Respected by her family (28). [From Dr. Bryan Webb's 2002 Mother's Day sermon.]

Food for Thought: A God-fearing mother is a wonderful asset. No family should be without one. My own mother taught me a lot about God just by the way she loved all people, regardless of race, finances, job, or age. Her generosity overflowed. She is called blessed by all who know her. Others always embrace a loving and generous spirit warmly. Those who don't reach out to others through giving of their time, talents, and money find themselves lonely and empty. God made us as social beings. His love is to be shared. Reach out to someone outside your family this week. Expend some effort to do something special for a shut-in or church member or friend. When you cast your bread upon the water, it does return to you with even greater blessings.

May 26
Bible Readings: Psalm 127; Song of Songs (Solomon) 1-8

In terms of its interpretation, the Song of Solomon, or Song of Songs, is the most controversial book of the Bible. Some of those controversies we will explore. First, Solomon may have been the author (a view held by Keil and Delitzsch[31]) or it may simply be a book written about Solomon. We certainly know that Solomon wrote more than a thousand songs (1 Kings 4:32). Second, it may be a single song or love-poem, or it may be a collection of songs or love-poems. Its very title indicates it is THE Song of ALL Songs, the best one. Often attributed to having been originally composed as a wedding song or songs, it would be appropriately sung at the weeklong wedding festival. In Syria today, the week ends with the bride and groom being crowned king and queen.[33] (Some believe it was Solomon's wedding song, but they differ on who the bride was.) Third, written much like a play (very obvious in *The Living Bible* version), it clearly has characters, settings, and drama. The eight chapters are divided into 6 or 7 stage settings; each would then represent a different scene in the play. As with all plays, it has a central theme that the plot builds around until it is fully developed, causing the audience to view its finale with awe and speechless appreciation. Fourth, the Jewish people view it as an allegory (a symbolic representation of an event having a much deeper meaning[8]) depicting God as the lover and Israel as the beloved. Christians are generally split on its interpretation. Some believe it is totally about the perfect love experienced in a courtship and marriage within God's Will. Others believe the lover is symbolic of Jesus and the beloved symbolizes his bride, the church. (Read Rev. 19:7-9 and 21:2). Many believe it is an allegory. On its face value, it unfolds the binding commitment of two lovers within the moral guidelines of God's law. On a deeper level, it is a glimpse at the perfect, sacred love between Christ and His people, 'the church'.[34]

Three books of the Bible are closely associated with Solomon. Song of Songs focuses on matters of the heart. Proverbs address wisdom or the intellect. Ecclesiastes mourns the loss of what was and what will never be. Hebrew tradition holds that each of these books represents a phase or stage of Solomon's life: Song of Songs is his courtship and love as a young adult, Proverbs comprise the wisdom of his middle years, and Ecclesiastes mourns the loss of youthful beliefs and ideals.[35] The ancient Hebrews held this song in such high esteem that it was included in the festal scrolls traditionally read at the annual festivals. The other festal scrolls were Ruth, Esther, Lamentations, and Ecclesiastes.[35] The Targum, or Hebrew translation of the Bible into Aramaic,[5] assigns it to the 8th day of Passover as a part of the public worship.[31]

I have chosen to view this as an allegorical play, using the scene subdivisions provided in the *Life Application Bible*.

Scene 1: The Wedding Day (Song 1-2:7) - The girl is depressed because she is tanned so darkly, an obvious sign that she had to do outdoor labor to survive. Kedar was a tribe of desert nomads who were well known for their tents of black goat hair.[34] Solomon responds that she looks more like his royal silken tents than Kedar's tents. She is like a bouquet from the semitropical oasis of En Gedi where a bountiful hot spring produced lush vegetation on the barren western shore of the Dead Sea.[5] All the fears of young women concerning their appearance is compared to the love-struck young man's perception of her. This is God's purest form of courtship, love, and commitment - innocent and unashamed. This scene may also picture God's view of His chosen people. He sees them as beautiful, a lily among thorns (pagans). They are as myrrh (precious perfume) near His heart. He spreads His banner over them.

Scene 2: Memories of Courtship (Song 2:8-3:5) - As with many girls on their wedding day, the girl thinks back over her courtship remembering the stolen moments and secret gazes. She has long dreamed of this day. Even in her dreams she was willing to face fear and danger for her lover. Her love was true. The stage setting is springtime, a time for love. Just as a young lover, God pursues His people, seeking a meaningful relationship with them. Frantically, the lost search through the darkness seeking the One who will fulfill their empty lives (3:2). Once God is found, Christians covetously hold on to Him, seeking a relationship for their family and friends, too (3:4).

Scene 3: Memories of Engagement (Song 3:6-5:1) - The lovers have committed themselves to an exclusive relationship. The beauty his eyes behold in her entrances the young man or king. This is their wedding night. This scene particularly mentions gold, frankincense, and myrrh, the gifts of the wise men to baby Jesus. The sweet savor of our love is greater than all riches (vs. 10) we could present. God's people are like a well of living water pouring from the source of its flow, Jesus (vs. 15).

Scene 4: A Troubling Dream (5:2-6:3) - The girl dreams that her lover came knocking at her door, but she delayed in answering. When she did answer, he was gone. Jesus comes knocking on our door, asking us to let him in. If we delay, it may be too late (5:2-6). The beloved remembers her lover in terms of richest value and beauty, highly sought after by other women. Many people, too, seek after God. But only through Jesus can God be found. When the time is right, God will retreat to His garden in Heaven and gather His children to Him (6:2). We will belong to each other, God and Christians; we will live in peace in a place of beauty (6:3). [Symbolic of this rare beauty, water-craving lilies are seldom available in a desert environment. In the desert of life, we find God.]

Scene 5: Praising the Bride's Beauty (Song 6:4-7:9) - Tirzah was a beautiful fortified city that became the capital of Israel (the northern kingdom) when the kingdom was divided.[5] Jerusalem, God's chosen city, became the capital of the kingdom of Judah. Some authorities believe this passage refers to Solomon and Abishag who was a beautiful Shulammite woman.[34] The number of other women available to the king emphasizes that the beloved is more lovely and loved than all these. [Ultimately, Solomon had 700 wives, mostly contract wives, and 300 concubines (1 Kings 11:3).] The girl begins to yearn for her previous life. Her husband once again focuses all his attention and love on her to convince her of his love. God's children often look back and yearn for their old lives. God loves us and is always focusing His attention on us.

Scene 6: The Bride's Tender Appeal (Song 7:10-8:4) - The bride is completely swayed by her husband's overwhelming love. She longs to be free, open, and uninhibited with her love. New Christians and 'revived' Christians experience this same euphoria when we are filled to overflowing with the Holy Spirit.

Scene 7: The Power of Love (Song 6:10-7) - The bride and groom share in an everlasting love commitment. Her own "vineyard" is dedicated to her husband, her king. Through the love of Jesus we have an eternal home, a permanent commitment. We long to be in His Presence and hear His voice. Compare Song 8:14 with Rev. 22:20. Enough said.

Food for Thought: Three of the festal scrolls have a woman as a main character, most unusual for the ancient Hebrews or any of the Arab/Asian nations. The woman's key role in Song is that of a lover and wife, in Ruth she is strength for maintaining the family, in Esther she is the heroine and hope of a nation. The Bible holds women in high regard. The decline of that status has occurred as a result of the decline in self-worth of today's women. Women need to make peace with God. In doing so, they make peace with themselves. Then they are ready to serve Him in all aspects of life.

May 27
Bible Readings: 1 Kings 11

Solomon is nearing the end of his life. The decades of acquiring numerous wives through contract, acquisition, or proposal were now reaping their consequences. God had forbidden the Israelites to intermarry with the pagan tribes of Canaan. Deuteronomy 7:2-6 warned Israel that foreign wives would turn their hearts away from following God. Instead they would turn to the idol worship of the pagan gods of their wives. Solomon had maintained peace with the neighboring peoples through contracts of marriage. He had been his own worst enemy. God had promised David He would love and protect Solomon provided he walked in the ways of the LORD. Was it Solomon's fear of these people or fear of war that caused him to compromise and sin? Was it his pride and ego that made him want to claim alliance with nations like Egypt that led him to defy God's law? As we have learned in previous lessons, compromise leads to tolerance that leads to sin. Sin starts as a small compromise of what you know is in opposition to God's Law. Then sin increases in a stair step fashion. Each one a small step away from God. At each level we become 'comfortable' with sin. Then when the consequences come we look back and see the long way we have come from God. The battle to get back to God is much harder than the little compromises we made initially. Now we have to overcome the evil that is within. Solomon had produced children through unions with pagans. His children would not have the godly influence he had. They would grow up in paganism. Solomon paid a high price for his compromises. What price have you paid?

God paid Solomon a visit. God commands that Solomon's kingdom will be torn from the hand of Solomon's successor (his son) except for one main tribe, Judah (Benjamin chooses to stay in Judah), which is dedicated to the righteousness of David. The city of Jerusalem was chosen by God (1 Chron. 11:4-9) to be the place where He met with His people in His temple (1 Kings 8:10-13). David had been dead many decades now, but God was still 'remembering' him. (You'll recall from earlier lessons that when God 'remembers' you, it is in the form of a blessing.)

The peace that Solomon had coveted was now dissipating. First Kings 11 tells us that God raised up two adversaries: Hadad the Edomite and Rezon of Aram. Both men had escaped death as boys when David's forces destroyed their people. To make matters worse, one of Solomon's officials, Jeroboam, rebelled against him. The prophet Ahijah had told Jeroboam that God would take 10 of the tribes of Israel away from Solomon and raise up Jeroboam as their ruler. The most amazing prophecy Ahijah delivered was God's promise to Jeroboam, "If you do whatever I command you and walk in my ways and do what is right in my eyes by keeping my statutes and commands, as David my servant did, I will be with you. I will build you a dynasty as enduring as the one I built for David and will give Israel to you."[1] (1Kings 11:38) Jeroboam was given a similar promise as David! Will Jeroboam rise to God's charge? Future lessons will reveal.

Just as with Saul, when God's favor was removed from Solomon, he chose to try to kill God's chosen man. Solomon's 'little' sins had so hardened his conscience that premeditated murder now seemed acceptable. Our lesson to learn is that every small decision makes a big difference in living for God, blessed by His favor.

Food for Thought: Second Samuel 7:12-16 tells of God's promise to David. God would always love Solomon and the house of David would endure forever. But God also promised to punish Solomon through the actions of other men when he did wrong. Have you experienced the "floggings of men?"

> Verse of the Week: **2 Chron. 15:2** "The LORD is with you when you are with him. If you seek him, he will be found by you, but if you forsake him, he will forsake you."

May 28
Bible Readings: Ecclesiastes 1:1-11; 6:10-12; 3:18-22; 2:12-16; 9:1-12; 8:16-17

Ecclesiastes means the teacher or sometimes translated as the preacher. It is thought to represent the last stage of Solomon's life. The tone is one of depression. Solomon surveys all the food, women, wealth, wisdom, and power he has and determines it all means nothing. Nothing materialistic, intellectual, or secular brings lasting happiness or peace. Only an on-going relationship with God can bring meaning to life, and even this revelation eludes the teacher until the end of the book.

Ecclesiastes is a book only sought out for reading when one is depressed or beaten down. In this state, you relate to everything the teacher says, as well as to the overall tone of helplessness. The teacher feels that all efforts in life are futile because your destiny was predetermined. In other words, life is one big pity party - poor me.

Undoubtedly Solomon is going through the grieving process over his lost youth and vitality. We all go through this, sometimes quietly, sometimes dramatically. It starts in those years when our youthful hormones begin to decline and the signs of aging show up in our physical appearance. (I'll never forget when I first looked down into a mirror and stared in horror because my face had slid off!) We refer to this stage as the mid-life crisis. In actuality it is denial. We desperately try to do all the things we had wanted to do in our youth but hadn't the money, time, or courage. Suddenly, we are frantic to squeeze all the 'living' we can get out of life. The clock of aging no longer dings in the recesses of our minds but rather pounds its incessant bongs. You are suddenly in the race against time and with each passing day you feel the victory slip through your fingers.

Solomon certainly must have been in denial when he married so many wives (pagans at that) and then proceeded to worship their gods. He was denying any consequences to his actions. Surely, he believed himself to be the golden boy, too blessed by God to be punished. Or maybe he believed he could skate through life on the coattails of his father's reputation and righteousness before God. (Is there a lesson here for us?) Then the anger stage of grief sets in as he tries to kill Jeroboam. Usually this stage is much shorter than the others because it requires a constant input of fuel to keep the anger burning. We wear down quickly to the relentless energy anger requires.

As we read Ecclesiastes, we are immediately struck by Solomon's depression. Ecclesiastes 6:12 declares, "For who knows what is good for a man in life, during the few and meaningless days he passes through like a shadow?"[1] He then proceeds to review all the things in life which had given him pleasure but were now of no importance.

Food for Thought: My parents are always telling me that they hardly see anything they really want anymore. Of course the statements that follow allude to the effort required to enjoy and/or maintain the 'want.' Solomon is discovering that the most important pursuit in life is not what you build externally but what you build internally. Do you have a sustaining relationship with God?

May 29
Bible Readings: Ecclesiastes 1:12-18; 2:1-11, 17-26; 4:1-16; 5:1-20; 6:1-9; 7:13-14; 8:2-15; 9:13-18

In Ecclesiastes 2:4-11, Solomon reviews all the 'things' in life he acquired to make him happy, only to realize they were all meaningless. He confesses in 2:10, "I denied myself nothing my eyes desired; I refused my heart no pleasure."[1] Sin always begets consequences. Verse 17 gives his judgment, "So I hated life, because the work that was done under the sun was grievous to me. All of it is meaningless, a chasing after the wind."[1]

As we read through the thoughts of the deeply depressed teacher, we find him questioning every aspect of life. Even God's plan for our lives seems to come under attack. The dead are proclaimed to be better off than the living, and the unborn better off still. After reaching this depth of his depression, we see a ray of sunshine gleaming through the darkness. The teacher remembers the value of the friends made in life. When he falls down, his friend is there to help him get up. Together, two can stay warm and two can defend themselves from life's attacks. But "a cord of three strands is not quickly broken" (Eccl. 4:12).[1] The strength of the church comes from its Christian ministry to each other in accordance with God's Will. You can feel the teacher is pulling out of his depression and is ready to once again praise God. The mercy of God is awesome when Solomon realizes the sin of abandoning his vow. He had received God's blessing of wisdom, wealth, honor, and a discerning heart, but Solomon had not walked in the ways of God and obeyed His commands. This had been the promise or requirement for God's blessing of a long life (1 Kings 3:14). God had been merciful and patient with Solomon, just as He is with us. Although God's mercy endures forever, His patience does not. Solomon knows he has been allowed to live and prosper even though he didn't deserve it. Isn't that what Jesus gives us? When we receive Jesus as Lord and Savior we receive eternal life in the city of splendor, basking in the glory of God.

Solomon warns us not to count on God's patience; don't test God. "When you make a vow to God, do not delay in fulfilling it.... It is better not to vow than to make a vow and not fulfill it. Do not let your mouth lead you into sin."[1] (Eccl. 5:4-6) Then, as all people coming out of depression, Solomon warns others not to make the same mistakes. Do not value the extrinsic material possessions of life but rather treasure the intrinsic pleasures of living in God's Will and enjoying His blessings.

Key verses of warning include:

1. Appreciate the blessings that God provides without always looking for something more. (6:7-9)
2. "Do not stand up for a bad cause... the wise heart will know the proper time and procedure."[1] (8:3-5)
3. "Wickedness will not release those who practice it."[1] (8:8)
4. "There is a time man lords it over others to his own hurt."[1] (8:9)
5. "Whoever loves wealth is never satisfied with his income."[1] (5:10)
6. "One sinner destroys much good."[1] (9:18)

All of Solomon's wisdom can be summarized in one statement. "Moreover, when God gives any man wealth and possessions, and enables him to enjoy them, to accept his lot and be happy in his work - this is a gift of God."[1] (Eccl. 5:19)

Food for Thought: What is smart? What is intelligent? I have found that most smart, intelligent people are limited in their expertise to certain areas of life. My brother is smart in numbers. I am the wordmonger. Neither of us claims to be talented enough to do what the other does. Thus is the plan of God. God created all people in His image. Just as Adam needed a helpmate, so we, too, need helpers. If everyone could do everything, we would have no need to be dependent on anyone for anything! How would we learn to depend on God? God designed us to NEED others. It is this need that draws us closer together. We learn to love out of need. We learn about God's love out of our need. Christians reflect God's love through their actions. Pray that God provides you opportunities to love someone today.

May 30
<u>Bible Readings: Ecclesiastes 12:9-10; 7:1-12, 15-29; 10; 11:1-6; 12:11-12; 8:1</u>

The sun has broken through the clouds of Solomon's life. The wisdom of his proverbs has returned. Almost immediately, he tells us "Do not say, 'Why were the old days better than these?' For it is not wise to ask such questions."[1] (Eccl. 7:10) Solomon has learned not to grieve for that which is gone but rather be grateful for what you have.

We have observed in the past lessons that wisdom is characteristic of God. Wisdom is knowing God; and knowing God brings wisdom. God living in us imparts wisdom to us. In Ecclesiastics 7:11-12, substitute the words wisdom or knowledge with God. Then it reads "God is a shelter [for Christians] as money is a shelter [for the worldly], but the advantage of God is this: that God preserves the life of his possessor [eternal life]."[1] [Brackets are mine.] The point to be made here is that one cannot be wise without God. But with God, His entire glorious kingdom is ours to inherit. God is our shelter through the storms of life. God is the power of our natural life and the sustainer of our eternal life.

Solomon makes an astute observation: "There is not a righteous man on earth who does what is right and never sins."[1] (7:20) It will be some 900 years before Jesus is born. Jesus was not just a 'righteous man' as some believe. Jesus was the Son of God. A thousand years from the time of Solomon's statement, the Apostle Paul will declare in his letter to the Romans (3:23) "all have sinned and fall short of the glory of God"[1] but "righteousness from God comes through faith in Jesus Christ to all who believe."[1] (3:22)

This world believes in 'eating, drinking, and being merry' as described in 10:19. The world also believes that "money is the answer to everything"[1] or as the Hebrew states, "but silver answers all."[20] Solomon has observed the futility of mankind. But Jesus told us to store up treasures of a different kind -- heavenly treasures (Matt. 6:20).

Ecclesiastes 12:12 issues a warning similar to Revelation 22:18-19. Nothing is to be added to the words of the Shepherd. Psalm 23 told us "the LORD is my Shepherd." Whenever various religions choose to add other 'books' as equal to the Bible, we must realize that the Old and New Testaments warn us of the danger. Revelation states they will receive "plagues."

Our lesson ends with Solomon in the final stage of the grieving process -- acceptance. He has come to accept the things he cannot change. The history of one's life is exactly that -- history. One can only change the present and, in so doing, impact the future. Solomon has realized that the joy and happiness in life must be tempered by the seriousness and responsibilities of life. "The man who fears God will avoid all extremes."[1] (Eccl. 7:18)

Food for Thought: We have all grieved over something or someone. Some go through a bargaining stage with God and others seemingly give up. Life is not about bargaining or giving up. Every day is a new day. Ask God to show you His blessings today. He blesses in ways we will only know about when we get to Heaven. Think of all the things that DID NOT happen to you today! You didn't die, you didn't lose a limb or vital organ, you didn't go insane. You may have had a bad day, but it could have been worse. It would have been much worse had God not been watching over you. Thank God now for His loving protection.

May 31
Bible Readings: Ecclesiastes 3:1-17; 11:7-10; 12:1-8, 13-14; 1 Kings 11:41-43; 2 Chron. 9:29-31

We start our lesson with the most widely known passage of Ecclesiastes (3:1-8). "There is a time for everything, and a season for every activity under heaven."[1] The list of activities that follows this opening statement contains pairs of equal but opposite events: a time to be born - die, kill - heal, weep - laugh, keep - throw away, silent - speak, and so forth. In 1966, The Byrds set this passage to music as a popular secular 'folk-type' song called "Turn, Turn, Turn". These verses give us a sense of the order and rhythm of life. God is in Heaven and is in control of an orderly world that functions according to His time. He controls a universe that can be clocked to a thousandth of a second or better. There is already a time known only by God when "God will bring to judgment both the righteous and the wicked...."[1] (Eccl. 3:17) Ecclesiastes 5:19 is presented in a different form in 3:13: "That everyone may eat and drink, and find satisfaction in all his toil - this is the gift of God."[1] A blessed person indeed has food, water, and work that give him or her satisfaction! The teacher continues with "I know that everything God does will endure forever; nothing can be added to it and nothing taken from it."[1] (3:14) One of the first principles I learned in physics was that mass can neither be made nor destroyed; it only changes forms. Genesis 1:1 tells us that God created the heavens and the earth and everything in it. God initially created everything and ever since that time we have not been able to make or destroy God's basic creation - just change its form and, in so doing, its path. An example is a tree that provides shade, shelter, oxygen, and beauty. We can cut it down and burn it but all we really do is change its protective, beautiful form into heat and fertilizer. We can change what God created, but we can't make or destroy His creation. God's plan is always the best plan. We are an impatient people. Our plans are designed to speed up God's plans. Our path always leads to self-destruction. Try as we might, though, God still has the final vote. "In his heart a man plans his course, but the LORD determines his steps."[1] (Prov.16:9) Therefore, you should "Commit to the LORD whatever you do, and your plans will succeed."[1] (Prov. 16:3)

Solomon advises young people to use their youth wisely. Altogether too soon, they will have cataracts (12:2), palsy and back trouble (12:3), retirement and hearing loss (12:4), fears and waning desires (12:5). Solomon's summation of his wisdom regarding life is found in Ecclesiastes 12:13-14. "Now all has been heard; here is the conclusion of the matter: Fear God and keep his commandments, for this is the whole duty of man. For God will bring every deed into judgment, including every hidden thing, whether it is good or evil."[1]

Solomon reigned 40 years and was about 60 years old when he died. Solomon did not live a long life because he did not walk in the ways of God and obey Him (as God's promise required)(1 Kings 3:14).

Food for Thought: Are you seeking God's Will in your life? As long as we are alive, God has a plan for us. In fact, God has a plan for us to live forever. Through the sacrifice of His only Son, Jesus, God planned for us to believe He sent His Son, believe His Son rose again, and by believing obtain eternal life. Do you believe?

The Divided Kingdom

June 1
Bible Readings: 1 Kings 12:1-33; 13:1-32, 2 Chron. 10:1-19; 11:1-4, 13-17

We have already learned that Solomon had judicial wisdom but not wisdom in all areas of his life. His insatiable appetite for grandiose buildings and cities left his nation virtually bankrupt and his citizens on the verge of rebellion. Solomon's forced labor from the citizens had taken its toll. While they were working for the king, their own fields and homes were neglected. After 40 years of high taxes and forced labor, Solomon's son Rehoboam is facing a hostile group of subjects. They seize the opportunity to demand lighter burdens. Instead of accepting the wisdom of his elder advisors, Rehoboam listens to his young, power-hungry friends and threatens the people with even harsher slave labor and higher taxes. His overbearing response results in rebellion of the tribes. The people return to their homes. For Judah (and the few Benjamites that are left) Jerusalem and its countryside is home. The other 10 tribes held a meeting at Shechem where they chose Jeroboam as king. Shechem has always been a key city. Joseph's bones were buried there (Josh. 24:32), Joshua renewed Israel's covenant with God there (Josh 8:30-35), God appeared to Abraham there (Gen, 12:6-7), Abraham and Jacob built altars there (Gen. 33:18-20). Shechem was located at the intersection of several major highways and trade routes.[5] Shechem was naturally the city of choice for the capital. The northern 10 tribes had effectively seceded from the tribal nation. They will be known throughout history as the northern kingdom or Israel.

Meanwhile Rehoboam decides to squelch the rebellion. Shemaiah, a man of God, intervenes with a message from God: this was His Will. The people of Judah decide to obey God. This kingdom would be called the southern kingdom or Judah hereafter. When the northern kingdom turns to idol worship, the Levites will flee to Judah, also.

Recall the promise God made to Jeroboam (1 Kings 11:38). Instead of claiming God's promise, Jeroboam immediately fortifies Shechem and makes two golden calves to be worshipped as god. (This was a well-known idol form of the Egyptians.) One was placed in Bethel and the other in Dan. Jeroboam has chosen alternative worship over God's leadership. Many believe Jeroboam intended these graven images to represent God, but this would still be in violation of the second commandment.[30] Jeroboam's motives were political. Israel had a history of civil strife (2 Sam. 15:1-12). The one cord that had prevailed was their worship of one god -- the one and only God. Their worship was concentrated in the sacrifices and festivals conducted in the Temple in Jerusalem. These events brought them together as brethren. Jeroboam had been a rebel and continued to think like one. He sought to break the bond to Jerusalem and effectively break the brotherhood of the worshipers. Jeroboam even goes so far as to create his own religious festivals.

In our churches today, we frequently find individuals seeking to rule over the other members by intimidation and power plays. The lesson of Jesus is that <u>Christians are servants not rulers</u>.[30] He who is greatest must be willing to wash the feet of those who are least (John 13:1-17). Jesus even washed the feet of His enemy.

God chooses a man from Judah to go up to Shechem and confront Jeroboam. He delivers God's message that Josiah will be born of the house of David. Josiah will sacrifice Jeroboam's priests on the altar (all Hebrews knew God detested and forbade human sacrifice) and as a sign that this would occur the altar would split, spilling out its ashes. This would definitely be a sign to Hebrews of God's rejection.

We are told the messenger was a "man of God." He was careful to follow God's commands as he entered what was now enemy territory to deliver the prophecy. He was careful to leave in accordance with God's commands. But before the task was finished, he let down his guard. The man of God was tricked into disobeying the command God had given him. Who could possibly trick a prophet? Of course, someone posing as another prophet could. This is a strong testimony to Christians. We must always be alert and mindful that all may not be as it seems. We must continually apply the measuring device of God's word. Our decisions and actions must be aligned with God's ways and commands. Even Jesus' betrayer came from within his disciples. The man of God disobeyed God's command and lost his life. God's church must not let itself be led astray.

Food for Thought: The name Jeroboam means: "May he plead the people's cause."[30] Jeroboam was given the right start in life. He was given the right promise and he had the right opportunity. Like many people today, the power of the position went to his head. When that happened, Jeroboam no longer needed God; he could do it himself. Or could he? He did something all right. He led the people into idolatry. Remember, God can put us in any position and he can remove us from any position. We are tools to carry out His Will. Whether we are used to build God's kingdom or to be a barrier to be destroyed depends on our choices. Have you decided to choose God? Are you building His kingdom? His kingdom is built one person at a time. Be God's tool today.

NOTES:
1. There is so much trouble in our world. Pray for your country, its leadership, and its people. God can deliver us, but only God can do it.
2. You should be encouraged at this point. There are only 4-5 weeks before we reach the halfway point! Then you will be on the downhill side -- headed toward reading the whole Bible this year! Just think of what meaning Christmas will have to you then! God's word in your mind and your heart will change your outlook on life.

June 2
Bible Readings: 1 Kings 13:33-34; 14:1-18, 21-31; 15:1-5, 6-8;
2 Chron. 11:5-12, 18-23; 12:1-16; 13:1-22; 14:1

We are told in 1 Kings 13:34 that the downfall of the house of Jeroboam came as a result of his sin in consecrating almost anyone to be a priest for the idol worship established on the high places. Jeroboam had ample time (almost two decades) to become thoroughly indoctrinated in idol worship during his period of refuge in Egypt when Solomon was seeking to kill him. The king of Egypt at the time was Shishak I[5] who saw an advantage to aiding any rebels from the domineering and powerful kingdom of Solomon. Jeroboam had been an official of Solomon's over the forced labor from the tribe of Joseph. Shishak I was glad to allow Jeroboam to return to Israel to split the kingdom after Solomon's death.[7] Jeroboam left believing Egypt to be his close ally.

Now Jeroboam, king of the northern kingdom, had firmly installed Egyptian worship. In our last lesson, a "man of God" had paid him a visit. Josephus tells us this man was Jadon from Jerusalem.[3] The message of condemnation for his idolatry sin only momentarily stunned Jeroboam. His heart was hardened by the power and wealth he possessed. The consequences of his sin soon began. Jeroboam's son, Crown Prince Abijah becomes ill. The condemnation message must still be ringing in Jeroboam's head for he sends his wife to the LORD's prophet Ahijah who lives in Shiloh. (You'll need to remember Abijah is the boy. B is for boy. Ahijah is the prophet. There are 9 different men in the Bible named Ahijah.[5]) Ahijah delivers a severe message to the mother - not only would the boy die, but all males in Jeroboam's lineage would perish. In fact, dogs would eat the bodies of those in the city and birds would eat those in the country. [Dogs were probably the first animals to be tamed. They were used for racing in Egypt and as pets in Greece. But in ancient Israel, calling someone a dog was one of the highest insults possible. Examples of its use are in naming Gentiles (Matt. 15:26), male prostitutes (Deut. 23:18), and unbelievers (Rev. 22:15). Dogs in Palestine were generally wild and ran in packs. They lived off the refuse from villages and towns.[5]] God's mercy is evidenced in the death of Abijah. Because God found goodness in him, Abijah was taken from this wicked environment and given a proper burial. This is a very good example of how God spares those He loves by taking them on to be with Him rather than allowing them to live in the devastating events to come. (Isa.57:1-2)

Meanwhile, Rehoboam realizes that Judah has a small population compared to the northern kingdom of Israel. This is significant because there will be fewer fighting men and fewer laborers and fewer people to pay taxes. If Judah is to survive as a kingdom, its defenses must be improved. King Rehoboam proceeds to fortify a large number of cities on his borders. Defense was weakest on his northern border. Perhaps he was hoping for reunification. Stores of food, supplies, and weapons were concentrated in 15 towns. He built forts to protect strategic points along the border with observation posts and signal stations filling in the gaps. Garrisons of soldiers were housed at each fort and defense city. Due to the mountainous land, chariots and cavalry were of little use.[7]

Rehoboam married two of David's granddaughters, Mahalath and Maacah, who were also his cousins. Maacah was Absalom's daughter. She will bear Rehoboam a son, Abijah, who will become king. Years after

Absalom's death, he finally has a descendant who is King of Judah. When Rehoboam believes he is safe and comfortable in his administration and family, he turns away from the LORD. (Isn't this typical of Christians today?) Judah is led into idolatry. Second Chronicles 12:2 says that because of this sin Shishak attacks Judah capturing the fortified cities. Josephus records Shishak as having 400,000 infantry.[3] Shemaiah, the prophet, told Rehoboam and his officials God had abandoned them. God no longer dwelt among them. The people of Judah humble themselves before God and they are made subservient to Egypt rather than killed. Shishak stripped the temple of all its treasures. Rehoboam reigned 17 years. Josephus says he was 57 when he died.[3]

[Now your text becomes very confusing because it talks about Rehoboam's son Abijah becoming king and waging war on Israel. But wasn't Abijah Jeroboam's son and didn't he die as a boy? As with people today, certain names became popular with each generation. The most frequent spelling of this new king of Judah is Abijam rather than Abijah. You will find this in your text footnote. To avoid confusion, I will refer to this king as Abijam.]

Abijam reigned for three years. War broke out between the north and the south. (Sounds like our own Civil War, doesn't it?) Abijam was outnumbered two to one. But Abijam and Judah were still following God. Judah not only survives but also soundly defeats Israel inflicting over 500,000 casualties. Judah was able to regain three large towns with their surrounding settlements. The sad final commentary on Abijam's rule is that he was not fully devoted to the LORD. Even a little waywardness is dangerous. But God remembered His promise to David....

Food for Thought: How will you be remembered? Will it be as a good person? Or maybe it will be as a good Christian? Worst of all, will it be as an evil person? Our lives are spent in battle: good versus evil. Our choices make all the difference. Every sin is seen or known by God and usually by other people. What will be the final commentary about your life? Are you fully devoted to the Lord?

June 3

Bible Readings: 1 Kings 15:8-24, 26-32, 33-34; 14:9-15, 19-20; 16:1-34; 21:25-26; 22:43-44, 46-47; 2 Chron. 14:1-8; 15:1-19; 16:1-34; 17:1-19; 18:1; 20:31-33

When contemplating the history of the Holy Land, it is easy to lose one's perspective of the small land area we are discussing. The northern kingdom or Israel is about the size of Delaware (the second smallest state in the U.S.[8]) and the southern kingdom or Judah is about the size of Rhode Island (the smallest state in the U.S.[8]). It just boggles my mind to think of the large number of soldiers these small countries could raise. Asa, king of Judah, had an army of 580,000 men. The northern kingdom had just lost over 500,000 soldiers in battle.

Asa enjoyed peace for a decade. He rebuilt the fortified cities and tore down the high places. Trouble began on his southern border as General Zerah attacked. Zerah is identified as a Cushite which was the name given to the Ethiopians who were descendants of Cush, the son of Ham who was considered the father of the Canaanites. Josephus states that Ethiopia should actually be interpreted as Arabia. He also recorded Zerah's army to be 900,000 footmen and 100,000 horsemen.[3] *The Living Bible* refers to Zerah's one million troops.[15] To say the least, this was a formidable enemy for Judah to face. Again Judah was outnumbered two to one. Again Judah called on the God of their land. Zerah's forces were wiped out. Judah was given the wealth of their enemy. Knowing Judah's history, Azariah the prophet warns King Asa not to forsake God stating, "The LORD is with you when you are with him. If you seek him, he will be found by you, but if you forsake him, he will forsake you.... be strong and do not give up, for your work will be rewarded."[1] (2 Chron. 15:1-7) Josephus adds a warning from the prophet that if Asa failed to follow God Judah would be broken up and its people scattered to many nations.[3] Asa decides to get serious and declares that anyone who doesn't worship God will be put to death. He even removed his grandmother, Maacah (Absalom's daughter), as queen mother because she worshipped Asherah.

Upon Jeroboam's death in Israel, his son Nadab became king but was soon assassinated. His assassin, Baasha, took the throne and established his capital at Tirza. (Baasha is the son of Ahijah from the house of Issachar -- a different man than the prophet Ahijah the Shilonite.) To say the least, Baasha is evil from the start. He forcibly prevented traffic between Israel and Judah. It wasn't long before he threatened war.

King Asa lets fear overwhelm him to sin. He takes the gold and silver he had dedicated to the LORD's Temple (this was part of the war plunder from the battle with Zerah) and gives it to the king of Syria as contract money to become Judah's ally. Syria is north of Israel so Israel would have to defend opposite borders. King Ben-Hadad immediately attacked Israel, capturing several large towns. Baasha retreats to his capital, Tirzah, to defend it and his kingdom. But it is a hollow victory for King Asa. He had allied himself with evil rather than depending on God. As you would predict, a prophet, Hanani, shows up on Asa's doorstep to condemn his guilty conscience. His sentence would be a reign filled with war. No more peace for Judah or for Asa. Sin is a terrible thief; it robs us of our joy. Unfortunately, Asa takes his anger out on some of his subjects. Our human side never wants to admit we are wrong. Often our inability to humble ourselves before God manifests itself in anger. An angry person is one who has turned the controlling reins of his life over to the devil. I often hear people use the excuse that their anger was justified and even Jesus had righteous anger when he cleared the merchants out of the Temple. We know nothing about righteous anger. It is a characteristic of God that humans cannot begin to truly comprehend. The truth is we just get mad and lose our temper, relinquishing control of our lives for a period of time. As with all sins, anger has its consequences.

Now God isn't letting evil Baasha off the hook either. The prophet Jehu (whose father is Hanani - a different man from the previous prophet) brings Baasha a chilling message. His family will have the same fate as Jeroboam's. Dogs and birds are in their future (1 Kings 16:4). After Baasha dies, his son Elah becomes king only to be assassinated shortly thereafter. The assassin Zimri becomes king for a week, but it was long enough to kill Baasha's whole family. The Israelites had an uprising and made Omri king. Zimri set the palace on fire, killing himself. (Doesn't this sound a lot like the evening world news?) Since Omri had to build a new palace anyway, he just moved the capital ten miles away to a hill he bought from a man named Shemer. The hill became Samaria. When Omri dies, his son Ahab, the most evil of all Israel's kings, takes the throne. Married to the wicked Jezebel, Ahab plunges the country totally into idolatry - worshipping Baal and Asherah. The Samaritans are destined to become the most hated enemies of the ancient Jews, even down through the time of Jesus.

Back in Judah, King Asa is sick. His pride is getting ridiculous. He is afflicted with a severe disease, but he refuses to turn to God for healing. After all, he's still mad at God for not approving his way of handling Israel's invasion. When Asa dies, his son Jehoshaphat takes over. Jehoshaphat was a good king who tried to remove idolatry from Judah with a measure of success. He reactivated the defense system, required the Levites to perform their duties in teaching the laws of Moses (the Pentateuch), and initiated peace with Israel (although this became a stumbling block to him).

Food for Thought: Fear is an enemy. When we become fearful, we do and say things we wouldn't otherwise. Like Asa, we tend to jump into sin. Few of us are brave in the face of great physical danger, especially if we are alone. Comrades and allies seem to reassure us. But God tells us we are never alone if we are obeying Him; He forsakes only those who forsake Him. The next time fear strikes, humble yourself before God. Peace soon replaces fear.

Verse of the Week: **2 Kings 6:16** "Don't be afraid . . . . Those who are with us are more than those who are with them."

June 4
Bible Readings: 1 Kings 17:1-24; 18:1-46; 19:1-21

Elijah is one of the most famous prophets. He followed God all the days of his life. He was from Tishbe in Gilead. Gilead was the land east of the Jordan River that was settled by Reuben, Gad, and the half tribe of

Manasseh. Elijah announces to King Ahab of Israel that a drought is coming. There will be neither dew nor rain except when Elijah requests it. (Now a person would have to have a great deal of confidence to make a statement like that! Elijah means "Yahweh is God."[7]) It is significant that Elijah includes dew in his proclamation. Dew falls one-third of the nights per year in Israel and is an important supplement to the rainfall.[7] It is also significant that Elijah chose drought as his pronouncement. Ahab and Jezebel were involved in worshipping the pagan gods Baal and Asherah (also called Baalath). These names actually mean lord and lady gods. They were gods of fertility of all types: humans, animals, and plants. As such they were responsible for producing rain and fertile fields for crops to grow. By a man of God controlling the rain, Elijah was, in effect, slapping the pagan gods in the face. Baal worship included a seasonal cycle. Baal was to have died in the fall that was marked by funeral rituals that involved cutting the body and tattoos (Lev. 19:28). These scars and tattoos were permanent symbols of one's devotion to Baal and pagan worship. In the spring, Baal was reborn. Therefore, Baal worship was characterized by all sorts of perverted sexual activities, generally in mass groups in the so-called shrines.[7]

As you would suspect, when the drought started Elijah became a hunted man - a fugitive. But God took care of him. God had the ravens bring him food and provided a brook for water. When the brook dried up God sent him to a widow in Zarephath. Zarephath was a Mediterranean coastal city between Tyre and Sidon in the land of Phoenicia.[5] The widow and her son were preparing to die from lack of food. She took Elijah in and the little flour and oil she had left never ran out until the LORD brought rain again. During Elijah's stay with the widow, her son became gravely ill and stopped breathing. Elijah took the boy to his room and stretched himself out on the boy three times asking God to return the boy to life. The boy was restored. When Jesus came to earth, the Jewish people were like this widow. They were oppressed and preparing to die. Their only hope was a Messiah to save them. For three years Jesus 'stretched himself out' over them ministering to their needs and teaching them God's word. Those who accepted Jesus as their Savior were restored to life eternal. The widow's response would be just as appropriate for the disciples of Christ. "Now I know that you are a man of God and that the word of the LORD from your mouth is the truth."[1] (1 Kings 17:24)

More than 3 years into the drought, God sends Elijah to talk to King Ahab. Ahab's Minister of the Palace was Obadiah. As Minister of the Palace, Obadiah would have been second in command, similar to a Prime Minister. He would have worn a special dignitary robe and sash (also called belt or girdle). Because he was keeper of the key to the palace gates, he controlled the beginning and ending of the official court day. Obadiah would have been well educated with his own official state seal to transact business.[7] Obadiah is recorded as being a devout believer in God. He had hidden 100 of God's prophets when Jezebel was killing them all. Ahab sent Obadiah out to search the land for grasses and water for the royal horses and mules. On his way, he runs into Elijah. Elijah sends Obadiah to tell Ahab to meet him. Elijah throws down the challenge to Ahab. Ahab is to bring 450 Baal prophets, 400 Asherah prophets, and summon all the Israelites to Mount Carmel. Mt. Carmel is part of a mountain range that juts out into the Mediterranean Sea. It is near modern day Haifa. The pagan Canaanites had built shrines for their weather gods on this mountain. It is 470 feet high.[5] Mt. Carmel was definitely not friendly territory for a man of God.

Elijah let the Baal prophets choose their sacrifice and perform their rituals from early morning until noon without interference. At noon he cannot hold himself any longer. He starts taunting them. By 3:00 p.m., there was still no response from Baal. Now it is Elijah's turn. Elijah cut up his sacrifice and placed it on the wood on the altar he had built using 12 stones for the 12 tribes of Israel. He had a trench made around the altar. Twelve jars of water were brought and poured on the sacrifice, wood, and altar. The trench was full of water. Elijah prayed and fire came down from the LORD. Everything was gone - the sacrifice, the wood, the altar, the water, and even the soil. The people believed and fell down worshipping God. Elijah had the prophets of Baal killed (Deut. 13:5) in the Kishon Valley on the northern base of Mt. Carmel.[5] Elijah begins to pray for rain. Seven times (symbol of completion) he sends his servant to look at the sky over the sea. When a small cloud appears, Elijah warns everyone to run for home. Elijah must have been very physically fit because he was able to run ahead of Ahab's chariot all the way. Now Elijah had a different worry. Jezebel was mad and seeking to kill him. He sought safety in Judah. By this time, Elijah's determination and perseverance begin to wane. He is discouraged and asks God to let him die, but God had other plans. God sent an angel with food and water to strengthen him. Elijah traveled 40 days and nights (or a long time) to reach Mt. Horeb in the southern Sinai Peninsula. He hid in a cave there feeling like we often feel, as if we are the only ones left trying to do what is right. God calls Elijah to stand on the mountain and experience His Presence. First, there is a great wind that shatters rocks and tears the mountains. The wind represents faith defined as a certainty of something we hope for but do not see (Heb. 11:1). Jesus taught that if we have faith the size of a mustard seed, then we can move mountains (Matt. 17:20). Second comes the earthquake, a visible show of God's power. He who has faith will see God's power. Fire was the third event. Fire always represents God's judgment (or God's acceptance of a sacrifice). If you have not faith, then you have not God's power and you come under God's judgment. After all of these events, Elijah still hasn't seen the LORD's Presence. All these other experiences had cleared the way for Elijah to concentrate on and hear a gentle whisper! The gentle whisper of the Holy Spirit speaks to Elijah. God tells him he isn't the only worshiper left. God has preserved 7,000 in the kingdom of Israel (people like Obadiah and the 100 prophets he saved). God gave Elijah a helper and a companion named Elisha.

Food for Thought: God doesn't want any of us to be discouraged and give up. When we seem to be so blue, God sends Christian friends to support us. We need to support and assure others. Our church family plays a key role in ministering to each other and witnessing for the Lord. Jesus is the eternal companion to those who are saved. The gentle whisper of God lives in Christians. We call it the Holy Spirit. There is nothing that chases away the blues like a long talk with God. Try it.

June 5
Bible Readings: 1 Kings 20:1-43; 22:1-28,51; 21:1-24,27-29, 2 Chron. 18:2-27

King Ben-Hadad of Syria is still in a fighting mood. When we last saw him he had conquered a sizable chunk of northern Israel. King Baasha of Israel had to leave off fighting Judah to run home to Tirza to defend the capital! It has been more than 20 years since that war, but Ahab's contract marriage to Jezebel was a clear threat to Syria. Jezebel was the daughter of the king of Tyre, a prominent commercial seaport for the trade routes through Syria. Tyre was in Phoenicia that bordered Syria's west side. Without Tyre, Syria would be economically and commercially destroyed. Ben-Hadad mounts an all-out attack on Samaria that is now the capital of Israel. Interestingly, God comes to Ahab's aid. Only 232 officers and governors of Ahab's administration are able to confuse Ben-Hadad's forces. The army of Israel then defeats their attacker. Why did God help the wicked King Ahab? Well, the answer is simple. The Israelites were still His chosen people. Even though they had sinned, the people had returned to God on Mt. Carmel. We are not told if Ahab returned to God, but we know Jezebel did not.

Ben-Hadad was not through yet. He assembled his military strategists and religious advisors. He was advised that the god of Israel was a god of the hills. If he fought Israel on the plains, their god would be powerless. So the next year, Ben-Hadad marches to the plain city of Aphek to attack Israel. The two armies size each other up for 7 days before doing battle. Again, God is with Ahab. God wanted the Syrians to know he was the omnipresent, or everywhere, God. Syrian casualties are 100,000 then a wall of the city of Aphek collapses and kills 27,000 more. The valley generally identified with this battle is only slightly larger than a football field for a long stretch. Ben-Hadad flees and hides out. When finally found, Ahab allows him to live in exchange for the cities he had taken during Omri's reign. As you would expect, a prophet shows up on Ahab's doorstep to condemn him for letting wicked Ben-Hadad live. The sentence is Ahab will lose his life and his people. (Is it any wonder kings thought prophets were troublemakers?)

At this point let's pause for a minute for an observation. First Kings 22:1 says there was peace for three years between Syria and Israel. Well, what happened to the prophet's prediction? If you have noticed throughout our studies of prophets, their condemnation prophecies do not occur quickly. God almost always delays final judgment to allow people to change their heart. How much time we have is unknown. Even now as we have lived in the end times prophecy for almost 2,000 years, God wants us to change our hearts. He does not choose for us to have eternal doom. Like any loving father, God prefers repentance and renewal. There are many examples in the Bible where people humble themselves after hearing their sentence and God lightened their judgment out of His mercy. As the final chapter of God's Will is unveiled in our world, will the people repent and humble themselves before God? We do not know how long God will delay.

Ahab begins to covet the land adjacent to his palace. When the owner refuses to sell, Jezebel has him killed. Ahab has no qualms about taking Naboth's land. But now he has really done it for here comes Elijah. Just like Jeroboam and Baasha, Ahab and Jezebel get the dogs and birds condemnation. Now we have an excellent example of God's mercy. Ahab is scared to death and immediately humbles himself and repents. God shows compassionate mercy and delays the sentence on the house of Ahab until after his death.

Ahab, king of Israel, strikes up a friendly relationship with Jehoshaphat, king of Judah. Ahab convinces Jehoshaphat to join him in battle against Ramoth Gilead. This was a very important town located on the King's Highway trade caravan route. The year is 853 B.C.[7] The King's Highway ran from the Gulf of Aqaba, which projected off the northeast corner of the Red Sea, to the land of Bashan that was far northeast of the Sea of Galilee in the country of Syria. Spices, ivory, exotic animals and other treasures from the Far East were transported inland along this route. The King's Highway was considered an international highway used by traders, travelers, armies, and nomads. Abraham, himself, traveled on this highway (Genesis 14).[5] (It is hard to realize that these ancient people had an interstate system, or more accurately an international system - and it was as good as ours today!) [I carried part of this long lesson over to June 6.]

Food for Thought: Ahab is considered the wickedest king of Israel. Yet, at one point, he repented and was treated mercifully by God. His ultimate downfall was his wife Jezebel. This should be a lesson to all adults. Spouses do make a difference, so choose carefully! There is no such thing as a perfect spouse. (Remember you aren't perfect either!) But your choice should be based on finding a Christian whose beliefs are in line with yours and whose values are compatible with yours. Likes and dislikes of worldly items make little difference. Over the years, you will come to enjoy many of the same things simply because the one you love enjoys them! You need to select a spouse that knows how to say, "I'm sorry." You also need to have a spouse who knows how to be humble before the Lord. Someone who can compromise is better than someone who is attractive. A spouse who seeks the Lord daily through prayer and Bible study will be one who is still by you when the going gets tough. Above all, ask God whom He has picked out for you. Often, it is the one you would have overlooked!

June 6
Bible Readings: 1 Kings 22:29-40, 48-49, 52-53;   2 Kings 3:1-5; 1:1-18;
2 Chron. 18:28-34; 19:1-11; 20:1-30, 35-37

Israel's false prophets predict a victory over Ramoth Gilead, but the prophet of God (Micaiah) predicts defeat and death of Israel's king. Poor Micaiah is punished for telling the truth. But the truth always prevails and Ahab is killed in battle. The dogs lick the blood from his wounds. The prophecy was fulfilled. Meanwhile Jehoshaphat has escaped and gone back home only to have Jehu, the prophet, pay him a visit. (I don't know about you, but these prophets could sure make a guy nervous!) Because Jehoshaphat had teamed up with wicked Ahab, he would be punished, but Jehoshaphat had some redeeming qualities. He immediately reforms the judicial system, charging the judges to fear the LORD as they represent Him in the court setting. The chief priest will be in charge of the religious judges, the leader of the tribe of Judah will be the 'Attorney General', and the Levites will be local officials.

Jehoshaphat warns the judges and officials that God does not abide injustice, partiality, or bribery.

In Israel Ahaziah is king now that Ahab is dead. Their subservient land of Moab sees this as a prime opportunity to rebel. They team up with the Ammonites and Meunites from the land of Edom. (These are all tribes residing in what is modern day Jordan.) Since they are located on the east and southeast sides of the Dead Sea, they first march on Judah. Jehoshaphat calls for fasting and praying. As he prays in the courtyard in the front of the Temple, he reminds God of His promise to Solomon's prayer for the dedication of the Temple. God promised to hear their prayers and save them. One of the Levites present prophesies a victory without even a battle! God even tells the Judahites exactly where to go to meet the enemy. Jehoshaphat is so confident of God's deliverance that he appoints men to march at the front of the column singing praises unto God! God so confused the invading army that the Ammonites and Moabites were killing the Edomites, their allies. By the time Jehoshaphat got there, the whole enemy army was dead! It took Judah's army three days to collect all the loot. (Mesha, king of Moab, inscribed what has come to be known as the Moabite Stone. It is a big, black monument-type stone that records the events marking Mesha's reign. Among these events are the wars with Omri and Ahab. The stone is 3 1/2 feet high, 2 feet wide, and 2 feet thick.[36] It was found in 1868 and is currently housed in the Louvre in Paris.[7])

Back in Israel, Ahaziah has injured himself in an accident. As expected, he sent messengers to inquire his fate from a pagan god. Elijah intercepts the messengers and condemns Ahaziah's action. The sentence is death. At this point a description of Elijah is given that is almost identical to John the Baptist (Matt. 3:4). In fact, the prophecy of Malachi 4:5 that Elijah would be sent before the judgment of the LORD is interpreted to be John the Baptist because of his great similarity in dress and lifestyle to Elijah.[5] Now Ahaziah decides to send a company of 50 men out to get Elijah. Elijah calls fire down from God and burns them up. He does the same for the next 50. The captain of the third company got smart. He approached Elijah on his knees begging. Elijah went with him and condemned Ahaziah to his face. Ahaziah died and his brother Joram became king.

Food for Thought: Jehoshaphat is a good king and basically a good person. He witnessed many miracles from God. But even when Israel is knee-deep in idolatry, Jehoshaphat wants to socialize with them. For some people, socialization seems to be more important than God's Will. Are you afraid of loneliness? If you spend your time in God's word and pray for Him to lead you, you won't be lonely. I realize that is a tall order for most people. Part of the problem is that we allow ourselves to participate in things that increase our distress, e.g., sad music, love movies, depressing phone calls to depressed friends. It is a cycle that feeds itself. When you are most alone is when God is easiest to find! Next time you are lonely, look for God. He is waiting for you. Don't disappoint Him.

June 7
Bible Readings: 2 Kings 2:1-25; 4:1-44; 8:1-2; 6:1-7

Elijah and Elisha have maintained the roles of mentor and protégé for many years; they also have become close friends and companions. Elijah knows it is time for him to leave this earth. Elisha must also know because he won't let Elijah out of his sight. First they walk from Gilgal to Bethel, a distance of about 15 miles.[4] The prophets of Bethel have been divinely informed that Elijah is about to go home to the LORD. You can just feel the undercurrent of whispers. Elijah seems almost like a caged animal. You can sense his anticipation. You feel he really wants to be alone and meet God one-on-one, but Elisha refuses to leave his 'pastor.'

Elijah is on the move again. They walk from Bethel to Jericho. The prophets there are whispering the news, too. This has been another 15-mile walk. They are now within a couple of miles from where they started at Gilgal. Why does God lead Elijah to make this 30-mile walk on his last day on earth? Maybe it was to see his friends, the prophets, one last time. Most of the religious training was conducted in these three towns, similar to our seminaries, thus the explanation for the groups of prophets that met Elijah and Elisha. Maybe he wanted to leave them with some last words or blessings. Elijah may have wanted to assure himself there were no 'loose ends' left for him to finish before departure. Elijah now proceeds to the Jordan River (another 5 miles). Elijah takes his cloak, folds it, and strikes the water. The Jordan parts and Elijah and Elisha cross on dry ground. Nothing like this has happened since the Hebrews crossed the Jordan to possess the Promised Land more than 600 years before! Now Elijah focuses on his last concern -- Elisha. What can he do for his long time companion, the man who will take his place of leadership? Elisha requests a double portion of Elijah's spirit or prophetic power. This request was in keeping with the Hebrew practice of giving the primary heir a double portion of the inheritance. Elijah only owns his clothes and the spirit with which God has blessed him. Only God could fulfill Elisha's request. As a sign, Elijah tells Elisha if he sees him depart, his request will be granted. Don't you know Elisha was afraid to even blink? Suddenly, Elijah is whisked away by a chariot of fire drawn by horses of fire. I have to believe that by sending a chariot of fire God was showing those watching (the young prophets) that He accepted Elijah's sacrifice in living his life for God. He owned nothing, but what he left behind (his teachings and witness) stood as a monument to guide all people to the LORD for centuries to come.

Elisha cried out at the awesome sight he beheld. He tore his clothes in mourning and picked up Elijah's cloak. As Elisha approaches the Jordan you know he must be wondering if his request had been granted. He did see Elijah depart, but he didn't feel any different. Now he has his first test. Elisha folds Elijah's cloak, calls out to God, and strikes the water. The water parts! Elisha has inherited Elijah's spirit! After the Jericho group of prophets spends three days verifying that Elijah wasn't set down somewhere else, Elisha performs his next miracle. He purifies the town's water.

Elisha is met by some jeering youths on his walk to Bethel. They are making fun of his baldhead. Apparently they are trying to anger him, possibly threatening him. He calls down a curse on them and two bears came out of the woods and mauled 42 of them. (These youths were equivalent to our modern day gangs.) From Bethel, Elisha walks all the way to Mt. Carmel by the Mediterranean Sea and back again to Samaria. This is over 120 miles (as the crow flies) since he left the Jordan and that doesn't take into consideration the mountains to cross!

A prophet's widow begged Elisha for help. Josephus tells us this is the widow of Obadiah, the Minister of the Palace who saved the 100 prophets of the LORD from Jezebel.[3] Her husband's creditor was going to make slaves of their two sons because she couldn't pay the debt. Again Josephus enlightens us about the debt. Obadiah had borrowed the money to provide for the needs of the 100 prophets.[3] Her appeal to Elisha, the spiritual leader, was justified. Elisha tells her to borrow as many jars as she can from all her neighbors and then shut herself and her sons up in the house. She is to pour her little bit of oil into the jars. She follows his instructions and amazingly the oil keeps flowing. It doesn't stop until the last jar is filled. When she sells her oil, she pays her debts and has enough left to live.

A couple in Shunem befriends Elisha. They were blessed by their comfortable living, but they had no children. They built a summer room on the roof for Elisha to use when he was in town. Rooms like this were usually made of branches and had a bedroll to sleep on. The roof was a cool place to sleep at night and the openness of the walls allowed air to circulate, rainfall occurred rarely and only in certain seasons. Therefore, Elisha's furnishings could be removed, if necessary, during the rainy season. Elisha's room was well furnished with a bed, table, lamp, and chair (most likely a little stool). In return for her kindness, Elisha promises the woman a son to be born in about one year. The promise is fulfilled.

Next Elisha performs two miracles involving food. First, his servant gathers some wild herbs and vegetables and prepares a stew for some company. It turns out one of the ingredients was poisonous. Elisha put flour in it and the poison was gone. Later Elisha takes 20 loaves of bread (these were usually small, short loaves) and feeds 100 men. This is a forerunner of the miracles Jesus did when He fed the 5,000 (Matt. 14:16-21) and the 4,000 (Matt. 15:32-38). The prophets fed hundreds, but Jesus fed thousands.

One day the Shunammite woman's son became very ill and died. She laid him on Elisha's bed and immediately left on a donkey to seek Elisha at Mt. Carmel. This would have been about a 20-mile trip by slow donkey. Elisha sees her in the distance and knows something is wrong. He sends his servant, Gehazi, out to meet her. When Elisha hears of the boy's fate, he tells his servant to take his staff and run and put it on the boy's face. (Now this servant runs 20 miles and then runs back to meet Elisha who is walking to Shunem. This man ran at least 30-35 miles!) When Elisha arrived, he prayed and then stretched himself out on the boy. The boy got warm. Elisha paced awhile and stretched out again on the boy. This time the boy sneezed seven times and came back to life. [This miracle is very similar to Elijah's miracle of raising a dead boy (1 Kings 17:17-24).] Elisha tells the couple that the land will have famine for 7 years and they need to go away with their son until it is over.

The student prophets at Jericho decide to build a meeting room beside the Jordan River. In the process, one of the ax heads comes off its handle and falls into the water. The prophet is frantic because he had borrowed the ax. By law the prophet would have to pay back the owner and, in some cases, the law required double the value of the lost item. (See Ex. 22:9, 14) Elisha cut a stick, threw it in the water, and the ax head floated to the surface!

Food for Thought: Elisha performed many miracles in today's lesson. They were all events in the everyday lives of ordinary people. Just as Jesus will minister to the needs of all people, Elisha provided assistance in ordinary situations. In the serious problems, like the boy's death, the mother who believed he could raise the boy back to life calmly sought Elisha. In our own lives, God provides for us and protects us in our day-to-day activities. We should praise God daily for His blessings, many of which we aren't even aware. In the serious problems of life, we should confidently seek the Lord in prayer. God hears our prayers and answers our prayers as He knows is best. Praise God today for His blessings!

June 8
Bible Readings: 2 Kings 8:16-22; 3:6-27; 1 Kings 22:45,50
2 Chron. 21:2-5; 20:34; 21:1,6-17,20

Elijah and Elisha both lived and served in the northern kingdom of Israel that was ruled by wicked kings who promoted idol worship. This was fertile ground indeed for men of God to proclaim the one and only God who sees all, knows all, and is all powerful. Prophets Jonah, Amos, and Hosea follow Elijah and Elisha. We serve a God who repeatedly provides opportunity to repent and turn to Him. God doesn't choose for us to be punished for our sins; He prefers we seek Him with all our hearts and walk in His Will so that we avoid sin. For 200 years God sends messengers called prophets to Israel, telling them to turn from their wicked ways. God loves us and patiently tries to turn our hearts to Him, until we reach the point where our hearts have hardened by sin. Then when we forsake God, He forsakes us (2 Chron. 15:2).

In the southern kingdom of Judah, Jehoram, the son of King Jehoshaphat, is given the kingdom by his father and becomes somewhat of an apprentice king. As soon as Jehoram is firmly entrenched as king, he has his six brothers killed. Jehoshaphat was still king, too, so why didn't he stop this killing? Possibly the reason is that Jehoram was already too strong to overcome. Maybe he realized the guilt was his own because of the poor choices he had made for his son. Regardless, Jehoram wanted to be sure no one else attempted to obtain the kingship. In addition to that, he would then inherit all the brothers' wealth given them by their father. Greed breeds wickedness.

Ahab has been known throughout history as the wickedest king of Israel. Likewise, Jehoram becomes Judah's most wicked king to date. What connection existed between these two kings? The answer lies in one woman named Athaliah. Athaliah was Ahab and Jezebel's daughter. Jehoshaphat arranged a contract marriage between Jehoram, the Crown Prince of Judah, and Athaliah. Athaliah was a case of 'like mother, like daughter.' She was every bit as wicked as Jezebel. Jezebel had killed the LORD's prophets and Naboth. She aggressively promoted idolatry. Athaliah influenced her husband to kill his brothers and turn the nation to idol worship. Before her death she would even kill all of her own grandsons, save one who was protected by God.

Jehoshaphat had been a good king during most of his reign. His downfall was his friendship with Ahab. First

Corinthians 15:33 says "Do not be misled: 'Bad company corrupts good character.'"[1] King Jehoshaphat is an excellent example. God even sent Jehu the prophet to warn Jehoshaphat against helping the wicked Ahab (2 Chron. 19:1-3). Jehoshaphat repented and turned back to the LORD. But Ahab's death apparently gave Jehoshaphat a false sense of being freed from the evil for he soon enters a shipping alliance with Ahab's son, Ahaziah. This time Eliezer, the prophet, condemns his actions and all the ships are destroyed. When Ahaziah dies with no sons to succeed him, the throne goes to his brother Jehoram. (Don't get confused here. This is the king of Israel, but at this same time the king of Judah is also named Jehoram who is Jehoshaphat's son. You may see either name written as Joram.)

God saw the goodness of Jehoshaphat and He remembered His promise to David: David would have a kinsman on the throne forever. Therefore, God warned Jehoshaphat but did not destroy him. Like us, Jehoshaphat would walk the 'straight and narrow' (behave himself) for a little while then he would get pulled right back into the wickedness. His last alliance with Israel was when he joined forces with Israel and Edom to fight Moab. They marched 7 days without finding water. Because they were near Elisha's house they sought his help. Elisha tells them to fill the valley with ditches for the water is coming. The next day finds the valley flooded with water! Additionally, Elisha promised God would overthrow Moab. The Moabites could see the valley of water in the distance, but it looked red like blood to them. (This may have been because the water came from Edom (the red earth) and contained a lot of soil as a result of the flash flood.) Feeling confident their invaders were dead, the Moabites rushed to the Israelite camp to take their loot only to be slaughtered by the Israelites. (Here is another example where greed is a sin that leads to serious consequences.) In accordance with Elisha's words, the army totally destroys Moab except for Kir Hareseth. The king of Moab sacrificed his own son, the Crown Prince, on top of the city wall. (Although some commentators believe the boy was sacrificed to the God of Israel as an appeasement effort not realizing human sacrifice was repulsive to God, most believe it was a sacrifice to the Moabite god Chemosh. Human sacrifice was common for Chemosh followers.) The Israelites withdrew upon witnessing this carnage and went home. Different versions of the Bible translate this verse (2 Kings 3:27) in opposing ways. *The Living Bible* says the Israelite army left in disgust.[15] The NIV indicates this act so infuriated the Moabites against Israel that the Israelites withdrew.[1] Moab is now under the king of Israel.

Elijah may be gone, but he isn't forgotten! Suddenly, Jehoram receives a letter from the same Elijah who had already gone up to Heaven in the chariot of fire! How this happened we are not told. Elijah, being informed by God of future events, probably wrote the letter and made arrangements for it to be delivered at a certain time. Nevertheless, it bears a condemnation of the wicked King Jehoram of Judah. Besides the mysteries behind the letter itself, Elijah had served as a prophet to Israel, not to Judah. Maybe in his adversarial role to wicked Ahab, Elijah realized a future marriage between Jehoram of Judah and Athaliah would be the downfall of God's people. Regardless of how events took place, King Jehoram will have a long agonizing death.

Soon the Philistines and Arabs attack and carry off Jehoram's wealth and all his family except his youngest son, Ahaziah, whom God saves for the sake of David. In this weakened state, vassal kingdoms Libnah and Edom seize the opportunity to revolt. Your lesson ends by telling us this all happened because Jehoram had forsaken The LORD.

Food for Thought: Have you forsaken God? It's never too late to repent and humble yourself before God. As in days of old, God is still willing to halt your condemnation, but **you must seek him**! Seek him now.

June 9
Bible Readings: Obadiah

The book of Obadiah is the shortest in the Old Testament and is not quoted in the New Testament. The Edomites (sons of Esau) and the Israelites (sons of Jacob) never liked each other. For example, the king of Edom refused Moses passage through his country during the days before the conquest of Palestine. There are many times in

Israel's history when such a prophecy against Edom might be uttered, but I believe the most likely time to be around 585 B.C. after the Babylonians sacked Jerusalem. The strongest argument for this time period is the prophecy's amazing similarity to Jeremiah 49:7-22 which was written near the time of the destruction of Jerusalem.

It appears that the Edomites had volunteered to assist the Babylonians in destroying Jerusalem. The Apocrypha book of 1 Esdras (4:45) indicates the Edomites were actively involved in destroying the temple. Their enthusiastic support of the Babylonians was self-serving in that the Edomites themselves had been plotting against Babylon only a few years before (Jer. 27:1-3). Thus, they were not only malicious but also turncoats. Jewish remembrance of Edom's treachery would be long lasting. "In fact, Edom would become a code name for 'the enemy' in Jewish rabbinic writings."[37] (p. 144) Verse three of the prophecy indicates that pride was the source of Edom's sin. These people lived in secure mountainous places; their capital city was such an impregnable fortress that one wonders even today how it could have ever been conquered. Edom was also very wealthy because a number of trade routes traversed her territory. The prophet declares, however, that Edom will be plundered; nothing of value will be left. Verse seven argues that Edom will suffer from disloyal friends. Thus, what she has done to Judah will be done to her.

The reasons for Edom's judgment are clearly enumerated in verses 10-14:

1. Unrestrained and openly expressed joy at the misfortune suffered by Judah.
2. Looting the city of Jerusalem as it is defenseless.
3. Intercepting the refugees from the conquered city and delivering them up either to Babylonian conquerors or slave traders.

Verses 15-18 introduce a common theme in Old Testament prophecy: The Day of the LORD. This doctrine is in nearly all the prophetic books (Joel 2:1-2, Amos 5:18-20, Zephaniah 1:10-13). It is carried over into the New Testament in what we as Christians refer to as the Judgment Day. That day is to be fearful for Edom. The people of God will be the fire and the Edomites the stubble. There will be no surviving remnant of this nation for its judgment will be complete.

In the last few verses Edom's lack of a future stands in contrast to the people of God who may be downtrodden at the present but will return and possess their land in the future.

Food for Thought: Always remember in the midst of your difficulty that the last page of the book of your life hasn't been written yet. As a Christian, your destiny is sealed, but the path you take to get to Heaven is based on choices.

June 10
Bible Readings: 2 Chron. 21:18, 2 Kings 6:8 - 7:20; 8:3-6; 5:1-27

An interesting observation of Elijah's political involvement compared to Elisha's becomes evident in today's lesson. We find Elisha repeatedly providing advice to the king of Israel concerning the movements of Syria's army. At one point, the king of Syria believes he has a traitor in his camp that is leaking military secrets to the enemy. Upon being told it is the man of God, Elisha, the Syrian king forms a commando squad to kidnap Elisha. Before we go any further, let's look at Elijah's years as a prophet to Israel. Elijah prophesied during the years of Ahab and Jezebel when Baal and Asherath worship was rampant. Therefore, Elijah was a lifelong foe of the royal family because of their paganism and murder of the LORD's prophets. God sent messages of condemnation by Elijah. Elijah lived and worked most of his life as a wandering nomad living off the land in the wilderness. He was often alone and a fugitive. Elisha, on the other hand, had a ministry to the people. He had a home in Samaria and performed miracles for the ordinary citizens. Elisha chose to work within the political system to become an advisor of God's Will to kingdom officials.[5] Elijah was a hairy, rugged man who wore garments of animal hair held by wide leather belts. He wore a mantle or cloak for protection from the weather. Most likely, this was also of animal skins. In contrast, Elisha wore the usual robes of a prophet in his day. We know Elisha was bald and seems to be more even-tempered and diplomatic. Elisha doesn't seem to be prone to the bouts of depression that Elijah occasionally experienced. As a whole, we have two very different people who chose to do the Will of God in two opposite ways, but both served God well. We all have different personalities, talents, and characteristics. God can use us all if we only yield our will to His Will.

Let us go back to the king of Syria's task force to kidnap Elisha. Elisha is apparently visiting Dothan. [You'll recall Joseph's brothers put him in a pit and sold him into slavery from the area of Dothan (known as Tell Dotha today).[5]] When Elisha's servant rises in the morning, he learns commando forces have surrounded the town. After his excited appeal to Elisha, a marvelous miracle occurs. Elisha prays that the servant's eyes will be opened to God's army. The servant stands in speechless awe as he sees the hills around the city filled with horses and chariots of fire. (In this case, fire represents the judgment of God. Chariots are only used for war and official functions. Elijah's chariot was on an official function assignment. The chariots of Dothan were those of war. Horses symbolize power and war. Only royalty owned horses, for personal use and for war. God uses them the same way. (See Rev. 6:2-8 and Rev. 19:11-16.) The common people rode on donkeys or mules. The use of mules by commoners is evidence of an improved economy. (You will recall in early Hebrew history, only royalty rode mules and the Hebrews had no horses.) Thus, Jesus rode on a donkey when He entered Jerusalem on Palm Sunday, a lowly animal of service. Ephesians 6:12 warns us of the spiritual warfare we must fight. We know this warfare is going on continually in the spiritual realm (Daniel 10:7-21).) Elisha causes the advancing army of Syria to be blinded. Elisha then proceeds to 'assist' the army by leading them to the 'right' city. When their eyes clear they find themselves captive in the capital city of Samaria! The king asks Elisha what should be done with the captives. Elisha's standing with the king is evidenced when the king refers to Elisha as 'my father,' inferring spiritual leadership. Elisha says to give them food and drink and send them home. This reminds me of Proverbs 25:21-22. Take the time to read these two verses. Israel's graciousness shamed Syria into stopping their invasions. Israel had suffered at the hands of the Syrians (Arameans) since King Asa of Judah first enlisted Syria's support (1 Kings 15:18-21).

When the Shunammite woman and her family return from their refuge from the famine, God provided for Elisha's servant Gehazi to be telling the king the story of how Elisha raised the woman's son from the dead. The king provided for the woman to regain her house, land, and all the income the land brought while she was gone. This would seem to be very unfair to the current tenant. But, in all likelihood, the king had seized the abandoned house and land for lack of taxes and in actuality the king was giving her possessions back out of his own treasuries.

To see how God's Will can be done by every person regardless of circumstances, a young Israelite girl is captured by Syria and made a slave in the house of the king's army commander Naaman. Naaman was a well-respected soldier, but he had a skin disorder (all of which are called leprosy in the Bible). The young girl tells Naaman's wife about the great man of God in Israel. Naaman requests a leave of absence from the king to go to Elisha. This king is probably Ben-Hadad II. Ben-Hadad had probably become a throne name of the royal family.[5] Elisha doesn't see Naaman but merely sends a messenger to him saying he should wash 7 times in the Jordan. If Elisha had come in contact with the leprous man, he would have been unclean and had to live outside the 'camp' for one week. When Naaman is cured, he returns to Elisha and this time gets to meet with him. Naaman, who was a high official in the pagan country of Syria, makes a profoundly insightful statement. "Now I know that there is no God in all the world except Israel."[1] (2 Kings 5:15) You'll notice Naaman asked to have some earth to carry back to Syria. These ancient people believed a god was god of a specific country or place. Naaman wanted to worship the God of Israel and needed to have a piece of Israel to assure God was with him. (The pagan god of Syria mentioned in this passage is Rimmon, god of rain, storms, lightning, and thunder.[5]) Naaman proceeds to leave with his entourage. Elisha's greedy servant, Gehazi, can't withstand the temptation of Naaman's gifts that Elisha declined. Gehazi runs after Naaman, tells a lie about why he wants the gifts, then goes home and lies to Elisha about where he has been. The same man who testified to Elisha raising the dead thinks he can get away with lying! Elisha sentences Gehazi and all his descendants to living with leprosy. We don't know what happens to Naaman after all this, but his king, Ben-Hadad II, mobilizes his whole army to mount a siege on Samaria (Elisha's town). Was Naaman still commander of the army? If so, how could he justify his actions with his faith? Do you wonder how Elisha felt to have helped heal the commander of the army of the enemy? A siege usually involved many months of war often turning into years. Embankments were built when possible against the city walls. Battering rams were used. Arrows, spears, and knives were the chief weapons making only close range targets possible. Starvation and water deprivation could take its toll on a city under siege, but it could also take its toll on the supplies for tens of thousands of hungry troops mounting the attack. Fortified Judean cities usually had casement walls. A wall of this type was made of two thick walls with storage rooms between to store supplies. Sometimes earth and rocks would be placed in the storerooms to reinforce the walls. If a battering ram broke through the outer wall, it just caused more rubble to deal with before the inner wall could be reached. Tunneling under such a thick wall would be extremely difficult, especially since most of these cities were built on solid rock hills. Often the city-gate was actually two gates. If the outer one was broken, the enemy was trapped. Soldiers on the walls above rained down spears and arrows on them.[7] In accordance with the census of Moses, military service was compulsory at age 20.[7]

The siege on Samaria apparently lasted several years. The citizens resorted to eating dung, donkeys' heads, and even their children. All these were detestable to the Hebrews but come as a fulfillment of the curses of Moses in Deut. 28:49-57 on the nation of Israel when it turns from God. The king was so distraught that he tore his robes, revealing the sackcloth underneath. This was probably more ritual than true remorse because he lets his anger prevail and sends a messenger to behead Elisha! Poor Elisha! What has he done? Commentators have several theories: (1) Elisha may have advised the king that he should humble himself before God and God would deliver them but it hadn't happened yet, or (2) There was a long history of animosity between the kings of Israel and the prophets and the conditions stir old dislikes, or (3) Maybe the king remembered that Elijah had ended a famine (1 Kings 18:41-46) and blamed Elisha for not ending this one.[15] God protects Elisha by showing him the danger so that he can bolt the door before the executioner arrives. Elisha refers to the king as a murderer (he was a descendant of Ahab who had the LORD's prophets killed). The sound of the king running to stop the irrational order can already be heard. When Elisha admits the king and predicts the siege will end the next day and food will be plentiful, an officer of the king expresses doubt and is condemned by Elisha. During the night four lepers decide to give themselves up to Syria so they could be fed or killed, either way was preferable to their current existence. They discover the Syrian camp is totally abandoned. Food and loot are plentiful. We are told the LORD had caused the Syrians (Arameans) to hear the sounds of vast armies coming. They supposed the king of Judah had somehow obtained assistance from the Hittites, northwest of Syria, and the Egyptians, southwest of Judah effectively trapping them between the advancing armies. The soldiers literally ran for their lives! When word of the discovery of food reached Samaria, there was such a great stampede that the 'doubtful' officer of the king was trampled. The king sent two chariots to track the Syrians to verify it wasn't an ambush. They tracked them about 22 miles finding the road strewn with clothing and objects that were discarded so they could run faster!

Food for Thought: The king's remorse and humbleness after his assault on Elisha is evident when he says, "This disaster is from the LORD. Why should I wait for the LORD any longer?" (2 Kings 6:33) His question is pleading for Elisha to give him hope the LORD will intervene. We often lose hope just before the victory. I sometimes wonder if God allows this just so I don't get too big for my britches and believe I had something to do with bringing about victory. Nothing humbles us like believing we are defeated. Nothing renews our faith like experiencing the intervention of the Lord. If you feel defeated today, don't despair. Humble yourself before God in prayer. Better to humble yourself before God than to be humbled by your enemy. God is merciful; the enemy is not. God loves us; the enemy hates us. More than 600 years went by before the curse of Moses was fulfilled, but God's word always prevails. The end of time is coming. Do you know Jesus as your Savior? God's word promises us eternal life if we repent and accept Jesus as Lord and Savior of our lives. Ask Jesus to come into your life today.

> Verse of the Week: **Joel 2:12** "'Even now,' declares the LORD, 'return to me with all your heart, with fasting and weeping and mourning.'"

June 11
Bible Readings: 2 Kings 8:7-15,23-29; 9:1-37; 10:1-17 2 Chron. 21:19-20; 22:1-9

Elijah's prophecy of Jehoram's (king of Judah) agonizing death is fulfilled. The Bible states that no one regretted his death! What a sad commentary about anyone's life. His son, Ahaziah (also called Jehoahaz), becomes king. His mother, Athaliah, is the daughter of Jezebel. Just like Jezebel, she encourages the king to do evil.

Meanwhile, in Syria Ben-Hadad II is ill and Elisha has told the king's servant Hazael that the king will recover from the illness, but will die nonetheless. (The illness did not kill him but the murderous evil of Hazael did.) An unusual event occurs at this point. Elisha begins weeping. When Hazael inquires as to the reason why, he is told it is because of all the death and destruction Hazael will bestow on the Israelites. Hazael asks how a mere servant could do this. Elisha responds that he will become king. And immediately Hazael goes back to the palace and smothers the ill Ben-Hadad II.

Parallels can be drawn between Hazael's betrayal of Ben-Hadad II, King of the Syrians, and Judas' betrayal of Jesus, King of the Jews. God condemned both betrayers. Both came from within a trusted circle of companions. The man of God, Elisha, mourns over the death and destruction of the Israelites. Jesus mourns over the death and destruction of the lost.

The kings of Israel and Judah unite to wage war against the Syrians who were attacking Ramoth Gilead. In the June 5 lesson we learned this was a key city on the north-south trade route. In the course of battle, Joram, King of Israel, is wounded. Ahaziah does what seems to be a normal show of good manners to me -- he visits the wounded Joram, his uncle. Second Chronicles 22:7 reveals it brought about Ahaziah's downfall. During the previous events, Elisha sent one of the student prophets to anoint Jehu as king of Israel. At the time, Jehu was one of the army commanders of the forces at Ramoth Gilead. Jehu was the son of Jehoshaphat (not the King of Judah). There is a charge that goes with the anointing. Jehu is to totally destroy the house of Ahab. The prophet reminds Jehu that the LORD condemned the houses of Jeroboam, Baasha, and Ahab to the dogs and birds. Then the prophet flees. (Notice these prophets deliver the news and then run like crazy!) Jehu immediately goes to the town of Jezreel, confronts Joram with the idolatry and witchcraft of his reign, and kills him. Joram's body was thrown on the land of Naboth whom his father had murdered. Ahaziah is wounded, too, but manages to escape. Jehu goes to get Jezebel. When he sees her in the window of the palace, he calls to her attendants to throw her down. And they do. Jehu goes in to eat. Then he orders Jezebel to be buried. When the servants went to get her body, nothing was left but her head, hands, and feet. She had received the curse of the dogs, just as Elijah had said.

Jehu is a man on a mission. He is to annihilate the house of Ahab. In Samaria, he orders 70 of Ahab's relatives beheaded. Jehu even had all of Ahab's friends, advisers, priests, and associates killed. (People who like to hobnob with those who are in power should think about this.)

Having wiped out the immediate house of Ahab, Jehu now turns his attention to Ahaziah, Ahab's grandson. He kills Ahaziah, his sons, his family, and his relatives. Ahaziah was accorded a burial in his family tomb in Jerusalem. (Only kings could be buried inside the city. All of the other citizens were buried outside the city. About 250 tombs, many with massive ornate fronts carved out of the stone mountains, have been found around Jerusalem.

These would not come into vogue, though, until the eighth and seventh centuries B.C. after the fall of Israel. Thus, none has been found in the Israel area.[7])

Food for Thought: My husband takes great comfort in thinking of death as being "gathered unto his people." I, on the other hand, cringe somewhat at the phrase. In the tombs of Jerusalem, benches were hewn out of the stone wall. The bodies would be covered with ointments and spices and placed on a bench. Years later (usually when another body needed the bench), the person's bones were gathered up and placed in hollows cut into the stone walls or under the benches. So being "gathered unto your people" had both a literal and spiritual meaning. Of course, spiritual bodies will replace our physical bodies until the Lord comes again. Isaiah 26:19 tells us our bodies will rise and shout for joy. First Thessalonians 4:16-17 says the dead in Christ will arise first immediately followed by living Christians. Our spiritual bodies will inhabit perfect immortal bodies. Christians will be the citizens of the New Jerusalem. Yes, we will be "gathered unto our people" -- the people of God.

June 12

Bible Readings: 2 Kings 11:1-21; 12:1-3; 10:18-31 2 Chron. 22:10-12; 23:1-21; 24:1-2

Our previous lesson sets the stage for the change in power in Judah. Athaliah didn't grieve the death of her son, Ahaziah. In fact, she was so power hungry she proceeded to kill the rest of her own grandchildren! Ahaziah's sister managed to save the youngest prince, Joash, by hiding him at the Temple. For six years, Athaliah ruled.

In Israel, Jehu has continued to zealously eliminate Baal worship. He set a trap by mandating all Baal prophets, ministers, and priests attend a special sacrifice in the temple of Baal. Jehu and his men killed them all and demolished the temple of Baal. The site was turned into a public outhouse. For his faithfulness, God promised Jehu four generations of kings would come from his house. But Jehu had one area of weakness; he did not destroy the golden calves. Isn't it strange that we can recognize the foreign gods among us but cannot see our own materialistic gods? Jesus said it best in Matt. 7:3-5. "Why do you look at the speck of sawdust in your brother's eye and pay no attention to the plank in your own eye? You hypocrite, first take the plank out of your own eye, and then you will see clearly to remove the speck from your brother's eye."[1] The problem with planks is that they consume so much of your vision that you can't see around them. But your vision soon adjusts to their presence so you don't even notice them anymore. Even when they are pointed out, you can't see them. Now were we talking about planks or faults? Jehu had a fault. He grew up with the golden calves. He never questioned worshipping them. They were a part of his life to which his spiritual vision had adjusted. They were so much a part of his routine and so widely accepted that he never saw they were planks. Does your life or your worship have planks in it? Have you reviewed all that you do or believe to see if it is in accordance with God's Holy Word? Not what someone told you or taught you to do. If you haven't read and studied God's word, then the answer is certainly "No." Many times we have read God's word but don't see how teachings from ancient people can apply to today's world. God's word is timeless. Ask God to show you how to apply His word to your life as clearly as Elisha's servant saw God's army of chariots of fire on the hills surrounding Dothan. God will reveal the planks.

When Joash was 7 years old (interesting number, huh?), his uncle Jehoiada, who just happened to be his guardian and priest, called on the Temple guards (made up of Levites) to stand guard in and around the Temple while he anointed Joash as king of Judah. This was definitely an act of treason against the reigning Queen Athaliah. But harboring a fugitive from the executioner was punishable by death, too. Jehoiada and his wife Jehosheba had preserved the lineage of David. Joash would become an ancestor of Jesus. God was certainly blessing this event. Joash was then crowned and proclaimed king by the people. When Athaliah came to check out the ruckus, she was dragged out of the Temple and killed. Burnt offerings and celebrating took place, followed by a royal parade to the palace where the king was seated on the throne. Joash would reign 40 years (another interesting number!). He did what was right in God's eyes as long as Jehoiada lived. (This last statement should be a clue as to what will happen!)

Food for Thought: As with us today, the kings in Judah went through a special coronation ceremony. First, the king was crowned in the Temple and presented with the 'testimony,' generally believed to be the regulations God laid down for his conduct as king (See Deut. 17:14-20), a copy of the law (the Torah), and the obligations associated with the office of king. Second, the priest (or prophet) anoints the new king. Third, the people proclaim him as king by shouting, "Long Live the King!" Fourth, there is a royal parade to the palace where the king is seated on the throne to symbolize his assumption of power. Fifth, the king receives the highest officials in the nation during which they declare their loyalty to the king.[7] These steps in the coronation process may not always be in this order. Frequently, kings were secretly anointed years before they were crowned. Even then a lapse of time may occur before the actual enthronement. We have all sorts of rituals we go through to recognize authority figures in our lives. What rituals do you have to show the world God is in authority in your life? Has He only been secretly anointed? Or maybe He has been publicly proclaimed? But has your spiritual life matured to the point that God is permanently enthroned?

June 13
Bible Readings: Joel

The book of Joel is one of the shorter books of the prophets, but it contains one of the most important announcements for the Christian faith: the outpouring of the Holy Spirit. The primary focus of the book is its description of an unusually severe plague of locusts, which have devastated the countryside. Because no king is mentioned in the book, most commentators have set the date for Joel either around 837 B.C. when Jehoiada the High Priest was ruling as regent for the boy King Joash (2 Kings 11:1-21) or after the exile around 400 B.C. Thus, depending on how one looks at it, Joel is either the first or last of the written prophets. Nothing is known about the prophet other than his name and his father's name. The name Joel means "Yahweh is God" and was fairly common in the Old Testament. Twelve other men by that name are mentioned in the Old Testament.

The book can be divided into two parts: 1:2-2:27 which focuses on the plague and the prophet's call to repentance, and 2:28-3:21 which comprises the prophet's vision of future events. In verses 1:2-12 the prophet asks if anyone can remember any devastation that has been as complete and awful as the present one. In verse 4 the locust is identified as the cutting locust, the swarming locust, the hopping locust, and the destroying locust. These four designations were likely local names "intended to denote four stages of development in their life cycle, or perhaps four successive hordes"[37] (p. 144) that swept across the land. The devastation is so complete that all areas of society are affected. The drunkard wails because the grape crop has been destroyed. The priest wails because there is such a scarcity of grain that the cereal offerings cannot be offered. In 1:13-18 the prophet sees in the dire circumstances a need for fasting and prayer. The chapter ends with yet another catastrophe: severe drought.

Chapter 2 opens with a description of the actual locust plague (up close and personal). Note the contrast of the language in verse 3, the garden of Eden (lush) becomes a desolate wilderness (barren). In verses 11-17 the prophet understands that the plague is not merely a natural occurrence and calls upon the people to repent and turn to God.

One of the things that doesn't seem to have emerged from the events of 9/11 is a call for national repentance. Yes, we have had our prayer meetings in public places where the week before many of the lost would have objected with the words "separation of church and state" (the last resort of the evil one if I ever heard one!), but has anyone attempted to understand why such a thing could have come upon us? Is there a connection between this tragedy and the moral decline of America's leaders? Many campaigns seem to emphasize, "Character doesn't count." Does the fact that it is easier to get into a prison to give out Bibles than to get into a school have anything to do with it? Joel was not one who was satisfied with the explanation: "Well, these things just run in cycles."

The prayers of the people were answered. God caused a strong north wind to blow that drove the locusts into the desert to the south of Judah and into the Dead and Mediterranean Seas.

Beginning in 2:28 and running through to the end of the book is the prophet's vision of future events. It begins with the prophecy of the outpouring of the Holy Spirit. Peter quoted this passage on the day of Pentecost. In verse 30 the vision takes a more ominous appearance as the doctrine of the great and terrible day of the LORD is introduced. Chapter three describes a scene of judgment, the Valley of Jehoshaphat. This valley has been identified with the Kidron Valley that lay between Jerusalem and the Mount of Olives. The name is only used here in the Old Testament and the term literally means "the valley of Yahweh judges." It seems to me that rather than being a proper name for a place, the term should be taken as "the valley where God judges." The imagery and tone of the passage are much like the Book of Revelation. The nations of the earth will gather in the Valley of Jezreel for a battle that in Hebrew is called Har-Magedon. I believe that Joel was getting a glimpse of this final event.

The book closes with an image of peace and prosperity for God's people. This likely is a picture of Christ's millennial kingdom.

Food for Thought: Joel 2:12-13 are a promise of hope. Return to God and He will return to you.

June 14
Bible Readings: 2 Chron. 24:3; 24:4-27 2 Kings 12:4-21 10:32-36; 13:1-4, 7-11, 14-20

I find it intriguing that the same priest Jehoiada that gave the king 'the rules for a king to live by' from Deuteronomy would then choose two wives for him. Why? Deuteronomy 17:17 says he must not take many wives. The only answer I have determined is that even priests (or ministers) are not above succumbing to peer-pressure -- everybody was doing it! A king's wealth and power were measured by the world, in part, by the number of wives he had. To Joash's credit, he did start repairs to the LORD's Temple.

In Israel, Jehu made a good start by eliminating Baal worship, but his failure to eliminate golden calf worship was about to have consequences. Israel loses territory to Syria to the point that all land east of the Jordan River is gone. Jehoahaz succeeds Jehu, his father, and likewise displeases God.

An unusual set of circumstances has taken place in Judah. Joash declared early in his reign that the LORD's Temple would be repaired from offerings and tax monies. Now, 23 years into his reign, the Temple is still in disrepair. As chief of the priests, Jehoiada has been in charge. It appears too much of the money has gone into the priests' support instead of the Temple repair. (Many of today's churches have the same situation.) A guarded chest was designated for the Temple offerings of money. Taxes were collected and counted by the Royal Secretary who represented the king and the Officer of the Chief Priest who represented the Temple. The Royal Secretary ranked just under the Minister of the Palace. He was responsible for all official correspondence, the official state archives, and other official duties as assigned.[7] After the Temple repairs were completed, articles needed for Temple worship services were made. Jehoiada died at 130 and was honored by being buried in the royal tombs in the City of David.[5]

After Jehoiada's death, Joash turns from the LORD. So many times people of every century have disciplined themselves and kept their lives in check because of an instrumental person in their lives who influenced them to do good. If God is not enthroned in their hearts, then their goodness dies with the one who inspired it. When Jehoiada's son, Zechariah, confronts Joash with his sin, the king has him stoned to death. Think of the irony. Jehoiada and his wife had saved Joash from being murdered (at great peril to their own lives). Now they are repaid by having this 'adopted' son kill their natural son. Obviously Joash had forsaken God. (This was not the Zechariah who wrote the Book of Zechariah.) Review 2 Chron. 15:2.

In the meantime, the Syrians repeatedly attack Israel. (King Asa really got his money's worth out of allying with them against Israel 100 years earlier!) Israel's army was reduced to less than three brigades with only 10 chariots and 50 cavalry. With Israel's army theoretically ineffective, Syria pushes on into Judah. Because the LORD had been forsaken in both Israel and Judah, God forsook them both. (America, are you listening?) God allowed a small Syrian force to overtake Jerusalem (the capital). King Joash of Judah took all the gold from the Temple and the royal palace and sent it to King Hazael of Syria as payment to call off the troops. It worked. When King Jehoahaz of Israel dies, his son Jehoash becomes king. He goes to visit Elisha who is terminally ill. The king cries out, "My father! My father! . . . The chariots and horsemen of Israel!"[1] (2 Kings 13:14) You will remember this was the same statement Elisha made upon seeing the fiery chariot and horses take Elijah to Heaven (2 Kings 2:12). Jehoash obviously knows Elisha is dying. Chariots and horsemen represented the strength and security of a country -- in this case Israel. It is used in relation to Elijah and Elisha as symbolic of their importance to the strength and security of the nation.[25] These prophets had been specially anointed by God and had imparted God's Will to the leadership of Israel. As a final prophecy, Elisha has the king shoot an arrow out the east window. East had double significance. It is the direction of the 'day of dawning' for the Hebrews. All other directions were based on orientation to the east (as we now use North on our compass). East also was the direction of where this particular Aphek (there were about 4 towns with this name) was located.[5] Elisha prophesies that Israel would be triumphant over Syria (Aram). Then Elisha told the king to take his arrows and strike the ground. Elisha became very angry when the king stopped at three strikes. (Don't you think a king would feel rather silly beating arrows on the floor, especially in front of this revered man? If someone had suddenly entered the room, it would appear the king was throwing a childish tantrum!) Elisha prophesies that Israel's victories over Syria would now be limited to only three. (See, humbleness is more blessed than pride!)

In a murder conspiracy, the King of Judah is assassinated in his sleep for killing Zechariah. It is interesting to note that each of the conspirators had a mother descended from Lot. Even though their motive had been right, their method was wrong. These people had the right motive: to worship their creator and sustainer. But they had the wrong method: worshipping pagan gods.

Food for Thought: Are your motives and methods right? Do you worship God when in church or is it a social event? One of my pet peeves is having my worship service diminished by the constant talking around me. On a recent holiday I was unable to hear the words of a mini-musical that had so painstakingly been prepared by the choir. Why? Because a deacon and his wife were too busy visiting with all their children and grandchildren sitting over several rows. Christian fellowship is a wonderful delight but worshipping God is my very reason for being. My soul needs that lift. Are your motives good but your methods askew?

June 15
<u>Bible Readings: 2 Kings 12:21; 14:1-16, 23-24; 13:12-13, 20-25, 2 Chron. 24:27; 25:1-24</u>

Amaziah now comes to the throne of Judah. He executes his father's assassins and reigns for 25 years following God but failing to remove the high places.

In Israel, Elisha performs a miracle from beyond the grave (or is that in the grave?). Moabite bandits often carried out hit-and-run missions on unsuspecting Israelites. During one of these raids, some frightened mourners threw the deceased into Elisha's tomb in preparation for skeedaddling (that's Southern for run like crazy). Upon touching Elisha's bones, the corpse sprang to life!

Ben-Hadad III, son of Hazael, is now on the throne in Syria. As Elisha prophesied, he was defeated three times by the king of Israel, who regained the captured Israelite towns. Judah's King Amaziah decides its time for him to regain Edom. He organizes an army based on drafting young men 20 years old and older. They were organized into five divisions: Judeans made up the 3 divisions that carried shields and spears, Benjamites made up the other two divisions that carried shields and bows.[7] To further ensure his success, Amaziah hired 100,000 mercenaries from Israel. In route to Edom, a man of God tells Amaziah that God will not bless any campaign that involves pagan mercenary soldiers. But Amaziah had already paid 100 talents for them. He gives a typical twenty-first century response to the man of God, "What about my money?" The prophet's answer is a simple statement of fact -- God can empower you or overthrow you. Amaziah sends the mercenaries home that are now angered by their lost potential of war loot. On their way home, they kill 3,000 Judean citizens between the towns of Beth Horon, Judah and Samaria, Israel. But Amaziah must worry first about his Edom campaign. Edom stretched from the southern end of the Dead Sea to the Gulf of Aqaba. When Judah lost Edom, Judah's commercial trade route had also gone. A large section of the King's Highway runs north from the Gulf of Aqaba through the length of Edom. Amaziah engaged the Edomites in the Valley of Salt. Sela, the capital of Edom, is located there in the Wadi Musa or Valley of Moses,[5] currently called Wadi al Arabah.[4] Sela was near Mt. Hor (where Aaron died) in the Wilderness of Zin. Petra now stands at the site.[5] Amaziah inflicted 10,000 casualties and captured 10,000 more that he subsequently threw off a cliff. His movement away from God is now obvious. Victory has gone to his head. Amaziah seized the Edomite gods and brought them back to Judah. As a result, God abandons Judah. But Amaziah is feeling powerful from his victory. Jehoash, King of Israel, was also feeling powerful from his Syrian victories. They march against each other in the Valley of Sorek, meeting at Beth Shemesh (about 15 miles west of Jerusalem).[7] God is so angered at Amaziah that Israel soundly routes Judah's army causing them to disperse and flee. The army of Israel advances on Jerusalem and breaks down 600 feet of the city wall. Jehoash plunders the Temple and palace. Apparently, Joash (the previous king of Judah) had so stripped them of valuables to pay off Syria to prevent further invasion that Jehoash is disappointed in his hope of great amounts of loot. As insurance to extract future wealth from Judah, Jehoash takes hostages back to Israel.[7] When Jehoash dies, Jeroboam II, Jehoash's son, succeeds him and proves to be an evil king.

Food for Thought: Are we sometimes disappointed because we don't get more of the loot? Do we take hostages? Certainly, we do. We just call it mind games. You know the kind parents play when they say, "You can do what you want, just remember you will be the one to pay for any mistakes!" Of course, you are too afraid to do anything then. Or maybe a gift giver who says something like, "You mean you are using that good stuff for everyday?" [Was I suppose to encase it in glass as a museum piece?] Well, there was a time when I was too particular about my material things. In some ways I still am. But now I realize it is because there is not enough strength or years left for me to work and purchase more. Before I was particular because the object meant too much to me. Now I am particular because of need. Loot has taken a back seat. When God moves to the forefront, materialism moves to the backfield. Invest in living for God -- a gift you'll use every day!

June 16
Bible Readings: Jonah, 2 Kings 13:5-6; 14:25-27

The book of Jonah is the most peculiar of all the books of prophecy. Most of these books contain very little information about the actual prophet and are dedicated almost exclusively to the prophet's words or visions. The reverse is true in Jonah. His message is short, "Forty days more and Ninevah will be overturned."[1] (Jonah 3:4) The rest of the book is concerned with Jonah's resistance to God's mission for him, Jonah's anger with God for pardoning Ninevah, and God's effort in teaching Jonah a lesson about being merciful.

The book is also unusual in terms of its author. All of the other books of prophecy are written by the prophet whose name the book bears. However, someone else wrote the book of Jonah. The prophet is always referred to in the third person and information is included that the prophet is likely not to have known (e.g., how could Jonah have known the details of the sailors' repentance since he was not present?). (1:16)

It is perhaps best to think of Jonah as a short story that has a spiritual meaning. Other Bible books of this nature are Ruth and Esther. This interpretation does not argue that the characters were not historical or that the action recorded in the narrative did not happen. We know that Jonah was an historical figure (2 Kings 14:25). What this interpretation wants to stress is that there is something far more important here than the big fish or the fast growing vine. Just as the book of Ruth shows that not all Moabites were bad and at least one could become part of the people of God, Jonah shows that God is concerned with the souls of all people everywhere.

Let's consider the author's intention. During the time the Jews spent in captivity in Babylon (around 605-535 B.C.), they developed a strong distrust of foreigners. They also felt that the varied national groups in Palestine after the exile hindered them from restoring a truly Jewish community. These attitudes are somewhat reflected in the books of Nehemiah and Ezra. The Jews were correct in being careful of foreign influence; after all, the influence of the Canaanites had corrupted Israel and brought about her judgment. Over time, however, this Jewish exclusivism, this 'we' versus 'them' mentality, caused the Jews to lose sight of God's original mission for Israel. In Exodus 19:5-6 God called Israel to be a kingdom of priests. No doubt, God intended to use Israel to win the world, but in the Old Testament, instead of Israel influencing others, others influenced Israel.[37] Ninevah was destined to become the capital of Assyria. Joppa was originally located in land given to Dan. Joppa served as the seaport city for Jerusalem. When Jonah fled God to board a ship to Tarshish, he was going in the opposite direction of Ninevah. In fact, he was headed 2500 miles in the opposite direction! Jonah's childish disobedience is contrasted to the sailors' faith and obedience. Jonah knew all about the one true God but flagrantly disregarded His Will. The sailors knew little about God but were obedient. Jonah, God's man, showed no compassion for the Ninevites, but the sailors had compassion for Jonah. Jonah's selfish concern over the dead vine is contrasted to God's concern for the souls of pagan Ninevah. The three days and nights Jonah spends in the great fish are symbolic of the death, burial, and resurrection of Jesus.[108]

The author of the book of Jonah exposes the narrow nationalistic attitudes of the Jews and reveals the redemptive design of God for all mankind.

Food for Thought: The sequel to disobedience is a growing inability to obey. When people will not do right, the time comes when they cannot do right. In fact, the ability to distinguish between right and wrong no longer exists. We often speak of our conscience as if it were an innate part of us that cannot be impacted by our actions. This is not true. God's Holy Spirit forms our conscience. It is by this guidance and the Word living in us that our conscience is shaped to do right.

June 17
Bible Readings: Hosea 1-3:5

The prophet Hosea is one of the earliest of the written prophets. Based upon his opening comments, we know that his ministry must have comprised a minimum of 40 years. He was a contemporary of Isaiah and Amos; likely coming a little after Amos and a little before Isaiah. He was a prophet to the Northern Kingdom of Israel although it is likely that he migrated to Judah before 722 B.C. when Israel was taken captive by the Assyrians and deported to lands in the east.

Hosea's prophecy is largely related to the tragedy of his own life. Through his unhappy marriage with Gomer, he was able to understand God's anguish and disappointment with the behaviors of Israel.

One of the most serious issues in understanding the book is how we are to interpret 1:2. Some commentators believe that the marriage story is allegorical, a hypothetical story told to illustrate a larger point. There is much merit in this view, but several elements in the story do not seem to fit. In an allegory, the names have symbolic meanings, and the various actions have symbolic values that are equated with meanings that lie outside the story itself and thus relate to the major point the prophet is trying to make: namely Israel's unfaithfulness to God. Thus, we would expect to find that Hosea's wife would have a name like "unfaithful" or "wandering." The name Gomer, however, means "to achieve." Also, given an allegorical interpretation it is difficult to understand what is the symbolic significance of the daughter's (Lo-ruhamah) weaning before the conception of the second son (1:8).

It seems best to understand the story as an actual experience but written from hindsight rather than foresight. Most of us see God's activity in our lives as we look back; the same was probably true with Hosea. Thus, we may understand that when Hosea married Gomer, in so far as he knew, she was a pure woman who may have been a little more interested in the Canaanite religion than she should have been. The early years of the marriage seemed to go well, and there is every indication that the first boy Jezreel belonged to Hosea. Sometime after the birth of their son, Hosea began to see a change in Gomer. When their second child, a daughter, is born, he suspects the child is not his. He calls her Lo-ruhamah meaning "unpitied" (1:6-7). By the time the third child is born, Hosea's previous suspicions have been confirmed. He knows this boy is not his and calls him Lo-Ammi meaning "not my people."

In chapter 2 we find suggestions that Hosea likely confronted his wife and considered exposing her for what she was. She must give up her sinful ways (2:2), "lest I . . . expose her." He even encourages the children to appeal to their mother. Gomer apparently left Hosea, or he divorced her. She finally ended up in the position of a slave.

After some time had passed, Hosea realized that he still loved Gomer. He finds her being auctioned off in the slave market and purchases her for 15 shekels of silver and 7.5 bushels of barley. The price of an average slave was 30 shekels; Gomer's price indicates that by the time of her purchase she was pretty well worn out. Also, the fact that her purchase price was a combination of currency and commodities indicates that Hosea was a poor man and may have had difficulty raising the purchase price.

Hosea's purchase does not bring immediate restoration with Gomer. She is separated from her lovers and must learn to live without them (3:2-4). The hope of regaining her position as Hosea's wife is promised (3:5). We will look at other issues related to the book tomorrow.

Food for Thought: As we look back upon our lives, we can see, like Hosea, mistakes that we have made. However, if we try to look at these experiences from God's perspective, they sometimes become doorways to understanding great spiritual truths. For this type of revelation, we usually have to spend much time in prayer and meditation. Don't just read God's word, ponder its message for you.

Verse of the Week: **Hosea 10:12** "Sow for yourselves righteousness; reap in mercy; break up your fallow ground, for it is time to seek the LORD, till He comes and rains righteousness on you." (KJV)

June 18
Bible Readings: Hosea 4-9

Anyone closely reading the book of Hosea will notice the strong sexual overtones of the book. Passages like 1:2, 2:2-3, 3:3, and 9:1 all evoke images of sexual promiscuity. These passages are partially inspired by the nature of Hosea's marital problems and the parallel that he sees between his experience with Gomer and God's experience with unfaithful Israel. Another factor that contributes to these images is the prophet's assault on Canaanite religion.

From the time of the wilderness wandering at Baal-Peor, the Jews had come into contact with the fertility cult of Baal. The Canaanites believed that Baal was the god of winter rain and was responsible for bringing, with his wife Anat, fertility to the earth. [Anat was one of many names (or wives) that have been used in connection with the female consort of Baal.] The religion was formerly introduced into the Northern Kingdom during the reign of Ahab through his wife Jezebel who came from a country where Baal was worshipped. Despite Elijah and Elisha's battle against the religion, its practice seemed to become more and more entrenched in Israel.

One of the major problems was that its beliefs and rituals degraded the people. One of its most degrading doctrines was how fertility was released upon the earth. The ancients, by means of causal reasoning, believed that sexual union was the source of fertility. Cows, ewes, and mares became pregnant as a result of a physical act. The Canaanites wrongly concluded that fertility would come to the natural world if the god and goddess likewise engaged in such an act. To encourage this action, the Canaanites had temple prostitutes in an official position within their religion. As part of the worship in the temple of Baal, a worshiper would engage in a sexual act with the temple prostitute in the hope that Baal and his consort Anat would likewise engage in such an act on a cosmic level.

Israel's false religions led them to practice human sacrifice and to worship an idol in the shape of a bull. In many places in Hosea, we can see the prophet attacking these degraded views of so-called religious faith.

1. He sees its theology as wrongly giving credit to Baal for what are rightly gifts of God. (2:5, 8-9)
2. He declares its sacrifices are futile, offered to the wrong gods in the wrong places for the wrong reasons. (4:19, 5:7)
3. He rejects its means of revelation as lifeless instruments. (4:12)
4. He deplores its sexual acts, brazen blends of lust and magic. (4:13-14)
5. He mocks its hollowness -- people kissing calves (13:2) adoring the products of their own craftsmen. (8:6)
6. He condemns its savagery -- the vicious sacrificing of little children (5:2).[38]

Food for Thought: People today still have idols. We call them movie stars. If you have even glanced at the magazine rack at the store or have seen a commercial or have seen a TV program/movie, then you know these are sexual idols. Just when I thought they couldn't be more perverted, I am always disappointed to find out they can. These are the people who demand large sums of money (who the world fights for the privilege of paying them) for the right to demoralize our minds and turn our hearts from God. You can't even watch public television anymore without making a moral decision about every program. Having followed closely after the Victorian period, those of my generation are still shocked by such behavior. But in the days of the ancient Hebrews, every conceivable perverted action was carried out in the name of religion, including mutilation and murder. As we view the powers of the Middle East now, the religious beliefs aren't much different, only less public. People of all countries need our prayers. Pray for a return to the one, true God. Lift up missionaries in prayer for God's strength and protection.

June 19
Bible Readings: Hosea 10-14, 2 Kings 14:17-22; 15:1-4, 2 Chron. 25:25-28; 26:1-15

When a Christian reads the Old Testament, he/she should always consider how the passage or book relates to the New Testament and how New Testament writers used the book. Although Hosea is a short book, it is quoted several times in the New Testament and a common metaphor used in the Bible to describe our relationship to God originates with Hosea.

1. Hosea's prediction of people calling the rocks to cover them from judgment (10:8) is repeated in Luke 23:30.
2. Hosea's appeal to the people in 10:12 to "sow with a view of righteousness" is reflected in Paul's comment in 2 Corinthians 9:10.
3. His idea of our praise to God as being the fruit of our lips is similarly expressed in Hebrews 13:15.
4. God's account of His care for Israel in the Exodus (11:1) is thought fulfilled in Christ's descent into Egypt (Matt. 2:15).
5. God's ransoming the people from the power of Sheol (death) (Hosea 13:14) becomes for Paul a cry of resurrection victory (1 Corinthians 15:55).
6. The changing of Hosea's children's names from negative (1:6, 9) to positive (1:11, 2:1, 2:23) becomes a prophecy of the inclusion of Gentiles into the church (Romans 9:25, 1 Peter 2:10).[38] (p. 47-48)

In addition to these quotations (or at least references), Hosea's metaphor of God's marriage to His people is repeated in later prophetic literature (Jer. 3 and Ezekiel 16) and influences the idea of the church being the Bride of Christ. This image of our relationship to God is mentioned in Ephesians 5:21-23 and is a dominant idea in Revelation 19 and 21.

Food for Thought: The Bible is the inspired word of God. From the beginning of mankind until today, God has been revealing His plan for us. As we continue studying together, ask God to reveal His plan for you.

June 20
Bible Readings: Amos 1-4

The prophet Amos is generally thought of as being the earliest of the prophets whose sermons were recorded. He preached during the reigns of Uzziah of Judah (783-742) and Jeroboam II of Israel (786-746). In both countries this time was a period of political stability and peace. The nations were prosperous and were transitioning from an agricultural to a more commercial way of life. Religious services were well attended (9:1), tithes and offerings were joyously and punctually given (4:4-5), and impressive festivals were being held (5:22-23). Beneath all this outward show was a darker side. The people weren't practicing what they professed. Amos was sent to warn them to "walk the walk" as well as "talk the talk."

The book consists of two subdivisions: the words of Amos (1-6) and the visions of Amos (7-9). The words of Amos take many forms. There are judgments (1:2), sermonettes (3:1-2, 4:1-3, and 5:1-3), a dirge (5:2), woes (5:18, 6:1), and doxologies (4:13, 5:8-9, and 9:5-6). There are 5 visions in Amos, more than any other prophet. Amos sees a vision of a locust plague, a vision of a great fire, a vision of a plumb line, a vision of summer fruit, and a vision of God standing beside the altar.

Concerning the person of Amos, nothing is known other than what we are told in the book. He was from Tekoa (1:1) a small town about 11 miles south of Jerusalem 18 miles west of the Dead Sea. Other biblical references to Tekoa are 2 Samuel 14:2, 23:26 and 2 Chronicles 11:6, 20:20. Amos is called a shepherd and a dresser of sycamore trees. A dresser of sycamore trees was involved in picking and processing the small cluster like figs from the sycamore trees. Because sycamores did not grow around Tekoa, it is logical to deduce that Amos was a poor migrant farm worker spending part of the year in the Jordan Valley or coastal plains harvesting fruit and the rest of the year tending sheep. Although Amos likely had very little formal education, he had a brilliant mind. In the first two chapters he weaves a web of logic that would have impressed the Athenian philosophers on Mars Hill.

The book begins with a bang: "The LORD roars from Zion." In the first two chapters, Amos delivers eight judgments upon the two Jewish states (Israel and Judah) and six neighboring nations. The judgments follow a common formula:

1. Each begins with the messenger formula (Thus says the LORD)
2. General accusation (for three transgressions, etc.)
3. A specific accusation introduced by "because"
4. Announcement of judgment
   A. God will not hold back punishment any longer.
   B. God will act in judgment.
5. Messenger formula (Says the LORD)

One should pay close attention to the order of the nations. Amos begins with Damascus, who surely had no sympathizers. He continues with Gaza and Tyre. No doubt, his listeners are really engaged in the message adding a hearty "Amen." Then Amos begins to condemn Edom, Ammon, and Moab, Israel's distant relatives; his crowd is less enthusiastic. Amos continues condemning Judah, Israel's brother state to the south. By now Amos can only get a meek Baptist "Amen" or a mere Quaker "nod." The sermon is much less enjoyable. Finally, Amos condemns them. He has laid a trap for his listeners, for how can they excuse in themselves what they have already condemned in others. Note also the formulaic "for three transgressions and for four." The idea is that three stands for enough; their sin is full and complete. The fourth is more than enough; it is the straw that broke the camel's back. We'll look at chapters 3-6 tomorrow.

Food for Thought: Amos was preaching during a time of prosperity. Life was good for the Israelites, maybe too good. Satisfaction had led to complacency. Complacency led to boredom that led to sin. Keep yourself busy and you can avoid boredom. The best way to stay busy is to be involved with Christian outreach activities. There are plenty of nursing homes or shut-in elderly who need errands run, chores done, or just want company to visit. In larger cities, there are many families of long-term sick children who need assistance with daily activities so they can stay near their loved one. Caregivers need to be relieved every week so they can have some time to get away and renew themselves. Simply sitting with an invalid can provide a much needed service for a caregiver. It also gives the patient a change. Hospital visitation is an important program. In short, there are numerous services that can be done if you CHOOSE to use your time for the Lord. Otherwise, boredom will lead to thoughts and often actions that aren't consistent with living for Christ. Serve God today.

June 21
<u>Bible Readings: Amos 5-7:9; 8:1-9:15</u>

In chapter three Amos begins to punch holes in some of his hearers' preconceived notions. They rightly believed that they were God's chosen people, but they wrongly believed that this special relationship would cause God to overlook their sins. Verse two punctures that notion. Verses 3-6 ask a series of rhetorical questions whose answer is obviously "no." His point is to show that neither will God bring judgment upon His people without first revealing His plans to the prophets.

In 9-15 Amos proclaims judgment upon the cities (Samaria and Bethel) of Israel. He also attacks the wealthy, whose superfluity of wealth and abuse of power are a privilege, who are a major source of Israel's problems. Her destruction is to be severe. Amos compares the remains of the destroyed city with the devoured remains of a lion's prey (12). His indictment against them (10) is particularly troubling, "They do not know how to do right." As has been said, "The sequel to disobedience is the growing inability to obey. When people will not do right, the time comes when they cannot do right."[37] (p. 103)

Chapter four provides numerous examples of the nation's depravity. The women here are light years away from the ideal woman of Proverbs 31. They are lazy drunkards who encourage their husbands to oppress the poor, so they can have more wealth to lavish upon themselves. In verses 4 and 5 Amos attacks the people's worship. Bethel and Gilgal were important religious sanctuaries in ancient Israel. The point Amos is making is that there is no such thing as right worship without right conduct. Remember, piously going to the Lord's House on Sunday is hypocrisy (and a sin) if you've been running with the devil all week.

Amos argues (6-12) that the people need to repent and refers to a number of recent calamities that God has sent on Israel to lead her to repentance. These calamities include (1) famine, (2) drought, (3) mildew, (4) locusts, (5) pestilence, (6) war, and (7) earthquake. (These last items would suggest that Amos' ministry spanned several years (See 1:1).) Chapter 4 concludes with a praise of God's grandeur.

Chapter five begins with a dirge (funeral song) for the house of Israel. She has been devastated with no hope of recovery. Some commentators suggest that Amos may actually have attired himself with the garb of a professional mourner and sung this song to the people. Verses 4-7 turn from the death of Israel to the means she can use to escape her death. Note that salvation was not to be found in Bethel or Gilgal but rather in justice and righteousness. The most memorable verse in Amos that best summarizes the prophet's theology is verse 15. "Hate evil, and love good, and establish justice in the gate."

In verse 18, Amos brings up the idea of the Day of the LORD. His concept of the day was different from his hearers. They believed that the Day of the LORD would bring judgment upon all their enemies. Amos believed that it was a day that all sin would be judged, and considering Israel's record, it wasn't a day she should be anxiously awaiting.

In chapter six, Amos attacks the leisure class in all their finery and play. They are proud of their accomplishments (vs. 13). Amos warns them that troubling days are ahead.

Amos 7 begins with a series of visions. The first is of a great locust plague and the second is a great fire. In both instances, Amos prays that the judgment might cease, and in each instance the prophet's prayer turns back the disaster. The great deep (vs. 4) was the primeval ocean that the ancients believed flowed under the earth. It is referred to elsewhere in Gen. 1:2, 7:1; Ps. 24:2, 36:6; Isa. 51:10.

In the third vision, God shows Amos why the judgment is necessary. Just as the plumb line shows that the wall is so crooked it must be torn down and replaced, a moral plumb line shows that the present nation is crooked beyond simple reform and must be torn down and replaced with something better.

The chapter ends with an exchange between a priest, who remembers the status quo, and the prophet. The priest is tired of this southerner (remember Amos is from Judah) criticizing the way things are done up north. Amaziah had heard Amos' words correctly but responds incorrectly. As a result he has condemned himself and his family.

Chapter eight also begins with a vision. Amos sees a basket of summer fruit and hears the voice of God pronouncing an end to Israel. Summer fruit represents an end to the harvest and fall, and the beginning of winter. Amos understands that this is the beginning of the end for Israel. As if in one last desperate attempt, Amos warns the people a final time in 8:4-14. He enumerates their sins in 4-6. In 7-14 he describes their punishments: earthquake (7-8), a type of disaster that produces an unrelenting mourning (9-10), and the departure of God's Presence from them (11-14).

Chapter nine begins with a vision of God standing beside the altar. The Temple is destroyed and, despite all of the efforts of the people to hide themselves, they are brought to judgment. The prophet concludes with the image of a brighter future. After the people face their judgment and learn to obey, they will be blessed with plenty. The statement in 13, "When the plowman will overtake the reaper," is an indicator of a great harvest. It takes about 3-4 times as long to plow a field as to harvest it. When the plowman overtakes the reaper, the harvest is indeed great. The book ends with a promise of security that all enjoy who put their faith in God.

Food for Thought: Have you ever had a vision? Boy, I have!! Every time I see a snippet of a horror movie (which I avoid at all costs) or even the news these days, I have nightmares. I will never forget the first episode of The Invisible Man. I had visions of invisible men for weeks (all night long)! Now I wonder, how did Amos know the difference between God's visions and the world's? After all, the items in the visions were recognizable from the world around Amos. Keep in mind one of the lessons we learned from the beginning of our year: God uses the ordinary occurrences of our existence to do extraordinary things. The world calls them "luck," "charmed," "fortunate," "good omens," "intuition," "good vibes," and "special auras." But believers recognize the handiwork of the Lord. Often it comes as a result of prayer. Proverb 15:29 says, "The LORD is far from the wicked, but he hears the prayer of the righteous."[1] Take time to pray every day. God wants to hear from you.

June 22
<u>Bible Readings: Amos 7:10-17; 2 Kings 14:28-29; 15:5, 8-18 2 Chron. 26:16-21</u>

Amos had come from Tekoa, Judah to Israel to prophesy against the golden calf worship that served as a substitute for worshipping God in His Temple in Jerusalem. (Now, imitation butter is still just margarine by a different name.) God is not an imitation nor can He be imitated. You either worship God or you don't. Amaziah, priest for the Bethel calf temple, was very upset by Amos' preaching. (This is a totally different Amaziah from the one who was king of Judah.) Why would Amaziah be upset? Especially, if he believed he was worshipping the one true God (which would be the right motive but the wrong method). To begin with Amos' third vision definitely threatened the future and security of the king and kingdom of Israel. By so doing, Amaziah's own future was in jeopardy. After all, the religious system of Israel had been designed, controlled, and maintained by the king. Therefore, it was in the political interests of the king to put down any insurrections, rebellions, or conspiracies.[37]

Amaziah verbally and openly attacked Amos personally and spiritually. He sneeringly calls Amos a "seer," in other words a 'professional prophet' or someone who prophesies for money or power rather than as a man of God. Amaziah further tells Amos to get out of town and never come back! Another way to phrase Amaziah's intent would be to "go hawk your wares elsewhere!" At this point, Amos could have easily taken off for home. But he didn't. He calmly stood his ground as a representative of God, delivering God's message. Amos promptly condemns every man, woman, and child in Israel. They will certainly be exiled to a foreign land.[37]

Israel's fate is sealed. God's love is infinite, but His patience is finite. The message is clear, "Repent and turn to God." Israel is spiraling downward. Jeroboam II dies and is succeeded by Zechariah who is assassinated 6 months later. (This is a different Zechariah than the prophet or the son of Jehoiada the priest.) The assassin, Shallum, reigns for one month before he is assassinated. Menahem, the murderer, becomes king.

In Judah, King Uzziah is so conceited that he decides he will offer incense to God himself. After all, he had been greatly helped by God (2 Chron. 26:15). Why wouldn't God want an offering made personally by the king? But, as always, God only wanted obedience, and pride goes before destruction (Prov. 16:18). Uzziah was leprous the rest of his life. He was quarantined in a separate house and most of his administrative duties were turned over to his son Jotham who became a co-regent.

Food for Thought: Think of a time when you were personally attacked. How did you feel? How would you have felt if you had been a stranger in another country? Amos was certainly doing God's work and he drew strength from God. God calls us to do many tasks for Him; some are not fun, some are not short, some are not easy, and many are not popular. If our faith is strong and our communication with God is continuous, then we are assured of the path we are to take. Being sure makes ALL the difference! Are you sure of your paths? Do you know God as your personal Savior, Friend, Redeemer, Counselor, King? Today is the day to be sure.

June 23
Bible Readings: Isaiah 1:1-26; 5:1-23; 2:6-18; 3:8-4:1; 32:9-11

BACKGROUND: Isaiah is one of four prophets commonly known as the Major Prophets: Jeremiah, Ezekiel, Daniel, Isaiah. In the 1990s, there was a movie called "Return of the Jedi." Not being a Star Wars fan, I know nothing much about it. But it did provide me with an excellent tool to use for remembering the Major Prophets -- JEDI. Each letter represents one of the aforementioned prophets. Jeremiah wrote both the book bearing his name and Lamentations. I've never forgotten the Major Prophets since.

Isaiah is one of the longest books of the Bible. More importantly, it makes the prophetic bridge between the Old Testament and New Testament by containing so many prophecies about the coming Messiah. Isaiah's Messianic prophecies are not clouded or obscured but are instead clearly and distinctly describing the birth, death, and resurrection of Jesus. Having the advantage of hindsight, we can only be awed at the accuracy of Isaiah's foresight.

Isaiah's ministry started the year Uzziah died, about 742-740 B.C. (Isa. 6:1). Isaiah preached for 40 years (until 700 B.C. approximately).[39] The book of Isaiah was written over a space between 740-681 B.C.[15] Isaiah was married and had two sons.[39] There is no dispute that chapters 1-39 were written by Isaiah. These chapters address the people of Judah during the time prior to their captivity. Chapters 40-66 are believed by some to be written by Isaiah's followers during the period of captivity in Babylon (around 550 B.C.). This would be two centuries after Isaiah died. Thus, these chapters are sometimes referred to as "Second Isaiah." Others believe these latter chapters were simply Isaiah's prophecies projected far into the future; therefore, Isaiah wrote them all. There are other interesting facts to be noted in the organization of the book and the life of the prophet. Isaiah 1-39 has the same number of chapters as the Old Testament has books: 39. Isaiah 40-66 has the same number of chapters as the New Testament has books: 27.[5] 'First Isaiah' addresses the fallen state of man and the impending judgment while

'Second Isaiah' addresses the Messiah and Savior who brings forgiveness and mercy to those who repent. These parallel the messages of the Old and New Testaments. Isaiah the prophet was probably a relative of the royal house of Judah and was most likely born in Jerusalem. He served in King Uzziah's court and was generally thought to have been a scribe. This would certainly have prepared him for the writing skills and religious training needed to be a major prophet during a turbulent time. Isaiah repeatedly refers to God as the "Holy One of Israel." He distinctly describes the location and birth of the Messiah over 700 years before Jesus was born! Subsequently, his description of Jesus' death on the cross as a Suffering Servant is more vivid and detailed than any account in the New Testament.[5] Commentators vary on the number of quotations in the New Testament from the Book of Isaiah with a low of 50[15] to a high of 400.[39] As you study, you may want to try to establish your own number.

It is not insignificant to notice that Isaiah preached 40 years. Certainly, this was 'a long time' as our number would indicate. But this was even more exceptional when we realize God's merciful patience and efforts to turn the people back to Him. Judah will soon stoop to child sacrifice (Jer. 32:35). God loves us always, but even His patience has a limit. For 40 years, Isaiah persevered; some of the people would repent and turn back to God, some would hold fast to God as they always had, but most would continue headlong into destruction. As you read 'First Isaiah,' you cannot help but compare it to our nation today. Won't you repent and turn back to God? Or maybe you are one who will continue to hold fast. Just maybe, you are the one God has called to preach repentance and salvation to His people! Many are called, but few will come.

One reader wrote this week and expressed a longing to get started in the New Testament, to enjoy the grace of God rather than the judgment period we are now studying. God does not leave His people long without comfort. As any good parent, God loves us even during our judgment. Before they go into exile, you will see God sending words of comfort to His people. God stands ready to provide us comfort even when we are suffering the consequences of our sin.

LESSON: Many parents can relate to Isaiah 1:2. Regardless of how well children are reared, they often rebel against their parents. God's children rebelled, too! (See, you can't always blame parents!) We are even told that the children of God had become corrupt from the top of their heads to the soles of their feet! Jerusalem is being ravaged by the devastation of the war.

God asks the question all parents ponder sooner or later, "What more could have been done . . . than I have done . . . ?" (Isa. 5:4) The children of God's delight have strayed far from their upbringing. Isaiah now elaborates on their specific sins.

1. Ritualistic Religion - Offerings and sacrifices were being done as a result of ritual (this is how we've always done it) instead of out of a repentant and thankful heart.
2. Injustice - The people were dishonest, took bribes, and oppressed the poor. They were murderers literally and figuratively.
3. Idolatry - Idols were everywhere and the Jews befriended the pagans.
4. Pride - They were arrogant in their wealth and power.
5. Sinful Leaders - Judah's leaders are compared to the open, rampant sin of the people of Sodom. The elders and leaders have led God's people astray.
6. Sinful Women - The women have become more interested in their apparel, riches, and appearance than in living godly lives.
7. Greed - God's people were increasing their own wealth rather than ministering in His Name.
8. Party Animals - Many of the young adults in our world gleefully categorize themselves under this label - - a label of condemnation.
9. Arrogance - Those who are arrogant will be humbled.

10. Excusing Sin - God's people were thinking up ways to present their sin so that they appeared righteous. Shakespeare said, "A rose by any other name is still just as sweet." (Romeo and Juliet) Likewise, stinkweed by any other name still stinks!
11. Drunkenness - Condemned.

Food for Thought: God didn't pull any punches. Each judgment was delivered squarely on the mark. As you read Isaiah, compare the sins of Judah to those of our world. Is there any wonder why we are seeing worldwide destruction?

June 24
Bible Readings: Isaiah 5:24-30; 1:18-20, 27-31; 2:1-5, 19-3:7; 4:2-6; 6:1-13
2 Kings 15:6-7, 19-28, 32-35, 2 Chron. 26:22-23; 27:1-6, 8

As Judge, God has enumerated Judah's sins and now His anger burns against the people. They are condemned and their punishment will be devastation at the hands of foreign nations. Isaiah's imagery is unnerving. God whistles and the foreign nations come running, ready to devour. Those who have backslidden into sin will be broken. But the lost will perish. No one can rescue them. God will prove just how worthless pagan idols are.

God calls the people to reason. Even after they have been sentenced, God appeals one more time; He offers one last chance to repent. You will recognize that Isaiah 1:18-20 is the basis for a well-known hymn.

Isaiah 4:2 starts off "In that day ..." This, of course, refers to the Day of the LORD or, as Christians generally call it, Judgment Day. The Branch of the LORD is Jesus who is also the "fruit of the land." Again we see fire and judgment used together. Fire can be used to 'judge' by purification or used to 'judge' by destruction. All will face Judgment Day. Some will be deemed as children of God and go to Heaven; others will be lost forever, continually burning in the flames of hell.

In the last days, Mt. Moriah will be raised above the hills (possibly by earthquake). The law of God will be administered from Jerusalem with Jesus as King. The swords of the people will be beaten into plowshares once more (compare to Joel 3:10).

We are back now to our history lesson. In 2 Kings 16, the kings of Syria and Israel decided to form an alliance against Assyria. King Ahaz of Judah refused to join. So the other two turned and attacked Judah. To get out of his bind, Ahaz paid the Assyrian king Tiglath-Pileser (also called Pul) to be his ally. Two or three years later, the Assyrians have taken Damascus and carried the Israelites into slavery. Judah always seems to get a big bang for their bucks! Remember Judah had hired Syria to fight Israel early in the history of the divided kingdom.

King Menahem of Israel dies and is succeeded by his son Pekahiah. Two years later, Pekah, who declared himself as king, assassinated Pekahiah. Pekah ruled for 20 years. All these kings were evil as we have come to expect in Israel.

In Judah, Uzziah died. His son Jotham reigned 16 years. Jotham followed the LORD, but the people did not. When Uzziah died, Isaiah received the call from God to preach. His response was one of despair. He declares himself a sinner living among sinners. A favorite verse is Isaiah's response to God's call. Isaiah offers no resistance, no excuses. He simply said, "Here I am. Send me!"

Food for Thought: King Jotham became powerful conquering the Ammonites and receiving much wealth from them. The Bible says this was because "he walked steadfastly before the LORD his God."[1] (2 Chron. 27:6). Are you walking steadfastly before God?

Verse of the Week: **Micah 4:1** "In the last days the mountain of the LORD's temple will be established as chief among the mountains; it will be raised above the hills, and peoples will stream to it."

June 25
Bible Readings: Micah 1-2

While Isaiah came from the royal court and ministered unto the officials and people of Jerusalem, Micah came from the common people. Micah is also a prophet to Judah, serving those outside Jerusalem. The Book of Micah is divided into three sections. The first consists of chapters 1 and 2. Section 2 contains chapters 3-5, and the final section is comprised of chapters 6 and 7. Micah begins by condemning Israel and predicting the total destruction of Samaria, Israel's capital. Then he moves his sights to Judah. As with naming people, towns had also been given names that reflected their nature or described their appearance. Micah uses a play on their names when he describes their fate as being like that of Israel. For example, Beth Ophrah means 'house of dust' so Micah says its people will roll in the dust. Write in the meaning of the following names and you will begin to understand Micah's message: Gath (wine press), Shaphir (beautiful), Zaanan (going out), Beth Ezel (adjoining house), Maroth (bitterness), Lachish (team), Moresheth Gath (possession of Gath)[Micah's hometown], Aczib (deception), Mareshah (summit), Adullam (refuge). We can't fully comprehend the extent of his puns because we cannot be certain of the meaning of each name, nor do we name our towns in this manner. To the people living in these small towns, we can be sure the meaning of Micah's prophecies was clear. (Adullam was fairly close to Micah's hometown.[40])

Micah, like Isaiah, condemns their greed. The people will not be able to save themselves with their land or houses. Micah further warns against believing in false prophets who only preach that all is well and there will continue to be plenty of wealth. Today's lesson concludes with Micah promising that as surely as the LORD will bring judgment, He will also bring deliverance.

Food for Thought: When the DOW Jones Industrials hit 9900 on the New York Stock Exchange, brokers said it was only a slump. When it hit 9600, it was at the bottom and things would be going back up. When it hit 9300, they ceased to crow any longer. They hid and prayed for relief. Stockbrokers are like the pied piper -- trying to lead people to buy stocks that are traded by their brokerage. Are we also led astray in our religious lives? Most people don't understand the stock market; therefore it is easy to lead them. Most people don't understand or even try to understand God's word; therefore it is easy to lead them astray. Be faithful in your study of the Bible and God will reward you.

June 26
Bible Readings: Micah 3-5

Section 2 of Micah covers the three middle chapters of the book. Micah immediately begins his rebuke of the religious and governmental leaders who have led the people astray. He accuses them of stripping the very flesh from the people, breaking their bones, and chopping them up. Although not literal, this is a vivid picture of the depth of sin the people had descended into by following the paganism of their leaders. Those who called themselves priests and prophets but only for the prestige, power, and/or wealth would be humbled to shame. The leaders at every level of society were corrupt. Micah prophesies that Jerusalem will be totally destroyed.

As in section one, section two begins with the condemnation judgment of Judah's leaders and people, followed closely by the promise of deliverance. As with Isaiah, Micah tells that the last days will see Mt. Moriah hovering over the other hills with streams of people making pilgrimages to it. The Word of the LORD will administer the law of the land from Jerusalem. John 1:1-2 tells us the Word of God is Jesus. Compare Micah 4:3 with Isaiah 2:4. Peace is foretold. Micah declares that other nations may walk in the name of their gods, but "we will walk in the name of the LORD our God for ever and ever."[1] (Micah 4:5)

Judah will eventually be enslaved; its people will be carried to Babylon. But a remnant will be preserved. For now, though, God will give Jerusalem victory over many nations who seek her destruction.

Micah 5:2 prophecy gives the birthplace of the Messiah. This prophecy is so well known that 700 years later the wise men quoted this verse when asked by King Herod where the Christ was born (Matt. 2:6). God's love is so great that we cannot even conceive of its height, length, width, and depth (Eph. 3:17-19). I find a lot of comfort and peace in Micah 5:4-5a that speaks of the time Jesus ascends the throne of David. "He will stand and shepherd his flock in the strength of the LORD, in the majesty of the name of the LORD his God. And they will live securely, for then his greatness will reach to the ends of the earth. And he will be their peace."[1]

When Assyria invades Judah, Micah prophesies that God "will raise against him seven shepherds, even eight leaders."[1] (Micah 5:5) The idea here is that 7 provide a complete defense but 8 are more than enough to defend Judah. They will not only defend but will invade Assyria and be victorious in battle. (Assyria is called the land of Nimrod. Nimrod was a mighty warrior who was the son of Cush, father of the Canaanites.[5]) The remnant of Jews will triumph over their foes in the Day of the LORD. Pagan worship and instruments of war will be destroyed. God declares, "I will take vengeance in anger and wrath upon the nations that have not obeyed me."[1] (Micah 5:15)

Food for Thought: A Roman Catholic priest in the 1850s, Frederick William Faber wrote this great hymn about God's mercy.

> *"There's a wideness in God's mercy,*
> *Like the wideness of the sea;*
> *There's a kindness in His justice,*
> *Which is more than liberty.*
> *There is welcome for the sinner,*
> *And more graces for the good;*
> *There is mercy with the Savior;*
> *There is healing in His blood.*
> *For the love of God is broader*
> *Than the measure of man's mind;*
> *And the heart of the Eternal*
> *Is most wonderfully kind.*
> *If our love were but more simple,*
> *We should take Him at His Word;*
> *And our lives would be all sunshine*
> *In the sweetness of our Lord."*[41]

June 27
Bible Readings: Micah 6-7

The third section is presented in the same format as the previous two: first there is judgment, then there is deliverance. It opens with a courtroom-like setting. The people are told to plead their case before God's creation because God had lodged a complaint against them. God then begins His case. God recounts the many milestones in the Hebrews' lives where He had intervened and blessed them. The people of Judah can't even begin to defend their actions. God, of course, is right. Starting in verse 6 they just simply ask what they can do to get out of this charge! As usual, they want to know what <u>works</u> can be done to erase their sin. God's answer is classic. "He has showed you, O men, what is good. And what does the LORD require of you? To act justly and to love mercy and to walk humbly with your God."[1] (Micah 6:8)

Lessons of Love

God gives the summation of His case against the people before pronouncing the sentence: they will forfeit all their material possessions, be put to shame, and be enslaved. Neighbor will turn against neighbor and family members against each other. Micah boldly declares his own stance, "But as for me, I watch in hope for the LORD, I wait for God my Savior; my God will hear me."[1] (Micah 7:7)

Finally, the people respond -- not to God's accusations but rather to those gloating over their downfall. They admit their guilt and accept their sentence, but now they declare that God will not abandon them. He will reconcile them to Himself. This lesson concludes with a prayer for restoration to their previous state. They beseech God to once again let them enjoy the bounty of the land as in Bashan and Gilead. The people of Judah remind God that He delights in being merciful.

Food for Thought: In Romans 3:23, Paul said, ". . . for all have sinned and fall short of the glory of God."[1] How would you defend your actions in God's courtroom? You know on the Day of the LORD you will be facing accountability. Your works do not save you, but the world judges you by them. James 2:26 tells us that "faith without deeds is dead."[1] If you believe in Jesus, then your life (and works) will show it.

June 28

Bible Readings: 2 Kings 15:29,30-31,36-38; 17:1-2; 16:1-4, 1 Chron. 5:23-26, 2 Chron. 27:7,9; 28:1-4

While Pekah was king of Israel (732 B.C.), the king of Assyria conquered and deported the Hebrew people who lived east of the Jordan and most of Naphtali. They were relocated to work on Assyria's building projects and cultivation of the land. Assyria was very much like Palestine (the Holy Land promised to Abraham[5]) in size, weather, and geography. For the most part, though, it was poorly settled. Having only four major cities (Arrapkha, Erbil, Ninevah, and Ashur), Assyria was in great need of laborers to build an empire. Assyria was located along the Tigris River, anchored by Ninevah in the north and Ashur in the south. It stretched eastward to the Zagros Mountains. The Assyrians took great care to maintain family and community groups of Hebrews during the deportation. They were given adequate food, clothing, and shoes. Carts and donkeys were provided for the women and children. For the people of Israel, the enslavement was as painless as possible for those who were cooperative when going from freedom to slavery. On the other hand, Assyrians were ruthless in punishing the rebellious. Their punishments were designed to ensure compliance from the masses. Basically these deportees found themselves in a land similar to their own but doing manual labor for a foreign king. Lengthwise, Assyria covered about 100 miles.[7]

[Review from June 24th.] Meanwhile Pekah allied with the king of Syria. When Judah refused to join the alliance, Syria and Israel turned on Judah. Shortly thereafter, Pekah's friend[3] Hoshea assassinated Pekah and claimed the throne. Twelve years[15] earlier, King Jotham had died in Judah and was succeeded by his son Ahaz, who promptly allied Judah with Assyria. Judah and Israel once again have something in common: evil kings who worshipped idols. Judah's King Ahaz was so depraved he burned his own sons as sacrifices.

Food for Thought: Even in their sentence, God had mercy on Israel. Hosea and Micah have reminded us that God delights in showing mercy to the penitent. The problem is that few people really humble themselves to the point of repenting. On the other hand, some spend a lifetime beating themselves up over the sins of the past and live in a state of anguish. God forgives and washes our sins away when we repent and turn to Him. Memories of past sins may haunt us because the devil makes us suffer every way possible when we turn our backs on him. If you keep your eyes on Jesus, you have a new life with a new joy.

June 29

Bible Readings: Isaiah 7-9

God sends Isaiah to wicked King Ahaz of Judah with a message. God intends to protect Judah from Syria and Israel's attack. Isaiah prophesies that Israel as a nation will be no more within 65 years. Ahaz is to stand firm and request a sign from the LORD. Ahaz refuses to ask for a sign. It is possible his refusal was because he did not want to know any god existed other than those pagan ones he worshipped. God decided to send a sign anyway. A virgin will give birth to a son whose name will be Immanuel. The prophet states that the boy will eat curds and honey. This is a sign that the land will be so devastated that it will no longer produce. The crude form of cheese called curds will be made out of the milk from the herds and the natural food honey will be used to eat with the curds. In the Hebrew culture, the time of knowing right from wrong occurs around the twelfth birthday. Jewish tradition says this passage refers to the birth of Hezekiah, Ahaz's son. [Tiglath-Pileser would destroy Demascus and invade Israel, making King Pekah of Israel an Assyrian vassal king along with King Ahaz of Judah.][39] Christians interpret verse 14 as prophecy of the birth of Jesus. The land of Judah will be in total decay at that time.

Isaiah prophesies that Syria and Israel will fall within two years. Assyria will sweep the country so that it will seem like rising floodwaters had engulfed them.

The LORD warns Isaiah not to fear men but rather fear the LORD and His judgment. For the LORD will be a stumbling block to many people because they will not be able to accept the free gift of salvation. People need only to seek God. No intermediary in the form of spiritists, mediums, priests, or prophets are needed. Jesus Christ is the only one we need to present us to the Father.

Chapter 9 definitely contains Messianic prophecy. First, Isaiah starts by saying that the land of Zebulun will be honored. The town of Nazareth is in Zebulun and Jesus will grow up as a citizen of Nazareth, always referred to as Jesus of Nazareth.[5] Next, the land of Naphtali will be honored as the center of Jesus' ministry (the land of Galilee). Jesus will shatter the yoke of religious oppression on the people. He will reign on the throne of David and establish His kingdom over which He will maintain justice and righteousness. He will be called Wonderful Counselor, Mighty God, Everlasting Father, and Prince of Peace.

Isaiah turns his prophecy to the destruction that is about to be unleashed on Israel. Her enemies will be many: (1) Rezin's army (Syria), (2) Arameans (Assyria), (3) Philistines. Israel will be attacked from the north, east, and west. God will eliminate all the governmental and religious leaders at one time. Brother will turn against brother. The people will not be satisfied because their wickedness was too great; therefore, their consequences will be great. In their discontent, they will attack Judah seeking to find the wealth, security, and joy they have lost. As in the last days, many will not recognize the Hand of God, nor will they turn to Him.

Food for Thought: You will notice our passage today mentioned several times that God's Hand was still upraised. Refer back to Exodus 17:10-13. What parallels can you draw between these two passages of scripture? Moses represents God. The Amalekites represent the pagan world. Joshua represents our spiritual leaders. We are the soldiers. The battle lines are drawn. God's Hand is raised.

NOTE: These Lessons are cumulative. We have steadily been building a knowledge base of Biblical facts and principles. This base is critical to a full understanding of the lessons to come. You have to understand 'where you have been' and 'where you are now' before you can see 'where you are going.'

June 30
Bible Readings: Isaiah 10:1-34; 11:1-16; 12:1-6; 2 Kings 16:5-6; 2 Chron. 28:5-21

God has unlimited mercy. In Matthew 18:21-35, Jesus told a parable about a servant who owed the king several million dollars. The servant couldn't pay his debt when the note came due so the king issued an order for the entire family to be sold as slaves to pay on their debt. (You can relate this to a lender foreclosing on one's property.) The servant begged for more time to pay. The king had compassion and canceled the debt. Later the servant ran into someone who owed him only a few dollars and demanded full payment. When the man begged for more time, the servant had him thrown into prison. When the king heard of this, he was furious and had the servant brought before him. The king told the servant that he should have given mercy to others just as he had received mercy himself. The unmerciful servant was then imprisoned. Just as God has extended mercy to us, we should show mercy to others. Isaiah warns those who oppress the less fortunate that a 'day of reckoning' is coming.

The king of Assyria had a throne title that meant 'the great king.' The commanders under his rule were equivalent to lesser kings, based on the extent of their authority. Some of these commanders had actually been kings before they were conquered.[39] This is an example of how Assyria treated conquered peoples. You will recall that even in King David's time conquered kings were killed or maimed. Several towns are mentioned in this passage. Calno was also known as Ctesiphon and was located on the left bank of the Tigris River. Carchemish was a city west of the Euphrates River and was the ancient capital of the Hittites. Hamath and Arpad are both Syrian cities even today. Arpad was about 100 miles southwest of Haran, the area where Abraham and his father Terah lived for a while. Calno, Carchemish, Hamath, Arpad, Samaria, and Damascus were all fortified cities on major trade routes; yet, they still fell to the Assyrian conquerors.[5] The Mesopotamia area where the first two cities were located had participated in idol worship since before the birth of Abraham. In Isaiah 10:10, God says they excelled at pagan worship and judgment came to them. Likewise, judgment would befall Jerusalem and Samaria with their idols.

God now proclaims that after He has used Assyria to bring judgment on Jerusalem, He will then judge Assyria for their pride and arrogance. God will send a wasting disease on the Assyrian army. The God of Israel will consume Assyria's army like a fire consumes a forest. Only a few soldiers will survive. Israel (the northern kingdom), too, will have only a few survivors after their judgment is complete. The remnant of Israel will no longer rely on Assyria but will turn to God. On the other hand, God assures Jerusalem not to be afraid of the Assyrians for soon the judgment against Jerusalem would be complete and their burden would be lifted. Then God will strike Assyria down just as he had done with Midian (See Judges 7).

The Assyrians will attack first at Aiath and march on through the cities of Benjamin's territory until they finally stop at Nob.[5] From Nob they will mount their attack on Jerusalem. Imagine these towns as being on the sides or top of these small mountains. As the enemy marched on one mountain, they could be seen from other mountains. Keil-Delitzsch gives the following moving account of the march of Assyria to Jerusalem.[42]

> "When the Assyrian[s] came upon Ayyath [Aiath], about thirty miles to the north-east of Jerusalem . . . in order to surprise Jerusalem, it takes a different route, in which it will have to cross three deep and difficult valleys. From Ai [Aiath] they pass to Migdron . . . situated about eight minutes' walk from Beitin [Bethel] . . . . Here they deposit their baggage, so far as they are able to dispense with it . . . . For they proceed thence through the pass of Michmash, a deep and precipitous ravine about forty-eight minutes in breadth. . . . the Assyrian army took up its quarters for the night at Geba . . . . Starting in the morning . . ., they pass on one side of Rama, situated half an hour to the west of Geba, which trembles as it sees them go by; and the inhabitants of Gibeath of Saul [Gibeah] . . . take to flight when they pass by . . . . The prophet . . . appeals to the daughter of Gallim, to raise a far-sounding yell of lamentation with their voice and calls out in deep sympathy to Laysha [Laishah] . . ., "only listen," the enemy is coming nearer and nearer; and then for Anathoth . . . about an hour and a quarter to the north of Jerusalem . . . : O poor Anathoth! . . . Madmenah flees in anxious haste: the inhabitants of Gebim carry off their possessions. There are no traces left of either place. . . . he [Assyria] will gather up fresh strength there [Nob] in front of the city that is doomed to destruction . . . . It was not long, however, before his hand was drawn out to strike, and swing over the mountains of the daughter of Zion . . . . The instrument he [God] employs is . . . his terrifying and crushing power. . . . the angel of the Lord, who is represented as destroying the hundred and eighty-five thousand in the Assyrian camp in a single night." (pp.277-281) [words are mine]

Now Isaiah switches from prophesying judgment to Messianic prophecy. The Messiah will come from the house of Jesse -- King David's father. The Messiah, or Branch of the tree of Jesse (family tree), will be filled with the Holy Spirit. He will judge in righteousness. When He rules the earth, there will be no more fear and no anger. Those who have been aggressive will become meek and those who were fearful will fear no longer. The Root of Jesse (Jesus) will stand as a banner to all people. Banners placed on the end of standards marked the rallying point or gathering point for a tribe or group. Banners were used in the exodus to mark the camp of each of the tribes of Israel. The banner or flag of a nation identified the place where its members or citizens were to group.[5] Likewise, Christians rally to the Banner of Jesus representing the House of God. Isaiah tells that on Judgment Day the LORD will reach out His Hand a second time to save the remnant of His people left in Assyria, the Upper and Lower Nile Valley area, Cush, Elam, Babylonia, Hamath, and the islands of the sea. The Israelite people would be exiled in all these places. The LORD will provide a highway for His people to come home by drying up great gulfs and breaking up rivers into streams. Then all the people will praise God.

Because of Judah's great sins in worshipping pagan gods, the LORD handed them over to Syria and Israel. Syria killed 120,000 soldiers and Israel captured 200,000 women and children.

In Samaria, Obed, a prophet, negotiated a release of the captives. The captives were fed and clothed. The wounds of the sick were dressed and the weak were put on donkeys to return to their land.

Now the towns scattered throughout Judah's countryside were easy prey for raiding attacks by the Philistines and Edomites. Instead of turning to God, Ahaz turned to Assyria for help. But Assyria saw a chance to increase its empire. Rather than aiding Judah, Assyria attacked.

Food for Thought: God can use every experience we have as a way to minister to others. I was able to provide comfort and guidance to an older friend of mine today as a result of my experiences with Daddy during his heart attack recovery. I cannot even begin to list all of the 'coincidences' that had to take place for me to be in the right place at the right time to bring comfort to one of God's children. I praise God for the opportunity to serve Him. I pray each of you have the fulfillment and joy of serving Him daily.

July 1
Bible Readings: Isaiah 34:1-4; 14:24-27; 15:1-9; 16:1-14; 17:1-14

Judah is crippled. To survive, they have to serve Assyria. (As I read Isaiah 34:3, I can't help but think of Afghanistan.)

God now announces a series of judgments against pagan nations: (1) Assyria, (2) Moab, (3) Damascus, (4) Edom, (5) Arabia, (6) Phoenicia, (7) Philistia, (8) Babylon, (9) Ethiopia, and (10) Egypt. The latter two are addressed in the July 9 lesson. Together, this is the largest collection of judgments in the Bible.[39] Let's look at each one.

(1) Assyria - God declares He will crush Assyria, removing the yoke of oppression from the Israelites. The mountains of Judah will be the site of their defeat. What God has decided, no man can reverse.

(2) Moab - You will recall that Moab was the land where Sodom and Gomorrah were located in Genesis 19. They were the most famous of the five "cities of the plain" that were to be destroyed: Sodom, Gomorrah, Admah, Zeboiim, Zoar. Archaeological studies show a giant explosion destroyed four of these cities.[5] (This was possibly due to the large asphalt and sulfur deposits in the area. God uses natural occurrences in supernatural ways.) God spared the small town of Zoar for Lot to dwell in. The Moabites were Lot's descendants as a result of an incestuous relationship with his oldest daughter. Moab is located on the eastern and southern sides of the Dead Sea; its territory extending north to the Arnon River and, at times, even further. Moab has conquered and been conquered, built and rebuilt. Many of the towns listed were once captured by the Reubenites, i.e., Elealeh, Medeba, Heshbon, Nebo, Jahaz, others were captured by the Gadites, i.e., Dibon, Jazer, and still others were assigned to both tribes jointly, i.e., Sibmah, or are unknown as to their history, i.e., Sela, Eglaim.[5] Isaiah reveals in horror the

cities of northern Moab will be destroyed in a single night. The people go to their temple of Chemosh to beg relief to no avail. A great wail and despair is heard throughout the country. The mourning practices are seen everywhere, e.g., shaving one's head, shaving off beards, wearing sackcloth. Even Isaiah is moved to despair over the widespread destruction. The pride, conceit, and wealth of Moab are completely wiped out. Not only are the cities gone but also the pastureland, orchards, vineyards, and fields. The women are fleeing like helpless young birds pushed out of their nest. The LORD declares judgment will come upon Moab within three years. Very few Moabites will survive. Those that do will be forever despised.[42]

(3) Damascus (Syria) - Damascus is at the crossroads of some of the ancient world's most important highways. It is "the oldest continually-inhabited city in the world."[5] (p.273) Damascus was well known for its export of a patterned cloth called damask. Aroer is the southernmost town of Israel located east of the Jordan River. It was often called the Beersheba of the East (Beersheba was the southernmost town of Judah west of the Jordan River).[5] In this passage of Isaiah, Ephraim is synonymous with Israel and Aram is synonymous with Syria. You'll recall that Israel and Syria allied to attack Judah (735-734 B.C.). Now God declares that both Israel and Syria will be devastated; the fat of their bodies, or wealth, will waste away. They will be like fields after the harvests -- nothing but stubble and a few missed gleanings. At that time they will turn to God. Terror will come upon them suddenly and be gone by morning. In 732 B.C. Tiglath-Pileser III invaded and captured Syria and Israel for Assyria.

Food for Thought: We have much for which to be grateful. We have a risen Savior who wants to wash our sins away so we will never face the wrath of God's final judgment. If you do not have the Savior's Grace, pray now that He will come into your life and reign forever.

Verse of the Week: **Isaiah 26:9** "My soul yearns for you in the night; in the morning my spirit longs for you."

July 2
Bible Readings: Isaiah 21:11-12; 34:5-17; 21:13-17; 23:1-18;
2 Kings 16:7-20; 18:1-7; 2 Chron. 28:22-27; 29:1-2

(4) Edom (Dumah) - Judgment will come in two waves to Dumah -- the land of the dead. Dumah symbolizes the future of Edom. The Edomites keep asking the prophet how much of the night is left or how much is left of this tribulation. This passage, too, is not a literal message to Isaiah but rather it is symbolic of the desperation of the Edomites. When morning comes it will still be night. In other words, daylight will bring a short respite from the first judgment, but it will quickly be followed by the second judgment. Only if they turn "and come back yet again" will they get relief from the judgment. This is obviously the prophet's way of saying, "Repent and turn from your wicked ways and come back to the LORD." (Recall that Edom descended from Esau who was raised in the God-fearing household of Isaac.) Judgment keeps rolling upon Edom as long as they reject God. History bears this out as Edom was invaded by: (1) Assyrians, (2) Chaldeans, (3) Persians, (4) Grecians, and (5) Romans.[42] But, Edom refused to come back to God.

The second wave of judgment not only reveals the people totally destroyed but now the land as well is devastated never to return to producing life again. (The capital city of Bozrah is destroyed.) At this judgment the LORD will have a day of vengeance (short time of terrible bloodshed) and a year of retribution (long time of tribulation). Edom was located in an area of mountains that were created by volcanoes. Previously dormant, they now come alive. The whole land will be continuously burning from the pitch and sulfur. (Imagine the odor of burning asphalt and rotten eggs mixed together!) Fire and brimstone become synonymous with hell. Brimstone means burning stone and refers to burning sulfur that is extremely combustible. There are large deposits of pitch and sulfur around the Dead Sea.[5] Historical reports detail the periodic spontaneous combustion of the Dead Sea, often referred to as the Lake of Fire and symbolically used in Rev. 20:14 as the place of eternal damnation. Only scavenger animals will be able to survive. Edom will always be a wasteland -- the LORD has decreed it.

(5) Arabia - Dedan was an area on the east side of the Red Sea. Caravans would cross the desert carrying goods between Egypt and Asia. Isaiah warns they need to bring water for there will be none fit to drink; they will be driven back to the southeastern desert as fugitives from the great war in Arabia. Within one year, Kedar (a name used for the collective tribes of Arabia) will lose its army; few will survive.[42]

(6) Phoenicia (Tyre) - Tyre was an extremely prosperous merchant city. It owned large fleets of commercial trade ships. Phoenicia, in general, had profited greatly from its seaports and trade routes. Isaiah prophesies that all vestiges of civilization will be destroyed in Tyre and the rest of the world will mourn the loss of trade. (Sounds like the New York City dilemma in 2001!) The LORD will bring down those in pride. The Phoenicians can seek refuge on the island of Cyprus, but war will come to them there, too. The Assyrians had managed to destroy the Chaldean or Babylonian land. For 70 years, Tyre will be forgotten. At the end of this time, God will restore her to international trade, but this time Tyre will be dedicating her profits to the LORD. (The rest of the judgments will be covered later.)

King Ahaz initiates a vassal agreement for Judah with Assyria to keep Syria in check. Tiglath-Pileser captures Damascus, kills the king, and deports its people. Ahaz increases his worship of pagan gods, renovating the LORD's Temple to suit his pagan needs. Ahaz took away the furnishings of the Temple. When Ahaz died, he was not buried with the other kings of Judah. His son Hezekiah began his reign and is well known for following the LORD. Hezekiah destroyed idols, including the bronze snake Moses had erected in the wilderness so the people wouldn't die from the snakebites. Apparently the snake had also become an idol among the people. Hezekiah was successful in what he did because the LORD was with him.

Food for Thought: Rev. 20:10 tells us the devil will be thrown into the lake of burning sulfur, a place the Israelite people would relate to their Dead Sea experiences. The odor, flames, barrenness, and general repulsion of the area are enough to repel most people. Today, the devil is trying to even make the Dead Sea out to be a resort where soaking in the brine will cure what ails you when all along the salts are siphoning the very water of life out of your cells. It is amazing that the world has stooped so low as to pay for a dip in the lake of fire. All they have to do is stay on the path of destruction and God will provide them with a free one-way ticket!

July 3
Bible Readings: Isaiah 14:28-32; 13:1-22; 14:1-23; 21:1-10

(7) Philistia - (After reading 4 different commentaries (repeatedly) on this passage, I was more confused than ever. They proposed two different versions of the same words! Finally, I looked at different Bible translations and settled on *The Living Bible* version.) King Ahaz died in 715 B.C., but the king who had broken Philistia was the king of Assyria, Tiglath-Pileser III, who died in 727 B.C. Even though Tiglath-Pileser had been a conquering king, he also had a degree of compassion on enslaved peoples. But from him would come a son, Shalmaneser V, who would be as fearsome as a poisonous viper. He would bring a new level of oppression to Philistia. God will care for the poor and needy of His people (Judah) although the remnant of Philistia will be destroyed by famine. Then a great, organized army will move down from the north. Sargon II was the king of Assyria and Babylonia who had succeeded Shalmaneser V as king. (Remember King Ahaz of Judah has given up independence to become a state under the jurisdiction of Assyria.) God will place Jesus on the throne at Jerusalem and all His people will find refuge.

(8) Babylon - The judgment against Babylon will be especially severe. God is mustering an army from the ends of the earth to the ends of the heavens, indicating both a physical and spiritual battle will ensue. Terror will seize the Babylonians when they realize the Day of the LORD is at hand. (God will be especially angered at the Babylonians because they will be the ones to conquer Judah and carry God's people into exile. Even though God allows this as judgment on Judah for pagan worship, He will not allow the perpetrators to go without

punishment.) All creation will shake and tremble before the anger of God. Like sheep without a shepherd, the Babylonians will be slaughtered. God will send the Medes against them. Even the women, babies, children, and youth will be killed. The Medes care nothing for gold and silver, only expansion.

Babylon will become the "jewel of kingdoms" and the "glory of the Babylonians' pride" (13:19), but God will wipe her out like He did Sodom and Gomorrah. Revelation 17:5 calls Babylon the "Mother of Prostitutes and of Idol Worship Everywhere around the World."[15] God will continue to care for the remnant of Jacob, though.

Next in our lesson is a lengthy passage that the remnant of Judah will use to taunt the Babylonians when judgment comes. God declares He will sweep Babylon clean with the broom of destruction. The Babylonians, who thought they were even above God, will go to their graves like any other mortals. Their idols will be smashed to pieces. Those who follow the practices of Babylon won't even lie in peace after death but will await the final judgment where they will be cast into the Lake of Fire.

Food for Thought: At one time Babylon was a beautiful walled city located on the land between the Tigris and Euphrates Rivers. It was the capital of the Babylonian Empire and was believed by its people to have been built by the pagan god Marduk. A large ziggurat and temple dominated its skyline. The gates of the city were decorated with colored enamel bricks. It is located in the heart of the Garden of Eden area -- just like the serpent was. Even in the Garden of Eden, evil came from within. Good and evil are in a battle for control of our lives. Prayer and Bible Study provide two weapons of defense. Build your spiritual defense armory today.

July 4
Bible Readings: 2 Chron. 29:3-36; 30:1-27; 31:1-21

Hezekiah was a king who sought God and did what was right in the eyes of God. He ordered the Temple of the LORD cleaned and repaired. All unclean items found were to be taken to the Kidron Valley and burned. Ever since King Asa used the Kidron Valley to dispose of idols, all unclean things associated with idol worship had been thrown there. It was a deep ravine that ran along the eastern side of Jerusalem. In the winter, it was full of fast-flowing water. In the spring, it was almost dry.[5] Hezekiah declared to the Levites, priests, and people that the anger of God was on them because they had failed to follow God's commands. If they wanted God to protect their wives and children who were in captivity, then they needed to covenant with the LORD so God would turn away His wrath.

The Levites sanctified themselves and the Temple. Then they set out to clean it up. It took 16 days which is an indicator of the depth of filth and decay into which the Temple had fallen. Remember from 1 Chronicles 23:3 David had counted 38,000 Levites 30 years old or older. Even if only 10% of that number were left, 3,800 men can still do a lot of work in a couple of days, much less 16 days. Hezekiah, though, is pleased the work was done so quickly and he praised the LORD. He brought 7 of every clean animal acceptable for sin offerings. Again we see a 'complete' number used to ensure full restoration with God. For the first time since Solomon, we get to experience the joy of worship in the LORD's Temple again.

Out of the fullness of Hezekiah's spiritual joy, he invites all Hebrews, from Dan the northernmost city of Israel to Beersheba the southernmost city of Judah, to come to a celebration of Passover. This would be the first joint celebration of Passover since the tribes had separated into two kingdoms. Hezekiah offered a 'peace offering' to his brothers by sending messengers throughout Israel and Judah to offer a personally announced invitation to the people. A hand-written invitation was also sent. Ephraim and Manasseh are specifically mentioned because they represented the largest number of people in the northern kingdom. Hezekiah's message is appropriate. ". . . Do not be stiff-necked . . .; submit to the LORD. Come to the sanctuary . . .. Serve the LORD your God . . .. He will not turn his face from you if you return to him." (2 Chron. 30:8-9) Unfortunately, most of the Israelites scoffed and rejected the invitation. Nonetheless, the celebration had prayerfully been set for the second month of the Jewish year. Passover was to be held the 14th of the first month of the year, but the consecration of the Levites and Temple was not completed in time.

Some of the Israelites did come to Jerusalem, though. Asher, Manasseh, Ephraim, Issachar, and Zebulun are represented besides the people of Judah. For seven days they celebrated and worshipped together. At the end of that time, the whole assembly agreed to extend the festival seven more days. Out of their renewed covenant with the LORD, they go into their communities and destroy pagan idols and worship places.

As life returns to its everyday pace, Hezekiah reinstitutes the priests and Levites into full-time service for the LORD. The people willingly and joyfully bring their offerings and gifts to the LORD. The Levites established a system for distribution of the food to the many Levites in the cities and countryside. All recorded Levite males from the age of weaning upward were given an allotment for themselves and all adult males received an allotment for their families. The descendants of Aaron were included in this system as well.

Food for Thought: We have the privilege of giving back to the Lord a portion of our blessings. Let us pray God is willing to give us more than we give Him.

July 5
<ins>Bible Readings: Isaiah 24:1-23; 25:1-12; 26-27:1; 32:1-8; 35:1-10</ins>

Isaiah 24 vividly describes the last days. The earth will be totally laid to waste. The devastation will not be a respecter of people; all will be equally affected. Because of the disobedience of the people, the earth is defiled and cursed by God. Most of earth's people will be burned up. The earth's water will dry up. There will be no laughter or joy. Every house will be barred. There arise some who will betray the people, luring them into false hope of God's deliverance from the scourge. For those who lead others astray, Isaiah says they will flee from terror only to fall into a pit. They will climb out of the pit only to find themselves in a trap. God's judgment will be most severe for them.

Then the floods will come. Floods and earthquakes will tear the earth apart. Both heavenly and earthly powers will come under God's judgment. The LORD will reign from Jerusalem. God's plan is in its final stages. The poor and oppressed are given relief. The ruthless are stopped in their tracks. Those who know the salvation of the LORD will sit down at a glorious banquet prepared for all Christians in the LORD's Banquet Hall. Jesus conquered death and now He conquers evil forevermore. God wipes away our tears and the disgrace of His people. Let us rejoice! Those who have steadfastly trusted in God are upheld and their paths are righteous, but those who have elevated themselves to lofty positions from which they oppressed others will be trampled. Even when goodness prevails, those who would do evil do not see the Hand of God lifted high until the fire of judgment consumes them. Righteousness will reign. Christians yearn to see their Savior who will destroy their enemies and secure their justice.

Isaiah 26:19 assures us that the earth will give birth to her righteous dead. The bodies will rise again. God's people are told to hide themselves from God's wrath while God punishes the wicked. (This passage quickly brings to mind the Passover that occurred in Egypt. The Hebrews marked their doors as God had commanded then they hid inside as the LORD's angel of death destroyed the firstborn of the land.) On Judgment Day the wicked will be swept from the land. The earth will rejoice. Condemnation will no longer rest on mankind. The blind will see and the lame walk. Deserts will become gardens. A highway will be there called the Way of Holiness. Only those who are clean can travel on it. Jesus is the way (John 14:6) and only those whose sins have been washed away by His blood can travel on the Way of Holiness. All who travel this road are secure and untouched by any fierce animals (wickedness) from the world. Fear and despair, pain and sadness are left behind as joy and singing fill the air. The Redeemed of God are coming home!

Food for Thought: Many believe they can work their way onto the Way of Holiness road, but Isaiah 35 plainly says only the redeemed can walk on it. Others believe their ritualistic worship will save them; it won't. Only Christians can walk on the Way. The requirement is simple -- accept the free gift of salvation from Jesus Christ. Ask Jesus to come into your life and wash your sins away. Ask Him to be Lord of your life and reign forever. Humble yourself before God, repent of your sins, ask for forgiveness and mercy, accept Jesus as your Risen Savior, and step onto the Way!

July 6
Bible Readings: Isaiah 28:1-29; 22:1-14; 29:1-21; 33:1

The messages in Isaiah 28 - 32:20 may be referred to as "The Assyrian Cycle of Prophecies." The prophecies predict the Assyrian invasions of both Israel and Judah.[39] Ephraim, the name of the largest tribe of the northern kingdom, is used here as synonymous with 'Israel.' The pride of Ephraim is Samaria. We know this prophecy was prior to 722 B.C. because that is when Israel fell to the Assyrians. Isaiah accuses the Israelites of drunkenness and false prophecies; they will be trampled. He doesn't stop at the people but continues on to the religious leaders who he accuses of staggering and stumbling through befuddled decisions. In the Day of Judgment God will be the crown of glory for the remnant of His people who survive. He will rule them with strength and justice.[39]

At this point, Isaiah's accusations anger the leaders and they lash out at him (28:9-10). They sneer that they aren't children and he can save his lectures for those who are children! Isaiah replies that he will save his message, but now they will learn their lessons from a foreign tongue (Assyria).

Isaiah makes fun of Judah's arrogance and self-righteousness telling them that when the armies sweep down over them, they can hide behind their pack of lies. Their agreement Isaiah calls "a covenant with death." The agreement referred to here was a treaty between Hezekiah and Pharaoh Shabako of Egypt. Isaiah was opposed to Judah depending on any power other than God. Assyria was gaining power every month and steadily encroaching upon and engulfing other countries.[39]

God's message comes to Isaiah. God's precious cornerstone, Jesus Christ, will be the foundation for a kingdom that is both just and righteous. The Hebrew word translated in 28:16 as tested stone or tried stone or stone of trial is used nowhere else in the Old Testament. It is of Egyptian origin meaning a fine-grained stone that is especially suitable for inscribing. God's cornerstone will come with a message.[39] The message is the last line of verse 16, "The one who trusts will never be dismayed." Lies will be useless and treaties eliminated. Every time the 'scourge' comes, Judah will be beaten down. Day after day, it will be pounded and broken. The people will be miserable like a man trying to sleep on a bed that is too short with a blanket that is too small. The misery will seep into their very souls. (One commentator said this was an example of "the inadequacy of Judah's foreign policy." (p.76)[39]) God commands they stop their mockery or their judgment will be even greater. (They're just having a temper tantrum!)

It is apparent that Isaiah 28:25-29 is in response to the complaints of the Judean people that the prophesied judgment is too great for their 'little sins.' God is treating them unfairly! (Can't you almost hear violins playing the funeral dirge as background music? These people are such whiners that I've already lost my patience with them! They're very fortunate God is in charge and not me!) Isaiah's response is very appropriate. Just like a farmer knows the various harvesting requirements for each type of grain produced, God knows the best method for 'separating the wheat from the chaff.' God will harvest when He knows is best. God sees us as individuals and He 'threshes' or judges us according to our individual differences. God is "wonderful in counsel and magnificent in wisdom."[1] (Isa. 28:29) He knows what is best for us.

The next section is a prophecy concerning the "Valley of Vision" referring to Jerusalem. Jerusalem is built on two hills with a valley between. Mountains surround Jerusalem. Isaiah lived on the lower of the hills. When he looked out, he saw the Temple Mount (Mount Moriah) and the Mount of Olives looming 300 feet above him on the east, Mt. Zion rising on the south, and a mountain backdrop on the other two sides. Jerusalem, from that viewpoint, looked liked a valley.[42] His vision was Jerusalem being taken without even a fight. The sheer size of the invading army is overwhelming. Government officials will flee. Judah's defenses are gone, but still they do not look to God. Instead they celebrate saying, "Let us eat and drink, for tomorrow we die!" (Isa. 22:13) In other words, they have a cavalier attitude toward life. The LORD's response is "Till your dying day this sin will not be atoned for."[1] (Isa. 22:14)

Ariel means the 'lion of God.' Isaiah (29:1) uses the name for Jerusalem because the lion was Judah's emblem.[5]

Jesus is often called the lion of Judah. Jerusalem's people will be humbled, lying in the dust. But God will not allow Judah's enemies to escape without penalty. The LORD's Judgment on those who dare to attack Jerusalem will be like a sudden earthquake with fire and wind and thunder. The enemies of Judah will be totally destroyed.

Man has his secret plans and hidden sins, thinking no one knows. Can the creation say to the Creator, "You do not know me." In the Day of the LORD, evil will be separated from good.

Food for Thought: People of the 21st Century have adopted a response that is generally given to any question requiring accountability, "Whatever!" It is modern society's version of the 20th Century's "Who cares?" In many ways, we are an apathetic society. Many people need to care; some do care. God cares for all. God loves us so much that He gave His only Son so that whoever believed in Him should not perish but have everlasting life. "Whatever!" "Who cares?"

NOTE: I am so pleased to inform you that as of this week we are half way through the Bible!! It is so exciting to be on the downhill side of our goal. And the BEST is yet to come! I hope you feel like you are learning something that will enhance your worship experience and improve your Bible experience.

July 7
Bible Readings: Isaiah 29:22-24; 27:2-13; 32:12-20; 33:2-24; 22:15-25

The LORD proclaims to the house of Jacob (all Hebrews) that the time is coming when being slaves -- a defeated people, will no longer shame them. When their eyes are opened to the new generation that is among them, their hope is renewed. In this verse (23), children refer to a new church. One that God made holy and sanctified unto Him. God's children (church) will worship Him with a willing spirit and eagerly seek His guidance and instruction.[42] This stands in stark contrast to their previous attitudes.

The church is depicted in this song (Isa. 27:2-6) as God's beloved vineyard. God, Himself, is the Keeper and Protector of the church (vineyard). God shows only love to his church, not anger. If only physical enemies (briers and thorns) attacked His church, then He would declare war on them and destroy them. But no, the attack is from spiritual enemies. God's church must seek refuge in Him. In the future, the Israelites will prosper and grow, filling the world with the fruit of the vine (the message of salvation in Jesus).[42]

Even though the LORD has punished the Hebrews, He has not destroyed them like He did their enemies, i.e., the various Canaanite tribes. Punishment on the house of Jacob will be complete when the Israelites realize God will not tolerate pagan worship in His people. Jerusalem is abandoned. Animals graze on the bushes growing in its once busy streets. Women of the area come there to collect firewood where only years before armies engaged in battle. The Hebrews had been a stiff-necked people (stubborn) and had refused to turn to God, so God showed them no compassion.[42]

In the Day of Judgment on the Hebrews' enemies, God will crush them like a thresher from the Nile River to the Euphrates River (from Egypt to Assyria). But the Israelites will be carefully hand-plucked and returned to Jerusalem.[42] Justice will come back to Jerusalem and righteousness will prevail. God's people will live in peace and security.

Every morning we arise to do battle with the world. Every morning we should ask God to be our strength and courage, for the enemies flee before the sound of God's voice. Pagan nations run for cover when God moves. Assyria conquered many nations including Babylon, Egypt, Syria, Israel, and Philistia. As Assyria did to their conquered nations, so God will do to Assyria.[39] God will be exalted in Jerusalem and He will be the foundation of all the riches of salvation. Most of the 7 gifts of salvation (Isa. 11:2) are repeated here in verse 6.

The brave men of Judah wail when they realize their treaty with Assyria has been broken. The old treaty between Ahaz, king of Judah, and Tiglath-Pileser, great king of Assyria, (745 - 727 B.C. reign) was disregarded when Assyria's new king, Sennacherib, decided to seize the land. Tiglath-Pileser had already forced Judah to give him annual payments and, in no position to disagree, Judah soon became a servant state to Assyria. But Sennacherib treats cities of Judah's countryside with contempt. He attacks and conquers them, destroying the vegetation. The land wastes away. Four specific geographic areas are mentioned. First is Lebanon that is an area along the seacoast that included most of Phoenicia. It was very rich and proud due to its strategic position for commercial trade. Lebanon is said to be ashamed and withered. Second is Sharon that is like the Arabah. Sharon was an extremely fertile area that ran for about 50 miles starting at the south side of the Carmel Mountains and ending at Joppa. It, too, was seacoast land. Arabah was the valley region that ran from Mt. Hermon to the Red Sea. This 'valley' included the Sea of Galilee, Jordan River, and Dead Sea. It is about 240 miles long and varies in width from 6-25 miles. Third is Bashan, the land so fertile and inviting that the half-tribe of Manasseh chose to stay there rather than crossing into the Promised Land. Bashan is about 1/3 mile above sea level and is a fertile tableland of rich volcanic soil with good rainfall. Finally, the Carmel Mountain range is about 13 miles long at a height of about 1700 feet. It is near modern day Haifa on the Mediterranean Sea. (Elijah challenged the prophets of Baal at the top of Mt. Carmel.[5]) Those four areas represented the richest farmland in Israel and Judah. All four had been destroyed and the land now was fallow.[39] The crops of grain, olives, grapes, and spices were only memories in the autumn of life. The reference to dropping leaves in verse 9 leads many to believe Isaiah wrote this in the fall of the year.[42]

God will now rise up and sift the people like wheat from chaff. The godless will be destroyed. Only the righteous and upright can withstand the process. They are the only ones with enough substance (Spirit of God) to remain while the chaff (godless) is blown away by the wind. The Israelites will anxiously look for their Savior. When the Savior comes, Jesus will rule from Jerusalem. The heavens will be His canopy. No longer will warships sail the rivers. There will be no more sickness.

Strangely, Isaiah changes course to prophesy against Shebna, Hezekiah's Minister of the Palace. (Shebna, demoted to secretary, would be one of the representatives to go out and speak to Sennacherib's commander when he marches to Jerusalem.) Shebna was guilty of refusing to acknowledge the hand of God raised above Judah. He had boldly begun to carve out a monument tomb for himself in the mountainside. God tells him to forget it. He won't he having the pleasure of dying in Judah. Assyria will be his final resting place. Eliakim will be his replacement. (He, too, will be an ambassador to Sennacherib's commander (2 Kings 18:18).) He will wear the robe and sash of his office and carry the keys to the palace and gates. All the glory and honor of his family will rest on Eliakim's shoulders, even down to distant cousins. But then -- the LORD will cut him off from the royal household and his family will fall with him.

Succession of Assyrian Kings During This Time
- Tiglath-Pileser III (745 - 727 B.C.)
- Shalmaneser V (727 - 722 B.C.)
- Sargon II (722 - 705 B.C.)
- Sennacherib (705 - 681 B.C.)
- Esarhaddon (681 – 669 B.C.)
- Ashurbanipal (669 – 627 B.C.)

Food for Thought: There is a special peace and contentment that comes from hearing God's voice. When He speaks, the whole world stands still and the fears and worries of the world disappear. Stop and listen to God today. When you seek Him, you will find Him.

July 8
Bible Readings: 2 Kings 17:3-41; 18:7-12

It is the year 722 B.C. Hoshea is king of Israel and he is under attack from Shalmaneser V, son of Tiglath-Pileser III, of Assyria. Israel was under the jurisdiction of Assyria, but Hoshea had betrayed Assyria by seeking an alliance with Egypt. Now all of Israel had to pay the price. For three long years, Samaria was under siege. At this time the Assyrians were good to conquered people who obeyed, but at the time of Ashurbanipal they were known to skin rebels alive as a warning to others. The people of Israel were separated and relocated into areas of northeastern Syria and current Iran. Israel had wickedly clung to pagan gods and idol worship. Now they had consequences to pay. Assyria brought in pagan peoples to settle in the abandoned cities of Israel; these were people who believed in divination, mythology, astrology, child sacrifice, and magic.[5] These people would intermarry with those Hebrews who managed to escape deportation and produce children who forever would be the hated Samaritans.

When God sent lions to attack the towns of Samaria, the king of Assyria sent one of the exiled priests back to Bethel to teach the people the ways of God. But the people only worshipped God as another one of their gods. Idols of many nations now prevailed in the former land of Israel. Isn't it interesting that the king of Assyria could recognize the mighty hand of God even from afar but not the people experiencing the trials? It's another example of not seeing the forest for the trees. The Bible tells us that even to this day the people worship God while serving idols -- good mixed with evil.

With today's Muslim practices and beliefs in mind, review 2 Kings 17:27-41. It is obvious to any Bible student that God is revealing to future generations of Christians to beware -- the Muslim faith is a mixture of Christian and pagan beliefs. **Do not be led astray**.

Food for Thought: The Islamic religion is the fastest growing 'religion' today. It is imperative that God's people take leadership roles in revealing the truth about this pseudo-Christian faith. It has mixed some of God's commands in with a lot of pagan practices in an attempt to give a hint of godliness to an otherwise misguided religion. God is not a sprinkle of salt; **He is the salt** of the earth. He is our Covenant of Salt. Salt is used to purify, preserve, and season. We are purified by His blood, preserved through His promise, and seasoned by His faithfulness and dependability. Take a stand for God today!

> Verse of the Week: **Isaiah 40:31** "But those who hope in the LORD will renew their strength. They will soar on wings like eagles; they will run and not grow weary; they will walk and not be faint."

Judah After Israel's Fall

July 9
Bible Readings: Isaiah 18:1-7; 19:1-25; 20:1-6; 30:1-33; 31:1-9

Now we will look at the last judgments of Isaiah (continuing from July 2 lesson).

(9) Ethiopia (Cush) - The land south of Egypt is called Ethiopia. It is a land of swarming insects, hot and tropical. Light boats were made of papyrus because they had to be carried around the many cataracts or waterfalls of the river. The tall, smooth skinned people spoke a language foreign to Isaiah. When Assyria reaches her pinnacle of power, others will harvest her and prune her branches. In other words, her far-reaching empire will be chopped up into smaller kingdoms, as God's prophet had predicted. Ethiopia will be so impressed that it will bring tribute to the God who dwells in Jerusalem. God will watch the collapse of the Assyrian empire and all the nations will observe.

(10) Egypt - Egypt will experience civil war. The idols and spirits they consult will not help them. During this time of strife, a powerful and cruel pharaoh will rule Egypt. History records a national revolution started in the city of Sais and resulted in the overthrow of the Ethiopian dynasty ruling in Egypt in 695 B.C. Egypt was split into 12 small kingdoms.[42] Isaiah also foretells of the hand of God striking the Nile, the center of life for Egypt. The drought was so bad that the river dried up. All families were dependent on the river for food, clothing, travel, and industry. This would be a devastating blow to the nation. Pharaoh (who was believed to be a god) and all his advisers are helpless to reverse the judgment of God. The leaders of two of Egypt's ancient royal cities, Zoan and

Memphis, are but fools led down the road of deception. Isaiah declares, "There is nothing Egypt can do . . .."[1] (19:15) The Egyptians will fear God and His chosen land of Judah. They will build an altar dedicated to God. When the Egyptians turn to God, He will answer their pleas. In that day, Assyria (Iraq), Egypt, and Israel will all worship the LORD.

Because of the Ethiopian dynasty in Egypt, Isaiah refers to the two countries as virtually one and the same. Isaiah 20:1-2 is rather startling. God commands Isaiah to go stripped and barefoot. Isaiah had been in mourning (as shown by the sackcloth) over the foreseen destruction of Judah. He now removes his sackcloth and sandals. For three years he is "naked" before the people or, to put it another way, he goes about in his underwear. Clothing was essential to an Israelite due to the scorching sun in the day and the frigid air at night. The prophets frequently used graphic words and visual demonstrations of their prophecies. Isaiah's actions symbolize the stripping away of Egypt's power. Judah had placed her faith in Egypt's strength instead of God. The object of their faith was going to be humiliated. The Egyptians would go into exile barefoot and stripped, except verse 4 says their buttocks will actually be showing.[43]

Judah has historically depended on the strength of an ally rather than God. They made a treaty with Syria to invade Israel. Even though that worked for many years, Judah soon turned to Assyria to protect them from Israel and Syria. Now they had depended on Egypt to protect them from Assyria. Judah was running out of potential allies. The fall of Egypt brought great dismay to Judeans. Their ambassadors had so thoroughly displayed their presence in Egypt that they were even known in the smaller judicial towns. There was no doubt in Assyria that Judah was associated with Egypt. With Egypt conquered, Judah would be the next target.

Egypt is called Rahab the Do-Nothing in our text. The Hebrew is translated "their strength is sit still."[20] Rahab is a term referring to a mythological sea monster or dragon.[5] Egypt was frequently called Rahab by the surrounding nations. Now she is mocked as 'sitting still' and a 'do-nothing.'

Even in the wake of despair, Judah refuses to turn to God for her protection. Judeans do not want to hear the prophecies of Isaiah and demand he stop 'cramming God down their throats.' When you silence the messenger, then you should expect to hear from the One who sent him. And so Judah does. God declares the judgment for their sins of rejection, oppression, and deceit would be total destruction. Destruction so complete not a portion will be left large enough to serve the people. Judah will be like a collapsing wall or broken pottery. Until destruction comes they will live in fear. Even a small threat will be enough to cause them to flee. All the Israelites have to do to stop this judgment is turn to God. He wants to protect them, guide them, and bless them. Many Bible students believe verse 26 refers to the establishment of God's Kingdom as seen in Rev. 21:23.

Judah's destruction will actually begin with the toppling of the Assyrian empire. (God will sift the nations that make up Assyria in His sieve.) Reference is made to the fire pit of Topheth in Judah. This was the location where infant sacrifice occurred. It is on the south side of Jerusalem in the Hinnom Valley and was used as a garbage dump. The dump burned continually, consuming the waste. Topheth came to be associated with the Valley of Hinnom, symbolizing eternal torment.[43] Ahaz had sacrificed both a daughter and son at Topheth. Ahaz was also responsible for the alliance with Assyria. God will consume Topheth with a stream of fire like burning sulfur. Judgment will be wrought on Judah and Assyria.[43] First, God will protect Jerusalem against the invasion by Assyria. The sword of God will strike down the Assyrians.

Food for Thought: Many people choose to spend their lives at the bottom of a gorge in a burning garbage dump. Others choose to live on the mountaintop with God, never acknowledging there is a garbage dump. God needs people who are willing to bring their testimony of living with God to those who are living with torment and despair.

July 10
Bible Readings: 2 Kings 18:13-37; 19:1-36; 20:1-21; 2 Chron. 32:1-33; Isaiah 36:1-22; 37:1-37; 38:1-22; 39:1-8

Sennacherib attacks the Judean cities scattered throughout the land. Hezekiah becomes increasingly worried about Jerusalem's safety as each outlying city falls. To prevent further attack, Hezekiah offers to pay Sennacherib whatever he demands. He collects all the silver and gold he can find and sends it to Sennacherib, king of Assyria, as a peace gesture.

Some time later Hezekiah develops an abscess and becomes bed-ridden from the infection. Isaiah delivers a message from God saying Hezekiah will die. Hezekiah prays that God will remember his faithfulness and will have compassion on him. God then sends Isaiah back to say God has granted Hezekiah 15 more years of life. (Hezekiah was 25 years old when he became king and he reigned 29 years. That would make him only 39 years old at this time.) To verify His promise, God gives Hezekiah a sign -- the shadow on the steps went back 10 steps. God turned time back (which has been proven with our advanced technological time measurement capabilities developed through the space program)! Upon recovery, Hezekiah pours out his story, praise, and thanksgiving in writing.

The LORD blessed Hezekiah so that he and Judah prospered. He set about building another wall that would stand outside the original city wall. The new wall was called the broad wall because it was 23 feet wide and stood 27 feet high. It tripled the size of Jerusalem. A town's weak point was always its water supply. Hezekiah commissioned a tunnel to be dug from Gihon Spring, at the base of the hill on the east side, through the solid rock under the city to the Pool of Siloam. It was 1700 feet long and varied from 3-11 feet in diameter. (Its course resembles a backward Z with the angles being 90 degrees each.) The tunnel was dug from both ends at once, meeting in the middle. For that time period, this water tunnel was one of the most remarkable engineering feats known. It is 60 feet underground and still exists today. Hezekiah increased the size of the army and updated his weaponry.[7] Hezekiah was considered the best king Judah ever had (remember, this was after the kingdom divided). But Hezekiah had a little problem. He was proud of what he had accomplished and was eager to show everything to the Babylonian ambassadors who came to call. Most of us would think this was normal, benign behavior. Apparently, Hezekiah failed to give God the glory and be humble in his blessings. Isaiah is quick to call his hand and prophesies that everything will one day belong to Babylon.

Kings went to war every spring and Assyria was no different. So Sennacherib began movement toward Jerusalem again. In an effort to make life as difficult as possible for Sennacherib, Hezekiah proceeded to block off all the streams and springs. Water was necessary to support a couple of hundred thousand soldiers with horses and pack animals. But water also facilitated the enemy's tactical (attack) plans. Siege ramps and towers could be built upstream and floated to the battle site. Other heavy equipment, i.e., mobilized battering rams, could be moved downstream on rafts rather than carted over and around the mountain.[7]

Being detained at the battle of Lachish, Sennacherib sent his field commander and a large portion of his army to Jerusalem. The commander called for Hezekiah to come meet with him. Instead, Hezekiah sent his three right hand men: Eliakim, Shebna, and Joah. The commander mocked God and ridiculed all who worshipped the God of Israel, making sure the people on the city wall could hear him. But Hezekiah had instructed the people to remain silent. They were not to fear "for there is a greater power with us than with him."[1] (2 Chron. 32:7) [This is quoted from Elisha in 2 Kings 6:16.]

The king's three representatives returned distraught, but Isaiah brought a message from God. The Assyrian army would withdraw and Sennacherib would be slain in his own country. Just as Isaiah prophesied, Sennacherib had a report that the Ethiopians were attempting an invasion. But before leaving, Sennacherib writes Hezekiah a letter meant to weaken Hezekiah's resolve and diminish his spirit. Sennacherib names off many of the Mesopotamian (Garden of Eden) cities he has conquered as evidence that Hezekiah can't stand against him. But he greatly underestimated the power of Hezekiah's God. Hezekiah prays and Isaiah delivers God's message. This is the year of briers and thorns that was prophesied (Isa. 7:21-25). The people had not been able to leave the safety of the city wall to sow crops. The Assyrian army crushed the land. Now the time for sowing was upon them and the land wasn't ready. But the third year would see them harvesting crops again. They were to plant vineyards with the assurance of eating the fruit. It takes many years for vineyards to mature to harvest. The people of Jerusalem would enjoy peace again.[43] The Jerusalem remnant of the house of Judah would survive. As far as Sennacherib is concerned, he will never invade Jerusalem. That night an angel of the LORD slay 185,000 Assyrian soldiers. Sennacherib takes the men he has left and goes back to Ninevah.

At the age of 54, Hezekiah dies.

Food for Thought: Hezekiah asked for his life to be extended. During his 15 extra years, he produced a son who was named Manasseh. From the best king of Judah came the worst king of Judah. Hezekiah had many good accomplishments for Jerusalem in that period, but you have to wonder how different life might have been in Jerusalem had Manasseh never been born.

July 11
Bible Readings: 2 Kings 20:21; 21:1-16; 2 Chron. 33:1-9, 33

Manasseh became king at 12 years old -- a bad age for any person. With his father dead, he apparently didn't have a godly influence in his life. He ultimately becomes the 'worst of the worst.' Unfortunately, he reigns for 55 years.

Manasseh plunges Jerusalem into paganism. Pagan idols and altars go up everywhere. Not satisfied with worshipping just Baal and Asherah, Manasseh adds worship of the sun, moon, and stars, too! Even that isn't enough, he brings in diviners (fortune tellers), mediums, and magicians. Then he reaches the pinnacle of evil and sacrifices his own son in the fire. The LORD's Temple is converted to a pagan worship center. Manasseh and the people's hearts were so hardened to God's voice that they didn't even know God had left the building! The key sentence of today's lesson is a very sad one. "Manasseh led them astray, so that they did more evil than the nations the LORD had destroyed before the Israelites."[1] (2 Kings 21:9) Verse 16 continues with Manasseh's wickedness. "Moreover, Manasseh also shed so much innocent blood that he filled Jerusalem from end to end . . . ."[1]

The LORD's prophets deliver His judgment. God will judge Judah with the same method and standard used for Samaria or Israel (Zech. 1:16 and Amos 7:7-9). The measuring line and plumb line were used to determine the 'truthfulness' of what was built but also to what was level to the ground. Thus, there was the "measure of desolation and the plummet of devastation."[25] (p. 471) When the measuring line was applied to Samaria and the plumb line to the house of Ahab, there was no truthfulness in them. Both were destroyed. God now warns Jerusalem will be measured likewise. Jerusalem will be wiped out, uprooted, and turned face down where God does not have to look upon her wickedness any more. God has rejected and forsaken the last of His people.

Food for Thought: You will also find the measuring line and plumb line used against Edom in Isaiah 34. Edom was totally devastated, never to recover. But the Edomites weren't God's people. Measuring lines can be used to build up or to tear down. Once built, though, the plumb line determines if it is true to its design and purpose. Our design is the 'image of God.' Are you ready for the plumb line measurement?

July 12
Bible Readings: Isaiah 40:1-31; 41:1-10

Now that Judah's judgment is definite, Isaiah prophesies about the future. Judah's punishment period will be completed. In God's compassion, He even states they have suffered double for their sins. In His wrath he condemned them, in His mercy He pardons them.[42]

Their Messiah will come, a Savior for their people. He will be heralded by a voice (John the Baptist) calling in the desert. When the Messiah comes, the playing field will be level. All people will be equal. Man's word withers under the least exposure, but God's word stands forever. Shout from the mountaintop above Jerusalem that God comes in power to rule Judah and be rewarded by her coming back into the shepherd's fold. Judah is carried close to God's heart.

God's power is unlimited and beyond anything we can imagine or comprehend. Nations are but specks of dust. Even the abundance of plants and animals found in Lebanon are not sufficient for an altar fire comparable to God's love. Idolatry has proven its worthlessness. God sits enthroned in Heaven with the heavens as His canopy. People are but grasshoppers. They are put in one place and then blown elsewhere. The nations are barely sown, her rulers are not even established, before God moves them elsewhere. If you think anyone is God's equal, then you must merely look to the skies at all the stars that God knows by name. They reappear each night; none is missing from the fold. God is an everlasting God, the Creator of all things. He is both first and last. All things depend on Him. The Israelites have seen God's handiwork and they fear the next stage of their history, their judgment. Cyrus will be aroused in the east and move toward Judah. Israel must learn that she is God's servant (Isa. 40:28-31). (Hereafter, the name Israel will refer to the surviving remnant of Hebrews.) God will strengthen, guide, and protect her through this 'learning' stage. Even though Judah is being punished for her sins, the outcome sought is that she learns her lesson and returns fully to the LORD's service.

Food for Thought: God is greater than all our enemies and fears. He is also our Protector, Redeemer, and Savior. When we fear, we need only to call on Him. The hard part is to actually turn loose and let God handle our problems. He will tell us how we should walk and how we should talk -- all without fear. My husband has a sign on his wall at work (right behind where the students sit in his office) that says "Fear God and you have nothing else to fear!"

July 13
Bible Readings: Isaiah 41:11-29; 42:1-25; 43:1-7

With God's guidance, Israel cannot be opposed or disgraced. God takes hold of Judah's right hand. You should have noticed by now that God frequently refers to the "right hand." God's right hand refers to His dominance and power (Ex. 15:6). His "righteous right hand" as seen in verse 10 indicates His power and judgment are righteous in their actions. God's hand is not only used for power and judgment but also for comfort and guidance (Psalm 37:24). Jesus is at the Father's right hand (Acts 7:55 and Matt. 22:44).

God declares that He will renew and rebuild Israel like a threshing sledge with new teeth. Then she will crush her enemies and reduce them to chaff. The lowly, weak worm, Israel, will now overcome and crush obstacles much bigger than it. God remains the champion of the poor and needy, in this case the reference is to the Israelites. In a land where little water was available, Isaiah's audience would have readily appreciated the blessing of having such an ideal environment that desert acacia and cedar could grow as well as wilderness cypress and elm trees. This entire passage is symbolic of the Israelites' search to satisfy their longing (thirst) for righteousness (living water). Notice 7 types of trees are named. All grew in Syria and Palestine. The areas that were barren before will now be fruitful. The restoration and blessings of the Israelites will be complete in the living water of Jesus Christ.[43]

You will find courtroom scenes scattered throughout the writings of the prophets. Consider the following examples:

- Hosea 4 - Charges against Israel
- Amos 3 - Witnesses summoned against Israel
- Isaiah 41 - Present your case Judah
- Micah 1 - Indictment against Israel and Judah
- Jeremiah 25 - Verdict against Judah
- Ezekiel 7 - Sentencing of Judah

God serves as the Judge, Prosecutor, and Jury. In the case of Isaiah 41, God is demanding that Judah's pagan gods present evidence of their power -- whether used for good or bad. Of course, nothing happens. God declares the pagan gods "are less than nothing" and, therefore, "worthless." (vs. 24) The decision rendered is "he who chooses you is detestable."[1] (vs. 24)

The prophet announces an enemy will come from the northeast (north and land of the rising sun - east). This enemy will tread on the people until they are thoroughly trampled underfoot. Did the prophets of the pagan gods foretell this? No, only God's prophets were able to bring the message of truth. Again the false prophets have failed.

Again Isaiah prophesies a Messiah. The Christ is God's chosen one who will have both God's support and the blessing of the Holy Spirit on Him. With Him will come justice in a quiet, persistent manner. Jesus will be bruised but not broken (none of His bones was broken at the crucifixion). He will be faithful and true to His mission. God will take the hand of the surviving remnant of Israelites and make a covenant with them. They are to bring the light of the world, Jesus Christ, to the Gentiles. The Jews are now told point blank that the God of their fathers will become the God of all people. The Jews will be responsible for spreading the gospel to the world. There is one God and only one as His prophets have shown repeatedly.

A new song of praise is given beginning in 42:10. Land dwellers as well as sailors are to sing this song. They are to shout it from the mountaintops. Let people at the ends of the earth praise the LORD. The LORD will march out and defeat His enemies at the sound of the battle cry (when the trumpet sounds). God declares He has been silent and restrained too long. Now He will strike out and devastate the land while leading those who are spiritually blind. The path will be smoothed and darkness turned to light for those who follow God, but woe unto those who worship idols for they will be put to shame.

Israel has refused to see or hear God's messengers. As a result the Israelites have become the plunder of those who serve other gods. Who among the Israelites will come back to God? Who among them even recognizes that their downfall is their judgment from God? God the Judge is also God the Redeemer. God will call forth His people when their time in captivity is complete. Once again the Jews will worship the Holy One of Israel. Afflictions and troubles will come, but the redeemed will pass through them unharmed! The water and fire of judgment (end of the world) will no longer threaten them.

Levitical law requires something else must be offered in the place of the one who is redeemed. We are told in verse 3 that Egypt, Ethiopia, and Seba (possibly the Sudan[5]) are to be given to redeem the Jews from their captors. God will gather His people from the four corners of the earth -- **everyone** who is called by His name.

Food for Thought: I am proud to be counted among God's Redeemed. One special Jewish man (Jesus) who died on a Roman cross, overcame death and rose victoriously has made all the difference. We have seen what happened to those who turned God away. Mylon R. LeFevre wrote the following song in 1963.

> Without Him I could do nothing,
> Without Him I'd surely fail;
> Without Him I would be drifting
> Like a ship without a sail.
>
> Jesus, O Jesus, Do you know Him today?
> You can't turn Him away,
> O Jesus, O Jesus, Without Him, how lost I would be.
>
> Without Him I could be dying,
> Without Him I'd be enslaved;

Without Him life would be hopeless,
But with Jesus, thank God, I'm saved.[44]

July 14
Bible Readings: Isaiah 43:8-28; 44:1-28; 45:1-13

God, the Prosecutor, demands the pagan worshippers present witnesses to prove they are right. The Israelites are to be God's witnesses. Not only are they witnesses but also servants. Our mission as Christians is two-fold: to witness to others about the saving grace of God, and to serve the one and only living God. God is the first and the last. Before Him there was nothing. "I, even I, am the LORD, and apart from me there is no savior."[1] (Isa. 43:11) "No one can deliver out of my hand. When I act, who can reverse it?"[1] (Isa. 43:13) By acting as Prosecutor of the pagans, God is actually defending the Israelites. He will not allow Babylon to continue its arrogant enslavement and fragmentation of the Israelites.

The Israelites had rejected God. They had not obeyed the commands of God since the days of Hezekiah. But God is merciful and loving. He forgives them stating, "I, even I, am he who blots out your transgressions, for my own sake, and remembers your sins no more."[1] (Isa. 43:25) [As Christians and God's church, He is still in the business of mercifully and lovingly forgiving us daily.] But Israel had consequences to pay. All sin brings consequences. They would have a period of enslavement by people who had been serving pagan gods before the father of the Israelites, Abraham, was even born. They would, in essence, have their fill of pagans. By the time this enslavement is over, they will thirst and hunger after God. But just as the deceitful Jacob had his name changed to Israel, or prince with God, God now gives a new name to His children[39] -- Jeshurun or the beloved one.[5]

Now God takes the stand as His own witness, "I am the first and I am the last; apart from me there is no God."[1] (Isa. 44:6) Has His proclamations not come true? What can an idol made by human hands do? It is nothing more than a whatnot. It can be burned or melted down and used for a totally different purpose. Is it truly a god then? Is a god so easily made or destroyed? Return to God, O Israel, the One who has redeemed you with His own sacrifice -- the promise of His own Son. Even now God's plan of salvation is in motion. He will use a Persian named Cyrus to free His people and rebuild Jerusalem and the Temple. He will also use Cyrus to dominate the Babylonians. God will lead Cyrus with His mighty right hand. Even though Cyrus worships the pagan god, Marduk, he recognizes the voice of God when he is told to rebuild Jerusalem. Cyrus goes down in history as one of the greatest 'friends' of the Israelites. The Persian Empire will spread from western Turkey to India. Cyrus will be known as 'Cyrus the great,' in fulfillment of all God promises in Isa. 45:1-7. God does not let our sins stand in the way of His plan for the world. He not only uses natural events in supernatural ways, but He also uses non-Christians to implement His plan when His children refuse.

Food for Thought: God foretold the future to the Jews through Isaiah. Cyrus was specified by name 150 years before he became king! Likewise, the fall of Jerusalem was prophesied 100 years before it happened and the rebuilding of the Temple 200 years prior to the reconstruction.[15] God warned His people, well in advance, as to what the future held. We, too, have been warned, more than 2000 years ago, as to what the future holds -- for those who accept Jesus as their Savior and for those who don't. The choice is ours.

July 15
Bible Readings: Isaiah 45:14-25; 46:1-13; 47:1-15; 48:1-15

The Egyptians, Ethiopians, and Yemenites will recognize the God of Israel. God has promised Cyrus that these peoples will be His subjects because they will recognize that God is blessing Cyrus. Isaiah 45:1 refers to Cyrus as the LORD's anointed. In the Old Testament this title has only been used for priests, prophets, and kings. "Cyrus is the only Gentile who is given this title."[39] (p. 133)

God declares those who worship idols will be put to shame and disgrace. Ignorant are those people who carry idols around. The One and only God carries us through trials and troubles, not the other way around. Idols only add to one's load, increasing the burden.

At the end of chapter 45, God reiterates His allegiance to the Israelites. They will be found righteous. This is the lingering promise given with the five affirmations in chapter 44. (1) His people are His servants. (2) He made them. (3) He will not forget them. (4) He has wiped out their sins. (5) They have been redeemed. I hope by now that you realize that the birth, death, burial, and resurrection of Jesus Christ has already been decided. It is a certainty -- a done deal. It will happen. God has not only promised, but He has already started wiping out the sins of His people through His sacrifice of His only Son. But what if Jesus had called down a legion of angels to save Him, then what? God already knew He wouldn't. Just as Isaac was willing to be sacrificed if it was the will of his father, Jesus is even more so. Jesus will do the Will of the Father. Isaiah has 4 Songs about the Suffering Servant -- Jesus. First is 42:1-4, second is 49:1-6, third is 50:4-9, and fourth is 52:13-53:12. These contain many of his prophecies of the coming Messiah.[39]

Bel and Nebo (chapter 46) are the main gods of Babylon. Bel means lord and was the title used for Marduk. Nebo was the son of Marduk. Marduk was the patron god of the capital city. He was the god of all arts, science, and literature. Nebo actually means elevation or elevated one. Names for the kings involved combining Nebo with other names. The best example is Nebuchadnezzar which means 'O Nebo, protect the heir (son) (king).'[39]

God reminds the people that He made it known from the beginning of time what would come about. As He has said, Cyrus will come. In Isa. 46:11, you get the feeling that God is reaching down and shaking the stubborn, blind Hebrews who prefer to feel sorry for themselves and give up rather than planning for the future. God says, "Listen to me!" Now when I was a child and my mother said that, I paid attention. Incredibly, God goes on to tell them He is going to bring salvation to them even if they are pig-headed and stubborn! (Well, He didn't say pig-headed, I did. Pigs, of course, were unclean animals not suitable for God's people to raise, eat, or sacrifice. The more you read about their stubbornness and rejection of God, the more you believe they were unclean and undeserving -- just like us.)

God promises Babylon will get what is coming to her. Babylon will be used to carry out the consequences of Judah's sins, but then Babylon will have its own consequences to pay. She will be reduced to servitude herself. Babylon's true condition will be revealed. Her regal coverings will be stripped away to show her decadence and decay. God had been angry with His people and had removed His blessing, allowing them to be enslaved. But Babylon had gone too far. Babylon had been cruel to the Hebrews, even to the elderly. On top of that she was arrogant -- so sure she was mightier than all other nations -- so smug. But God will bring such a disaster on them that they won't know what hit'em. Then let the magicians and astrologers try to get them out of it! The fire of judgment will consume them.

Again God tries to get the attention of His people, "Listen to this!" (48:1) You think you're so special because you are a citizen of Jerusalem. Rather, you are so stubborn your neck is made of iron and your forehead is bronze. (Maybe that's where those mechanical bulls lost their heads!) God revealed everything to you Israelites. Why did you ignore His warnings? God has tested you with affliction so you would not continue to slander His name. "Listen to me," God declares, "I am he; I am the first and I am the last."[1] (Isa. 48:12) With His own hands, God made the heavens and the earth. Now God has chosen a pagan to carry out His judgment against Babylon.

Food for Thought: One of my favorite verses is the Verse of the Week. I have it on my wall at work. When I am feeling especially old and tired, I stop and read it and thank God. Put up some of your favorite verses on the refrigerator, bathroom mirror, or office wall. Let God's word remind you (and your loved ones) of His love.

> **Verses of the Week: Isaiah 57:1-2** "The righteous perish, and no one ponders it in his heart; devout men are taken away, and no one understands that the righteous are taken away to be spared from evil. Those who walk uprightly enter into peace; they find rest as they lie in death."

July 16
Bible Readings: Isaiah 48:16-22; 49:1-26; 50:1-11

Israel now has to listen. God gives them a stern lecture. (Sounds just like a parent lecture.) "I'm the one who brought you into this world, taught you right from wrong, and directed you in the way that you should go. If you had only listened to me, you wouldn't be in this trouble, instead you would have been given more than your heart could even desire!" When you are facing punishment, those famous last words seem to always be ringing in your ears —"If only . . . ."

God will not abandon His children, for they have been redeemed. God has decided. Redemption will happen. Isaiah's second Servant Song begins in chapter 49. Parallels can be drawn from the literal description of the relationship of Jesus to the Israelites and the implied relationship of Jesus to the church. Again the Israelites are told they are to bring salvation to the Gentiles, to the ends of the earth. Their mission is clear: they are to preach the gospel.

The time of Judah's exile is coming to an end. This second 'exodus' will be ever more glorious than the first. In the first exodus, they left to escape into a wilderness with the promise they would receive a land of milk and honey. They had been slaves in Egypt so long that none was still alive who could remember living in freedom. They weren't prepared to face the hardships of the unknown. In this second exodus, though, the people have been enslaved only 70 years, not so long that they can't remember their homeland and freedom. This time God will be their shepherd instead of Moses. He will provide food and water and turn the mountains into roads. God's people were going home!

A promise even greater is that God will never forget them. As evidence, He has engraved their names on the palms of His Hands. Remember the significance of God's Hands? His Hands create, protect, strengthen, guide, lift up, dominate, comfort, and draw us to Himself. As Christians, we share in this promise. God's people are ever before Him!

The children of Isaiah 49 again refer to the church. God even foretells in verse 21 that the Jews will be taken off-guard and surprised by the Gentile Christians (church). "Who are these people worshipping our God? Where did they come from?" Amongst the Gentiles, God will raise His banner or flag. Many of these heathen people will come to know Him and proclaim their allegiance to Him. They will humble themselves before the Jews out of respect for their position as God's chosen people and out of gratefulness for their inclusion in God's family. Verse 23 states, ". . . those who hope in me will not be disappointed."[1] Remember that hope in the Bible always implies trusting in Jesus.

Isaiah's third Servant Song is presented in chapter 50. This song contains a prophecy about the character of Jesus. As I read verses 4 and 5, I asked the Lord to bless me with these characteristics, but as I read verses 6-9, I thanked God that someone much better than I (Jesus) had faced these trials. Indeed, God provided Jesus with the ability to carry His message to the people. Jesus had a heart dedicated to the Father and a mind disciplined through faith and prayer. He was not rebellious or untrustworthy. Verse 6 is a chilling, vivid picture of how Jesus will be tortured. (1) He will be beaten. (2) His beard will be pulled out. (3) He will be mocked. (4) He will be spit on. At no time will He flinch or cry out in pain or defend Himself. God gives Him the strength to be the sacrifice. His accusers hide behind the Romans, the government, the rioters. The devil lurks and hides. Jesus' accusers walk in eternal darkness. Those who depend on the world's light are condemned to torment. John 1:4-5 says, "In him was life, and that life was the light of man. The light shines in the darkness, but the darkness has not understood it."[1] Those Jesus came to save, the Jews, would not understand Him. Those who were told He was coming and who should have been looking for Him didn't recognize Him. In John 8:12, Jesus said, "I am the light of the world. Whoever follows me will never walk in darkness, but will have the light of life."[1]

Food for Thought: Can you think of a blessing you missed because you failed to follow God's call to you?

July 17
<u>Bible Readings: Isaiah 51:1-23; 52:1-15; 53:1-12; 54:1-3</u>

As poor as some of our memories are, God expects us to remember how He has helped us in the past so we can gain encouragement to face the future. An elderly lady I once knew lost all of her memory of family, friends, and events, but even on her deathbed she still sang hymns! God provided memories that could comfort and guide her into Glory. We, too, need to cherish the memories of past battles won. My husband once preached a sermon at the Friends Church in Alva, Oklahoma about remembering the milestones of one's life. This sermon was given to him as he listened to his father reading journals kept from years before, recalling the trials and the answers to prayer. Many of our church leaders now advocate written prayer journals -- even dated listings of prayer needs and answers -- where we have been and how God brought us through. In this way, we don't let the 'forest' of the problems loom over us so that we can't see the 'trees' of God's answers. The children of Israel are reminded that the God of their past is also the God of their present who is more than capable of fulfilling His promises. Moreover, He is the God of the future and He is sending salvation (51:5) so that all who will listen and accept His free gift will have eternal life. (Again you see Egypt referred to as Rahab. With the exception of Rahab of Jericho who became part of the lineage of Jesus, Rahab is used as a name for an evil power force often in reference to Egypt.)

God comforts the Jews in 51:12-16, urging them not to fear because their numbers are so few. The words of Elisha are so appropriate here, "Don't be afraid. Those who are with us are more than those who are with them."[1] (2 Kings 6:16) Babylon is the same land that Abraham left so many centuries before on a promise from God that He would make Abraham into a great nation, and He did. Leaders have come and gone, but Israel has no leader to console them now. When they rejected God, they rejected the only true Leader they ever had! Verse 23 seems to depict my position in life, "And you made your back like the ground, like a street to be walked over."[1] (And my back says somebody had on high heels!) God promises that He has removed the cup of their iniquities (or the consequences of their sin); never will they drink from it again. Jesus will pay the price.

Isaiah prophesies the joy in Jerusalem will be overwhelming when the captives have been freed and peace has been proclaimed. God truly reigns. Never again will heathen people take Jerusalem. (See Rev. 21:27.) God returns to His dwelling place -- Zion or Jerusalem. (Zion was the name of the fortress manned by the Jebusites on the southeast hill of Jerusalem. After David captured Jerusalem, Zion also referred to the "city of David." When the Temple was built on Mt. Moriah, the term Zion was expanded to include the Temple Mountain. By the time of Isaiah, Zion referred to all of Jerusalem.[5])

The last Servant Song begins with Isaiah 52:13. It starts with a gruesome depiction of Jesus' crucifixion. He will be (1) raised up, (2) highly exalted, (3) disfigured beyond that of any man, and (4) marred so as not to even look human. His death will be such a revelation of who God is that even kings will be speechless but will know the truth. The Messiah will come as an ordinary child, with an ordinary appearance, growing up in an ordinary home, but He will be despised and rejected because of the message He brings. He will be a man of sorrows who suffers under the weight of our sins; He will be pierced and crushed (bruised in Isaiah 42:3) so that we can be healed of our sins. "We all, like sheep, have gone astray, each of us has turned to his own way; and the LORD has laid on him the iniquity of us all."[1] (Isa. 53:6) Like a lamb to the slaughter, He is silent. He was killed along with the wicked by His oppressors. His grave was with the rich. No deceit was found in Him. He carried out the Father's Will for Him to be the sacrifice, the guilt offering (See Lev. 5:14-19 and 6:1-7). Keil and Delitzsch explain that Jesus met the requirements for this guilt or trespass offering by (1) being an unblemished male of God's flock, (2) chosen by God, (3) presented by Himself, God's High Priest, (4) not presented on a holy day, (5) shedding of His blood, (6) consecrated by God, (7) accepted even after it is wounded, and (8) as restitution or compensation for sin.[42] He poured out His life for us, the sinners. God awarded Jesus the place at His right hand.

Food for Thought: Jesus willingly offered Himself for you and me. To accept His gift, you

(C) confess that you are a sinner in need of forgiveness,

(B) believe Jesus died for your sins and rose again to eternal life, and

(A) accept Him as Lord and Savior of your life.

July 18
Bible Readings: Isaiah 54:4-17; 55:1-13; 56:1-12

The prophet uses the metaphor of the estranged wife (Jews) of the husband or Maker (God). The wife was deserted and distressed in her youth (obviously as a result of waywardness) as a necessary judgment from God in order that she might be redeemed back into the relationship, never to be separated again.[39] God's promise never to rebuke the Jews again is as binding as His promise to Noah that floodwaters would never cover the earth again. God also promises to rebuild Jerusalem with precious stones (See Rev. 21:18-21). Peace and righteousness would be supreme. No weapon or attack raised against Jerusalem will ever prevail.

Isaiah issues an early plea that the Jews come home to Jerusalem when they are freed. He realizes under the peace and security of Cyrus' reign Babylon will look like a beautiful city of plenty when the yoke of captivity is removed. Choosing the beautiful, seemingly easy road of becoming a free person in Babylon versus the long walk to a city of ruins would be a great temptation to many of the Jews. Rebuilding Jerusalem would not be a quick or easy task. Isaiah prophesies that those who come home to the LORD will be richly blessed. They are to seek God while He can be found (Isa. 55:6). This is a warning to us today. There comes a time that even if we seek Him, we can no longer find Him. Our wickedness can become too great and our hearts hardened too much to be capable of true repentance any more. Those who believe a deathbed confession or a dying religious rite can alter the course of eternity will be severely disappointed. Repentance must come from one's heart and soul. Rejecting God for years hardens one's heart so that even the face of death is unlikely to change one's soul.

God's thoughts and ways are not that of mortal men. We do not understand God's ways because we are limited to our earthly experiences. God is the God of the universe, Maker of all things, Redeemer of those who turn to Him. All those, Jews and Gentiles alike, who serve God, love Him, and worship Him will be bound to Him eternally. ". . . for my house will be called a house of prayer for all nations."[1] (Isa. 56:7)

Food for Thought: The term Jews was not used until the kingdom of Israel divided. At that time the people of Judah were referred to as Jews to distinguish them from the Israelites of the northern kingdom. After the fall of the northern kingdom in 722 B.C. and the southern kingdom (Judah) in 587 B.C., the surviving remnant of the Hebrews was referred to collectively as Israelites. Realizing that it was the Jews of Judah who were sent back by Cyrus to rebuild Jerusalem, it becomes easy to understand how the name Jews has been retained.[5] Descendants of the Israelites from the northern kingdom were frequently of mixed race having intermarried with the people in the areas where they were deported. Today the Jews live in the nation of Israel and are, thus, also Israelites. In New Testament times, people were classified as a Jew or a Gentile (anyone who wasn't a Jew).

July 19
Bible Readings: Isaiah 57:1-21; 58:1-14; 59:1-21

Isaiah 57 contrasts the righteous with the wicked. Verse 2 provides comfort for those who suffer grief from loss of a loved one. We are told, "the righteous are taken away to be spared from evil."[1] The righteous ones enter into peace when they die. This serene scene is contrasted with the descriptions of the evil-hearted. The condemned of Jerusalem included those who sacrificed their children at Topheth; their reward was the idols discarded in the Kidron Valley. The wicked also included those who maintained pagan symbols in their homes and gave offerings to pagan gods. Even though the wicked tired of their lives, they didn't look to God to help them make the changes needed. Idols and religious rituals can't save them, but God can. He revives and renews the hearts of those who are penitent and humble. But, "There is no peace for the wicked."[1] (Isa. 57:21; 48:22)

Apparently the Jews were back into worshipping God but had added four more days of fasting to their rituals. God had only commanded fasting on the Day of Atonement. God's people were to fast and pray as they repented of their sins and resolved to live closer to God. As with the Pharisees of the New Testament, the Jews found out that more outward show of religious ritual did not invoke God to bless them more. God knew their hearts. He saw their quarreling, back-biting, gossiping, slandering, anger, and oppression of others. True fasting involves soul searching, repentance, and changing of one's ways.[39] True Christians seek to free the oppressed, share their bountiful blessings with those less fortunate, provide for those in need, and care for those in their own families as well. When these practices are part of our daily lives, we can expect to enjoy God's approval and blessings.

Our sins separate us from God. To draw close to God, we must repent and turn to Him. [The armor described in Isaiah 59:17 will be seen again in Paul's letter to Ephesus. (Ephesians 6:14, 17)] "The Redeemer will come to Zion"[1] (59:20) and all men everywhere will fear the name of the LORD.

Isaiah 59:21 is God's promise to His church of the new covenant. The Christians of the church will be founders of the new heaven and new earth. God's Spirit will rest on His church that is endowed with the mission to carry His message to the entire world. Never again will God's people forsake Him.[42]

Food for Thought: When I started Lessons, I had one lady who wanted to be a participant until she found out I wasn't using a Catholic Bible. Later, I had a participant who thought it heretical that I wasn't using a King James Version. John 1:1, 14 says, "In the beginning was the Word, and the Word was with God, and the Word was God . . . . The Word became flesh and lived for a while among us. We have seen his glory, the glory of the one and only Son, who came from the Father, full of grace and truth."[1] Jesus is God's word. Jesus didn't come in a Catholic version or a King James Version. Jesus came as the Truth, the Word of God. God's word is so marvelous in that the same verse will speak to us in a different way each time we read it based upon our individual need at the time. "Ask and it will be given to you; seek and you will find; knock and the door will be opened to you."[1] (Matt. 7:7)

July 20
Bible Readings: Isaiah 60:1-22; 61:1-11; 62:1-12; 63:1-19; 64:1-12

In chapter 60 Isaiah describes the glory Jerusalem will have. It will be illuminated like a spotlight surrounded by utter darkness. (Compare Isa. 60:3 with Rev. 21:24.) People of all nations will bring tribute to her. The images of the Middle Eastern culture are depicted in the camel caravans bringing supplies over inland trade routes while ships bring riches from other parts of the world. All manner of riches and wealth will be brought to Jerusalem as offerings to the Holy One of Israel.[39] Foreigners will rebuild the city; peace will prevail (as pictured by the city gates never closing.) The nation or kingdom that doesn't serve God will perish (60:12). Those who despise Jerusalem will ultimately be forced to bow down before her, recognizing it as The City of the LORD (See Isa. 45:22-25). The Jewish people will be blessed with great wealth, peace, and righteousness.

Isaiah 60:19-20 foretell Rev. 21:23. There will be no sun or moon in the New Jerusalem for there will be no night because God will be our Light. The least of the Jewish survivors will multiply to a thousand or the smallest to a nation. In other words, God will greatly increase their numbers. Chapter 60 ends with a warning. "I am the LORD; in its time I will do this swiftly."[1] (vs. 22)

Everything that has been predicted in chapter 60 will happen suddenly at a time known only to God.[42] The recipients will be all believers.

After Jesus' temptation for 40 days in the wilderness, He returned to Nazareth and attended the synagogue. He stood up and read Isaiah 61:1-2 (Luke 4:14-19). Jesus was about to start His short ministry of only three years, a ministry that would be for all ages and all people in the world. The Jews of His hometown were furious. They didn't want the outcasts of society in their religion, much less their synagogue! Jesus was proposing to minister to the prisoners, poor, downtrodden, and enslaved!

The Jews would be God's special plantings, His mighty oaks of righteousness. Isaiah prophesies that foreigners would do the manual labor leaving the Jews to be the spiritual ministers to the world, the ambassadors of God.[39] They will be rewarded with a double portion of God's blessings. (In a letter to Timothy, the Apostle Paul says those who do a good job of directing the affairs of the church will be given double honor (1 Timothy 5:17).) God will clothe the Jews in the garments of salvation and adorn them with a robe of righteousness. They will be dressed like a bride (Jews) waiting to meet her groom. Jerusalem will be given a new name. As with other name changes in the Bible (Gen. 17:5; 32:27-28; John 1:42) a new name depicts a new character and personality. Instead of being Desolate, Jerusalem will be Beulah land -- meaning married to God. The LORD swears by His powerful right hand that no foreigners will ever plunder Jerusalem again.

Isaiah 63 opens with a mighty warrior coming from the capital of Edom. His clothes are red with blood. God is the warrior and He has trampled Edom to death.[42] The Edomites had rejoiced at the downfall of Jerusalem. In fact, they were so anxious to gain the territory originally belonging to Israel, they actually aided the Babylonians by capturing or killing any Jews escaping across the Jordan River (Obad. 10-14). The Edomites were the closest blood relatives the Israelites had. Jacob and Esau were fraternal twins who fought in the womb; Jacob's descendants became the Israelites and Esau's descendants became the Edomites. Both descended from a common set of ancestors -- Isaac and Rebekah. Jacob and Esau were grandsons of Abraham -- one chosen, one not.

Isaiah recounts all the miracles and blessings God bestowed on His people during the greatest single event of their heritage -- the exodus from Egypt. The details of the exodus have been preserved in song, poetry, history, and religion. The Feast of Tabernacles and the Passover served as annual reminders of God's miraculous provisions for His people. With this background, Isaiah proceeds to offer a prayer to God.

Isaiah's prayer asks for mercy and compassion, reminding God they were His chosen people. For a while they had held a place of honor, but now they were trampled. Isaiah calls for God to return to His people as in days past. He confesses the sins of the nation, asking "How then can we be saved? All of us have become like one who is unclean, and all our righteous acts are like filthy rags; we all shrivel up like a leaf, and like the wind our sins sweep us away."[1] (Isa. 64:6) Isaiah refers to God as "our Redeemer" (63:16), our Father (64:8), and "our potter" (64:8). These titles clearly depict God's redeeming power, His love, and His sovereignty.[39] All the material things "treasured" by the Jews are now nothing but ruins. (In Matt. 6:21, Jesus reminds us "For where your treasure is, there your heart will be also."[1])

Food for Thought: In the fall of 1861, Julia Ward Howe was reading Isaiah 63. In the early months of America's Civil War, she was deeply moved to convey the message of God to the tune of "John Brown's Body Lies A-Moldering in the Grave." This had become a marching battle song of the South. Her new song was titled "Battle Hymn of the Republic." She knew the contrast of brother against brother and the judgment of God with the joyous southern song about a northern defeat would not fall on deaf ears.

"Mine eyes have seen the glory of the coming of the Lord,

He is trampling out the vintage where the grapes of wrath are stored;

He hath loosed the fateful lightning of His terrible swift sword --

His truth is marching on."

Lessons of Love

July 21
Bible Readings: Isaiah 65:1-25; 66:1-24; 37:38, 2 Kings 19:37, 2 Chron. 33:10-17, 21c

God has always been near, inviting us to seek Him. A people who never sought Him found him and He chose the Israelites to be His people. The Israelites were willing to believe in a God they could not see. Other nations insisted on deifying animals, places, heavenly bodies, kings, or the dead. God will measure out the full payment of judgment to the pagan nations. Those who believe in Fortune and Destiny will be slain. The descendants of Israel will possess God's holy mountain. God's servants will be given many blessings -- materially, emotionally, and spiritually.

Again the new heaven and earth of Revelation 21 are foretold in Isaiah 65. There will be no crying, premature death, toiling in vain, and no strife. The earth, animals, and mankind will live in harmony. In essence, there is a reversal of sin's destructive forces and a return to the Garden of Eden.

Jesus tells us in Matt. 5:34-35 that heaven is God's throne and earth His footstool. This word picture comes from Isaiah 66. Those who will live in Heaven with God will be the humble, repentant faithful. The enemies of the Lord will receive all they deserve. They will be the footstool of Jesus, the Redeemer of the saved (Heb. 10:12-14).

Isaiah 66:7 tells of a son born before the woman goes into labor. Rev. 12:4-5 tells of a woman delivering a son while the beast of evil waits to devour him. The son is delivered and taken up to God before the beast can get him. One interpretation of these rather strange passages is that the woman (the nation of Israel) gave birth to a Son (Jesus) before her pains came (the tribulation). Isaiah goes on to talk about Jerusalem giving birth to her children or, put another way, God's servants (believers) being brought home to a New Jerusalem, His chosen city. She will have peace like a river and the wealth of nations.

The Book of Isaiah ends with a passage about the judgment and destruction of the wicked. The LORD is coming with the fire of judgment to slay the wicked. Believers are streaming into Jerusalem in such large numbers that some will be selected to serve as priests or ministers to the others. The new heaven and earth will endure forever. All mankind will bow down before God to be judged. Those who rebelled against God will be in eternal torment. The last verse of Isaiah implies hell can be seen from Heaven; if Jerusalem represents Heaven and the Dead Sea represents hell, then they are only 15 miles or so apart. A New Jerusalem will be lit up by the Glory of God like a bright light in a world of darkness. The parable Jesus told of Lazarus and the rich man (Luke 16:22-26) plainly states the rich man who was in hell could see Lazarus with Abraham. When the rich man begged for relief from his torment, Abraham told him there was a great chasm between the two places that could not be crossed.

Today's lesson ends with the assassination of Sennacherib of Assyria by two of his sons. A third son, Esarhaddon, succeeds him. Meanwhile Manasseh and his people are captured by the Assyrians and taken into captivity. (Now Isaiah's prophecies are coming to life.) During his captivity, Manasseh repents and turns to God. I am reminded of Prov. 22:6 that says, "Train a child in the way he should go, and when he is old, he will not turn from it." Parents should be ever mindful of this charge. God hears his prayer and returns him to Jerusalem as a subservient king to Assyria. Manasseh eliminates idols and pagan altars. He restores the altar and worship of God. Even with these great reforms, Manasseh could not change the bondage of the Jews; bondage his earlier evil leadership had produced as judgment for their sins.

Food for Thought: When Abraham talked to the rich man in hell, we are never told if Lazarus could actually see the rich man. Some believe that part of the torment of hell is being able to see Heaven but not able to go there. Some believe this parable was a story Jesus told to make a point rather than an actual occurrence. One thing is sure: Christians don't have to worry about hell or torment. Have you secured your place in Heaven?

July 22
Bible Readings: Nahum

Like Jonah, the Book of Nahum is exclusively directed towards a foreign nation: Assyria. We know almost nothing about the prophet. The name Nahum means to console or to comfort. He was from Elkosh that likely is in Judah, but because it is referred to nowhere else in the Old Testament, we have no idea as to its exact location. The theme of judgment is pervasive in Nahum. Perhaps no book of the Old Testament is so singular in its topic.

Judging from the style of the book, Nahum was a bit of a poet. In chapter three he combines the sensations of sight and sound in staccato word flashes as he depicts the advance of the attack on Ninevah, the Assyrian capital.

Crack of whip and Rumble of wheel, Steed rearing and Chariot lurching.

The time of the prophecy is between the fall of Thebes (663 B.C.), also called No-Amon that is described in Nahum as already fallen, and the fall of Ninevah (612 B.C.) that is spoken of as a future event. If the words of Nahum appear to be rather vitriolic, keep in mind that the Assyrians at this time were the most brutal of all conquering empires when it came to rebellious captives. Suffice it to say that their court annals openly boasted of acts worse than any sane man's most horrible nightmares.

The book begins with a visitation of God upon the earth. His purpose of judgment is so serious that the wettest parts of Palestine wither before Him. The Assyrians are described as plotting against God. This attitude can be seen in Isaiah 36:14-20 where the Assyrian officials try to insult the God of Israel.

God first speaks to His people in Nahum 1:12-2:2. Numbers do not impress God. He plans to break the yoke of Assyria. Verse 15 is practically a direct quotation of Isaiah 52:7. The idea is how beautiful is the news and the feet of him who brings the news of Assyria's end.

Chapter 2 describes the end of the city in graphic terms. Nahum's description is very accurate. Note verse 6: the river gates are opened. The Greek historian, Diodorus Siculus, indicates that the fall of Ninevah was assisted by a series of heavy rains that swelled the Euphrates, flooded parts of the city, and washed away about two miles of its wall.[45]

In Nahum 2:11-12, we have a taunting riddle aimed at the Assyrians who like to compare themselves to lions. In verses 2:13 and 3:5 a most fearful judgment is announced. Can any reader imagine a statement more sobering or a prospect more terrifying? Yet anyone who rejects God throughout his life is embracing the same judgment. In the latter part of chapter 3, Nahum is pointing out to his hearers that tall and thick walls do not guarantee security. After all, the entire great Egyptian city of No had them and all can see what happened to her.

The book ends with a taunt song over the city of Ninevah. Her destruction is inevitable. Despite her large population that resembles the locusts in sheer numbers, she will disappear. The last verses are aimed directly at the king.

The books of Nahum and Jonah are alike in many ways. A final similarity they share is that they are the only books of the Bible that end with a question. The questions reveal the mercy and justice of God. The penitent Assyria deserves mercy, but the Assyria that persists in her sins deserves judgment.

Food for Thought: God is love. Today show love to someone who only God could really love!

Verses of the Week: **Jeremiah 1:7-8** "'You must go to everyone I send you to and say whatever I command you. Do not be afraid of them, for I am with you and will rescue you.' declares the LORD."

July 23
Bible Readings: 2 Kings 21:17-26; 22:1-2; 23:25-27, 2 Chron. 33:18-25; 34:1-2

This lesson is especially short. It gives you some historical background of the happenings in the royal household in Jerusalem just before the fall of Judah. Manasseh has tried to undo all the evil he has done and eventually dies a natural death. His son Amon, who only reigns two years before he is assassinated by some of his officials, succeeds him. Manasseh's poor example for his son is evident in that Amon is an evil king who reinstituted pagan worship. After the conspirators are executed, Amon's son Josiah comes to the throne. Josiah walked in the ways of the LORD and is considered the most righteous king of the divided kingdom era. But, Josiah was only 8 years old when he became king and God's judgment on Judah had already been decided as a result of Manasseh's wickedness in the early years of his reign. Josiah reigned 31 years as king of Judah, a subservient to Assyria.

Food for Thought: One life does make a difference. Hezekiah was a good king but let pride get in his way at the end. His son Manasseh was an evil king who repented near the end of his life. Manasseh's grandson is the most righteous king Judah ever has. [Hezekiah was the best king in building Jerusalem as a city and he was a good spiritual leader. Josiah was the most righteous king, although his powers of development are not evident.] People do make end-of-life conversions to Christ, but they leave a wake of evil behind them that takes generations to overcome. Someone is watching you today. Be an ambassador of Christ.

July 24
Bible Readings: Zephaniah, 2 Chron. 34:3-7

Zephaniah is a most singular book among the prophets. In most instances we know nothing or next to nothing about the prophet. In Zephaniah we are not provided with much more than that, but if we pay attention to subtle clues and consider the time in which the prophet was preaching, much becomes clear. The book has a traditional beginning, the message is God's word that is delivered through a particular prophet. The book then traces Zephaniah's lineage through four generations. Of the sixteen prophets who wrote books, eight have no family history recorded, six mention the names of their fathers, and one refers to his father and grandfather. Only Zephaniah traces his lineage this far back. The likely reason is the name mentioned in this fourth generation: Hezekiah, which was a relatively rare name. It is likely that Zephaniah was a descendant of the famous king, and thereby a relative of Josiah during whose reign Zephaniah preached.

In 2 Kings 21 we learn that a religious revival occurred during the reign of Josiah that was largely precipitated by the discovery of a lost book during an effort to remodel the temple. This lost book gave serious warnings of what would happen to the people if they were unfaithful to God. Most scholars believe that this lost book is Deuteronomy.

If a reader compares Zephaniah's preaching to Deuteronomy, it becomes clear that the prophet is very familiar with the book. In fact the similarity in expressions in Zephaniah and Deuteronomy is quite remarkable.

Note the following examples.

"And they shall build houses, and they shall not dwell in them." Zeph. 1:13

"And a house you shall build but you shall not dwell in it." Deut. 28:30

"They shall plant vineyards but they shall not drink their wine." Zeph. 1:13

"Vineyards you shall plant and you shall serve but their wine you shall not drink." Deut. 28:39

Other examples include Zeph. 1:15, Deut. 28:53, 55, 57; Zeph. 1:15, Deut. 4:11; Zeph. 1:17, Deut. 28:29; Zeph. 1:18, Deut. 32:21-22; Zeph. 3:5, Deut. 32:4; Zeph. 3:17, Deut. 28:63; Zeph. 3:19-20, Deut. 26:19; and a host of other references.[45]

Thus, it is likely that Zephaniah and his relative the king were working together to bring about reform and revival. Zephaniah was the preacher of righteousness calling for repentance; Josiah was the king exerting pressure for reform in the political realm.

Zephaniah's three chapters largely fall in a three-part outline. Chapter one proclaims a great day of judgment when creation shall be reversed and the covenant people will be cut off. Chapter two consists of judgments upon the nations surrounding Judah. Chapter three looks forward to a purified people returning to the LORD.

Food for Thought: A memorable verse from Zephaniah, which speaks to our affluent society is 1:18.

> "Neither their silver nor their gold
> Will be able to deliver them
> On the day of the LORD's wrath;
> And all the earth will be devoured

In the fire of his jealousy,
For he will make a complete end,
Indeed a terrifying one,
Of all the inhabitants of the earth."

July 25
Bible Readings: Jeremiah 1-3:5

Jeremiah was born in the Levite city of Anathoth, a small town 3-4 miles northeast of Jerusalem. As the son of a Levite, he would have received training from early childhood in the laws and practices of God as a matter of course. It is so important that children be trained in God's word so that they will be prepared when God's call for service comes. And we all do have a place for service. We are to worship Him and prepare ourselves to hear and act on His call to service. Jeremiah's call came in 626 B.C. when he was but a youth. This statement about Jeremiah's immaturity may simply mean he was less than 25 years old which was the age that priests entered the service of God, probably as an apprentice or assistant to gain experience and training before actually having the grave duty (at 30) of handling and accounting for the Temple worship services and offerings and maintaining its furnishings (1 Chron. 24:3-7.) You will recall that Abiathar, a priest of David, was banished to Anathoth for his role in usurping the king (1 Kings 2:26-27). Jeremiah was probably a descendant of Abiathar who descended from Eli.[47] You will also recall from Num. 3:1-4 that Ithamar was one of Aaron's sons; thus he was of the high priest lineage. In 1 Sam. 2:27-36, Eli's family is judged by God for the sins Eli allowed his sons Hophni and Phinehas to continue to practice before the people. Eli was of the lineage of Ithamar. Therefore, being of the lineage of Ithamar, Jeremiah's family could no longer serve in the high priest position. This probably fostered some natural resentment toward the current priests serving in the Temple and living in the splendor of Jerusalem as well as a sense of shame and embarrassment. Jeremiah was human just like us. At the time of his call, like Moses, he pleaded an inability to do public speaking (an excuse still used today). God provides for those who are willing to obey and serve; God's Hand touched Jeremiah's mouth and God's words were placed there (1:9).

Jeremiah receives two messages in the form of visions. First, Jeremiah sees the branch of an almond tree. In Hebrew, the name almond means awakening because its blossom was the first to bloom in the spring. The almond blossom image decorated the lampstand of the Temple. In Jeremiah it clearly depicts God's dependability in watching His people but also His message through Jeremiah to 'awaken' them to turn from their wickedness.[5] Second, Jeremiah saw a boiling pot tilting "away from the north" or spilling its contents toward the south (Judah's direction). God commands Jeremiah to get prepared because obeying God includes fighting against evil forces, but God will support and rescue.

Again we see a courtroom scene in action in Jeremiah. God, the Prosecutor, declares charges against the Jews: (1) They forsook Him, and (2) They devoted themselves to serving worthless gods. Their guilt was so great that regardless of the number of purification washings, they could not remove the stain of their sins.[46] But when trouble hit they always went looking for God, not out of true repentance but rather out of desperation. Instinctively they knew their pagan gods were worthless, but those gods provided them with a way to rationalize their evil practices and morals. Yet in spite of these charges against them, the Jews refused to acknowledge their sins. In fact, they have no remorse or shame. God, the Judge, pronounces them "Guilty." (Compare Deut. 24:1-4 to Jer. 3:1.)

Food for Thought: The greatest compliment Jeremiah could ever receive came years after his death when many people compared Jesus to Jeremiah (Matt. 16:14). We all should strive to live like Jesus. Apparently, Jeremiah's life continued to be a witness over 500 years later! How long will your Christian example be remembered?

July 26
Bible Readings: Jeremiah 3:6-5:13

King Josiah was Judah's most righteous king, but Manasseh's reign of evil had carried the people too far from God. Judgment was sure and certain. Even when Israel fell, Judah did not take heed. The LORD's pronouncement was "Faithless Israel is more righteous than unfaithful Judah."[1] (3:11)

It is hard to believe that the powerful and awesome God is willing to beg unworthy sinners like us for time and attention. God does just that in Jer. 3:12-22. He pleads with Israel to confess, repent, and turn back to Him before it is too late. Verse 14 reminds me of Abraham's plea for the cities of the plain (Gen. 18:16-33). God says that if He can only find one righteous person in a town or two from any one family group, He will spare them. God's plan was to take those righteous seeds, plant them in Jerusalem (after the Jews are removed), and give them new righteous leaders. God's covenant with the Israelites (Ark of the Covenant that contained the Mercy Seat of God) would be gone and never needed again because He would sit on the throne in Jerusalem. Israelite and Jewish exiles would return to Jerusalem to inherit the land. Of course, this whole passage is a depiction of the exiles from the lands of Assyria and Babylon returning to Jerusalem.

In a flashback to our original courtroom scene, we have the confession of Israel presented with God declaring the conditions for commuting their sentence: return to Him, remove all pagan idols, trust in Him solely, and pledge allegiance to God. Now God calls Judah to present their confession, but no confession is forthcoming! God announces the judgment: Judah will fall to Babylon.

The only side of Judah where attack was feasible was the northwest side. The Hinnom Valley was on the south and wrapped around much of the west and the Kidron Valley was on the east. Directly north was the Temple Mount. Most of the roads into Jerusalem (to accommodate a huge army) will be in the northwest sector. Due east of Judah, Babylon would have to circle to the north to invade.[47] The shear size and power of the invasion will leave Judah's government and religious leaders speechless with fear.

In Jeremiah 4:10, we see Jeremiah acting as the Defense Attorney. He accuses God of deceiving the people by telling them they will have peace in Jerusalem if they only turn back to Him when actually they are about to be cut down with the sword. (Remember King Josiah has eliminated idols and declared God be worshipped, but the people never truly repented nor did they worship only God! They only made a show of changing instead of really repenting. This could easily describe many church members today.) God's reply is that He will devastate the land. The wind in Judah normally came from the West, originating over the Mediterranean Sea. An eastern wind off the desert was excessively hot, dry, and contained much sand. [47] In essence, you had a sand storm. Once in Albuquerque, New Mexico, I was in a sand storm. It was awful. You couldn't see for the blinding sand -- all in your clothes, mouth, and hair. You couldn't turn on the windshield wipers or roll down a window because of the sand gritting and scratching the glass. In some cases the paint was stripped from cars. The next day people were cleaning up piles of sand from inside the buildings! It had even penetrated all the ventilation shafts! Therefore, I can relate to the damage a desert sandstorm can do. Judah had nothing pleasant to anticipate!

The northernmost city of Israel is Dan. The new inhabitants hear the vast army coming long before they are visible. Messengers are dispatched with the alarm (You may recall that even though Assyria removed the Israelites from their land and deported them to various Assyrian locations, they also imported large groups of pagans into the Israelite cities. Owning a wasteland would be of little use to them. It would take new inhabitants many decades to rebuild to the point of feeling secure enough to rebel.)

God mourned the lost relationship with His people. He looked at what would be left of Judah. God's chosen land had reverted back to its state at the time of creation -- without form and void. This scene reminds me of when a volcano blows its top. All life for miles around, in air or on land, ceases -- no plants, no animals, no people. The thick soot and ash choke out all glimmers of light. The land shakes and the hot molten rock levels the landscape. Devastation is everywhere.

In one last effort to save Judah, God tells Jeremiah (5:1), "If you can find but one person who deals honestly and seeks the truth, I will forgive this city."[1] Alas, there was none. Now you may ask, "What about Josiah?" Well, Josiah was taken home to God by way of an arrow during a battle at Megiddo (interestingly this is the same area as the great battle of Armageddon in Revelation). The Judean army was trying to keep the Egyptian army from marching north along the seaport road. Pharaoh Neco of Egypt was going to help the remaining Assyrians after the fall of Ninevah in 612 B.C. But I am getting ahead of the story. You will learn more about this in the August 3 lesson.

Our lesson today has been a prophecy of what is to come as well as a look back at what has happened.

Food for Thought: This has been an unsettling week - a week of troubles, some of my own and some of others. Several times I reached the breaking point and was reduced to tears. Every time God provided Christian people to stand in the gap. Other times I let God move through me as I stood in the gap for others. Friday brought much physical pain and distress on top of watching others suffer. Then the Lord brought this verse to me. "For just as the sufferings of Christ flow over into our lives, so also through Christ our comfort overflows."[1] (2 Corinthians 1:5)

July 27
Bible Readings: Jeremiah 5:14-6:30

Even after their prolonged wickedness, God could not bear to completely destroy every one of His people. He reserved a remnant for Himself. The remnant, though, would find out how it felt to serve foreign people with their foreign gods. They must pay the consequences of their sins.

Judah has been smug in its sin. After all, the Jews were God's chosen people, living in God's chosen city, with God's chosen Temple (house). God wouldn't dare leave them! Now they are selfish, greedy, and wicked to the point that "their evil deeds have no limit."[1] (5:28) Judeans are so 'into themselves' that they don't even realize the horror of the coming judgment. Scholars believe Jer. 5:14-17 refers to the raiding party made on Syria and Palestine in the late Seventh Century B.C. by the Scythians. These were a barbaric people who lived on the land between the Caspian Sea and the Black Sea in the current country of Georgia, formerly a part of the Soviet Union. They were allies of the Assyrians (for about 30 years) to help subdue northern kingdoms.[5] (With friends like these, you sure don't need enemies to fight!) Scythians were only interested in taking plunder. Because they were a nomadic people, they weren't interested in land expansion[5] -- the Assyrians could have the land. Based on Russian archaeologists' excavations in Georgia, "The Scythians wore garments made from the tanned skin of their victims. Women were not considered old enough to marry until they had killed a man. They even used the skulls of their victims to decorate their saddles."[47] (p. 31) (Centuries later Joseph Stalin would come out of Georgia, the Scythian homeland, to similarly oppress the people of Russia.)

God's people had purposely rebelled against Him because lying prophets and priests misled them. We should take this as a warning today! If we do not read and study God's word and pray for His guidance, we cannot discern the truth or reject lies. The devil is crafty and knows our weaknesses better than we do. When we become secure in our church or denomination, he attacks us from within, at the very time we allow our defenses to rest because we are 'secure.' God designed His church to provide a respite to His disciples from the world's storms, but as disciples we must be alert to any invasion of ideas, actions, or people who are juxtaposed to the Word of God.

In chapter 6 we see the warnings go out that invaders are coming. Tekoa was a signal station town about 10 miles south of Jerusalem. Its elevation half a mile above sea level made it a particularly good fortified city. The name Tekoa means trumpet blast,[5] obviously named for its trumpet signal that would echo for miles through the valleys and mountains. From Beth Haccherem (a village about 2 miles south of Jerusalem[5]) signal fires would go up. Now the interesting note here is that the invaders were coming from the north so why are these southern fortifications announcing the alarm? The answer is relatively simple. The Jebusites had held Jerusalem until David conquered it. Jerusalem was a border town between Israel and Judah. Because it had not belonged to any tribe, David was able to make it a good, politically neutral capital city to unite the tribes.[7] When the northern kingdom fell, Jerusalem was left exposed to potential invasion from the north. Tekoa, being some 150 feet higher than Jerusalem, had a good view of Jerusalem and the hills beyond. So southern fortified cities which once watched for Egyptian, Ethiopian, and Arab invaders now had to watch for northern invaders as well. Verse 3 talks of "shepherds with their flocks" invading. This obviously means foreign kings with their armies.[47]

God makes it clear (vs. 8) that His judgment does not involve actual punishment but rather the simple removal of His Presence. Jerusalem would be left to follow her own sinful ways. God's wrath towards His people is allowing them to do as they please but without any protection or blessings from Him. The Judeans quickly find out what it means to see God's back. Verse 17 tells us God sent His prophets to warn them, but they flatly rejected God's message. All the religious rituals, burnt offerings, sacrifices, and religious festivals would not save them because their hearts were not right with God. The devastator will come on them quickly. God sent Jeremiah to refine them in the crucible of fire (like precious metals are purified), but the impurities could not be separated out. They rejected God; like rejected silver, they were worthless.

Food for Thought: Have you allowed God to remove the impurities in your heart and life? Or have you stubbornly clung to them? Even Christians are refined and purified. "Those who sow in tears will reap with songs of joy."[1] (Psalm 126:5)

July 28
Bible Readings: Jeremiah 7-9

The people of Judah had become so brazen that they would worship all their pagan gods and then go to God's Temple and reassure themselves their God-in-a-Box (Ark) was still there! As with their pagan gods, they limited God to a 'place' also. Jerusalem, at this time, reminds me of Salem, Massachusetts. Amongst the evil witchcraft in Salem, there are still some Christian churches. Likewise, amongst the evil pagan worship in Jerusalem, there was still God's Temple. Just as I felt the breath of evil breathing down my neck while visiting Salem, Jeremiah must have felt very threatened being an out-of-towner preaching against paganism in a town that had rejected God. He surely claimed his promise from God (1:8) repeatedly in prayer.

Chapter 7 begins with Jeremiah standing at the gate to the Temple and boldly proclaiming to the arriving 'worshippers' to repent and turn from their evil ways. He goes on to say, "Has this house, which bears my Name, become a den of robbers to you?"[1] (7:11) Hundreds of years later, Jesus will quote a portion of this verse when he drives the money-changers and merchants out of the Temple (Matt. 21:13). He also quoted Isa. 56:7 saying God's house should be a house of prayer. Keep in mind that Jeremiah's priestly lineage had been permanently stigmatized by their humiliation and removal from the high priest position because of the sins of Eli and his sons. Therefore, Jeremiah (from a fallen priest lineage) was standing at the Temple telling these rich and powerful citizens of Jerusalem that their priests and officials had led them down the path of destruction! (Surely it looked like a case of jealousy to most who heard him.) Can you imagine the danger he was in? The Jews no longer had God as their conscience. Murder was part of their worship now (child sacrifice). Why would they restrain from killing Jeremiah? Of course, God promised to rescue Jeremiah from danger as long as he obeyed God's command. Jeremiah's message was that the Temple couldn't protect the Jews, only God could do that, but they must truly repent and turn to Him or even their Temple would be destroyed.

Next, Jeremiah tells the Jews to recall the destruction in Shiloh (during the days of Eli and Samuel). Shiloh had been the first home of the tabernacle. (Later, when the kingdom divided, the Israelites made Shiloh one of their main worship centers.) The Philistines had destroyed Shiloh and the same would happen to Jerusalem if they didn't repent and turn to God.[47] In fact, the Philistines had carried off the Ark of the Covenant. Jeremiah was reminding them that they were once again placing their trust in an icon rather than God! Regardless of the dynamic message Jeremiah delivers to the people, the Jews still turned their backs on God.

Now Jeremiah prophesies judgment. Their destruction will be so thorough that even the bones of the dead will be removed from their graves. Any people surviving the destruction will wish they were dead. There will be no food, no leaders, no wisdom, no safety, no one who can be trusted, and no God to turn to for help. God declares, "I will make Jerusalem a heap of ruins . . . and I will lay waste the towns of Judah so no one can live there."[1] (9:11) The mournful wailing for Jerusalem will be heard throughout the nations. Too late, the survivors will teach their children that "Death has climbed in through our windows and has entered our fortresses."[1] (9:21) We need to teach our children this today. Death (evil) is climbing into their fortresses (hearts, souls, bodies, minds) through their windows (eyes, ears, mouth). We have become a nation of complacent, apathetic people. God is sending His spiritual leaders, but we are rejecting His message. As Christians, we must take a stand against evil. We must not allow evil in our homes and cars, schools and workplaces via radio, television, pornography, and filth. When we pass off foul language, violence, and perverted filth as commonplace, then we are, in essence, giving our stamp of approval. God is not going to accept the excuse, "Well, everybody was doing it!" nor the one "You can't live without any pleasure in life, and everything has some bad language or violence in it." What started in the 60s as shocking nudity, violence, sex, and drugs in the news is now merely an accepted daily state of affairs. The world has not only come to expect but rather to insist upon the most barbaric sex, violence, and language the devil can devise in every aspect of our daily lives. God is sending His messengers, but we can't even hear His message over the din of our iniquities. Take a stand with Jeremiah. Boldly tell the world to repent and turn to God!

Food for Thought: God says it best:

> "Let not the wise man boast of his wisdom
> or the strong man boast of his strength
> or the rich man boast of his riches,
> but let him who boasts boast about this:
> that he understands and knows me,
> that I am the LORD, who exercises kindness,
> justice, righteousness on earth,
> for in these I delight."[1] (9:23-24)

July 29
Bible Readings: Jeremiah 10-12

Jeremiah is preaching during the reign of Josiah.[47] Josiah has instituted religious reform and is in the process of destroying all the idols. Jeremiah tells the people they can adorn their idols with silver and gold, but they are still just scarecrows! Likewise, we can adorn our church buildings with crystal, plush carpet, gold, and carved wood, but they are still just scarecrows if God isn't there! As with all scarecrows, there can be a lot of flash on the outside but still have no living substance on the inside. In contrast to dead idols, God is living, true, and eternal. God is alive and working. His people who are His church must be alive and working on His behalf.

Jeremiah reminds the Jews that the one and only God is Creator of the universe, Maker of all things, and the Portion of Jacob. God is described as power, wisdom, and understanding. Again Jeremiah condemns Judah's priests and prophets. He says the "shepherds are senseless and do not inquire of the LORD."[1] (10:21)

During Josiah's reforms, the Temple was cleaned up and repaired. In 622 B.C. a book of law was found stored in the Temple. The book was brought to Josiah and read before him. Bible students believe this was the Book of Deuteronomy.[47] (Also mentioned in the lesson on Zephaniah.) Jeremiah 11 refers to the covenant four times. The covenant between the Hebrews and God at Mt. Sinai after the exodus is contained in Deuteronomy. You will recall that the covenant ended (Deut. 27) with a list of curses that will befall the people if they did not keep their promise to God. Just imagine the righteous King Josiah hearing these curses for the very first time! There it was in the people's own contract with God! The Jews had condemned themselves by violating the contract. Who knows -- he may have even been able to hear Jeremiah's preaching from his palace door! Josiah must have been frantic in his destruction of the idols and pagan shrines by this point. The covenant was read to the people and Jeremiah had new sermon material! He accused Judah of having as many gods as they had towns and as many altars for Baal as Jerusalem had streets. As you would suspect, Jeremiah was becoming a very unpopular man. After all, the pagan priests and idol makers were now unemployed not to mention the whole town was condemned to death and destruction! Now it seemed to them everything was going along just fine until this ole Jeremiah came along. For a pagan people, the answer to their woes was easy -- kill Jeremiah! As always, God was true to His promise and warned Jeremiah of the plot to kill him by the men in his own hometown -- Anathoth! [Remember Anathoth was a city given to the Levite priests. Here some of God's own priests were plotting murder of another priest! Again we see scarecrows without the Word in them. As you recall, the Levites were set aside or consecrated as the redemption price for the firstfruits (first male child) of the Hebrew families. Their primary purpose in life was to serve God. Now they were leaders of sin. Think of the large number of scandalous news stories today about the corruption of priests and preachers claiming to carry the banner of God.] God is so incensed by this sin of the men of Anathoth that He declares not even a remnant will be left of that town! (This must have been a shattering, sad time for Jeremiah. First, he discovers his friends and relatives plan to kill him, then he hears God say his whole hometown -- all he has known for so many years -- will be totally wiped out -- no one and nothing left.)

Jeremiah, in his despair, asks the questions we all do at times. "Why does the way of the wicked prosper? Why do all the faithless live at ease?"[1] (12:1) Next he launches into his own pity party. He's obeyed, he's been faithful, he's been proven through trials -- why isn't he successful? No one is listening, no one is turning to God, and now everyone wants him dead! (It seems like a good case to me!) God, in all His mercy, replies, "If you have raced with men on foot and they have worn you out, how can you compete with horses? If you stumble in safe country, how will you manage in the thickets . . .? Your brothers, your own family -- even they have betrayed you."[1] (12:5-6) (Hummm -- as usual, God has a better case!) As disciples we have to learn to overcome the smaller problems or obstacles in order to be experienced enough to tackle the big jobs God has for us.

God tells Jeremiah the people must bear their shame -- the consequences of their sins. But God will not allow the invaders to go free. They, too, will pay. Their sin will be in oppressing God's chosen people and taking the land from the Hebrews, the land God gave them.

Food for Thought: Isaiah (40:29) had some words about God that would have encouraged Jeremiah -- and still encourages us. "He gives strength to the weary and increases the power of the weak."[1]

Verses of the Week: **Jeremiah 17:7-8** "But blessed is the man who trusts in the LORD, whose confidence is in him. He will be like a tree planted by the water that sends out its roots by the stream. It does not fear when heat comes; its leaves are always green. It has no worries in a year of drought and never fails to bear fruit."

July 30
Bible Readings: Jeremiah 13-15:9

The demonstration that God calls Jeremiah to perform in chapter 13 is so full of symbolism that my main concern is not being able to convey it properly. First, let's look at the three main symbols.

(1) Jeremiah represents God (as God's ambassador, he represents God to the people).

(2) A belt was a key piece of utilitarian clothing. It was used for beauty on holy days when one wore a highly

embroidered belt with the standard tan or near white clothing to worship and praise God. Belts were also used in battle to carry the needed weapons. Daily life required a belt for 'girding up the loins' (tucking the loose ends of the robe up in it) to do manual labor or to run. Scribes used belts to carry writing tools and ink. Linen was the material used to make the priests' garments. Ordinarily, linen belts were white (unless embroidered). Thus, the white linen belt Jeremiah buys represents the pure and innocent nation of Israel -- the children of God, a holy people, a kingdom of priests.

(3) Perath represents the Euphrates River that runs through the land of Babylon. Of course, this represents foreign bondage.[46]

Let's analyze this story one scene at a time. First I will tell the story line and then I will give one interpretation.

1. Jeremiah buys a linen belt and puts it on.
   - God binds the children of God -- the infant nation of Israel -- to Himself with the covenant at Mt. Sinai. They are to praise, honor, and serve Him.
2. Jeremiah wears his belt daily expecting it to serve him well. He never separates himself from his belt.
   - God supports and binds Himself to His people at all times, expecting them to serve Him and only Him. The people are never separated from God.
3. Jeremiah's belt has become very dirty over time, but it is never removed for washing.
   - God's people became dirty with sin, but God had never removed them from Himself to scrub out and eliminate the filth of sins, their moral decay. He continued to hold them to Himself even when they became a source of shame.
4. Jeremiah goes to Perath and hides the belt in a crevice in the rocks.
   - God exiles His people to Babylon, hiding their shame in the hardness of the Babylonian servitude.
5. Many days later, Jeremiah returns to Perath to retrieve the belt.
   - Seventy years later God seeks His people in Babylon.
6. Jeremiah 'digs up' the belt, but only a little is left. Most is decayed, ruined, worthless.
   - God now has to dig up out of the mire the remnant of His children. The rocks have worn down over the years to sand and mud. The consequences of the sins of the Hebrews were physical decay, ruin, worthlessness -- a rejected object of disgust.[46]

Jeremiah preaches against the pride of Judah, knowing pride goes before destruction. If the people do not turn to God they will be taken into captivity. The king will be exiled and the fortified cities in the Negev (south) will be abandoned. The rain will be withheld. The ground will be unproductive. When the judgment comes, the people will cry out to God. It will be too little, too late. They will be destroyed by sword, famine, and plague. The remainder will go into captivity.

The siege on Jerusalem will be so long that those who don't die by the sword will die by famine. The LORD goes on to say that even Moses and Samuel together couldn't convince Him to extend any more compassion to these wicked people. The trial is over; the sentence has been given.

Food for Thought: Jeremiah's belt demonstration reminds me of Fanny Crosby's song "A Wonderful Savior is Jesus My Lord." Jesus is our Rock who was broken so the filth of our sins could be washed away. We are hidden in the cleft of the rock (in the arms of Jesus) and protected by God's own hand, not left to our own ruin.

"A wonderful Savior is Jesus my Lord,
A wonderful Savior to me;

He hideth my soul in the cleft of the rock,
Where rivers of pleasure I see.
He hideth my soul in the cleft of the rock,
That shadows a dry, thirsty land;
He hideth my life in the depths of His love,
And covers me there with His hand."

July 31
Bible Readings: Jeremiah 15:10-21; 16:1-21; 17:1-18

Jeremiah is depressed. He has devoted his life to trying to save his countrymen, but they would not listen. Instead they mock him, beat him, and ridicule him. They have even plotted to kill him! His friends, his relatives, his loved ones have turned their backs on him! Did I say Jeremiah or Jesus? When we get to feeling sorry for ourselves, we need to remember that whatever we are enduring, Jesus had it worse.

Jeremiah complains that he had neither been a borrower nor a lender. Because the love of money is the root of all evil, most strife in life has money as its basis. God's answer is to say, "Okay, so that's the way you feel? Well, you can be enslaved with the rest of them!" Now that gets Jeremiah's attention! Immediately he begins to backpedal, asking the LORD instead to avenge him by striking his foes. Now Jeremiah pleads his own case before God. He's not really rebellious. He had been separated from everyone else -- all alone because of God's mission for him. He had obeyed God and performed his preaching duties, but Jeremiah was indignant, grieved, and sorrowful of his lot in life. Why had God caused him so much pain? Why had God deceived him into thinking his preaching could make a difference? (Jeremiah is pretty bold to accuse God of being deceitful! Above all, this should be a clear sign that Jeremiah had reached his breaking point. Everybody has a breaking point. I pray none of us has to find out just where that point is in life. The breaking point is easily defined -- its that point in time when your level of desperation overrides your discipline, logic, and conscience. The closer one gets to that point, the greater prayer is needed to prevent a disaster.)

Out of God's deep love and mercy comes His call to repentance. "Jeremiah, look at yourself. If you want to again experience confidence, courage, zeal, and hope, then repent of this sin you just brought on yourself. Turn to Me for help and I will rescue you and sustain you."

Jeremiah comes back to God only to find his life will be even lonelier than he imagined. God commands that Jeremiah must never marry or have children. In addition, he can never participate in community events, i.e., funerals, celebrations, festivals. Because God has turned His back on these people, Jeremiah must do so, too. These commands had far reaching implications for Jeremiah. In the Hebrew culture, one's hope in the future was in their children, primarily their sons. Having no wife meant having no one to share the trials or joys of life. No children meant the end of the lineage -- no hope.[47] Clearly, I see the picture of a suffering world seeking companionship, meaning to life, and hope. The Jews placed their companionship in the tribe's rituals and festivities; they continually searched for meaning to life by going from one pagan god to another seeking answers, but their hope was in their children. The continuation of their nation was in the hands of their children. Moreover, the great emphasis placed on genealogy meant children had to be produced to keep the lineage intact. Apparently, not once did they realize that the continuation of a lineage, nation, or mankind was at the pleasure of God. When they became a stench unto God, they no longer brought Him pleasure. When they rejected God, they rejected their true hope for the future.

Many of the Jews would die by sword or famine. Many more would die of disease. The survivors would be exiled, but God will not abandon them. He will return to them and bring a remnant of His people back to the Holy City. For now the hearts of the Jews are so hardened that even engraving tools couldn't write God's word on them. The person who places trust in mankind is cursed to doom and destruction from the beginning, but a person who trusts in God is blessed with hope and life. In the Old Testament, God is the Rock from whence comes the spring of living water: water for a dry and thirsty land, water for a dry and longing people. In this example we can see an even deeper meaning to the Numbers 20:1-13 event. Even though initially we realize Moses disobeyed God by striking the rock instead of speaking to it, we now can see that as a symbol of God (rock), Moses was rejecting God and striking out at God as a result of his anger at the people. Moses had reached his breaking point. God brought forth the water anyway because His people were in need; Moses took credit for it. Now God took Moses aside and told him what the consequences would be for his sin. Obviously, God could not depend on an earthly servant to give water to His people. God had a Holy Rock in mind that would eternally produce life-giving water to a dry and thirsty world.

Food for Thought: When the world is kicking you in the teeth, and it seems like God is too far away to hear you, that is the time you realize what faith means. Faith keeps us doing what is right even when we feel alone. A favorite hymn of mine says it well.

> "When my wavering faith, in trials, falters,
> When His guiding hand I cannot see,
> Then in wondrous love and tender mercy,
> Through His Word He says to me,
> My child, just
> Trust me, try me, prove me, saith the Lord of hosts, and see
> If a blessing, unmeasured blessing,
> I will not pour out on thee."[44]

August 1
Bible Readings: Jeremiah 17:19-27; 18:1-23; 19:1-15; 20:1-18

Jeremiah is preaching again. This time the sermon topic is 'Keep the Sabbath Holy.' The 4th commandment was "Remember the Sabbath day by keeping it holy . . . . On it you shall not do any work . . . ."[1] (Ex. 20:8-10) God told Jeremiah to preach this 'open-air' sermon at the gate of the people where the king and his family go in and out. There are many conjectures as to which gate this was, but I have chosen Keil and Delitzsch's [46] as being plausible to me. Most likely, the primary entrance to the outer court of the Temple would be entered by common men as well as royalty, all come before God equally. On the other hand, the priests and Levites entered the area through side entrances that allowed them easy access to carry out their duties. (Remember there were thousands of Levites and priests on duty at a time. They literally transported hundreds of gallons of water a week and unlimited numbers of cords of wood for sacrifices.) The gate of the people then would be the eastern gate. The reference Jeremiah gives to loads being carried in indicates the many business transactions that took place in the Temple courtyard area. His message brings hope, if they keep the Sabbath holy then destruction can be avoided! (The first four commandments are how people should respond to God and the last six are how the people should respond to each other.) God was down to His last commandment regarding the people's worship of Him. They had already rejected the other three. As a result of turning away from God, the last six commandments were blatantly thrown aside as the people plunged headlong into evil. If Jeremiah could only get them to agree to keep the Sabbath holy, then they would be taking the first step in the right direction. Only one day out of seven, surely they would agree to that!

Next, Jeremiah goes <u>down</u> to the potter's house. This was probably located in the Hinnom Valley. Clay would be easily accessible in the valley earth, as well as the water needed in production of pottery. As Jeremiah watched the potter work, a hard lump of clay deformed the vessel. The potter stopped, kneaded it down, and started again making a new vessel. Likewise, God molds His people. When a lump of resistance appears, the whole vessel becomes ruined and must be destroyed so a new vessel can be formed from the clay. Again, the warning comes that destruction is imminent.[47]

Jeremiah is instructed to ask two questions of the people:

1. Does the snow of Lebanon ever vanish from its rocky slopes?
   (This would be the snow on top of Mt. Hermon in the territory called Lebanon.[46])
2. Does its cool waters from distant sources ever cease to flow? (vs. 14)
   (The melting snow on the mountain constantly runs down to the valleys below.)

The answer to both questions is "No." All nations knew of these facts because they could depend on obtaining water in this area when traveling the highways. God's creation provided life sustaining water, but the people turned away from God. Now God will turn away from them.

Jeremiah had managed to make big enemies in high places. The people of Jerusalem have tolerated him, most likely because Josiah is their righteous king who is also calling for reform. Since they can't legally kill Jeremiah, they decide to talk him to death! An old children's rhyme goes "Sticks and stones may break my bones, but words will never hurt me!" All of us recognize that as false. It should more correctly read, "Sticks and stones may temporarily hurt me, but words will permanently do damage!" The slander campaign begins. In Jeremiah's anger, he calls on God to pour out judgment on them! Isn't this strange? God's prophet sent to try to turn the people from destruction is now praying for God to "bring on the sword and famine!" This is only human for us to want deliverance from our persecutors. King David was a man after God's own heart, but even he prayed for relief from enemies (read Psalm 109 as an example). Jesus was holy, and through His holiness, He could ask for forgiveness of His enemies. We need to strive to be like Jesus.

Early in Jehoiakim's reign,[47] Jeremiah is called to go to the Hinnom Valley again and this time he is to buy a clay jar. He takes it to the Potsherd Gate. Potsherd refers to pieces of pottery, sometimes broken pieces, other times small whole pieces.[5] So the Potsherd Gate goes to the pottery-making compound in the valley -- the same valley of Topheth where child sacrifice took place. Then Jeremiah launched into another sermon. Previously called the Valley of Ben Hinnom, it would now be called the Valley of Slaughter. (Ben Hinnom means son of Hinnom, an unknown person who may have been the original Jebusite owner.[5]) Judah and Jerusalem are condemned to fall by the sword. Birds and animals will eat their rotting flesh. They will become so demented that they will turn to cannibalism during the siege. Now this is a powerful sermon, especially where it is located. The Hinnom Valley also served as the town's garbage dump. All unwanted refuse, including dead animals, were thrown in the dump. The stinking garbage burned day and night. Their garbage dump had no plastic or paper products but rather decaying animals (and discarded animal parts), feces, wood, and food scraps. The odor must have been vile. The smog of the smoldering garbage must have hung over the valley like an unwanted shroud. For certain, at some point a person from every household had to pass through the Potsherd Gate daily to carry out the unpleasant chore of taking out the garbage! What a setting for a 'hell, fire, and brimstone' sermon! With his listeners enthralled by his commanding sermon, Jeremiah suddenly smashes the pottery jar to pieces. His listeners startled and shaken are now told they are the jar. They are the worthless piece of clay that was hardened by sin. Of no value, they will be smashed to bits.[47]

Upon leaving the Potsherd Gate, Jeremiah goes to the Temple courtyard to resume his sermon. Pashhur, the son of chief priest Immar, calls the Temple police to beat Jeremiah and put him in the stocks. This is a good example of the power the Temple Levites have built over time. The High Priest's family calls the shots on Temple ground. But Jeremiah has guts! He tells Pashhur to his face that his name is now Magor-Missabib, indicating he will live in constant terror. Pashhur's punishment will be to see his friends slaughtered and his whole family exiled to Babylon. Worse yet, he will die and be buried there. To a Hebrew there is no worse punishment than to die and be buried in foreign soil forever. God forever rejected Pashhur. Not even his bones would find rest on holy soil again. The highest religious official and his family were permanently banned from God's land. (The Pashhur discussed in chapter 20 is a different Pashhur than the one mentioned in chapter 21.)

Now that King Josiah has been replaced by a series of evil kings, Jeremiah again sinks into despair. He turns to his only companion, God. Jeremiah confesses to God that he feels deceived. This passage is most notable in that the word form of deceive is the same as that used in Exodus 22:16 to describe sexual seduction. Jeremiah apparently envisioned himself as being married to God, but now he feels God has overpowered him or forced him to be involved in events outside his will. In essence, Jeremiah's language is that he feels violated![45,47] Poor Jeremiah! He has been preaching for more than 20 years and no one has walked the aisle, no one has been discipled, no one has been converted, no one has seen the light. What perseverance! He confesses he wanted to quit many times, but he couldn't quench the fire of God's message within himself. Now the people are mocking him, nicknaming him "Magor-Missabib" or terror on every side! Jeremiah ends his confession with a recommitment of his allegiance or vow to God.

Food for Thought: Many years ago I visited Paris. While there, I made a special trek along the river to see Notre Dame. It is an impressive building indeed! But surrounding the building and in the other areas of its neighborhood were panhandlers, beggars, collectors for charities, and souvenir hounds. All were hoping to make a fast buck off the temporary glint of compassion of the visitors, or simply just selling the impassioned proof of their visit. These are the types of people Jesus drove from the Temple (John 2:13-17). Unfortunately, they are there because we allow them to be; nay -- we demand them to be! We do not want to be inconvenienced by the guilt of our compassion or the hardness of our desire for plunder.

August 2
Bible Readings: 2 Kings 22:3-20; 23:1-24, 28; 2 Chron. 34:8-33; 35:1-19, 26-27

Our lesson jumps back a few years to pick up our historical records during the time of King Josiah's religious reforms. Keeping track of the timeline since we began Jeremiah has been a challenge. Because Jeremiah preached during the reigns of five kings, the action is sometimes difficult even for Bible scholars to assign to a particular period, especially those times of transition from one king to another.

Josiah appointed a committee of three to administer the Temple repair plans: Shaphan, Maaseiah, and Joah. Shaphan was the son of Azaliah and grandson of Meshullam. He was a scribe who was most likely the father of Ahikam and Elasah.[5] Shaphan's family was a great help to Jeremiah during difficult times. Ahikam protects Jeremiah (Jer. 26:24) when the people seek to kill the prophet. In Jer. 29:3, Elasah carries a letter from Jeremiah to the exiles in Babylon. Josiah's committee is composed of a scribe to represent the interests of the Temple, the governor of Jerusalem to represent the interests of the town, and the royal recorder (the king's accountant) to represent the interests of the king. They designated two supervisors from each of two Levite clans: Kohathites and Merarites. King David appointed both of these clans as gatekeepers. "All these . . . were capable men with the strength to do the work . . . ."[1] (1 Chron. 26:8) A third clan, the Gershonites, had the responsibility of being treasurers of the house of God. Good sense dictates that those who collect the money not to be the ones who also spend the money! Additionally, more than one from each of the two supervisory clans provided for equal peer monitoring of the books preventing any one person from capitalizing on the power of the position. Thus, an excellent system of checks and balances was in place. So, it was quite easy for the king to "entrust" the money to these supervisors who would act "faithfully."

When the money was brought out of the Temple 'vault,' the Book of the Law was discovered. Obviously, a valued possession that had been placed in the 'safety deposit box.' As we have discussed in previous lessons, the book was probably Deuteronomy. Shaphan read it to King Josiah who was deeply moved by the judgment that lay before them as a result of the breech of contract. Note that the king put together a committee of 4 Temple priests and Levites and 1 personal servant. Their charge was to "inquire of the LORD," a task that should have been simple for the High Priest alone to do had he been doing the LORD's Will all along! Instead, they have to find a prophetess to reveal God's message. (Sorry fellas, but I just have to say this. Five men were assigned a job that it took only one woman to do!) The message is simple -- Judah will suffer the consequences of their sins, but Josiah will be buried in his family tomb in the Promised Land without having to witness the destruction.

Josiah proceeded to stand in his official position by his Temple pillar and read the covenant to the Jews. He announced his nationwide reforms to commence immediately. Pagan idols, shrines, and worship sites were not only destroyed but also desecrated so that they were permanently defiled and unsuitable for religious purposes. The pagan priests, mediums, and spiritists were executed.

Amazingly, Josiah leaves his nation of Judah and proceeds to destroy the pagan idols, altars, and worship centers of the old northern kingdom (Samaria) that is now ruled by the Assyrians. Why? How does he get away with what amounts to a declaration of war against another nation and especially the huge, powerful nation of Assyria? First, let's look at why. Josiah clearly saw himself as the religious 'missionary' and 'guardian' of those few Israelites who had been left behind in Samaria. After all, they, too, had been a part of the covenant. Josiah must have felt almost a parental desire to turn the last few of his northern brethren back to God. Maybe, just maybe, it could mean a reuniting of the tribes, a renewal of their faith, a re-secured allegiance to the Jerusalem leadership. (Alas, this was not to be.) Next, we see that Assyria is rapidly disintegrating from within. Assyria is too big to control all areas and suppress all rebellions.[25] The conquered nation of Babylon is growing stronger. Besides, this was an attack on religious sites not on official government sites. Also, Josiah only attacks the pagan worship centers and idols that had been built by the Israelites. The implication is that he was cleaning up the sins of the Israelites but not attacking the pagan worship images and centers of the imported peoples.

Josiah destroyed the worship sites of the golden calves, the primary one being at Bethel. He had the tombs (caves) opened up and the human bones in all of the little cubbyholes were brought forth and burned on the altar to defile it. At one point Josiah spots a special tombstone marking the grave of a man of God from Judah and another from Samaria (Israel). (Read 1 Kings 13 to recall the story.) These bones were spared burning. All the prophecy of the man of God from Judah was now fulfilled.

At Passover time, Josiah invited all of his Hebrew brethren in Israel and Judah to the great celebration. The priests and Levites consecrated themselves in preparation. Josiah donated 30,000 sheep and goats and 3,000 cattle. The administrators of the Temple gave 2,600 lambs and 300 cattle; the leaders of the Levites gave 5,000 lambs and 500 cattle. That is a total of 41,400 animals to be slaughtered! Just think, they didn't have refrigerators or freezers either! Can you imagine how many priests and Levites were needed to make the sacrifices? On the evening of Passover, the male head of the family killed the Passover lamb. Passover preceded the 7-day Feast of Unleavened Bread. Imagine all the firewood and water that was needed! Not since the time of Samuel has such a great Passover festival occurred. Sadly, though, that's all it was -- a great festival. Rituals can't take the place of true repentance. Josiah tried, but you can't force others, no matter how much you love them, to come to God. If they choose to continue in the ways of the world instead of following the ways of God, you cannot stop the consequences.

Food for Thought: Think of someone you know who 'talks a good game' or 'goes through the motions' of religion. No, you aren't judging them because Jesus tells us in Matt. 12:33 that we will recognize the true Christian by the products of his/her life. Likewise, we can determine a lack of Christian faith by observing a person's life. Matt. 12:36-37 says, "But I tell you that men will have to give account on the day of judgment for every careless word they have spoken. For by your words you will be acquitted, and by your words you will be condemned." Pray for those who are 'faking it' for Judgment Day is coming.

August 3
Bible Readings: 2 Kings 23:29-37; 2 Chron. 35:20-25; 36:1-5; Jeremiah 22:10-17; 26:1-24

Here is a short timeline to help keep us on track with the kings and events of the major Middle Eastern powers of this period. Dates vary somewhat among references.

Assyrian Empire	**1000 - 625 B.C.**
Assur-nasirpal II	883-859 B.C.
Shalmaneser III	858-824 B.C.
Shamshi-Adad V	823-811 B.C.
Adad-nirai III	810-783 B.C.
Shalmaneser IV	782-773 B.C.
Assur-dan III	772-766 B.C.
Assur-nirari V	754-745 B.C.
Tiglath-Pileser III	745-727 B.C.
Shalmaneser V	727-722 B.C.
Sargon II	722 - 705 B.C.
Sennacherib	705 - 681 B.C.
Essarhaddon	681 - 669 B.C.
Ashurbanipal	669 - 627 B.C.

New Babylonian Empire (Chaldean dynasty) established by Naboplassar - 625 B.C.	
Nebuchadnezzar II	605 - 562 B.C.
Fall of Ninevah, capital of Assyria	612 B.C.
Fall of Babylon to Cyrus	539 B.C.
Persian control	539 - 332 B.C.

Egypt	
Libyan Dynasty	950-710 B.C.
Ethiopian Dynasty	710-671 B.C.
Assyrian rule	671 - 652 B.C.
Pstamik I liberates Egypt	652 B.C.
Pharaoh Neco	605 - 593 B.C.
Cambyses conquers Egypt	525 B.C.
Persian rule	525-404 B.C.
Amyrtaeus frees Egypt	404 B.C.[48]

Other major events of the time period are listed below.	
King Ahab dies	853 B.C.
Elisha called as a prophet	848 B.C.
Jehu is king in Israel/Athaliah becomes Queen in Judah	841 B.C.
Joel called as a prophet/Joash is king in Judah	835 B.C.
Jehoahaz is king of Israel	814 B.C.
Jehoash is king of Israel	798 B.C.
Joel ends his ministry	796 B.C.

Jeroboam II becomes king/Jonah becomes prophet	793 B.C.
Uzziah becomes king of Judah	792 B.C.
Shalmaneser IV becomes king of Assyria	783 B.C.
Ashur-dan III becomes king of Assyria	772 B.C.
Amos becomes a prophet	760 B.C.
Jonah preaches to Ninevah	759 B.C.
Ashur-nirari V becomes king of Assyria	754 B.C.
Jonah's ministry ends/Hosea becomes a prophet/Zechariah dies	753 B.C.
Jotham becomes king of Judah	750 B.C.
Tiglath-Pileser III invades Israel	743 B.C.
Micah becomes a prophet/Pekahiah becomes king	742 B.C.
Isaiah becomes a prophet to Judah	740 B.C.
Ahaz becomes king of Judah	735 B.C.
Israel falls to Assyria	722 B.C.
Hosea's ministry ends/Hezekiah becomes king of Judah	715 B.C.
Sennacherib surrounds Jerusalem	701 B.C.
Micah's ministry ends	687 B.C.
Isaiah's ministry ends	681 B.C.
Nahum becomes a prophet	663 B.C.
Josiah becomes king of Judah/Zephaniah becomes a prophet	640 B.C.
Jeremiah becomes a prophet	627 B.C.
Habakkuk becomes a prophet	612 B.C. (Ninevah falls)
King Josiah dies	609 B.C.
(Assyria completely conquered)	609 B.C.
Daniel taken captive to Babylon	605 B.C.
(Battle of Carchemish)	605 B.C.
Ezekiel captive in Babylon/Zedekiah becomes king	597 B.C.
Habakkuk's ministry ends	589 B.C.
Fall of Judah - Jerusalem destroyed	586 B.C.[15]

The Assyrians attacked Egypt in 671 and 664 B.C. completely conquering them. Under Assyrian dominance, the Egyptian army was called to assist Assyria in defending itself against the Babylonians.[5] The Babylonians were marching on Carchemish, one of Assyria's fortified cities. Pharaoh Neco marched his army out of Egypt and up the seacoast plains. Neither he nor his father before him (Psammetichus I) wanted domination by the fierce Babylonians. When he reached the area of Megiddo, "where the Iyron Pass opened out into the Jezreel Valley"[7] (p. 290), he was met by Josiah and the Judean army. Neco sent a messenger to Josiah that he had no quarrel with Judah but desired only to march through to his destination on the Euphrates River. Josiah would not listen but engaged the Egyptians in battle. The barrage of arrows from the Egyptians not only severely routed the Jews, but one arrow mortally wounded Josiah. The Egyptians now controlled Judah for four years before being conquered by the Babylonians in 605 B.C.[5]

Josiah's son Jehoahaz succeeded him. When Neco returned after being defeated by the Babylonians, he sent for Jehoahaz to meet him at Hamath in Syria. When Jehoahaz arrived, he was arrested and imprisoned. Neco made Jehoahaz's half-brother Eliakim king, changing his name to Jehoiakim.[3] Neco also taxed Judah 100 talents (3.75 tons) of silver and a talent of gold (75 pounds). Jeremiah proceeded to launch an attack of prophecy against

Jehoahaz first (Jer. 22:10-12) and then continued with his successor Jehoiakim (22:13-17).[46] He denounces the expansion of the palace when there is no justice for the poor. Jeremiah declares the king is guilty of dishonesty, murder, oppression, and extortion.

One very good possibility for Jeremiah 26 is that it is actually the people's response to Jeremiah's sermon in chapter 7.[47] If that is the case, then chapter 7 should precede this chapter historically. If you read over chapter 7 again, you can understand how Jeremiah's rather scathing comments about the Jews could evoke this powerful reaction. The Temple priests, false prophets, and people riot, seizing Jeremiah and demanding he die. The city's riot squad arrives to squelch the mob's actions before Jeremiah is killed. At this point, we remember Jeremiah hasn't been the only preacher pronouncing judgment on Jerusalem. The city officials remind the people that Micah brought the same pronouncements during Hezekiah's reign. Ahikam, Shaphan's son, stood by Jeremiah and defended him. Shaphan's family had both political and religious power. You have to wonder if Jeremiah wasn't scared silly when he was released. The criminals all seemed to be on the <u>outside</u> of the prison rather than inside!

Uriah was also a prophet delivering the same condemning messages as Jeremiah. When faced with a threat against his life, he ran. When your trust in God falters, your human reactions get you in trouble. Even Egypt was not far enough away to protect Uriah. He was extradited to Judah and executed.

Food for Thought: My boss reminded me this week that there were only 8 more paychecks until Christmas. I guess panic set in because I rushed out and bought several Christmas presents! Uriah reacted just like I did; he panicked. Without thinking about his calling to obey God and preach His messages, he succumbed to human fears. Without thinking of the joy and blessedness of Christmas, I succumbed to human stress. Start preparing your heart now for the real celebration of Christmas -- the birth of our Savior.

August 4
Bible Readings: Jeremiah 46:1-28; 47:1-7

Jeremiah has spent so much time prophesying to Judah and Jerusalem that we have almost forgotten his original call from God. In Jer. 1:10, God appointed Jeremiah "over nations and kingdoms to uproot and tear down, to destroy and overthrow, to build and to plant."[1] Starting in chapter 46 and continuing through chapter 51, we hear Jeremiah's prophesies to the Gentile nations, nations where little (if anything) was known about the God of Israel.

It is the year 605 B.C.[49] Pharaoh Neco has just been defeated by the Babylonians under Nebuchadnezzar at the Battle of Carchemish on the Euphrates River. You will recall that Babylon was one of the oldest cities in the world, first mentioned in Gen. 10:10. It was the site of the building of the tower of Babel that was to reach to the heavens and be a gateway to God. At the top of the tower were zodiac charts, indicating their worship of the heavenly bodies. The developer and first king of the city of Babylon was Nimrod, a mighty warrior and grandson of Ham, father of the cursed Canaanites. Nimrod means 'let us rebel' and is viewed by many scholars as a depiction of the antichrist. Isaiah 47 prophesies the actual fall of Babylon, particularly making reference to the worthless astrologers in verse 13. Rev. 18 also prophesies the fall of Babylon, but the actual fall of Babylon occurred over 500 years <u>before</u> Revelation was written. So what does this chapter 'reveal' -- just a past history lesson? No! Rev. 18 tells of the fall of the devil's kingdom, symbolized by Babylon. Now you can see why Nimrod is viewed as the antichrist. Babylon is seen as the great prostitute who lures people away from the ways of God and into the ways of the devil (Rev. 17). Bible scholars believe Babylon was used as a code name at the time John wrote Revelation. It stood for Rome, which was the famous capital of the Roman Empire and responsible for the oppression of many nations.[5]

Starting in verse 3, a vivid picture of the battle scene is laid out in poetry. Egypt is compared to the Nile that rose to flood stage every year covering the Nile delta with water. Egypt, too, wanted to have command of a vast territory. Mercenaries from nations south, west, and east of Egypt are hired to help with the attack on the Babylonians. But God put Egypt to the sword, a sacrifice for their sin of killing Josiah. Even the famous balm or healing ointment of Gilead would not cure Israel's wound from the loss of Josiah. [The Virgin Daughter of Egypt in verse 11 refers to the Hebrews when they were still innocent people who were living in the land of Goshen at the time of Joseph.][49]

Nebuchadnezzar will attack Egypt in its homeland. (After the Battle of Carchemish in Assyrian territory, the Egyptians fled back toward Egypt followed by Nebuchadnezzar on their heels. The Babylonians routed the Egyptians again at Hamath, Syria. Because of his father's death, Nebuchadnezzar had to leave without the complete destruction of the Egyptian forces so he could go home to be crowned king in 605 B.C. By 604 B.C. the Babylonian army was on the way to Egypt again, conquering all in its path.) The city of Ashkelon in Philistine country is captured in 604 B.C. Judah was so weakened and frightened at this point that it pledged allegiance to Nebuchadnezzar, still hoping Egypt would ride to its rescue. Remember, Judah had been under Egyptian rule prior to this.

Verse 14 lists some cities in northeastern Egypt that contained large colonies of various people who had sought refuge from the invading Assyrians and Babylonians over the years. Many of the colonies were Israelites. Pharaoh Hophra (Apries) was just a big windbag -- all talk and no substance. Nebuchadnezzar is compared to Mt. Tabor and Mt. Carmel (both 1700-1800 feet high) that towered over the plains. Egypt is derogatorily called a heifer because of their worship of the bull. But Nebuchadnezzar is like a biting gadfly that stings and wounds cattle. The well paid fattened mercenaries would flee when the battle becomes heated. Another derogatory comparison is made to Egypt being a snake. The Egyptians were enthralled with snakes as a sign of power. A snake was always seen on the royal families' jewelry and headpieces. [Thebes, also called No, was the capital of southern Egypt (often called the upper Nile because the river flows south to north). Amon-Re was the god of the Egyptian rulers. The area of Thebes is most famous for its Valley of the Kings where the infamous King Tut's tomb is located. The Assyrians conquered Thebes in 663 B.C.[5]]

God now says He will bring judgment on Egypt and all those associated with Egypt because of their pagan worship. But Egypt will return to its vitality as a nation once again. Alas, the same cannot be said of Philistia. The Plain of Sharon will not rise to glory again. The Philistines (Gaza) and Phoenicians (Tyre and Sidon) were seacoast nations that often provided aid and protection for each other.

Food for Thought: Tyre and Sidon are just south of modern day Beirut. The Gaza Strip comprises a large portion of old Philistia, the rest being poorly organized and settled. Surely, you see the prophecy still revealed in the continuing devastation of pagan peoples trying to build up these areas. The homeland of the Philistines has been in turmoil for centuries. According to Jeremiah, they will never return to their glorious state. World events today were predicted thousands of years ago. God gives His people ample warning, if they would only listen. Pray for those who are lost and without God in our world. Pray for our soldiers in other lands, too.

August 5
Bible Readings: Habakkuk

Like many of the other Minor Prophets, Habakkuk has a number of unique characteristics. Whereas most of the prophets contain preaching meant to warn its readers of coming judgment, the Book of Habakkuk is the meditations of a sincere believer trying to come to grips with the dire days that lie before the nation. Habakkuk is in the position of a child of God living in a perverse and sinful land. He realizes that much of the behavior of sinful men seems to go unpunished (1:2-4). When making it a matter of prayer, Habakkuk learns that God is about ready to punish the nation. This news brings little comfort because the chastisement will come at the hands of the Babylonians who are worse than the Jews (1:5-12). Habakkuk likewise realizes that these invaders are not going to differentiate between him and the sinners next door.

In verses 12-17, Habakkuk questions God's action. He just can't understand how God can permit this to occur. In chapter two the prophet waits for God's answer. God responds by telling Habakkuk to write the answer and to do so using big print so that anyone can read it at a glance. The prophet first declares (2:3) that God's timetable is not ours. We want action now; God's judgment is not immediate, but it is absolutely certain.

The prophet then declares an important truth that is thrice repeated in the New Testament; it is so profound that it inspired Martin Luther to begin the reformation of the church. That truth is "the just shall live by faith." It basically means that in the midst of life's uncertainties and problems, we put our trust in God. Trust is the very thing that God has required of man since the Garden of Eden. The unpardonable sin is not murder, rape, or pillage. It is to die believing and acting as though God and His Word are not trustworthy.

The rest of chapter two focuses on the men of violence. Habakkuk utters a number of woes against these people. A woe is a type of taunt song expressing dismay or misfortune. The prophet pronounces woes upon aggression 2:6-8, upon exploiters and extortioners 2:9-11, upon the cruel and violent 2:12-14, upon those guilty of inhumanity to man 2:15-17, and upon the idolater (2:19).[37]

Chapter three consists of Habakkuk's prayer and the theophany that inspires it. A theophany is "any direct, visual manifestation of God." The person does not actually see God Himself but rather the effects of God's unmediated Presence.[5] It would seem that God's Presence was manifested in a great storm that arose out of the southeast. Note the imagery suggesting a storm (vs. 3) "His glory covered the heavens, (vs. 4) "rays flashed from His hand," (vs. 10) "the raging waters swept on," and (vs. 11) "light of thine arrows as they sped at the flash of thy glittering spear."

Habakkuk's prayer (3:16-19) is an affirmation of faith. He is not going to let circumstances control him, for he knows that God is the ultimate source of strength and meaning in life.

Food for Thought: Hebrews 11:1 defines faith as "the substance of things hoped for, the evidence of things not seen." If we intend to live for God, we must be willing to trust Him without demanding immediate material evidence of His activity.

Verses of the Week: **Jeremiah 29:11-14a** "For I know the plans I have for you," declares the LORD, "plans to prosper you and not to harm you, plans to give you hope and a future. Then you will call upon me and come and pray to me, and I will listen to you. You will seek me and find me when you seek me with all your heart. I will be found by you," declares the LORD, "and will bring you back from captivity."

August 6
Bible Readings: 2 Kings 24:1, 7; 2 Chron. 36:6-7; Jeremiah 25:1-38; 35:1-19

Judah is now under the control of the Babylonians. Nebuchadnezzar takes the best of everything, people and material possessions, back to Babylon. The young man Daniel is among the captives. For 23 years Jeremiah has preached without any converts. The warnings landed on deaf ears. Now the Jews could look forward to 70 years of captivity (a multiple of 7). But at the end of that time, God promised to destroy Babylon. The Babylonians are a good example of how God can use a pagan nation to exercise His Judgment, but He then brings judgment on the pagan persecutors. All the pagan nations will have to drink the 'cup of God's wrath' or will receive God's Judgment. Their drunkenness symbolizes their sinful state. The nations under judgment are Judah - God's people are without excuse; Egypt and its associates (Libya, Ethiopia, Sudan, and others[4]); Uz - Syria[4]; Philistia - Philistine nation on the southeastern seacoast - (Gaza Strip); Edom, Moab, Ammon - east of the Jordan River - Jordan[4]; Phoenicia - Tyre and Sidon on the northeastern seacoast - Lebanon[4]; Mediterranean coastlands - Turkey[4-5]; Arabia - Saudi Arabia; Zimri, Elam, and Media - Iran, Iraq, and Kuwait[4]; Babylon.[49] Their time had come; judgement would not be delayed. They could not escape.

Jeremiah now uses the family of Recab as an example of obedience. Jonadab, the son of Recab (1 Chron. 2:55), had commanded that all his descendants must always live in tents, never drinking wine or farming. (Jehonadab ben Recab was a zealot for the LORD assisting Jehu in destroying the house of Ahab (2 Kings 10:15-17).) Ahab died in 853 B.C. It is now 605 B.C. The Recabites had faithfully obeyed their forefather some 250 years! Yet the Jews had found it difficult to obey God beyond the lifetime of each righteous king. God blessed the Recabites but condemned the Jews.

Food for Thought: People are quick to make covenants but slow to fulfill them. In fact, covenants requiring much effort and time are doomed to failure from the beginning -- unless you rely on God. God supplies us with the strength and determination to fulfill our commitments and do His Will. Where do you stand in your commitment to read the Bible through this year? God gives us all the same amount of time, but you determine how you will use it.

August 7
Bible Readings: Jeremiah 36:1-32; 45:1-5

In 605 B.C. the LORD instructs Jeremiah to write down all the messages He had given Jeremiah over the years. Jeremiah engaged Baruch, a member of a prominent Judean family, to serve as his scribe. This does not mean Jeremiah couldn't read and write but rather the process of writing on a scroll was tedious and required much concentration, so much that it detracted from the speaker's thought process. Judeans, in fact, were probably more literate than the general population is today. Pottery pieces were inscribed with the owner's name, tombs were inscribed, inscriptions were left in the Siloam water shaft by Hezekiah's workers, ostraca (pieces of pottery written on in ink) were used to maintain a business's accounting for bills of laden and sales, and bullae (papyrus documents tied up with string which were secured by a lump of clay pressed with a personal seal) were used to record deeds.[7] Two important bullae from the Bible are that of Baruch (Jer. 36) and Gedaliah, who became governor of Jerusalem under the Babylonians (Jer. 39:14).[7]

Baruch obviously works steadily at his task for many months, complaining at the end that not only had his task been physically trying, but it was also anguishing to dwell daily on the coming judgment. God rewards Baruch's efforts by assuring that his life would be spared.

After Jeremiah's last commotion at the church (Jer. 26), he had been barred from the Temple. So Baruch is sent to read the scroll to the people on a fast day. These days of fasting were declared during emergencies and most Jews participated. The service was for the people to present petitions to God for divine intervention on their behalf. This fast day occurred in December 604 B.C. most likely when the Babylonians attacked Ashkelon in the Philistine plains.[49] You recall that Shaphan's family was supportive of Jeremiah. Shaphan's son, Gemariah, allowed Baruch to read the scroll from Gemariah's upper courtroom overlooking the courtyards below. All the people in the Temple area could hear him. Gemariah's son Micaiah reported the content of the messages to the state officials who were in session in light of the state emergency. The Royal Secretary was Elishama. Several officials are mentioned by name, but the most interesting is Elnathan, son of Acbor. Acbor was one of the 5 men King Josiah had assigned to "inquire of the LORD" after hearing the Book of Law (2 Kings 22:12).[49] With the Babylonians attacking only 50 miles away, the state officials are alarmed at the words of Jeremiah. (Where have these people been for 23 years?) They tell Baruch to take Jeremiah and hide. The scroll is taken to King Jehoiakim. As it is read, Jehoiakim cuts pieces off and throws them in the fire, much to the dismay of the officials. Remember, Jehoiakim got his position from the Egyptians who ruled the land. Jehoiakim placed his faith and trust in Egypt to protect Judah instead of God. God tells Jeremiah to dictate another scroll. God also reveals Jehoiakim's judgment. He and his household will be punished for Jehoiakim's wickedness. He will have no descendants on the throne and his own body would not even be buried. During the writing of the second scroll, the king has an arrest warrant out on Jeremiah and Baruch.

Food for Thought: My pastor made a comment today that really struck me (even though it wasn't a new comment). You and I may be the only Jesus some people will ever know. We are ambassadors of Jesus Christ, as such we represent Him to the world. Can others see Jesus in you and me?

August 8
Bible Readings: Daniel 1:3-20; 2:1-49

We start the Book of Daniel today. It is divided into three main sections: introduction to Daniel, stories of Daniel and his three friends in captivity, dreams and visions of Daniel. This latter section is referred to as apocalyptic literature. Apocalypse is a Greek word meaning to uncover or reveal in the form of a vision.[5] Various pieces (chapters 1-7) of the Book of Daniel may have been recorded and passed down as a part of Jewish tradition. Scholars debate when the actual book was compiled. One school of thought is that it was actually written during the time of the exile that was during Daniel's lifetime.[51] The other school of thought is that the book was compiled close to the end of the Maccabean revolt in 165 B.C.[50] Regardless of who wrote it or when, it has been repeatedly verified as consistent with Bible prophecy, Jewish history, and world events. In other words, all scholars accept it as God's inspired message.

Daniel was one of the first exiles deported in 605 B.C. when Nebuchadnezzar took control of Jerusalem. Only the royal family, the nobility, and many of the priests were included in this deportation; then only selected physically fit, attractive, intelligent young men were trained in the language, science, and literature of the Babylonians.[50] The training would last three years under a eunuch named Ashpenaz, chief of Nebuchadnezzar's court. Daniel was probably a teenager at this time, but he will be close to 90 years old by the end of the Book of Daniel.[51] Ashpenaz changed the names of Daniel and three of his friends to Chaldean names. All four young men had Hebrew names referring to God. All four were given Chaldean (Babylonian) names referring to their pagan gods: Bel, Nebo, Marduk, to name a few (some or all of these may have been different names for the same pagan god).

Daniel ----->	God is my judge -------->	Belteshazaar ---->	may Bel protect his life[5]
Hananiah --->	Jehovah is gracious ---->	Shadrach -------->	command of Aku[5]
Mishael ----->	Who is what God is? -->	Meshach --------->	(associated with Marduk)
Azariah ----->	Jehovah has helped ---->	Abednego ------->	servant of Nebo[5]

Marduk was the primary god of the city of Babylon, but the conquered territory of Babylonia worshipped many gods. Nebo was a god of science and literature. This must have been terribly upsetting for these 4 religious youths from the tribe of Judah. They were to be forced to eat the same food as the Babylonians, too!

Daniel asked permission to eat only water and non-meat foods, but Ashpenaz refused out of fear for his life. Daniel didn't give up. He convinced a guard to let the 4 boys eat only Jewish-type foods for 10 days as a trial. (The Babylonians ate a lot of pork and other unclean meat. Refer to the dietary laws of the March 4 lesson on Lev. 11 and 17.) The guard agreed to Daniel's proposal and after 10 days of eating non-meat foods and water, Daniel and his friends were more robust than the other captives. God blessed these men for their faithfulness allowing them to excel in their studies and Daniel was given the gift of understanding visions. The Babylonians heavily believed in magic, exorcism, and divination, but Daniel and his friends were found to be 10 times better than the exorcists, magicians, diviners, and enchanters.

One night Nebuchadnezzar had a troubling dream. Being crafty, he asked the wise men of the land to first reveal his dream and second to interpret its meaning. If they failed, they would be executed. When no one could do it, the king decreed that all the wise men should die. This included Daniel and his friends. Daniel told the king that he could do it. Daniel and his friends were allowed to spend the night praying to God for the answer. During the night Daniel had all revealed to him through a vision.

Daniel revealed to the king that the dream was about a large statue that had a head of gold, arms and chest of silver, thighs and abdomen of bronze, legs of iron, and feet made partially of iron and partially of clay. God cut a rock out and rolled it down on the statue, smashing its feet. The statue collapsed into a pile of powder that was totally blown away by the wind. The rock then became a huge mountain and filled the whole earth. Daniel's interpretation was that the head of gold represented Nebuchadnezzar as King of Babylon, the silver represented an inferior empire that would arise, the bronze represented a third kingdom that would rule the world, and the iron was a fourth kingdom that destroyed all others. The iron and clay feet represented a divided kingdom having both strengths and weaknesses. The divided kingdom would not be able to stay united. During that time, God would establish His kingdom that would last forever. There is much controversy as to the identity of each of the remaining empires. One school of thought is that after the Babylonian Empire came the Median Empire that was followed by the Persian Empire and the Greek Empire. The Greek Empire had many weaknesses. There was resentment between the Ptolemies of Egypt (clay) and the Seleucids of Syria (iron). During the reign of the disgusting, cruel Antiochus IV, God would rescue His people.[50] Other scholars believe the silver empire was the Medo-Persian, the bronze empire was the Macedo-Grecian, and the iron empire was the Roman that was broken by its mixture of 10 strong and weak nations. The Rock cut out of a mountain is a Holy God sending His Holy Son to establish His Kingdom forever.[51,15]

As a result of his display of wisdom, Daniel was given many gifts and made a ruler over Babylon. Daniel's three friends were appointed as administrators. Daniel's rise to power in a foreign land from a position of captive parallels Joseph's own story in Egypt. Joseph, too, interpreted a king's dream to be made second-in-command of an empire (Gen. 41).

We know very little about Daniel's personal background other than his devotion to God. Josephus says he was of the royal family of Zedekiah, but this could be supposition rather than fact (based on Dan. 1:3).[3] We are not told anything about Daniel's lineage, marital status, or of any possible descendants. We do not know for sure that Daniel died in Babylon or was buried there. Based on Isa. 39:7, some scholars have proposed the idea that Daniel was castrated and made a eunuch in the king's court, many court officials were but not necessarily all. This would account for no mention of wife and children as Joseph had. Personally, I don't believe Daniel was a eunuch. First, he was a prophet. Even though probably not a priest or Levite, he did commune with God. Levitical laws were very specific about no one serving before God who was blemished nor any burnt offering being brought to God that was blemished (Lev. 21). Eunuchs were not even allowed to worship in the assembly of God's people (Deut. 23:1). Next, Isa. 39:7 says that some of Hezekiah's descendants would become eunuchs. We are not told whether Daniel is from the royal family or the nobility. Some versions translate 'descendants' as 'sons.' The Jews kept very good lineage documentation and it certainly seems that a royal who had escaped death would be noted in the documentation if he became a statesman for the Babylonians. The very obscurity of Daniel from the historical documents of Judah seems to indicate he was from lesser nobility than the royal family. Regardless, God protected Daniel and his friends from the fiery furnace and the lions' den. I don't believe God allowed castration to beset Daniel.

Food for Thought: Daniel remained obedient to God all his life. He was in a foreign country where the focal point (visible for miles around) was a gigantic ziggurat built to the pagan god Marduk. Separated permanently from his family and culture, Daniel persevered in his faith. How many times do we waver and doubt in the face of far less danger?

August 9
Bible Readings: 2 Kings 24:1-6; 2 Chron. 36:8; Jeremiah 48:1-47; 49:1-33; 22:18-23

Judah's neighbors have served dual roles as both relatives and bitter enemies. Both Moab and Ammon were sons of Lot, Abraham's nephew. For a while, Israel conquered Moab but was unable to maintain control.

Likewise, Judah conquered Ammon but could not retain control. The Arameans and Babylonians were from the Mesopotamian area, the land of Abraham's birthplace. The Middle East was like one big quarreling family (Was? More like is!). Above all, Manasseh's sins stand out because God was not willing to forgive him for what he had done -- not even if Moses and Samuel pleaded his case (Jer. 15:1).

God's judgment against Moab begins by naming the fortified cities of Moab along with their individual sentences. The Moabite pagan god Chemosh will helplessly go into captivity along with the people. The people of Moab will be as ashamed of their pagan god as Israel was of their golden calf at Bethel. Moab will be salted to guarantee all will be destroyed. Still God mourns over Moab. The land flowing with wine will be drunk from the cup of God's wrath. The cities of the plain (Zoar) over 3,000 feet below will be able to hear the cries of Moab. This is especially meaningful when you realize Zoar was the only one of five cities of the plain God spared when He destroyed Sodom and Gomorrah. Zoar was the city saved for Lot to inhabit. The city of Lot will be in deep mourning.

The eagle swooping down symbolizes God's judgment and is used in several places in the Old Testament. Moab's sin was defying God. Heshbon, meaning stronghold, was the former capital of Sihon, a king of the Amorites.[5] Sihon was the king who refused Moses and the Israelites passage through his land during the exodus. Moab's judgment ends with a hope of future restoration.

The Ammonite pagan god Molech will also go into captivity along with the people. Ammon and all its surrounding suburbs will be destroyed by fire -- the judgment of God. Ammon's guilt was in trusting in its wealth. Ammon, too, will be restored. (Rabbah-Ammon is the capital of Jordan today.)

The Edomites were Israel's closest relatives, the descendants of the patriarch Israel's twin brother Esau. The Book of Obadiah is devoted to judgment against Edom. The Edomites were so heartless that they actually helped Babylon capture escaping survivors crossing the Jordan into Edom. Edom is given no hope for the future. It will be stripped bare with no place to hide. The eagle of judgment will carry off the children and destroy the land. For unknown reasons, Edom was known for wisdom in earlier days. Teman is a symbolic name for Edom. Dedan, on the other hand, was a wonderful oasis southeast of Edom in the area of Arabia.[47]

Damascus, Hamath, and Arpad are all primary cities of Syria that were captured by Assyria and later by Babylon. The wars between Syria and Israel (northern kingdom) had been especially fierce under Hazael, Ben-Hadad, and Rezin. Now Syria was condemned.

Kedar was located between Judah and Egypt. It was actually a tribe of Arabian people who settled in this northeastern Sinai Peninsula area. They were excellent sheep breeders (Isa. 60:7), traders (Ezek. 27:21), and archers (Isa. 21:13-14).[49] Hazor may have been the title awarded their kings as the kings of Egypt carried the title Pharaoh. Alternately, Hazor may have been a town or 'tent city' where the tribal business, religious activities, and social functions occurred. Babylon will totally destroy the Kedarites' community.

Remember King Jehoiakim of Judah? He was the one who defiantly cut up Jeremiah's scroll. In accordance with Jer. 36:29-31, Jehoiakim will die and his body will be thrown on the garbage heap of Jerusalem -- the burial of a donkey! No one in modern day Lebanon, Syria, or Jordan will mourn him. Verse 22:21 is an eye-opener. Jehoiakim had always been rebellious even as a child. I think most baby boomer parents reared children believing the primary impact on children was the environment, nurturance, and culture of each child. Possibly verse 21 reveals that adults are products of inherent qualities such as temperament, self-discipline, aggressiveness, and personality.

Food for Thought: My Daddy tells of a time during World War II when he was assigned to the detail of picking up the bodies and loading them on a truck. Daddy started out trying to handle the body with care, dignity, and respect. Soon his sergeant was screaming at him to just throw those bodies in the truck, after all they were dead and didn't know the difference. My Daddy was upset, but he had to follow orders. The next week the body he threw on the truck was his sergeant's! What goes around comes around. Every word and deed should be prayerfully considered <u>before</u> it goes into action. God knows your heart.

August 10
Bible Readings: 2 Kings 24:6, 8-20a; 2 Chron. 36:8-16; Jeremiah 22:24-30; 37:1-2; 52:1-3; Daniel 1:1-2

Upon the death of Jehoiakim, his son Jehoiachin becomes the vassal king. This is not viewed as a contradiction of Jer. 36:30. Jehoiakim may have been assassinated and his young son was placed as the figurehead leader to face Nebuchadnezzar. When he got there, Jehoiakim was dead, but Nebuchadnezzar had a point he wanted to prove to rebellious kingdoms. The siege was on. (It probably started in January 597 B.C. and the city surrendered on March 15 or 16, 597 B.C.[7]) Jehoiachin knew he could not win and soon surrendered, possibly hoping to be treated favorably by Nebuchadnezzar. Instead, he and all his family and servants are deported along with 9,000 men capable of supporting a war effort through their physical prowess, and 1,000 skilled craftsmen and artisans. The 3 Ss were deported: strong, skilled, and smart. Only the poorest people are left in Jerusalem. Notice verse 14 says 'poorest' not 'poor.' A poor person is only one who has little or no property of value. The poorest people are those who are morally and spiritually deficient as well (Jer. 24).[25]

Nebuchadnezzar appointed 21-year old Zedekiah as king. Zedekiah was inexperienced in leadership and had no desire to assume the responsibilities of king, a perfectly weak ruler for the poorest of people. Nebuchadnezzar should have no more rebellion problems, but this line of thought will prove to be untrue. According to Josephus, Zedekiah was inclined to listen to his young friends' advice rather than the prophet Jeremiah.[3] Zedekiah reminds me of Rehoboam, King Solomon's son. When Rehoboam took the throne, he, too, listened to the advice of impetuous, immature, inexperienced 'friends' over the sage advice of experienced elders. Rehoboam, like Zedekiah, lost most of his subjects as a result (1 Kings 12). Even today, young people value the opinions of peers, regardless of the grave consequences, more than they do those of the experienced.

Food for Thought: Jerusalem has a habit of rebelling. This is only one of several deportations and only one of several 'falls' for the city! Finally, the ultimate total destruction of all primary structures in the city will stop the rebellions, both against the conquering kings and against God. What does it take to stop us from rebelling? How many warnings does God give us? Why are we so stubborn? Pray that your stubbornness be broken so you can do God's Will in your life.

August 11
Bible Readings: Jeremiah 24:1-10; 29:1-32; 27:1-22; 28:1-17

Zedekiah will reign 11 long, miserable years. He is the last vassal king of Judah. Only the poorest people are left for him to rule (some select leaders were left behind to maintain order). The Temple and palace have been stripped of treasures and the gold items Solomon made and dedicated to God. And then there is that troublesome Jeremiah! That man keeps going like the Eveready Bunny! I can just imagine ole Jeremiah is more wound up than ever. His prophecies are being fulfilled and his time until the destruction of Jerusalem is growing short.

First God gives Jeremiah a vision of two baskets of fruit. One contained figs gathered at peak harvest; the other contained figs that were too bad to eat. The good figs represented the exiles in Babylonia. God would preserve them and bring them back to Jerusalem. (Hum--fig preserves!) They had redeeming qualities. The bad figs represented those who were left behind in Jerusalem. They would die by sword, famine, or disease. They had no redeeming qualities. God has separated the wheat from the chaff.

Jeremiah sent a letter to the exiles in Babylon by Elasah ben (son of) Shaphan, and Gemariah ben Hilkiah. Both were from priestly families who had been prominent in the reforms of Josiah. Their mission was to carry the annual tribute money to Nebuchadnezzar. Jeremiah's letter they would also deliver in 594 B.C.[49] Jeremiah tells the people to make the best of their situation for they will be there 70 years. They are to build houses, plant gardens, marry and have children, continue with usual family events. This is the last third of Jeremiah's 3-part call to be a prophet. God put him over nations and kingdoms to (1) uproot and tear down, (2) destroy and overthrow, and (3) build and plant (Jer. 1:10). The exiles are charged to increase in number (as they did in Egypt) in preparation for their second exodus experience. Astonishingly, Jeremiah even tells the Jews to pray for their captors, wish them well, for the future of the Jews is dependent on the well-being of the Babylonian Empire for the next 70 years! Furthermore, Jeremiah warns against the words of the false prophets among them who were predicting Babylon's quick demise. In fact, he prophesies the false prophets Ahab and Zedekiah would be roasted alive! (Note the names. Ahab bears the same name as Israel's (northern kingdom) most wicked king (but so weak that Jezebel practically ruled the kingdom) and Zedekiah bears the name of Judah's weakest and most indecisive king. Jer. 23:14 declares the false prophets guilty of adultery and lies. Jer. 23:15 says they spread ungodliness throughout Judah.) These two false prophets probably tried to lead a rebellion against Nebuchadnezzar, one of the few offenses that would receive the fiery furnace judgment. (Daniel 3)

Next, we find Jeremiah in the famous face-off with Hananiah over the 'yoke of the people.' God instructed Jeremiah to make and wear a wooden yoke held by leather straps. It was to symbolize the yoke of Babylon on the Jews. (Remember, Jeremiah is now preaching to the poorest left in Jerusalem.) If the people would yield to the king of Babylon, God would protect and preserve them and restore Jerusalem. Those who insisted on remaining in Judah would die. This depicts the people yielding their stubborn will to the Will of God. They must bow themselves under God's yoke (represented by the king of Babylon whom God used to carry out His Will). Six hundred years later, Jesus says, "Come to me, all you who are weary and burdened, and I will give you rest. Take my yoke upon you and learn from me, for I am gentle and humble in heart, and you will find rest for your souls. For my yoke is easy and my burden is light."[1] (Matt. 11:28-30)

Hananiah decides to grandstand for the crowd. He prophesies that God will break the yoke of Babylon within two years and all will be restored! Here stands old Jeremiah wearing this wooden yoke preaching 70 years captivity and now this young whippersnapper is saying it will only be 2 years! Both of them claim to have their prophecies from God. If you were part of the crowd, which would you believe the old tried and proven true prophet of God or the younger prophet preaching what you want to hear? Weary Jeremiah says, "I sure hope you are right! But the proof is in the pudding." This makes Hananiah mad and he marches over and breaks Jeremiah's yoke into! (Can't you hear the crowd hollering, "Fight! Fight!") Well, Jeremiah got the last word. He told Hananiah he would die before the year was out! (Remember what happened to the hooligans who taunted Elisha about his baldhead?)

Food for Thought: Decades ago, before the days of instant pudding, making good tasting pudding with a creamy thickness was an art. Few accomplished this feat consistently. It would burn, lump, or be too thin, or be too sweet, or not sweet enough. Definitely the proof of one's knowledge and experience was in the outcome of the pudding. Hananiah's pudding was about to fail the test. To those who heeded Jeremiah's words, the pudding would be creamy and tasty -- life would be much better for them. The decisions we make in life will result in our own 'proof of the pudding' on Judgment Day. Will your life be a series of scorched places and lumps or will it be sweet and creamy under the yoke of God's Will?

August 12
Bible Readings: Jeremiah 23:9-40

Today's lesson is strictly addressing the false prophets. God declares His heart is broken, His bones tremble, and He is overcome by the agony of His people's sin. God squarely places blame on the priests and prophets who have worshipped Baal and led the Jews astray. They have pronounced prophecies and visions from God when they knew not God! But these religious leaders have not sought the counsel of God. God's judgment is permanent removal from the Promised Land and everlasting disgrace. Notice God doesn't have them killed but rather allows them to live under the yoke of shame, disgrace, and rejection. They could live through years of rejection just like God had done.

Food for Thought: Do we have false prophets today? You bet'cha! How can we tell the real ones from the false ones? We must "stand in the counsel of the LORD," meaning we must seek Him in prayer and Bible study. We must not take everything we hear, see, and read at face value. Everything must be measured against God's word. If it doesn't measure up, then it is not from God. Don't let popularity, charisma, charm, wealth, appearance, smooth talking or any other of mankind's earthly characteristics lead you astray. Jeremiah told the ancient people Judgment Day was coming for their land. **Jesus** told us Judgment Day is coming!

Verses of the Week: **Ezekiel 18: 30b-31** "Repent! Turn away from all your offenses; then sin will not be your downfall. Rid yourselves of all the offenses you have committed, and get a new heart and a new spirit."

August 13
Bible Readings: Jeremiah 51:59; 50:1-40

Seraiah, the quartermaster to Zedekiah,[5] was the bearer of Jeremiah's next letter to the exiles. It contains a prophecy concerning the future of the exiles, both of Israel and Judah. I suppose Zedekiah did not know about the letter or possibly he put so little credence in Jeremiah's prophecies that he didn't even care that Jeremiah was writing the exiles. Nevertheless, God tells Jeremiah to lift the banner of the LORD and proclaim His message. (You almost find yourself listening for the trumpet call!) The message is direct: Babylon will be captured and its pagan gods rendered helpless for all to see. A northern nation (Medes) will destroy Babylon. An alliance of nations (called the Medo-Persian Empire or the Medes and the Persians) will plunder Babylon's wealth. The children of Israel (northern kingdom) and Judah (southern kingdom) will soon be participating in the exodus home. They will come with tears of repentance, seeking God, reuniting the tribes, and making a new covenant commitment.

In verse 6 God again condemns the shepherds (priests and prophets) who led His people astray. (Those whose goal is to milk the wealth of the people under the guise of praying for and ministering to their souls had better take notice -- God will punish them more harshly than the people.)

Babylon has no hope for a future. No one will ever inhabit it again. Even its name will elicit horror. This is fulfilled in Revelation by the name of Babylon being used symbolically to identify the capital of the antichrist! Babylon has been destroyed before (by Sennacherib of Assyria) and rebuilt (by Esarhaddon, his successor[5]). This time rebuilding would not be in Babylon's future. Today, the ruins of Babylon stand as a monument to God's judgment.

The people of the northern kingdom of Israel have been scattered over many lands. First, Assyria deports most of them to many different places, then Babylon takes what is left. Their plight and grief were worsened by pagan groups of foreigners being imported into Israel to live. God's remnant of people from Israel will return to the pastures of Carmel and Bashan, the northwest and northeast portion of Israel's land and the hills of Ephraim and Gilead, the southern and eastern land of the former Israel. The people of the southern kingdom of Judah had also been deported. The time of Israel and Judah's judgment is over and God forgives the remnant that survived.

Jeremiah calls for an attack on Merathaim and Pekod. Both are symbolic names for Babylon. Merathaim means double rebellion and is a play on the Hebrew words meaning Land of the Double Rebellion,[5] or rebel of rebels. It was located in southern Babylonia[15] where the Tigris and Euphrates Rivers met. Pekod means visited by judgment and is used here to indicate God's judgment on Babylon.[5] Pekod was located in eastern Babylonia.[15]

God summons all of Babylon's enemies to battle. Babylon is guilty of opposing Jehovah God. Its sentence is complete annihilation. All of Babylon's sources of arrogance will topple: pagan gods, false prophets, warriors, horses and chariots, gold and silver, water, cropland, city walls, pagan temples. Babylon's future was to be the same as Sodom's and Gomorrah's -- never more to be.

Food for Thought: Jer. 50:15 calls to Babylon's enemies to "do to her as she has done to others."[1] I have often heard people of today say, "Do unto others before they do unto you!" In other words, assume all are out to get you, but you get them first. This is a modern day Babylonian attitude! In the case of Babylon, God was making the consequence fit the crime. Galatians 6:7 states, "Do not be deceived: God cannot be mocked. A man reaps what he sows. The one who sows to please his sinful nature will reap destruction; the one who sows to please the Spirit, from the Spirit will reap eternal life."[1]

August 14
<u>Bible Readings:</u> Jeremiah 50:41-46; 51:1-58, 59-64; 49:34-39; 34:8-22

The Medes attacking from the north will be made up of many nations with many vassal kings. They are armed and without mercy. The king of Babylon is gripped with fear; the attackers are more numerous and powerful than he. The Medes will carry out God's justice on Babylon. God has not forsaken His people. He urges His people to run for their lives. Stop and think about God's people. They have built homes and reared families in this place. Daniel who is also a Hebrew is counselor to the king. Other Jews are court administrators. The hanging gardens of Babylon were one of the 7 wonders of the ancient world. The gates of the city are enameled in beautiful colors and patterns. The ground is fertile and water is plentiful. The Jews had been given much freedom to live in their own communities, to hear the words of their own prophets and worship, and to be locally governed by their own elders. Why leave now? There are some who do not leave -- Daniel, for one. Fear of the attacking mass compels most to flee as soon as Babylon is breached. You can hear the longing for the city that had provided for the exiles in verse 9. They wanted to redeem her, but her judgment was too great. God is avenging the destruction of His Temple. God swears by Himself that the Babylonians will incur the consequences for He is the Inheritance or Portion of Jacob, the Creator of the universe.

Jer. 51:20-23 is controversial in terms of its subject. There are many different opinions as to the identity of God's hammer (or war club); our Bible defines it as Israel or God's people who are true to Him. Other commentators identify the hammer as (1) Cyrus, the king who destroyed Babylon, (2) an 'ideal' person who obeys God, or (3) Babylon who was used earlier in time to destroy and uproot kingdoms.[46]

Jer. 51:26 declares to Babylon, "No rock will be taken from you for a cornerstone."[1] Obviously, this looks to the future when Jesus, the cornerstone, will come from the Jews. The cornerstone will be hewn from the Rock (God) who lives on the mountain in Jerusalem.

God commands the nations be summoned against Babylon. Three specific nations are mentioned: Ararat, Minni, and Ashkenaz. These three kingdoms were located in modern day Armenia[49] (southern and southwestern Georgia, the old homeland of the Scythians). Babylon will be completely overwhelmed by the attack. It will become a heap of ruins. Verse 42 refers to the sea rising over Babylon. This is not a literal sea but reference to a mythological sea the Babylonians believed Marduk (their pagan god of creation) subdued to form the land of Babylonia. Its destruction would be quick and fierce like a wall of water, in essence reversing the work of Marduk. God will cause Bel to spew forth or vomit up the nations of people it has captured. The city wall of Babylon will fall. That will be quite a feat! The wall was actually two walls 23 feet apart. The outer wall was 12 feet wide and the inner wall was 21 feet wide! Rows of chariots could travel on top of the wall simultaneously! Additionally, there were guard towers every 60 feet. Outside the double walls was a canal that was filled with water from the Euphrates.[49] The ziggurat shrine to Babylon's pagan god was about 70 feet tall,[5] providing a good view of the land beyond the walls. One can easily see why Babylon felt so smug and impregnable.

Now we come to a part of Jeremiah that makes me laugh! Jeremiah has this long scroll letter of condemnation describing the terrors to come on the Babylonians that he has just finished, and he calls for Seraiah the quartermaster. Jeremiah tells Seraiah that <u>when</u> he is captured and taken to Babylon he is to stand up in the crowd, read the words of the scroll aloud, proclaim "LORD, you have said that you will destroy Babylon so that not a living creature will remain, and it will be abandoned forever," then tie a rock to the scroll and throw it in the Euphrates River declaring, "So shall Babylon sink, never more to rise, because of the evil I am bringing upon her." Now this guy would not only have to be the poorest in possessions and spirit, but he would have to be the poorest in brains to boot! Anybody with any sense would reply, "Sure! I'm going to be a captive of war who loudly reads a condemning letter about my captors in the middle of their capital then throw away all evidence that would implicate you [Jeremiah]? Right, and I'm a monkey's uncle!" (See, it's a good thing the Lord can use all of us in different ways for His Will because some of us would rebel!)

God now (597 B.C.) pronounces judgment on Elam.[49] Elam lies directly north of the northern end of the Persian Gulf. It is in the southwest of modern day Iran with the Karun River running through it.[4] The Elamites descended from Elam who was the son of Shem and grandson of Noah.[5] The Elamites first appeared in the Bible in Gen. 14:1 where they joined forces with other kings scattered from the Mediterranean to the Tigris to battle the 5 cities of the Dead Sea plains. These cities had been subject to Elam for 12 years. They rebelled in the 13th year. Elam thoroughly plundered the cities, taking Lot and his family with the captives. Gen. 14:17 tells us Abraham and his household men (318) did battle with the Elamites and got all the captives and plunder back! (Never underestimate the power of one God-fearing man, even against the strength of many nations.) Isa. 22:6 tells us the Elamites were archers and charioteers. Ezekiel (being a captive in Babylon) writes a funeral dirge for Elam in Ezek. 32:24-25. Ezekiel's dirge is a prophecy of Elam's downfall to the Persians. The verses point blank say Elam will descend to the pit (hell). By now, you can readily determine Elam had been fierce enemies of the Israelites. History doesn't provide us with all the details. We know from Isa. 11:11 that many of the deported Israelites were relocated in Elam. Likewise, Elamites were sent to live in Israel (northern kingdom) (Ezra 4:9). Daniel 8:2 describes a time when Daniel is in Shushan or Susa, capital of Elam, which became the winter quarters of the Persian kings.[50] The vision predicts the rise and fall of the Medo-Persian Empire. Elam was obviously controlled by the Persians at this time as evidenced by Esther 1:2. This would have fulfilled Jeremiah's prophecy that the Elamites would drink the cup of God's wrath (Jer. 25:15, 25). Verse 39 of this section of our lesson is God's promise to restore Elam in the future. Acts 2:9 lists Elamites as one of the foreign participants in the receiving of the Holy Spirit at Pentecost.

Back in Judah, King Zedekiah decides to obey the Book of Law (Deut. 15:12-18) and free all Hebrew slaves. This may not have been out of the goodness of his heart but rather for a more practical reason. Slaves had to be fed. Being under siege (588 B.C.), Jerusalem's fields were destroyed; thus, slaves had no productive work. Zedekiah needed these people in the battle efforts and the owners needed them to be self-supporting.[49] The siege lifted for a while because Nebuchadnezzar had to fight the Egyptians who had marched out against him. So only months after freedom was declared for the Hebrew slaves, the owners reneged and took their slaves back. At this point, God is really angry. These people had made a covenant with Him in His Temple agreeing to free their Hebrew slaves. They had no fear of God because they didn't even recoil from the idea of breaking a promise to God. God had been used as an insurance policy! If they made peace with God, then He would be obligated to end the siege. When the siege was lifted then they quit paying their premiums. They broke the contract! Jeremiah uses an example from ancient Hebrew custom to describe their consequences. (See Gen. 15:9-17.) Anyone who broke a sacred covenant would be treated like the sacrificial animal – conquered and divided. Even though Jeremiah (34:22) prophesied the Babylonians would be back, the people of Jerusalem still weren't listening. Sure enough, the Babylonians returned and the siege was on. Jerusalem fell to Nebuchadnezzar's army in 586 B.C.

Food for Thought: We now have another fall of Jerusalem. They never give up rebelling! This time the punishment by the Babylonians would be more severe. During all this time, I have to wonder what Daniel thought. Did he mourn, even privately, for the captives? Did he try to alleviate their pain? Did he stay in his place of service to the kings of Babylon and later Persia because he could better serve God there? We know so little about him, but we must assume that he was in the center of God's Will. The Bible records his faithfulness even at the age of 90 -- a long time to be a captive. Will we be recorded as faithful all our lives?

August 15
Bible Readings: Ezekiel 1-7

The Book of Ezekiel was written by a member of a priestly family that likely had participated in Josiah's reforms of 621 B.C. Ezekiel may well have been a Temple priest during the reign of Jehoiachin or was at least in training for the priesthood at that time. According to Ezekiel 1:1 the prophet was deported to Babylon in 597 B.C. In 592 B.C. Ezekiel received his call to be a prophet, and Ezekiel 29:17 would seem to suggest that his ministry was at least twenty years. Unlike Jeremiah, Ezekiel was married. His wife's death that occurred in connection with the news that Jerusalem had fallen is an important part of the book[53]

The book is divided into two equal subdivisions. In the first part (chapters 1-24) Ezekiel explains why the nation is being subjected to its present turmoil. The second part of the book (chapters 25-28) looks forward to a restored Israel, after she has served her sentence for unfaithfulness. The event that changes the content of Ezekiel's preaching is the fall of Jerusalem.

Like many of the prophetic books, Ezekiel contains visions. There are, however, far more visions in Ezekiel and much more detail is provided concerning them. Ezekiel was a highly developed mystic who possessed abilities not commonly manifested. An example of this was his understanding of what was going on during the siege of Jerusalem (24:2) even though he was physically hundreds of miles away from the city at the time. Another even more graphic example is chapter 8.

Ezekiel also is known for acting out his sermons. In chapter 4 he draws a map of Jerusalem on a stone and explains how the Babylonians are besieging it and preparing to batter down the city's walls. In chapter five he shaves his beard and head and disposes of the pile of whiskers and hair in a variety of ways symbolic of the plight of Jerusalem's inhabitants. Ezekiel's purpose was to make an impact upon his hearers. As a teacher of language, I often realize that words are a weak means of communication. Quite likely Ezekiel's audience was in such a state of mind in their worry over their friends and family back in Jerusalem and what was going on there that pantomime was the only possible means of communicating with them.

Ezekiel's call with its angelic being is similar to Isaiah's call (Isaiah 6:1). The scroll that Ezekiel eats (3:1-2) is similar to John's little book in Revelation 10:9-11. Ezekiel's description of the four living creatures and the throne above them in chapter 2 is similar to John's vision in Revelation 4.

In Ezekiel's vision each creature had each of the four faces whereas in Revelation each creature has only one face and each is different. In each instance the four faces are a man, lion, ox, and eagle. These four creatures may stand for everything that is noblest, strongest, wisest, and swiftest in nature. Each has preeminence in its own area. The lion is supreme among beasts; the ox, with its great strength, is supreme among cattle; the eagle is supreme among the birds; and man is supreme among all creatures. Irenaus, an early church father, in commenting on the creatures in Revelation, argued that they represented four aspects of the work of Jesus Christ. The lion represents his leadership and royal power. The ox symbolizes the priestly side of His work, for it is an animal of sacrifice. The man symbolizes His incarnation. The eagle represents the gift of the Holy Spirit, hovering with His wings over the church.[54]

Food for Thought: What would you think if someone today related having such a seemingly bizarre vision? Would you be skeptical, maybe even scared, of that person? Remember that Ezekiel is relating to the people in a way that was actually familiar to them. We have a hard time imagining being separated from our loved ones like Ezekiel's audience was. When you put yourself in their places, it is hard to understand how they even survived the great anguish. Praise God today for your freedom.

Lessons of Love

August 16
Bible Readings: Ezekiel 8 - 11

Even though Ezekiel is very precise in dating many of his visions, it is difficult to be exact in the year because the Jews usually counted even a part of a calendar year as one year. We begin in September 591 or 592 B.C.[50] The elders of Judah paid Ezekiel a visit. As they were sitting before him, the power of God came upon Ezekiel and he saw the Glory of the LORD. (Note here that Ezekiel was of the high priest lineage of Zadok and Eleazar. Jeremiah, Ezekiel's contemporary, was of the priestly lineage of Abiathar who had been barred from ministering in the Temple. Ezekiel ministered before the Glory of the LORD through God's revelations to him whereas Jeremiah delivered the messages of God.) The Spirit of the LORD lifted Ezekiel up, suspending him between heaven and earth. In his vision, Ezekiel was in Jerusalem at the north gate of the inner court of the Jews. There he saw a pagan idol (probably Baal, Tammuz, or Asherah). Our God is a jealous God who wants our complete love and devotion. By setting up this pagan god, the Jews had kicked out the owner of the house (Temple) -- God! God had been evicted!

Next Ezekiel digs a hole through a wall by the entrance to the court. When he broke through to the 'secret' chamber, he saw 70 elders of Jerusalem involved in various forms of idol worship. Jaazaniah son of Shaphan is specifically named. We do not know if this is the same Shaphan who is listed as the Royal Secretary in Jeremiah and the ruler of the city in 2 Kings 22. More than 20 years have passed since Shaphan read the newly found Book of Law to King Josiah. We know Shaphan had two righteous sons who assisted Jeremiah. We do not know if he had another son, namely Jaazaniah who secretly worshipped idols. I believe it is the same family, mainly because Jaazaniah was the only one mentioned by name of the 70 elders (notice the multiple of 7 given here).

Ezekiel was whisked back to the entrance to the north gate. He saw women mourning for Tammuz. Now don't take this statement to mean they thought their pagan god was gone forever. On the contrary! Mourning was an integral part of Tammuz idol worship ritual. Tammuz was a Babylonian fertility god of love and war[5] that extended to vegetation and the underworld. He was the male counterpart to the goddess Ishtar who was well known by the elaborate Ishtar gate that framed the Procession Way (main) entrance into Babylon. (A reproduction of this gate can be seen in the Archaeological Museum in Berlin.) The gate was covered in blue enamel glazed bricks with bas-relief images of lions (holy animal of Ishtar) in red, yellow, and white. A paved road over 200 yards long led to the gate. Sixty lions (statues) lined each side of the road. The gate itself stood over 70 feet high. In Nebuchadnezzar's remodeling project he added bulls and dragons in glazed brick to the gate (symbols of Adad and Marduk). The gate pierced the double wall system around Babylon. (Wall dimensions are given in the Aug. 14 lesson.) That means the 'gate' was over 56 feet deep! It was like a great hallway in a palace! On the inside exit from the gate, one walked on imported white limestone on Procession Way which was 65 feet wide at some places and was lined by red breccia borders. (Babylon didn't have any stone. It was a marshland area. Thus, mud bricks were used for construction and faced with enamel when decoration was desired.) The Way was parallel to the Euphrates River that ran through the center of town. Along the Way was located the temple dedicated to Marduk, the ziggurat (some people believe to be the tower of Babel), and the famous North Castle with its hanging gardens.[7]

Let us turn our attention back to Jerusalem now. Weeping was usually done at the end of harvest when fertility was gone and vegetation died. Ancient pagans believed their god died, too, only to be reborn in the spring. Thus, springtime with its new vegetation brought worship in the form of sexual orgies.[52]

In Ezekiel's next scene, there are 25 men worshipping the sun, bowing to the east (many eastern religions continue to do this). To make matters worse, they turned their backs to the Temple -- 180 degrees away from God. The meaning of verse 17 is obscure. Putting a branch to one's nose may have been a pagan ritual[52] or it may be a phrase meaning this was the 'straw that broke the camel's back' or added fuel to God's wrath (judgment).[51]

Ezekiel 10 returns to the image of the Glory of God depicted in Ezekiel 1. One of God's men of judgment goes in among the wheels and obtains coals of fire (destruction) from among the cherubim -- the center of God's Glory -

- the judgment seat! The sound from the furious beating of the cherubim's wings was like the mighty voice of God. The coals of the fire of judgment were scattered over Jerusalem. The faces of the beings have one change -- the face of an ox is now given as the face of a cherub, possibly **the** cherub who had gathered the coals of destruction. (*The Living Bible* translates it as the face of an ox.[15]) Ezekiel gives us more detail of the Glory of God stating that it was entirely covered with eyes. This symbolizes God's Omniscience (all knowing and all seeing). The wheels symbolize His Omnipresence (everywhere).

The Glory of God crosses the threshold, leaving His dwelling among the people of Judah and Jerusalem. Outside the eastern gate, the Glory of the God of Israel (a name which reflected the corrupt covenant people) could be seen. God left Jerusalem and went to be with His people -- the exiles in Babylon. It was Ezekiel's job to show the people that the God of Israel was not confined to one country or one Temple. He was a God who could be found and worshipped anywhere. The sacrificial system of worship was now over. The remnant must learn to repent and seek God's face in a foreign land without benefit of the visual manifestation of sin, repentance, and forgiveness found in the sacrificial system. God would restore them, but first they must learn to trust and worship an unseen God. God promises to take away their hearts of stone and give them spiritual hearts of tenderness. With this Ezekiel's vision was complete. He revealed his vision to the exiles.

Food for Thought: For a people so ingrained in the sacrifice of animals, it must have been a very unsettling time. Ezekiel had a huge job ahead of him. My husband reminds me regularly that I have undertaken a task with Lessons that only a crazy person would try to do in one year! Many times I have felt he was right! But God has helped me get through the tough times and has provided for my needs along the way. Just like Ezekiel did, I am trying to be trusting and faithful, obedient and trustworthy. But I daily feel the pressure, time constraints, and fatigue that Ezekiel must have experienced to such greater levels. After all he was a captive in a foreign land. Thank God that others have fought to keep you free!

August 17
Bible Readings: Ezekiel 12 - 14

Ezekiel is instructed by God to act out a scene where an exile digs through the wall and under the cloak of darkness sneaks out of the city; his face is covered and he carries only the bare necessities. He does this in full view of the exiles already in Babylonia. This demonstration is a prophecy of what is to come for King Zedekiah (Jehoiachin is specified by some scholars[52]) and the people left in Jerusalem. Ever since the first deportation, the exiled captives had been hoping Jerusalem would once again become a great city, possibly freeing them from Nebuchadnezzar. Ezekiel's drama clearly predicts the fall of Jerusalem. God further instructs that Ezekiel is to eat and drink with trembling, as if in terror of imminent danger. The exiles say that Jeremiah has been preaching the destruction of Jerusalem for nearly two decades and it hasn't happened yet. So why should they think anything is different now? God says, "It is time."

God now calls on Ezekiel to prophesy against the false prophets of Israel who are prophesying a short period of captivity with the Babylonian Empire soon coming to an end. They are speaking their own words, not God's words. Not only do they stand condemned by God for leading the people astray, they will be blotted from the historical records of Israel and will not enter the Promised Land again. (These lineage records were very important. Only those who could prove full and pure Jewish lineage could participate in ministering before the LORD, as well as in other positions in the community.) These false prophets have thrown up a wall of false beliefs for the Jews based on a foundation of their own feeble, worthless words and whitewashed with lies. Their false prophecies have formed a wall of sin covered with cheap, fake paint. God will unleash violent winds, torrents of rain, and hailstones to destroy the wall and reveal the lies.

Now God's attention is turned to the prophetesses. These women remind me of the voodoo priestesses of New

Orleans and the witches of Salem. They predict the future and offer magic charms and potions for good and evil outcomes. In 1971, Cher recorded a song called "Gypsies, Tramps, and Thieves." It told of men who preached just to obtain a little money and women who read palms or sold 'favors' for income. God makes it clear -- both are under condemnation.

Chapter 14 was a warning to the people of Ezekiel's time and continues to warn us today. <u>Anyone</u> with idols (obsessions) in the heart will experience the judgment of God. By setting your hearts on a passion other than God, you cut yourself off from God and His Hand will be stretched out against you. Most religions set aside a time for self-evaluation, repentance, and turning aside from pursuits that come before God. Take this time seriously. When God sends judgment upon a country for unfaithfulness, even the righteousness of Noah, Daniel, and Job could not save anyone else. The point here is that a righteous man can only stand for himself on Judgment Day. Each person will be judged according to his or her own sins. No one will be judged based on another's record. God will send 4 judgments on Jerusalem: sword, famine, wild beasts, and plague. Four judgments indicate more than enough: Jerusalem's fate would be severe.

Food for Thought: Today we think people have been preaching the 'end times' so long that life will just continue on as it is for another 1,000 years. Most people think very little about the end times, believing there is plenty of time left to make changes. God does give us plenty of time and plenty of warnings before judgment comes. Have we had eyes that didn't see and ears that didn't hear? Isn't 2,000 years plenty of time? God's warnings are in His word, the number one best selling book in the world for more decades than we can remember. We've had time and we've had warnings. What preparations have you made to face God on Judgment Day?

August 18
Bible Readings: Ezekiel 15 - 18

Ezekiel plunges into a series of three allegories. First, Judah is depicted as a useless vine -- no good for fuel or lumber or even as a peg. To Hebrews a vine was always thought to be a grapevine; thus a vine was only good to produce fruit. (To us Southerners, vine always brings to mind Kudzu that covers parts of the South.) A vine that could not produce grapes was worthless. Judah's 'fruit' was in serving God. If they didn't serve God, they had no reason to exist. The vine (the nation of Israel) was burned at one end (the capture of the northern kingdom's 10 tribes) and then at the other end (the capture of Judah) and finally was scorched in the middle with the surrender of Jerusalem under Jehoiachin.[51] This useless vine Judah will undergo the fire of destruction (literally when Jerusalem is burned and spiritually/physically/emotionally when the fire of God's judgment consumes them).

There are three ways this allegory is commonly interpreted. The bride is seen as the nation of Israel,[51] or as the kingdom of Judah, or as Jerusalem.[52] [I have chosen the latter.] Second, Ezekiel confronts Jerusalem with its despicable practices. Throughout the Old Testament, we see God's people presented in the image of a bride with God as her husband. In this passage, Jerusalem, the capital and crown jewel of the kingdom, is seen as a wayward unfaithful wife who through adulterous relationships has defiled her covenant or marriage agreement with God. Jerusalem, with its rich and ornate Temple and palace, with the high ground location and massive city walls, with its secure water supply, was the pride of the kingdom -- and pride goes before destruction (Prov. 16:18). Jerusalem had nothing to be proud of on its own. It was originally a city governed by Hittites who were later ruled by an Amorite king at the time David attacked. Through David, God selected this town as His Holy City and had His Temple built there. The prophets Hosea, Isaiah, and Jeremiah saw Israel as a pure nation who was defiled by the Canaanite religious practices. Ezekiel, though, sees Jerusalem as being corrupt from birth. Jerusalem was nothing more than an unwanted abandoned baby (the illegitimate child of a Semitic father and a non-Semitic mother[52]) until God adopted her. He provided for her and protected her until she became a city of mature believers. He established His marriage covenant with her (spreading His garment over her is given in Ruth as a marriage proposal) and chose to dwell in her midst in His Temple. She would be His queen. Jerusalem was given the finest blessings as evidenced in Solomon's reign. Instead of being grateful, obedient, and joyful over her elevation from illegitimate child to queen, Jerusalem broke her covenant with God to pursue other relationships. (Can't you just hear the Jews complaining? "He just doesn't understand us!") The downfall of mankind seems to be our continuous quest for something more than what we have. We're never satisfied. Lust has always brought despair, sadness, and rejection. Jerusalem was worse than a prostitute. Prostitutes are paid, but instead Jerusalem paid her lovers (pagan gods) by giving them the gifts that God had provided her! She did not even bother to remember the days when she was a rejected city. God stretched out His Hand against her and His judgment was allowing her to plunge headlong into her own way, but Jerusalem still did not repent. She left no passing pagan god unmolested under the reign of Manasseh. She forced herself upon the gods of her neighboring nations, even to the point of sacrificing her firstborn (who had been redeemed by God through the dedication of the Levites to His full-time service) to the detestable Ammonite god Molech. The gifts God reserved for Him were given to pagan gods. Even when other nations seized portions of her people and wealth, Jerusalem still did not repent. God will strip her bare of her wealth, pride, and beauty. All her lovers will see her wickedness revealed. She is even more demented than her sisters (Samaria and Sodom) were. God says that her sisters even seem righteous when compared to Jerusalem. God has condemned Jerusalem, exposed her sins, and now is divorcing Himself from her. Jerusalem must bear her shame and disgrace before the world. Those she had scorned will now scorn her. Jerusalem must bear the consequences of her sin. But, she is offered one ray of hope. When she remembers the God who elevated her, she will repent and turn back to God. In that day, God will make atonement for her and bring her back home.

Third, Ezekiel has a vision of two eagles and a vine. The great eagle Nebuchadnezzar swooped down and plucked the top out of the regal cedar (King Jehoiachin who surrendered Jerusalem). Along with 10,000 exiles, the regal cedar was taken to Babylon. The exiles put down roots in the land of fertility, flourishing greatly. They turned their hearts to God even though their roots were still confined to Babylonia. Next, the young man (Seed of the royal family) Zedekiah was placed on the throne of Jerusalem. His covenant with Babylon allowed him much freedom to grow and flourish as a nation again. Zedekiah was inexperienced, weak, and irresponsible. He turned away from God, broke his covenant with Babylon, and placed his faith in Egypt. Now he would pay the consequences for his sin and the payment would be great. His sons will be slain in front of him, then he will be blinded, and finally, he will be carried a prisoner to Babylon to live and die in disgrace on foreign soil.

Ezek. 17:19-24 is considered by some to be a primitive Messianic prophecy at best[52] but by others as a definite depiction of the Messiah.[51] Jehovah God will pluck a shoot from the top of the cedar (the cedar represents the house of David). He will plant it on Zion where it will produce branches and fruit. (In other words, there will be many offshoots of Christians who spread the gospel throughout the earth winning others to the Kingdom.) All types of people throughout the earth will find both food (for the soul) and protection. All the kings and royal families of the earth will know the LORD will bring down the tall tree (lofty governments) and raise up the lowly tree (the suffering servant Jesus).

In Chapter 18, Ezekiel fractures the beliefs of the Jews in exile that they were paying for the sins of their ancestors. He emphatically states they are paying for their own individual sins! Repeatedly he warns them that the one who sins will die for those sins. Each individual will bear his or her credits for righteousness and charges for wickedness. Ezek. 18: 21-32, particularly verse 26, is interpreted many different ways among religious denominations. Those who believe in 'once saved, always saved' would say the man in verse 26 was not saved from the beginning; therefore, he died in his sins. Others believe that salvation begins with one's belief in God and then is borne out by one's continual walk in faith. If one slips back into a pattern of iniquity, then one dies in his deliberate decision to return to the sinful life. My thoughts are that God knows our hearts. He knows when we are truly saved, he knows when we are truly repentant, and he knows when we are completely rebellious.

As humans we sin. No matter how hard we try to walk faithfully, sin still finds our weaknesses. As Christians we should be deeply sorry for our sins, ask forgiveness, and determine to avoid that pit again. Salvation is not only personal but also emphatic. If you are saved, you know it and the guilt of sin will become a burden you cannot bear but must give over to God. If you 'wonder' if you are saved, then you aren't. When the Holy Spirit fills you, there is no room for the king of doubt (devil).

Food for Thought: There is no time like the present to dedicate your life to the Lord. Salvation is so easy to obtain that many people refuse the gift. We simply must humble ourselves and recognize that we are sinners. Then we realize that all others are sinners, too. There is only One who was without sin and He died so that you and I can have eternal life. Accept His love and mercy. Make Him Lord of your life today.

August 19
Bible Readings: Ezekiel 19 - 22

Chapter 19 is written in the Hebrew dirge meter called kinah. Judah is the lioness in the first lament, and the vine in the second one is either Jehoiachin or Zedekiah. The laments mourn the death of the Israelite nation.[52]

Laments for the Kings

Judah was an impressive nation among the other nations. Judah had a special tie to the God of Israel that bound Judah together as a pure and holy nation unto God. Judah lay down among the Gentile nations and produced her royal princes of Israel. One of her princes, Jehoahaz, became strong and began to devour other peoples. The Egyptians caught him and took him back to Egypt as a captive.[51]

Judah then took another prince and made him strong. He, too, learned to capture other people and conquer towns. Sadly, he went much further by devastating the towns and imprisoning defenseless widows so that the inhabitants were left desolate. Other nations feared him and set a trap for him. When trapped, King Jehoiachin was brought to Babylon and imprisoned.[51]

Judah was like a choice vine planted in fertile land with plenty of water. It became thick with branches and fruit. Judah produced powerful kings. (See Psalm 80: 8-11.) It towered high above its territory. God's fury uprooted it causing the hot wind off the desert to wilt it. Judah was stripped of its wealth and its people. The fire of God's judgment consumed it. Now the Jews are exiled in the desert, a land dry and thirsty for the love of God. Judgment on Zedekiah spread throughout Jerusalem and consumed the whole city. No noble family is left in her.

On August 14, 591[50] or 590 B.C., some of the elders of Israel again came to visit Ezekiel. [Note: You will notice Ezekiel is called 'Son of Man' throughout this book. Ezekiel and Daniel are the only other people in the Bible called 'Son of Man' besides Jesus. Ezekiel, being a priest in the lineage of Aaron, was consecrated to commune directly with God. Thus, Ezekiel is called 'Son of Man' and given his vision directly from God, whereas Daniel receives his call and vision from an angel. According to Keil and Delitzsch, the address from God as 'Son of Man' "furnishes an evidence that Ezekiel does not, like the false prophets, utter the thoughts and inspirations of his own heart, but, in all that he says and does, acts under a *divine* inspiration, and serves to impress the rebellious nation more and more with the conviction that a prophet of the LORD is in their midst, and that God had not departed with His Spirit from Israel."[51] (p. 13) About Daniel, Keil and Delitzsch likewise state, "he was deemed worthy of receiving high divine revelation." (p. 310)] God lashes out at the elders, refusing to allow them an audience with Him. God swears with an uplifted hand (Do you recognize our courtroom oath practices are modeled from the Bible?) on the day He revealed Himself to the Israelites in Egypt, to be their God if they rid themselves of their pagan gods and devoted themselves to Him. But, they rebelled against Him. God wanted to pour out His wrath on these rebellious Israelites, but Moses intervened. (See Num. 14: 11-19, 21.) God brought them out of Egypt so that His name would not be profaned among the pagan nations. Ezek. 20:12 specifies that the Sabbath observance was given as a sign of recognition by the Israelites of the Holy God they served, but the people rebelled even more -- utterly desecrating the Sabbaths! Again God wanted to destroy the Israelites, but again Moses intervened. (Remember those lessons when we felt sorry for Moses?) Then the Israelites' children grew up to be rebellious to the extent they were murdering their firstborn for paganism. (You can easily feel God's pent-up anger of all those centuries is bursting forth against these sinners, no longer restrained.) Now God points out that He has slain the worst of the offenders and handcuffed the others marching them into confinement. Judgment has been executed upon them because their proud and stubborn hearts would not be humbled to obey God. Each one must pass under the rod of the Shepherd. (See Psa. 23.) A shepherd lets the sheep pass under his rod so that each one is individually inspected, counted, and evaluated as to physical condition. In this way the shepherd binds himself to his flock. (Now you can feel that God's anger has wound down for this encounter and His compassion is kicking in.) God reveals that the Israelite people will again serve him when they have completed the time of their sentence. The exiles will repent and turn back to the God of Israel and will hate themselves for the vile sins they have committed. Ezek. 20:44 decidedly points out that God will deal with the Israelites as His namesake (children, inheritance) NOT as they deserve.

Ezekiel 20: 45-49 is so full of symbolism that it is probably best I delineate the various components first.

    (1) South = Judah
    (2) Forest = population or people
    (3) Trees = individual persons
    (4) Green tree = righteous man
    (5) Dry tree = ungodly man
    (6) Fire = war[51]

If you read this passage substituting the interpretation for the symbols, you quickly see the passage as a prophecy of the coming war upon Jerusalem. Verse 21:4 indicates God's sword will start in the south (Judah) and go to the north (Ammon) slaying all in its path. Ezekiel is ordered to mourn loudly so the people will ask about his grief. (It will give Ezekiel an opportunity to witness -- something we all should seek.) He grieves over the destruction of Judah.

Ezekiel launches into a song. The Hebrew people are very musical and their heritage and culture have been passed down through songs. Also, words set to music are much harder to forget. The tune and the words play over and over in their heads and their hearts. The song tells how the sword is coming against the King of Judah and the Jews. Striking the hands together three times indicates the strength or force of the sword. It will slash all those on both the left and the right and the center. A triple-edged sword will Babylon be! Ezekiel even predicts the details of how Nebuchadnezzar will cast lots with arrows to determine where he attacks first; he also consults his idols and examines the liver. (Putting arrows, each with the name of a town or country to be attacked, in a quiver and shaking the quiver until one falls out constitutes the first inquiry. The second method was to consult Penates, the pagan god of good luck. How the god supposedly responds is unknown. The last method was to literally examine the liver of a sacrificial animal. Both the Babylonians and Romans put a lot of faith in this method.[51] The liver and its attached gall bladder are frequently depicted in pictorial graphics of the era.) The weapons of war mentioned are arrows, battering rams, ramps, and siege works. Battering rams and siege works were pre-fabricated, brought to the battlefield, and assembled. Battering rams were long iron poles with sharp pointed spearheads on one end and were on wheels surrounded by a protective chariot with full frontal shield. The shield was covered by leather that was watered down to prevent it from burning from fires of the destruction.[7] A crew of men rolled the ram into place and charged the walls or gates. The pointed spearhead would lodge between the stones or mud bricks (they had no cement or mortar). The ram would have been wiggled and charged until a stone was dislodged. Then, like a house of cards, the wall would tumble down. A siege works could easily be developed over the slope of stones. Ramps were also assembled on site and rolled into place.

God issues a special warning to Zedekiah: "The lowly will be exalted and the exalted will be brought low."[1] (Ezek. 21:26) God also issues a prophecy of the destruction of the Ammonites who are destined to be remembered no more. Their guilt is bloodshed and pagan worship. (These are descendants of Lot's son.) Jer. 49 promises their fortune will be restored -- and it will be but under the name of Arabia.[51]

Our lesson returns to the condemnation of the house of Israel and Jerusalem. Their sins are listed.

- Despised the holy things of God
- Desecrated the Sabbaths
- Slandered
- Committed lewd acts
- Participated in pagan worship
- Violated women
- Committed adultery
- Committed incest
- Took bribes
- Charged excessive interest
- Employed extortion
- Committed murder
- Committed robbery
- Oppressed the needy
- Denied justice
- Mistreated foreigners

God sees the house of Israel as dross among the few remaining faithful (silver). He is about to put them all in the fiery furnace and melt the dross away. The priests were no better than the people. They, too, will be purified. All will feel the consequences of their sin.

Food for Thought: Before you start thinking that the people of Judah and Israel in general are such horrible sinners, take a good look at the newspaper or TV news. All of these same sins are with us today. Many are more extensive than in Ezekiel's time. Except by the Grace of God go all of us. Be careful not to believe that you are above such deeds yourself. Without God, we are all the same. Praise God and thank Him for the great sacrifice He made so that we could be forgiven!

Verse of the Week: **Jeremiah 33:3** "'Call to me and I will answer you and tell you great and unsearchable things you do not know.'"

August 20
Bible Readings: Ezekiel 23, 2 Kings 24:20; 25:1, Jer. 52:3-4; 39:1; 52:4, 2 Chron. 36:13

To illustrate the sin and unfaithfulness of the Jews, Ezekiel tells an allegory of two sisters Ohlolah, representing the northern kingdom of Israel, and Oholibah, representing the southern kingdom of Judah. In their youth (time spent as slaves in Egypt) they learned prostitution (became familiar with Egyptian idolatry). In spite of their marriage to God, they continued to be unfaithful (practiced Assyrian and Babylonian idolatry). For those reading a modern translation, Ezekiel is quite blunt and graphic in describing the sisters' vulgar lechery. His purpose was, no doubt, to fill his listeners with loathing disgust for these two awful women. Through the story though, Ezekiel is describing how God looks upon our sin and unfaithfulness.

One of the great follies of our day is the belief that modern man doesn't practice idolatry. The physical objects of adoration have changed, but the practice of worshipping things has remained. Mark Twain astutely observed that the chief religion of his day was "Get money, get it quickly, get it in abundance, get it in prodigious abundance. Get it dishonestly if you can, honestly if you must." Is the twenty-first century any different? How many of us allow material things to get in our way of serving God and worshipping him? Do things serve you, or do you serve things?

This passage certainly shows that Ezekiel was a man who could call a "spade" a "spade." Oh, that there were more of these in this age of political correctness!

Food for Thought: Ezekiel was a man in times that were desperate and dark for the nation of Israel. Few survivors remain from the once well-populated country. A nation to be feared in David's day and to be envied in Solomon's day, Israel as a nation was now just to be pitied. Ezekiel as God's messenger spares no words nor softens any sin. The people who did not understand God's message now were truly beyond hope. God was being very blunt; not what we like to hear, but what we sometimes need. Talk to God now and listen for His responses. The more you converse with Him, the more you will hear His voice guiding you.

August 21
Bible Readings: Ezekiel 24

On Jan. 15, 588 B.C.,[50] God announces to Ezekiel that the siege on Jerusalem has started. It will last about 18 months.[50] God's message to the Jews comes in the form of a song. Again I will identify the components of the song before we look at its message.

(1) Pot = Jerusalem
(2) Pieces of flesh and the bones = inhabitants of Jerusalem
(3) Fire = fire of war
(4) Setting pot on fire = commencement of the siege
(5) Choicest pieces of flesh and pieces of bone = strongest and ablest of the population
(6) Wood = judgment
(7) Encrusted/rust = shameless sin with no repentance

The walled city of Jerusalem is seen as a large pot where its inhabitants will be boiled by the fire of war. As the intensity of God's judgment increases, the number of fatalities increases; person-by-person they die. The people of Jerusalem had so shamelessly sinned that their murders had been done openly, spilling the victims' blood on the rock (pagan altars) without even the decency of being covered and buried. Now it was consequence time. The spices of death are evident in the pot. The wrath of God is piled high and even the strongest of the survivors are diminished to worthless waste. They are being judged in accordance with their sins. The pot will have the wood and fire piled under it until it is burned clean and all impurities are gone.

Ezekiel now receives devastating news of his own. God informs him the love of his life is going to die. Ezekiel has less than 12 hours with his wife. To make the situation even more difficult, God commands Ezekiel not to mourn or display any signs of mourning. Hebrew mourning consisted of tearing one's clothes, wearing sackcloth, periods of fasting, eating special foods, not combing one's hair, no make-up, loud continual wailing, and throwing dust on one's head. Ezekiel is also forbidden from going barefoot and bareheaded. For the average citizen's death, mourning lasted 7 days. But Ezekiel is not to mourn because he will demonstrate to the Jews that they are not to mourn their beloved Jerusalem either. When Jerusalem falls, they will know that there is only one divine, holy Sovereign LORD.

From the time Ezekiel's wife is buried until the fall of Jerusalem, God makes Ezekiel mute. It is a time the Jews will spend in silence, reflecting on their sins, contemplating their judgment, and repenting. It will be a time of silent introspective soul-searching, a time to fully realize the sovereignty of the God they rejected, a time for remorse and returning to the God of the Covenant.

Food for Thought: Be silent before God. Concentrate on His great power, mercy, love, and compassion. Look carefully into your own life. What are your idols? What are your sins? Is God first place? Determine today to turn from sinful habits and ways, place God first in your life, and lead your family and friends to a closer relationship with the Savior. Pray for God's strength.

NOTE: The term Israel is used many times now to refer to the remnant of Judah in exile and the remaining population left in Jerusalem. It may also mean the old northern kingdom. Keep in mind as you read, Israel may mean any of these. A review of history would be the northern kingdom, but a concern about the period of the exiles would be the remnant of Judah. Those deported from the northern kingdom were thoroughly scattered and integrated into other nations. After a while they intermarried and few pure blood northern kingdom Israelites remained. The nation would be called Israel again but with Judah as the primary tribe of ancestry.

August 22
Bible Readings: Jeremiah 21; 22:1-9; 34:1-7; 32; 33:1-9

Zedekiah now decides to inquire of God as to what to do next. (Personally, I believe he is doing the same thing all of us have done before -- asking God when all else has failed. God is last on his list. Even now he can't humble himself to do God's Will.) Notice in Jer. 21:2, Zedekiah acknowledges that God has performed great wonders in the past. Maybe Zedekiah thought he was too bad for God to help him. Again, this would be a common concern of many of today's people. After Jeremiah relates the famine, plague, and sword that are coming, he offers Zedekiah a chance to avoid the loss of life. All who surrender to the Babylonians will not die. Many of Jerusalem's citizens would abandon the city and surrender to Nebuchadnezzar. How many were desperate versus how many believed Jeremiah is unknown. God's warning takes on a greater sense of urgency as Jeremiah pleads with the royal household to "Do what is just and right." The palace will be destroyed if they do not heed God's Will. God sends this message to Zedekiah: (1) he won't escape, (2) he will see the king of Babylon, (3) he will speak to the king face-to-face, (4) Jerusalem will be burned, (5) Zedekiah will die peacefully, and (6) the Jews will honor and mourn his death. As Jeremiah is speaking, the last three fortresses of Judah are under siege: Jerusalem, Lachish, and Azekah. These three towns are about 20-30 miles from each other, roughly the points of a right angle. Zedekiah becomes so angry at God's message to surrender that he imprisons the messenger in the guard's courtyard.

During his confinement, Jeremiah is instructed by God to buy a piece of land in Anathoth, his hometown. Land was to remain within the family originally receiving the allotment. As nearest relative, Jeremiah had both the right and obligation to buy the land. Now Hanamel was visiting his nephew in a prison situation in an area under siege. First, how did he get in and out of town? Second, wasn't he concerned about getting his money from someone obviously outside the king's favor and obviously without any means of income? In the August 14th lesson, we learned that the siege lifted for a short time while Nebuchadnezzar fought the Egyptians. Thus, Hanamel could get into Jerusalem unimpeded. Towns around Jerusalem remain under siege. Regarding the money situation, Jeremiah was from a priestly family and, as such, received an allotted portion of the sacrifices just as any other Levite did. Additionally, his confinement was more of a restriction as to where he could preach within the palace. Jeremiah signs the deed to the land and seals it (bullae[7]). He gives his secretary instructions to store it for long-term preservation -- a time when Judah will be restored.

God's promise to destroy Jerusalem and its wicked people is now in full swing.

God comes to Jeremiah with messages on two occasions while the prophet is confined. First, Jeremiah is to warn the people that God is angry about the idol worship. Therefore, the city will be burned down. But at a future date, God will restore the Jews in their homeland and once more they will be blessed with prosperity. The second message from God is that He will heal His people. God promises to (1) cleanse, (2) forgive, and (3) bless them in response to their obedience and praise.

Food for Thought: Our verse of the week comes from Jeremiah's first message from God. God longs for us to call to Him so He can tell us the secrets of a fulfilled life. Call God today. His line is never busy or out-of-service. He's waiting to hear from you.

August 23
Bible Readings: Jer. 33:10-13; 30; 31:1-25; Jer. 31:26

When the exile is over, God will restore the land and fortunes of His people. The Hand of the Shepherd will again protect each of the sheep. God will gather the remnant of exiles from both Judah and Israel, reuniting His family. No longer will they be in bondage. Freedom, peace, and security will be theirs. God will discipline with justice. Life will return to normal. Jerusalem will be rebuilt. God will raise one of their own from the lineage of David to rule over them. This King will be near to God and God will be near to Him. (This is obviously referring to Jesus.)

Jeremiah reassures the people in Jerusalem that those who survive the war will find favor among the Babylonians because that is God's Will. Now, I can imagine them thinking, "Yeah -- IF I survive the war!" Keep in mind, God has already told them what is required to survive: surrender! All who surrender will be spared when the city is destroyed. Those whose hearts are devoted to God will flourish and increase in Babylon.

Jerusalem will fall during the summer. Making the long trek of the captives to Babylonia will be difficult. A short distance north of Jerusalem is the remains of Ramah, the border town that had protected the route into Jerusalem from the northern kingdom. Nebuchadnezzar will halt the captives' march at Ramah long enough to kill the old and weak who are not able to make the long march.[5] Thus, Jer. 31:15 talks of "Rachel weeping for her children." As Israel's favorite wife, Rachel is used symbolically to represent the mother of Israel's children. (Poor Leah is still ignored.) Those who are killed are Jews of Judah's tribe (Leah's child) from the southern kingdom. (Most of Rachel's descendants were the northern tribes of Ephraim and Manasseh. Only the small tribe of Benjamin was in the south.) This verse from Jeremiah will be quoted in Matt. 2:18. Jeremiah is looking forward and Matthew is looking backward at the time Herod has all the children two and under killed in an effort to eliminate the Messiah. This extermination of the infants of Bethlehem is said to rouse Rachel from her grave to mourn and weep. (Remember Rachel was buried near Bethlehem (Gen. 35:19)). So Jeremiah is predicting an attempted extermination of the beginning of a new nation through the mourning of the passing away of the old nation.

God declares they must not mourn for there is hope for the future. God has heard Ephraim's moans. (Ephraim, as the blessed tribe of the northern kingdom, is used symbolically to represent those, now scattered, people.) The people of Israel were deported almost 135 years earlier. They have had plenty of time to self-evaluate and repent. Memories recounting the power and splendor of the united nation of Israel under kings David and Solomon have been passed down through the generations. The exiled Israelites mourn for a home they no longer remember. They long for the God of Israel to return to them. Jeremiah declares assurance of God's longing and compassion for them. God calls for their return to Him. Verse 31: 22 is especially controversial in interpretation. Some believe it refers to the birth of Jesus. Others believe it represents the loving relationship of God to His children, like that of a mother and child.[46] Still others believe the woman is faithless Israel who will return to her husband (God) and surround Him with love and devotion -- certainly a new thing![52] God promises to "refresh the weary and satisfy the faint."[1]

Food for Thought: Surrender is still the message for survival today. We need to surrender to God's Will just as the people of Jerusalem were told. We are a world of stiff-necked people, puffed up with pride. On a daily basis, we need to replace our pride with humility. Try it. You'll find much joy and happiness (not to mention a lot more friends) when you become humble.

August 24
Bible Readings: Jer. 23:1-8; 33:14-26; 31:27-40

Today's lesson presents three directives Jeremiah had on the future return of the remnant to the Holy Land and the restoration of their nation. The three directives have the themes of (1) blessings of deliverance, (2) promises of the future, and (3) their new covenant with God. First, he starts by condemning the leaders who led the people astray initially. When the people return from exile, God will select their new leaders. A song is sung at this point about the King who will come from the lineage of David, a righteous branch of the family tree. This King will do what is just and right. He will save and protect both Israel and Judah. He will be called LORD of Our Righteousness or Jesus Christ. Jesus is frequently referred to as the branch or root of Jesse (Isa. 11:1,10). The Hebrews used to mark time based on the number of years since their exodus from Egypt. Many of their holiday celebrations were to immortalize the events of the exodus and to provide an easy way to teach future generations the history of the people. 'The exodus' was referred to on a daily basis. Jeremiah says it will wane in comparison to the second exodus of the Israelites and Jews who will be returning home from the Middle East nations where they have been scattered.

Second, Jeremiah again sings his song about Jesus being raised up from a branch of David. He further declares God will fulfill His promise to David that a descendant will always be on the throne of the Hebrews and the Levites will always have a man to stand before God. God's new covenant or contract with His people will be more binding than the last. It will be as integral a part of God's plan as the orbits of the heavenly bodies are. The Hebrew descendants will increase innumerably. God hears the jeering comments made by other nations. They believe the exiles are proof God rejected both the northern and southern kingdoms. But God says His promise of restoration for the Israelite nation is more binding and permanent than His promise to maintain the laws of the universe.

Third, Jeremiah talks about the future of the reestablished nation of Israel. Under the new covenant each and every person will be judged and disciplined for personal sins rather than corporate sins of their ancestors. The law of God will be placed in the hearts and minds of the people. They will have a soul that is capable of distinguishing right from wrong. They will have a conscience that will cause them to condemn themselves with the guilt of sin or rejoice in a victory over sin. All of the people will innately know God, but those who accept Him as LORD of their lives will be forgiven of their sins. No record or remembrance of their sins will exist. God will wipe their accounts clean. In the past, the Day of Atonement allowed the people to have a zero-based account with God yearly. This accounting principle is simply that each year's budget is based on zero credits and debits rather than on historical data. In essence, those who truly repented and turned from their sins on the Day of Atonement would start over with a clean account. The problem developed when very few of the people heartily repented. Instead, it became another empty holiday. God's new covenant will provide a means whereby we can repent anytime and ask forgiveness directly from God. God knows each one's heart and each one's account of sins will be purged based on the repentance in the heart. [Because we are all sinners, our overall account is always in the red unless we believe in Jesus, and then the red blood of Him covers our red ink debts!]

Jerusalem will be rebuilt and never again will it be destroyed. The landmarks mentioned in verses 38-40 are as follows:

Tower of Hananel - NE corner of city wall
Corner Gate - NW corner of city
Hill of Gareb - West of city
Goah - West of city

Valley of dead bodies (Hinnom Valley) - south of city
Horse Gate - east side of city[46]

Obviously, if the Hinnom Valley is included then the city will be larger than it was. You'll recall the Hinnom Valley was also the garbage dump -- outside the city wall. Also, it was the most despicable of places to the LORD. Child sacrifices to Molech were conducted there. Jeremiah tells us that the whole city will be holy to the LORD. Therefore, the unclean will become clean. How can that be? Aha! Jeremiah is talking about the kingdom of the Messiah who will reign in the New Jerusalem! The sacrifice of God's Son will wash all sin away. You notice there is no mention of rebuilding the Temple that Nebuchadnezzar burns when the city falls.[51] Find the reason by reading Rev. 21:22.

Food for Thought: Praise God! Praise God! I am a child of the King! Today we have read about God's promise of deliverance from the bondage of sin, restoration to a place in His family, and hope for eternal salvation. If you don't know Jesus as your personal Savior, right now is the time to turn to Him. It is as simple as:

C = Confess that you are a sinner,
B = Believe that Jesus is the Son of God who died for you to have eternal life, and
A = Accept Jesus as Lord and Savior of your life.

Just talk to God like you would to your best friend. After all, He already knows the worst and the best about you! If you are already a Christian, then tell someone else about Jesus.

August 25
Bible Readings: Ezekiel 25; 29:1-16; 30; 31

Yesterday we were in Jerusalem under siege with Jeremiah. Today we are in Babylon with Ezekiel preaching to the earlier deportees from Jerusalem. These exiles are hearing the judgments God has in store for their old pagan neighbors. If they had listened to Jeremiah 15-20 years earlier, they would already know what Ezekiel is going to say. On the other hand, we do not know exactly when Jeremiah preached his judgments on the nations sermon. It is believed to be around 600 B.C. The first exiles were deported in 597 B.C. Therefore, it is quite possible that Jeremiah's sermon was preached after the first 3,000 plus captives were taken to Babylon. If so, this would be new information for them.

Ezekiel pronounces judgment on 7 of Judah's enemies: (1) Ammon, (2) Moab, (3) Edom, (4) Philistia, (5) Egypt, (6) Tyre, and (7) Sidon.

(1) Ammon - Because the Ammonites rejoiced and celebrated over the fall of Israel (northern kingdom) and Judah (southern kingdom), God will give the land to Babylonia. Why did they rejoice? See 1 Chron. 19-20:3. Ammon will be plundered and its capital will become pastureland. No longer can Ammon be proud of its wealth. The Ammonites are destroyed around 600 B.C.

(2) Moab - Moab's sin involved mocking the God of Israel as being no different than any other nation's god. The three frontier towns named are all northern towns (above the Arnon River), which had been taken from Moab by the Amorites and then were taken by the Israelites when they were preparing to enter the Promised Land after their 40 years in the wilderness. Consequently, these towns were given to Reuben who was one of the tribes wanting to settle east of the Jordan. (Recall that Moab hired Balaam to curse the Hebrew people of the exodus (Num. 22).) Moab is captured by the Babylonians in 582 B.C. Their nation is destroyed. Bedouin tribes pasture their sheep in what used to be Moab's towns. At some point, Nabateans settle the land. It is believed some Moabite survivors may have been absorbed into the Nabatean people. (Nabateans were possibly descendants of Nebaioth, son of Ishmael (Abraham's son by Sarah's handmaid) and brother-in-law of Esau (Gen. 28:9). Their power grows into a land-controlling nation as a result of the fall of the Ammonites, Moabites, and Edomites. Nabatea spreads

into these lands and controls the King's Highway until 106 A.D. when the Romans conquer them.[5])

(3) Edom - By mentioning the northern area of Teman and the southern area of Dedan, God's message is that the whole land from north to south will become wasteland. Edom took revenge on the Jews by capturing their refugees as they fled the land and turning them over to Babylon. God's wrath is upon the Edomites.

(4) Philistia - The Philistines have always been enemies of the Hebrews. (Everyone remembers David and Goliath.) The Philistines had been defeated so many times by David that they were bitter, resentful, and malicious. They, too, rejoiced at the fall of God's people. The Philistines have a heart filled with hatred. God says He will 'cut off' or destroy the Kerethites (Cherethites). These people are believed to be Cretans who moved to the coastline from the island of Crete. They had formed David's personal army in 2 Sam. 15:18.[5]

(5) Egypt - This section begins 7 words or messages of God against Egypt. These messages were probably delivered during the winter months of 588-587 B.C.[50] God says Pharaoh (who thinks he is a god) is nothing but a crocodile (Job 41) that has been hooked in the jaws and pulled upon land to die in the desert. All the people (fish) of Egypt will die with him. Repeatedly, God has referred to Egypt as a reed (See Isa. 36:6). Reed is a symbol of weakness.[5] [Jesus refers to them as shaking in the wind (Matt. 11:7). As a form of mockery, the Romans put a reed in Jesus' hand during His persecution (Matt. 27:29).] Over and over the Hebrews have allied themselves with Egypt, believing they had a strong, courageous friend when actually Egypt was a weak, brittle, hollow reed that broke every time Judah needed them. Egypt's weakness had allowed Judah to be invaded. Egypt will become a wasteland from Migdol in the northeast to Aswan in the southeast (the first cataract on the Nile). God extends that judgment even further to the very border of Ethiopia in the south. Not even a few miles of Egypt will escape judgment! For 40 years (a long time) the Egyptians will be scattered among other nations. After then, God will restore their remnant to the Upper Egypt region. Now Jeremiah breaks into a mourning song or dirge for Egypt. (This would be the spring of 587 B.C.[50]) Even the mercenary soldiers who fought in Neco's army (Jer. 46:9) will be destroyed. They are given here as Cush and Put, Lydia and all Arabia, and Libya, which are on the south, west, and east of Egypt. The fire of God's war will come upon the land. The streams of the Nile will dry up (See Isa. 19:4-6). The idols of Memphis, the capital of Upper Egypt, will be destroyed. (Later it is rebuilt as Cairo, Egypt's modern day capital.[5]) Other royal cities are identified for destruction: Zoan in upper Egypt; Thebes in upper Egypt; Pelusium, the eastern gateway into Egypt (it was surrounded by marshes); Heliopolis, city of the sun god; Bubastis, the city of Diana's temple; and Tahpanhes, a fortified city where Pharaoh had a palace (Jer. 43:9).

God will break both of Pharaoh's arms or his might (power). Babylon will conquer Pharaoh, the man who thinks he is a god. Pharaoh's subjects will be scattered among all the nations of the Middle East. God reminds Pharaoh of the fate of Assyria. Assyria was a mighty tree, towering over all other nations, but it was felled. The sin of pride brought it down.[51] It had been the envy of all kingdoms but was now cast into the pit of hell. God dealt with Assyria in accordance with its wickedness (sin). The vassal states that had grown strong under Assyria now withered in its defeat. Assyria now lies in hell with the rest of the pagans.

Food for Thought: I heard an interesting Bible teacher say this week that we are saved by our faith in Jesus Christ as our Savior, but we will be judged on our adherence to the commandments. His definition of commandments included all of God's word. That's a lot to think about.

August 26
Bible Readings: Ezekiel 26; 27; 28

The judgments against the pagan nations continue in today's lesson.

(6) Tyre - Tyre was used in Isaiah and Jeremiah as a symbol for Phoenicia. Tyre was proud of its wealth obtained by its extensive fleets of trade ships. The business district and the homes of the wealthy were on an island only a short distance from the mainland where other businesses and residences were located. Not only proud of its

wealth, Tyre was also proud of its natural defense and believed itself to be secure from invasion. It had the sea to its west, mountains to the east, and several precipitous cliffs around it.[5] Tyre rejoiced at the fall of Jerusalem. The plan was to draw the nations that had streamed into Jerusalem for worship and training in the law, into Tyre. This would increase the trade and wealth of Tyre. (For 13 years, Nebuchadnezzar besieged the mainland city before destroying it in 572 B.C. Alexander the Great destroyed the island city in 332 B.C. after 7 months siege.[5]) Tyre's pride and greed caused its demise. It will never be rebuilt. Alas, it, too, will go to the pit of hell.

Again Ezekiel presents a funeral dirge. Remember it is hard to forget songs. He wants the people to have his words ever before them. This lament begins by describing the glorious magnificence of Tyre. Tyre is viewed as a ship built out of the best materials. The pines of Senir are probably cypresses from Hermon. The tallest cedars of Lebanon were the masts. Cypress and cedar resist invasion by worms and bugs (attacking forces). The sail of fine embroidered linen was a symbol of wealth and superiority; the awnings of blue and purple indicated royalty. (Tyre had a good commerce business in the rare and expensive purple dye.) Oars were oak from the forests of fertile Bashan and the deck was cypress inlaid with ivory. Only skilled master craftsmen were aboard. Hired professional soldiers served in the army. Thus was the beauty and splendor of Tyre. Every nation from Egypt to Arabia to Greece traded with Tyre. But, God was sending the east wind (Nebuchadnezzar) to break Tyre. The mainland shore will quake from fear. They will mourn intensely: shaving their heads, wearing sackcloth, and rolling in ashes. Traders will have disdain for Tyre and horror will fill the nations. Tyre, the impregnable, will fall.

God never lets wicked leaders off the hook. The king of Tyre is condemned for the sin of pride. (Have you figured out yet that for many people the gate to hell is labeled 'Pride'? Pride lets in a host of sins, i.e., greed, lust, hate.) The king is so full of himself; he thinks he is as wise as a god! An interesting insight is found in 28:5, "By your great skill in trading you have increased your wealth, and because of your wealth your heart has grown proud."[1] Being the best horse-trader is not always the best avenue for your life. Jesus did not ever get the best deals in life, nor did He try to gain wealth because He was wiser than other men. Jesus died a poor man by earth's standards but a King in God's eyes! Ezekiel goes on to describe the king of Tyre as being wise in his own eyes. His wisdom led to wealth that led to pride that led to self-importance. He will die with the rest of the pagans. The king of Tyre had everything anyone could ever want (or did he?): wealth, fame, wisdom, luxury, gold, jewels, and beauty. But, his greed led to bargains and business deals with pagans. Soon, the pagans were his friends. Shortly thereafter, they were all pagans. The Apostle Paul says it best in 1 Corinthians 15:33, "Do not be misled: 'Bad company corrupts good character.'"[1]

(7) Sidon - Sidon was another city-state of Phoenicia. It was the oldest city and was well known for its purple dye and blown glass. Ezekiel prophesies a plague will come upon Sidon that will make blood run in the streets. This prophecy came true in 351 B.C. when the Sidonians rebelled against the king of Persia. The Sidonians had been constant agitators of the Hebrews. For their sin of ill will toward God's people, they will be punished. No longer will Sidon oppress the Jews. (Recall that Jezebel was the daughter of the king of Sidon.)

Sidon (Saida today) is about 30 miles south of modern Beirut, Lebanon and 23 miles north of ancient Tyre. Sidon was the eldest son of Canaan. Thus, they were pagans. Notice that God does not condemn Sidon to total destruction. He will "gain glory within" it. Today, Sidon (Saida) has over 20,000 people who are of three basic religious types: Catholics, Christian (generally Russian and Greek Orthodox), Islamic. Sidon, indeed, has had a "sword against her on every side." The Greeks, Ottomans, Romans, Crusaders, English, Turks, and French have all ruled Sidon. It even suffered a terrible earthquake in 1837 A.D. Sidon is greatly reduced in its population but still survives.

Food for Thought: Pride is a violation of the first commandment. We are told to hold no other gods above The God. Pride puts self in front of God. According to legend, Benjamin Franklin developed a list of 12 virtues to attaining moral perfection. A Quaker friend of his pointed out an important omission -- humility.[50] What pride do you need to root out of your life?

> **Verses of the Week: Lamentations 3:22-23** "Because of the LORD's great love we are not consumed, for his compassions never fail. They are new every morning; great is your faithfulness."

August 27
Bible Readings: Jeremiah 37:3-21; 38

Let's return to Jerusalem for an update on the news. Zedekiah is no longer sending messengers to Jeremiah requesting he inquire of the LORD (21:1-2), now Zedekiah asks Jeremiah to "Please pray to the LORD our God for us."[1] (Jer. 37:3) Note Zedekiah's change of attitude. Every word shows he has been humbled and forced to recognize the authority of God. The siege had lifted for a time while Nebuchadnezzar fought the Egyptians who had come to defend their claim on Jerusalem. (Have you forgotten that Jerusalem is under Egyptian rule at this time?) Jeremiah sends the king some very bad news, "It's too late!" God says that Nebuchadnezzar will return to capture the Jews and burn down Jerusalem! This is a revealing situation. We always think we can do everything our way and then run to God to save us when all else fails. Jeremiah makes it clear that the consequences are already determined, but God will be with them through their time of discipline. The Hebrews writer said, "No discipline seems pleasant at the time, but painful. Later on, however, it produces a harvest of righteousness and peace for those who have been trained by it."[1] (Heb. 12:11)

Jeremiah seems to be rather unconcerned about the siege around him. He even tries to walk out of the city just so he can go claim his land in Anathoth! This action was mistakenly perceived as desertion and landed him in prison. Even though Jeremiah denied the accusation, the anger and fear of the city officials resulted in Jeremiah being beaten and imprisoned in the dungeon of Jonathan, one of the officials. King Zedekiah sent for Jeremiah to see if God had changed His mind! Jeremiah finally says, "I told you so" when he inquires as to what happened to all the prophets who prophesied peace for the city. Obviously, Zedekiah figured out Jeremiah had the upper hand here. He ordered Jeremiah to be under courtyard arrest rather than going back to the dungeon, and he also ordered that Jeremiah be fed as long as Jerusalem had food. Now the city officials aren't too happy that they have been overruled. The fact that Jeremiah is telling everyone to surrender to the Babylonians in order to live is not making them any happier either! When they confront the king, he gives in to their wishes. No more dungeon time for Jeremiah! Now he is put in the cistern (underground water cavern) belonging to one of the princes (officials). All that remains in the cistern is mud -- but, oh so much mud! Jeremiah sinks like a rock! An Ethiopian servant of the king hurries to report this atrocity to Zedekiah. Again, the king rescues Jeremiah and puts him back in courtyard arrest. (At this point, it is the safest place for him.)

For the third time, Zedekiah seeks advice from Jeremiah. For the third time, Jeremiah tells him to surrender in order to save the city and the people. For the third time, Zedekiah lets his fear and pride overwhelm him. (Keep in mind -- captured kings were usually killed.) Jeremiah warns that if the king doesn't surrender, he will not escape. The city will burn and he will be captured. The women of the harem he inherited from previous kings will mock him. (Zedekiah's fear of surrendering was in being mocked by the deserters. Now he will have concubines mocking him!) The song they sing to humiliate him starts with a verse from Obadiah (1:7). Rather interesting because Obadiah's prophecy was against Edom. (The house of Jacob and the house of Esau have something in common again.) Zedekiah's friends (the false prophets and counselors) have deceived him. In fact, they have abandoned him like a stick in the mud!

Food for Thought: I had an interesting experience last weekend. I attended a colloquium where imminent scientists (a surgeon, an anesthesiologist, and a psychologist) all provided scientific evidence that there was a God! Jeremiah would have thrown up his hands in frustration. How long had he been saying that? Nevertheless, I was in a room filled with skeptics and unbelievers, but they didn't squawk! In fact, they were enthralled by the lectures (an hour and a half each). These scientists veiled much of what they said under the title of "consciousness," but they did actually credit God. God works in powerful ways.

August 28
Bible Readings: 2 Kings 25:2-22, Jeremiah 39:2-18; 52:5-30; 40:1-6, 2 Chron. 36:17-21

July 18, 587 B.C.[50] -- The day the wall was breached. [Note: Your Bible gives the date as 586 B.C. The year is based on whether you count the year Nebuchadnezzar ascended the throne or start counting at the next full year of kingship.[15]] The famine in the city had been severe. I can even imagine the smell of the Babylonian army's food cooking must have pushed some of the Jews to a mental breakdown. I'm sure the soldiers taunted the Jews with their food whenever possible. The siege had lasted 18 months. Now the chief generals of Nebuchadnezzar's army added insult to injury. They all took seats in the Middle Gate, setting up a military command post. The Middle Gate may have been the gate between the lower city (the original city of David) and the upper city (added by Hezekiah).[46] I imagine Jerusalem's 'old town' or lower city as somewhat like a right footprint. The heel is south, the Temple is at the arch, and the ball of the foot is north. The north has the higher elevation. (Remember the heel sinks in deeper.) The upper city was added at a later date, making it the 'new town.' It is to the southwest of the Temple area and serves to bulge the footprint out from behind the bunion to below the heel. At the Middle Gate, both the upper and lower cities could be viewed. When Zedekiah and his royal bodyguards saw the Babylonians in the Middle Gate, they fled through a palace garden wall gate that led outside the city. They headed east toward the Jordan River, but the Babylonians caught them in the Jericho plains.

Zedekiah and his family were taken to Riblah, Syria, 65 miles north of Damascus.[5] There he met the king of Babylon. There he watched while they slaughtered all his sons. Bound and shackled, they put his eyes out. The rest of Zedekiah's life was spent in a Babylon prison. The last memories he has are of a starving Jerusalem and his slaughtered sons. Just think, humbleness could have saved him from this outcome. August 14, 587 B.C., Nebuchadnezzar's commander Nebuzaradan returned to Jerusalem to kill, plunder, and burn. All the treasures left in the Temple (mostly bronze) were removed and broken into smaller pieces for transporting to Babylon. The other buildings were plundered as well. Then Nebuzaradan burned the palace, Temple, and all other important buildings. All the officials from the city and religious governing groups were killed. The commander of the army and the royal advisers were taken to Riblah to be executed.

The surviving citizenry were gathered together for deportation to Babylonia. A few of the poor were left behind in Jerusalem. After all, they could contribute nothing to Babylonia nor did they have any resources left to outfit even a small rebellious force. Most of the city walls and building walls were knocked down. In 597 B.C. Nebuchadnezzar had taken 3,023 captives, now he took 832 people, in 581 B.C. he will take 745 more. Altogether, 4,600 Jews went into exile.[47] There they will remain until the Persians conquer Babylon.

Nebuchadnezzar appointed Gedaliah as governor of Judah. We are told he is the grandson of Shaphan, the same Shaphan whose family helped Jeremiah. God rewards everyone who has assisted in the deliverance of His messages. The Ethiopian slave who had secured Jeremiah's rescue from the cistern was assured his life would be spared because of his trust in God. Apparently because Jeremiah had advocated surrender to the Babylonians, Nebuchadnezzar orders his release from courtyard imprisonment. We find out later, though, that he has accidentally been rounded up with the other captives and taken to the first deportation stop at Ramah. (I just imagine Jeremiah was too busy preaching to everybody to hightail it to safety.) Here he is recognized and released again. This time he heads back to the governor's house to live. Again Shaphan's family provides for Jeremiah. Just think what sermons those poor Jews got now!

Food for Thought: The Babylonian officials who sat in the Middle Gate area included Nergal-Sharezer, son-in-law of Nebuchadnezzar who becomes king in 560 B.C.; Nebushazban, the chief of the eunuchs; Samgar-Nebo, an unknown officer; another Nergal-Sharezer, the chief magician; and Sarsechim, another unknown officer.[5, 46] Nebo was a pagan god of literature, wisdom, and the arts. Nergal was a pagan god of war.[5] The Hebrew believers had named their children names that honored God. What motivates us when we are naming our children?

August 29
Bible Readings: Lamentations 1-2

A man experiencing a combination of life's most extreme circumstances wrote the Book of Lamentations. Many of his family were either dead or deported to a place where he would never see them again. Any material possessions were either destroyed or permanently lost. The most serious circumstance was that major premises upon which his religious faith was based had been destroyed. His problem is a circumstance most Christians can't grasp. For instance, if Washington, D.C. had been destroyed by an atomic bomb on September 11th my heart would have been seriously grieved, but my religious faith would not have been destroyed. The Jews, however, viewed themselves as God's chosen people; Jerusalem with its Temple was the city of God. The destruction of Jerusalem caused many to question if it was possible to believe in God anymore.

The author of Lamentations is most likely Jeremiah. Throughout history the book has always been associated with him. Second Chronicles 35:25 tells us that Jeremiah made a collection of laments. In terms of its structure, it is a collection of five separate songs or poems. The first four are complete acrostics. This type of poem uses all 22 letters of the Hebrew alphabet in successive order as the first letters of lines and stanzas (chap. 3) or of stanzas only (chap. 1,2,4). Chapter 5 is not an acrostic but does contain 22 verses.[52]

Now let's look at the first two of these songs. In each instance the chapters begin with "how" which is not meant as a question but as a moaning statement. The emphasis of chapter 1 is the tremendous contrast between what was and what is. In verses 5,8,9, and 18, the author readily admits that the nation's sins have brought it to this situation.

The emphasis in chapter 2 is on the anger of the LORD in dealing with His disobedient people. In fairness we should keep in mind that for centuries God delayed His judgment, sending prophet after prophet to warn His people. Jerusalem's circumstance is like Judgment Day around God's great white throne (Rev. 20), there is no mercy nor is there any time for decisions to be made. Each of us should realize, like Jerusalem's people, that there is a Heaven to be gained and a hell to be shunned. Eternity is a long time and hell is hot; make your peace with God today!

Food for Thought: There are many countries around the world that can relate to everything Jeremiah has to say in these chapters. Those of us who cannot relate are blessed indeed. War veterans have seen much of this suffering, but few still living have experienced it in their own towns. In recent years we have witnessed this type of destruction in natural forces, i.e., earthquake, tornado, and hurricane. God has sent many prophets to warn us. Some were sent thousands of years ago, but still we go our own way. Pray for insight into God's Will for your nation, your state, your town. As a Christian, you have a responsibility to do God's Will in these places, too.

August 30
Bible Readings: Lamentations 3-5

In chapter 3 of Lamentations the mourning becomes more personal. Here the focus is on the prophet's personal travails. Like everyone, Jeremiah would have preferred to live during a time of peace and security. Like everyone, Jeremiah would have preferred to have a nice church with nice people where he could have preached nice sermons. Instead he was called to deliver a message of judgment to a people who didn't care and wouldn't listen. Because he suggested surrendering to the Babylonians, he was persecuted and reviled. Unfortunately, God sometimes has to lead his children through the fire and flood to accomplish His purposes. Jeremiah is at one of those moments when he is bitter about the mission he was given, but in verses 22-36 Jeremiah realizes that God is faithful.

In chapter 4, Jeremiah returns to the plight of Jerusalem's people. The reference to the ostrich in verse 3 no doubt is alluding to the infamous reputation of the females of that species in caring for her brood. She takes no trouble to disguise her nest and she forsakes it at the least alarm.[55]

In the midst of all this suffering, Jeremiah feels that the people would be better off dead than alive (4:9). He also calls for judgment upon the Edomites who have hunted down those trying to escape and have delivered them over to the Babylonians.

In chapter five the prophet enumerates everything that the nation has lost. These include the following:

(1) Our inheritance - that is the land,
(2) Our houses,
(3) Our parents,
(4) Our husbands and wives,
(5) The necessities of life (water and wood),
(6) Our freedom,
(7) Our honor,
(8) Our children,
(9) Our joy, and
(10) Our king.

The book closes with an appeal to God to renew the nation as it was in the days of old. Subsequent lessons will show that prayer was answered.

Food for Thought: Jeremiah feels the same way many of us do. "Even when I call out or cry for help, he shuts out my prayer."[1] (Lam.3:8) But in verses 22-23, Jeremiah remembers that the LORD has great compassion that never fails and we must wait for Him. Faith is the belief that God is still there and still cares for you and loves you even when you don't see Him at work. Our grief, fear, anger, depression, or loneliness often masks the workings of God. But He is still in charge. We must be patient and continue to seek Him.

NOTE: Dates are always debatable. I have chosen some because they are plausible but also because I like to have a certain date to 'hang my hat on.' It removes some of the uncertainty when I read. Feel free to disagree with the dates and interpretations. After all, there are plenty of scientists and archaeologists who do!

August 31
<u>Bible Readings: 2 Kings 25:23-26, Jeremiah 40:7-16; 41-44; 51:64</u>

Within weeks, a committee forms to warn Gedaliah of a plot by Ishmael to assassinate him. Although from a priestly family that should have been politically savvy, Gedaliah doesn't demonstrate even average caution as a result of being forewarned. In fact, he denies the possibility of such an event and admonishes the committee of army officers to settle down and serve Babylon without a fuss. Gedaliah seems to interpret their warning as battle anxiety, implying they need to allow themselves to once again become a part of a peaceful, trusting community. They are to plant, harvest, and store for a good future.

Seven months after the fall of Jerusalem, Gedaliah entertains Ishmael and ten of his men at Mizpah. Mizpah is now the Babylonian capital set up for Judah. Mizpah has a rich history as the place where Saul was first presented to the people as their king. Samuel visited there regularly as their judge.[5] Gedaliah prepared the traditional Middle Eastern welcome in the way of food to eat. While eating, Ishmael and his men killed Gedaliah. Why? One reason, Ishmael was of the royal lineage and Gedaliah wasn't. Ishmael probably felt he had been cheated out of a position that should have been his. Secondly, Ishmael was a terrorist at heart. Like the terrorists today, he worshipped pagan gods, envied others of what they had, was angered by a downturn in events, and placed blame on the most visible entity. Followers of pagan gods become extremely demented. Their worship practices require extreme tasks be performed over long hours of concentrated effort. The pagan leaders are just men devoted to Satan and, as such, are filled with hatred. These groups prey on people who are angry and feel they are "owed" whatever they want just because they wanted it!

As with all sin, one murder isn't enough. Now Ishmael and his men fall upon 80 men who are traveling to the house of the LORD to bring offerings and worship. [Note: The Temple had been destroyed, but some were still trying to make an effort to worship there.] Seventy are murdered, but ten talked their way out of the jam by promising stores of food for the band of criminals. We don't know how many Jews were with Gedaliah at Mizpah, but all in his household were killed. I believe we could safely say that close to 100 people were killed and their bodies were thrown in the cistern. Ishmael forces the remaining citizens to march out toward Ammon. Now we see the real leader behind the terrorism -- Ammon. As senior remaining officer, Johanan and his band of officers go after Ishmael, catching up with him two miles away at Gibeon. In the ensuing fight Johanan rescued the Jews and killed two of Ishmael's band of murderers. There are probably no more than 2,000 Jews in the whole group. Fearing the Babylonians would return to avenge the death of their governor, Johanan and his men decide to make a run to Egypt. They lead the surviving Jews southwest, stopping at Geruth Kimham (believed to be a caravanserai designed as an 'inn' for travelers, founded by Kimham, son of Barzillai (2 Sam. 19:38-40)[46]). Now near Bethlehem, they take a lengthy rest to refresh and regroup.

The decision was made -- they would continue on to Egypt. All they needed was God's blessing. So the group turns to Jeremiah, requesting he solicit God's direction on how they should proceed as to their future. (Don't read these verses as 'looking' for roadmap directions!) Read their request carefully. Notice they refer to "your God" twice when presenting their request to Jeremiah, but Jeremiah doesn't let this 'Freudian slip' go by. He jumps right on it! When he agrees to the petition he responds with "your God," subtly reminding the group that all of them were to worship the same God. The group's reply first uses "your God" before changing to "our God." Even this victory is short-lived. They promise to follow God's direction for their lives regardless of what it may be. (Does that sound like all of us?) Jer. 42:7 tells us there is a lapse of 10 days before God gives His response to Jeremiah's prayer. This is not because God didn't know, nor is it because He wanted them to sweat. God's answers often come after we have had a span of time to self-evaluate, repent, surrender, and generally become more humble and open to His Word. God's answer is, "Stay in Israel and rebuild and I will bless you. Go to Egypt and die." The leaders do not seem to have done much repenting. In fact, we are told they arrogantly called Jeremiah a liar. Apparently, their intention was for God to 'rubber stamp' His approval of the plans they had already! (We'd never do that!) They even go so far as to blame poor Baruch, Jeremiah's scribe and sidekick, as the treacherous one who instigated this negative response. Johanan was determined to go to Egypt. The group didn't rest until they reached Tahpanhes.

The refugees from Judah had insisted on continuing their worship of the queen of heaven. Their short-sighted view of God's plan for their nation and their lives resulted in them associating the deaths and destruction to the stoppage of their pagan worship rather than as a result of their paganism. At this point, Jeremiah seems disgusted. He tells the Jews to keep their vows to paganism but rest assured that there would be few survivors.

Pharaoh had a second palace at Tahpanhes. While on the brick road to the palace (which probably extended from the palace to well outside the city), God instructs Jeremiah to take some large stones and bury them in clay in the brick pavement, while the Jews watched. Then he is to tell the people that Nebuchadnezzar (the tool the LORD is using to carry out His Will) will set up his throne there. The fact that God had Jeremiah to bury large stones is significant. Obviously, there are bricks and mortar (clay) available, so why use heavy, odd-shaped stones? The building materials are symbolic of the strength and power of the two kingdoms. Babylon's kingdom would be powerful and permanent, whereas Egypt's would be crumbly and weak -- easily broken.[46] In fact, Egypt will be demolished and their pagan gods destroyed by the Babylonians. Our verses particularly mention the destruction of the sun god's temple at Heliopolis, famous for its magnificent building. Several obelisks were used to adorn the temple site. The two largest obelisks were 150 feet high; Emperor Augustus carried one to Rome and the other was broken in 1160. The removal of these obelisks signified the end of the ancient kingdoms of the Pharaohs.[46]

So that you can maintain the proper perspective concerning time and place, notice Jer. 44:30 indicates Pharaoh Hophra was reigning at the time of Babylon's invasion. Nebuchadnezzar attacked Tyre soon after the fall of Jerusalem. We know it took 13 years to conquer mainland Tyre. Most likely Nebuchadnezzar did not invade Egypt before 573 B.C. Even during Babylon's campaigns against Phoenicia, the Egyptian Pharaoh Hophra kept sending attack forces against Nebuchadnezzar. In other words, Egypt became a real pain to Babylon. So after the Pharaoh decides to interfere repeatedly, Nebuchadnezzar makes Egypt his next battle. Hophra died in 570 B.C. as a result of his defeat at the hands of the people of Cyrene.[46]

Food for Thought: One of the great mysteries of the Bible is the reason for the enormous animosity between the Israelites and the Ammonites. The Ammonites were always teaming up against Israel, all for control of the Holy Land. Interestingly, God brought about confusion in their ranks so that they self-annihilated (2 Chron. 20:1-23). Over time, the whole nation self-destructed. They missed God's long-term plan. Are we shortsighted, too? Stop and think of the hurdles you have overcome with God's guidance. Appreciate God for being always available and always dependable.

The Exiled Nation

September 1
Bible Readings: Ezekiel 33:21-33; 34-36

Ezekiel's period of silence entices debate by Bible scholars as to how long it continued and whether or not it was uninterrupted silence. The *Life Application Bible* states in a footnote, "Near the beginning of his ministry, Ezekiel was unable to speak except to give specific messages from God."[15] (p. 1168) Other schools of thought include the following.
- Ezekiel was silent from the time of his wife's death until the messenger announcing the fall of Jerusalem arrived[50] and the period of silence was 1.5 years[51] to 2 years[15] rather than the short time stated in the Bible commentary introducing today's lesson.
- The judgments were given after the messenger arrived with the news of Jerusalem's fall.[51]

If we go back to Ezekiel 3:26-27, we see that God, Himself, gives us the answer <u>before</u> the question ever arose! (Read it now. What do you think?)

Ezekiel point blank asks the exiles why God should let them possess His land. After all they are still worshipping idols and ignoring God's laws at this point in the exile. The news of the fall of Jerusalem will cause them to stagger under the realization that Jeremiah and Ezekiel have been right all along. Until now they have agreed with Ezekiel to his face but kept on with their same daily habits. In other words, God tells Ezekiel they are no more than 'groupies.' Ezekiel takes the Jewish leaders to task again. His judgment is leveled against the Levites and priests. They have feasted on the best of the offerings to God and clothed themselves with the best wool, but they have failed to minister to the spiritual needs of God's people. Basically, they were paid for work they didn't do! Now they are accountable to God, and He fires them! God will just do it Himself, seeing as how He can't depend on any of the hundreds of Levites and priests that were left. Notice in Ezek. 34, God emphatically states He will lead the sheep. He will rescue them; He will protect them. God refers to Himself 15 times as "I" in the first 16 verses not counting the numerous "my" and "myself."

Then God turns His focus on the flock. They haven't been blameless, either. God is certainly taking on the characteristics of a new shepherd, one with authority to make needed changes. God will judge between the fat sheep and the lean sheep (fat sheep were symbolic of oppressors and bullies who were taking advantage of the lean sheep who were the oppressed). God will also judge between the rams and the goats. In Matt. 25:31-33 Jesus tells us He will sit on His throne with all the nations before Him and He will separate the sheep from the goats. The sheep will be placed at His right hand -- a place of honor, the goats at His left -- a place of rejection. On Judgment Day we all want to be counted as God's sheep, His flock, His children. How do you get to be a sheep? Read the rest of Matt. 25:34-46. Jesus will be our Shepherd. Ez. 34: 23 states David will be their Shepherd. This refers to Jesus being of David's lineage. We need to develop His lineage somewhat at this point. You will recall in Jer. 36:30, Jehoiakim is cursed by God and told he will no longer have a royal lineage. Thus the lineage of David through Solomon ends with the 3-month reign of Jehoiachin. Nevertheless, God still has a way to preserve David's lineage. He will use the descendants of a different son, namely Nathan. Nathan was Solomon's full brother. From Nathan we see Mary descend (Luke 3:23 -- although it lists the males only here, Joseph was actually the son-in-law of Heli, Mary's father). Jesus is the son of David through Mary. He is the legal son of Joseph, but we know His Father is God. Thus, Jesus was actually the 'adopted' son of Joseph. Through Jesus, a new covenant would be established. God's people would have peace and security. Their roles as either victims or slaves would be no more.

Even though God singles out Edom for Ezekiel's special condemnation in chapter 35, Edom is both a pagan nation and a symbol for all other pagan nations. The chief judgment against Edom is its antagonistic, hostile, enmity and bloody hatred towards Israel.[51] As you read this, remember God's word is true. There are many neighbors of Israel who are currently engaged in bloody wars and raids on Israel. There are many other people who harbor ethnic hatred. God condemns it all. They who oppose Israel stand condemned before God -- a goat. God curses Edom with constant bloodshed and wasteland. Rejoicing in the harm that comes to God's people is sentencing you to the same fate.

Ezekiel 36 is an interesting chapter. God's prophecy is to the land of Israel rather than to the people. The land will be restored. Fertility will return. No longer will Israel be scorned but rather the nations around her will be scorned. Israel's towns will again be inhabited. Her people and her crops will be fruitful and multiply. Again the land of Israel will be the treasured inheritance of God's people. To the exiles Ezekiel says that God will make His name holy again among His people. God's Holiness will then be seen by all nations through His children. When Jesus comes to bring salvation to the Gentiles, too, all of us who are Christians will represent God's Holiness to the world. Do others see Jesus in you?

Jesus will bring salvation through His personal sacrifice for all people who come to Him. His blood will wash away our sins. We will be clean and pure before God. We will be given a new heart. We will be God's people and He will be our God forever. Once you turn from a life of sin to living for Jesus, your desolate, lonely life becomes filled with hope and joy and peace -- even during trials.

Food for Thought: Psalm 24 offers an appropriate hymn of praise that was incorporated into this song by Georg Weissel in the early 1600s.

> "Lift up your heads, ye mighty gates:
> Behold, the King of glory waits!
> The King of kings is drawing near,
> The Savior of the world is here.
> O blest the land, the city blest,
> Where Christ the ruler is confessed!
> O happy hearts and happy homes
> To whom this King of Triumph comes!

Fling wide the portals of your heart:
Make it a temple, set apart
From earthly use for heav'n's employ,
Adorned with prayer and love and joy.[41]

September 2
Bible Readings: Ezekiel 37-39

Ezekiel 37 contains perhaps the best known of all Ezekiel's prophecies -- the valley of dry bones. The LORD takes Ezekiel's spirit to a valley filled with very dry bones. God asks Ezekiel a simple question, "Son of man, can these bones live?" Let's think about this. The only other people called Son of Man are Jesus and Daniel. At this point, Jesus is still with God. Ezekiel is here in spirit with God. As God looked out over His people whose lives and hearts were like brittle, lifeless, worthless very dry bones, can you imagine God saying symbolically to Ezekiel but actually to Jesus, "Son of Man, can these bones live?" Can you hear Jesus replying, "Yes, Father, I will go so they can live."?

Now Ezekiel tells the dry bones that God is going to breathe new life into them. They will be given new bodies. With a rattling sound the bones came together and flesh appeared on them. There stood a vast army, symbolic of the army of God -- God's people. In Babylon, they had lost all hope. Jesus Christ will be the new Hope of all people. (In the New Testament, Hope is synonymous with Jesus.) The Spirit of God will be placed in His people.

Next, God has Ezekiel take two sticks. On one he is to write "Judah" (referring to the southern kingdom) and on the other "Ephraim" (referring to the northern kingdom). Now Ezekiel is to bind the two sticks so that they become one united unit. God will take all the survivors of both kingdoms and bring them back to Israel to be one united nation again. They will have only one king (Jesus) and will never be divided again. No longer will they be defiled, for God will cleanse them. "They will be my people, and I will be their God."[1] (Ezek. 37:23) They will follow God's laws, keep His decrees, and live in the land of Israel forever (New Jerusalem of Rev. 21). God will make His dwelling place among them.

Chapter 38 is apocalyptic describing the war between good and evil in the last days. Gog is the ruler of the land of Magog, but he is also the symbol of all evil. Ezekiel is told to prophesy to the north, to the land of Magog. Read 1 Chron. 1:5. You will see the sons of Japheth listed. Magog is Japheth's second son. Naturally, the people of Magog would ally themselves with their brethren.

Tubal - 5th son of Japheth, whose descended people lived in Turkey[5]

Meshech - 6th son of Japheth, whose descendants were known as Moschi or Moschoi[5]

Ezekiel 27:13, 19 indicate Javan, Japheth's 4th son, also traded with Tyre, as did the brethren of his two brothers. Javan was the father of the Greeks. Therefore, Javan may have played at least a minor role in this drama. Gomer was Japheth's eldest son whose descendants are believed to have settled in Russia (or possibly Europe).

The allied forces of Magog will include Ethiopia, Libya, Turkey, Iran, Georgia, Russia and possibly the Ukraine. All of these people descended from Japheth. (It may be that Greece is included as well as other countries.) The invasion from the north will be like a cloud. A cloud of evil descending on God's righteous kingdom with the purposes of plundering their land and gaining control of the continental span from Russia to Africa.[51] But God's "hot anger" will be roused against the invaders. A great earthquake will occur in Israel. (A large fault line runs the length of the Jordan.) All the natural resources of God will enter the battle: hail, fire, burning sulfur, torrents of rain, crumbling cliffs. God's name will not be profaned! The war ends quickly. (Stop and read Rev. 20:7-10. It takes only 3 verses to describe the whole war.) The enemy will be defeated. For 7 years the weapons of the invaders will be burned as firewood by God's people. The flesh of the corpses will serve as an enormous sacrificial meal prepared for the birds of prey and the wild beasts before the remains can all be buried. Seven months will be required to bury the dead. Seven represents the completion of God's divine judgment.[51] Both righteous Israel and faithless pagans will know that there is only one God -- the God of Israel.

Food for Thought: As children of the King, we, too, will be counted among the righteous of Israel. We will live with God in New Jerusalem. I have longed to see the Holy Land and walk where Jesus walked, to see the sun rise over the Mount of Olives. I may never get to do that but one thing is sure and certain, I <u>will see</u> the New Jerusalem! Will I see you there?

Verses of the Week: **Job 5:8-9** "But if it were I, I would appeal to God; I would lay my cause before him. He performs wonders that cannot be fathomed, miracles that cannot be counted."

September 3
Bible Readings: Ezekiel 32; 33:1-20

In the spring of 585 B.C., Ezekiel sings this sad song over the impending demise of Egypt. It is a throwback to the judgment against Egypt in Ezek. 29. Again Egypt is represented as the crocodile monster thrashing about in the water (See Job 41). Egypt has been a constant source of threat and aggravation to all nations within the Mediterranean and Middle East. (Pharaoh Hophra even managed to turn his own people against him because of his relentless, and often unwarranted, attack on multiple nations. Finally, he sails out to fight the Cretes where he is killed.) Again we see Egypt captured in God's net and hauled onto dry land where it is eaten by birds of prey and wild beasts. (Have you noticed throughout the Bible that the really bad guys are sentenced to this end?) God will snuff out the Egyptians and put out their heavenly lights, another way of saying He will demolish their pagan worship of the heavenly bodies. The nations will be startled and appalled by Egypt's downfall. The king of Babylon will easily conquer the land of Egypt. All the cattle of Egypt will be destroyed. (Remember Egyptians also worshipped cows, calves, and bulls.) Thus, more pagan gods will fall. The land will be stripped and all who live there will experience the power of God.

A couple of weeks later, God's word came again to Ezekiel to prophesy the sentence of Egypt -- it is condemned to hell. But, Egypt has a lot of company in hell. There, too, are Assyria, Elam, Meshech, Tubal, Edom, Sidon, and all the princes of the north. This list would include the modern day areas of Iraq, Turkey, Iran, Jordan, Lebanon, Syria, and Georgia. Obviously, "princes of the north" could include a whole lot more countries like the Balkan nations.

Ezekiel now presents a word from the LORD to the leaders of nations. Leaders are endowed to be the watchmen of their countries. When danger comes, they have the responsibility to sound the alarm. If the people choose to ignore the alarm, then their blood is on their own hands. If the watchman fails to sound the alarm, then the blood of the people must be born by the watchman. Ezekiel is again reminded that God has ordained him as the watchman for Israel. Those ordained by God have the responsibility of sounding the alarm when spiritual danger arises. If they don't, the condemnation of the flock is on their heads. God hates the condemnation of sin. He gave His only Son so that no person would have to stand condemned before Him. All we must do is turn from our wicked ways, repent, and seek Him. Yet, many do not.

Ezekiel 33:12-20 is a misunderstood passage by many people and many religions. (Take the time to read it before we go on.) If a righteous man (one who keeps **ALL** the commandments and decrees of God) cannot save himself, then certainly the wicked cannot save themselves. First, we are told in Romans 3:10, 23 that no one is righteous in his own right. Second, if a man lives a good life and keeps all the commandments outwardly, then he stills stands condemned for the unrighteous thoughts he has entertained. Third, if any person, whether living righteously or wickedly, truly repents and turns to God, that person will be saved. (Under no circumstances should you leave this passage without reading Matthew 19:16-30!) Every person will die and be condemned for each one's own sin UNLESS they have been washed in the blood of the Lamb.

Food for Thought: "If we confess our sins, he is faithful and just and will forgive us our sins and purify us from all unrighteousness."[1] (1 John 1:9) 1 John 2:1 tells us we have our own defense attorney -- Jesus Christ. I hear advertisements by many law firms urging people to develop "a relationship" with their attorney before they need him. Have you developed your relationship with Jesus?

September 4
Bible Readings: Daniel 3

In Babylon, King Nebuchadnezzar erects a 90 foot tall and 9 foot wide gold image (most likely a version of himself or one of his gods) in Dura, commanding that all should fall down and worship before it whenever they heard any music. The instruments listed are from several nations. The horn and pipe are Jewish. The lyre, harp, and bagpipe are Greek, and the trigon is Oriental. The kingdom of Babylon included many nations ranging from present day Iran to the Mediterranean Sea to Ethiopia.[52] This was heresy for the Jews! The Babylonians complained that they had to worship the image, but three Jews didn't comply. (There may have been more, but because these three were administrators over portions of the land, they were held accountable.) Shadrach, Meshach, and Abednego were named. King Nebuchadnezzar had them brought before him and he gave them one last chance to comply. These three young men refused. They would follow the commands of the God of Israel. Their accusers were the political officials of the land who were envious of the official positions these young foreigners had been given.

The furnace was heated 7 times hotter than usual. In fact, it was so hot the soldiers who pushed Shadrack, Meshach, and Abednego in were consumed themselves. Suddenly, Nebuchadnezzar jumps to his feet! Not only are the 3 young men walking about easily in the furnace, but now there was a fourth man with them! This fourth man appeared to be a "son of the gods." Nebuchadnezzar calls for them to come out. Miraculously, not a hair on their heads was singed, not a piece of clothing was scorched, nor was there any hint of smoke about them! Nebuchadnezzar is so amazed that he offers praise to the God of Israel, acknowledging that an angel had been sent to rescue these men. Then the king surprises his officials by decreeing that all people of Babylonia who said anything against the God of the Jews would be mutilated and their houses destroyed. Nebuchadnezzar's last statement is revealing of his changing attitude toward God, "for no other god can save in this way."

In some ancient Greek and Latin versions of this story, the Pray of Azariah is inserted after verse 23 and followed by the Song of the Three Young Men. These verses say the men sang hymns while in the furnace. The fuel was naphtha, pitch, tow, and brush. Certainly, strong enough fumes that the men should have reeked from the odor.[52]

Shadrack, Meshach, and Abednego were three very faithful men of God who will always be remembered by their pagan names. Why this was the case with them but not with Daniel is at least interesting to ponder. Even though the Babylonians refer to Daniel as Belteshazzar, he is not remembered today by that name. Where is Daniel, the chief magician, during this event? Why wasn't he part of the furnace story? After all, Nebuchadnezzar's officials were there. One proposal is that Daniel's high office allowed him the privilege of being represented by his Jewish lower officials. This effectively kept him from having to openly rebel before the king. Maybe Daniel believed his position too great an asset for protecting the Jews to risk compromising it. For whatever reason, we know Daniel wasn't there.

Food for Thought: There were many Jews present at this ceremony. How did the others respond to the command to bow? The story implies everyone bowed but these three men. Who left with their integrity intact?

September 5
Bible Readings: Ezekiel 40-44:3

Twelve years go by without any recorded visions of Ezekiel. In the year of the 25th anniversary of the first captives being taken into exile, Ezekiel has a vision where he is taken in spirit to a mountain outside Jerusalem (likely the Mount of Olives[51] in April[15] 573 B.C.[50]). There waiting for him is an angelic type of man, bronze in color. Probably this is the same man that was Ezekiel's guide in chapter 8 where he witnessed the terrible defilement of the Temple. This man is holding a linen cord in preparation for measuring the visionary Temple. Linen was the cloth used by the high priests. Many believe this man was Jesus who preceded God to measure righteousness and mete out justice and serve as the doorway for people to come to God. In chapter 9 we saw the destruction of the Temple. In chapters 40-43 we see the rebuilding of a Temple that is more grandiose in size than that of Solomon, but architecturally very similar. Although, it does not have the beauty of Solomon's Temple lined with gold. This is a vision of a temple that has never been built. Now we must become investigative reporters to figure out the story.

Let us start by addressing some immediate questions.

(1) Why did God give such an exacting blueprint to Ezekiel for a Temple that wasn't built? First, we must remember that Ezekiel was a priest. As such, his whole life revolved around the LORD's Temple and its sacrifices and rituals. He could relate to a Temple structure that represented God better than to an abstract concept of God who was omnipresent (always present everywhere). Second, Ezekiel could give the exiled Jews more concrete hope of Israel's restoration if they knew of the grand plans for God (represented by the Temple) to be in their midst. The exiled generation could understand the sacrificial worship system. They would have rejected the idea that they could all be priests and come directly before God in a personal relationship. (Hundreds of years later, their counterparts rejected this idea and crucified Jesus.) To the Jews, the Temple's blueprint meant God planned to live among them again. They could not have understood Jerusalem without a Temple as in Rev. 21:22.

(2) What was God's purpose in Ezekiel's Temple blueprint vision? First, the acknowledgement of all nations that the God of Israel was the one and only God of the universe was uppermost. In the future, the Gentile nations would be offered salvation and eternal life with the God of all mankind. Second, the holiness of God is an overriding theme. The Glory of God will fill the Temple and assure Ezekiel (and the Jews) that God has returned to Jerusalem to dwell. All gates and stairs led to the central Essence of the Temple -- God's Presence signified by the Holy of Holies. Third, the complete restoration of Israel would come to pass. God and His people would be restored in their relationship. Fourth, the ritual purification of God's people is emphasized. Remember, Jesus will not come for another 580 plus years. The people must be cleansed of their sins. They must trust and depend on their God.[52]

(3) If this isn't a real Temple, then what is it? Ezekiel's vision was a visual example of God's perfectness (perfectly square, perfectly laid out), His grandeur, His holiness, His glory, His Presence, His coming back to Jerusalem, and His permanent dwelling among His people. You'll recall in Ezek. 10:19 that God left the Temple of Jerusalem through the east gate. When God returns to Jerusalem, He'll come through the east gate and close it behind Him as a symbol of His permanent dwelling in Jerusalem. Only the Prince of Peace -- Jesus -- will use the east gate. Many Jews believe that this Temple will someday be built on Temple Mount, directly on top of the original Temple site. Today, Muslims control that site. If it is built, the time will be prior to the New Jerusalem when God establishes His kingdom on earth.

(4) Who will build this Temple? Some believe Jesus will build it (based on Zech. 6:12-13) or cause it to be built by the Jews in the future. Its purpose would be to prepare those who will minister during the millennium. Others believe it will never be physically built but rather carries a much greater symbolic representation of God. The size of this Temple complex is much larger than the present Temple Mount site. Thus, the site would have to be 'shored up' on all sides or the site would have to change or God would have to modify the landscape (Zech. 14).

Just as there are many similarities between Solomon's Temple and Ezekiel's Temple, there are also many differences. In Ezekiel's Temple:

There is no wall to separate the Jews from the Gentiles,

There is no separation of the women from the men,

There are no lavers, Table of Shewbread, lampstand, incense altar, veil, or Ark of the Covenant, and

The altar is approached from the east by stairs instead of a ramp. The top of the altar is now called the hearth of God.

Now I come to the point of what I believe. But first, I will be upfront in saying these last chapters are extremely difficult to interpret as to reality versus symbolism: (1) the details are so minute as to be overwhelming for mere symbolism, (2) living after the resurrection gives me a viewpoint the Jews could not have had, and (3) I have the advantage of the New Testament's gospel. We have to be careful we don't condemn the Jews for having a more concrete image of God associated with the Temple and the actual land that made up the Holy Land. Had we lived then, I shudder to think how we would have toppled to the least danger or influence. Because I have the words of Jesus and those Apostles who lived and ministered beside Him, I choose to form my personal beliefs on the New Testament. Here we go.

Matt. 24:27 tells us Jesus will come "as the lightning comes from the east and flashes to the west."[1] We know from God's plans given to men, the Temple always gave the front as facing the east, even though that was looking away from the actual city of Jerusalem. Luke 1:76-79 depicts Jesus as "the rising sun" who will come to us from Heaven. The sun rises in the east. Jesus IS the eastern gate through which God enters the Temple. In John 14:6 Jesus said, "I am the way and the truth and the life. No one comes to the Father except through me."[1] Jesus is our High Priest (Heb. 8:1). The outer court accepts all people of all ages and both genders. There is no wall of separation. Eph. 2:14 says, "For he himself is our peace, who has made the two one and has destroyed the barrier, the dividing wall of hostility, by abolishing in his flesh the law with its commandments and regulations."[1] *The Living Bible* translates this passage as Christ made peace between the Jews and the Gentiles.

The perfection of this new Temple plan is evidenced by (1) exactly equal sides yielding a perfect square, (2) 7 steps up to the entrances that show completion of the transition from the world's view of God to the Heavenly view of God, and (3) 8 steps into the inner court depicting God as being more than enough (8 represents covenant) for our lives. As we enter the inner court, we must leave behind our stained worldly garments of sin. We must put on the linen garments of priests. The altar contains the sacrifice God made so we could be in His Presence -- the blood of Jesus, and the lack of a veil clearly invites us to experience God's Presence continually. In Psalm 23:6, David talked of dwelling in the house of the LORD forever. Jesus said, "In my Father's house are many rooms; if it were not so, I would have told you. I am going there to prepare a place for you."[1] (John 14:2) The Temple clearly has many rooms for the priests of God. Peter told us that Christians "are a chosen people, a royal priesthood, a holy nation, a people belonging to God."[1] (1 Peter 2:9)

Jesus said, "I tell you that one greater than the temple is here."[1] (Matt. 12:6) Paul admonished Christians, "Don't you know that you yourselves are God's temple and that God's Spirit lives in you? If anyone destroys God's temple, God will destroy him; for God's temple is sacred, and you are that temple."[1] (1 Corinth. 3:16-17) God has made us in His image (Gen. 1:27) and given us the mind of Christ (1 Corinth. 2:16). "And this is how we know that he lives in us: We know it by the Spirit he gave us."[1] (1 John 3:24)

Food for Thought: If Jesus were visibly by your side, how would your actions or reactions change? How much more they should change knowing that Jesus lives within you 24 hours a day. How many times a day do we say, "I shouldn't say this but . . .." Then we follow that with "Do you know what I mean?" Unfortunately, we know all too well what is meant.

Temple Complex

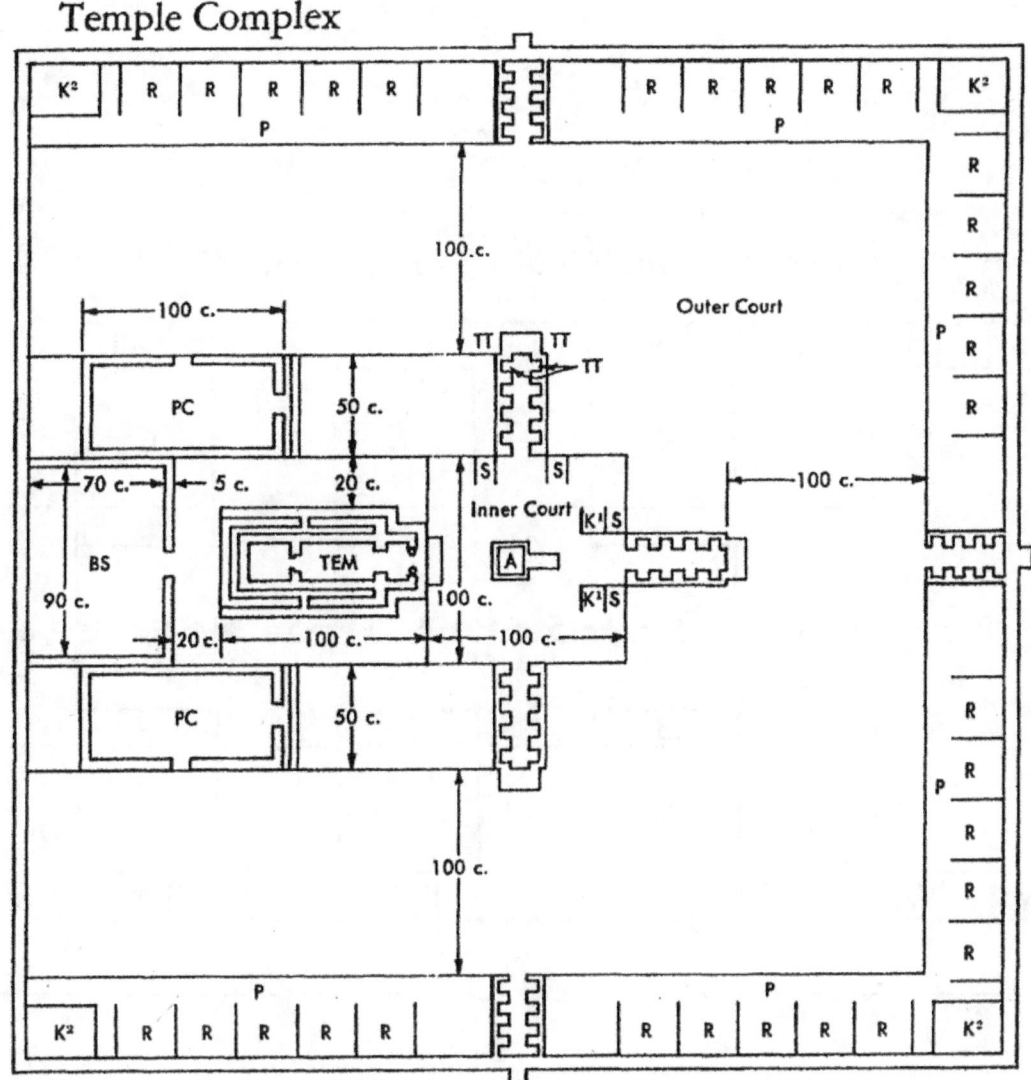

KEY

A	Altar (Eze 40:47b)
BS	Building of separation yard (Eze 41:12-13b, 15)
K¹	Kitchens for priests to boil sacrifices (Eze 46:19-20)
K²	Kitchens for priests to boil people's sacrifices (Eze 46:21-24)
P	Pavement (Eze 40:17-18)
PC	Priests' chambers (Eze 42:1-14)
R	Rooms in outer court for storage or priests (Eze 40:17)
S	Rooms for singers (priests) (Eze 40:44-46)
TT	Tables for slaughter of sacrifices (Eze 40:39-43)
TEM	Temple proper (Eze 40:48—41:11, 13a, 14, 16, 23-26)
	Inner court (Eze 40:4-7a)
	Outer court (Eze 40:17-19, 23, 27, 39-43)
	Width from outer gates to inner gates (Eze 40:19, 23, 27)

Gate System for All Gates of the Outer Court

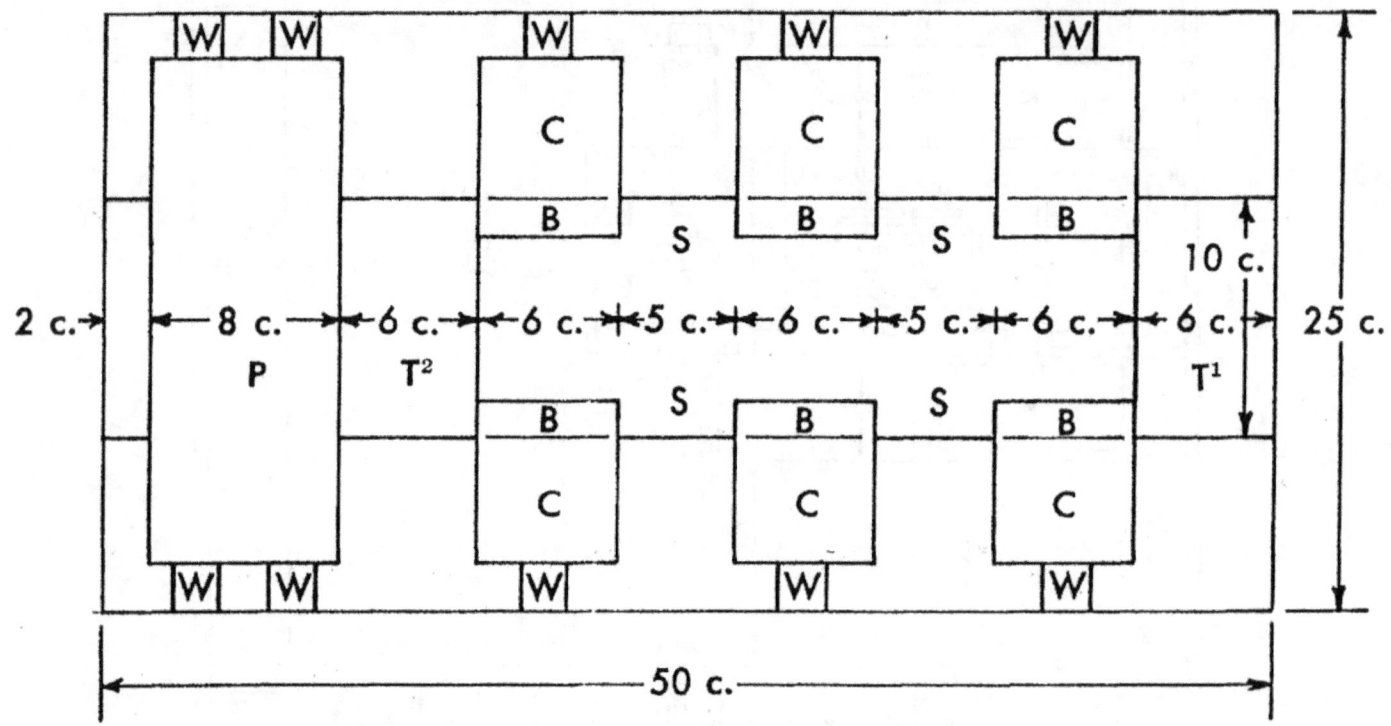

KEY

B	Borders (barriers, space) (Eze 40:12a)
C	Chambers (side rooms, guard rooms) (Eze 40:7a, 10a)
P	Porch (vestibule) (Eze 40:7c, 8-10b, 14)
S	Space between chambers (Eze 40:7b, 12b)
T^1	Threshold of the gate (Eze 40:6, 11)
T^2	Threshold of the porch (Eze 40:7c)
W	Windows (Eze 40:16)
	Overall height, length, and width of the gate (Eze 40:13-15)

Lessons of Love

Altar of Sacrifice

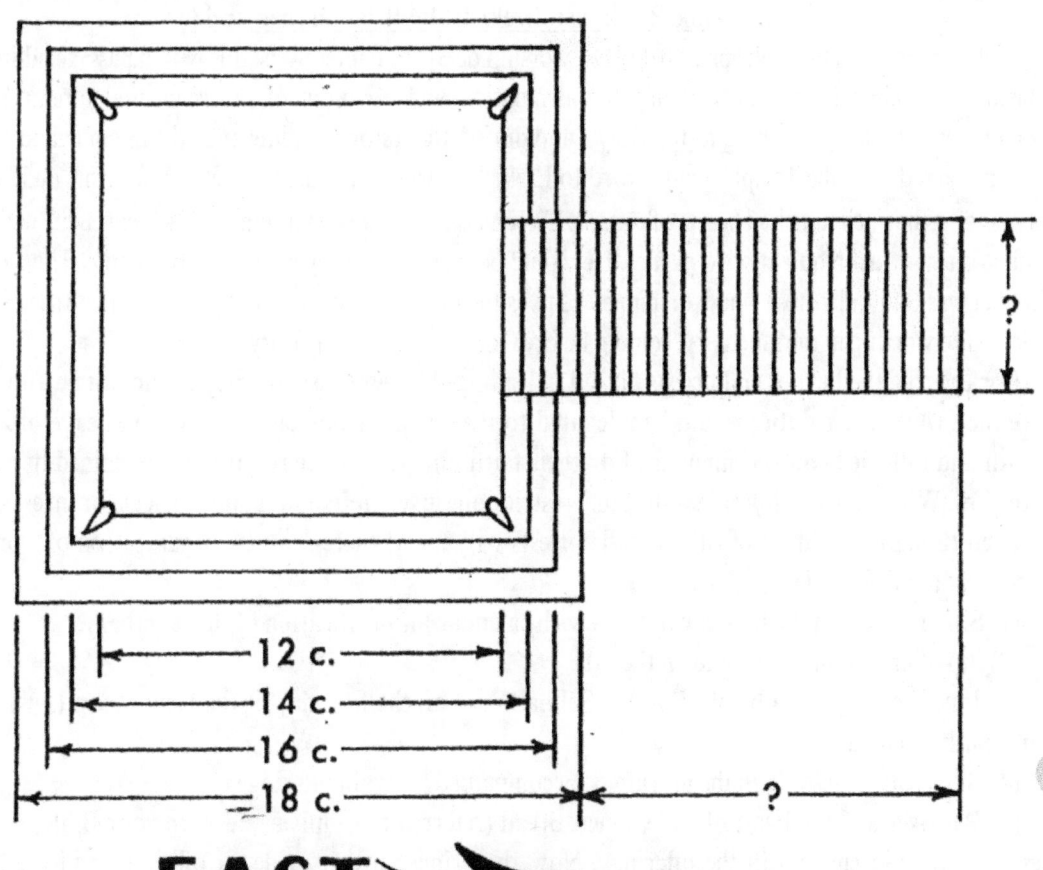

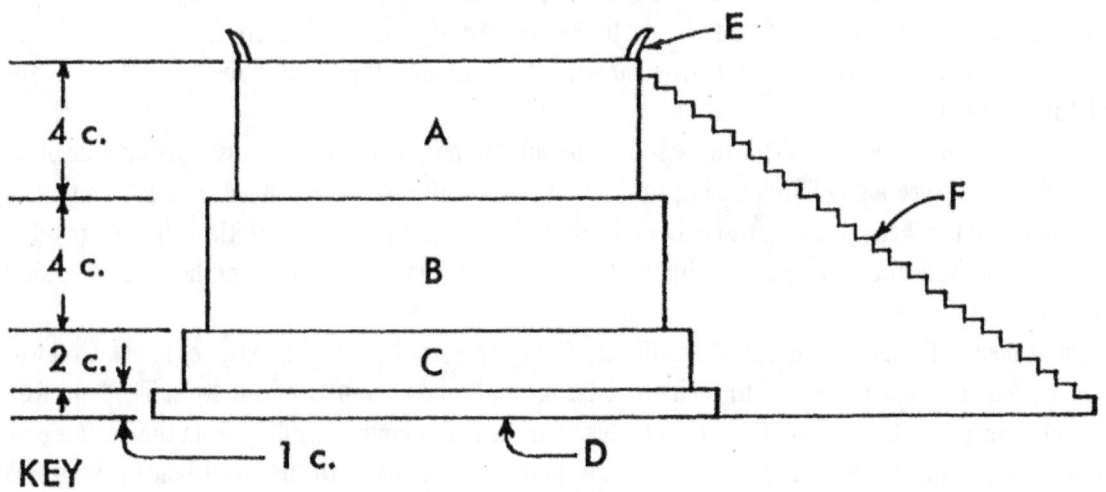

KEY

- A Altar hearth (Eze 43:15-16)
- B Enclosure (Eze 43:14, 17)
- C Interior (Eze 43:14, 17)
- D Bottom (Eze 43:13)
- E Horns of the altar (Eze 43:15)
- F Steps (Eze 43:17)

September 6
Bible Readings: Ezekiel 44:4 through chapter 48

Ezekiel now turns from blueprint details to worship details. Chapter 44 begins with a passage addressing exclusion of the uncircumcised from the sanctuary. Condemnation and exclusion of uncircumcised foreigners is mandated. Unfortunately, the Jews returning to the Holy Land during the restoration interpreted this command to mean all non-Jews were barred from the Temple. God's word to Ezekiel is very specific in specifying "uncircumcised" foreigners. God is referring to the uncircumcised hearts of pagans. Circumcision was always a sign of God's covenant with His people.[5] A covenant is a contract requiring two parties. He would be their God. They would be His people. Thus, God's command to Ezekiel was that only those who worshipped Him as the one and only God and demonstrated true repentance would be allowed to worship in the sanctuary, coming before God's Presence and Glory.

For the role the Levites and priests played in leading the people astray, they would not be allowed to minister before the LORD. Their duties would be relegated to the manual labor tasks. Only the lineage of Zadok had kept the faith and followed God's commands. For their faithfulness, they are rewarded -- ordained by God to minister before Him. With consecration comes the same restrictions given in Exodus and Leviticus for priests.

Even though the old set of rules for the priests will apply, there is a new organization of worship activities. The new protocols include:

(1) Sin offerings on the first day of the Jewish calendar for purification of the sanctuary,

(2) Sin offerings for the people on the 7th,

(3) Inner court gate to be open on the Sabbath and on the first day of the New Moon (Jewish calendar is a lunar month calendar),

(4) Burnt offerings only in the mornings, accompanied by grain offerings,

(5) Passover and the Feast of Unleavened Bread (referred to simply as Feast in your Bible) remains the same dates but with big changes in the offerings. Now the prince must provide all offerings and the quantities have dramatically increased. For a burnt offering seven bulls and seven rams must be provided each day (notice there are no longer any lambs). Originally the Feast required ten animals be sacrificed as burnt offerings in addition to the daily sacrifice and the sin offering. The first Passover looked backward to God's first covenant with His people. Ezekiel's Passover looks forward to God's last covenant with His children -- the gift of Jesus. (Ezk. 45:25 is about the Feast of Tabernacles.)

Prince is a term that carries three definitions: son of the ruler (king), Son of God (Jesus), city or state official. I believe the Prince of Peace is the holy offering to God on our behalf. We are humbled, made repentant, and washed in the blood of His sacrifice. But I also believe the prince's land allotment refers to the country's royal land set-aside for the king. This allotment would contain the official government buildings and house some officials, i.e., the Royal Secretary.

The arrangement of the land allotment is significant. The Temple would be in the center of Israel. God would be the center or heart of the land, central to their lives. He must also be the center of our lives. The land will be allotted in layers like a cake. God's Temple is in the center with the king's lands extending from the Temple east to the Jordan and west to the Mediterranean Sea. God's dwelling layer (along with the royal land) is sandwiched between Judah and Benjamin (the two primary tribes of the old southern kingdom). Reuben is no longer east of the Jordan River but is layered above Judah. Ephraim, Manasseh, Naphtali, and Asher are allotted land in roughly the same order as they always had but are now much further north. You will recall Dan never could fully conquer his original allotment of land from Moses and finally gave up, moving to the extreme northern border. In Ezekiel's design, Dan gets the northernmost layer. Traveling south from the Temple layer you have Benjamin, Simeon (tribe originally absorbed into Judah), Issachar then Zebulun (both have made extreme moves from north Israel to south Israel), and finally Gad (also removed from the east side of the Jordan). The outstanding theme depicted here is the centrality of God. Another theme is the equal inheritance God gives His children in the new Promised Land. An interesting observation is that Leah's sons will be layered to the immediate north and south of the Temple. Benjamin's stand to do what was right by staying with Judah when the kingdom split provided him the reward of land in the midst of Leah's sons. (Of course, Leah had reared Benjamin since his own mother died in childbirth.) Rachel's remaining son, Joseph, has two tribes who are located north of Leah's sons. The land allotted to the extreme north and extreme south were the sons of handmaids.

Notice that the people were required to enter the Temple by one gate and leave by the opposite gate. Because no one but God and Jesus could enter the east gate and God's Temple has no west gate (there is no rear entrance or back way into God's Presence), the worshippers had to come and go through the north and south gates. Why were they required to use different gates for entering and leaving? Think about a large department store where you have been. You went inside because there was something you wanted. You entered a door marked "Entrance" and you found what you wanted. You took it before the open register (which has recorded the price of your desired object) where the price was announced. You paid the price and left by the door marked "Exit." What if you discovered the most valuable treasure ever was available to all people (at no cost to yourself) and all you had to do was go in and ask for it? Jesus paid the price for us. When we leave His Presence we leave behind our sins. We should also leave behind our sinful ways. Therefore, we should exit different people than when we entered.

The Temple's River is our last topic, but a very important one. Compare Ezek. 47:1-12 to Rev. 22:1-5. Revelation tells us clearly that the water is from the throne of God and Jesus, giving further support to the possibility that Ezekiel's Temple is symbolic of the future. Ezekiel sees the water flowing from the inner court where God's Presence would be, flowing past the altar of the sacrifice, crossing the outer court, and flowing under the southeast corner of the wall. It is flowing in abundance into the desert of Judah! The water at first was only ankle deep, but as Ezekiel got further away from its source, it got deeper until finally he had to swim. (The farther away from God we are when we accept Him in our lives, the greater His Grace is to cover our sins.) Because Jerusalem is on a mountain facing east (Jordan valley is east), the water flows downhill to the southeast. The water flows into the Jordan and finally reaches the Dead Sea -- BUT the sea is NOT dead anymore! The living water has given a new life to the sea. The trees on both sides of the river are continuously fruitful and their leaves provide healing. God provides us with food and healing, both physically and spiritually. The swamps and marshes along the edges, though, will remain salty and dead. What does this mean? During the rainy season the sea overflows into these low-lying areas. (We have our season when we overflow with blessings.) When the water recedes (when trials come), a residue of mineral salts remains in the stagnant pools. Unlike seasoning salt that enhances, these salts are deadly, killing all it touches.[51] Think of the people you have known who have had mountaintop experiences with religion only to experience extreme disillusionment when the people or events that gave life to their emotions were no longer around. The residue of bitterness, anger, loneliness, and maybe even hatred killed their desire for any real relationship with God. They saw the Promised Land but never committed to it.

Food for Thought: In chapter 46 Ezekiel talks about the kitchens of the Temple complex. Why is this topic so important? What do we do in kitchens? Well, the kitchen is the hearth of the household. Good food, good fellowship, good memories come from the kitchen of a home. God's Temple provides holy food prepared in the kitchens of His house for those who minister before Him. God takes care of those who do His work, both physically and spiritually. As a girl I often made hot homemade cinnamon rolls for my Daddy late at night while we watched some cowboy or war movie. A lot of love and happiness came from the kitchen. We weren't rich, but we worked hard and were happy. My Mother has always been an excellent cook and many of our happiest hours have been spent stirring some 'new' dish for the ones we loved. Do the work of the Lord so you, too, will have happy, loving memories of the times spent in the kitchen of God.

September 7
Bible Readings: Ezekiel 29:17-21, Daniel 4, Jeremiah 52:31-34, 2 Kings 25:27-30

Ezekiel's Temple vision was 12 years after the exile and another two years pass before his word from the LORD concerning Tyre. King Nebuchadnezzar attacked Tyre after Jerusalem fell and after 13 years of siege, only mainland Tyre has fallen. Soldiers received the spoils of war as compensation for their labors. Nebuchadnezzar's army had toiled hard without being able to capture the rich booty of the island. God blesses the king instead with the riches of Egypt "because he and his army did it for me." Nebuchadnezzar was only the tool of God at this point, not a believer. Had he been a praying worshipper, I believe God would have given him Tyre. To Ezekiel, the fall of Egypt symbolized the destruction of heathenism and the fall of the last world power outside Babylon.[51]

Horns are a symbol of might and strength. God promises to make Israel strong after Egypt falls. The promise that God will open the mouth of Ezekiel among the Jews actually refers to the mouths of all the prophets. In other words, God's word will be fully taught among the Jews of the restored Israel. The horn of Israel will be salvation, the power and might of God. The Spirit of God would be poured out to all nations from its source at Jerusalem.[51]

In the last years of his reign, Nebuchadnezzar has a disturbing dream. Of course, he calls for Daniel to interpret. Compare his dream in Dan. 4 to Ezekiel's word from the LORD in Ezek. 31. The same prophecy of the mightiest, tallest tree in the forest is given to Nebuchadnezzar as was given to Egypt depicting the fall of the world powers of Assyria and Egypt. Babylon had been responsible for the fall of the first two world powers, now it was Nebuchadnezzar's turn. (See Jer. 50: 17-18.) He would be felled from his lofty height. But God saw his redeeming qualities and promised to leave a stump from which he could sprout a new man. When we become Christians, our 'new person' sprouts from our 'old person.' In other words, we receive a new heart reflecting Jesus in our lives, but we still carry the vestige of our old way of life in our earthly bodies. Becoming a Christian does not eliminate the consequences of sin but allows us to sprout a new 'heart' out of the old earthly body. The king will spend 7 times (a period of completion of judgment) living in the wild. Some commentators interpret the iron and bronze binding the stump to be shackles holding the insane man, others see it as binding to keep the nation together after its king goes insane, and still others discount both these ideas but offer no suitable alternative. Personally, I believe the bronze represented the common people of Babylon, those who used bronze utensils everyday for daily functions, i.e., food preparation, farming tools, household items. I believe the iron represented the Babylonian army and government officials. Iron was the metal of choice for defense weapons. The two metals binding the stump **and** its roots symbolize the support of both the army and government officials as well as the common people for Nebuchadnezzar during his illness. If this had not been the case, they could easily have replaced the king. Commentators also want to discount the idea that "times," as used in this prophecy, does not mean years because it would be incredible for a man to recover after 7 years of insanity, not to mention having a powerful kingdom like Babylon without a king. To me, this is a gross underestimation of God's power! God can do anything, including restoring sanity after years of insanity and putting a large, powerful nation in a holding pattern until its king is restored.

Daniel has worked for this king all his life. He is stunned and almost speechless at the prospect of this dream coming true. He pleads with the king to acknowledge the God of Israel as the one and only God. (Daniel is presenting the plan of salvation (Old Testament version) to Nebuchadnezzar, King of Babylon!) God gave the king a year to turn to Him, but Nebuchadnezzar let pride be his downfall. The king was given the heart of an animal. (Again we see sentencing involves animals. God is definitely making the distinction between people and animals. The hearts of mankind were to belong to God, but the hearts of animals belonged to the wild.) At the end of his sentence, Nebuchadnezzar is restored to his throne with a new heart, one that knew God personally. He issues a letter of testimony to all the people under his rule, praising and exalting the one and only God. His letter closes with a warning. God is a god of righteousness and justice "and those who walk in pride he is able to humble."[1] (Dan. 4:37)

His son, Evil-Merodach, succeeds Nebuchadnezzar after a long reign. Evil-Merodach had Judah's imprisoned king Jehoiachin brought out of the guardhouse and into a place of honor at the King's table. Of course, to come before the king, he had to be well groomed and well dressed. So at the end of his life, Jehoiachin was given a place of honor and respect, but the consequences of his sin remained. He was a captive in a foreign land. This sentence was most severe to a Jew. To have to live outside the Holy Land was terrible, but to die and be buried on foreign soil was to be cut out of the inheritance of God. Yes, Jehoiachin died a prisoner -- a prisoner of his own sin. Jeremiah's prophecy (22:24-30) was fulfilled.

Food for Thought: We generally remember Nebuchadnezzar as the king who destroyed Jerusalem and took the Jews prisoners. Seldom do we remember that he was the tool of God. The sins of the Jews destroyed Jerusalem and brought about captivity of its people. Nebuchadnezzar obviously had a receptive heart -- receptive to God's influence. He also had a heart willing to believe as evidenced by his reaction to the salvation of the three young men from the fiery furnace. Do you have a heart receptive to God? Do you want one? Start by expelling the evil influences from your life -- cursing, drunkenness, pornography, violence, immorality, lust, greed, and let's not forget pride. Ask God to fill those empty places with His Spirit and then walk in the footsteps of your Savior.

September 8
Bible Readings: Job 1-3

Job is a man to whom we all can relate. His story, as revealed in the Book of Job, addresses grief, depression, loss, and discouragement. More importantly, it shows the actions and reactions of a righteous man to earthly trials and troubles. The date of Job cannot be established because many authors wrote the book over several centuries. You might have called it a "work in progress" over many decades. It consists of both prose and poetry. It is included in the Bible with the wisdom literature of Proverbs, Ecclesiastes and part of the Psalms. Similar stories about good men who experienced severe trials can be found in many Near Eastern ancient cultures from Egypt to Mesopotamia (land of Abraham's birth). Job is mentioned in Ezekiel 14:14, 20 indicating the story of Job was well known at this point in history. It is difficult to determine if all of Job's authors were even Israelites. All other books of the Bible make reference to Jewish historical accounts, i.e., the exodus and the exile, except Job. Only one time is the Jewish name for God, Yahweh, mentioned (Job 12:9 of the original Hebrew). Conversely, no other text of Job has been found in any language other than Hebrew.[56]

The Book of Job addresses the age-old question of "Why do righteous people suffer?" It is basically a story without an ending. You are left to interpret Job's story based on your own life experiences and to derive a conclusion consistent with your own beliefs. I recall a fascinating series of television shows called "The Twilight Zone" where Rod Sterling introduced the audience to a staged situation that paralleled our fears and dreads of the unknowns in life. The end of the story was always left open so that each person in the audience would surmise the worst based on their own innate fears. In contrast, Job leaves us with our own faith and values to stimulate us to intuitively come to an appropriate conclusion about the ways of the righteous during trials.[56]

Over centuries Job has been held up as the epitomy of patience, perseverance, and righteousness under fire. Hopefully, as we traverse the life of Job, you will recognize that he represents all Christians struggling from day-to-day to live righteously and keep the faith. Job experiences the stages of grief and dejection. Job believes God is mighty and just, but Job's continual suffering finally brings him to the very brink of unbelief. His wife apparently gives in to her grief telling Job to "Curse God and die!"[1] (Job 2:9) All Christians come to the brink of unbelief. None of us wants to talk about it for several reasons.

1. We fear if we talk about it we will be heard by God and condemned or, at the very least, punished for our faltering (like God didn't already know our thoughts and our hearts!).
2. We fear talking about it might actually give rise to our embracing unbelief. In this regard, you could say we're superstitious which isn't consistent with righteousness either.
3. We don't want other people to know we are not the Rock of Gibraltar. (The famous half-mile high rock in the strait between Spain and Africa that had a fortress town perched on top as guardian of the inlet to the Mediterranean Sea.[8]) As Christians, we think we should never have doubts or stumbles. We seem to forget that Christians are still humans. Eph. 6 reminds us we are to put on the armor of God so we are prepared to do battle with evil. Sometimes we lose a battle, but Jesus has already won the war! Jesus tells us (Matt. 16:24-25) that our battles are on earth, but Heaven is our reward. If you have come to the brink of unbelief, read the Book of Job -- all of it. Let Job's grief, frustration, and bewilderment represent your own feelings. Follow his responses to friends who are not true, to scorn, to rejection from the world. Continue with Job as he recalls God's righteousness and justice. Then come to your own conclusion about the reward that awaits those who are faithful and persevere in trials.

Job is from the land of Uz. Its exact location is unknown, but it is presumed to be east of Edom in the Syrian or Arabian Desert.[5] Job is referred to as **the** greatest man of the East (meaning peoples beyond the plains east of the mountains of the Jordan River area). Job had the perfect blessings from God -- 7 sons plus 3 daughters to give 10 (considered the perfect number in Bible numerology[57]). He had 7,000 sheep and 3,000 camels for a perfect 10,000 (multiple of 10). Both of these animals were considered very valuable. Plus, Job had 500 oxen and 500 donkeys for a perfect 1,000 (multiple of 10) work animals. Job seems to be the perfect man with the perfect family leading the perfect life. What changes all that?

The next scene of the chokma or play presents God talking to Satan about His faithful servant Job. This is not a literal scene but is representative of the forces of good and evil that impact our lives. Ancient people believed the gods talked, fought, and manipulated their subjects as in a board game. Therefore, it is characteristic of these extremely early manuscripts to describe good and evil in human or superhuman terms. Someone who lived near Mesopotamia but was included in Solomon's large kingdom may have written Job 1 possibly during King Solomon's time. In the prologue to Job's story, Satan challenges God to a duel with Job as the weapon. God's divine assurance of Job's unfailing faith makes Satan the adversary in an effort to wound Job to the point he will denounce God, making Satan the victor. The battle of evil trying to overcome good is at hand.

Job is reduced from extreme wealth to utter poverty. [Note: Sabeans (an Arab tribe) and Chaldeans (a southern Mesopotamian tribe) steal Job's wealth.[56]] When he accepted that as the right of God who owned everything anyway, then Satan took all of Job's family except for his wife who turned her grief and anger on Job! (Don't we often lash out at the ones we love the most when we are hurt?) [Note: The loss of lives came from natural forces: a lightning storm and a cyclone.[56] Job was hit by humanity and nature.] When Job accepted the loss of his children as God's Will, Satan declares it is because Job's physical body had been protected. Now Satan afflicts Job with painful sores. Throughout it all Job maintains his faithfulness, integrity, and innocence. (Remember, people of this time associated troubles with sin.) Job's three friends hear of his problems and come to check it out for themselves. (Were they just nosy? Disasters always seem to draw crowds. They don't appear to be faithful, true-blue friends.) They participate in the Jewish mourning period that required torn clothes, shaved heads, dust on the heads, no grooming, no talking, only bland food for 7 days. When the mourning period is over, they address Job. (Different authors, possibly one author for each of the speakers, may have written all the poetic speeches.) But Job, as custom, is the first to talk.

Job is in the classic stages of grief. Chapter 1 where he so easily attributes his loss to God's Will is the stage of denial. Many people go through this stage early in a long-term illness. But in sudden death situations, denial takes place immediately upon learning of the death(s) and usually lasts until after a period of mourning. Denial is a refusal to believe what has happened. People often busy themselves with as many activities as possible so as not to have to face reality. This only serves to prolong the inevitable. Job 3 is stage 2 of grieving -- anger. Job curses the day of his birth. Wishing we had never lived is a natural response to deep-seated emotional pain. Invariably someone has to say, "Better to have loved and lost than to never have loved at all!" And you strain to refrain from hitting them! At some point (at least for women), you cry it all out until you are totally limp, weak, beaten (or you think you are). (Sometimes men are more destructive with their anger.) Read Job 3:25. Job has found himself in "The Twilight Zone."

Food for Thought: Anyone who says they cannot relate to Job's feelings in chapter 3 is certainly less than 10 years old! In today's world, even many young children are in grief counseling. Victims of crimes are often 'stuck' in the anger stage and are never able to function in a normal lifestyle again. The one and only answer to overcoming grief is to turn to God. Grief simply means loss. Loss can be experienced in material items (house burns, car is stolen, etc.) or in loss of life (death of comrades, friends, loved ones, self). Is grief your victor or is God?

September 9
Bible Readings: Job 4-7

The first friend to speak is Eliphaz. As a Temanite, he was probably a descendant of Esau's son by his Hittite wife, Adah.[5] This is additional evidence that links the story of Job to a location close to Edom, close enough for three friends to arrive in time for the mourning week. As Job's oldest friend, Eliphaz has the floor to speak first.

ELIPHAZ'S SPEECH: Eliphaz reminds Job of all the teachings of God that he has proclaimed in his lifetime. Job's innocence and humbleness should be his hope for justice and restoration from God. Only those who sow trouble reap it. Righteous people are never destroyed. Eliphaz continues by saying a supernatural message has been brought to him to reveal to Job. A mortal cannot be more righteous than God. If God will judge His angels (Satan was a condemned angel), how much more will He judge mortal men? Men, by their very nature, are born to experience trouble. Eliphaz gives the wisest counsel of all in verses 8-9 of chapter 5. God is Job's only hope. He is capable of miracles. Seek Him. God will lift up to safety those who humble themselves or are humbled through circumstances before Him. "Blessed is the man whom God corrects; so do not despise the discipline of the Almighty."[1] (Job 5:17) God's children do not have to fear condemnation (beasts of the field). They have security and peace. Eliphaz ends his speech with the classic adage, "Physician heal thyself!"

JOB'S RESPONSE: [Any heart patient I've ever known could have written the first seven verses of Job 6! Even in Job's misery you have to get a chuckle out of these verses.] Job is able to claim a victory over pain at this point by declaring that even in unrelenting pain he has not denied God. All people fear persecution. At some point in their Christian lives, all Christians fear losing a spiritual battle where pain is the weapon. Many older people come to the end of their lives with the attitude that they have earned the right to say whatever they are feeling or thinking. None of us has that right! God did not give us the Great Commission as 'Go you into all the world and offend as many people as possible so they will never turn to Me.' Jesus said, "All authority in heaven and on earth has been given to me. Therefore go and make disciples of all nations, baptizing them in the name of the Father and of the Son and of the Holy Spirit, and teaching them to obey everything I have commanded you. And surely I will be with you always, to the very end of the age." (Matt. 28:18-20) That is to say, the end of your life or the end of time, whichever comes first. Job seems to have gotten a second wind in defending himself by the end of chapter 6. He tells his friends that they have kicked him when he was down rather than being supportive. (Keep in mind the custom of Job's day was that the elder ruled. In this case, Eliphaz's words represented all three friends.) Job obviously resents being told that the righteous man is not destroyed. After all, Job is proof that righteous people are afflicted with serious troubles, too! Job compares his friends to the wadies or streams of Edom that have flash floods in the rainy seasons but dry up in the dry season when they are most needed. Seeking renewed hope and refreshment for the body, the sight of a streambed on the horizon can fool travelers. If they allow themselves to turn aside and seek the stream, they will die in the dry and thirsty land. Similarly, Job was hoping for encouragement for his soul when his three friends arrived, but he got a disappointment instead. Only by keeping his heart and mind on God was he able to sustain himself. He challenges them to specify his sins and not talk in generalities. Again Job launches into his own defense, asking his friends to relent and change their minds about his guilt. His integrity is at stake.

In chapter 7 Job addresses the futility of his life as it is now -- only pain and suffering. All of us reach a point somewhere in our lives where we say, "Why go on?" In Job's depression, he feels life goes by swiftly and then it ends in misery and pain. Job's spirit is in anguish and bitterness fills his soul. He finds no rest even when he lies down. Job is plunged into depression (another stage of grief) feeling he would prefer to die rather than live like this. He asks God, "Why? Why do You not take this burden from me?"

Food for Thought: "Do not let any unwholesome talk come out of your mouths, but only what is helpful for building others up according to their needs, that it may benefit those who listen."[1] (Eph. 4:29)

Verses of the Week: **Job 19:25-27** "I know that my Redeemer lives, and that in the end he will stand upon the earth. And after my skin has been destroyed, yet in my flesh I will see God; I myself will see him with my own eyes – I, and not another. How my heart yearns within me!"

September 10
Bible Readings: Job 8-10

BILDAD'S SPEECH: Bildad was a Shuhite who were descendants of Abraham and Keturah. The Shuhites may have lived in northern Syria.[5] Bildad really lets Job have it. He hits Job with a verbal onslaught of accusations declaring that IF Job is innocent then God will come to his aid and restore his prosperity. Does Job think they were all born yesterday? Certainly not! They have lived long enough to discern the ways of the world. Those who turn away from God depend on the fragile weakness of themselves. They will be cut down and left to die in the heat. But the innocent will find joy and laughter.

JOB'S RESPONSE: "How can a mortal be righteous before God?"[1] (9:1) God has wisdom, power, and control of the earth, control of the heavenly bodies, creative powers, miraculous powers, and omnipresence. God is omnipotent (all-powerful). How can mere people defend themselves before God? (Verse 19 mentions Rahab that often refers to Egypt, but in this case, it refers to a mythological dragon of chaos.[56]) God is a god of order, not chaos. How can mortal man plead his case before God, the Judge? Man can only beg for mercy. Even a man who believed himself innocent could not defend himself to God. If this is a contest, then I, Job, give up! In a burst of passion Job shouts, "It doesn't make any difference if I'm guilty or innocent, the result is the same!" (Poor Job. It is so hard to remember the sunshine in one's life when the rain has fallen for so long. Even Job had doubts. We often equate doubt with sin, but doubt is a sign of weakness in our faith, not in itself a sin. Faith grows stronger through victory in trials and temptations.) When life flies by, if we stand guilty before God, who will be our mediator? (Job visualizes an arbitrator will speak for him. Of course, we know Jesus and the Holy Spirit are our intercessors. See Hebrews 7:25 and Romans 8:26-27.) Job despises his existence so that he doesn't fear asking God what the charges are against him nor does he fear declaring that God knows he is innocent, even though he is at the mercy of God. Defending his case before the Judge, Job reminds God that He was Job's Creator. Would He now be his executioner? Job knows God would punish him if he were guilty, but even in his innocence he cannot face God. As mortal man his life is shameful before the righteous God. Job presents four pictures of his persecution:

(1) stalked like a lion, (2) awesome power brought against him, (3) witnesses called against him, (4) vexation from God's anger. Again Job wishes he were never born. He begs God to turn the persecution away so he can have a few moments of joy before he dies.

Food for Thought: Haven't we all had times where we felt like the whole world was against us? Did it ever seem fair? Was it a depressing time? The very best cure I have ever found for depression is songs of praise. You cannot be sad and sing praises to God at the same time. Invest in Christian music. It will change your outlook on life.

September 11
Bible Readings: Job 11-14

Before we start, spend some time in prayer for all families who have lost loved ones as a result of terrorism. Ask for God's guidance and protection for them, our world leaders, and our homelands. Ask God to eliminate the terrorism and persecution against His children all over the world. If it is not in His plan, ask that He sustain and strengthen those under attack.

ZOPHAR'S SPEECH: Zophar was a Naamathite, a descendant of Naamah, who lived in northern Arabia.[5] (Zophar means "twittering bird."[5] Think about what a self-assured strutting bird he is during this speech!) He accuses Job of being a "talker" rather than a "doer." He even accuses Job of mocking God! Zophar is sure if God would only speak, Job would find out his sins are so numerous that God couldn't even remember all of them! (Now, how would you like to have a friend like this come to visit right after you just lost all your children!) Zophar sounds like a prosecuting attorney. He questions Job's knowledge of the mind of God. Surely God knows deceitful men when He sees them! Zophar even stoops to call Job a witless man! (I believe if I were Job I would have made dog-meat out of this guy by now! Maybe tolerance of Zophar is the real reason Job is called patient.) Now Zophar gives Job a lecture on putting away his sin so he can live without shame and troubles. Verses 13-20 are very personal with "you" being used repeatedly. You can almost imagine Zophar shaking his finger in Job's face!

JOB'S RESPONSE: Job again defends himself; this time with more fury. There is sadness in the reality of 12:4. Job realizes his friends are voicing what others are thinking. Job, in disbelief, recounts how the wicked seem to be safe and prosperous while the innocent suffer. How can this be? Job draws his answer from nature. God holds the life of mankind and all creatures in His Hand. God's universe is ordered and predictable. Earthly wisdom and understanding come with age, but all knowledge and power belong to God. God builds up and tears down in accordance with His master plan. All men and nations are subordinate to His Will.

Job now takes more of a courtroom setting. He charges his friends with speaking wickedly on God's behalf. Also, he accuses them of taking God's side against him. Then Job turns the tables. How would they come out if God examined their lives? What they say doesn't hold water. It's time for them to be silent and let him talk! Then Job emphatically states the foundation of his defense in verse 15 of chapter 13. Even if God chooses to slay Job, Job's faith and trust will remain in God. He is sure God will hear his defense and vindicate him. Now Job asks his friends, "Can anyone bring charges against me?"[1] (13:19)

Job turns to God and presents his case. First he asks God to grant him two requests: don't abandon him and don't terrify him with God's awesome Presence.[15] Job faces his accuser (viewed to be God). He demands to know with what he is charged. Why has God hunted him down and shackled him like an enemy? Is it for the sins of his youth? Man's life upon this earth is short; God decrees every day. Man lives and dies, never to live again until the end of the age. Even trees and plants have hope; they can put up new shoots and sprouts. If only God would hide him in the grave for a while but bring him back at a later date! (This is a foreshadowing of the death, burial, and resurrection of believers.) Read Job 14:14-17. Through all the hard, painful days of life that we serve Him, we have the hope of being called by God to our reward. Surely God will keep an account of our righteousness and cover our sins. (And God does cover our sins with the blood of His Son -- Jesus.) But while we wait for that great reckoning day, our lives are filled with pain and sorrows and troubles.

Food for Thought: Bargaining is another stage in grieving. We may bargain with ourselves or with God. Bargaining usually consists of some proposed exchange. "If you will take away this pain, then I will attend church every Sunday." Bargaining occurs even in our thoughts and even when we aren't grieving. Mankind cannot get away from the concrete philosophy of "Nobody does anything for nothing!" But who can appraise the value of peace, joy, hope, love, and encouragement? God gives us these for free. All we must do is accept Jesus as Lord and Savior of our lives. "May the God of hope fill you with all joy and peace as you trust in him, so that you may overflow with hope by the power of the Holy Spirit."[1] (Romans 15:13)

September 12
Bible Readings: Job 15-17

Job's three friends have all spoken in turn and he has responded to each one. Now we start round two of the speeches.

ELIPHAZ'S SPEECH: He immediately tells Job that his folly has undermined and hindered his and others' devotion to God. Eliphaz accuses Job of condemning himself by his own defense arguments. Why does Job think he's so special? Is he on God's council? Was he counted among God's original creation? So why does he dare to question God? If God does not even trust His angels but calls on them to account for their actions, how much less trust does corrupt man deserve? (Read Rev. 12:7-9.)

Eliphaz decides to enlighten Job on the wisdom his years have produced. (Remember Eliphaz is believed to be the eldest of the friends and, thus, the wisest.) Then he proceeds to give his life's philosophy. In a nutshell, his philosophy is the wicked are judged and sentenced to troubles all the days of their lives. (This is the same philosophy he espoused in his first speech. He's just more hurtful this time.)

JOB'S RESPONSE: Job tells them off! "Miserable comforters are you all!"[1](16:1) Are your lectures never going to end? It's easy to accuse and lecture others, but their attitudes would change if they were in Job's shoes. Except Job wouldn't talk to them so viciously. He would console and comfort them. Now Job turns downtrodden and disheartened to God. He recounts all his miseries: loss of health and family, scorned by friends, crushed by grief, loss of wealth. Still Job maintains his purity and innocence. Job's advocate and intercessor is in Heaven. Only that Holy One knows of Job's innocence and pleads his case before God, the Judge. Job is broken and weary. Even though his friends have talked to him harshly, he will not denounce them. The righteous will continue to do what's right and grow stronger in their faith. His friends have refused him bail, and, all others have reviled him. Death seemed to be his only hope for rest.

In the Book of Job, God is cast in three different roles: Adversary, Judge, and Defender. As New Testament Christians, we understand that Jesus is our Mediator and Defender (Rom. 8:34). We also know that Satan is the adversary, not God. (Satan means adversary.[5]) Job did not have this advantage.

Food for Thought: Several times in my life I have experienced pain both physical and emotional that brought me to the same point as Job. I found my solace and comfort in God's word. I learned the meaning of Rom. 8:26-27, 38-39. In 1 Peter 1:6-7, we are assured "though now for a little while you may have had to suffer grief in all kinds of trials. These have come so that your faith -- of greater worth than gold, which perishes even though refined by fire -- may be proved genuine and may result in praise, glory and honor when Jesus Christ is revealed." "Cast all your anxiety on him because he cares for you."[1] (1 Peter 5:7)

September 13
Bible Readings: Job 18-21

BILDAD'S SPEECH: Bildad tells Job it is time he started being reasonable and talk sensibly. After all, does Job think they are stupid? They can see the destruction Job has experienced. Only a wicked man would have such calamities! Bildad's description of the wicked paints a picture of there always being justice on earth (which we know isn't so). According to Bildad's philosophy, the wicked have their places in the community (lamp) and their influences (light) snuffed out; they are physically weakened; traps, snares, and nooses lie in wait for them; terror is on every side and calamity is stalking them; their security is snatched from them; their descendants are all killed; no memories remain of them; burning sulfur of judgment destroys all hope of renewal; men everywhere are horrified by the fate of the wicked.

JOB'S RESPONSE: Job's frustration is evident. How long will his 'friends' keep attacking him? Job has spoken 5 times and they have spoken 5 times and still they continue to attack Job's character. Job replies that IF he had sinned it would be none of their business! They should quit looking down on him. He has called to God for help but to no avail. Job has been stripped of his honor and righteousness; his enemy tears him apart. He is under siege with enemies camped on every side. Both brethren and friends have abandoned him. Even his servants have only disdain for their master. Physically, Job has wasted away to skin and bones. [Note: Verse 20 is the origin of the phrase "escaped by the skin of my teeth." Scientists have learned that the mucosal lining of the mouths of land mammals is almost identical to the external skin of porpoises and killer whales. (A freebie bit of information!) Job may have meant his teeth had fallen out and only his gums remained or that he was so thin his cheeks barely covered the internal mucosa of his mouth.[56]]

Job's faithfulness to God is growing even more confident and assured as he says, "I know that my Redeemer lives and that in the end he will stand upon the earth. And after my skin has been destroyed, yet in my flesh I will see God; I myself will see him with my own eyes -- I, and not another. How my heart yearns within me!"[1] (Job 19:25-27) In the face of great trial and adversity, Job had taken a prominent, definite, permanent stand. He no longer has any doubts or fears. He will see God! All Christians have this testimony, if only we were all this bold!

ZOPHAR'S SPEECH: Zophar is bristled over the rebuke he has received from Job. Zophar proceeds to reiterate his stance that the wicked always suffer destruction. Their joy is fleeting as well as their prosperity. The children of wicked parents have no inheritance except trouble and dishonor. Surely the wicked are struck down in their youth and go down to their graves. They have cherished evil as a sweet delight, unwilling to give it up, only to have their very souls soured with bitterness from its bite. The disgust of their own sin will poison and sicken their hearts. All that is gained by the wicked cannot fill the emptiness of their lives. Despite any treasures they obtain, in the end, they are still without salvation. Distress and terror fill their lives as evil waits to attack them. The fire of judgment will expose their guilt and the inhabitants of the earth will serve as witnesses against them. Such is their fate.

JOB'S RESPONSE: 'Listen to me while I speak, after which you can resume your mocking!' Job has become thick-skinned by now. His friends' accusations no longer rattle him. After all, he is standing on the solid foundation of God! Job states his complaint is with God, not with men. He wants God to answer his questions concerning why the wicked prosper and the righteous are afflicted. This question has plagued billions of people through the ages. Where is the justice? Why continue to be righteous? Death comes to all men, wicked and righteous alike. Who repays the evil man for all the damage he has done? Let God punish him while he is yet living where he can be properly humiliated! Instead, he is buried with the same dignity and honor as the righteous. (Job chastises his friends, as their answers have all been a pack of lies.)

Food for Thought: Christians know the answer to these questions! Wickedness receives its empty, shallow rewards here on earth only to endure great torture in eternity. The righteous endure persecution by the devil while they are earthbound, but when God calls them home their souls are set free to live eternally in Heaven. When you feel you can no longer bear the pain of the world, remember Paul's statement, "I can do all things through Christ who strengthens me." (Phil. 4:13) Commit it to memory and claim its promise in every moment of weakness!

September 14
Bible Readings: Job 22-24

ELIPHAZ'S SPEECH: 'What pleasure does man bring to God? Is it for your humbleness that you are being punished? Your wickedness must be great and your sins endless to be dealt so much trouble.' (At this point, Eliphaz just makes up a bunch of sins to assign to poor Job! Eliphaz lies boldly and without shame.) After all that Eliphaz has said, it is ironic that he is the one to declare that wickedness cannot be hidden from God! Now Eliphaz proceeds to insist that Job humble himself before God in hopes of being restored. 'Surely if Job repents and turns to God, he will be forgiven and delivered from his troubles.'

JOB'S RESPONSE: Job replies he would be glad to turn to God if he only knew where God was! Job is anxious to put his case before the Judge. God is just and would set the record straight. Job declares, "When he has tested me, I will come forth as gold."[1](23:10) Job is sure of his innocence for he has kept the commands of God and treasured His word. Job is weary in waiting, not knowing when his case can be scheduled on the docket. God charges no one with doing wrong; yet so many suffer. Why? (Aren't you glad you know the answer?) Those who rebel against the light (God), live in fear of the light (God's judgment). Their days are spent hiding while their nights are devoted to evil. They are but scum on the surface of water, cursed and without a future. They prey on the helpless that are without defenders. The lives of the wicked will be cut off without even a memory left behind.

Food for Thought: Chapters 24-27 of Job show a marked digression from the writing style, consistency, and messages of the previous chapters. Some of the ideas presented are contrary to all Job has fought for to this point. Therefore, the possibility of various authors or an adulteration of the original text exists. As an example, in chapter 24 Job addresses God's indifference to wickedness. The first 4 to 6 verses of chapters 26 and 27 are unclear in the original text as to whether Job or Bildad is speaking.[58] Some scholars believe the discrepancies extend on through chapter 31. Nevertheless, your translation has adopted a reasonable order for the characters.

September 15
Bible Readings: Job 25-31

BILDAD'S SPEECH: All power and dominion is God's! He, alone, is responsible for establishing order. Bildad expresses God's sovereignty through His power while emphasizing man's low esteem by associating man with maggots and worms.[58] The lack of purity by the heavenly bodies may refer to God's repulsion of paganism where these bodies are worshipped.

JOB'S RESPONSE: Job sarcastically mocks Bildad's self-imposed loftiness. 'How nice Bildad could stoop enough to advise one as stupid as Job! Was Bildad a prophet? If so, of whom?' Job now launches into a lengthy lecture addressing his religious principles, view of God, righteousness, and troubles, finishing with yet another declaration of innocence.

First, Job discusses images of God. God sees all, knows all, and is all-powerful. God has the power to save or destroy. His awesome power suspended the planets in space, yet also the nebulous clouds over the earth. In His wisdom, God destroyed chaos. In His power comes forth the thunder.

Next, Job states his personal faith and principles. "As long as I have life within me, the breath of God in my nostrils, my lips will not speak wickedness, and my tongue will utter no deceit. I will never admit you are in the right; till I die, I will not deny my integrity. I will maintain my righteousness and never let go of it; my conscience will not reproach me as long as I live."[1] (27:3-6)

Third, Job presents his philosophy on the wicked. They will be cut off from God, never to delight in God's Presence. Their children will experience death through violence; their families will always hunger. Plagues will kill them, but nobody will mourn. The wealth gained by the wicked will be given to the righteous. The house of the evil man is as fragile as a cocoon. His prosperity is temporary, swept away by the wind.

Fourth, Job establishes his philosophy on wisdom. The mine referred to in 28:1 is actually a silver smelter as there are no silver mines in Palestine. The reference to gold being refined further enhances this interpretation.[56] For those men who do mine ores, who dangle in the earth, wisdom is still not found. The same earth that provides food on its surface forms sapphires in the fire below. Wisdom cannot be found in the sky above the earth, on the surface of the earth, or in the tunnels below the earth. The price set on wisdom is beyond that of precious jewels and pure gold. Where, then, is wisdom found? God, and God alone, understands wisdom and knows the way to find it. Those who have not God, have not wisdom. Understanding is hidden from them, "the fear of the LORD - that is wisdom, and to shun evil is understanding."[1] (Job 28:28) Wisdom comes from recognizing the awesome power of God and consequently humbling ourselves before Him in worship.

Fifth, Job discusses his former days of prosperity and health. He longs for the 'good ole days.' In those days God protected him and all he touched seemed to prosper abundantly. Those who knew him respected him. He was given a place of honor in the seat of judgment. Job had carried out God's commands, ministering to all God's children. Righteousness and justice engulfed him. When all was well, he thought he would die in peace leaving a heritage of a respected and righteous namesake to a long line of descendants. In those days, he thought his blessed life would not end. When Job talked, everyone listened for the community held him in highest esteem.

Sixth, Job takes account of his present state of affairs. Now, the sons of men he would not have let lie down with his dogs were mocking him. They were the sons of the lowest of lowlife. Their fathers were so lazy and worthless they had been banished from civilization. Job is now viewed as too detestable for even these to spit on. Job must be on constant guard for attacks. These opportunity seekers are anxious to close in for the kill. Job's dignity and safety are gone. Suffering and pain are his companions. They have reduced him to dust and ashes, the basic building block of God's creation (dust) as well as His destruction (ashes). The great power of God completely engulfs Job like clothing. God supports Job like the neck of his garment supports the clothing. (The long, very loose tunics required a neck opening large enough for the head to go through but small enough to support the garment from the shoulders. The rest of the tunic hardly touched the body.) Job has bared his soul to God and God has clothed and supported him.

Seventh, Job completes his discourse by restating his innocence. He cries out to God for an answer. (Haven't we all done this?) But Job's adversary has tossed him about, pounding him with recurrent, relentless storms. The pain never subsides. His skin grows black with decay and sloughs off. His body is racked with fever. Job's life was lived in obedience to God's commands. He did not lust or cheat or lie or commit adultery. His servants were all treated no worse than he, for hadn't the same God made them all? Job had given to the needy and fought for justice for the oppressed. His security was in God, not in earthly treasures. No idols could be found in His possession nor did he ever worship anything other than God. Job had been careful not to sin with his mouth, his eyes, his mind, his heart, or his soul. He treated his neighbor as he wanted to be treated himself. Job rests his defense and awaits any indictment from the Almighty.

Food for Thought: Wonder how long a period of time this story covers? At least long enough for Job to waste away. His 'friends' must have stayed around just to watch him die or they delighted in argument. Praise God for your faithful friends!

September 16
Bible Readings: Job 32-37

Elihu seems to suddenly appear out of nowhere during a period of deafening silence. The three friends have exhausted all their arguments that Job's troubles are a result of sin. You have an almost eerie sense that Elihu has been there all along, just hidden in the shadows of his elders, even taken for granted. You can imagine the surprise all registered, and especially Job, upon Elihu's sudden burst of pent-up anger and frustration. But I'm getting ahead of the story. First, let's meet Elihu.

Elihu was the son of Barakel, the Buzite from the family of Ram. Elihu means, "He is my God;" Barakel means "God has blessed;" Ram means "Exalted."[5] This was obviously a family who worshipped God. Buz was the brother of Uz (Gen. 22:21), an Aramean tribe living in the land of northern Arabia.[5] You recall from Job 1:1, that Job is living in the land of Uz. Therefore, it is very likely that Job and Elihu were relatives. The meanings of Ram's family names may well indicate wealth as ancient people equated wealth with blessings and righteousness. (The Book of Job is testimony to those beliefs.) All of this said and done, we find one sharp reversal of these facts and assumptions. Jer. 25:23 denounces the Buzites as being one of the peoples to drink the cup of God's wrath! Beyond this mention, we do not know any specifics about this tribe.

Elihu has waited respectfully, although not patiently, while the elders have argued with Job. At this point, Job has emerged the victor because his three friends have been unable to sway his convictions of personal innocence. Elihu's speech begins with an apologetic overture for his youthfulness, but he quickly assures his audience that he is very wise anyway. Indeed, his opening statement asserts that the Holy Spirit of God breathes understanding into a man. In Paul's letter to the Ephesians (3:4), he states, "In reading this, then, you will be able to understand my insight into the mystery of Christ."[1] (Eph. 3:6 gives you the solution to the mystery.) Thus, Elihu was wise in realizing that true understanding comes from the indwelling of the Holy Spirit in mankind.

Elihu says his anger has been kindled for two reasons: (1) Job justified his own actions and thoughts rather than justifying God's Holiness in executing His master plan and (2) the elders have failed to present a persuasive argument to sway Job's convictions. Elihu immediately sets out to address these concerns. After verifying his own righteousness, Elihu declares that Job went astray in his argument by not basing it on the principle that "God is greater than man."[1] (33:12) God speaks to man through dreams to warn him and pain to discipline him, both to preserve man's soul from the danger of hell. (This is based on Job's assertion that God was his Adversary and Judge.) Out of a thousand angels, for sure one would come forward to serve as mediator between God and man. Again, we see a distinct picture of the coming Messiah to serve as Mediator and the Ransom for Christians. (Read Psalm 49:7-9.) God warns man repeatedly not to stray into wickedness.

In his opening statement Elihu shows respect for his elder, Job, urging him to speak up if he has any comments. Elihu uses good psychological technique in making Job his partner in discerning right and together learning what is good. The parallel to this in the New Testament is found in 1 Thess. 5:21, "Test everything. Hold on to the good."[1] (34:9) With maturity, we realize that one's perception of a situation is not always the reality. This is true of Elihu's youthful perception of Job's arguments. Elihu sees Job as challenging God's authority to govern as He sees fit when actually Job is expressing his own bewilderment. All ancient Near Eastern religious beliefs equated blessings with righteousness and troubles with sin. Job had done everything known to man to obtain righteousness but had been sorely afflicted.

As chief defense counsel for God, Elihu launches into his case. God is just and merciful. He shows no partiality. He creates and destroys with discrimination. God's omnipotence provides protection and His omnipresence assures He is always with us. God's omniscience proves He sees all and knows all. No evil escapes His sight. God doesn't need to hear judicial cases in order to judge mankind. Elihu believes Job was presumptuous to have even suggested such a situation. The cries of the poor and oppressed, God can hear. God hears the cries of the smallest baby while judging the sins of a whole nation. Both good and evil are sentenced justly based on their own righteousness or wickedness.

Elihu presents a theoretical situation to Job to evoke a deeper level of thought processes. Suppose a man confesses to be guilty before God and agrees not to do the offensive thing again. Should God reward this man? Basically here is an evil man who has decided to be a good man hereafter. Will he get eternal life? NO! One must repent of their evil and turn from wickedness. In Elihu's fictional situation, the man makes a conscious decision to change without any regret or repentance of the evil he's already done! He stands condemned before the Judge for those sins committed. Elihu declares that Job has added rebellion to the sins he already has and apparently never repented. Again Elihu accuses Job of having served God merely to receive the profits (blessings). Now Elihu really steps off into the realm of ignorance. He restates Job's argument: righteousness or wickedness done by man does not affect God -- only man is impacted. Only man pays the consequences, not God. Of course, Job didn't say this, but Elihu continues to paraphrase his perception of Job's defense. Men cry out looking for God when they are oppressed, but God doesn't listen to empty pleas. Elihu accuses Job of empty talk -- babble to God without knowledge of God's Holiness. There are greater things to ask of God than just relief from trouble. (In agreement with this latter statement, Jesus provides an answer, "Therefore I tell you do not worry about your life, what you eat or about your body, what you will wear. Life is more than food, and the body is more than clothes .... Who of you by worrying can add a single hour to his life? Since you cannot do this very little thing why do you worry about the rest?"[1] (Luke 12:22-23, 25-26) "Do not be afraid, little flock, for your Father has been pleased to give you the kingdom."[1] (Luke 12:32) But Jesus also reverses the idea that God isn't affected by mankind's ways. "There is more rejoicing in heaven over one sinner who repents than over ninety-nine righteous persons who do not need to repent."[1] (Luke 15:7) God cares for all His children, but He is deeply grieved over those persons who have chosen to be orphans instead. Jesus grieved over the lost people of Jerusalem, "O Jerusalem, Jerusalem, you who kill the prophets and stone those sent to you, how often I have longed to gather your children together, as a hen gathers her chicks under her wings, but you were not willing!"[1] (Luke 13:34) Elihu concludes this portion of his attack on Job's testimony by declaring that in wisdom, he [Elihu] is perfect! (Remember, pride goes before destruction!)

The core of Elihu's defense of God is now ready for presentation. Elihu has begun his case by tearing down Job's testimony (although not credibly). He turns his argument to the characteristics of God. God is mighty, just, eternal, protective, paternal, authoritative, healing, comforting, exalted, holy, loving, forgiving, and merciful. Elihu warns Job to beware of turning to a life of sin in order to avoid troubles. Great lessons can be learned from God's creation. As Elihu watches the coming storm, he is awe-struck by the magnificence as God's curtain rises on the spectacular light show appearing on the horizon stage. God's power and might are evident in all of nature. One can only marvel at the cycle of water that refreshes all life. Elihu marvels at the power of lightning and the roar of thunder. With His voice of thunder, God controls the pouring rains and halts all the labors of man. In His master plan, each season of the year is carefully orchestrated. As winter arrives in Arabia, so also come the cold winds, frozen seas, and swirling snow. One simple substance so vital for life that God has provided it in many forms is water: running spring streams, steamy summer humidity, cool fall showers, freezing ice and snow storms of winter. Can anyone other than God perform these miracles? Read Psalm 24:1-5. The heavens and earth are the continuously changing canvas of God.

Food for Thought: Living on the Gulf Coast, we get a wide range of weather changes even from one block to another. Recently I left work for the day and when I reached the parking lot a sudden, deafening bolt of lightning shot from the sky and hit the ground only a mile or less from me. Car burglar alarms were going off everywhere. Never have I heard the crack of lightning so loud. I literally jumped several inches and screeched involuntarily! Even after I got to my car and started home, it continued, one bolt after the other -- but no rain! When I got home, I found my husband sitting in the back yard watching God's light show. Every bolt was large, loud, and driven straight into the ground. The awesome power of God is both beautiful and fearful.

Verse of the Week: **Daniel 7:18** "But the saints of the Most High will receive the kingdom and will possess it forever -- yes, for ever and ever."

September 17
Bible Readings: Job 38-42

From the midst of the storm, the LORD's voice is heard. He speaks directly to His servant Job. God is now acting in His own defense. He intends to ask the questions and Job shall respond.

God's presentation addresses 3 wonders of creation: (1) earth and seas; (2) universe; (3) animals: lioness, raven, mountain goat, doe, donkey, ox, ostrich, horse, hawk, and eagle (a perfect 10).

(1) Earth - Where was Job when God was busy creating the earth? Does Job know how the earth's dimensions were laid out and how it was formed? Where are its footings and its cornerstone? God's defense portrays Him as the engineer of all creation. Where was Job when God marked off the limits of the seas? Can Job explain how a cloud is made or determine how the seas are kept in place?

(2) Universe - Maybe Job would rather explain how the sun rises and sets? Or how the earth's topography was decided and formed? Can Job round up the wicked and break their might? Has Job determined the origins of the sea or waded along its bottom? (Now Job's idea of a sea is limited to the Mediterranean. He really would be dumbfounded over the sight of an ocean!) Where does darkness come from and where does it go? How does God replenish lightning? Has Job seen the storehouse of snow and hail? Can Job control the paths of the storms? Maybe he could bring water to the wasteland or make the dew? Is creating frost beyond his power? Maybe Job's power is more cosmic, how are the starry constellations suspended in the heavens? Who cues the heavenly bodies in their daily performance? With a spoken word, can Job bring forth rain? Can he count the clouds? Maybe Job will explain how wisdom and understanding are given a man?

(3) Animals - Well, let's see if nature is where Job's expertise lies. How does a lioness know how to hunt her prey? Who provides food for the birds to survive? Is Job the creator of new life? Can he determine when the time is right for each species to bring forth its young? Maybe Job knows how the infant animals are protected in the wild? Do the mountain goats and deer depend on Job for directions? Maybe Job knows the ways of the wild donkey and ox? Can Job harness the wild beasts and trust them to till and harvest? Consider the ostrich: a bird whose wings are useless yet she can run faster than a horse! Being land bound, she lays her eggs on the ground, caring little for their survival or the young's survival. Wisdom and knowledge are not hers, but in physical strength she excels! (Doesn't God provide all of us with different gifts and talents that complement and supplement each other for the work of His Kingdom?) Maybe Job was responsible for endowing horses with great strength or great courage? Can Job control the migration of birds? Can Job perch the eagle's nest on a rocky crag of the mountain? Maybe Job can endow the eagle with eyesight keener than man's? Job, can you correct the Almighty? "Let him who accuses God answer him!"[1] (40:2) (I sure am glad Job is on the stand and not me! You can almost hear ole Job's knees knocking, lips quivering, and mouth stuttering. He is paralyzed with fear!)

JOB'S RESPONSE: "I am unworthy -- how can I reply to you?"[1] (40:3) Job is now in the last stage of grief -- acceptance. He recognizes his unworthiness to question or challenge God's authority in any aspect of life. (Have you ever told God how angry, disappointed, grieved, or sick you were and insisted on knowing why? All of us have, even if only in our thoughts. After a few minutes, did guilt and shame fill you as a great awareness of your many blessings swept over you? When God makes His Presence known, our unworthiness is overwhelmingly apparent.)

GOD CONTINUES: Again God will question Job and Job shall answer Him. Does Job believe God is unfair? Would he condemn God in order to justify himself? God now starts His two final discourses: large land animals and large water animals. God chooses the behemoth as representative of large land animals. The description given in this passage best fits the hippopotamus that lies under the lily plants and hides in the tall grass of the marshes. The hippo was found in the Nile River back during the ancient days of Egypt and was known as the "Nile horse." With civilization, the animal retreated to the Amazon. Who can make an animal with such power and strength that only eats grass? In his great bulk and might only God can challenge him, yet even small animals aren't afraid of his gentle ways. Can Job capture a hippo?

The crocodile represents large water reptiles. In Job 41:1, the crocodile is called a leviathan that is often translated in other books of the Bible as sea monster or gliding serpent (Psa. 74:14, Isa. 27:1). Can Job capture a crocodile? Will a crocodile have mercy on him? Who can tame the creature? But all creation belongs to God and is under God's control. Who else would dare to approach the creature whose impregnable armor and fearsome teeth strike terror in the hearts of men? He churns the water, threshes the mud, and snorts warnings to all near and far. No weapon can match the strength and ferocity of the crocodile! What hope would man have against him?

JOB'S RESPONSE: Job admits God is in control and has authority over all life. He also confesses to speaking of things beyond his true understanding, things too magnificent for mere man to comprehend. Job repents of his boldness in questioning God. Again we find Job in dust and ashes, a fit image of the beginning and the end! God is our Alpha and Omega, our beginning and end. Job's doubts and weaknesses were now made strong through his personal relationship with God.

GOD JUDGES THE THREE FRIENDS: God expresses His anger at the men for their attack on Job. He restores the relationship of the men to Himself and to Job by appointing Job as the mediator or intercessor for the men. Job takes the complete sacrifice of 7 bulls and 7 rams and offers them as burnt offerings to God. Job also offers intercessory prayer and does not bring judgment on the men for their sins. The men did not do what was right, as Job had done. This passage is clearly a picture of Jesus Christ. It shows Job as intercessor between men and God. Job is also the High Priest who offers the complete sacrifice that is capable of covering all sin and restoring the relationship of God and mankind. God accepts the prayers of Job who symbolizes Jesus, the Son of God and Son of Man who did what was right.

Job's blessings in the last decades of his life were even greater than the first. He again had 7 sons and 3 daughters and twice as much wealth as before. Job was given a double blessing. (This reminds me of Elisha who received a double portion of the Spirit when he saw God's chariot come for Elijah. You don't see God's Presence without an overflowing of blessings.) Job lived 140 years.

Food for Thought: The speech by Elihu has all the benchmarks of being written by a different author and 'dropped' into the text of Job. Elihu mysteriously appears and disappears without being acknowledged elsewhere in the text. Scholars have debated on whether Elihu's speech should be retained in Job because they don't agree about whether it makes any great contribution or clarification of the text of the book. Try reading Job without Elihu's long speech and determine what you think. Others believe that Elihu's presentation offers a needed and appropriate reminder of the awesome magnificence of God and the splendor of His intricately ordered creation.

September 18
Bible Readings: Psalms 44, 74, 79, 80, 85, 89

We return again to the songs of the Hebrews. Psalm 44 was a song possibly written during the reign of King Joash.[59] A 'maskil,' this song is generally sung at an annual festival.[5] It was written as a commemoration to the fallen people of Israel, a national lament.[56] Under Joash, the Jews worshipped God. Thus, their claim to following the covenant, but they worshipped other gods, too. Both the Philistines and Phoenicians had plundered Jerusalem and sold many of the Jews as slaves to the Greeks. (Read Joel 3:6-8.) Another possibility is that this song was written to honor the thousands who died in the revolt of the Maccabees (Apocrypha). The Maccabees engaged in a religious war against the Greeks to prevent a pagan temple to the Greek god Zeus from being built on the Temple Mount (about 162 B.C.). Still others believe it was written during the time of King Jehoshaphat because it is placed with other psalms of that period.[59] The commentary guide in your Bible places it as a song of the exiled Jews.

Psalm 44 is the counterpart to Psalm 85. It was probably sung as a litany with the congregation singing alternate stanzas with the king. As with all national festivals, the history of the nation of Israel is recited by the people. The king responds in the second stanza that he does not trust in his weapons and army but in God. The people respond in stanza 3 with a cry of anguish over their defeat at the hands of their adversaries. In stanza 4 the king mourns the disdain and reproach on the nation and professes his own disgrace in the situation. Stanza 5 specifically indicates the people's beliefs that they are innocent keepers of the covenant. (This is not what you would expect to hear from exiles in Babylon. If it is a psalm written by the exiles, then they were in deep denial of their sins against God.) Verses 20-22 give the king's declaration of the nation's innocence. Finally, the people cry out for God to act on their behalf.

The poetry and verse of this psalm pair well with Psalm 85, with the king starting the litany. He reminds God of previous times when God had restored the people. Then the people refrain with a plea for restoration and revival (something we all need). The king continues by promising his allegiance to God in keeping the people within God's covenant. Surely, God will save them soon. The people respond that faithfulness comes from man, but righteousness comes from God.

Psalm 74 mourns the rejection of the people by God, resulting in the fall of Jerusalem and the destruction of the Temple. Lam. 2:5-9 provides a similar picture. Your Bible's commentator has placed this with the exiles' songs. As you begin to read, it definitely seems to be describing the fall of Jerusalem to Babylon until verse 9. At that point, the decision to contribute this song to the Babylonian defeat becomes shaky. God had certainly provided prophets after the fall of Jerusalem in 587 B.C. Jeremiah was still in what was left of Jerusalem until Johanan takes the remainder of the citizens to Egypt. Ezekiel was in Babylon with the exiled Jews. A later time when the Temple was destroyed and defiled was in 167 B.C. when Antiochus IV Epiphanes sacrificed pigs on the altar of burnt offering (See Dan. 11:31), hung the circumcised babies, killed their mothers and fathers, and destroyed every copy of the Torah, God's laws (all the books of the Bible available to Jews at that time) (1 Maccabees 1:54-64). In 1 Maccabees 4:46, we are told there were no prophets left in Jerusalem. Additionally, Psalm 74:9 states that the length of the Jews' travail is unknown. Again, before Babylon ever captured Jerusalem, Jeremiah told the people they would be exiled 70 years. So, this verse seems to totally relate to the attack by Antiochus. Beginning in verse 12 mourning and grief are exchanged for worship and praising God. The psalm ends with a plea for God to remember His people and send salvation.

Psalm 79 is a song of outrage about the atrocities committed against the Jews. They were slaughtered and their bodies left to the birds and beasts of the wild. This is desecration of God's creation. Even today rabbis will scrape every bit of flesh and blood they can find on rocks, vehicles, buildings, earth or anywhere else into a plastic baggie for proper burial. (Life was in the blood and God had commanded them to treat all life with respect and dignity, set aside as holy unto God and then portions of the offering were eaten only by those designated by God. Even then, all blood had to be removed first and offered to God.) The song requests that God pay back their enemies 7 times what they have dealt the Jews.

Psalm 80 is a song of prayer asking God to restore Israel to its former glory. (Recall the vine prediction of Ezekiel 15?) The bountiful grapevine of Israel had been planted in the Holy Land. Now the vine had been cut down and burned. As Ezekiel predicted, Jerusalem was destroyed. Babylon forces had returned to totally destroy all buildings of importance and pull down its wall of protection. The useless vine of the Jews was burned in the fire of judgment. Verse 17 would seem to refer to Jesus, but instead "the man at your right hand" refers to the king. The Bible frequently comments that God raised a leader for His people. In this psalm, the people are asking for God's blessings on the king and restoration of the nation.[56]

Psalm 89 is attributed to Ethan the Ezrahite. Ethan from the tribe of Judah (1 Chron. 2:6) appears to be confused with Ethan from the tribe of Levi who were the musicians (1 Chron. 15:17). It probably should have been copied as Ethan the Merarite.[59] Both Psalms 88 and 89 recognize an Ezrahite as the composer. This song is a hymn of praise to God. It recounts God's covenant with David, a man after God's own heart. God fought for the Israelites and built a great nation. The God of all creation was the strength and protection of Israel. God is righteous, just, loving, and faithful to all who walk in His Presence. The song reminds God of His promise to make David's lineage eternal (verse 29). God swore by His Holiness that He would keep His promise to David. Suddenly the tone of the prayer changes in verse 38 with "But . . . ." Now the nation of Israel has been rejected and the royal lineage cursed from the actions of Jehoiakim. The psalmist sees God's rejection and anger as a reversal of His promise to David. But how can that be? God promised in His own Holy Name. The psalm has changed from one of praise to one of accusation! God is accused of supporting the enemies of Israel, of defiling the crown of the king, and of breaking down the walls of Jerusalem so it could be plundered! (Of course, the thought is that God removed His protection and blessings from the Jews, allowing all these things to happen.) Verses 44-45 are more obviously pointing to a specific king -- Jehoiachin, the king who surrendered to Babylon. He was taken to Babylon at 18 years old. The throne of David was gone, or so it seemed.[28] (Remember Jesus is of the lineage of David.) Now that the anger and pain of the people have been vented, the humbleness and broken nation is pleading for God's mercy. This psalm ends with the blessing and double Amen.

Food for Thought: In several songs, poems, and prayers, God's children "remind" Him of His promises or past actions. God doesn't forget what He has done or said, but we need to "remind Him" as a way of remembering our own blessings and to keep the faith. As a parent likes to hear children say "Thank you!" God likes to know His promise was taken seriously -- you remembered. Talk to God about the promises He made to you. It will warm your heart as you realize He has kept His promises all along.

September 19
Bible Readings: Psalms 102, 106, 123, 137

Psalm 102 is one to which we can all relate. This is the prayer of one who is afflicted to the point of feeling broken and beaten. The psalmist is so distraught; he feels God doesn't hear him. His life is rapidly waning; his body wastes away. The first 11 verses sound like the life of Job. He eats ashes for food and tears for drink. The psalmist is completely alone to fight enemies who curse him. Verse 12 suddenly turns from the wailing of man to the urgent request for God to act 'now' to restore Jerusalem. This prayer calls upon the God of Israel to arise and take pity on Jerusalem, to make her strong and respected again. The hope of all future generations lies in the Hands of God. In verse 23 the psalmist briefly returns to the lament of sinful man who has come under judgment. His strength is broken; his life is shortened. Finally, the tortured soul recognizes God as Creator. The created will exist but for a while; God will be the same forever.[56]

As in many other psalms, Psalm 106 is a prayer that revisits many of the milestones of the great exodus march out of Egypt. It opens with a stanza of praise for a just God. Stanza 2 begins with the confession of the Hebrews' sins but switches from the personal 'me-you' relationship to the impersonal third person pronoun 'he.' At this point the history lesson in the sins of a nation begins for the Jewish people. Remember that songs were used for teaching everything from history to repentance to the coming salvation. This historical account is introduced by the crossing of the Red Sea with the drowning of the Egyptian army (Ex. 12-14). The judgments of the exodus, which serve as the themes for each stanza, are as follows.

- The plague visited on the grumbling Hebrews after greedily stuffing themselves with quail (Num. 11:4-35)
- The greed of Dathan that resulted in his family being swallowed into the earth (Num. 16:1-35)
- The golden calf worship at Mt. Horeb (Ex. 32:1-35)
- Rejection of the Promised Land which resulted in 40 years of wilderness wandering (Num. 13-14) (Deut. 4:25-31)
- Their turn to paganism, worshipping Baal and bringing prostitutes into the camp (Num. 25)

Moses bringing water from the rock at Meribah (Num. 20:2-13)
Contamination of the Hebrews with the Canaanite people and their pagan religions (Judges 1, 17-20)
The many times the Israelites were oppressed as a result of their sinfulness (Judges)
The prayer of Solomon (1 Kings 8:49-50)[56]

This psalm is a chronicle of the Hebrews' rebellion and rejection of God with each resulting judgment. It is a poem of warning against defilement by sin. Beginning with praise and confession, it ends with a plea for salvation and restoration and an offering of thanks.

A song of ascents was sung as the priests climbed the mount to the Temple. Psalm 123 is a prayer for God's relief from contemptuous people. At some time in our lives, all of us have been singled out as the subject of gossip or derogatory comments. The sin for such contempt rests on the attacker not the victim. But that doesn't stop the victim from experiencing much mental and emotional anguish. Psalm 123 is a prayer close to the heart of anyone who has endured ridicule and contempt. Many have walked in the shoes of the oppressed, and all who have become better people for the experience found their solace in God.

There is no doubt that Psalm 137 was written by the exiles in Babylon. As captives, some of them would have been conscripted to be musicians for the king and his officials. Their heavy hearts made joyous songs a painful experience. The jeers and mirth of their captors made the pain intolerable. The hills and valleys of Zion were emblazoned in their memory in the midst of the marshy flatland of Babylon. We see the idea of the worship of God being tied only to Judah in verse 4. In this state of mind, the bitterness and vengeance toward the Edomites, who assisted Babylon in capturing the Jews, is paramount in their song. The last stanza expresses the joy the Jews will feel when Babylon is conquered and destroyed.

Food for Thought: Eventually, the Jews turn their hearts and lives back to God. At that time, they will realize that "when we are judged by the Lord, we are being disciplined so that we will not be condemned with the world."[1] (1 Corinthians 11:32) "No discipline seems pleasant at the time, but painful. Later on, however, it produces a harvest of righteousness and peace for those who have been trained by it."[1] (Heb. 12:11)

September 20
Bible Readings: Daniel 7-8

587 B.C.	Jerusalem fell
573 B.C.	Ezekiel's Temple vision
539 B.C.	Cyrus of Persia takes the throne of Babylon
538 B.C.	Cyrus ordered the Temple rebuilt in Jerusalem, 1st group of exiled Jews return
522-486 B.C.	Darius I reigns
486-465 B.C.	Xerxes reigns as King of Persia
458 B.C.	Ezra
465-424 B.C.	Artaxerxes on throne -- Nehemiah
423-404 B.C.	Darius II reigns
404-359 B.C.	Artaxerxes II reigns
359-338 B.C.	Artaxerxes III reigns
356-323 B.C.	Alexander the Great of Macedonia rules the Greek Empire -- Hellenism
336-330 B.C.	Darius III King of Persia- Macedonia ruled by Alexander the Great's generals, effectively dividing up the kingdom
323 B.C.	Ptolemy becomes King of Egypt and rules Palestine
321 B.C.	Seleucus rules Babylonia area and establishes Antioch-on-the-Orontes in Syria

	as his capital--Hundreds of years later believers were first called Christians at Antioch.
279 B.C.	Antigonus II Gonatas rules Macedonia
232 B.C.	Antiochus III (the Great) becomes King of Seleucid Empire
176 B.C.	Antiochus IV takes the Seleucid throne
168 B.C.	Antiochus IV attacks Jerusalem[6]

Chapter 7 of Daniel is an apocalyptic vision that foresees hundreds of years into the future. It is no surprise that this vision occurs in a dream at night. Belshazzar is co-reagent to his father and serves as King of Babylon (not to be confused with Daniel's Babylonian name Belteshazzar). The first scene is "the four winds of heaven churning up the great sea." Four represents all four corners of the earth, or better put as the whole of earthly civilization. The entire heathen world is in a great commotion and upheaval. Four different beasts emerge from this commotion: a lion with eagle wings, a bear with ribs between its teeth, a leopard with four wings and four heads, a beast with iron teeth and ten horns.

First Beast - Winged beasts were popular symbols in Babylon, being found decorating their city gates. Even now, lions and eagles represent the kings of the animal world. This first beast is believed to represent the kingdom of Babylon. Back in chapter 2, Babylon was seen as a gold head on the large statue. Gold is the king of metals. Thus, Babylon is depicted as the King of everything powerful or best. The first beast (Babylon) will have its eagle wings plucked off so that it can't hover over and attack other lands anymore. The beast is then set upright and given the heart of a man. This transformation into a man symbolizes the conversion of Nebuchadnezzar from a pagan to a believer.[5]

Second Beast - The bear is the second strongest animal of Daniel's world. Chapter 2 tells us the statue had a chest and arms of silver, the second most precious metal. One interpretation of the statue is that the two arms represent two parts of one kingdom. One part came before the other. This would represent the Medes and the Persians. Daniel 8:20 would seem to confirm this theory. There are many interpretations about the three ribs. My preference is that the three ribs represent the three kingdoms conquered by the Medo-Persians: Babylon, Lydia, Egypt. The kingdoms will be devoured.

Third Beast - The leopard is more agile than the other two beasts but less strong. The leopard has 4 wings like those of a bird, but not eagle wings. Thus, he will be able to obtain greater agility with four wings but not with the royalty of an eagle's wings. The kingdom of the leopard will spread quickly.[51] The identification of this empire is difficult. If the previous beast represented only the Medes, then this empire is the Persians with its four successive kings.[50] If the second beast represents the Medo-Persians (as I prefer), then this beast is the Macedo-Grecian Empire ruled by Alexander the Great of Macedonia, Greece. At the time of Alexander's death, he had no heirs yet born. His empire was divided into four smaller kingdoms ruled by each of four of his generals: Cassandra (Greece), Lysimachus (Anatolia), Seleucus (Syria and Mesopotamia), and Ptolemy (Egypt).[50]

Fourth Beast - No animal is named because this is so terrible a beast that no known animal could represent it. Its iron teeth will crush and break and devour. Anything that is left over will be trampled and crushed by its bronze claws. This beast has 10 horns representing 10 kings. If the four beasts were interpreted as Babylon, Mede, Persia, then this would be the Greeks (Alexander's empire). On the other hand, if the four beasts represent Babylon, Medo-Persia, Greece then this is the Roman Empire (my preference). A horn symbolizes strength or might; therefore, 10 horns symbolically mean perfect or total power. The fourth beast devours the whole civilization. The interpretation of this being the Roman Empire is futuristic in that the 10 kingdoms that arise are still in the process. See Rev. 17:12-13. The 10 kingdoms will last 1 hour (or a short time by God's measurement). They give power and authority to the beast. The Revelation of John uses much of the same imagery as Daniel to describe the end times. When I think of possible kingdoms that have risen to power since the Roman Empire, the following come to mind: the Spanish colonization, United Kingdom, Third Reich, Japanese Empire, U.S.A., U.S.S.R., Chinese dynasties, not to mention the Arab (Middle East) possibilities. The horn that uproots is the coming antichrist. Daniel also saw God who is pure and holy (white clothing) and has all wisdom without end (white hair). He has authority (throne) to judge (fire) the world. Thousands of angels serve Him while enormous numbers of people await judgment. The court being seated indicates finality. The books are opened. (Notice that books is a plural word. See Rev. 20:11-15, 21:27. There is the Lamb's Book of Life and the Book of Judgment. Which one is your name in?) The beast is slain (Roman Empire representing the evil one) and its body (representing all evil people) is thrown in the fire (Lake of Fire - Rev. 19:20, 20:10). The beast of Rev. 13 seems to be a compilation of all the evil beasts given in Daniel 7.[51]

Jesus is seen coming in the clouds (Second Coming of Christ). His kingdom is eternal; the Ancient of Days (God) gives His authority, glory, and sovereignty. The Saints of God (all Christian believers) are awarded eternal life with Christ in His kingdom.

Then Daniel asked further questions about the fourth beast. In this explanation, the 10 horns are 10 kings who come to power; one will rise and overcome 3 of the others. Christians will be persecuted for 3.5 years (corresponding to half of the tribulation). (Rev. 17:12-14)

Two years later Daniel has another vision. He sees himself at the Persian capital of Susa beside the Ulai Canal. The vision begins with a ram with 2 long horns. One horn came up later than the other, but it grew longer. The horns represent the Medes and the Persians. The ram attacked north, south, and west. It did not attack the east. The ram was indomitable. Then a goat with a horn between its eyes came from the west. The goat is Greece and Alexander the Great is the first great horn or king. The Greeks and Persians engaged in a great war. Persia (ram) was defeated. At 33 years of age, Alexander the Great died and the Greek Empire was divided into 4 smaller kingdoms (4 horns). From one of these kingdoms (Syria) came a king who grew in power (Antiochus IV Epiphanes). In the south he gained power over Egypt.[51] In the east, he ruled Babylon. The Beautiful Land he overpowers is the Holy Land. Antiochus throws down some of the starry host and tramples them. These hosts are the people of God. God is often called the God of hosts, which may mean the heavenly beings, but the Hebrews were known, too, as the "hosts of Jehovah" (Ex. 7:4, 12:41). King Antiochus IV Epiphanes (the horn) took away the daily sacrifice, desecrated the Temple, and set himself up as ruler of the Jews. As noted in the Sept. 18th lesson, 1 Maccabees 1:39-46, 3:45 tells that Antiochus destroyed, forbad, or desecrated everything used in Jewish worship, including sacrificing pigs on the altar of God. The persecution will last 1,150 days or about 3 years and 2 months. This number may actually be symbolic, indicating the persecution will last a long time but will have a definite beginning date and ending date known only unto God. This would then make the little horn symbolic of the great tribulation period when God's children (Christians) are persecuted.[51] [Note: Daniel 7:25 gives 3.5 years, but Dan. 12:11-12 gives 1,290 days from the time the daily sacrifice is abolished until the abomination is set up. Blessed are those who persevere and survive 1,335 days. This is a difference of 45 days. According to 1 Maccabees, the time from the beginning of the Temple desecration to its re-consecration took more than 5 years.[51] Thus, 45 days may be the time for cleansing the temple prior to resuming worship.]

The Archangel Gabriel stood before Daniel. The angel calls Daniel "son of man." (God called Ezekiel "son of man." Thus, Ezekiel is still the only prophet called that by God.) The interpretation that follows is a picture of the antichrist: a wicked, stern-faced king; a master of intrigue (he will draw people to him mesmerized); very strong by the power he has been given from Satan; devastation will be integral to his strength; deceitfulness will be perfected in him; superiority describes his view of himself; killer of many; and the enemy of Jesus Christ. Yet God will destroy him (Rev. 20:7-10).

Food for Thought: There are seven archangels in Hebrew writings: Gabriel, Uriel, Michael, Remiel, Raphael, Saraquel, and Raguel.[50] Which ones are named in the Bible?

September 21
Bible Readings: Daniel 5, 9

The King of Babylon gave a banquet for 1,000 of his leading citizens. Apparently on an ego trip, he has the gold and silver goblets that belonged to the Jerusalem Temple brought in for their use. Of course, these vessels have been consecrated to God. Now drunken pagans were using them! To add insult, they were toasting the gods of construction materials! Now you know the king must have thought he was having alcoholic hallucinations when the fingers of a human hand started writing on the wall. (The inception of Power Point!) In fact, he collapsed! He called for his magicians, offering a reward of purple clothing, a gold chain, and third highest ruler of the land. Only Daniel could interpret the writing.

Daniel starts by reminding Belshazzar that his ancestor, Nebuchadnezzar, was thrown into insanity to live like an animal when he became too arrogant and proud. After his humbling experience, he recognized the one and only God. Daniel uses some political finesse by telling Belshazzar he had not humbled himself rather than telling him he was arrogant and proud! (Otherwise he might have been wearing burial clothes instead of purple!) Daniel points out that using God's consecrated vessels so sinfully had made him an enemy of God. God had judged Belshazzar and his reign was coming to an end. The Medes and Persians would get the kingdom of Babylon. Daniel was given his reward and that night the king got his -- death -- both earthly and eternal. At 62, Darius became king for the Medes.

A few months later, Daniel was reading Jeremiah when he discovered the prophecy that the desolation of Jerusalem would last 70 years (10 x 7 = 70 perfect completion). Daniel fasted, repented, and prayed for forgiveness for the Jews. His prayer confesses the sins of all the people in rejecting God and His prophets. Daniel begs for God's mercy on the Jews. He acknowledges that all the curses of Moses have been borne by the Jews for their sin in following other gods. Daniel knows God is righteous and he prays that God's wrath will be turned away from Jerusalem without delay. Then Gabriel appeared before Daniel, bearing an answer to his prayer. There are 3 common theories as to the interpretation of these verses: (1) The reference is to the time of oppression of the Jews by Antiochus IV Epiphanes, (2) It prophesies the time until Christ is born, or (3) It is a prophecy of the end times from the exile to the Second Coming of Christ.[51] The phrase "70 weeks of years" is used in several different types of Jewish records to represent 70 years. Gabriel may be reinforcing Jeremiah's prophecy that the judgment on Jerusalem will last 70 years. The Jews had failed to provide the land the required rest every 7 years (Lev. 25:2-7). As a result, God took the land back and allowed it to be dormant and desolate for 70 years (2 Chron. 36:20-21). The 70 years served as a time for the people to turn from sin and repent. It was also a time for the Jews to reconcile themselves to God through their penitence.[60]

The phrase "from the issuing of the decree to restore and rebuild Jerusalem" could mean (1) the decree Cyrus issued to let exiles return to Jerusalem (536 B.C.) (Ezra 1:1-4; 6:1-5), (2) the decree of Darius to complete the restoration of the temple (519 B.C.) (Ezra 6:6-12), (3) the first decree of Artaxerxes in 457 B.C. (Ezra 7: 11-26), or (4) the second decree of Artaxerxes to rebuild Jerusalem's walls (445 B.C.) (Neh. 2:4-8).[60] Both 1 & 2 refer to rebuilding the Temple. To determine which decree is the right one, you count forward 483 years (69 x 7). The only one that coincides with an important event is the 457 B.C. decree that precedes the resurrection of the Messiah by 483 years. This decree to rebuild Jerusalem resulted in the second mass exodus of the Jews out of Babylon. By this theory then, the first decree of Artaxerxes is the correct one. Thus, Daniel 9 is the only prophecy to predict the exact birth of Christ.[61] The anointing of the "most holy" is believed to be Jesus at the time of the resurrection. (Although some believe it is the anointing of a high priest for the first time in 70 years after the Temple was rebuilt. Remember that a priest could only enter full service at 30 years of age. The age Jesus entered His ministry, our High Priest. The only age at which He could enter the synagogue as a Rabbi or teacher.) Your Bible counts the period of exile from the time the first captives were taken into exile (605 B.C.) to the time the Temple foundation was laid (536 B.C.).

The 70 years interpretation is debated, too. Some scholars believe it is 7 years times 7 to equal 49 years, from the time of destruction of the Temple until the time of the fall of Babylon.[52] Using this theory, verse 25 may then be interpreted to mean there will be 49 years from the time the Temple is begun until the Temple is rebuilt (plus the Jubilee year for a total of 50 years) plus 62 times 7 (434) more years until Jesus is resurrected, fulfilling Messianic prophecy. This gives a total of 484 years. Jesus was crucified in the middle of a year of ministry. Therefore, His ministry was 3.5 years long. A 'half-week of years' is 3.5 years or the length of Jesus' ministry.[52] As you can tell, the big disagreement is not only when the time begins and when it ends but also whether it is 49 years, 490 years, or 484 years. (Of course, there are at least a hundred other opinions and theories, too.) Additionally, a problem exists concerning the time being broken up in verse 25. Does that refer to the years not being continuous but in two parts? Other scholars believe that the 62 'sevens' represents all of the subsequent Jewish history from the destruction of the last Temple by the Romans in 70 A.D. until the Second Coming of Jesus when the last 7 years of tribulation will be served. Still other scholars believe this verse should be interpreted as 490 years from the end of Old Testament prophecy until Herod's Temple is burned in 70 A.D. This vision occurred in the first year of the reign of Darius, about 522 B.C. Jesus was born about 6-5 B.C. It may possibly be the time of his death 33 years later. Finally, the 7 year-weeks may be futuristic in the 6 millenniums of mankind (about 4000 B.C. - 2000 A.D.) with the 7th being the 1,000 years Satan is bound (Rev. 20).[51] Obviously there are many interpretations, many questions, but no definite answers -- at least not at this point in time.

The Anointed One is usually interpreted to be one of two people, dependent on which of the above theories you are examining. Isaiah 45:1 refers to Cyrus, King of Persia, as the LORD's anointed one. He would free the Jews and decree the restoration of Jerusalem. Of course, the second Anointed One is Jesus who would set free all believers from the bondage of sin and restore the kingdom of God, the New Jerusalem.

Daniel 9:26-27 may refer to Antiochus IV desecrating the Temple and destroying Jerusalem or it may refer to Satan running amuck after the crucifixion of Jesus. In either case, wars follow continually, particularly in the Holy Land.

Again, verse 27 could refer to Antiochus IV or to the 7 years of the tribulation. The "middle of the seven" may refer to either. Antiochus persecuted the Jews 3 years and 10 days.[52] The last half of the 7 years of tribulation will bring unbelievable persecution. Antiochus, the symbol of Satan, desolated and destroyed until he was defeated and died a madman.[5]

Food for Thought: After all these decades of reading the Bible, Daniel 9:20-27 still leaves me "scratching my head" trying to decide what I believe it means. I actually believe it was a true historical event that foretold of a greater event to come. God sent His children a drama picture of the tribulation in the future, much like Jeremiah and Ezekiel acting out their prophecies. What do you believe? (Read *The Pre-Wrath Rapture of the Church*.)

September 22
Bible Readings: Daniel 6; 1:21

King Darius of Babylon set up a satrap system for the country, appointing 120 officials to the new role. The new satraps or governors ruled their provinces and reported directly to the king's administrators. Daniel was one of these administrators. He so far excelled the others that the king wanted him to become head of the government, a plan that made Daniel unpopular with his fellow administrators. Because Daniel was always upright and honest, the jealous governors had to figure out something they could develop to trap him. So they asked the king to write out a decree declaring for 30 days everyone was not to pray except requests to the king. Anyone not doing so was to be thrown in the lions' den. The king's ego led him to comply with this request and the law was sealed as a binding law of the Medes and Persians. (The Medes ruled Babylon.) Daniel continued to pray three times a day in front of an open window facing Jerusalem. Of course, the envious governors soon had him arrested. The king was very distressed because he liked Daniel and now realized he had been used in a plot against Daniel. Upon putting Daniel in the lions' den, the king said, "May the God whom you serve continually, rescue you!"[1] (6:16) Daniel was sealed in for the night. Meanwhile, the king had a miserable night. His sin in this sham law must have gnawed at his very soul. At the first sign of dawn, the king rushed to the lions' den and called out to Daniel. The king's question is revealing of his being under conviction for his sin. "Daniel, servant of the living God, has your God, whom you serve continually, been able to rescue you from the lions?"[1] (6:20) Daniel replied that God had sent an angel to shut the mouths of the lions. When he was lifted out of the pit, Daniel had no wounds. All of the evil men who plotted against Daniel, along with their wives and children, were thrown into the lions' den and killed.

Darius sent out a decree to all the land that the people must fear the power of God and show reverent respect to the God of Daniel. Darius describes God as living, eternal, having an indestructible kingdom, sovereign, protector, savior, and creator. Even the lost recognize (but don't accept) the one and only God. Daniel continued to find favor and prosper well into the reign of Cyrus the Persian.

Food for Thought: Would we have had the calm assurance that Daniel had when placed in a situation that guaranteed we should have been killed? Many have been killed so that we could have religious freedom. Don't let a day pass without utilizing your freedom to worship. Use it or someday you may lose it!

NOTE: I am looking forward to the New Testament! Prophecy gets heavy when you engage the JEDI!

Period of Restoration

September 23
Bible Readings: Ezra 1-4:5; 2 Chron. 36:22-23

Cyrus ascended the throne of the conquered Chaldean (Babylonian) Empire in 539 B.C. During his first full year as King of Persia, he decreed the rebuilding of the Temple at Jerusalem. Any Jew wanting to return to undertake this task was free to go. There are several important points to remember about this event.

(1) Cyrus was an instrument of the LORD. He was God's anointed one for carrying out God's master plan (Isa. 45:1). Ezra 1:2 provides the opening statement of Cyrus' decree, which declares that the God of heaven had given Cyrus the vast Persian kingdom and had appointed him to rebuild the Temple. Cyrus knew he was God's tool in a master plan.

(2) Nebuchadnezzar was referred to as God's servant. He, too, played an important part in the Will of God (Jer. 25:9).

(3) The Jews had been living in the wealthy, fertile land of Babylon for 49-67 years, based on the different years groups of captives were deported. They had taken Jeremiah's advice to marry, build homes, and have families (Jer. 29:5). Those less than 49 years old had never known any other homeland or any other lifestyle. Many of the Jews had acquired great wealth and slaves (Ezra 2:65). They and their families would have to give up all they had accumulated to return to a desolate wasteland of ruins and start all over in worse shape than before they were deported. Now they would have no powerful king to protect them, no city walls to protect them from the hostile settlements of pagan peoples living around Jerusalem, and the ruins would have to be cleaned up before reconstruction could even begin.

(4) The trip to Jerusalem was long and dangerous. Many raiding parties attacked people on the ancient highways to steal their gold, silver, purple cloth, and other trade goods. Even though the distance between Babylon and Jerusalem was only 530 miles 'as the crow flies,' it was about 900-1,000 miles by road. The trip would take 4 months.[62]

(5) Cyrus wanted all his subjects to be as happy as possible so there would be no rebellions to overcome. This

turned out to be a good strategy; one Cyrus had been successful with before. Cyrus had managed to overpower the Median overlord and unite the Medes and Persians on an expansion campaign through Asia Minor. Babylon was his last stop. On Oct. 12, 539 B.C., Cyrus and his army marched into Babylon virtually unopposed. Cyrus had diverted the Euphrates River so that Babylon no longer had the water between her and the enemy.[7] The Persians then marched into the city through the water canal that ran north and south through the city and under the walls. Without water, it became a large tunnel into Babylon.

Cyrus asked for volunteers to return to Jerusalem; 42,000 decided to go, although the future would be filled with hardship and danger. Cyrus also decreed that those living around the returning Jews throw them a big going away (Temple Rebuilding) party! Talking about the gifts! Given to the Jews for restoration of their Temple was 1,100 pounds of gold, 3 tons of silver, plus 100 fine linen embroidered robes for priestly functions. Even in the poor economy of 2002 A.D., the value of this much gold is $5.67 million, and for this amount of silver, it is $27,720. In addition to that, they received livestock and household goods to help them get reestablished. With all this 'stuff,' it is amazing the Jews made the long trip in just 4 months! They traveled north along the Euphrates River into Syria before turning back south toward the Holy Land.[63]

Those who chose to return included the heads of the houses of Judah and Benjamin, as well as some Levites and priests. The list of priests is identical to the one given in Neh. 7: 39-42. Only parts of the other figures coincide with the Nehemiah list. Cyrus returned 5,400 vessels that were taken from the Jerusalem Temple. The 1,000 goblets used by Belshazzar at his banquet for nobility would have been included and issued by the designated Persian treasurer (Mithredath) to Zerubbabel, named Sheshbazzar by the Babylonians.

When the exiles arrived in the Holy Land, they split up and went to resettle their respective hometowns. But on the 1st day of the seventh (Sept.-Oct.) month they reassembled in Jerusalem for a special day of rest and worship. Prior to the 1st, the restored Jews rebuilt the altar to God "despite their fear of the peoples around them." These would be the pagan people who had been relocated on the surrounding land by the Assyrians before the Jews were exiled. This Feast of the Trumpets tradition would continue to become the Jewish New Year celebration of Rosh Hashanah, the Day of Judgment. On the 10th of the seventh month is the Day of Atonement when the Jews atoned for their sin and reconciled themselves to God. On the 15th-21st was the Festival of Tabernacles (Booths) when the Jews were reminded of the time when God freed their ancestors from Egyptian slavery and led them forth to the Promised Land. It also served as a harvest celebration. Afterward, the people began assembling construction materials for the Temple as Cyrus had authorized. The Temple foundation was laid 2 years later in 536 B.C. This was a day of great celebration and great tears of sadness over the result of their previous sin. It would be 515 B.C. before the Temple was completed.[5]

The enemies of the Jews seize the opportunity to lie about their intentions and try to infiltrate the Jews with offers of labor assistance. But the Jewish leaders turn them down. When this deceit didn't work for the pagans, they used psychological warfare -- discouragement. They even **hired** people (for 21 years) to discourage the Jews! This should be a lesson for us today. Many Christian churches would be appalled at turning down anyone who presented for membership, but many pagans are on the church rolls casting votes of dissension among its members.

Food for Thought: The Festival of Trumpets has a rich history. You remember Moses called assemblies by using two silver trumpets. One trumpet meant only the leaders came; two trumpets meant everyone came. The Festival of Trumpets is a foreshadowing of the day when Israel will have its final regathering with God.[62] God will be celebrating His harvest on that day. The Messianic Jews believe the Second Coming of Christ will occur on Rosh Hashanah. We should be ready every day. Are you ready?

> Verses of the Week: **Daniel 11:35, 12:13, Zech. 4:6** "Some of the wise will stumble, so that they may be refined, purified and made spotless until the time of the end, for it will still come at the appointed time.... At the end of the days you will rise to receive your allotted inheritance.... 'Not by might nor by power, but by my Spirit,' says the **Lord** Almighty."

September 24
Bible Readings: Daniel 10-12

In 536 B.C., Daniel received another vision; this time he is beside the great river. The text states it is the Tigris that runs through Persia. It is interesting to note that two of Daniel's apocalyptic visions involved scenes by water and two occur in his bedchambers. This probably means these were Daniel's favorite types of places for quiet time, worship, and prayer. God talks to those who talk to Him. Daniel is now about 88 years old. Daniel had received a revelation involving a great war. His spirit was so saddened that he mourned and prayed for 3 weeks. The last half of which should have been a great joy because of the Passover celebration. A man in linen appeared before Daniel, possibly Gabriel[52] as in an earlier vision, an angel (Rev. 15:6), or one "like a son of man" as in Rev. 1:13. The actual description of the heavenly being most closely depicts the one in Revelation who represents Jesus. The heavenly being in Daniel 10 refers to a common depiction of Daniel, the "highly esteemed." Daniel is told to stand up, to arise. When Jews are told to stand, it is significant; they are being told to rise up, be watchful, and take a stand against evil. Notice what the heavenly being tells Daniel, "Since the first day that you set your mind to gain understanding and to humble yourself before your God, your words were heard."[1] (Dan. 10:12) We should remember this. It is the formula for direct communication to God. First, we must decide or "set our minds" to worship God. Second, we must humble ourselves before God. Third, we must study His word to gain understanding. Finally, we must pray. Keep in mind, Daniel is especially in the Spirit as this is the first week after the Festival celebration. Ten days before this vision had been one of the two most sacred religious assembly days of Passover. (Daniel may have worshipped privately).

The heavenly being reveals a glimpse of the heavenly warfare so often talked about in passages such as Ephesians 6:12. This being had been sent to bring this interpretation to Daniel three weeks earlier (the time Daniel had been mourning and praying) but had been delayed by the evil spirits supporting the pagan gods of Persia. Although pagan gods have no power of their own, evil spirits fight to keep paganism thriving by attacking the followers of God, both earthly and spiritual. The Archangel Michael came to the heavenly being's assistance. The being says he was assigned to protect Darius the Mede who had brought God's sentence on Belshazzar. Darius (though not known to be a Christian) was a part of God's master plan. This heavenly being was protecting God's interests. Now Daniel is admonished to be strong in the face of evil.

Soon the prince of Greece (Alexander the Great) will come. He will conquer as he pleases. Then the kingdom will be divided out unto the 4 corners of the earth (north, south, east, and west). Now we have introduced two key characters: the king of the South (Egypt and its conquered territories in Palestine under the rule of Ptolemy I) and the king of the North (Syria and Asia Minor ruled by Seleucus I). These were the two most powerful kingdoms to come out of Alexander the Great's empire. Alexandria (first established by Alexander the Great) was the capital of the South and Antioch was the capital of the North. The Greeks started the Age of Hellenism (Hellenes is Greek for Greece).[6] Greek became the language of choice and Greek culture was "haute couture" (high fashion). Aristotle had been Alexander's teacher, instilling a thirst for knowledge in the boy.

Ptolemy II acquired a great library with books and records from all the great philosophers and scientists of the time. Alexandria had a very large population of Jews who had lived there so long they could no longer speak or read Hebrew fluently. To preserve their religious teachings, they started translating parts of the Hebrew Old Testament into Greek. Paul refers to the Hellenists, or Grecians, in the Book of Acts when referring to Greek-speaking Jews.[5] When Ptolemy II came to the throne of Egypt, he had the High Priest in Palestine send copies of

Moses' books in Hebrew along with 72 learned men who could translate them. Thus developed the Septuagint or Greek version of the Old Testament. Septuagint means "the seventy."[64]

The Seleucids become stronger than the Ptolemies. In an effort to secure peace, Ptolemy II (285-246 B.C.) gave his daughter Bernice in a contract marriage to Antiochus II, king of the North. Laodice, Antiochus' divorced first wife, got so mad she had the king, Bernice, and their son murdered. One of Bernice's brothers (Ptolemy III) was on the throne of Egypt and attacked the king of the North, Laodice's son Seleucus II (246-227 B.C.). This set the stage for a long history of war between the two countries. Seleucus III and later Antiochus III (known as Antiochus the Great) reigned in the North. Palestine was the key piece of ground between them and belonged first to the South, then to the North, and back to the South. Finally, Antiochus III won back Palestine and arranged the marriage of his daughter Cleopatra to Ptolemy V of the South. (There were many Cleopatras. This is not the famous Cleopatra.) Antiochus III was killed in a war. Later, Heliodrus, a tax collector, assassinated Seleucus IV. All this history gets us up to Antiochus IV Epiphanes coming to the throne of the North in 176 B.C. [By 165 B.C. he has murdered many of the Jews and desecrated the Temple. (He even plotted to assassinate the High Priest Onias in 171 B.C.) Antiochus IV is a picture of the antichrist.] Antiochus IV made two attacks on Egypt, one in 170 B.C. and another in 168 B.C. The first was successful, but the latter wasn't. Roman ships commanded by Popilius Lasenas defeated him. After this disappointment, he takes out his anger on the Jews. They were divided into those who knuckled under to Antiochus IV and became known as Hellenizers (represented symbolically as Edom, Ammon, and Moab) and those who stood up for their religious faith even under persecution, the Hasidim. The revolt of the Maccabees occurred in 168 B.C. led by Mattathias in Modein. This is said to be "a little help" (Dan. 11:34).[50]

Antiochus thought himself a god above all others, including the gods of his fathers (Greek gods) and the god desired by women (Tammuz-Adonis, the Syrian god of vegetation[52] who died in the winter and was reborn in spring). Antiochus seemed unstoppable, but God's prophecy concerning his end was about to unfold. Troubles come from the east, from a town called Elymais. Antiochus had donated many gold vessels to his pagan temples, some weighing 500 pounds. In need of more money, he planned to plunder a temple in Elymais (located southeast of the Tigris River in Elam) but failed. [This statement gives credibility to the fact that Daniel's vision was at the Tigris River that some commentaries discount in favor of the Euphrates.] Both Antiochus III and IV attempted raids on its temples. Antiochus IV tried to raid the temple of Artemis (in a town now called Anahita). Meanwhile, the Maccabees defeated his governor, Lysias. Antiochus was so distraught; he got sick and died in 164 B.C.[50]

Daniel's vision jumps from the death of Antiochus to the end times. Daniel is told Archangel Michael will arise to save all whose names are in the Book of Life. Those who have already died will awake (resurrection of the dead). This is a very controversial point among religions, namely: "Does the soul go immediately to be with God and the body go later or does the soul fall 'asleep' with the body until the day of the rapture?" Technically, it makes no difference if your name is in the Lamb's Book of Life. When we fall asleep at night, eight hours pass in the twinkling of an eye. If we fall asleep in death, we will awaken in Heaven in the twinkling of an eye, regardless of how much time elapses. (See John 5:28-29.) If we know Jesus Christ as our Lord and Savior, we don't have to worry about anything eternal; he has already prepared everything. Our place is reserved and the price has been paid! On the other hand, if you know <u>NOT</u> Jesus as Savior, then eternal condemnation is your fate -- your reservation is in torment. Accept Jesus as your Savior today.

Daniel now sees two other beings, one on the left bank of the river and one on the right. Daniel asks how long it will be before this vision is fulfilled. The man in linen is above the river; he lifts his right hand and then his left in a solemn oath. The man answers, "It will be for a time, times and half a time. When the power of the holy people has been finally broken, all these things will be completed."[1] (Dan. 12:7) The phrase "time, times and half a time" is generally understood to be 3.5 years, which is the length of Jesus' ministry, but it is also the length of the great tribulation. In the first, Jesus who is the power of the Jews was crucified, at that time the holy dead came forth from graves (Matt. 27:52-53). In the case of the great tribulation, the physical strength of God's holy people will run out and the harvest of the remaining righteous will occur.[51] (Read Rev. 14.)

Food for Thought: I have said before that the plan of salvation is summed up in a single Bible verse. "'If you confess with your mouth, "Jesus is Lord," and believe in your heart that God raised him from the dead, you will be saved.'"[1] (Rom. 10:9) CONFESS -- BELIEVE -- ACCEPT

September 25
Bible Readings: Ezra 4:6-6:13

The restored Jews are facing much opposition from the pagan leaders around Jerusalem. Ezra 4:6 is controversial as to its date and present location in the text. [The problem arises in that Xerxes (son of Darius) ruled from 486 B.C. to 465 B.C.] King Cyrus died in battle in 530 B.C. Cyrus had two sons: Cambyses and Bardiya (also known as Smerdis). Cambyses ascended to the throne and reigned from 529-522 B.C. The news of a coup by his brother sends Cambyses racing home from battle. In his haste, he wounds himself with his own sword. Was it suicide or an accident? No one knows. Darius was an aspiring military leader who put forth the rumor that Cambyses murdered his brother and that Guamata (a Mede) had impersonated Smerdis to get the throne when Cyrus died. Some believe Darius was the one who killed Smerdis and no impostor existed.[7] Others believe the impostor reigned for a short time. Verse 6, then, falls into one of these possibilities: (1) It is out of place in the text based on its address to Xerxes who ruled 36 years after this complaint to the king, or (2) The recipient was actually the impostor who was reigning and called Xerxes as a royal title.

Several years later, the Persian officials living in Samaria wrote a letter of complaint to King Artaxerxes. These officials were technically administrators over the people who had been displaced by the Assyrians and brought into Samaria to recolonize. They intermarried with some of the Israelites who were left to become the despised Samaritans. The officials' letter to the king requested a review of the archives to prove what a rebellious people the Jews had been. It urged the king to stop the restoration of Jerusalem or he would risk losing their tax monies in another rebellion. Of course, Jerusalem did have a history of rebellion, so King Artaxerxes issued an order to stop the restoration. The Samaritans were only too happy to use force in stopping the rebuilding. It is of interest to note that Zerubbabel of the royal lineage was the recognized leader in Jerusalem. Cyrus had officially made Zerubbabel responsible for returning the gold and silver vessels to the Temple. But these paranoid Persian officials decided to stick their noses into Jerusalem's happenings! They surely knew Cyrus had sent the exiles home, but they wanted to take advantage of a weak political time to advance (or at least maintain) their own political power. The evil one uses lots of people and situations to try to hinder or stop God's work. If you are doing the work of the Lord, then you're in battle against the enemy.

In 520 B.C., Tattenai, the governor of Trans-Euphrates, and other officials petitioned King Darius concerning the rebuilding of the Jewish Temple that was now going up rapidly. Apparently Zerubbabel had become very discouraged by the constant opposition to the restoration of the Temple and Jerusalem. God sent two prophets, Haggai and Zechariah, to encourage the Jews. As Christians, we should always take the time to encourage those who are doing God's work. The governor's letter encouraged the king to search the archives to determine if Cyrus really had decreed the rebuilding of the Temple. The search uncovered the decree at Cyrus' summer palace in Ecbatana, Media. Court had been held in the summer of 539-538 B.C. in this palace, which was located 230 miles southwest of Tehran at an altitude of 5,500 feet. It was made of cedar and cypress plated in gold and silver.[7] The decree was very specific. The Temple was to be 90 feet high and 90 feet wide with three courses of large stones and one of timber. All costs were to come from the royal treasury. Tattenai was told not to interfere with the reconstruction. In addition, Tattenai was to pay for all the costs of the construction and provide any and all materials and sacrifices needed for the Jewish worship! When God provides, He really provides abundantly!

Furthermore, any person who tried to interfere would be impaled on a beam from his own house and then his house would be destroyed. This was certainly a strong enough deterrent to make even the staunchest opposition wane. The Temple was completed on March 12, 515 B.C.[7]

Darius was an assertive military leader who launched many campaigns in the early years of his reign to increase the size of Persia. It soon became as large as the U.S.A. is today. He reopened the canal between the Nile and the Red Sea. It was 80 feet wide and allowed two ships to pass each other. The three river valleys that were heavily populated were once again easily accessible: Indus, Tigris-Euphrates, and Nile. Darius also built a royal highway that ran from Susa to Sardis, over 1,600 miles! His organizational skills were excellent. The Persian Empire was divided into 20 satraps (possibly 23) that were similar to large provinces. Palestine (the name now given to the Promised Land) was in the 5th satrap along with Phoenicia, Syria, and Cyprus. A system of standard weights and measures and standard currency was established. Land was surveyed and annual taxes were assessed. Satraps were responsible for civil and military functions in their jurisdiction.[7] Darius was a follower of Zoroastrianism, worshipping Ahura Mazda, a god of light, truth, and goodness. This god required man's good deeds to help win the war against the spirit of darkness. Zoroastrianism still survives today in Iran but with only a few thousand followers. In India it is known as Parseeism and has many more followers, descendants of Persian immigrants.[5]

Food for Thought: While I was wrangling with the visions of Ezekiel, I became rather discouraged myself. My Sunday School class sent me a bouquet of five roses, each one a different color. One rose became especially dear to me. It was white with a double crown (center). Although white roses are usually the first to turn brown and die, this one lasted three weeks in perfect condition! In fact, it lasted until I finished Ezekiel! God sent me a special message through a single rose sent by His encouragers. It represented purity of purpose, lasting endurance, and a double blessing. Praise God from whom all blessings flow!

September 26
Bible Readings: Haggai 1-2; Zech. 1:1-6

The books of Haggai, Zechariah, and Malachi are all written to post-exile Israel. All three, at least in part, deal with a common theme: the lack of commitment the people have demonstrated in practicing their faith.

We know very little about Haggai. He is also mentioned in Ezra 5:1 and 6:14. His name means festival, which probably means that he was born on a feast day. His known ministry is short, lasting from late August to mid-December of 520 B.C. The book largely consists of four sermons: 1:1-15, 2:1-9, 2:10-19, and 2:20-23. Haggai dates each of his sermons. The first is on the first day of the month, which was a religious feast day of a new moon. The second sermon comes 51 days later, the third 63 days later, and the fourth later that same day.

To appreciate Haggai's messages, it is essential to understand what was happening in Israel at the time. After Cyrus' decree allowing the Jews to return to their homeland, very few Jews elected to return with Zerubbabel in 537 B.C. With so few to do the work, the task of rebuilding the nation was daunting. To make matters worse, the first few crops were rather poor. As a result, the people's morale was low.

In his first sermon, Haggai challenges the people to begin building the LORD's house. Astonishingly, they have been in the land seventeen years and have not performed this essential task. He points to their paneled homes and compares them with the ruins where they worship. In 5-6 and 9-11, the prophet declares that their lack of success is because they have failed to put first things first. The spirit of his words reflects the command of Jesus in Matthew 6:33.

By the time of Haggai's second sermon, the construction of the new Temple is well underway (2:1). Because of their limited resources, the people's work does not compare favorably with Solomon's Temple. Haggai reminds them that God will fill the house with splendor. We must always remember that we have our work that we must faithfully perform. God has His work to which He will always be faithful.

The third sermon possibly takes place on the day the new Temple was dedicated. In 2:10-11 the prophet asks the priest two questions concerning ritual uncleanness. His purpose is to show that holiness can't be transferred from one object to another, but uncleanness can. For example, health isn't contagious, but sickness is. He then notes that previously the people were not blessed by their sacrificial offerings because they had failed to rebuild the LORD's house. Now, however, in light of their recent efforts, God is going to bless them.

Haggai's fourth sermon is directed at Zerubbabel, the governor of Judah. Zerubbabel was the grandson of Jehoiachin who had been a king of Judah before the exile. In calling Zerubbabel a signet ring, God is saying that he is a valued possession. Most interpreters believe that the blessing God extended to David was also extended to Zerubbabel, who also had a zeal for God's house. God promised David that his lineage would reign forever: a promise fulfilled in Jesus Christ. One should notice that in Matthew 1:12, Zerubbabel was an ancestor of Jesus.

Food for Thought: What work has God called you to do? Are you doing it?

September 27
Bible Readings: Zechariah 1:7-6:15

Zechariah's grandfather Iddo was one of the returning exiles from Babylon. As patriarch of his family, all descendants and their families probably returned with him. Zechariah was of priestly descent and some believe his father was dead. The name Zechariah means "he whom God remembers." In the first 8 chapters, Zechariah is a very young man (most likely he is at least 30 for his word from God to be accepted by the Jews) who encourages the restored exiles to rebuild the Temple and to have hope.[65]

In the late fall in 520 B.C., the word of the LORD came to Zechariah, "Return to me and I will return to you." The people repented and acknowledged they had received what their sins deserved. Three months later, Zechariah received a series of 7 visions all in one night. The first was a man riding a red horse. He was in a myrtle tree grove in a ravine. There were red, brown, and white horses behind him. Myrtle trees are ornamental and lovely. The wood is very fine grained and highly prized. As such, they represent Judah. The ravine represents the low state to which the Jews had fallen. The color of the horses is significant. Red is the color of blood and white depicts the heavenly and divine glory. The color of the third horse causes more debate. A comparison with Rev. 6 would indicate a pale (possibly speckled or light brown to blonde) horse represents death by famine. So the horses represent death by sword, famine and plagues, or divine judgment. Therefore, this vision indicates an angel of the LORD who was standing among the Jews received the report of the horsemen who had gone throughout the earth assessing the situation. They report that all Judah's neighbors are at peace. The Temple can be rebuilt in safety. It has been 70 years since the destruction of the Temple. God promises His house will be rebuilt, He will return to Jerusalem and be merciful, and they will once again enjoy prosperity.[65]

In the second vision, four horns appear followed by four craftsmen. Horns are symbols of power and strength. For every evil empire that arises, God will raise a craftsman to dehorn it. (Recall Dan. 2 and 7.)

In the third vision, a man measures Jerusalem. The reference to a city without walls with large numbers of people and livestock is to the future Jerusalem that will be open and much larger. It will be blessed with numerous people and livestock. God, Himself, will surround Jerusalem and provide its protection. Those Jews left in Babylon are told to flee before the judgment comes for these pagans. Zion is the apple, or pupil, of God's eye, the center of His people. He will uproot those nations who have enslaved the Jews and make the slave owners into the plunder of the slaves (Jews). People from all nations will join the Jews as God's people. He will dwell in the land He claims for Himself.

The fourth vision refers to the Branch, Jesus. Joshua the High Priest symbolizes Jesus. He stands before God, but Satan tries to find fault with him. The High Priest serves as the intercessor between God and man. Representing man's sins are Joshua's filthy clothes. Jesus takes away man's sins and puts on man the robes of royalty fit for children of the King. Joshua is charged to walk in the ways of the LORD and keep His commandments. He is to uphold the official duties of the priesthood on earth so that he will also be able to serve before God in Heaven. The kingdom of God (stone) is laid before Joshua to serve as an administrator to 'keep the courts' or sit in judgment. The complete (7) eyes of God will protect and watch over His kingdom. The stone will be inscribed (their version of cut and polished) to make it the most precious, sought-after gem. God is sending Jesus to die for the sins of the people and the land. God's purified church will invite all to come and worship with God's people.[65]

The fifth vision is of a gold menorah with an olive tree on each side providing a continuous flow of oil so the light never goes out. This obviously is a picture of the golden lampstand of the tabernacle, neither of which the Jews have any more. The lamp symbolized understanding (2 Sam. 22:29), guidance (Prov. 6:23), and life (Job 21:17).[5] The church will bring the Light (Jesus) to a world of darkness. Many people interpret verse 7 to mean that in the future the mountain of Zion will become a level plain by the might of God. God laid the foundation of the church through the Jews and He would place the finishing stone (capstone) in place. This stone not only completes the structure but also holds all the others in place. God's people will rejoice when they see the plumb line of justice. God's supply of Holy Spirit on His people will be seven-fold, complete and continuous. God's anointed olive trees are the high priest and the king.[65] Jesus is both our High Priest and our King.

Vision six contains a flying scroll 30 feet long and 15 feet wide, the same size as the porch on Solomon's Temple and the Holy Place of the tabernacle. In this case, though, it represents the Holy Place of the tabernacle just as the lampstand did. It symbolizes the measure by which this curse will be dispensed: the measure of the Holy Place. In other words, all sinners will be banished before God. You recall the 10 commandments were divided into sins against God and sins against man. One of each is given here to represent them all. The sins man commits will destroy him.[65] Your Bible lists the next vision as 7, but most records indicate it was part of vision 6 giving a total of 7 visions instead of 8. A basket (ephah) used for measuring is seen that contains the sins of the people throughout the land. When the lead cover is raised there is a woman inside called "wickedness." She is quickly pushed back into the basket and the lead lid is replaced. The woman is Jezebel who represents all that is wicked. Just as individual grains are piled in the basket to be measured, individual sinners will be, too. Two women are needed to carry such a heavy measure of sin. Their large stork wings help them lift the basket so that it is suspended in air and they fly away to Babylon with it. It is a curse on the land of Nimrod (Babylon). Sin is carried away permanently from God's people (through the blood of Jesus) and deposited squarely on the wicked forever (represented by those who built the tower of Babel).[65]

The last vision consisted of four chariots coming out between mountains of bronze. Each chariot had a different color of horses: red, black, white, and dappled. The two mountains are Zion and the Mount of Olives, making the Valley of Jehoshaphat the place of judgment (Joel 3:2). The colors of the horses mean the same as in vision one, but black (the color of grief) has been added. The judgment on God's enemies will be red indicating the blood lost in war. The dappled or speckled horses bring pestilence and plagues. The black horses carry famine. (See Rev. 6.) The white horses represent the divine victories over sin accomplished by the ministers of judgment. The Spirit of God goes with the chariots. Famine goes to Judah's enemy to the North -- Babylon. Pestilence and plagues go to the southern enemy of Egypt. The white horses go west to cover the whole earth with complete victory over the power of the world. The red horses represent war and stand ready to fight for God's people.[65] All the enemies of the Jews are having trouble. God was giving peace to the Jews so the Temple and Jerusalem could be rebuilt.

Zechariah is to take some silver and gold brought from Babylon and fashion it into a crown. Keil and Delitzsch interpret this crown of two metals to represent many diadems. Christ will be given a crown consisting of several diadems twisted together (Rev. 19:12), the insignia of his reign over all kingdoms.[65] Joshua is an Old Testament Hebrew word for Jesus.[5] Thus, Joshua will be crowned symbolically for Jesus and will be clothed with royal robes to sit on the throne and rule over His people. He will be both the High Priest and the King. The crown will be kept in God's house as a symbol of what is to come.

Food for Thought: When we are overwhelmed by troubles, God gives us peace, too. How many times have we said the situation couldn't get any worse, only to realize it really could be much worse. Stop and count your blessings. Thank God for always being there for you.

September 28
Bible Readings: Zechariah 7-8:23, Ezra 6:14-22

In chapter seven, messengers came from the settlement at Bethel concerning questions about the continuation of the fast of the fifth month. This fast remembered the breaching of the wall of Jerusalem by the Babylonians in 586 B.C. Of special significance is the fact that it is now 516 B.C. These Jews figure that the 70 years of captivity prophesied by Jeremiah are at an end.

Zechariah answers their question by asking one of his own. Did you fast for God? That is, did you lay aside your physical needs so that you could concentrate on building a relationship with God? The answer was "No." Their fast was a kind of pity party that brought to remembrance this extremely unhappy judgment. In 7:8-14, Zechariah tells the messengers that to serve God they must be honest and kind toward other people. We must always remember that personal conduct represents the majority of faith. When we obey God's word, we declare in the strongest possible way that we believe it.

Chapter eight contains ten separate messages from God. Each begins with "Thus says the LORD of hosts."

1. He loves and has a zeal for Zion. (Verses 1-2)
2. He will return to the city and dwell in it. (Verse 3)
3. The signs of normal city life will return to its streets. (Verses 4-5)
4. He marvels at Jerusalem's changed fortune. (Verse 6)
5. He will bring His scattered people back to Jerusalem. (Verse 6)
6. Because the people have started to rebuild the Temple, the land will be fertile, and the people will be prosperous. (Verses 9-13)
7. God declares that He has a changed attitude toward Jerusalem and lays down requirements for His continued favor. (Verses 14-17)
8. Their previous fasts associated with Jerusalem's destruction will become feasts of gladness. (Verses 18-19)
9. People will come to Jerusalem to seek the LORD. (Verses 20-22)
10. In the future, others will respect the Jews. (Verse 23)

Food for Thought: We often feel 'put upon' by responsibilities at our churches. We need to serve Him with gladness. On the other hand, those who are not actively serving need to volunteer to relieve those who serve so faithfully. God blesses every effort. Lend a helping hand.

The Restored Nation

September 29
Bible Readings: Psalms 78

The psalms we begin today are songs of praise written by the Jews who have been freed from their captivity in Babylon. Psalm 78 is almost a journal of the first exodus from Egypt. A fitting memory to set to music so that miracles from God will not be forgotten and the penalty of sin will serve as a warning. First, children of present and future generations are told to heed the teachings of the song. God, who is praiseworthy and powerful, performs great wonders. Like their forefathers, those who rebel against God will be judged. The men of Ephraim are specifically identified. As the largest tribe, the Ephraimites were seriously jealous that Judah had been selected for the capital and for the royal lineage. After all, the Ephraimites were descendants of Israel's favorite son, Joseph. Jeroboam was the Ephraimite who split Israel into two kingdoms by leading the northern ten tribes to rebel.

The miracles God performed during the first exodus are remembered with joy, but joy turns to sadness when the rebellions are recounted. Rebellion equals sin which equals judgment. When troubles came, they (Jews) turned to Him. When mercy came, they went their own way. God was loyal; they were not. God was faithful; they were not. The Hebrews repeatedly put God to the test. They had forgotten the Almighty God who brought the plagues on the Egyptians. Part of the namesakes of Ham was destroyed. (Mizraim, the grandson of Noah and son of Ham, settled Egypt.[5] The death angel took the firstborn sons of Egypt.) But His faithful servant led out God's people like sheep. God went before them and dispossessed other nations so that His children would have the inheritance of His Promised Land, a land sanctified and made holy by God. But they rejected God's gift and God's anger was kindled against them. God rejected them. The judgment of war swept their once blessed land. The country was rent between good and evil. Ephraim rejected God, but Judah held fast to God's laws (at the time of the split). Then God called David the shepherd to lead the people of Jacob (Israel). David led with integrity of heart, a man after God's own heart.

Food for Thought: We need to count our blessings, but it is also good to remember the sting of judgment, never to go that way again!

September 30
Bible Readings: Psalms 107, 116, 118, 125

Psalm 107 begins the Fifth Book of the Psalms. (If you have forgotten the origins of the psalms divisions, go back and read the April 21st lesson on Psalms.) Verse 1 is identical to Psalm 118:1 and 29. This psalm describes four groups of captives in the Babylonian exile marches. We can relate these to our spiritual march in life. Praise is given to God and His love is declared eternal as He gathers and redeems His people from the four corners of the earth. When the Jews marched or wandered, homeless in the desert, they called out to God in their distress. He made their paths straight in His Way and provided a place for them to dwell. They received water and food from a heavenly Provider. God is your Bread and Water of life, the Giver of rest and peace.[28] Let us break bread together.

Some of God's people had existed as prisoners of guilt in darkness and gloom. They had rebelled against God and paid a price. They, too, cried out to God in their distress and He led them to safety, breaking the chains of their bondage. Praise God for His unfailing love. He broke the gates of bronze and bars of iron that sin placed between man and God. He arose! He arose! Hallelujah, Christ arose!

Some had denied God and gone their separate, worldly way. The pain of their judgment brought them near to death. In their sickness, they called out to God. He healed them spiritually, snatching them from the eternal grave. To God be the glory, great things He has done!

Others escaped on the seas of life, adrift on the waves, free to go as they willed. Then God commanded the seas and stirred the waves. God demonstrated His control. As they pitched to the crests of the walls of water and fell back into the troughs below, they called out to God. He answered and quieted the storm. It is well with my soul.

God can turn rivers of water into dry beds and desert wastelands into oases. He can make productive land worthless from salt wastes and wasteland productive from springs of water. In God, those who believe themselves great are brought low, and those who believe themselves worthless are elevated. Justice comes to the needy and the upright. "Consider the great love of the LORD."[1] (107:43) Love lifted me.

Psalm 116 is a very personal poem from someone God rescued. In the joy of the moment, praise and thanksgiving gush forth. This person makes his worship public. He proclaims the great miracle that God heard his prayers and had mercy on him. The man even seems astonished that God would listen to him. In the second set of verses, the psalmist tells of the trouble and sorrow he was experiencing when God saved him from the eternal darkness of the grave of sin. His praises bubble forth. God is gracious, righteous, compassionate, protective, and Savior of those in need. From death and sorrow and waywardness, He delivers. Mankind deceives us, but God rescues us.

The psalmist vows to always call on the name of the LORD for his salvation. His vow will be given openly to all who hear, a public declaration of his God. The death of one of God's saints (people) is a loss of great value to His work. This worshipper vows to be God's servant for life, to present offerings of thanksgiving, and to praise the LORD forever.

Psalm 118 begins and ends with a refrain concerning the goodness of God and the endurance of His love. God's holy people, His priests, and any others who fear God's judgment should lift their voices in agreement. In great distress the psalmist cried to the LORD and God answered. Now, with assurance man can say, "The LORD is with me; I will not be afraid. What can man do to me?"[1] (118:6) The enemies have already been beaten as God's people find refuge in Him. In the heat of battle, the saved can say, "The LORD is my strength and song; he has become my salvation."[1] (118:14) Victory is proclaimed everywhere for righteousness has won. By the mighty works of God's right hand, salvation has come. Though we walk through the valley of the shadow of death, we fear no evil. Jesus has become the gate of righteousness, the way to salvation. "The stone the builders rejected has become the capstone. . . . This is the day the LORD has made; let us rejoice and be glad in it."[1] (118:22, 24) "Blessed is he who comes in the name of the LORD."[1] (118:26) For He is the Light in our darkness and the mercy in our troubles. He is worthy of our praise for His love endures forever.

Psalm 125 is a short psalm that proclaims God's faithfulness and dependability. We can count on the fact that "Jesus Christ is the same yesterday and today and forever."[1] (Heb. 13:8) As enduring as Mount Zion and as comforting as the mountains of Jerusalem that surround the righteous with security and peace, God is eternal. The wicked reign but for a short time on earth, never to rule again. But the righteous ones have eternal life with God.

Food for Thought:
> "Praise Him! Praise Him! Jesus, our blessed Redeemer!
> Sing, O Earth, His wonderful love proclaim!
> Hail Him! Hail Him! Highest archangels in glory;
> Strength and honor give to His holy name!
> Like a shepherd Jesus will guard His children,
> In His arms He carries them all day long:
> Praise Him! Praise Him! Tell of His excellent greatness;
> Praise Him! Praise Him! Ever in joyful song!"
>
> Fanny Crosby

Verse of the Week: **Psalm 129:2** "They have greatly oppressed me from my youth, but they have not gained the victory over me."

October 1
Bible Readings: Psalms 126, 128, 129, 132, 147, 149

Today's lesson completes the Book of Psalms. It is fitting that we should finish with such joyful and hopeful songs of praise. Psalm 126 tells of the great blessings God has bestowed on the restored Jerusalem. Those who have persevered and sowed in times of great sadness have reaped great blessings from God at harvest. This is also true of soul winners. When seeds of the gospel are sown, even in times of great persecution and adversity, God will provide a harvest of blessings. We must sow in faith in order to reap the rewards.

Psalm 128 is a blessing a father might give his son upon his departure to find a bride or upon his wedding. Likewise, it is a blessing God bestows upon His children, a blessing of joy, fruitfulness, peace, and prosperity. "'For I know the plans I have for you,' declares the LORD, 'plans to prosper you and not to harm you, plans to give you hope and a future.'"[1] (Jer. 29:11) May the God who reigns from Zion bless you with prosperity and long life. The psalmist ends with a common closing prayer line: Peace be upon Israel.

Psalm 129 celebrates the victory of perseverance. Even though greatly oppressed and under much hardship, the surviving Jews can joyfully declare freedom. The fullness of their joy can only be understood from the viewpoint of great bondage. Troubles seem insurmountable and overwhelming at the time, but when victory comes it is that much sweeter. Our sojourns on earth are filled with troubles and bondage, but when we see Jesus our rewards will be that much greater!

David's dedication to bringing the Ark to Jerusalem from Kiriath Jearim (city of Woodlands) is commemorated in Psalm 132. Unlike the exiles that returned to Jerusalem, David vowed that he could not lay his head down in a comfortable house while the LORD's Ark was still in a temporary dwelling. Those in David's ancestral home of Bethlehem (Ephrathah) heard of his vow. Caleb's wife was named Ephrathah and they had a son named Hur who became the father of Bethlehem. Hur's son was Shobal who became the father of Kiriath Jearim. Thus, the community surrounding Bethlehem became known as Ephrathah.[59] The Ark was at the home of Obed-Edom in Jaar (meaning woods[5]) for 3 months after David's first attempt to bring it to Jerusalem resulted in a death. (See 2 Sam. 6.) The psalm asks for God's blessing on the transfer of the Ark to Jerusalem and on His anointed one, King David. May God's priests be righteous and His church full of praise. God's promise that David will always have a descendant on the throne is reiterated here. But it is followed with the condition that God's laws must be kept. God has chosen Zion and David for His own. Both will be blessed with physical and spiritual abundance.

The infinite blessings of God the Creator are recounted in Psalm 147. Not only does God name and number the stars but He also administers justice to the people, heals the brokenhearted, provides for the needs of all creation, delights in all who worship Him, and maintains the seasons and cycles of all life. The psalm presents alternating passages on man and nature. As a tribute to God's greatest creation, this psalm starts and ends with God's blessings on His people.

Our last psalm is 149. The people of Jerusalem are singing praises to their God, the King of Zion and Ruler of all nations. This is a picture of the church who brings offerings of praise to God, whether in public worship or in private rooms. God has brought salvation to His children. The church of God is to battle the enemy, Satan and his followers. The church is to prevail over the wicked and demented. But the church is also to carry out all sentencing God assigns on the wicked. "Do you not know that the saints will judge the world? . . . Do you not know that we will judge angels?"[1] (1 Cor. 6:2,3) Praise the Lord if you are a believer and free of sin's bondage. God gives eternal life to His saints.

Food for Thought: Psalm 147 summoned all creation to praise God. Psalm 149 summoned God's people to praise Him. Together they are the perfect invitation to lift up praises to God with one of Fanny Crosby's songs written about 1872.

> "Praise the Lord, praise the Lord,
> Let the earth hear His voice!
> Praise the Lord, praise the Lord,
> Let the people rejoice!
> O come to the Father through Jesus the Son,
> And give Him the glory -- great things He hath done!"[41]

October 2
Bible Readings: Zechariah 9-14

The last prophecies of Zechariah are the most exciting! They reveal the coming Messiah. These 6 chapters are divided into 2 oracles: (1) chapters 9-11, and (2) chapters 12-14. The first oracle, or prophetic declaration, begins with the condemnation and destruction of the heathen nations: Hadrach (Lebanon), Damascus and Hamath (Syria), Tyre and Sidon (Phoenicia which is now Lebanon), Ashdod and Ekron and Ashkelon (Philistia which now belongs to Israel), and Gaza (Gaza Strip).[4] For some of the judgments against these nations, you can review Isa. 10:5-11; 14:28-32; 17; 23; Jer. 47; Ezek. 25:15-28:26; Amos 1. The locations slated for defeat are prophecy of Alexander the Great's victories. After defeating the Persians, he also conquered Hamath, Sidon, and Tyre. Alexander conquered Tyre in only 7 months, a feat which the Assyrians and Babylonians had not been able to do in 18 years of siege! He then marched south, taking each town until all the towns listed in Zechariah 9 had fallen to Greece. But when he gets to Jerusalem, he decides to spare the city from destruction and slavery. The people of Jerusalem were allowed to govern themselves as a colony of the Greek Empire.[66] Israel will never again experience total defeat (until the end of this earthly kingdom) because God has chosen to watch out for her. In 1967, the armies of Israel's surrounding nations marched on her at one time from all sides (Jordan, Syria, Egypt, Lebanon). Now known as the Six-Day War, Israel defeated them all!

Rejoice believers, you who are the children of God! Your eternal King brings righteousness and salvation. He (Jesus) will come as a gentle man riding on the colt of a donkey. (This is in direct contrast to the warrior king and savior the Jews were expecting.) Jesus will rule over all the earth with peace and justice. His rule will extend from the Euphrates River to the ends of the earth. The old land of Judah will enlarge to encompass the surviving Israelites from the old northern kingdom. Judah and Ephraim together become a strong bow in the hands of God. His arrows will be so mighty and powerful that they will flash like lightning. God will sound the trumpet call to march against the violent storms from the south -- the Arabian Desert area. God's people (all believers) will be filled with the blood of the holy sacrifice, as they are victorious over their enemies. In other words, when believers are washed in the blood of the Lamb, they are filled with the Holy Spirit and from that point throughout eternity; they are victorious over death and their enemy Satan. Believers will be the jewels of God's crown!

Zechariah, as with his predecessors, denounces evil leaders. Those who lie and deceive people by predicting bright futures and hope for evildoers, who provide false comfort, and who, in general, lead the people astray will be punished.

Judah will produce the Messiah. God and Judah together will form a fierce army and trample their enemies underfoot. Judah's military power will be strengthened and salvation will come to the Israelite survivors as well. Worshippers of God will be reunited into the kingdom of God's children, represented as the nation of reunited Israel. The Hebrew children who have been scattered to other lands will return to the Promised Land. The pride and haughtiness of pagan nations (like Assyria), as well as the oppression of peoples by dominating nations (like Egypt), will pass away. Only those who walk in the LORD will remain forever.[65]

In Zech. 11, we begin with the prophecy that all, which is exalted and lofty in the ancient land of Israel, will be destroyed. This actually happens when the Romans conquer the land. Verse 4 starts a passage of symbolism where the prophet Zechariah is the shepherd of the flock. Zechariah represents God and the flock represents the Jews. Keep in mind this is Messianic prophecy, so it is looking forward in time from Zechariah's day. The leaders of the Jews are only concerned about the money they can make; so they spare not the people nor have any mercy on the people. God gives the flock to the prophet to feed in order to stop the senseless slaughter (those destined to die without God). As the shepherd, Zechariah took 2 staffs; one he called Favor and the other he called Union. With his staffs, or rods of correction and accountability, he led the flock. But they would not follow him! Disgusted, he left them to their path of destruction and broke his staff Favor that symbolized his covenant with the people. As a result, the flock became afflicted (oppressed). When they rejected the shepherd, he asked for his pay. The Jews paid the shepherd 30 pieces of silver -- a pittance. The shepherd threw them into the house of the LORD to the potter. Then he broke his second staff called Union that represented the reunited nation of Israel. A new shepherd will be raised up for the land that will rule with force and power. The interpretation of this passage is that, in the future, evil leaders would again lead the Jews away from God. God would sever His covenant or promise to make them His holy people. (That promise would be extended to believers of all nations.) For only 30 pieces of silver the Jewish chief priests and elders would obtain the betrayal of Christ -- the owner's compensation required for the killing of a slave (Ex. 21:32), also for the cost of the purchase of a slave (Hosea 3:2). God's work on behalf of the nation of Israel was worth no more than the price of a slave! The money was thrown to the potter. All potters worked in the Hinnom Valley that was an unclean area because of the child sacrifice that had taken place there in previous years. The pottery was sold at the potter's gate to the city (Jer. 19:2).[65] The potter, or unclean one, was in the house of the LORD when the money was thrown in. Matthew 27:5-10 describes how Judas Iscariot threw the money into the Temple after Jesus was condemned. The chief priests (bad shepherds) picked up the murder-for-hire sum and bought the potter's field (Jewish writings indicate it was in the eastern end of the Hinnom Valley[5]). The land was only fit to bury those foreign to the God of Israel, the eternally unclean. The nation of Israel would be forever broken into 2 groups: those who believed in God and those who didn't. The Romans would devour the best of the land and the bad shepherds would be eternally condemned.

    Chapters 12-14 make up the second oracle. The time designated as "on that day" is used 16 times in these chapters, obviously leading up to the last days before the establishment of God's kingdom on earth. Chapter 12 begins by stating a time will come when Judah and Jerusalem will be besieged by all the nations on earth. But God will make Jerusalem an immovable rock -- a solid foundation. The armies of the nations will be thrown into chaos (as we saw with Senaccherib in 2 Kings 19:35-36) and will injure themselves (Judges 7:22). God will empower and shield those living in Jerusalem. The leaders of Jerusalem will be like a consuming fire, devouring the attacking nations. The weakest among them will be as brave and strong as David. The house of David (Jesus) will be like God, marching out to war against the enemy with the Angel of the LORD going before them. (Do you remember the words to "Onward Christian Soldier?") Notice that LORD is spelled with all capital letters in your Bible, indicating God the Father. This is the first reference to the house of David. The second reference follows in verse 10: a spirit of grace and supplication will be poured out on David and the inhabitants of Jerusalem. Another way of saying this is that mercy and humbleness will come out of Jerusalem through the lineage of David. Jesus fulfilled this prophecy.

    The eyes of the Jews will be opened. They will realize they were responsible for the crucifixion of Jesus, God's Son. The Jews were no longer God's covenant people, but now believers from all nations were part of a new covenant. The mourning of the Jews will be great when they realize their sin. The mourning is compared to that of Hadad Rimmon where Josiah was killed in battle in the plain of Megiddo. Remember this is the location where Armageddon will take place (Rev. 20:7-10).

    The third reference to the house of David is in 13:1. Jesus is the fountain of Living Water that cleanses believers of their sins. All pagan idols and prophets will be destroyed. The false prophets will try to deceive and hide. Two-thirds of the population will perish as a result of following the false prophets. (See Rev. 13:11-13.) The one-third who belong to God will be tested in the fire of judgment and all impurities removed. They will be God's people and He will be their God. (See Jer. 32:38.) (This is what the first covenant with the Jews was.)

    Chapter 14 addresses the last siege of Jerusalem. All nations will attack and conquer Jerusalem. The city and its people will be broken. (See Dan. 12:7.) On that day God will stand on the Mount of Olives and a great earthquake will split it into from east to west. Half of the mountain will move north and half will move south. The valley formed between will serve as an escape route. Salvation has come from the east. (See Rev. 16:17-21.) The prophecy jumps in time to the establishment of the New Jerusalem (Rev. 21) where no sun or moon is needed (Rev. 21:23). Living water will flow from the throne of God to all the believers of the earth (Rev. 22:1-6). God will rule over the earth and He will receive all the praise. Jerusalem will be raised up like a plateau above the plains that will surround Jerusalem (Geba representing the north and Rimmon the south[4]). (Benjamin Gate represents north, Corner Gate (NW) represents the west, Tower of Hananel (NE) represents the east, and the royal winepresses were on the south.[65]) (See Jer. 31:38-40.) [This is the only place the First Gate is mentioned in the Bible but may be identical to the gate of the old city mentioned in Neh. 3:6 and 12:39. If so, it is in the northeastern corner.[65]] Jerusalem will be secure forever.

A plague will strike the nations that fought against Jerusalem. The bodies of the enemies will rot while they are still alive! In a great panic, they will turn on each other. A similar plague will strike all their animals. (Does this sound like germ warfare?) Great wealth will be the plunder for Jerusalem. Judah will defend against those who come to attack Jerusalem. The survivors from the pagan nations will worship the Almighty God, making annual pilgrimages to Jerusalem to celebrate the Feast of Tabernacles (Booths) in the fall. If they do not come, their land will have no rain. Egypt is singled out as a well-known example of the plagues God can bring as a result of disobedience.

Holy to the LORD was the inscription on the gold plate worn on the turban of the high priest (Ex. 28:36). Now that God's reign is permanent, even the animals are holy. In fact, everything in God's kingdom is made holy. There will be no more pagans in God's world.

Food for Thought: If you haven't gotten excited about the unfolding of all this prophecy in the New Testament, then you need to check your pulse to see if you are dead! It is impossible to study the Old Testament and not get excited about the New Testament. It is also impossible to study the New Testament and not get excited about what is yet to come! Prepare yourself for victory, not for plague.

October 3
Bible Readings: Esther 1-4

Esther is an unusual book about a young woman who risked death to save her people, the Jews. It is also unusual because the Book of Esther does not mention God anywhere in the book, yet you have an overwhelming sense that God is the central theme.[67] The Book of Esther presents a drama, complete with heroine and villain. It ends with victory for good and death for evil. The setting is in Susa at the winter palace of King Xerxes of Persia in the year 483 B.C. Susa was a city of 175 acres surrounded with a great wall and possibly a moat. It was situated about 150 miles north of the Persian Gulf. Xerxes occupied this winter palace from October-May each year. The palace was built around a series of elaborately landscaped courts. The north side contained a great audience hall that contained columns 65 feet high topped with bulls' heads. Adjacent to this hall was a terraced garden 50 feet high containing 35 acres. The east gate of the city wall was close to the palace. The gate was 131 feet by 92 feet and had a central room that was 69 feet square. This is where we find Mordecai, Esther's cousin and kinsman redeemer.[7]

Our story takes place in the great palace of Susa. Xerxes has invited all his military leaders, nobles, and province officials to a huge display of his wealth and power. (He has 127 provinces in 20-23 territories governed by satraps and ranging from India to Ethiopia to Asia Minor, in other words, the whole Middle East and northeast Africa.) This is not just arrogance and pride. Xerxes has a plan. In the winter, kings planned their spring military campaigns. Xerxes' campaign strategy was long range and magnificent. Persia would invade Greece! This 180-day celebration would convince his nobility that Xerxes had the wealth and power to pull this war off. The celebration would culminate in a huge banquet where Xerxes would make his final presentation for support. More than two years would be required for all the preparations to be made for the invasion.[7] That was a lot of up-front money and effort without any war plunder for payment. The full backing of all his nobles was vital to the effort. The satraps were responsible for the preparation, training, and strategy details. The civil leaders would be needed to rally the citizenry to the cause. The palace was ready. The huge marble columns had blue and white linen flags trimmed in purple and hung with silver rings. The gardens were perfectly manicured. The rich detailed mosaic marble tiled floors were sparkling. Chaise lounges of gold and silver dotted the banquet hall. The best wine and gold goblets stood ready. It would be a 7-day banquet that no one could forget over the next two years. While the hundreds of men talked business, Queen Vashti would entertain the women with their own banquet and activities. You can imagine King Xerxes smiling smugly and thinking, "I love it when a plan comes together!" Well, almost together. Xerxes went one step too far while under the influence of alcohol and the "wheels came off the buggy." His plan had not included dignity and self-respect -- especially on the part of the Queen!

On the last day of the banquet, an inebriated king decides to traipse his last piece of beauty before the nobles -- his wife, Queen Vashti. Even though the Bible doesn't specify, Jewish writings state that Xerxes' request was that the queen appear wearing nothing but her crown! Vashti refused! A decision that was certain to bring severe punishment, if not death.[68] Now the king had to think fast. If he couldn't maintain command of his household, how would he prove he could orchestrate a huge campaign against Greece? Quickly, he asks for the advice of his cabinet of seven wise men that always accompanied him for just such emergencies. Surely, the other women Vashti was entertaining knew of her refusal. Surely, these wives and concubines waited with bated breath to hear the response. All the eyes of the men were on the king. How should he respond? To prevent any further show of independence by the other women, the cabinet decided Vashti should be removed as queen and never come into the king's presence again. In that way the dominance of the men would be upheld.

A search throughout the kingdom for a new queen was declared. A beauty contest would be held. The kingdom's most attractive young girls would be brought to the palace for 12 months of beauty treatments and training. Then one at a time they would go in to the king for one night each. The one who pleased him the most would become queen.

At this point, let's look at the backgrounds of our main characters. Esther was an orphaned Jewish girl. Her next of kin, Mordecai has reared her. Mordecai was from the tribe of Benjamin, a descendant of Kish. You recall that King Saul of Israel was the son of Kish. Thus, Mordecai was from the rejected royal lineage of Israel. Saul made several mistakes, but the one that brought about his rejection was the sparing of Agag the king of the Amalekites (1 Sam. 15). When Samuel found out, he personally killed Agag. In the text of Esther, Haman is said to be an Agagite. This may mean that an Agagite was out-of-town or escaped on the day of Saul's raid. Or, it may be a title of reproach given to any Amalekite descendant. Either way, Haman was clearly the enemy of God and the Jews. Mordecai's ancestors had been deported to Babylon in 597 B.C. when Jehoiachin surrendered to Nebuchadnezzar. Obviously, Mordecai was one of the Jews who had chosen to remain in the land of Persia rather than go to a Jerusalem he didn't know. Mordecai had gained the respect of the people of Susa and sat daily in the eastern gate. Generally, only the most esteemed leaders were allowed to sit in the gate to hold a type of civil court. They settled disputes, witnessed deed exchanges, and gave advice. Mordecai's cousin Hadassah or Esther was one of the beautiful girls brought into the king's harem. She gained favor with all who saw her. As she proceeded with her beauty treatments, she was advanced to the top group in the harem. When her time came to go to the king, she won his favor, too. Four years after Vashti was deposed, Esther was crowned queen in a great celebration. Esther kept her family background a secret, as Mordecai advised. Shortly after, Mordecai learned of a conspiracy between two door guards (to the king's bedroom) to assassinate the king.[63] He informed Queen Esther and the conspirators were hanged.

Meanwhile, Haman had managed to get himself elevated to a position of honor. In fact, he was elevated to the point that the king decreed all should bow to Haman. But Mordecai refused. Probably Mordecai's own respected position was all that kept him from being executed on the spot. Nevertheless, Haman hated Mordecai and that hate was transferred to Jews in general -- anti-Semitism at its worst. Haman went before his gods and cast lots (pur) to determine a date for annihilation of the Jews. The date was the 12th month. Since it was now the first month of 479 B.C., Haman would have to wait a year to kill the Jews. Xerxes was still reeling from his naval loss to Greece the previous summer. He had to maintain watch over the Greek cities he had conquered in Asia Minor to keep them from rebelling during his time of defeat. Now Xerxes must plan his strategy for the coming spring engagement.[7] He couldn't afford any more problems. So Haman's suggestion to decree an annihilation order for a group of people refusing to obey the king's orders was a measure to thwart further rebellion. The king gave Haman his signet ring and Haman had the decree issued throughout Persia that the Jews would be destroyed on the 13th day of the twelfth month -- the month before the Passover celebration started! Did the Jews escape Pharaoh only to be killed by the Persians? Even the citizens of Susa were bewildered. After all Daniel had been one of the royal officials up until about a decade prior. Mordecai tore his clothes and put on sackcloth and ashes. Weeping and wailing, he went to the king's gate and requested to see Esther. He apprised Esther of all that Haman had done. He urged her to plead for mercy before the king. But the king had not called for Esther in 30 days. It was the king's policy that anyone entering his inner court without being summoned would be put to death -- unless the king was pleased and extended his scepter. Esther had an even chance to survive versus die. Mordecai assures she will suffer the fate of her people and deliverance of the Jews will come from another if she does not try to intervene. (Mordecai obviously believes God will protect the Jews.) Then Mordecai makes the famous statement, "And who knows but that you have come to royal position for such a time as this?"[1] (4:14) Esther requests that all the Jews in Susa fast (which indicates petitions to God) with her and her maids for three days. Then she will go to the king.

Food for Thought: Have you been put in a position to do something special for the Lord? God has a calling for each of us. Our commitment to Him determines our response. Will you reap the reward, or will you let it go to another?

October 4
Bible Readings: Esther 5-10

On the third day, Queen Esther put on her royal robes and entered the inner court. (Don't you know she was terrified?) But the king was pleased to see her and extended his gold scepter. He offered to grant her request up to half the kingdom. (Have you ever wondered why kings would say this? Mark 6:23 records King Herod as making the same remark.) Her only request was for the king and Haman to attend a banquet she planned. What was her strategy? First, the way to a man's heart is through his stomach (with his ego as a runner up). The king and Haman would relax their guard over a pleasurable meal. Second, by delaying her request, the king would spend time contemplating what her request could be that she would risk her life. The more he thought about her instead of war, the better. Third, it gave her a chance to assess the relationship between the king and Haman and determine the best course of action. After the meal, the king again asked for Esther's request. (She needed more time. She needed the 'right time' to make her case against Haman.) Would the king and Haman come to dine again tomorrow? Of course, Haman's ego was so pumped up that he had to brag to all his friends. But Mordecai remained a thorn in his side. His wife and friends advised Haman to go ahead and have Mordecai hanged. Why wait? Immediately Haman ordered a 75-foot high gallows be erected. (Hangings were commonplace. The gallows may have been stored in pre-fabricated sections.) That night the king couldn't sleep. He sent for a sure-fire sleeping material -- the court records. In the process of the reading, the record of Mordecai's exposure of the assassination plot came to light. The king discovered nothing had been done to reward Mordecai. The next day the king asks Haman how he should reward the man who delighted the king. Haman's ego assumed the man was himself and he came up with all kinds of honors that would be public. But it was Mordecai whom the king wished to honor and Haman was ordered to personally carry out the public recognition! Haman rushed home from the public ceremony humiliated. Then the king's servant came to take him to Esther's banquet. (The time was right!) After the meal, the king again asked for Esther's request. To his surprise, she only asked for her life and the lives of her people to be spared! Esther announced she was a Jew! (Can't you just feel Haman's heart pounding like a trapped animal?) The king had been so involved with his military concerns he didn't even know Haman had ordered the Jews be killed. In a rage the king goes to the palace garden to think. Meanwhile, Haman falls down over the chaise lounge Esther is lying on to beg for mercy. When the king walked in, the sight of Haman draped over the queen sent the wrong signal. Haman was hanged on the gallows he had built for Mordecai. Esther was given Haman's estate. The king's signet ring was taken from Haman's possessions and given to Mordecai. Again Esther begs the king to spare the Jews. The king gives Esther and Mordecai permission to decree a law in the king's name that would supersede or offset the one Haman issued. The real problem was that any law issued in the king's name and sealed with his ring was a Law of the Medes and Persians and could not be repealed. (Recall the honoring of Cyrus's decree to rebuild the Temple out of the royal treasury years after Cyrus's death.) Mordecai must be careful and crafty in the decree he wrote. Mordecai granted the Jews the right to assemble and protect themselves. They were to kill and plunder their enemies. Note that it doesn't specify killing anyone other than "enemies." The date of this uprising was the same day Haman had decreed as the Jews' annihilation -- the 13th of the twelfth month. The edict was carried throughout the land. Mordecai was honored with royal garments, a gold crown, and a purple linen robe. The Jews' mourning turned to great joy.

On the designated day, the Jews fought their enemies. No one could stand against the Jews. All of the nobles helped the Jews because they feared the power Mordecai had. In Susa, Haman's 10 sons were killed. At the end of the day, 500 men had been killed in Susa and 75,000 were killed in the remainder of Persia. When the king asked if Esther had further requests, she asked for Haman's dead sons to be publicly hanged and the Jews of Susa be allowed to kill their enemies for one more day. (The Bible doesn't mention that Haman's decree had only been for one day. The presumption being the enemies could not present arms longer than the 13th.) Thus, the 14th and 15th days of the twelfth month became the Jewish Festival of Lots called Purim.

Haman is viewed as a picture of the false messiah -- the antichrist. The antichrist will be deceptive and will try to annihilate God's children. He will probably be someone who rapidly rises to a high position. We are told he will set himself up as a god, expecting everyone to bow before him.

The Festival of Purim is a very joyous, happy celebration that is extremely noisy. The Jews rejoice over deliverance from their enemies by reading Esther in its entirety. The congregation all wear costumes, mostly representing characters out of Esther. Interspersed with the Bible readings are skits by children who act out the drama of Esther. The noisy part comes when one of the three main character's name is mentioned. The congregational response to each name is as follows.

Esther - Ah-h-h-h-h-h-h!   Mordecai - God bless you!   Haman - (Boos, hisses, noise)

The purpose is to drown out Haman's name so that it cannot be heard. Anything is acceptable: fog horns, tubas, rocks in coffee cans, noisemakers. The Jewish congregation will often write Haman's name in chalk on the bottoms of their shoes.[68] On the Sabbath prior to the Festival of Purim, the Jews observe a "Sabbath of Remembrance" when they read Deut. 25:17-20 and 1 Sam. 15. Families share a meal together and collect money for the poor and needy.[63]

Food for Thought: The Festival of Purim is decreed nowhere else in the Bible except Esther. The question of whether Esther should be included in the Bible was swayed by this fact. The festival could not be justified otherwise. The only two festivals not founded in the Laws of Moses are Purim and Dedication or Hanukkah. Hanukkah originated from the time of the Maccabees.[9] We are almost upon that time. Learn something about the celebration of Hanukkah today (through the Internet, dictionary, books, friends).

October 5
Bible Readings: Malachi

Our Old Testament traditionally ends with the Book of Malachi. We know nothing about the writer. The term "Malachi" means 'my messenger,' which causes many to wonder if the term, which is used nowhere else as a name in the Bible, is actually a title instead of a name. Some authorities, such as Jerome and Calvin, believe that the author of the book is Ezra. We do know that the sins of the people condemned in Malachi were problems also in Ezra and Nehemiah. These include divorce and a general lack of devotion and enthusiasm for the things of God.

Malachi has a number of unique features that separates it from the other prophetic books. Malachi's style of delivery is original. He makes great use of questions and answers to try to get his audience to think. His method is to make a charge against the people. This accusation is followed by a "but you say" expression that proposes an objection on the part of the audience. Finally, Malachi refutes their excuse using precise detail and reasserts his original charge. Examples of this pattern are included in 1:2-5, 1:6-8, 2:13-15. There are seven such cases in all.

A number of points in Malachi's message are rather unique or at least new in the emphasis he gives them. Note 1:11. This verse has frequently been interpreted as a prophecy of the Messianic Age and the universal worship of the Christian church.[37] The future sincere worship of the nations is contrasted with their current insincere worship. Malachi also prophesies of the return of Elijah (4:5-6). The New Testament picks up on this prophecy seeing the ministry of John the Baptist as its fulfillment.

Malachi is concerned with the subject of divorce (2:14-17), a topic not frequently mentioned in the Old Testament. Malachi views divorce as a sin against God and a treacherous act directed at one's spouse. His words anticipate Jesus' teaching about divorce.

Finally, Malachi stresses the fatherhood of God (2:10). If God is our Father, then we are all brothers. If we are all brothers, then let us deal honestly with our fellow men.

Malachi and the Old Testament end with a somber warning, "... else I will come and strike the land with a curse."[1] (Malachi 4:6) The New Testament begins with the birth of the One whose mission was to take away the curse.

Food for Thought: Mother once asked me what I thought happened to the Ark of the Covenant. With all its gold and ornamentation, why hasn't it been found? Read Rev. 11:19 to find the Ark, which is symbolic of God's covenant with His people. Second Maccabees 2:4-8 credits Jeremiah with hiding the Ark on Mt. Sinai in a place known only to God. Will we see it again? Discover for yourselves.

October 6
Bible Readings: Ezra 7:1-28; 8:1-36

One of the big debates about Ezra is whether he returned under Artaxerxes I or II. Most commentaries use Artaxerxes I.[63,25,15] This makes Ezra's trip to Jerusalem 57 years after the first exiles.[25] Chapter 7 opens with a list of Ezra's genealogy. Six names are missing between Azariah and Meraioth.[69] It is not uncommon in long genealogies to skip names of lesser-known members for the sake of time and space.[25] The primary point of the genealogy is to show that Ezra was a direct descendant of Aaron, the first high priest. Ezra was a learned teacher and scribe in the Law of Moses. The passage particularly notes that the hand of the Lord had been upon him and the king had given him all he asked.

Artxerxes gave Ezra a letter declaring that any Israelites in the Persian kingdom may freely return with Ezra to Jerusalem. Additionally, freewill offerings of gold and silver could be raised from the community. The only stipulation for the gold and silver was that it should first be used to purchase sacrifices for the God of Israel. Anything left after that would be used in accordance with the will of God. Any other supplies needed for the Temple may be obtained from the royal treasurer. The royal treasurers were authorized to provide whatever Ezra requested up to 3.75 tons of silver, 600 bushels of wheat, 600 gallons of wine, 600 bushels of olive oil, and unlimited salt! (Now I believe all of us would like to have a generous sponsor like this!) The king also ordered that no taxes would be levied against persons working in the house of God. Ezra was given the authority to set up a justice system in Jerusalem in accordance with the Law of God.

Ezra assembled his entourage by the Ahava Canal where he camped for 3 days making preparations. The first exiles had left from Babylon with Zerubbabel. Ezra would be leaving from Susa and taking a less northerly route. But Ezra is distressed that no Levites have responded to the call to go to Jerusalem. Enlisting Iddo's help, many Levites were recruited. Over 250 agreed to go, all were able to produce written records of their priestly or Levitical lineage.

Ezra prays that God will protect. He had told the king that God's blessings were on those who did His Will. Now it was time to take a step in faith. The trade routes were well known for their raiding parties and bandits. Ezra and his group begin their 4-month journey to Jerusalem. They are carrying 25 tons of silver, 3.75 tons of gold, 3.75 tons of silver articles, 19 pounds of gold articles plus 2 fine bronze articles. They arrive in Jerusalem unharmed in the 5th month of 457 B.C.[1] For three days, they rested, unpacked, and set up camp. On the fourth day, the gold, silver, and sacred articles were counted, weighed, and turned over to the Temple priests. Then burnt offerings were made for the exiles: 12 bulls for all the tribes of Israel, 96 rams, 77 lambs, and 12 goats (a sin offering for each tribe). The royal letters to the satraps and governors concerning treatment of the exiles, Temple restoration, and tax relief for the Levites and priests were delivered. Over 1,755 exiles had completed the journey to Jerusalem with Ezra.

Food for Thought: Ezra is an excellent example of how stepping out in faith can be frightening. If I had been responsible for that much gold and silver, even in a bank vault, I would be terrified, much less on an open road. The "What ifs . . .?" must have been endless. Ezra shows us all that when we follow the Will of God, we will be blessed beyond our expectations. Are you ready to be blessed?

October 7
Bible Readings: Ezra 9-10

Ezra arrived in Jerusalem in 458 B.C. and Nehemiah arrived in 445 B.C. Some interpreters believe the same person wrote the Books of Ezra and Nehemiah. Further, the passage of Nehemiah that presents Ezra reading the Law of Moses to the people (Neh. 7:73b-9:37) is believed by some to better fit between Ezra 8 and Ezra 9.[69] Notice the timeline supports this idea. Ezra 7:9 reports his arrival in Jerusalem on the first day of the fifth month. Neh. 7:73b indicates the Law of Moses was read on the first day of the seventh month. The princes of Jerusalem made their report to Ezra concerning intermarriages on the 20th day of the ninth month. Thus, we can see now why the restored Jewish citizens of Jerusalem suddenly come forward with a confession of sin. Additionally, we are told in Ezra 9:2 that "the leaders and officials have led the way in this unfaithfulness."[1] It is important to realize that the pagan nations mentioned are not literally still organized around Jerusalem but are mentioned here as a reference to those nations identified in the Torah or Law of Moses. Of course, Egyptians were still in existence and probably tribes of Ammonites and Moabites. Basically, any non-Jewish population was included in the pagan nation reference.[69] The emphasis is on maintaining a nation holy unto God and not contaminated with pagan worship.

Ezra enters a period of great mourning upon discovering that many of the Jews, including the priests and Levites, had married spouses from the surrounding pagan nations. You can tell his grief goes beyond normal mourning in that he pulls out hair from his beard and his head -- ouch! He was stunned. Had he brought all these people to Jerusalem just so they could experience the punishment of the Israelite citizens for this great sin? What if his group turned to pagan spouses as well? Would this be the end of the holy remnant of God?

At the evening sacrifice, it was time to meet with God. Ezra fell to his knees before the house of God, too ashamed and disgraced to go into the Temple. The sins of the restored Israelite group were great and numerous. He prayed fervently for God's remembrance and mercy. God had not deserted the survivors during their bondage and exile. But now they had abandoned God's laws -- again! Would God destroy even the few Jews who remained?

A large crowd of Israelites gathered outside the Temple, weeping and mourning for their sins. Shecaniah, a descendant of Elam (the Jew) and member of the first exile group to return to Jerusalem, comes forward with a possible solution: the Israelites would separate themselves from their pagan wives and children. They would put their promise to God in writing and seal it with their tribal symbol. Ezra retreated to one of the priest's quarters to fast and pray. Apparently, God revealed His acceptance of this solution to Ezra for he emerged to call an assembly of the people. Every Israelite male was required to attend or lose his property. They had three days to comply. On the 20th day of the ninth month, they all came together on the town square by the Temple. The covenant was presented and the men sealed it with their unique family seals. Because each case involving the separation of a wife and children had its own individual circumstances, the elders and judges would review each one as presented. Due to the constant rain, the people returned home to await their turn in civil court. Sin has so many consequences. Imagine how these women and children must have felt knowing they were about to be separated from their husbands and homes, not to mention the stigma attached to women and children who were alone. Sin is never a private, personal encounter. It **always** affects others; it's just not always so evident. God's people had sinned, and now many others would be included in the consequences. (Only two men supported by one Levite and one leader opposed the covenant but were outvoted. They obviously complied as the covenant was signed and no further mention is made of the men.) The civil court decisions were completed in three months. The list of those who signed the covenant seems very short for almost 50,000 Israelite males to be represented. Most likely this is only a remnant of the actual list that hasn't survived. One suggested possibility for the civil court sessions is that the Jewish men had taken daughters of wealthy aliens in the area in order to overcome their poverty status in the ruins of Jerusalem. If this was the case, separation of these wives and their wealth could have been a very delicate task.[69] Besides, cases involving the families of nobles from surrounding nations could prove to be political hotbeds. If not handled correctly, war could ensue.

Food for Thought: The key component of a marriage blessed by God is that the husband and wife share their belief in God. The Apostle Paul warned us, "Do not be yoked together with unbelievers. For what do righteousness and wickedness have in common?"[1] (2 Cor. 6:14) If you want a marriage made in Heaven, then you need to find a spouse who believes in God. Where do you find this person? In the house of God, of course, and in doing the Lord's work. Be about your Father's business and blessings will be yours.

Verse of the Week: **Nehemiah 8:10c** "...Do not grieve, for the joy of the LORD is your strength."

October 8
Bible Readings: Nehemiah 1-3

Nehemiah was a Jew who had become a trusted servant to King Artaxerxes I. As cupbearer, Nehemiah was responsible for selecting the best wine for the meal and for tasting it to assure it wasn't poisoned! In this respect, he was accustomed to placing himself in great danger. He also had the opportunity to witness the administrative practices, negotiating strategies, and organizational skills of the king of the largest empire in the world. I believe this is a classic example of how God uses all our situations in life, both large and small, to prepare us for carrying out His Will. But the bottom line to being used in God's plan is our willingness to serve. There is a famous post-Civil War line by General William Tecumseh Sherman that states, "If nominated, I will not run! If elected, I will not serve!" Do we ever take that stance with God? Nehemiah was both prepared and willing, not just once but twice. His first call came in 445 B.C. with the mission to rebuild Jerusalem's wall and serve as governor. His second mission in 433 B.C. was to resume service as governor and institute spiritual reforms.[63] This two-step process is our key to bringing others into the spiritual light of God's Will. Without the protective wall of Jerusalem, the Jews had no security, peace, or courage. Until this uppermost need was met, nothing else could be addressed. When security was restored, Nehemiah and Ezra could turn their time and efforts to leading the people back into the Will of God -- a new secure and receptive people. When we go to minister to others, their physical needs must be met before they can be receptive to spiritual food. Psychologists have long known that the primary concerns of all human beings are first, body needs; second, security; third, social; fourth, personality/self-actualization; fifth, emotional/mental; and finally, spiritual.

Nehemiah received word from a "brother" in late November or early December that the wall of Jerusalem had still not been repaired. In this first verse, the implication is that Hanani is simply a fellow Jew called brother because of the ethnic relationship. However, in 7:2 one gets the sense that Hanani may have been Nehemiah's actual brother. My main premise for this line of thinking is that Nehemiah never refers to anyone else by this term of endearment, even though many Jewish "brothers" surround him.

Nehemiah is in the winter palace of Susa when Hanani arrives with other Jews. The story indicates this trip was not for the purpose of soliciting Nehemiah's help but rather more of a trip for visiting old friends and relatives. In catching up on the news from Judah, Nehemiah is distressed to learn that the city is in trouble because it has no wall for protection from its enemies. It is disgraced by the exposure of its 'nakedness' or vulnerability. Nehemiah mourned, fasted, and prayed before God. Nehemiah's prayer begins with confession of sin then moves to reminding God of His promises (Deut. 30:1-5) and concluded with asking God's blessings on him as he sought to do God's Will. This is a model format for any prayer: confess and repent, remind God of the promises of His word, request blessings as you do God's Will. In order to pray effectively we need to humble ourselves to repentance, have God's word stored in our hearts for ready access, and seek God's blessings on the mission we are assigned.

Nehemiah mourns and prays for a long time because it is the month of Nisan, or March-April, before Artaxerxes asks about his countenance. Now Artaxerxes has a history of distaste for walled or fortified cities. His experiences with rebellion from these cities had established a steadfast aversion to aiding any rebuilding of city walls. For ten years, he had refused to allow Jerusalem's wall to be rebuilt. Nehemiah had four months of prayerful thought about his presentation of the problem and solution.[63] Nehemiah was careful to address the king respectfully and proceed with explaining his sadness in a manner that would be acceptable to Artaxerxes. Persian kings had a great respect for their dead ancestors and for their tombs. Many of these elaborate tombs and sepulchers are still well preserved today. Therefore, Nehemiah explains his sadness as being caused by the lack of a protective wall around the city where the tombs of his ancestors are located. (Tombs of the house of David were in the old city of David section of Jerusalem.) Artaxerxes was in an especially good mood for a banquet was in progress. When Nehemiah asked to go back to Judah to rebuild the wall, the king only asked how long he would be gone. We are not told how long Nehemiah reported, but it would take several months just to travel to and from Jerusalem. It took a little less than two months to rebuild the wall. However, we find that Nehemiah was gone 12 years (5:14). If you read 2:1-8 carefully, you have noticed that Nehemiah never mentions Jerusalem by name, only that he wants to go to a city in Judah (most all Jews living in the old land of Babylon were from Judah). Nehemiah takes advantage of the king's benevolence by asking for letters for safe passage, for timber to be issued from the king's forest for the wall and for his dwelling. The king puts his final stamp of approval on Nehemiah's mission by making him governor of Judah (5:14) and sending him off with an army/cavalry escort. We are never told just how or when the king discovered Nehemiah was going to Jerusalem. I have to wonder if he felt deceived, or had a decade of time made him complacent toward the prospect of a rebuilt wall around Jerusalem, or possibly his trust and respect for Nehemiah made all the difference. (Artaxerxes was the step-son of Esther the Jew.)

This official entourage from the King of Persia obviously upset Jerusalem's enemies: Sanballat from Beth

Horon, Samaria[5] and Tobiah the Ammonite. By this time in history, there were no organized Ammonite tribes left. The few survivors had integrated into other nations.[5] After a 3-day rest, and surely some interior inspection, Nehemiah takes a few men and does a nighttime reconnaissance. His mission must be kept secret until the strategic details of his plan are completed. First, he must know where and to what extent the wall was damaged. The entire wall had not been pulled down, primarily the portion hardest to reconstruct -- the mountainsides that overlooked valleys below. Nehemiah left by the Valley Gate on the southwest side of Jerusalem, the least populated side. (Jerusalem at this time looks like the outline of South America. The location of the Amazon River is about where the old southern city of David wall met the newer Solomon expansion.) He travels south past the Dung Gate and starts up the eastern side to the Fountain Gate. At this point, the rubble is so bad Nehemiah has to dismount and walk. He walked to the southeast end of the newer Solomon wall where it connected to the older city of David wall that had been destroyed. Solomon's expanded wall around the northeast side of Jerusalem still had large sections intact.[25] Retracing his steps, he and his men silently reentered the city.[63] It was time to form a plan.

The time had arrived for Nehemiah to announce his plan and gain the support of the people. Nehemiah calls upon the Jews' national pride and dedication to God's Will to rally support for rebuilding the wall. To complicate matters we now see another enemy has joined in the opposition -- Geshem of the nomadic Arab tribes to the south and east of Judah.[63] The enemies did not dare make an open attack on Jerusalem because Nehemiah had been sent with the king's blessing on this mission. Therefore, they hurl insults and mockery as psychological warfare. Nehemiah assigned each family to rebuild the portion of the wall nearest to their dwelling. Solomon had extended Jerusalem's wall to almost double the size of the original city of David. David's (old Jebusite) wall was built on the terraced slopes of the Kidron Valley mountainside on the southeast side of Jerusalem.[63] (One of my Bibles has a map in the back outlining Nehemiah's wall.[1]) The old city wall (of David's time) had been totally destroyed by pushing the stones off down the hills. The Solomon extension primarily housed governmental buildings, community squares for public meetings, the priests' dwellings in Ophel, and the palace. (You can imagine the city as a squared off figure 8 in Solomon's time. Hezekiah added the large northwest section to the wall.) The southern area of Jerusalem was the city of David and primarily the residential area of old Jerusalem. Hezekiah's enormous expansion of the wall on the northwest side of the city had been left standing, although it had sustained damages and breaches on the north side. Thus, all the southern outside wall was gone, starting at the southwest Valley Gate around the southern tip where the Valley of Hinnom met the Kidron Valley northward to the middle of the eastern side of Jerusalem. The northeastern and north portions of the wall were largely intact but damaged and breached in several places. The west side of the wall was in good shape down to the point of the Valley Gate. (Reviewing the Aug. 28th Lesson may help.) Nehemiah was a man on a mission. He had walls to build: first physical, then spiritual. Even though the workers were few, each had his assigned duty and the completed project was dependent on all sacrificing and serving diligently. Isn't this a picture of our work for the kingdom of God? It takes all of us, each dutifully working and sacrificing, to carry out God's work on earth. No one is listed as a construction expert or engineer. They had a master plan; they had their assignment, now it was up to them to complete the work.

Food for Thought: What has God assigned you to do? Have you put your 'neck to the yoke' or your 'shoulder to the wheel?' God's master plan includes you. Notice in 3:5 that the nobles of Tekoa (the birthplace of Amos 10 miles south of Jerusalem[5]) refused to work. God's plan was carried out, but they missed the reward.

October 9
Bible Readings: Nehemiah 4-6

Sanballat and Tobiah begin to step up their verbal assaults. Nehemiah responds with prayer. He asks God to turn their insults back on them. In the meantime, more enemies arrive. Jerusalem is under verbal attack from Sanballat and the Samaritans to the north, Tobiah representing the Ammonites' old territory to the northeast,

Geshem and the Arabians to the south and southeast, and the Ashdodites from Philistia in the west. We are reminded that Jerusalem is surrounded by evil, hostile nations. The attacks are still verbal because they don't dare risk a major physical assault on the King of Persia's governor. Work on the wall was progressing. The wall was half way up. Archaeologists have excavated portions of this wall. It was roughly constructed by non-craftsmen but was eight feet thick![63]

The building process is slowing down. The workers are exhausted and now the stones had to be hoisted to the top of the wall. Constant ridicule and chiding from the enemies was taking its toll on their morale. Men from throughout Judah have been commuting to Jerusalem daily to participate in the work. Some of those living near the enemy nations report the enemies' plan to attack with multiple raiding parties. Not enough to be deemed a full-scale revolt against the King of Persia, just enough to weaken, damage, and delay the work. Isn't this just like the devil to try to wear down God's workers and frustrate and confuse the work? Nehemiah posts 24-hour guards. Stationed behind every low spot in the wall and fully armed, those on guard duty protected the workers. Nehemiah, himself, wore his sword continually. He kept a trumpeter with him to sound a call to arms should any trouble occur along the wall. The commuters now had to stay inside the wall at night for protection. The work was taking its toll. Families were starving because crops were abandoned. Some families had even sold their children as slaves and mortgaged their land for food. Were the enemies going to take over after all? No, it's not the enemies but the Jewish officials who are oppressing their own people! Nehemiah is appalled. He quickly calls the officials together, properly chastises them, and demands reparation. This is followed by an oath to carry out their promises of repayment.

Neh. 5:14 jumps to the end of Nehemiah's story. We feel as if we have suddenly discovered we were merely listeners to a history of Nehemiah's actions in Jerusalem rather than observers. Nehemiah, the storyteller, states that in his 12 years as governor, he never demanded his rights to food allotments from the people. In fact, he regularly fed 150 Jews and officials at his table with limited quantities of food.

In chapter 6 we are returned to where we left off building the wall. The southeastern portion of the wall has been reconstructed on the crest of the hill or mount rather than on the terraced slopes. With a smaller population, the extra space wasn't needed and building along the crest was easier on the workers. Meanwhile, Sanballat and Geshem are up to no good. They devise a scheme to trap Nehemiah so they can kill him. They invite Nehemiah to a small village 30 miles away for a meeting.[63] (Some meeting -- your body meets our sword!) God provided Nehemiah with the discernment to realize it was a trap and he declined the invitation, but Sanballat was persistent. He sent four more invitations and finally, with the last one, he sent an open letter for the people accusing Nehemiah of treachery. Sanballat claims Nehemiah is planning a revolt and then will declare himself king! Nehemiah coolly and slickly calls Sanballat a liar and then proceeds to ask God to strengthen his own hands. If all this weren't enough, one of the Jews (Shemaiah, a Levite musician) tries to trap Nehemiah by enticing him with fear to hide out in the Temple. Nehemiah knew that only priests could enter the Temple and therefore, this man was trying to discredit him through sin (and a sentence of death - Num. 18:7). Don't evil beings often use fear to draw us into sin? Why did one of Nehemiah's own become a traitor? Well, Tobiah the Ammonite had intermarried his family with several of the noble families of Judah. They had been sending letters among the families, allowing Tobiah to know everything that went on in Jerusalem! Moreover, these Jewish nobles had tried to influence Nehemiah's opinion of Tobiah. (Shecaniah was Tobiah's father-in-law and may be the same person who is listed as a priest under Zerubbabel[5] (12:1).) Again, Nehemiah asks God to reward Sanballat and Tobiah with what their actions deserve. On the 25th of the 6th month (late August[5]) the wall was completed, just 52 days after the reconstruction began!

Food for Thought: Jesus tells us in Matt. 10:16, "I am sending you out like sheep among wolves. Therefore be as shrewd as snakes and as innocent as doves."[1] I think this appropriately describes Nehemiah. Does it describe you and me?

October 10
Bible Readings: Nehemiah 7 and 11-12:26

With the wall complete, Nehemiah appoints his brother Hanani and Zerubbabel's son Hananiah as co-mayors of Jerusalem because they were men of integrity who worshipped God. They were charged to maintain guards at the city gates from mid-morning until dark. After dark, the Jerusalem neighborhood watch went into action.

The population of the city was so small compared to the land within the wall that the citizens had difficulty performing all the duties. Nehemiah had the citizens to register by families. During that time, he found the original registration of those first exiles to return under Zerubbabel. Only a few families were unable to produce their family records. The determination of their qualifications for the priestly functions was decided by casting the Urim and Thummim by the High Priest (See Ex. 28:30). The completed census included work animals, too.

Jewish Males	42,360	Horses	736
Servants	7,337	Mules	245
Temple Singers	245	Camels	435
		Donkeys	6,720
Total Registered People	49,942	Work Animals	8,136

The following wealth was given to the treasury of the Temple, beyond the items returned by Cyrus.

	Gold	Silver	Bowls	Garments for Priests
Governor	19 lbs		50	530
Heads of Families	375 lbs	2,667 lbs		
People	375 lbs	2,500 lbs		67
TOTALS	769 lbs	5,167 lbs	50	597

The value of the precious metals based on Sept. 20, 2002 exchange rates is shown below.
Gold = $3,963,118   Silver = $381,945

The total Jewish males donated $103 each to the Temple treasury. Many of today's church members give less than this amount. For people who had spent 90 years trying to rebuild their city and property from ruins, this was a large, sacrificial donation. Remember some of them had mortgaged farms and sold their children as slaves to survive during these years. Even if their mortgages were canceled, they were still without wealth. Also, any male children would have been counted in each family. Thus, the sum from a single family could have been quite large. (Note the census list is almost identical to Ezra 2 and 1 Esdras (Apocrypha).) Keil and Delitzsch give the following comparison table (p. 45).[25]

	According to Ezra	According to Nehemiah	According to 1 Esdras
Men of Israel....................	24,144	25,406	26,390
Priests...............................	4,289	4,289	2,388
Levites..............................	341	360	341
Nethinim/servants of Solomon	392	392	372
Those with no proof of origin	652	642	652
TOTALS	29,818	31,089	30,143

The differences are attributed to clerical errors.[25]

In order for a city the size of Jerusalem to be fully functional, more citizens were needed. Nehemiah cast lots to determine which 10% of the families of the countryside would move to town. You might call this a 'tithe' of the people. Those who moved were honored for their sacrifice. (A list is given in Neh. 11.)

Food for Thought: The Book of Nehemiah is commonly called the "Leadership Manual" of the Bible. Anyone can be a godly leader if (s)he is dedicated to doing God's Will. Maybe God is calling you to lead in Sunday School, worship services, family ministry, youth ministry, senior adult ministry, care groups, Bible study, or any number of other positions. Pray about how you may serve.

October 11
Bible Readings: Nehemiah 8-10

In the seventh month, the people assembled in the public square. This was not a random assembling without an intended purpose. This was a special month for the Jews -- and a special day. The 1st day of the month began with the Feast of Trumpets. During this month, the Feast of the Tabernacles (Booths) was celebrated because the Jews discovered that God's law called for a 7-day festival to commemorate the first exodus. This discovery came about when the assembled people requested Ezra to read the book of the law to them. For two days he read the Torah from dawn to noon. For two days the people **stood** reverently listening to God's laws. They lifted their hands to God shouting, "Amen! Amen!" which is a double affirmation of their request, prayer, or covenant with God.[5] "The God of Amen" was the original meaning of the Hebrew word for Amen.[5] Amen simply means 'truth.' When you close a prayer with "Amen" you are taking an oath before God that your words and thoughts were truthful. Thus, "Amen! Amen!" is a double confirmation that truth is your bond and you will not forget your covenant with God. (Today's world thinks the Old Testament is too boring to listen to even a few verses. Can you imagine how hungry the Jews were for the word of God to stand 6 hours two days in a row listening intently to the Laws of Moses being read? Oh, if only the world hungered that much for God today. But then, I think they do. They just don't know where or how to find God. Why don't you show them the way?)

Then the Jews bowed with their faces all the way to the ground. Have you ever been humbled to the point of being prostrate before God? Times like these are usually the result of great, unbearable anguish and pain of the soul. Romans 8:26 tells us, "In the same way, the Spirit helps us in our weakness. We do not know what we ought to pray, but the Spirit himself intercedes for us with groans that words cannot express."[1] If you have ever been prostrated before God from the pain of life, then you fully understand this verse. Nehemiah saw the great grief of the people over their sin. He then reminds them that this is a great day set aside for God -- a day of rejoicing and wiping away the tears. What day was this? It was Rosh Hashanah, the Jewish New Year. God declared every 7th day of the week as a day of rest, every 7th month was a month of sacred assembly and rest, and every 7th year the ground was to lie fallow. The trumpets were to be sounded calling all God's people to rest in Him. On the 10th day of the 7th month, the High Priest would make his annual sprinkling of the blood sacrifice in the Holy of Holies as atonement for the sins of the nation.[9] After this, he would lay his hands on a goat and send it into the wilderness -- the scapegoat. This was a vivid picture for all the people to see God's provision for taking away of sins through the blood of the sacrifice and the transfer of guilt to the scapegoat. The Day of Atonement is Yom Kippur.[5] Rosh Hashanah may be viewed as the Day of Judgment and Yom Kippur as the Day of Sentencing. As New Testament Christians, we know we face the Day of Judgment, but on the Day of Sentencing we will be found 'not guilty' for our sins have been washed away by the blood of Jesus Christ. The Jews set aside the 7th month for rest and reflection on their relationship and covenant with God. The harvest was done, the time of judgment was at hand, and the atonement for sin was to be celebrated. We know that "on that day" Jesus will harvest and judge. I'm "not guilty." How about you?

Food for Thought: The Jews, once again, renewed their covenant with God. They promised to bring the first portion of all their bounty to God. Never again would they neglect the house of God. We are just like the Jews. We make promises to God, we break them, and then we renew our promises. Only by keeping our eyes and hearts on God can we keep our promises to Him and abide by His laws. The devil will try mightily to dissuade us. Keep the faith. God rewards obedience.

October 12
Bible Readings: Nehemiah 12:27-13:31

Nehemiah returned to Susa in 432 B.C. to resume his duties as cupbearer for King Artaxerxes. His 12-year term as governor was completed. While he was gone, Eliashib, the High Priest, allowed Tobiah to use one of the Temple storerooms. This action was wrong for several reasons: (1) Foremost is that only the tithes and equipment consecrated to God were to be stored in these rooms, (2) Tobiah's presence desecrated the Temple because Gentiles were not allowed, and (3) Tobiah was the archenemy of Jerusalem and Nehemiah. [Verse 4 of chapter 13 implies that Tobiah may have been related to Eliashib, probably because of his marriage to the daughter of Shecaniah (also a priest). Also, Neh. 6:18 identifies another of Tobiah's sons Jehohanan as married to the daughter of Meshullam, son of Berekiah, a priest (3:28-30).] The news of this sin eventually reached Nehemiah in Susa. Nehemiah was incensed by this evil and requested the king allow him to return. As soon as he got back to Jerusalem, Nehemiah purged the Temple. We have a foreshadowing of Jesus purging the Temple 460 years later.

In addition to the evil perpetrated by the priest, Nehemiah discovers the people had also violated their covenant with God. The people had not donated as promised to the Levites and they were not keeping the Sabbath holy. Because trade goods were hauled into Jerusalem from the countryside, returning the sanctity of the Sabbath was an easy problem to solve -- the city gates would remain closed on the Sabbath. We are not told how Nehemiah solved the offering problem, but as governor he could merely demand the people honor their covenant. To make matters worse, though, some of the Jewish men had married foreign wives. Again, these foreign wives and children had to be separated from the Jews. Wonder where Ezra was during all this? His allowance of any of these violations of the covenant is unfathomable. In fact, things had gotten so bad that one of Eliashib's (High Priest) grandsons had married Sanballat's daughter! Nehemiah had to conquer his enemies a second time.

There were so many economic, spiritual, and enemy problems at the time the Jerusalem wall was reconstructed that it had never been officially dedicated. Now with the renewed cleansing of the Temple and the people, a dedication celebration seemed the right activity to unite the citizens. For the celebration, Nehemiah divided the leaders and singers into two groups. They stood on top of the wall (Remember, it was eight feet wide!) and Ezra led one group in a southerly direction before turning northeast while Nehemiah led the other group northwest. The two groups started just north of the Dung Gate. They played handheld musical instruments and sang praises to God. The two groups met in front of the Temple. At the Gate of the Guard, they descended and entered the Temple complex. All that day, the people sang, praised God, and offered sacrifices. People from all over Judah brought their tithes and offerings into the storerooms of the house of God. The Book of Moses was read aloud and the curse on the Ammonites and Moabites was discovered. From that day forward, all people of foreign descent were excluded from the people of Israel, not just the Ammonites and Moabites. This policy of exclusivity will develop into one of elitism.

Food for Thought: Isn't it wonderful to own a copy of the Bible? Just think about these ancient Jewish people. Even the priests had to share the one fragile papyrus copy they had. Rarely did Temples have multiple copies. The copying of the Torah was very time intensive. Synagogues still have hand-copied texts in gold protective cases. Years are required to produce a copy. Each page must be perfect. No corrections are allowed. Praise God that we have His precious gift of Jesus who can forever erase our imperfections!

NOTE: As you may know, our section of the Gulf Coast is frequently evacuated for hurricanes. While writing this in 2002, we were under evacuation status, but we didn't leave town. I knew God didn't intend to send a Category 4 hurricane our way. I told my husband that God would not see us through telling the story of the Old Testament and then let the devil rob us of the witness of the gift of Jesus! I truly believe with all my heart that at the time the hurricane went from Cat 2 to Cat 4 was the time the devil tried to change the outcomes. I sat down and prayed that the storm would return to a Cat 2 before it came on land. We went to bed at midnight on Wednesday night and I woke up 8 hours later to my husband saying, "Guess what! The hurricane became a Cat 2 before it hit land!" I don't know why he was surprised!

October 13
Bible Readings: 1 Chronicles 1-2:55, 3:10-4:23

The Chronicles serve an important purpose: the genealogical tracking of the Hebrew tribes that will ultimately prove that Jesus is a descendant of David and the fulfillment of prophecy. Originally the information was contained in only one book, but at the time the Septuagint was developed, Chronicles was divided into two books.[69] The genealogy lists given are not part of one long continuous record but rather are a grouping of short family or tribal records. In some cases, only those individuals who played key roles in Jewish history or were part of the lineage of David are mentioned. Other lists target specific tribes, i.e., Levi, for the purpose of maintaining a pure high priest lineage.[25]

Many scholars believe the same author who wrote Ezra and Nehemiah also wrote the Chronicles. Some believe Ezra is that author, but others do not. Regardless, the Chronicles were written somewhere between 400 B.C. and 333 B.C. Japheth had 14 grandsons, Ham had 30, and Shem had 26. Totaled, there are 70 male descendants of Noah responsible for the 70 nations of the earth.[69]

First Chronicles begins with a list of mankind from Adam to Noah. Notice only those who are ancestors of the Hebrews are mentioned. For example, Cain and Abel are not mentioned, only Seth. The source for chapter 1 is Genesis. Noah's descendants represent the geographical regions of civilization at the time: Japhethites located in Europe and Asia Minor, Hamites located in Africa and Arabia, and Shemites located in Palestine and Mesopotamia. When the generalized list reaches Abraham, though, it branches out to cover both of Abraham's children, even including Abraham's concubine wife's descendants. Notice Isaac is listed first although he was the younger son. Isaac was the one with the birthright, though. Interestingly, this order of listing doesn't hold true for Isaac's children. Esau was the oldest but sold his birthright to Jacob (Israel). But Esau is given the first listing in this genealogical list. Also, the extensive record given testifies to the historical part played by the Edomites (Gen. 36). The dynasty of the Herodians would come from Edom. Herod Antipas would behead John the Baptist and ridicule and mock Jesus.

Chapter 2 lists the sons of Israel by those of each wife with the exception of Dan who suddenly appears before Rachel's children. Why are Bilhah's two sons split with Rachel's sons interjected between them? The Mesianic Jews believe the antichrist will come from the tribe of Dan. This is based on his "blessing" from Israel that he would be a serpent who causes mankind to stumble (Gen. 49:16-18), and that the tribe of Dan is omitted from the 144,000 sealed servants of God (Rev. 7:4-8). His prominence in future history may account for this placement. Of course, the chronicler wouldn't know how the future was to unfold except through the prophets. Another possible reason for the aberration in listing is that at the time of Rachel's barrenness, she had wanted the son of Bilhah to be counted as her own (Gen. 30:3-6). If this were the case, then Dan would be counted as Rachel's eldest.[25]

The sons of Tamar and Judah are given prominent genealogical listing. Of course, Jesse, as father of David in the lineage of Jesus, is Tamar's descendant. David is listed as the seventh son of Jesse although 1 Sam. 16:6-11 states Jesse had 8 sons. It is possible that Elihu and Eliah are actually the same person but was translated differently (See 1 Chron. 27:18). In this listing, we have a family tree of David's sisters and nephews, realizing their key roles in the history of David's reign as king.

The prayer of Jabez has been given much attention (1 Chron. 4:10). Jabez's birth had been painful and, as is the case for ancient names, he was named according to the situation. Jabez means pain. We are told he is more honorable than his brothers, although we don't know if his brothers were honorable or scoundrels. Jewish names were to depict one's character. As such, we assume Jabez is anticipating a painful existence. The prayer is both primitive and immature. Jabez asks only for selfish, materialistic blessings. Primitive religious thought was that God's blessings on mankind were demonstrated in wealth and abundance (land, children, animals, food, clothes). In ancient times God granted these requests anticipating the maturity in spirit that would evolve. Hundreds of years after Jabez's prayer, we meet Jesus, the most unselfish, non-materialistic man who ever lived. Jabez's prayer in today's Christian world is totally unacceptable. Jesus taught us to forego wealth and comfort in order to bring others to know Him. Jesus said, "If anyone would come after me, he must deny himself and take up his cross and follow me."[1] (Mark 8:34) This does not mean that Christians can't have wealth and health. It does mean that following Jesus is our most important mission in life even if it is in poverty and pain. Jesus is our Living Water, Bread of Life, Judge, Savior, and Brother. Our Christian inheritance is eternal life in an eternal land with no sadness or pain.

Food for Thought: Today's version of Jabez's prayer should read something like, "Oh, that You would bless me by increasing my opportunities to serve You! Let Your Hand protect and guide me as I do Your Will and carry the Good News of Jesus Christ to as many people as possible."

October 14
Bible Readings: 1 Chronicles 4:24-5:9; 5:11-17; 6:1-9:34

The descendants of the tribe of Simeon are listed even though Judah had absorbed the tribe of Simeon by the time of the Chronicles. According to one commentary, the Simeon who recognized the young Jesus as the Messiah was likely a descendant of the tribe of Simeon (Luke 2:25-35).[69] Although possible, there are no available records to prove it.

The tribe of Levi has an extensive genealogy as would be expected of a purified, consecrated tribe who served God. The Kohathites represented the priestly lineage that became the gatekeepers of the Temple. The Gershomites were the treasurers and part of the musicians. The Merarites were the smallest of the three clans of Levi. They also served as musicians in the Temple. At the time of the wilderness Tabernacle, the Merarites were assigned to carry the supporting framework, posts, crossbars, bases, ropes, and tent pegs. This clan has always been dependable support personnel, proving there is a place for everyone in God's master plan. The sons of Aaron, the High Priest, are listed separately.

Benjamin's importance to Israelite history is obvious in the detailed genealogy of Saul. The list of Naphtali's descendants comes from Gen. 46:24. Ephraim's list covers the half-tribe on each side of the Jordan River. There are some statements here that are introduced for the first time, specifically in verses 21-24 of chapter 7. These verses are very controversial due to inability by scholars to determine if and when these accounts occurred. The genealogy of Asher is more detailed than in any other place in the Bible. Many of the names are given nowhere else. Apparently, the chronicler used ancient family records.

Chapter 9 is devoted to the exiles restored to Jerusalem. A general summary of the heads of families from Judah and Benjamin is given. Much more information is given concerning the Levites who returned. Some insight is afforded by the description of gatekeeper assignments and rotation, as well as the assignments for preparation of the cereal, drink, and incense offerings. This passage culminates with a note on the job description of the musicians.

Food for Thought: Congratulations! You've made it to the end of the Old Testament! For many of you, this will be the first time you have read the Old Testament in its entirety. But, the Good News is yet to come! Praise God for the highway of history that led mankind to the gateway of Jesus.

> **Verses of the Week: John 1:1-4** "In the beginning was the Word, and the Word was with God, and the Word was God. He was with God in the beginning. Through him all things were made; without him nothing was made that has been made. In him was life, and that life was the light of men."

Intertestamental Period

October 15
Historical Readings to cover this Period: The Greeks

Nehemiah's wall was dedicated about 425 B.C. We know very little about the history of the Jews for the next 75 years, but we do know that a monarch named Philip II was building an empire to the west composed of the coastlands of the Mediterranean Sea. Every year his boundaries moved further inland. The empire was called Macedonia. Pella was its capital. The Persians had been a pain to Macedonian growth throughout the years of Artaxerxes III. Philip II wanted revenge. His goal was to conquer the Persian Empire! Upon Philip's assassination in 336 B.C., his twenty-year old son Alexander, who set about making his father's dream come true, inherited his throne. Even though Alexander's army contained only 35,000 men, they were well trained and had extremely capable generals. Being a coastal empire, Macedonia had a navy of 180 ships and 38,000 men. Alexander led his troops into battle. With only two-thirds the fighting force of the Persians, Alexander conquered area after area. In 334 B.C., the only Persian army in Asia Minor met Alexander at the Granicus River. The Macedonians soon outsmarted the Persians and all Asia Minor was theirs for the taking. By fall of 333 B.C., a young Darius III met a now experienced Alexander at Issus, the virtual gateway to all Persia. Darius fled after taking heavy losses. Soon his family was captured along with a huge sum of cash. Alexander now had the one missing ingredient he had needed to insure success -- money. In a short 7 months, Alexander manages to conquer the island of Tyre, but the people of Tyre are massacred. Alexander moved on down the coast to conquer Gaza and at Gaugamela, he met Darius again. With only half as many troops, Alexander manages to outmaneuver the Persians a second time. Escaping the battle, Darius is assassinated by one of his own men. Alexander has become King of Persia. By 326 B.C., his eastern frontier is the Indus River of India. His vast empire only lasts until 323 B.C. when Alexander the Great dies. With no living heir to take the throne, the Macedonian/Greek Empire becomes the prize of the strongest.[7]

Alexander had been educated in Greece by some of the foremost scientists, mathematicians, and philosophers in the world. When he came to power, he spread this Greek culture throughout his empire. Great cities were developed throughout the empire as centers of culture. The best known was Alexandria, Egypt. Other cities included Tarsus, Rhodes, Cos, Athens, Samos, and Cyprus. Men such as Epicurus, Zeno, Eratosthenes, Copernicus, Aristarchus, Heracleides, Herophilus, and Euclid were scattered through the empire creating the great theories and practical application of mathematics, physics, astronomy, anatomy, and philosophy. Physical competition was instituted and great gymnasiums were built. Additionally, the value of the arts, theater, and music were also appreciated and encouraged. Alexander managed to spread Greek culture (Hellenism) from west to east. Travel was no longer limited to the borders but was actually encouraged. More goods were both imported and exported with the advantage of a singular monetary system. Everyone sought the Greek way of life. The homes of the wealthy had baths, courtyards, great rooms, banquet halls, and two stories with an additional basement. Alexander was young, athletic, very handsome, intelligent, and a charismatic, capable leader. His subjects rushed to emulate his culture and society.[7]

Upon Alexander's death from unknown causes, the Macedonian-Persian empire was caught in a power struggle among the army's four generals. The two weaker generals were Cassandra who got Greece and Lysimachus who got Anatolia. By far the two strongest and most noteworthy were Seleucus and Ptolemy. Ultimately, Ptolemy got Egypt and the northern African countries and Seleucus got Syria and the area north of Palestine. Palestine was between the two and became the 'land of struggle' for preeminence. Fighting was almost continuous as each general (now ruler) conquered and then lost the territory of Palestine. Each ruler sought to gain the sympathies of the Jews. The dynasty of the Ptolemies was responsible for the Torah (Hebrew) being translated into the Septuagint (Greek). As a result, many more people were able to read God's laws and promises. On the other hand, the Ptolemies greatly taxed the people to support their excesses. The famous Cleopatra was the last of this dynasty. The Seleucids, too, were autocrats greatly Hellenizing their land. Under their rule, the Jews had citizenship and all the rights accorded the Macedonians living in the area. Altogether, the Greek empire had provided valuable avenues for the spreading of the gospel when Jesus came.

- There was one primary language and all who conducted business could read, write, and speak the language. Now there was a translation of the Old Testament that all could read.
- The concept of traveling freely across thousands of miles without detention was planted.
- The philosophy that there is a better eternal world yet to come was introduced.
- Travel was greatly improved, both by land and by sea.

The greatest negative impact of Greek culture has to be the mindset that all things could be explained through science and mathematics. Thus, a movement was sparked to explain and recreate creation without the need for God.

Food for Thought: Charles H. Gabriel wrote this famous song pleading for the gospel to be carried to all countries. It is based on Acts 16:9 where Paul receives his call to the mission field of Macedonia. I couldn't help but sing this song as I wrote of the rise and fall of the Macedonian Empire.

> "We have heard the Macedonian call today,
> 'Send the light! Send the light!'
> And a golden off'ring at the cross we lay,
> Send the light! Send the light!
> Send the light! The blessed gospel light;
> Let it shine from shore to shore!
> Send the light! The blessed gospel light;
> Let it shine forevermore."[44]

October 16
Historical Readings to cover this Period: The Maccabees

In 198 B.C., Antiochus III (a Seleucid) took possession of Palestine as a result of conquering the Ptolemies. The Seleucids initiated a state religion and increasingly sought worship for themselves as deities. Of course, orthodox Jews would never agree. Those Jews who had come to love and revere 'all things Greek' would compromise, resulting in dissension within the Jewish people.[7] By the time Antiochus IV came to power, the Jews were experiencing great persecution. Realizing the power of the Jews' belief in a single God who ruled the universe, Antiochus IV (royal name of Epiphanes) decided that elimination of the Jewish faith would halt all opposition to his own deification.[5] The atrocities against the Jews have been discussed in earlier lessons.

The office of high priest was now a political contest of bribery and lies. Joshua, a brother of Onias III who was an orthodox Jew, replaced Onias III as high priest. Joshua accomplished this promotion by promising a huge bribe to Antiochus IV. Joshua then changed his name to the Greek name of Jason to show his loyalty. Jason stole money from the Temple to pay the bribe, supported the building of a gymnasium for nude athletic competition, and three years later, brought war to Jerusalem by trying to regain his position after Menelaus offered Antiochus IV an even larger bribe! The orthodox Jews banned together, calling themselves Hasidim (pious).[7]

In the small town of Modin, west of Jerusalem, a priest named Mattathias killed a Jew who was about to perform a pagan sacrifice by royal decree. Mattathais and his family fled to the mountains as fugitives. Shortly thereafter, he died leaving his third son Judas "the Maccabee" (the hammer) as leader. He led a bloody, fierce revolt against Antiochus's forces known as the Maccabean rebellion. On the 25th of the 9th month on the Jewish calendar (December) 165 B.C., Judas marched into Jerusalem and cleansed the Temple of all the pagan defilement from Zeus worship. This date has been celebrated among Jews as the Rededication or Lights or Hanukkah festival.[7] (NOTE: From the Babylonian exile until the Macedonian Empire, the calendar in usage by the Jews changed. Both the Babylonians and Macedonians had their own unique calendar system that was extremely accurate for their time periods.[5] As a result, you will have difficulty relating months and years from the Apocrypha or other ancient writings to today's translation. I suggest accepting the origin and relationship of events during this time without trying to explain date discrepancies.) Judas ruled as a general of the army until he died in 161 B.C. Then his brother Jonathan took over until 143 B.C. Upon his death, Palestine's leadership went to Simon, Jonathan's son. Simon was able to secure independence of Palestine from Syrian control. The Jews gave Simon and his descendants permanent authority as high priests. Simon's family's rule was known as the Hasmonean dynasty. Simon conquered several surrounding towns increasing the size of his territory. One of these was the harbor town of Joppa. Simon and two of his sons were murdered, leaving his third son John Hyracanus as high priest. Hellenism itself disappeared, but its principles and philosophies continued in a group called the Sadducees. This group believed all things could be explained logically and scientifically; therefore, they did not believe in resurrection. The orthodox Hasidim group also disappeared leaving their views intact with a newly organized group of Temple scribes known as the Pharisees. With roots traced back to the orthodox Jews, Pharisees saw themselves as "more pious" than even the Hasidim. They not only insisted Jews follow the Law of Moses but also hundreds of 'interpretations' of that law as well as many oral traditions.[7] This two-party system would soon become the ruling powers. Together they would make up the highest ruling body among the Jews during Jesus' time: the Sanhedrin. Their limited power would extend to civil, religious, and criminal matters with maintenance of their own police force.[5]

Upon the death of John Hyracanus, his eldest son Aristobulus came to power. Aristobulus was very insecure and proceeded to kill all potential threats to his throne. One brother was executed, his mother was imprisoned and starved to death, and his other brothers were imprisoned. The Hasmoneans devoted themselves to seeking out anything Greek and adopted the Greek culture for themselves. Thus, they took the title of king.[7]

When Aristobulus died (reportedly from alcohol and disease), his wife Salome Alexandra released his brothers from prison and married the eldest, Alexander Jannaeus. (Does this make you wonder if Aristobulus had some assistance dying? The reason kings had cupbearers was because so many kings were poisoned.) Jannaeus extended the borders of the kingdom almost to the same territorial area Solomon had ruled.[7] Alexander's rule is one of continuous battles with invading nations. But he was also very cruel to the Jews. Josephus states Alexander received 6,000 Jews who approached him in goodwill and had them slain. Then he fought the others in the area until he had captured 800 of the best of the Jewish fighting men. Alexander crucified these men and, while they hung dying, he cut the throats of their wives and children in front of them. Is it any wonder God wanted barbarians like these destroyed? Alexander Jannaeus reigned 27 years and died at 49 years of age. Salome is widowed again. (Sounds to me like she is better off, too!) Salome ruled 9 years before dying at age 73 (so she had been 15 years older than her last husband). Shortly afterwards, in 63 B.C., the Romans conquered Palestine.[3]

Food for Thought: There is only one known instance where the Jews forced their religion on another nation. It happened to the Idumeans. They were conquered under the rule of John Hyracanus and forced to accept Judaism and circumcision. Herod was an Idumean. Herod would expand God's Temple and allow freedom to the Jews to move about the country and celebrate their festivals. But Herod was also a cruel man who would play an important role in bringing salvation to the world. "And we know that in all things God works for the good of those who love him, who have been called according to his purpose."[1] (Romans 8:28)

October 17
<u>Historical Readings to cover this Period: The Romans</u>

Pompey is credited with the conquest of Palestine. The area was subdivided into city-states. Those east of the Jordan were formed into the Decapolis or League of Ten Cities. Three of those had civil officials that were Jewish: Judea, Perea, and Galilee. Antipater was made Roman ruler of all Palestine. His son, Herod the Great, was appointed governor of Galilee and another son, Phasael, was appointed over Judea. Antipater was murdered in 43 B.C., after which Herod the Great fled to Rome and was able to convince the Roman Senate to make him "King of the Jews." His territory included Judea, Idumea, Perea, and Samaria. He later conquered Galilee and the city of Joppa. Upon Herod's death in 4 B.C. (after he has tried to find and kill the baby Jesus), his kingdom is divided primarily among his three sons: Herod Antipas (Galilee and Perea), Philip (northeast and east side of the Sea of Galilee), and Archelaus (Judea, Idumea, and Samaria). Archelaus is so brutal and incompetent (Matthew 2:22) that he is removed in only ten years and his territory is given to a Roman official. Herod Antipas ruled more than a decade after Jesus' crucifixion. Philip died of natural causes in 34 A.D. Agrippa I was eventually given almost all the land originally ruled by Herod the Great.[7] You recall the Herodian dynasty is composed of Idumeans who descended from Edomites (Esau). Acts 12:20-23 records Herod's gruesome death. Agrippa II takes over as a 17-year old ruler. He was steadily given more territory and power. With control over the high priests, the procurator (called prefect but similar to governor) asks him to judge the case of Paul in Caesarea (Acts 25-26). (Three procurators mentioned in the New Testament are Pontius Pilate, Felix, and Festus.) Agrippa II created a public scandal when he became involved in an incestuous relationship with his sister Bernice (Acts 25:23). Bernice later becomes the mistress to another ruler. With Agrippa II's death around 100 A.D., the Herodian dynasty ended.[7]

Now let's return to the time of Herod the Great. Herod was fearful of his position, as most kings were. He had Aristobulus drowned because of his popularity as well as for his grandeur. Herod embarks on many huge, expensive building projects. The most outstanding is the rebuilding of the Temple. The Temple would double in size. Its western wall is the longest at 1,590 feet and is now known as the Wailing Wall. The southern wall is the shortest at 912 feet. The eastern wall is on the side of the mountain (1,536 feet long) and must be stabilized with huge foundation stones weighing an average of 2-5 tons each. But the greatest strength was needed in the southwest corner where the stones weighed 50 tons each. The Court of the Gentiles was separated from the Courts of the Jews by a 4.5-foot high railing. A warning was on the railing to the effect that any foreigner proceeding beyond this point would lose his life. Due to the low railing, Gentiles were able to view the Courts of the Jews. Jewish women in the Court of Women could see over the heads of the men in the Court of Israel by means of a gallery. An 18-inch high stone fence separated the Court of Priests from the Court of Israel (men). The Holy of Holies was empty. The Ark disappeared with the Babylonian invasion of Jerusalem. The Temple doors were covered in gold. The priests' quarters along the sides of the Temple were three stories high. The actual Temple work was finished in 1.5 years, but the porticos and courtyards took 8 years. Apparently, the project grew and continued for 46 years (John 2:20).[7] The Temple was completed in 64 A.D. and was subsequently destroyed in 70 A.D. by the Romans. On regular festival days, a possible quarter of a million people crowded the Temple grounds,[7] swelling to over 2 million on Passover.[72]

Herod's other building projects included the following:

Caesarea
- A sewer system that was continuously flushed by the wave action of the sea
- Six miles of high-level aqueduct that funneled fresh water from Mount Carmel
- The first concrete breakwater to protect a harbor
- A huge pagan temple
- An amphitheater 290 x 190 feet

Herod's Palace
- Herodium built 7.5 miles south of Jerusalem on the site of his greatest victory
- Resembled a cone mound of earth with the top lopped off
- Double wall protected fortress
- Four towers, one on each compass point
- Hot bathhouse on west inside half
- Garden on east inside half

Jericho
- Site of winter palace which straddled wadi (river plain)
- Five room bathhouse
- Sunken garden
- Hippodrome
- Theater

Jerusalem
- Theater
- Hippodrome

Masada
- Fortified
- Casement wall (4,250 feet long and 110 rooms)
- Four palaces
- Built on a mesa 1,500 feet in elevation

Samaria
- Rebuilt 2 miles of walls
- Basilica
- Roman Forum
- Stadium (750 x 195 feet)
- Pagan temple

Machaerus
- Fortified palace (360 x 195 feet)
- Paved courtyard
- Baths

Obviously Herod's building projects were scattered throughout the kingdom and included community entertainment buildings.[7] Herod was quite the politician, trying to be all things to all people.

Food for Thought: The Temple was at its largest and greatest during Jesus' time. How appropriate that Jesus would walk the steps and courts of earth's best Temple. In all its glory, it wanes in comparison to the glory that is to come! Praise God you will see the New Jerusalem with all its splendor!

NEW TESTAMENT

Jesus the Christ

October 18
Bible Readings: Mark 1:1; John 1:1-18; Luke 1:1-4

Mark was not an apostle but was a follower of Peter's gospel message. In fact, the Book of Mark sometimes reminds one of the "Memoirs of Peter." The Gospel of Mark is believed to be the very first book to be written in the New Testament. Mark came from a well-to-do family in Jerusalem. His mother was named Mary. Mark's family home was often a meeting place for the early church (Acts 12:12). Mark's relative was Barnabas. Mark was included on Paul's first missionary journey with Barnabas. When the group reached Perga, Mark left abruptly and went home (Acts 13:13). After that Paul refused to have anything to do with Mark (Acts 15:37-40), perhaps believing him to be too fickle and undependable. Oral tradition says Mark started a church in Alexandria, Egypt. Toward the end of Paul's life, he was obviously reconciled to Mark, requesting that Mark come and minister to his needs in Rome (Philemon 24; 2 Tim. 4:11).[71]

The original version of the Book of Mark ends at 16:8. None of the remainder of that book appears in the same style of Greek in any manuscripts. We do not know who wrote the last 12 verses of the book. Matthew quotes 51% of Mark's actual words and Luke uses 53%. Only 24 verses of Mark are not quoted in one of these two books. This leads scholars to believe that the gospels of Matthew and Luke were based on the first account ever written: Mark.[71]

John was the apostle Jesus loved like a brother. The Book of John gives a personal, humble testimony of the early years of Jesus' ministry. In John's writing, the apostles emerge as different personalities. The Book of John differs greatly from the other three gospels. John gives Jesus' crucifixion as the day before the Passover while the other three gospels give it as the day of Passover. John's gospel was not written until about 100 A.D. Assuming Matthew and Luke's gospels are based largely on Mark (Oct. 19th lesson), we actually need only to compare the Books of John and Mark: Mark being the first gospel and John the last. Mark wrote accounts of Jesus based on Peter's preaching. John wrote about the Jesus he knew, the One he served alongside Peter. At the time of John's writing, his audience, the church, was primarily composed of Hellenistic (Greek) Gentiles. These church members could not relate to the long Jewish genealogies or royal lineages, e.g., King David's lineage. The Greeks had two great concepts that John used to reach his audience. First was the concept of *Logos* that meant both word and reason. Thus, John 1:1-2 gives Jesus as the Word and the Reason for all life. Second was the concept of the present world or life being only a hazy foreshadowing of a greater perfect world or life to come. Utilizing this concept, John presents Jesus as the link, bridge, or gateway between the two worlds. John's presentation of Jesus' miracles is to show the glory of God rather than as acts of compassion as presented in the other gospels. John was not interested in writing an historical account but rather a spiritual gospel. John sought to discredit the heresy of Gnosticism which was a doctrine based on the premise that God was good and the world was bad, therefore God could not have created the world because He could not be involved with anything bad. John counters with "The Word became flesh." (1:14) Other versions of Gnosticism held that (1) Jesus was a created being not divine and that (2) Jesus became divine when the Spirit entered Him at baptism. Given this background, you can easily see the impact John's first three verses would have on his readers![72]

John, James, and Peter made up the inner circle of Jesus' closest friends. James and John apparently had a temper being nicknamed Boanerges, translated as 'Sons of Thunder.' Their mother, Salome, went so far as to ask that her sons be given places of honor when Jesus came into His kingdom. Was this request a result of her ambition or theirs? We do not know. In Acts 4 we see John standing courageously before the Sanhedrin. On the Isle of Patmos, John sees the Revelation, the future Kingdom. Jerome reports John's dying words to be, "Little children, love one another." In John we have a picture of an assertive, ambitious, courageous man who is loving and beloved.[72]

John 1 implicitly states that Jesus existed from the beginning as God and with God. Or put another way, God the Son always existed with God the Father. All things were made through Jesus who is the Light to the world of sin (darkness). John clearly states John the Baptist was not God but was a witness to the coming of God as man to dwell among men. This statement was to dispel the beliefs of some that John the Baptist had been the actual Messiah. The law was given to Moses under which mankind was judged and condemned. No one was able to continuously keep even the basic Ten Commandments. Jesus brought grace and truth. God's grace is the free gift from God to us. We cannot earn it or buy it. Jesus paid the price. We must simply believe in Jesus as Lord and Savior of our lives.

Luke was a Gentile writing to Theophilus who was also a Gentile. Luke uses Greek terms and reasoning to address a Hellenistic (Greek) audience in both the Books of Luke and Acts. Theophilus is believed to be a high official in the Roman government because of Luke's address of "most excellent Theophilus." Oral tradition is that Luke and Theophilus were originally from Antioch, Syria. Luke was a friend of Paul, sharing a Caesarea prison cell for two years. Luke's Greek grammar was very good and his research was detailed. In fact, Luke is the book we traditionally turn to for the Christmas story of Jesus' birth. The prayer life of Jesus is revealed in Luke. As well, Luke shows us the equality Jesus gave women, Gentiles, slaves, lepers, the poor, the depraved, and the immoral. Luke presents Christ as the Savior for all people.

Food for Thought: Jesus took His ministry to the humble and lowly in heart. They were ready to receive His grace. Don't be a Pharisee. Welcome the lowly into His Kingdom!

October 19
Bible Readings: Matt. 1:1-17; Luke 3:23-38

There are two genealogies of Jesus given. The first account begins with Abraham and goes forward to Joseph. This is the lineage of Joseph (Jesus' adopted father) given in Matthew. The second genealogy is given in Luke and counts backward from Joseph (Mary's husband) to God, the Father of all mankind. This is actually the lineage of Mary. You will notice no female names in this lineage, only males. Thus, Mary herself is even replaced with the name of Joseph, head of the family. Luke was a physician and more inclined to write technically and objectively with less personal emotion involved. Matthew was a tax collector who was accustomed to making lengthy accounts of situations involving husband and wife, as well as children. Matthew had seen the atrocities and oppression of his people, the Jews. His writings particularly target the Jews for announcing the gospel or Good News.

The lineage of Joseph is broken into 3 segments of 14 generations each: Abraham to David, David to the exile, and the exile to Jesus. Again we see 7x2=14, twice the number of completion or a double confirmation that each segment of the Israelite nation's history was completed. Obviously Matthew's lineage account starts with Abraham because that is the patriarch that received the promise of becoming a great nation. He was the father of the Israelites. Recall that at the time Jesus was born, the ruler required all taxes to be paid based on the town of the father's tribe (Abraham being the father of all tribes). This was part of the regular 14-year census.[70] Today the census takers come to us. In Jesus' time, the people went to them. Luke, being more scientific, goes back to the origin of the species: God. Both genealogies are the same through King David. After David, Matthew's genealogy traces the lineage of Solomon through Joseph. You will notice the kings of the old southern kingdom of Judah in this lineage. Manasseh, considered the wickedest of all Judah's kings, is on this list that ends the second segment with the exile of Jehoachin and all his family. It is through his eldest son Shealtiel that we see the lineage continue to Zerubbabel who becomes governor of Judah, but not king. The curse on Jehoakim prevents any more "kings" from arising out of Solomon's lineage. Therefore, the King of Kings, Jesus, would be a blood relative through Mary traced back to Nathan, Solomon's brother. Only two names appear the same on both Matthew and Luke's genealogies after David: Zerubbabel as the father of Shealtiel. Because of the practice of intertribal marriage, the limited number of Jews in the preserved exile remnant, and the reoccurrence of the same names, it is impossible to know if these are the same or different families in the genealogies. My thought is that the two lineages may have crossed at this point during the Babylon exile. Because Luke lists no female names, it is impossible to know.

Food for Thought: Jesus came to elevate the lowly and humble in spirit and to bring low those full of pride and self-worth. Few were lowlier than women. But Jesus loved and protected His mother, counted Mary and Martha among His friends, brought salvation to the woman at the well, revealed His resurrected body first to Mary Magdalene, and traced His lineage to David through His mother (definitely not done by the Jews of His day). Jesus elevated women to the same position as men: co-heirs in the Kingdom. Our God does not discriminate or segregate. Thank you, Jesus!

October 20
Bible Readings: Luke 1:5-80, 2:1-38; Matt. 1:18-25

Today we have the traditional Christmas story. Only weeks before our celebration of Jesus' birth, now is the time to start preparing our hearts for the event. What better way than pondering the miracle of His birth?

Zechariah and Elizabeth were both of the priestly lineage of Aaron. All their lives they had kept the commandments and regulations of the LORD. Now they were childless and quite old. By rabbinic law this would be grounds for a divorce at worst and disgrace at a minimum. As a priest Zechariah was one of about 20,000 who were divided into 24 groups. Each group served one week twice a year in the Temple, except on major festival days when all served. Of the 900 or so in Zechariah's group, few would ever have the opportunity to enter the Holy Place to burn incense before the LORD.[70] Lots were cast. Zechariah was chosen. The greatest day of his life was here. As he burned the incense to represent an offering of the people's prayers to God, Archangel Gabriel appeared. Zechariah's own prayers had been heard and he and Elizabeth would have a son to be named John. From birth he would be a Nazirite, set aside for announcing the coming Messiah. Zechariah's doubt resulted in his consequence of silence until John's birth. The greatest day of his life -- offering the incense and being told he would have a son who would help fulfill prophecy -- and he couldn't tell anyone. The worshippers waited anxiously for Zechariah had been in the Temple too long. Was he dead? Had something gone wrong? There he is! But what is wrong? He does not bless us. He cannot speak! What miraculous event happened in the Temple? The people would have a long wait for Zechariah's story, but Elizabeth soon conceived.

Shortly thereafter, Gabriel visited a humble maiden (about 16 years old). Mary was betrothed or legally married to Joseph (probably about 40 years old) although the religious marriage ceremony had not yet taken place. Mary was to be blessed by God for she had been chosen to be the mother of Jesus, the Messiah and the Son of God. You'll notice her response was not one of disbelief as Zechariah's had been but rather one of acceptance of her destiny and inquiry into what she must do. Mary is a woman on a mission to serve God and seeks only His guidance in how to do that. The angel realizes what Mary will undergo from the 'well-meaning' public gossip. He provides comfort by announcing her much older cousin Elizabeth is with child. Two women with miraculous births could comfort each other.

After preparation, Mary hurries off to visit Elizabeth. Both Elizabeth and her unborn son realize Mary is the mother of the Messiah. Elizabeth is filled with the Holy Spirit and speaks prophetically and blesses Mary for her belief in God's word.

Luke 1:46-56 is known as the Magnificat. It is a hymn of praise that contains Old Testament prophecy. This hymn is said to address the three revolutions of God: moral, social, and economic. Verse 51 refers to moral disruption of the proud of heart. Verse 52 speaks to the social segregation of races, genders, and classes of people. Verse 53 addresses the feeding of the poor with Living Water and the Bread of Life while the rich (and proud) are rejected.[70] Mary stayed with Elizabeth 3 months. It was almost time for Elizabeth to deliver and be separated as unclean from the family.

Elizabeth gave birth to a son who was circumcised on the eighth day. He was named John, short for Jehohanan meaning Jehovah's gift.[70] Immediately Zechariah could speak. How very much he had to tell! The birth of a male child meant music and celebration with relatives and friends. (If everyone is kin to you then that must have been one big party! Of course, those who had 'to see it to believe it' were there, too!) Zechariah is now filled with the Holy Spirit and prophesies. This song recognizes the Messiah is about to come, the salvation of the Jews, fulfillment of prophecy, and descendant of David. John will be a prophet of God preparing the way for Jesus. John would tell the people that salvation existed through the forgiveness of sins out of God's mercy. Coming from the east, Heaven would send forth its Messiah to bring Light to a world of sinful darkness. The steps of the Christian way are shown as (1) preparation (76), (2) knowledge (77), (3) forgiveness (77), and (4) a new walk in Christ (79).[70] John would be a Nazirite all his life. Malachi 4:5 was well known to the Jews. They had expected Elijah himself to return, not one 'like Elijah.' The Old Testament ends with a curse on all who will not be turned to a relationship with God. The New Testament ends with the grace of the Lord Jesus on God's people -- confirmed with a final "Amen." There is no need for a double confirmation from God.

Now Joseph must be told of his wife's condition. How did Mary do it? You can imagine her fear, her preparation for the worst. After all, Joseph could legally divorce her. Joseph would have to think about this stunning news! Before he could decide on taking action, an angel of the LORD visited him in a dream. Mary was to give birth to Jesus (the Lord saves) -- Immanuel -- God with us. He would bring salvation and fulfillment of prophecy (Isa. 1:1, Jer. 35:15, Ezek. 37:24, Hosea 3:5).

The year is 6 B.C. and the Emperor Caesar Augustus has called for a census. Joseph must return to his hometown of Bethlehem, Judea, (city of David, home of Ruth and Boaz, and burial site of Rachel) to register with Mary who is close to delivering. Appropriately, the Messiah's first and last trip to Judea are on a donkey, a lowly animal of service. While in Bethlehem, she gave birth to Jesus, wrapped Him in cloths, and laid Him in a manger. The manger may well have been a stone bin projecting across a corner of the stable rather than a wooden one.[7]

An angel of the LORD, likely Gabriel, announced to shepherds keeping watch of their flock by night the news of the Messiah's birth. Shepherds were outside acceptable Jewish religious practices because they could not possibly maintain the purification regulations, given their profession. They were the impure custodians of the flock, the pastors. Shepherds only slept in the fields at night during the warm months of March - October.[73] Some believe Jesus was born April 1 and the devil has tried to obliterate His birthday by making it a joke day. If so, All Fools Day is a condemnation of a true fool -- one who lives without Jesus as Lord. The announcement is followed by a performance of the heavenly choir. The shepherds at once sought the baby Jesus and spread the word to all Jews -- the Messiah had come! By God's law, Jesus is circumcised and consecrated to God. At the time of purification (offering of two doves or pigeons for poor people) Simeon (a worshipper) recognized the baby as the LORD's salvation prophesying that He will bring glory to the Jews and truth to the Gentiles. But he adds that a sword would pierce Mary's own soul. (Mary would stand at the foot of the cross of Jesus as the Roman soldier pierced His side with a spear to confirm His death (John 19:34).)

Food for Thought: The Altar of Incense is the only one mentioned in the Bible as being in the New Jerusalem. (See Isa. 6:6 and Rev. 8:3-4.) The prayers of God's people will ever be before Him. Is your prayer life a daily offering of sweet savor to God?

October 21
Bible Readings: Matt. 2:1-23; Luke 2:39-52

The Magi or Wise Men of the east follow a bright star in the sky to find the king of the Jews. These Wise Men are often thought to be Medes from the old land of Persia who knew the laws and teachings of the Jews. Abraham's sons by his concubines had been given gifts and sent away "to the land of the east." (Gen. 25:6) Likely, the Wise Men were descendants of Abraham. Naturally, they first go before the man in charge of the land to inquire where they can find this newborn king. Feeling threatened by a new king who could lead the Jews (3 million in Palestine alone[7]) against him, Herod sends for the chief priests and scribes. They quote Micah 5:2, the king would be born in Bethlehem. The Magi went to Mary and Joseph's house in Bethlehem. (They were apparently putting down roots there.) The Magi bowed before Jesus and presented Him with three expensive gifts, each with its own significance. (1) Gold was the gift of a king. Its abundance was seen among all of the royal families. (2) Frankincense was used for incense signifying a gift to a High Priest before God. (3) Myrrh was one of the two primary embalming agents, used with aloe. Myrrh announced His death.[74] (Now what would you think if your baby was given a bottle of embalming fluid?) The Magi were warned in a dream to avoid Herod and they returned to their land by a different route. After their departure, Joseph has a dream where he is visited by the angel of the LORD warning him to flee to Egypt with his family. He got up immediately, packed, and left during the night! He must have been terribly frightened to leave in darkness and travel dangerous highways unprotected. Joseph stayed in Egypt until Herod died in 4 B.C. The prophecy of Hosea 11:1 was fulfilled.[74]

Meanwhile Herod had ordered the slaying of all males in Bethlehem less than 2 years of age. Herod was a murderer at heart. His murders would also include the members of the Sanhedrin of his coronation year, his 'beloved' wife, his mother-in-law, his oldest son, two other sons, and 300 court officials.[74] (Herod's infanticide reminds me of the same type occurrence at the birth of Moses.)

Upon Herod's death, Joseph heads back home with his family but is warned in a dream to avoid Judea. Herod's cruel son Archelaus is now ruler there. So Joseph takes his family far north to Nazareth, Galilee. As a result Jesus would be called a Nazarene. (Though Matthew says this is fulfillment of a prophecy, Nazareth was never mentioned in the Old Testament. The closest word is nezer, which means branch and could refer to Isa. 11:1.[74])

At 12 years old (just prior to the time of Jewish males 'coming of age' or Bar Mitzpah), Jesus went with his parents to the Passover festival in Jerusalem. When the festival was over and the crowd from Nazareth was walking home, Jesus could not be found. Joseph and Mary return to Jerusalem. They search for 3 days before finding Jesus in the Temple courts. (Jesus will spend 3 days in the tomb before all believers find Him at His resurrection. For 3 days His followers will seek Him, bewildered.) Even as a young boy, Jesus knows He must prepare for the work of God. He returned to Nazareth with his parents "and was obedient to them." Jesus grew in knowledge, in physical body, and in spiritual relationship with God, but He also grew socially with mankind.

Food for Thought: There is a children's story legend that when Joseph, Mary, and Jesus were fleeing to Egypt, they spent the first night in a cave. It was very cold. A little spider saw Jesus and wanted to do something to keep Him warm. So the spider spun his web across the entrance to the cave to form a curtain to keep out the wind. Later that night Herod's soldiers came seeking children to kill. When they went to enter the cave, the captain stopped the soldiers. Pointing to the hoar frost on the spider's web, he declared, "No one could have gone in there or the web would be broken." So the soldiers went on. The holy family was left in peace. To this day, we put tinsel on our Christmas trees to represent the glittering strands of the spider's web, a gift to Jesus.[74]

> Verses of the Week: **John 3:16-18** "For God so loved the world that he gave his one and only Son, that whoever believes in him shall not perish but have eternal life. For God did not send his Son into the world to condemn the world, but to save the world through him. Whoever believes in him is not condemned, but whoever does not believe stands condemned already because he has not believed in the name of God's one and only Son."

October 22

<u>Bible Readings:</u> Matt. 3:1-17; 4:1-11, Mark 1:2-13, Luke 3:1-18, 21-23; 4:1-13, John 1:19-34

Characters:	Emperor - Tiberius Caesar
	High Priests - Annas and Caiaphas
	Evangelist - John the Baptist
	Messiah - Jesus
Rulers of States:	Judea - Pontius Pilate
	Galilee - Herod
	Iturea and Traconitis - Philip
	Abilene - Lysanias
Stage:	The Jordan River just north of the Dead Sea at Bethany
Message:	Repentance for the forgiveness of sin
Year:	24 A.D. (possibly as late as 27 A.D. depending on what year you assign to Jesus' birth)
Background:	John the Baptist was a Nazirite. As such, he would only eat "clean" food as approved by Levitical law. Lev. 11:22 identifies the locust (grasshopper) as approved food. The locust bean (carob bean) was considered hog food. No Jew would eat locust beans unless they were the only hope for surviving from starvation. In Luke 15:16, we find the prodigal son "longing" for the pods (locust beans) being fed to the hogs. This would have been a clear message to the Jews that the boy was near death by starvation. The only recorded case we have of the Israelites eating locust beans is in 2 Kings 6:25 at the end of the siege of Samaria. The famine was so great that the people were eating donkey's heads and locust beans. After that they went to cannibalism -- all despicable foods before God. [Note: Locust (carob) bean was nicknamed St. John's bread after John the Baptist through confusion of the locusts (grasshoppers) he ate with the locust bean.[8]] A Nazirite abstained from wine and worldly material possessions. We know from several places in the Bible that they dressed rather ruggedly, ate off the land, and generally looked 'unmanicured.' In our day we would say this was not someone we wanted to meet on a dark street!
Storyline:	It has been 30 years since Jesus was born, 20 years since Herod the Great's death. Where was the Messiah? The One the angels announced to the shepherds? Many people wondered if John was the One. John's response was always the same. He only baptized with water; the Christ would baptize with the Holy Spirit. Until now, the Holy Spirit had only filled those who prophesied or had visions. John was preaching the Christ or Messiah would give this holy gift to all. But John adds that the Christ will baptize with fire or judgment, too. He will separate the

people, gathering believers to Himself and burning non-believers in eternal fire. John is careful to remain humble and project his unworthiness to do even the meekest and lowliest tasks for Christ.

Jesus presented Himself to John to be baptized. In expected humbleness, John responds that he is the one in need of Jesus' baptism. Jesus insisted His baptism was to fulfill righteousness. Why was Jesus baptized? He had no sin in need of forgiveness. The reasons are many:
- To endorse John's preaching,
- To relate to the common people rather than being associated with the Pharisees who only watched but did not participate in baptism,
- To confess the sins of the nation as we have seen prophets of the Old Testament do,
- To serve as an example for the people demonstrating obedience to God's Will,
- To initiate or begin His public ministry and have it anointed by God,[15]
- To give a picture of His death, burial, and resurrection.

After Jesus was baptized, He "went up out of the water" (Matt. 3:16) indicating He was actually on shore when the Spirit of God descended on Him "like a dove." The dove was a rabbinical symbol for Israel but also for the Spirit.[75] It was a dove that was sent out three times by Noah to survey the earth for a permanent dwelling (Gen. 8:8-12). Jesus was sent out for 3.5 years to the people of earth to lead them to an eternal home. A voice from Heaven (assumed to be God), "This is my Son, whom I love; with him I am well pleased."[1] (Matt. 3:17) Jesus was 30 years old and now anointed to begin His ministry as High Priest. (See Ex. 40:12-15.)

Immediately the Spirit moves Jesus to seek the solitude of the desert for 40 days of prayer and fasting. Before embarking on the call from God, Jesus knew a concentrated, focused period of prayer time was critical to victory over evil. All believers are called to a particular work in God's master plan. Jesus showed us the importance of being 'prayed-up and studied-up' for the task. When He is at His weakest physically (but strong in the Spirit), the devil comes to tempt Him. A law of physics is well applied here, too. "For every positive experience, there is an equal but opposite negative experience." Although nothing equals the experience of becoming a Christian, the devil tries hard to ruin the experience with as much force as he can muster!

Satan tests Jesus in the 3 areas most common to all men: physical desires, power, and prestige/pride. In each case, Jesus responded by quoting scripture from Deuteronomy. You will notice that Satan tries to use scripture to support his position, but Jesus counters with scripture that proves Satan has misapplied a portion of scripture taken out of context. Knowing the scripture and standing firm on its premises, is one of our main weapons against evil.

At this point, we go back to John the Baptist and see him being questioned by the Jews of Jerusalem who have been sent by the priests and Levites. They have only one real question of John, "Who are you? Christ? Elijah? A prophet?" John adamantly denies all. He is the one to fulfill Isaiah's prophecy. The Christ is among them, but they do not recognize Him. The next day John sees Jesus coming toward him and announces to all, "The Lamb of God who takes away the sin of the world!"[1] (John 1:29) John now discloses succinctly his own mission, "The reason I came baptizing with water was that he might be revealed to Israel." (John 1:31) John concludes with "I testify this is the Son of God."[1] (John 1:34)

Food for Thought: Hide the scripture in your heart. Daily it can be used to protect you. The word of God is our sword to defend. Read Eph. 6:16-18.

October 23
Bible Readings: John 1:35-51; 2:1-25; 3:1-36; 4:1-54; Luke 3:19-20

Two of John's disciples heard him identify Jesus as the Lamb of God. They turned and followed Jesus. One of them was Andrew. John 1:41 says, "The first thing Andrew did was to find his brother Simon and tell him, 'We have found the Messiah.'"[1] This should also be the first thing we do. When we come to know Jesus as Savior, we should tell all our loved ones about the Christ and how to have eternal life. If we cannot lead those we love so much to Christ, how will we lead those we don't know at all? If you have members of your family who are lost, then you should be so burdened that you fast and pray fervently for their souls and witness to them daily. Jesus also said that you couldn't be a prophet in your own land. Too many people take this to mean they shouldn't even try to reach their loved ones for Christ. If your children, brothers, spouse, sisters, or parents were in physical danger, would you not do all within your power to rescue them? Why then would you not tell them about an eternal Savior? Rev. 20:15 tells us, "If anyone's name was not found written in the book of life, he was thrown into the lake of fire."[1] The Jews knew and understood what the lake of fire was. The Dead Sea was covered in blobs of oil. Periodically it would spontaneously combust in the desert heat. It also had a high sulfur and salt content. A person thrown in the Dead Sea could not sink but bobbed on the top of the water (because the salt content of the water is so high). When the sulfur and oil would combust, the person could not even dive under the fire to get relief! They just bobbed up and down in the midst of the lake of fire, unable to escape. Because the Dead Sea was created from an earthquake (Remember Sodom and Gomorrah?), the bottom is a deep crevice pit. Already the sea is the lowest spot on earth, but its bottom is the 'bottomless pit' or the earthly abyss. What are you going to do to prevent your loved ones from spending eternity in the lake of fire with the devil? (Read Rev. 19:20 and 20:1-3, 15.) The least we are expected to do is pray and witness.

Jesus had His three apostles: Andrew, John, and Simon. Immediately Jesus changes Simon's name to Cephas or Peter in the Greek translation. Jesus knew Simon's heart. He would be a rock in the storms of this world, serving His Savior. Next, Philip joins the group. First he goes and brings back Nathanael, possibly his brother. Nathanael's famous comment to Jesus of Nazareth being the Christ is, "Nazareth! Can anything good come from there?"[1] (John 1:46) This comment shows Nathanael is familiar with Old Testament prophecy that does not mention Nazareth at all. It also shows a willingness by Nathanael to see for himself. A willing heart is a receptive heart. Many scholars believe that Nathanael is the same man as Bartholomew the Apostle (Matt. 10:3).[5] Jesus called Bartholomew a true Israelite, one who was not false. He went on to say He had seen Bartholomew under his fig tree. Why did this touch Bartholomew so deeply that he recognized Jesus as Christ? The fig tree symbolized peace and security to the Jews (See 1 Kings 4:25, Micah 4:4). A Jew sat under his leafy, cool fig tree to meditate and to pray. Bartholomew may have even been praying for the Messiah to come forth. Jesus had seen his private place, his intimate thoughts. Surely, this was God! Jesus then tells Bartholomew that the Son of Man will be the ladder (referring to Jacob's ladder in Gen. 28:12-13) that will lead to Heaven, another picture of Jesus as the "Way" or the "Gate" or the "Ladder" to God.[72]

Jesus' first public miracle is turning the water into wine in Cana, Galilee, at a humble family wedding. Cana can be seen from Nazareth. Mary seems to have been a close friend or relative of this family for she was assisting with the refreshments. She also had authority to give orders to the servants. Jesus appears to be His family head at this point. His father probably died years earlier, being much older than Mary. Mary looked to Jesus to save the host family from disgrace -- no wine for the wedding feast. Notice the symbolism here. Wine is symbolic of Jesus' blood shed for us and the wedding feast symbolizes the heavenly feast of the bride (believers) and the bridegroom (Jesus). Jewish law required all virgins be married on a Wednesday. We are told this wine shortage occurred the third day of the feast or the Sabbath. For one week the newlyweds would dress in their bridal robes, wear crowns, and hold open house for all well-wishers. They would be treated as a king and queen. The wine would have been consumed as 2 parts of wine to 3 parts of water to ensure no one disgraced himself through drunkenness. The water used for ceremonial washing referred to the washing of (1) feet on entering the house and (2) hands before every meal and between courses of a meal. There were 6 jars holding 20-30 gallons each. Six was a number symbolizing imperfection or unfinished. It was the number of man, made on the 6th day. There needed to be 7 to be complete. Jesus came to save the people from the imperfections of the religious laws. He came to finish God's victory over sin. And He did it with much more than enough! (No party could consume 180 gallons of wine!)[72] Additionally, He filled each water container (human body is more than 90% water) to the brim with the wine of His saving grace. Jesus will be more than enough. He will fill us to the brim. I don't know much about wine except that connoisseurs talk about the clarity, fullness, and bouquet of the wine. The most highly sought after wines have excellent ratings in all three areas. The blood of Jesus Christ will ceremonially (and literally) cleanse us of all sins, purifying us to meet God. His blood also fills our lives with the fullness, joy, and bouquet of life that can never be experienced otherwise. Without Jesus, you can only experience the colors of the facade of the sunrise. With Jesus, you can experience the miracle of the sunrise!

Passover is approaching and Jesus goes to Jerusalem for the festival. When He arrives, He finds livestock and crooked businessmen working out of 'shops' in the Temple courtyard. He makes a cord whip and runs out the livestock, overturns the tables, and runs out the crooked traders. The Jews demanded to know what miraculous sign Jesus could do to **prove** it was His Father's house. He told them if the Temple was destroyed, He could raise it in 3 days. Jesus was referring to His body as it served as the Temple of His deity. After the resurrection, His church would become the body of Christ. The Jews interpreted it to mean Herod's Temple, which had taken 46 years to remodel. Why was Jesus angry with the merchants? First, they were desecrating the Temple. Jewish pilgrims could not bring unblemished sacrificial animals over long distances. They had to purchase them in Jerusalem. The priests had established themselves as 'animal inspectors' for the Temple. Probably for a cut of the money, most animals brought from the outside were disqualified as not suitable. Only those sold inside the Temple for inflated prices passed inspection. Also, these animals were frequently blemished. (See the early history of sacrifice in Zerubbabel's Temple in Malachi 1:6-11. The building had been improved, but not the hearts of the people.) Moneychangers were needed for several reasons. (1) A half-shekel Temple tax was required of all Jewish males over 19 years old. This amounted to almost 2 days' wages. The moneychangers were adding fees that amounted to another day's wage![72] (2) Pilgrims came from all surrounding nations to Passover. The Jews strictly kept the second commandment forbidding graven images. Coins minted by governments usually carried the images of emperors, kings, or pagan gods. The approved Temple coin had only the pomegranate and lampstand on it.[76] Government coins had to be exchanged for Temple coins. (3) By Jesus' time, the Passover crowd could easily have been larger than 2 million.[72] No town the size of Jerusalem could 'make change' for even a portion of that crowd through regular merchants. So those having larger currencies needed to obtain smaller denominations. The final desecration of the Temple involved noise. With all the people, animals, and merchandising going on, the Temple was anything but a peaceful house of prayer and worship. All the builders (even Herod) had been careful to keep construction noise away from the Temple by dressing stone and preparing wood outside of town. But greed had replaced reverence. Jesus would not reveal He was the Messiah for He knew the hearts of these treacherous men!

One of the Pharisees on the Sanhedrin came to Jesus under the cloak of darkness. He dare not let others see him! His name was Nicodemus and he acknowledged that God sent Jesus. Nicodemus came seeking to know how one obtained eternal life. Jesus told him that anyone coming to God's Kingdom must be born in the flesh and then reborn in the Spirit. As a Pharisee, Nicodemus was an expert in prophecy. His parameters for God were so fixed by Pharisaical interpretation that he could not comprehend the complete acceptance of things unseen. Jesus asked how he would understand the things of Heaven if he couldn't even understand the things of earth. The Son of Man had come to be lifted up even as Moses lifted up the serpent in the desert (Num. 21:4-9) so that all may have eternal life. (See Feb. 10 lesson.) Jesus would take on all the sins of the people brought into the world through the serpent. He would be lifted up for all to look unto Him and be saved.

The Pharisees heard that Jesus' disciples were baptizing more people than John. To prevent any controversy that would attempt to place Him in opposition to John, Jesus left and headed north to Galilee. The territory of Samaria lay between Judea and Galilee. Jesus sat down by Jacob's well located outside Sychar, Samaria. A Samaritan woman came to draw water and Jesus asked for a drink. Jews and Samaritans had a history of strife and dislike of each other, so the Samaritan woman was surprised. Jesus went on to tell her He could provide her with Living Water where she would never thirst again. Jesus then proceeded to reveal the woman's life history. She was shocked to discover a total stranger knew so much about her (today, we'd just assume the man had computer Internet access!). The woman recognized Jesus was a prophet. Her next question was where she should worship: Mount Gerizim or Jerusalem? The Samaritans had glorified Mount Gerizim because they incorrectly taught (1) Moses had first built an altar there for sacrifice, (2) Melchizedek had encountered Abraham there, and (3) Abraham had been willing to sacrifice Isaac there.[72] Jesus explained that the time would come when they would worship in neither place, but salvation would come from the Jews. The woman at the well accepted Jesus as Christ and immediately went to tell the people of the town. As a result of one woman's (who was considered an unsavory character) testimony, many believed. Jesus spoke to His returning disciples saying the fields were ripe for harvest. Some will sow the gospel and cultivate it in the people. Others will come and harvest. All who do the work of the Father will be rewarded.

John the Baptist has begun chastising Herod for his sins, especially the sin of an affair with his sister-in-law, Herodias. Herod imprisons him.

Food for Thought: One interesting interpretation of the woman at the well story is that the woman represented Samaria. The five husbands represented the 5 different ethnic peoples brought in by the Assyrians to repopulate Samaria. Each set of people had brought in their own pagan god. The sixth common law husband represented the one true God that the Samaritans had never fully accepted.[72]

October 24
Bible Readings: Matt. 4:12-25; 8:1-4,14-17; 9:1-8; Mark 1:14-45; 2:1-12; Luke 4:14-44; 5:1-26

John the Baptist was now in prison in the dungeons of the Castle of Machaerus. When Jesus heard the news, he moved permanently from His home in Nazareth to a new operational center in Capernaum. Jesus' ministry was now in full swing. Galilee was chosen for its vast population in a small area. In 1,250 square miles there lived over 3 million people.[74] The message of Jesus was repentance. He went to their synagogues to teach in every town. The synagogue was usually arranged in a semicircular room that looked much like their amphitheaters but smaller. Stone benches arranged in step-style around the room provided an excellent view and sound acoustics. I call them 'pit auditoriums.' The speaker is at floor level and the students sit in tiers around the walls.[7]

Luke tells us of an incident that happened in Nazareth apparently before Jesus left. He had gone to the synagogue and read Isa. 61:1-2. Afterward, He simply stated He was the fulfillment of that scripture. Inflamed, the people rose up against Him with the intent of killing Him by throwing Him off a cliff! At this point, Jesus said the famous line "No prophet is accepted in his hometown"[1] (Luke 4:24) for even Elijah and Elisha had to travel to other towns to perform miracles. Jesus walked through the crowd and escaped unseen.

By comparing Matt. 27:56, Mark 15:40, and John 19:25, we can determine that Salome was probably Jesus' aunt. As the wife of Zebedee, she was also James and John's mother. Thus, James, John, and Jesus were cousins.[79] They knew each other well. Nazareth was about 20-25 miles from the Capernaum and Bethsaida area. No doubt Jesus and Mary visited her sister's family throughout Jesus' childhood and young adult years. Peter was both a fisherman and a business partner of Zebedee's (Luke 5:8-10). It is quite likely that Jesus, Peter, and James were about the same age. John had come to love Jesus for the spiritual fruit evident in Jesus' life: love, joy, peace, patience, kindness, goodness, faithfulness, gentleness, and self-control (Gal. 5:22). This tight circle of cousins embraced another friend and companion -- Peter. The question that always comes to my mind is, "Why wasn't Andrew (Peter's brother) included in Jesus' inner circle?" I do not have an answer other than Peter, James, and John were rather bold and adventuresome whereas Andrew seems to be more meek and timid among strangers.

Zebedee would have known Jesus all His life. I feel sure Mary and Joseph talked of their miraculous gift from God. The lack of any outcry on the part of Zebedee at his sons leaving to follow Jesus can be better understood when you look at their lives from the viewpoint of relatives. Even Peter and Andrew's parents probably knew the story of Jesus' birth and marveled at the man He had become. Had these parents and relatives known what it truly meant to "follow Jesus," fear would have gripped their hearts! Their life's choice would entail ever-present danger, scorn, and a minimalist lifestyle that had them always on the move.

At the Sea of Galilee, Jesus recruits the fishermen Simon, Andrew, James, and John as disciples. Then in Capernaum, He cast a demon out of a possessed man. The demon announced that Jesus was the Holy One of God, but Jesus rebuked it to be quiet. The news spread rapidly. Here was a man learned in the law, capable of healing, and now casting out demons. Jesus left there to retreat to Peter's home for rest. Upon finding Peter's mother-in-law sick, Jesus healed her. (Wonder where Peter's wife was all this time? Did he have children?) [I always wondered why Jesus wouldn't let the demons tell who He was. Now we see that it was because His 'time' had not come yet to die. He still had to teach and preach more about repentance and salvation. If the Jews had heard any announcements of His deity, then they would surely have tried to kill Him earlier for blasphemy. God had a time for everything, including the announcement that Jesus was King of the Jews, a title Herod would kill to keep, too.]

In the evening, people thronged the house with the sick, lame, and paralyzed. Jesus healed them all but would not let the demons identify Him. (Look at the irony of this situation. Demons recognized God among them, but God's own creation -- mankind -- didn't!) The crowd was there to get physical healing; they didn't come for spiritual healing. Jesus had healed in the synagogue, a private home, and now in the streets. We find the disciples taking their problems to Jesus early in His ministry. We also see a woman healed who is obviously a believer, and she gets up immediately to begin to serve. We should do so, too. Jesus saved us; we must serve Him.

Jesus, who is God, felt the necessity of withdrawing to be alone with His Father. Our strength comes from God. Prayer is the intravenous feeding from the source of our strength. When we falter and fall, it is because we have discontinued our feeding. Jesus cleanses and purifies our soul, the Holy Spirit dwells within us and guides us, and God the Father calls us His children.

Two other cases of healing are given in today's lesson: the leper and the paralytic. When Jesus healed the leper, He told him to follow the religious law and present himself to the priests to be pronounced clean but not to tell anyone else. Like us, the man was compelled by his joy to tell everyone. Those seeking a physical miracle thronged Jesus to where He could no longer teach repentance and forgiveness. The paralytic was lowered through a hole in the roof. When Jesus forgave his sins and he was healed, the scribes wanted to declare blasphemy. Because disease was associated with personal and family sin, Jesus asked the scribes what the difference was between telling the paralytic he was healed versus telling him he was forgiven. True healing comes from joy in the soul from the Presence of the Holy Spirit.

Food for Thought: God, cover us with the cocoon of Your love and suspend us in Your peace. Fill our lives with the joy of Your Presence. Protect us in a world of evil and guide us on our journey to an eternal life with You. Amen.

October 25
Bible Readings: Matt. 9:9-17; 12:1-21, Mark 2:13-28; 3:1-19, Luke 5:27-39; 6:1-19, John 5:1-3, 5-47

Matthew, the tax collector, is called to be the Lord's disciple. Tax collectors were notorious for gouging the people. Considered no better than common thieves, tax collectors gathered at Matthew's house to eat with Jesus.

When those who saw this complained, Jesus noted it was for sinners that He came. Though hated by many, Matthew had a receptive heart. He was looking for a Savior.

Next, the Pharisees ask Jesus why He and His disciples do not fast and pray as other great spiritual leaders have done. Fasting is a sign of deep spiritual concern. One fasts and prays to God for His intervention in the trouble. Jesus was 'God with us.' His disciples took their problems directly to Jesus. There was no need to fast as a sign of deep concern. Jesus was with them and knew their hearts. He supplied their needs. The time of prayer and fasting would come -- when He was no longer with them.

The parable of putting a new cloth patch on an old garment was to show the Pharisees how unacceptable it is to try to force the teachings of Jesus into their detailed religious rituals. It wouldn't work. The old and the new would be damaged. It is also likened to putting newly made wine into old wineskins. When the new started to enlarge and expand (as Christianity did), it would burst the old wineskin of the Pharisaical laws apart. The old ways would no longer apply to the new spirit. Once the new wine has matured, no one wants to drink the fresh wine again. This was said to show that a mature believer in Christ has come so far in Christian growth that there is no desire to return to the time when (s)he was only a babe in Christ.

The Pool of Bethesda was located north of the Temple.[1] A subterranean stream that occasionally bubbled up filled it.[72] The locals superstitiously believed this bubbling to be caused by an angel bringing healing to the first person who entered the water. This pool is what we might call an artesian well. Jesus healed a man who had been lame 38 years and had placed all his hope in the bubbling pool. Later Jesus warned the man to quit sinning before something worse happened to him. Key points of this story include

- Jesus asked the man if he "wanted" to be healed. (You must <u>want</u> Jesus to receive His gift.)
- The man trusted Jesus and obediently followed His commands.
- The man had sinned by placing his faith in superstition rather than God. (Now that he knew Truth (Jesus), he was to turn from his evil way.)
- Fear drove the man to betray Jesus to the Jews.[77]

The devil tries to steal our joy after every mountaintop experience. With new Christians, sin still comes easy. Old habits are hard to break, but they can and must be left behind with the old sinful life. The year is already 28 A.D. Wonder how this man will feel when the Jews finally crucify Jesus?

The Jews never referred to God in any way that would presume familiarity. They never even spoke God's name because of their unworthiness to do so. Now here comes Jesus claiming God to be His Father! Jesus makes some statements that reveal our future.

(1) All judgment will come from Jesus. God the Father doesn't judge.
(2) Believers in the Word (Jesus) of God have eternal life in Heaven and will not be found 'guilty' at judgment.
(3) All who die will rise to eternal life -- some will live eternally in Heaven and some will live eternally in hell.
(4) The judgment will be just -- in accordance with the sins of the evil.
(5) Knowledge of scripture will not save you, only accepting Jesus as Lord and Savior will do that.

The Jews repeatedly condemn Jesus for two reasons: working on the Sabbath and claiming God as his Father. The Pharisees had hundreds of petty laws detailing the definition of 'work' on a holy day. One could hardly do any more than lie on a mat all day (and couldn't even pick that up or roll it out) on the Sabbath. Food was not prepared; water was not drawn. Healing of the body or soul was not allowed on the Sabbath! But Jesus said, "The Sabbath was made for man, not man for the Sabbath."[1] (Mark 2:27-28) Jesus takes the opportunity to remind the Jews that it was permissible to save a lamb in danger on the Sabbath and man was much more valuable. Jesus' logic and skill at revealing the obvious faultiness of the Pharisees' regulations only served to rile their anger. Their hearts were hardened. Pride and power would be their undoing.

Jesus chose 12 men to be His apostles. Disciples are merely followers, but apostles were special messengers commissioned by God to carry His word to the world.[5] Missionaries and pastors are apostles. To help remember the Apostles' names use a jingle: The **5 J**s bring **P**ublic **B**ible **T**eaching to the **MASS**es. The Apostles were James, James, John, Judas, Judas Iscariot, Philip, Bartholomew, Thomas, Matthew, Andrew, Simon, and Simon Peter.

Food for Thought: How would you respond to a miracle from God?

October 26
Bible Readings: Matt. 5:1-48; 6:1-34; 7:1-29, Luke 6:20-49

Our lesson begins with a passage referred to as the Beatitudes. I remember it as the "Be-Attitudes." Jesus is taking a positive psychological approach, emphasizing the rewards when you determine to BE His follower. Being a believer means being a humble servant.

Blessings

Attitude	Reward
Humbleness	Kingdom of Heaven
Mourning	Comfort
Meekness	Inherit the earth
Seekers of righteousness	Filled with the Spirit
Merciful	Shown mercy
Pure/innocent of heart	See God
Peacemaker	Called sons of God
Persecuted for righteousness	Kingdom of Heaven

Woes

Attitude	Reward
Haughty greed	Without the Spirit
Excessive possessions	Hungry for the Spirit
Carefree irresponsibility	Spiritual mourning and weeping
Prestigious power	Hollow praise

Believers are the salt that enhances the sensual and spiritual appreciation of creation. They bring light (Truth) into a dark world of sin. Jesus made it clear: He will judge your heart -- your intent -- not your works, possessions, appearance, or token charity. The tormented spirit continues to wash the body (as the Jewish ritual washings) when the heart needs cleansing instead.[75] Jesus came to fulfill the prophecies of the Old Testament. But He also came to fulfill the Law. How? He became the sacrificial Lamb whose blood would wash away our sins. He also became our High Priest, the One who represented us before God. Jesus proved that one completely pure in heart could keep the law. Sin begins in the heart, is nurtured in the mind, and is activated by the body. Sin is not static or dormant. It grows vociferously until it has consumed its victim. The devil uses our 5 senses, gifts from God, for planting seeds of evil. How blessed people are who do not have to constantly keep sins at bay. A perfect example is the song, advertisement, or movie that planted a sinful idea that you can't seem to forget. Better to never have seen an advertisement or a movie nor heard a song than to be lured into a constant battle with sin.

Jesus challenges us to love others as we love ourselves. Unfortunately, we have turned this wonderful commandment into "I gave you a $20 gift for your birthday, now you owe me a $20 gift for my birthday!" We have forgotten the famous charity (meaning love) chapter 13 of 1 Corinthians. The Apostle Paul ends the chapter reminding us that charity is the greatest gift of all. Jesus tells us plainly how we should live in relationship to other people:

(1) Be merciful and kind,
(2) Share material wealth and possessions with others selflessly,
(3) Keep your charitable deeds private and be rewarded by the righteousness of the act,
(4) Be meek, humble, and mild-tempered,
(5) Never retaliate for persecution,
(6) Keep your promises,
(7) Forgive others,
(8) Be a Christian example,
(9) Recognize good versus evil people by their words and actions, then avoid evil,
(10) Repent and turn from your sin and help others do the same, and
(11) Do not worry, for it shows a lack of faith.

Build your life on the solid foundation of Jesus Christ, the Word of God.

Food for Thought: Spend some time in self-evaluation. How do you measure up to the teachings of Jesus? How can you change? Where is the glory in the number of funerals you attend when you did not provide for or assist others while they lived? To have a friend, you must first be a friend in Christ. Your actions speak louder than words.

October 27

Bible Readings: Matt. 8:5-13; 11:2-19; 12:22-50; Luke 7:1-50; 8:1-3.19-21; 11:14-36; Mark 3:20-35

We have two great miracles recorded by Luke. The first takes place in Capernaum. A Centurion was the equivalent of our American military Sergeant except Centurions commanded 100 men. Centurions also served as policemen for the local community.[5] The astounding point of this story is the faith a Roman soldier has in God in stark contrast to the lack of faith that had been displayed by the Jewish leaders. He understood authority and obviously believed Jesus was the Son of God. Because the Centurion felt unworthy to come before Jesus, he had sent esteemed representatives to request his servant be healed. His great act of faith was in his message. The Centurion only requested that Jesus "say the word" and heal his servant. Even Jesus was amazed at such great, total faith. It was a 'no doubt' request. Jesus turned to the crowd and testified to the Centurion's faith, followed by a statement addressing the Gentiles inclusion in the Kingdom of God. In the New Jerusalem, the Gentiles would supplant the non-believing Jews.

In the second event, Jesus shows great compassion towards a widow who has lost her only son to death. Now 20 miles southwest of Capernaum in a town called Nain, Jesus touched the coffin and commanded the young man arise. To compare, the first event was a request for help by a believer, desiring only a spoken word from a great distance and the second event was seemingly a moment of overwhelming compassion towards a stranger who appears to be a non-believer. I have to wonder if Jesus was thinking of the grief His own mother would soon endure.

John the Baptist is still in prison. His disciples report all the news of Jesus' miracles. John was now a depressed man. His life had been the wilderness with all its freedom, beauty, and, yes, danger. John had been a man at the center of a vibrant and growing work for God. He had a long mountaintop experience. John had been faithful and true to his calling. Now he was trapped in a small, dark cell. There were no crowds, no light, no freedom, no life. The devil was hitting John with all he had. John was at the lowest point of his life. He wondered if he had completed God's mission for him -- or had he mistaken God's revelation that Jesus was the Messiah? Had John lived in vain? Had he failed in his mission by identifying the wrong man as Christ? He had to know for sure. John no longer trusted his own judgment. The effects of his confinement were beginning to prey on his mind. John sent his disciples to ask Jesus if He truly was the Messiah. Jesus simply took a 'let me show you' position. After a day of John's disciples getting to see Jesus' miracles up close and personal, they are told to go and tell John what happened.[70] Then Jesus praised John. He told the crowd that John was the Elijah they had expected to prepare the way for the Messiah. If John were not a great man, then why had they gone into the wilderness to see him? Then Jesus makes an astonishing statement -- John is the greatest of those born in the flesh, but the least of those born in the Spirit is greater than John! What does this mean? John represented the last of the prophets who foretold the coming of the Messiah and His kingdom. Jesus brought in the Messianic Age. The gift of salvation and the new covenant in Jesus was much greater than believers who were under the laws of Judaism. In Heb. 11:13, many of the patriarchs are named with the statement, "All these people were still living by faith when they died. They did not receive the things promised; they only saw them and welcomed them from a distance."[1] You and I are greater than John the Baptist but only because the blood of the Lamb of God has cleansed us, we have become a temple for the Holy Spirit, and we have been bound in the new covenant of Christianity. Jesus fulfilled the old laws and became the foundation for the new promise or covenant in His blood -- the free gift of eternal life if you only believe in Him as your Savior and make Him Lord of your life. You will see John the Baptist in Heaven, but He will have gotten there by his faith in God as he lived under the Mosaic Law. John longed even for the glimpses he had of Christ. Even the least Christian would receive a gift much greater than any John had received -- the Holy Spirit.[70,73] Then Jesus makes a statement we will hear in all the early chapters of Revelation, "He who has ears, let him hear."[1] (Matt. 11:15) Jesus' words are a warning to the people. In other words, "Pay attention, be receptive, and be obedient." God's master plan is proven right as it is borne out over time.[70]

Jesus is invited to the home of Simon the Pharisee. First, you wonder if it is a trap. The Pharisees were opposed to Jesus. Second, you wonder if he was like Nicodemus, a secret admirer. Third, was Simon patronizing Jesus to win the popularity of his disciples? Of the three possibilities, the last one is most suitable. Simon probably wanted to gain influence with Jesus' followers and maybe be able to find a fatal flaw in Jesus' teaching as well! Then he would have prestige among the Pharisees. Simon, like all the Pharisees, was wealthy. His house would have contained a central courtyard probably with a fountain and a garden. In warm months, meals would be taken in the courtyard. Diners would recline on low couches propped on their left elbow using their right hand to eat. Their feet would be bare because sandals were usually removed, and their legs would have been stretched out behind them. When a Rabbi came to your home, it was customary for the town's people to be allowed to come and go so they could hear the teachings and wisdom of the teacher. Good manners dictated 3 rituals occur at the time a guest arrived: (1) A slave would remove the guest's sandals and wash his feet, (2) The host would lay his hand on the shoulder of the guest and give him a greeting kiss, and (3) A drop of a perfumed oil would be placed on the guest's head or incense would be burned. Any guest considered a Rabbi would have been given the 'red carpet' treatment.[70]

We find Jesus and Simon in the courtyard eating. A prostitute from the town enters. Like all Jewish women, she carried a vial of perfumed oil around her neck called an alabaster. As she stood behind Him, she began to weep and her tears fell on Jesus' feet. Then she knelt and unbound her hair. All Jewish women bound their hair up when they were no longer virgins. Their hair was only loosed in the presence of their husbands. Again we have a picture of the bride and bridegroom. Many from all walks of life will claim Jesus as Savior. She took her hair and wiped away the tears and dirt from His feet. Then she opened the vial of perfume and poured it over His feet. Simon was shocked. Such intimacy between a prostitute and a Rabbi! Simon doubts Jesus thinking a prophet would know what kind of woman was touching him. Jesus points out that the person who sinned the most has the most to be forgiven. Therefore, she loved Jesus even more. Simon had failed to offer even the customary good manners toward Jesus, but this sinful woman had gone beyond basic good manners to welcome Him! She had given her personal items of value to Jesus.[70] Jesus turns to the woman and tells her, "Your faith has saved you; go in peace."[1] (Luke 7:50)

Three women are identified who have been cured of disease or demon possession: Mary Magdalene, Joanna, and Susanna. These women would become followers and benefactors of Jesus. Mary Magdalene is identified as having had 7 demons cast out.

Jesus now identifies one sin that will not be forgiven in this life or eternity: blasphemy against the Holy Spirit. The Holy Spirit is God dwelling in us. It is bad enough that we drag God with us into sin daily, but it is unpardonable to then slander, revile, curse, or speak irreverently against the Holy Spirit.[5] You can understand the seriousness of the charge the Jews made against Jesus of blasphemy. It was a violation of the third commandment and a crime punishable by eternal death. "But I tell you that men will have to give account on the Day of Judgment for every careless word they have spoken. For by your words you will be acquitted, and by your words you will be condemned."[1] (Matt. 12:36)

The Scribes and Pharisees are becoming patronizing, taunting groupies trying to push Jesus to the point of weakness. Now they ask for another miracle to prove His deity. These religious leaders in every town want proof. By now His miracles were well known to all who lived in Galilee. Requests for more was an effort to try to 'unmask' some magic trick or fake healing to expose Jesus as a false prophet. But Jesus responded that as Jonah had been in the belly of the huge fish for 3 days and 3 nights, so would He be in the earth. The men of Nineveh would condemn these Jews at judgment because of their unbelief for even the wicked Gentile city of Nineveh (located in hated Assyria) repented at the preaching of Jonah. [Note: You can understand Jonah's reluctance to preach the message of His God in the streets of a major city of a pagan ruling nation.]

Jesus tells a story about an evil spirit being driven out of a man. The man removes all sin from his life and walks uprightly before God. Notice, though, throughout the New Testament evil spirits are driven out of people but are not destroyed. They only seek other living beings to inhabit. Evil may be restrained or conquered but not eliminated.[78] Evil is only bound when Satan is bound in the last days. Satan, of course, likes nothing better than to attack those living righteously and to regain the foothold he once had. In the case of the man in the story, that is what happened. He had managed to remove all evil from his life as a result of following Judaic laws but was left empty because he wasn't filled with the Holy Spirit. Therefore, when he could not keep all the oppressive Pharisaical laws, he gave in to even more evil than he had originally.[78] Victory over evil can only be accomplished through salvation from Jesus Christ. When Jesus cleans away all our sins, the Holy Spirit takes up residence to guide us and shape our consciousness so that evil may be kept at bay.

Food for Thought: Notice that the prostitute had provided tears to wash Jesus' feet. She kissed His feet and then poured perfumed oil on them. She had provided everything the Pharisee had not. Her gift was to anoint His body in preparation for His death.

October 28
Bible Readings: Luke 11:37-54; 12:1-59; 13:1-17

A Pharisee rebuked Jesus for not washing His hands before eating. The Pharisaical law was so detailed on ceremonial washing that special water had to be used and poured over the hands in a proscribed manner, much like a physician scrubbing for surgery but only to the wrists. Additionally, the hands had to be washed between every course of the meal and after the meal. Personally, I don't know how they had any skin left to wash! On the other hand, they probably ate a lot less than we do and certainly had no drive-in fast food! Jesus admonished the Pharisee for concentrating on minute external details while his soul knew not God. Legalistic ceremonial washing was more important than oppression, hatred, and abuse of their fellow men.[70]

Jesus launches into a sermonette of woes or curses on those who are evil.

- Woe to those who ritualistically tithe to the last cent but neglect justice and love (charity) to mankind.
- Woe to those who desire prestige and personal recognition. You will be like unmarked graves and defile all who touch you even unawares, infected with misconceptions about God. (See Num. 19:16.)[70]
- Woe to scribes who burden the people with detailed laws but fail to help them with trying to live under their laws.
- Woe to those who build monuments to the ones their forefathers murdered for then they glorify the sin of their fathers. (We are Civil War buffs but as I look at the monuments erected, I wonder if our nation has simply glorified war.)
- Woe to the Pharisees who know the scriptures but have not accepted their simple lessons and have obstructed the masses from coming to know God.

Jesus concludes with a warning that even a little sin pervades the entire mass. As I have said before, sin always impacts other people. No sin is confined only to the sinner. All pay consequences. Remember Ezekiel's vision of the 'secret' paganism going on in the hidden chambers of the Jerusalem Temple? (See Aug. 16th lesson.) Fear not those who can kill the body, fear only the One who has the power to condemn you to hell.

Jesus is even asked to arbitrate the inheritance issues of two brothers. Instead He warns against greed. The things one treasures reflect the heart. A heart that belongs to God stores treasures in Heaven. A heart centered on earthly treasures receives only earthly rewards.

Be watchful for Jesus will return when you least expect Him. Be prepared with your work for Him completed and at peace with your fellow man. Those who think their lives are their own and they can do as they please will be disappointed in their future.[70] Christians know their lives belong to God, bought and paid by Jesus. All we are and all we own are His. The Old Testament law teaches tithing (10%) of one's gain to God. The New Testament teaches that all (100%) we have is God's. The early church members even sold possessions to donate money to the poor. How selfish we are compared to those believers! (See Acts 4:32-37.) Putting the work of the Lord off until tomorrow or until the kids are grown or until retirement means Jesus will return when you have run out of time and your work will not be done. Those who know Christ as Savior and know God's Will for their lives will be held to a higher level of accountability than those who act in error out of ignorance of God's Will. Now you might say, "Well then, ignorance is bliss! If I don't seek God's Will, I won't be held accountable!" Not true! Jesus is speaking to teachers, leaders, priests, and preachers who know God's Will for mankind but lead the people astray. They will be more accountable than the poor deceived people.[73]

Luke 13 mentions two events we know little about and what we do know is supposition. First, there is an account of Pilate murdering some Galileans during their sacrificial ceremony. This is possibly during the time Pilate proposed a new water system for Jerusalem. The money to build the aqueduct would be taken from the Temple monies. The Jews were enraged. Roman soldiers with cudgels were cloaked and sent disguised among the crowd to disperse the uproar. Their orders were to break up the crowd, not to kill. The soldiers were overzealous and many people lost their lives. One assumption is that this incident caused the rift between Pilate and Herod that continued until Jesus' trial.[70]

The second account given is of a tower in Siloam that fell and killed 18 people. These may have been workers on the overhead aqueducts Pilate was building. The Jewish community believed Pilate stole the money from God to make the aqueduct; therefore, all wages earned from its construction belonged to God. They surmised the men were sinners (because of their work on the aqueducts) who got what they deserved. Job 4:7 presents the popular thought, "Who ever perished being innocent?" Jesus declared that only those who repented of their sins were ever innocent.[70]

Repeatedly we are told of Jesus' Sabbath healings. Why so many accounts from the same day? Remember, one of the Pharisees' main charges against Jesus was breaking Jewish law and working on the Sabbath. In this miracle, the woman had something similar to spinal degeneration or spinal curvature. She had been crippled 18 years. The synagogue ruler declared there were 6 days to heal (work) but not on the Sabbath. Jesus lashed back, "You hypocrites!" The Jews would untie their donkey and take it to water (provided that was less than 1,000 yards) on the Sabbath (because a donkey was valuable) but denied mankind healing. Examples of Jewish Sabbath laws include (1) tying a knot in a rope was forbidden, but you could tie one in a woman's girdle (belt), (2) carrying a load on the back or against the chest, or with the hand or shoulder was forbidden, but one could carry anything on the back of the hand, in the mouth, with the elbow, with the ear, with the hair, with the money bag turned upside down, between the money bag and shirt, in the shoe, or in the fold of the shirt![70] Praise God we don't live under the law!

Food for Thought: If one needed water on the Sabbath, (s)he couldn't tie a knot in a rope to lower the bucket. But a woman's belt could be used without any repercussions! If one needed to go further than 1,000 yards, then a rope could be stretched across the street and that declared to be the point of their residence. Then travel 1,000 yards beyond the rope was acceptable! I'm afraid I would be punished to the point of death because I couldn't remember all these laws. Could you?

Verse of the Week: **John 6:29** "Jesus answered, 'The work of God is this: to believe in the one he has sent."

October 29
Bible Readings: Matt. 13:1-52, Mark 4:1-34, Luke 8:4-18, 13:18-21

Today's lesson might be titled "Preparing for the Harvest." We have a series of parables Jesus told, all related to the harvest of believers in the end times, those who comprise the Kingdom of Heaven. Why did Jesus use parables? First, it was fulfillment of prophecy in Isa. 6:9-10 and Ps. 78:2. Second, it was because those who were believers would understand and grow in the Spirit so they, too, could teach God's message. But non-believers would not comprehend and, thus, would not cause trouble for believers because of the parable's message.

The classic parable is that of the sower. The sown seeds fell on four different types of ground: (1) hard path, (2) rocky, (3) thorny, and (4) good soil. These seeds of the gospel fell on 4 different types of people each represented as a type of ground. The hard path person was so hardened to God's word that it could not even penetrate the outside barrier. So it was quickly gone 'like water off a duck's back.' The rocky soil person had a thin-layer of receptiveness on the outside but a hardened heart. The word of God impacted him for a moment, but the effect was soon gone. You often see this happen at evangelistic meetings where all types of people come forward, but some are just 'caught-up' in an emotional moment. It was touching at the time, but there was no true understanding of the Truth, no true repentance, no true acceptance of Jesus' gift of salvation. The person represented by the thorny ground is one who wants to believe and wants to be saved but puts off to a time when he is less tired, not traveling so much, or under less stress. The cares and worries of the world swallowed up the good seed that was planted in the heart. Sometimes I think these people are the saddest of all. They completely missed the joy of knowing and living for Jesus because they were too busy. If they died today, their company would soon have their replacement and within a month they would no longer be remembered. Their job was too important to make room for God; their life was too full to squeeze in the time for an eternal life. But Jesus will not be too busy to pronounce their judgment. Not to despair, though, the sower must remember that some seed will fall on good soil. These people will, in turn, sow the seeds of the gospel to others so that each one's work is multiplied many times. This parable is for believers to understand why some come to Christ, but many don't. It is also for teachers and preachers of the gospel to remember when discouraged over the seemingly poor success their messages have garnered. God multiplies His children's efforts. Any message of salvation will produce fruit, some quickly, and some decades later.[78]

The second parable discusses the good seed sown by Jesus. The good seed are the believers. The enemy Satan comes along and sows weeds or evil people among the good. Notice the devil sneaks in at night or when you have let your defenses down, when you aren't alert to danger. The devil comes in when all seems to be going well. The sower doesn't even know the devil was there until evil starts growing amidst the good. The servants of God would like to wipe out all evil but in doing so some believers would be harmed, too. Evil has become too well integrated in the population. How would you go about destroying all evil in the world? Jesus states that the weeds will be plucked out and burned in the fiery furnace at harvest time. In other words, at the end of time Jesus will do a true sorting of good and evil. The evil ones will be in torment eternally while the righteous ones bask in the heavenly Light.

Other Parables about the Kingdom of God

Symbol of Kingdom	Action	Reward
Lighted lamp	take the gospel to all the world	harvest of believers
Mustard seed	plant the seed in faith	smallest on earth becomes greatest in Heaven
Yeast	a little gospel mixed in the masses	spreads throughout the world
Treasure	salvation is discovered & buried in the heart	all is sacrificed for Jesus
Pearl	valuable gift of salvation is found	all is sacrificed for Jesus
Fishing net	all fish are caught & sorted	believers go to Heaven non-believers to Hell
Owner of home	has new & old believers in storehouse	all believers will go to Heaven

Food for Thought: More than two decades ago, a Christian by the name of Margie had a Bible dictionary on her desk at work that she often read. My mother frequently ate lunch with her friend and was introduced to her book. Mother told me of the wonderful information in this book. As I recall, Mother even bought the book for me. I used it some during the first years I had it. Then a series of events shattered my earthly existence and I retreated to the solace of my Bible. Now I determined to truly study the words of God. I spent hours each day looking up each name and place in the Bible dictionary. Sometimes the hardest task of the day was stopping my study to go to work. My love for studying God's word multiplied rapidly. As a result of that effort, I have taught God's word in many ways over the years. Now I bring it to you. You take it unto all in your world.

October 30
Bible Readings: Matt. 8:18-34, 9:18-34, 13:53-58 Luke 9:57-62, 8:22-56 Mark 4:35-41. 5:1-43, 6:1-6

During Jesus' teaching, several people wanted to become disciples, but they had family concerns they wanted to handle first. Jesus comments that only those committed to the Kingdom of God are fit to serve Him. Everything else in life is worthless without Jesus. I am reminded of Lot's wife who was told to flee with her family in order to avoid the destruction coming on Sodom and Gomorrah. Their orders from the angel were, "Flee for your lives! Don't look back, and don't stop anywhere in the plain!"[1] (Gen. 19:12) Lot's sons-in-law thought it was a great joke. (Joke's on them!) Lot was very hesitant, to the point the angels had to take his hand and the hands of his wife and daughters and lead them out of evil, giving them the above instructions. But Lot's wife couldn't resist looking back to the old way of life. She lost out on a new life in God's Kingdom because she couldn't give up the old life of the world. She was not fit for service.

At one point, Jesus gets in one of a group of boats to set out across the lake. Jesus lies down to get some much-needed rest. A terrible storm arose and the disciples woke Him. They show their lack of true understanding in several ways: (1) they call Him teacher rather than Lord, (2) they ask if He doesn't care -- the One who is about to give His life for all sinners, (3) they are terrified at His power over nature, and (4) they even ask, "Who is this?" making it obvious they don't recognize the Lord.

When the boat reaches the Gerasenes (also called Gadarenes and located on the eastern shore[5]), Jesus meets a man having evil spirits. The spirits were called Legion because there were so many. The man displayed supernatural strength. This is evidence that all supernatural events are not from God; many are the devil's work. Again we see the demons instantly recognize "Jesus, the Son of the Most High." They beg for mercy. Notice they ask that He not torture them. Already they know their final destination will be torment. We always want to picture Jesus as the kind, compassionate, loving Savior. We need also to remember that He will be the stern, unyielding Judge. Even demons fear His judgment. We need to take heed. This demon possessed man lived among the tombs, symbolizing those dead to Christ -- the lost. From the Old Testament (Isa. 45:23) through the New Testament (Rom. 14:11; Phil. 2:10-11), we are told that "every knee will bow before me; every tongue will confess to God." The demon-possessed man gives us a picture of what is to come. The man fell on his knees before Jesus and the evil beings confessed Jesus as the Son of God; they begged for mercy while awaiting His judgment. They were sentenced to inhabit pigs, the most despicable, unclean animal the Jews could name. The 2,000 pigs are being raised by Gentiles and represented much earthly wealth. Even the despicable pigs could not bear the presence of the demons. They commit suicide! The man is left a believer and ecstatic over his deliverance. He begs to go with Jesus, but again we see one sent to carry the gospel to his family. Always be sure you aren't so busy telling others about Jesus that you fail to tell your family.

Jesus crossed the lake again trying to escape the crushing crowds seeking miracles. He is met by Jairus, a synagogue ruler. This title means he was responsible for obtaining teachers, maintaining schedules, monitoring order, and generally overseeing synagogue activities. The synagogue is likened to a community center. It was used for teaching the law to the common man but also for celebrations and other community events. Jairus' daughter was very sick and about to die. He asked Jesus to come and heal her. While on the way, a woman reaches out and touches the tassel of Jesus' cloak. He felt the power go out from Him. (Don't you wonder what the feeling was like?) The woman was healed of her 12-year hemorrhage. But she had been detected. Her act was known. Jesus was looking for the "one who touched Him." The woman fell at His feet, filled with fear, and spilled the truth. Jesus simply stated that she should go in peace for her faith had healed her. Now keep in mind this situation: (1) the woman had little or no power or authority to address a Rabbi, (2) she was unclean by Jewish law and, as such, not allowed to contact other Jews (for 12 years she had been separated from friends and family), (3) she had not been permitted to worship in the Temple nor participate in the festivals, (4) she had a very embarrassing problem (Imagine having to tell Jesus in the middle of a huge crowd all about this problem!), (5) she faced terrible punishment for touching the Rabbi in her unclean state. We have a picture of Jesus healing and forgiving us even in our worthless state of "filthy rags" (Isa. 64:6). He asks only for our faith. Meanwhile, Jairus' daughter has died. Jesus assures him all is well. Jesus takes the two parents and his inner circle of apostles (Peter, James, and John) into the girl's room. He takes her hand and commands her to get up. She immediately stands up. All who witness this are told to keep it secret. Why? Again the answer is to avoid the crowds seeking displays of miracles and the Jewish leaders seeking His death, for His time had not come.

Mourning rituals were detailed in Jewish law (39 rules). A mother was to tear her undergarment on the left neckline down to the level of the heart. Then she wore it backwards and put on her outer garment that she also tore to the heart. A father tore his garment from the left neckline to the level of the heart. All others tore their garments on the right neckline. The tear had to be big enough to insert a fist. The gaping tear had to be exposed for 7 days; it was basted loosely and worn for the next 30 days; finally, it was repaired permanently. A minimum of two flute-players would be hired and professional mourners engaged to wail loudly. By Roman law, ten flute-players were the maximum for a funeral. Because of the climate and lack of embalming, the bodies were buried quickly usually within hours, even in the middle of the night. Frequently, the person was not dead but rather in a coma. Often they awoke in a dark, cold solid rock tomb. Evidence of their desperation to get out has been found in several tombs.[74]

Food for Thought: Are we afraid to embrace a life committed to Jesus because we aren't willing to give up the familiar? Do we want to forego eternal joy for momentary relaxation? Anxiety has good points. It makes us pay attention and be involved. Be anxious about your eternal future.

October 31
Bible Readings: Matt. 9:35-38, 10:1-42, 11:1, 14:1-13 Mark 6:6-33, Luke 9:1-11, John 6:1

Jesus tells us there are many souls to save but few to go witness -- and time is running out. "Like sands in the hourglass, so are the days of our lives." (I guess you recognize this line from the soap opera commercial -- Days of Our Lives.) Jesus multiplies His outreach by commissioning His Apostles to go to all Israel, healing, casting out demons, and, of course, telling them about salvation. They are to take no material possessions. The people of the harvest are to provide for them. The homes and towns that welcome them should be blessed and those that reject should be cursed. A clear picture of the separation of the saved and the lost is found here. The startling outcome of rejecting Jesus' messengers is told in the statement that Sodom and Gomorrah will have a better fate than those who reject! Why is that? Remember it was evil men who were primarily ignorant of the scripture who committed Sodom and Gomorrah's sins, but those rejecting the Apostles could not plead ignorance. After all, every Jew alive was talking about Jesus and His miracles. Jesus warned the Apostles of the danger they will incur. They are to be alert and wise. There is an old country music song made popular by Kenny Rogers that goes, "You have to know when to hold'em, know when to fold'em, know when to walk away, know when to run." This sums up what Jesus was telling His Apostles. They were not to let danger, pride, compassion, or any other emotion, cloud their wisdom and good sense. Then a foretelling of their actual future is chilling: flogging, betrayal, arrest, hatred, persecution, and death. The sacrifices will be great, but the rewards will be even greater! Evil will be uncovered in the long-term. Revenge is the Lord's territory; the Apostles job is to stay the course, firm in their belief to the end. In Matt. 10:34 Jesus tells us He did not come to bring peace (for we are told there will always be wars and rumors of wars (Matt. 24:6)), He came to bring a sword. Eph. 6:17 states that we should use the "sword of the Spirit, that is the word of God" to defend ourselves. John 1:1, 14 says Jesus is the Word who became flesh and lived among us. We are to use the teachings and examples of Jesus to enrich and defend our souls from attack by evil. But no good deed will go unrewarded by Jesus. His Apostles were sent out in pairs and Jesus went alone. They were inexperienced and would face doubt and fear. Each would need another believer's encouragement. But Jesus had a single-minded focus on the task at hand -- the fields were ripe for harvest.

Now Herod had come to respect and fear John the Baptist. He knew John was a righteous and holy man. John's messages were enjoyable even though Herod did not understand their simple principles. Herod is an example of one who heard but did not understand. John's messages were interesting and enticing, but a free gift of eternal life was not logical. Then at his birthday banquet Herod made the ultimate mistake. After having his stepdaughter dance for the group, he promised her "whatever you ask I will give you, up to half my kingdom."[1] (Mark 6:23) Her evil mother told her to ask for the head of John the Baptist on a platter. Can you think of anything so barbaric? And the girl had no better sense than to do it! Herod's true character is revealed. His pride would not let him renege. Pride overruled his fear of killing a righteous man. As I have said in the past, the gateway to hell for many people will be labeled 'Pride.' Salome and her mother Herodias have also revealed their true hearts. They belonged to Satan. There is an old Jewish saying that a man is either good or bad based on the character of the woman with him.[71]

Jesus was deeply moved by John's death, His own drawing closer. When His Apostles returned, they crossed the Sea of Galilee seeking a solitary place for rest and renewal. But they could not escape the crowds. Alas, the fields are ripe for harvest, but the workers are so few.

Food for Thought: How can you work in the harvest? Can you teach, write, sing, lead, witness, or minister? Are you doing it? To he who has been given much, much is demanded (Luke 12:48).

November 1

Bible Readings: Matt. 14:14-36, 15:1-20; Mark 6:34-56, 7:1-12; Luke 9:11b-17; John 6:2-71, 7:1

On a remote hillside outside Bethsaida, Jesus preached to 5,000 men plus women and children (and without a sound system, too!). His Apostles urged Him to take a break for lunch! They were worried about having to feed a hostile crowd faint from hunger (sounds like today's eat'en-meet'en). Well, one little prepared scout brought his lunch, but he wasn't counting on feeding thousands! Jesus had the people sit in groups on the grass. He took the 5 loaves and 2 fishes, looked up to Heaven, gave thanks, and broke them, and broke them, and broke them! After feeding the whole crowd, twelve basketfuls were collected. (Shame they weren't in cars so they could just throw the trash out the window, right? Never!) They pressed for Him to be king. Jesus sent the disciples to Bethsaida via boat. He would catch-up with them later. A beautiful night in April provided solitude for Jesus to spend some much needed quiet time with the Father. Herod Antipas was getting worried about his title "King of the Jews," the scribes and Pharisees were ready to lynch Him but for their political careers, and the masses wanted a national king-Messiah who would end all their problems.[71] Yes, Jesus needed to be alone with His Father. About 3 a.m. Jesus is walking on the water across the Sea of Galilee. The wind had detained the Apostles and they saw Him! Was this Jesus, or a ghost, a spirit? Peter was never one to whisper when truth was for the asking. He shouts, "Lord, if its you, let me walk on the water, too!" Peter was always very sure of himself and his impulsive reactions humbled his pride. The situation always looks better through rose-colored glasses, but when you realize the world isn't rose-colored, the letdown can be your defeat. Just ask Napoleon about Waterloo! Peter walks out on the water and then starts looking around. "Oh, my stars, where am I and what do I think I'm doing?" When we take our eyes off Jesus and look at the world around us, we falter. Peter will have an even greater come-uppance when he denies Jesus (See Matt. 26:33-35, 69-75.). Jesus rescued Peter (who is just like us) and they get in the boat to land at Gennesaret. The crowds were evaded but not discouraged. They searched for Him (like we should do). When they found Him, they asked what 'work' did God require? They obviously still don't understand. Jesus responds that all they must do is believe in Him. How simple! He is the Bread of Life, the Living Water. We are promised that whoever comes will not be driven away. The Will of God is that none shall be lost that God has given to Jesus but rather they will be raised up to eternal life. God's Will is that all of mankind should be saved, that all should live eternally with Him. Then Jesus makes a statement that greatly offends the Jews, further evidence of their lack of understanding. They must be willing to eat His flesh and drink His blood! Remember Jews staunchly refused to ingest blood. Life was in the blood and the blood belonged to God. Mosaic law condemned those who ingested blood (pagans). Eating the flesh of a man was certainly despicable. How could Jesus teach this in the synagogue?

Obvious to Christians, Jesus was referring to His body and blood as the spiritual rebirth. We must completely internalize Jesus. His body and blood must be our bodies and blood. Our life (blood) and strength (flesh) must be drawn from Him. Otherwise, we are lost to evil. Jesus goes on to forecast His own ascension and His death. Only those who are invited by the Father through the Holy Spirit may come to Jesus. How can you get invited? By having a heart receptive to the Word. You must want to come to be invited. All who want to come will not be turned away. After this sermon, many of Jesus' followers left. They were willing to give up their traditional laws for a new covenant, but when the crossroads of life came and one path promised a new tough life while the other promised a familiar life, the lost souls took the wrong one. They chose the path most traveled. They turned their backs on Jesus. Jesus looks at His Apostles and asks if they want to leave, also. Then He announces that even though He chose these men, one was a devil (meaning Judas Iscariot).

The Pharisees never give up. This time they saw some of Jesus' disciples eating with unwashed hands. Jesus responded with a quote from Isaiah calling them hypocrites. They clung to tradition while letting go of God's commands. Nothing entering a man makes him unclean. It is what comes out of a man's heart and soul that make him clean or unclean. "For from within, out of men's hearts, come evil thoughts, sexual immorality, theft, murder, adultery, greed, malice, deceit, lewdness, envy, slander, arrogance, and folly."[1] (Mark 7:21-22)

Food for Thought: Peter was much like us, rushing headlong, impulsively into action, often butting our heads on brick walls. Nevertheless, Peter became the primary 'missionary' to the Jews. Peter's willingness to tackle the difficult tasks made him a perfect missionary. May we all be Peters!

November 2
Bible Readings: Matt. 15:21-39, 16:1-12 Mark 7:24-37, 8:1-26

Jesus left Galilee for Phoenicia (Gentile country). It was now time to show His Apostles that He came to save all men, even Gentiles. Orthodox Jews would never contact a Gentile; it was considered unclean. The area of Tyre and Sidon was originally included in Asher's allotment of Israel (Joshua 19:28-29), but the people of Asher had been unable to overcome the residents of the land. What man could not do with war, Jesus comes to conquer through love.

A Greek Canaanite woman came to Jesus begging for her daughter to be healed from an evil spirit. Jesus' response seems harsh. "I was sent only to the lost sheep of Israel."[1] (Matt. 15:24) Jesus said this for the sakes of those listening. Then He says, "It is not right to take the children's bread and toss it to the dogs."[1] (Matt. 15:26) No matter how you look at it, this sounds like an insult. Jesus though softened the comment by using a Greek diminutive word for dog that meant He was referring to their pet lap dogs. Doubtlessly, His tone of voice was a loving one. This woman was helping Him teach His Apostles a valuable lesson about the faith of Gentiles. Her response was "Yes, Lord, but even the dogs eat the crumbs that fall from their masters' table."[1] (Matt. 15:27) Her faith was strong and her daughter was healed.[71]

Jesus left there and returned to the Sea of Galilee, to the area known as the Decapolis or Ten Cities ruled by Syria. The Decapolis was a large Greek area of population on the east side of the Jordan. The ten cities were identified as Damascus, Dion, Gadara (where the demon possessed man was healed in Mark 5:20), Gerasa, Hippos, Canatha, Pella, Philadelphia (Ammon, Jordan), Raphana, and Scythopolis (only city on the west side of Jordan). Here Jesus heals a man deaf and almost mute. The people were amazed and praised the God of Israel.

The word spreads rapidly. Jesus soon has a crowd of 4,000 men plus women and children listening to Him teach on a hillside. They have been 3 days without food. Jesus is concerned about their needs. (When was the last time your congregation went 3 **hours** without food?) He asks the Apostles for food and seven loaves of bread and a few fishes are found. Jesus gave thanks and broke the food. Of course, we know what happened. He fed the whole crowd and 7 basketfuls were left over. As with all things, Jesus takes what we have to offer and multiplies it manyfold. One witness may lead to thousands saved. One person led Billy Sunday or Billy Graham to salvation.

These men were able to do what that one person could not do -- reach millions. But had it not been for the one person who was instrumental in leading them to Christ, millions would have waited to hear the Word of God. One witness makes a difference.

Jesus and His Apostles got into the boat to cross over the sea. The Apostles had brought only one loaf of bread. Jesus said, "Be on your guard against the yeast of the Pharisees and Sadducees."[1] (Matt. 16:6) The Apostles thought He meant He was concerned about the lack of food. Jesus reminded them of the food God had provided to feed the 5,000 and the 4,000. No, food was not His concern. Then they understood they were to guard against the teachings of the Pharisees and Sadducees. We still have Pharisees, Sadducees, and pagans among us, many in organized religions as ministers, priests, and teachers. Question everything you are told. Look for it in the Bible. Don't accept anything you can't prove is Biblical.

At Bethsaida, Jesus healed a blind man. This is an interesting miracle in that it is in two stages. First the man sees blurrily; then his eyes are fully healed. First we see God shallowly; then we mature in our faith. Blindness was frequent in the Middle East because of the glare from the sun. A commonplace occurrence was to see flies on the crusted eyes of the blind. Jesus led the blind man out of the village before He healed him. Why? So the miracle wouldn't draw a crowd of gawkers. Spit was a commonly used method of healing. So Jesus' use of spit was not shocking.[71]

Food for Thought: Matt. 15 tells of Jesus leaving Tyre and traveling to Sidon and on to the Sea of Galilee and into the region of the Decapolis. He would have walked 168 miles at an average pace of 14 minutes/mile. Now I have done a lot of walking and working on my speed, but Jesus far exceeds my capabilities. He was an extremely physically fit man. To sustain a 14 min/mile walk is a very hard workout. To do that for 12 hours is amazing! Most Jews walked from sun-up until sundown. Remember this was hilly country around the Sea of Galilee. Had Jesus not been so physically fit, He would never have survived the beating and torture He received prior to the cross.[109] Our Savior stayed fit to serve us. Do we stay fit to serve Him?

November 3
<u>Bible Readings: Matt. 16:13-28; 17:1-27; 18:1-35, Mark 8:27-38; 9:1-50, Luke 9:18-50; 17:1-10</u>

In Caesarea Philippi, Jesus started preparing His Apostles for His arrest and crucifixion. Caesarea Philippi was on the southwestern side of Mount Hermon. It was as far north as Jesus' ministry would go.[5] Jesus asked His disciples who men say He is. They replied, "John the Baptist, Elijah, Jeremiah, a prophet." Then Jesus asked the Apostles straightforward, "Who do you say I am?" Peter, quick to respond, answered, "You are the Christ, the Son of the living God."[1] (Matt. 16:16) Jesus gives Peter the ultimate blessing, the church will be built upon Peter's Christian faith and witness to the world about the salvation of God. Hell could not prevail against the church. The keys to the kingdom of Heaven will be given to him. Peter will be able to perform miracles as Jesus had done. Jesus warns them again not to tell anyone He is the Christ. Jesus had taught, preached, and performed miracles. Now, He finally saw His true identity revealed to one of His own. Only after Jesus' mission was complete could Peter reveal his knowledge to the world. Jesus did not want to be an earthly king but a heavenly one.

Jesus must now reveal His true mission: in Jerusalem He will be arrested, persecuted, and killed on the accusation of the scribes and Pharisees, but on the third day He will rise again. Again Peter impulsively responds, "Never!" Jesus who so generously blessed Peter just minutes before now rebukes him with a crushing statement, "Get behind me, Satan!" He goes on to explain that it is the Will of God and God's master plan is more important than earthly desires. At this point a crowd is forming and Jesus turns to them saying, "If anyone would come after me, he must deny himself and take up his cross and follow me. For whosoever wants to save his life will lose it, but whoever loses his life for me and for the gospel will save it."[1] (Matt. 16:24-25) A wonderful earthly life with all its pleasures is but a moment in time, but a life as a prince or princess in Heaven is for all eternity. The latter is more desirable than the former. Jesus continued to tell His followers that whoever was ashamed of Him would suffer a like experience in Heaven. We must never be too embarrassed to tell someone about Jesus. Embarrassment comes from our own weakness and inability. We should pray for courage and skill in presenting salvation!

Jesus makes a comment that many have found difficult to interpret. He says some of those in that crowd would not die before seeing the Kingdom of God come with power. There are two common interpretations. (1) They would see Jesus die and be resurrected, the point in time which marks the beginning of the new covenant between God and all mankind. (2) This new covenant would be carried throughout the world by Jesus' disciples. Churches with Jesus Christ as their foundation would be prominent from Egypt to Greece to Palestine within 30 years. Many of those in the crowd would live to see the establishment of God's kingdom on earth -- the body of believers He lovingly calls His church.

Six days later the three inner circle Apostles went with Jesus up Mt. Hermon. Jesus became transfigured. His face was shining and His clothes were white as light. (See Rev. 1:12-17 and Dan. 7:13.) Moses and Elijah appeared with Him. Peter quickly offers to erect three booths or shelters for them. This offer has been interpreted to indicate it was the time of the Feast of Tabernacles, which occurred in the fall. Then from a cloud a voice says, "This is my Son, whom I love; with him I am well pleased. Listen to him!"[1] (Mark 9:7) This is an exact repeat of the statement made at Jesus' baptism with one addition -- **"Listen to Him!"** (See Matt. 3:17.) This affirmation was reassurance from God the Father to His Son: go on Son, I am proud of you. Jesus and the Apostles had surely retreated to this quiet place for prayer. Jesus had been telling them of His own death that lay ahead. Certainly, He poured His heart out to His Father. He would want to be sure He had chosen His path wisely and fulfilled God's mission. Now He had God's approval. Also, His key Apostles had witnessed the event. They would never forget what had happened on that mountain. It would remain a driving force in their lives to take the Word of God to all people. The Apostles knew the situation was now grave; their own training was in its critical final stage. At all costs, they must listen! Jesus warns them not to tell anyone what they have seen until He has risen from the dead. John the Baptist had prepared the way, now Jesus would suffer and die.

Upon returning to the other disciples, Jesus discovered a crowd surrounding some scribes who were arguing with the disciples. A man had brought his son who was an epileptic. The boy frequently convulsed, often falling into the fire. Jesus' disciples had been unable to drive out the evil spirit. The father asked, "If you can do anything . . .." Jesus replied, "If you can? Everything is possible for him who believes." The boy's father responded, "I do believe; help me overcome my unbelief!"[1] (Mark 9:23-24) We, too, can ask God to strengthen us and help us overcome doubt. Doubt is one of the attack weapons of Satan. Among "good" people, it is the most frequent one used besides pride and greed. Jesus rebuked the spirit and it left the boy. Weak from the experience, he lay limp on the ground. Jesus took his hand and lifted him to his feet, whole again. Jesus will do the same thing for us. When the overwhelming troubles of the world leave us weak, limp, unable to fight anymore, Jesus will take us by the hand and lift us up -- whole in His Love.

In private the disciples inquire as to why they couldn't drive out the evil spirit. Jesus simply responded that they had too little faith. He goes on to explain that faith the size of a mustard seed can move mountains. This kind of faith is only revealed through prayer.

Leaving there they travel through Galilee to Capernaum. On the way, Jesus tells the disciples again that He will be betrayed, killed, and will rise on the third day. On reaching Capernaum, the Temple tax collectors come seeking to collect from Jesus and Peter. Jesus explained to Peter that as the Son of God, Jesus was exempt from paying taxes to God, but He would do it so as not to offend the Jews. Peter was instructed to go fishing. The first fish he caught would contain a coin in its mouth of the exact denomination needed for the Temple tax. It was so.

On their trip to Capernaum, the Apostles got in an argument over who was the greatest. Jesus replied, "To be first, you must be last and serve all the others." After having done everything God gives us to do, we are still unworthy servants who should be so humbled that we are like little children.

Jesus loved children. He warns that anyone who causes a child to sin would be better off with a millstone around his neck and drowning in the deepest part of the sea. The Jews were afraid of the sea. They thought of Heaven as having no sea (Rev. 21:1). Jews were terrified of drowning. Anything cast into the salt sea would be utterly destroyed. The Romans would drown people as punishment but not the Jews.[78] Our newspapers are full of stories of priests, pimps, and gang leaders who have led little children into sin. There will be a terrible price to pay in eternity for these sins. Then Jesus makes an interesting statement, "See that you do not look down on one of these little ones. For I tell you that their angels in heaven always see the face of my Father in heaven."[1] (Matt. 18:10) The Jews had raised angelology (study of angels) to a great height. They had angels for every leaf and blade of grass. Nations and people had angels. Even the weather had angels. So the Jews definitely believed every child had a guardian angel. These angels had direct access to the God of Heaven at all times. Jesus is telling them the importance or value God places on children. Their angels always have access while others have to wait. Each child is given enormous potential. It is the responsibility of all who come in contact with children to mold them into vessels for the Lord, tools to be used for God.[78] God is not willing for any child to be lost. We are entrusted with their care.

Now Jesus moves to a more severe picture of sin in our lives. It is better we remove the limb or body part than to allow it to drag us into sin. If we took this literally, there would be millions of eunuchs and blind people but few to marry and reproduce. The point of Jesus' story is that we need to eliminate sin from our lives regardless of how painful it is, in order to ensure our heavenly reward.

Matt. 18:16 quotes Deut. 19:15, "every matter may be established by the testimony of two or three witnesses."[1] We are wise not to make decisions with only one witness.

Peter asked how many times he should forgive his fellow man for offenses against him. Jesus' response was 77 times or until perfectly complete. Anytime you forgive someone that many times, you will have reached a level of perfectly complete grace. I don't know of anyone who has accomplished this but Jesus. That doesn't mean we shouldn't try.

Jesus tells a parable about a king who demanded all his servants pay up their debt accounts. One servant owed millions of dollars. He could not pay but begged for mercy, not wanting his wife and children to be sold into slavery. The king had mercy and canceled his debt. Soon that servant goes out and finds a fellow servant who owes him a few dollars. The man couldn't pay and begged for mercy. But he received none. He was thrown into prison until the debt was paid. When the king heard, he was furious with the wicked servant. Had the king himself not been merciful and forgiven millions? How could the recipient of such mercy be so ungrateful as to oppress another who owed so little? The king was so angry he turned the wicked fellow over to the jailers to be tortured until his debt was paid in full. Jesus finished with, "This is how my heavenly Father will treat each of you unless you forgive your brother from your heart."[1] (Matt. 18:35)

Food for Thought: Our senses are the doorways to letting sin into our hearts and minds. First we sense the sin, then we think about it, and finally we act upon it. Any time we know we are looking or thinking about something God forbids, we must pray God will remove the thought. We must also do our part and remove ourselves from situations that bring the thought to mind. Years ago, I gave up country music because of the lyrics that only talked about sin. My television watching is limited to some home decorating, weather, and public broadcasting shows. Unfortunately, there are getting to be very few television programs fit to watch. What our eyes see, our ears hear, our skin touches, our mouth tastes, or our nose smells becomes a part of our mind -- a part that we can only erase with God's help.

November 4
Bible Readings: John 7:2-8:11

Jesus' own brothers (James, Joses, Judas, and Simon -- Wonder why his name didn't start with a J?) made fun of Him. They teased Him rather unmercifully about going to Jerusalem and making a big display of His miracles. The reason behind this suggestion was that Jesus had only performed one miracle in Jerusalem -- the healing of the lame man at the Pool of Bethesda (John 5:1-15).[72] Even this great miracle had been overshadowed by the fact that it occurred on the Sabbath. Now His brothers showed their disbelief in Him, too. Anyone other than Jesus may have given in to despair. After all, Jesus was hated by the Jews, taunted by His brothers, and pursued by the crowds. Even a joyful festival was now a time of great danger. After His brothers had gone to the festival with the crowd from Galilee, Jesus went up alone. Jesus didn't have to shrewdly evade the public, He had the authority to call angels to protect Him, blind others to Him, or even kill His enemies. But God had sent Him to live as a man among common men. He was holy; He was not to be goaded into rash judgment. The Father's work must be done in the right way and in the right time.

The Feast of Tabernacles lasted a total of 8 days. Halfway through the festival, Jesus began to teach in the Temple courts. This Temple complex is so large that a thousand or more could sit on one set of the steps. Jesus had a large audience in the courts. The people of Jerusalem had heard of Him, but few had heard Him speak. They were amazed at His knowledge and insight into the scripture. But Jesus gave the honor to His Father. He also attributed all authority for His work to God. Jesus now has the opportunity to defend His actions. He reminds them that they are so steeped in Mosaic Law that all male babies are circumcised on the 8th day even if it is the Sabbath! Why then have they condemned Him for making a man well on the Sabbath? These people couldn't see the forest for the trees. Jesus reminds them and us that good judgment in line with the word of God should be our guide, not believing everything others tell us. We should verify our beliefs.

The crowd is now whispering and mumbling among themselves. "Isn't this the man the scribes and Pharisees are trying to kill? Why, then, do they let Him teach? Isn't this the Jesus from Nazareth?" Jesus goes on to say. "Yes, you know me, and you know where I am from. I am not here on my own, but he who sent me is true. You do not know him, but I know him because I am from him and he sent me."[1] (John 7:28-29) Now He had really done it! Telling God's chosen people they didn't know God was a slap in the face! Furthermore, saying that He alone knew God and that He was from God (or a part of God) was considered to be blasphemy from one the crowd knew as the son of Joseph. Now the Temple guards were sent to arrest Jesus. They had Him in the midst of Judea and the Galilean disciples wouldn't be able to protect Him here. Jesus declares to the crowd that He will only be among them a short time and then He will return to God. They will seek Him but not find Him. Why? Matt. 7:7 promises, "Ask and it will be given to you; seek and you will find; knock and the door will be opened to you."[1] But now Jesus is telling the Jews the exact opposite! The answer may be found in Isa. 55:6, "Seek while he is near." There is a time when God beckons us to come to Him. If we repeatedly refuse His call, then our hearts grow hardened. Ultimately, we will be so comfortable with sin that we no longer seek God then God will no longer seek us. John 6:36-37 reminds us, "But as I told you, you have seen me and still you do not believe. All that the Father gives me will come to me and whoever comes to me I will never drive away."[1] God knows who will accept His gift of salvation and who won't, but He offers the gift to all. Just as we become hardened, bitter, and angry towards telemarketers who keep calling us, the lost take on the same attitude toward repeated invitations to accept salvation. Their hearts become hardened to God. The scribes, Pharisees, and Jews were seeking a Messiah. Here He was before them, but they could not find Him.[72] Their eyes could not see, their ears could not hear, and their hearts could not receive the Christ. They were seeking but could not find. Again, only a humbled, receptive heart can find Jesus Christ. We must only Confess and repent of our sins, Believe that Jesus is the Son of God who died for our sins and rose to eternal life with God, and Accept Him as Lord and Savior of our lives. Eternal life with God is so simple that it is a great stumbling block for many people.

The first and last days of the feast were great assembly worship days. These were the most joyous and holy days of all the festival. If the Jews couldn't make the whole festival, they made every effort to attend one of these days, the last day probably garnering the most attendance. On the last day of the feast, "Jesus stood and said in a loud voice, 'If anyone is thirsty, let him come to me and drink. Whoever believes in me, as the Scripture has said, streams of living water will flow from within him.'"[1] (John 7:37-38) This referred to the Holy Spirit that would live in Christians and flow from its source (God) into all aspects of our lives. Throughout time, the Holy Spirit had only come upon those who were prophets or had visions from God. When Jesus rises from the grave and ascends into Heaven, the Holy Spirit will be given to all Christians beginning at Pentecost (See Acts 1). The conversation among the Jews following Jesus' announcement indicates they know the Messianic scripture of the prophet but they do not know much about the life of Jesus. But do we need to know that to accept Him as Messiah and receive salvation? No! People who have never seen or heard of a Bible can receive eternal life by accepting the gift of salvation through repenting of their sins and accepting Jesus as Lord and Savior of their lives. Missionaries witness this miracle continually.

The scribes and Pharisees brought in a woman who had been caught in adultery. The Law of Moses commanded she be stoned to death. (Wonder what, if anything, happened to the man?) In an effort to trap Jesus, the Jews presented the woman and demanded Jesus' judgment on her. What was the trap? From the Jews' standpoint, Jesus could make only two decisions: kill her or pardon her. In the first, He would be going against all He had taught about love, forgiveness, and mercy. Thus, He would be exposed as a liar. In the latter, He would be opposing the Law of Moses and appearing to condone adultery, a direct violation of God's commandment. Additionally, to sentence her to death would violate Roman law. Although the Jews were free to rule themselves in most civil and religious areas, they were not allowed to kill anyone; only Roman law could do that. What they didn't expect was for the Rabbi Jesus to stoop down and draw in the dirt. Why did He do that? Barclay lists four reasons.

1. It was a 'time out' to allow tempers to cool and good sense to return to the crowd.
2. Some manuscripts of this passage indicate Jesus acted as if He had not heard them. This would force them to repeat their charges against her, losing some of its force and crowd appeal on repetition. At the least, much of their anger would be transferred to Him for ignoring them.
3. Some have suggested that Jesus wanted to hide His own feelings of agony and pity over the shameful way this was becoming a game and a circus to the Jews.
4. The Armenian translates Jesus' actions as writing the sins of the Jews around Him on the ground where all could see them (just as this woman's sins had been exposed).

This last reason comes from the translation of the Greek word meaning "to write." (Remember the New Testament is written in Greek.) The Greeks normally used the word *graphein*, but in this passage the word *katagraphein* is used. *Katagraphein* is actually translated as "to write down a record against someone." Therefore, it is logical to understand that the doodling Jesus did was actually a list of sins the woman's accusers recognized as their own! When Jesus stands up, His judgment is what they never expected! "If any one of you is without sin, let him be the first to throw a stone at her."[1] (John 8:7) The word *anamartetos* translated as "without sin" may actually mean "without a sinful desire." Jesus forgave the woman and bid her go in peace and never sin again. It was not Judgment Day, but a day of mercy. But Judgment Day **will come** for those who never repent and turn from sin.[79]

Food for Thought: Jews, who lived outside Palestine, or the Holy Land, were known as the Diaspora, or the dispersion. Diaspora is still used today. In Jesus' day, these people were generally thought to be Greek-speaking exiles and immigrants who no longer maintained Jewish laws and customs (at least not to the detail the scribes and Pharisees required).[72] Those who are dispersed will again be gathered together.

> Verses of the Week: **John 8:12, 31-32** "I am the light of the world. Whoever follows me will never walk in darkness, but will have the light of life. . . . If you hold to my teaching, you are really my disciples. Then you will know the truth, and the truth will set you free."

November 5
Bible Readings: John 8:12-10:21

Our memory verse for this week is an appropriate beginning for today's lesson as Jesus switches analogies from being Bread and Water (needed to sustain life) to being the Light of the world (needed for growth and maturity). We see Jesus moving his teaching from the basic components of being a babe in Christ to the revelation of Truth found in growing, maturing Christians. His time is very short now and He must turn His primary focus from gaining converts to developing mature workers who can carry on the work after Him. Again He testifies that His decisions are justified as the Son of God, the One who sent Him. Again, He tells the Jews they do not know Him or His Father. But still no one harmed Him because His time was not yet up. Jesus warns that those who do not believe that He is the Son of God will die eternally in sin. Jesus refers to His own death on the cross and tells the Jews they will know who He is then. Jesus declares that He is the Truth and He can set them free. Now they are incensed! After all, they were descendants of Abraham and had never been slaves to anyone. For starters, we know this is a lie! The children of Israel were slaves to the Egyptians, Assyrians, Babylonians, Persians, Medes, and Romans. Granted they were not always conscripted slaves, but they also were not free to do as they pleased. Jesus goes on to say that a slave has no permanent place in the family but a son does. As slaves to sin we had no place in the family of God, but as sons (children) of God we have eternal life with Him. Biologically the Jews were Abraham's descendants, but they were not his spiritual descendants for Abraham had worshipped and followed God. The Jews were hung up on man's legalism and dictated moral laws. They had become the children of the devil, the master of lies and murder. Those who believe his lies are murdered for eternity. The Jews now hurl insults at Jesus. They called Him a Samaritan and demon-possessed. In calling Jesus the name of their most hated neighbors, they were saying that He, too, was a despised lawbreaker and heretic. One could say they were accusing Jesus of being a false prophet -- an antichrist! How could Jesus possibly want to die for the sins of any of these people? How could He mourn over them? (Luke 12:34-35) The answer is simple: He was the Son of God. Jesus responds that God has glorified Him and that Abraham rejoiced at seeing the day of the Messiah. Some Rabbis taught that Abraham had been given a vision of the time when the Messiah would come. Others taught that Abraham knew that the Messiah would come from his lineage (based on Gen. 12:3). Either way, the Jews would understand that Jesus was saying they should be glad to see Him - the Messiah - instead of denouncing Him. The Jews retaliate with "You aren't old enough to have seen Abraham!" Jesus answered, "I tell you the truth, before Abraham was born, I am!"[1] (John 8:58) This really incited the Jews to charge Jesus with blasphemy. After all, God had declared His own name was "I Am." (Ex. 3:14) Therefore, this man Jesus was saying He was God! At this Jesus became 'unseen' by the crowd and slipped away.[79]

Jesus was leaving with His Apostles when they encountered a blind man. The Apostles asked whether he or his parents were the sinner. Jesus responded, "Neither one." He went on to say that the man's blindness had happened just so God's work could be displayed to a lost world. The Apostles were learning a valuable lesson. Many troubles in this world are allowed so that God can be glorified to the lost people who are watching. Jesus spit on the ground, made mud, and put it on the blind man's eyes. Then He told the man to go wash in the Pool of Siloam (located in the southeast corner of Jerusalem[5]). First, we must note that the blind man had faith in Jesus for he immediately goes and washes in the Pool of Siloam. Second, we see he witnesses to his family and neighbors. Third, we pick up the story with the man being persecuted for his faith. The Pharisees heard of this miracle that had again occurred on the Sabbath. First, the man and then the parents of the man are questioned. Fearful of the punishment of the Pharisees, the parents transfer the burden of response to their son. His response was simple and truthful. "I did not see who healed me but I do know I was blind and now I see!" Recognized as a disciple of Jesus, the Pharisees hurled insults at him. He then uses their own theological teachings to discredit them. Now the Pharisees really were infuriated! They can only reply that he was filled with sin from birth (obvious to them because of blindness being associated with sin). The man is thrown out of the synagogue. When Jesus heard this, He sought the man and confirmed he was a believer. Jesus declared that He had come into the world so that the blind will see and those who claim they see (religious leaders of the Jews) will become blind to God's revelation of His Son.

Now Jesus moves to the analogy of believers being like sheep with Jesus as their Shepherd. We know already that Jesus is the Way, the Truth, the Ladder, and the Gate to God the Father. No man comes to the Father except through Jesus, the Gate. Jesus tells the Jews that only the Shepherd enters by the Gate. Those who try to get to the sheep in any other way are thieves trying to steal the sheep of God. The sheep know the voice of their Shepherd and follow Him. All the sheep that go through the Gate will be saved. They will be at peace and the Good Shepherd will provide for them. The Good Shepherd lays down His life to save the sheep. Jesus knows those who believe in Him. He also knows the Will of the Father. Other sheep not of this flock (in other words, Gentiles) also belong to Jesus. All believers will belong to one flock led by one Shepherd. As our Good Shepherd, Jesus chose to follow the Will of His Father and give His life for us. He had the authority to lay down His life or to save His life -- the decision was His. Praise God that Jesus chose to lay down His life so that we could live!

Food for Thought: Read Psalm 23 and imagine yourself being led by the Shepherd.

November 6
<u>Bible Readings: Matt. 11:20-30,19:1-2; Mark 10:1; Luke 9:51-56; 17:11-19; 10:1-42; 11:1-13 John 10:22-42</u>

Jesus is now leaving His 'second home,' Galilee. He is beginning to make His way to Jerusalem and the cross. Samaria lay between Galilee and Judea. The Samaritans were considered enemies of the Jews. Therefore, Jews would walk the long way around Samaria, but not Jesus, although Jesus was not always received well either. Not surprising, a Samaritan would refuse to shelter a Jew overnight. His fellow townspeople would likely have harmed the citizen. When no accommodation was found, James and John wanted to call down fire on the village in righteous indignation. Jesus rebuked them.

As they came to another village, ten lepers stood at a distance and cried out for Jesus to have mercy on them. You recall that lepers were not allowed to contact those who were 'clean.' They also were put out of the 'camp' or village and had to warn all passers-by by shouting, "Unclean! Unclean!" Jesus simply responded, "Go show yourselves to the priests." They, in turn, had the faith to go to the Temple. This was truly an act of faith because otherwise they might be killed for going into the village. One came running back to fall at Jesus' feet and give Him praise. The other 9 had what they wanted and went away with their gift. Notice it was a Samaritan who came back to praise Jesus. We don't know the nationality of the others (although the rest of the passage indicates the others may all have been Jews), but a Samaritan would normally hate a Jew, much less fall down and praise one. Jesus asks where the other 9 are. Then He sends the man on his way, enforcing that faith had healed him. How often do we beg God for mercy then fail to thank Him for His answer? Are we as ungrateful as the other 9 lepers? As Christians, do we take our positions as children of God with all its rights and privileges for granted? After all, we get to read God's Holy Word, pray to a living God, and call Jesus both our Savior and our Brother! We have been blessed beyond words and should thank God daily for His mercies.

Jesus appoints 72 of His disciples as missionaries in the field. The harvest is ripe and the workers are few. These men are given the same instructions as the Apostles were given when they went out (Oct. 31 lesson).

Although, this time a curse is pronounced on Chorazin (Korazin) which is called Khirbet Kerazeh today, Bethsaida which is believed to be a different town than the one several of the Apostles came from, and Capernaum which had been Jesus' headquarters in Galilee. All of these towns are within a couple of miles of each other north of the Sea of Galilee. Jesus reflects that the Gentiles would have readily believed in Him had they seen the miracles He performed. By contrast, the Jews only wanted to kill Jesus. So why did He spend His time on the Jews? God had made a promise hundreds of years before that these would be His holy people and He would send them a Messiah. God always keeps His promise. He never lets any efforts made in His name go unrewarded. The Jews would still carry the message of salvation to the whole world. Rest can be found in Jesus for all those weary and burdened. His gift is easy to accept and His requirements are only to repent of sins and believe in Jesus as the Son of God, making Him Savior of your life. To the Jews this should have been welcomed greatly. The burden of the Pharisaical laws was a heavy yoke to bear.

In Luke 10:25-37, Jesus tells a scribe the story of the Good Samaritan. The scribe asked whom his neighbor was that he should love as himself. Jesus told the story of a man traveling down from Jerusalem to Jericho. If you look at a map, you will find that Jericho is northeast of Jerusalem. So how was it the man was going **down** to Jericho? Well, Jerusalem is on a mountain and Jericho is in the Jordan Valley. The traveler was descending the mountain. In a 20-mile stretch of road, the elevation dropped 3,600 feet. The road to Jericho was famous for its danger.[70] Robbers attacked the traveler on the road, took his clothes, and beat him up. Left half-dead (down but not out!) in the ditch, three potential rescuers eventually come upon the scene. First was a priest who crossed to the other side to avoid the whole scene. Second was a Levite who did the same. But the third man was a hated Samaritan who had compassion on the victim. He poured wine and oil on the victim's wounds and bandaged them. (Wine killed the infection and oil sealed the wound.) Then the Samaritan placed the man on his own donkey and took him to an inn. The Samaritan paid the innkeeper to care for the man and promised to pay any additional expenses on his return visit. Who was the neighbor to the victim? Of course, it was the Good Samaritan.

Now let's look at the Good Samaritan story with a different eye. The label of Samaritan was given to anyone who didn't keep the ceremonial laws. In John 8:48 the Jews called Jesus a Samaritan. If you look at the Samaritan as representing Jesus then the victim represents the lost that have been beaten up by robbers who represent the devil. We see the love and compassion of Jesus pouring the wine of His blood on the wounds of sin in the lost. His blood kills evil's infection in their lives. After being cleansed by His wine (blood), then He pours the oil of His consecration over them and seals the wounds for healing. The cleansed have been consecrated as part of Jesus' church. Jesus binds (represented by bandages) the cleansed, sealed Christian Himself. In Matt. 18:18, Jesus gives authority to the church such that whatever is bound on earth is bound in Heaven. Jesus binds the devil on earth and he will be bound in the spiritual world, also. Likewise, Jesus binds those He calls His own so that none can be taken from Him. Jesus the servant who rode the lowly donkey (life of service) now places the repentant sinner (believer) on His own donkey (life of service). [Jesus is our example of living a life of service.] Jesus not only leads the donkey (life) but also walks beside him (us through life). Jesus paid the price to ensure those who believe and depend on Him have eternal life. Unlike the Samaritan, when Jesus comes again, there will be no need for further payment. The price was paid in full.

Jesus is moving toward Jerusalem again when He and His Apostles come to Bethany. He seeks the solace of His friends' home. Martha, the worrier, was running around everywhere trying to prepare food for 13 extra guests! Meanwhile her sister Mary was sitting at Jesus' feet listening to the teachings of the Rabbi. When Martha complains because Mary isn't helping her, Jesus reminds her (and us) that the real priorities of life should be spiritual.

Jesus taught His Apostles to pray. We know His model prayer as the Lord's Prayer. It acknowledges the holiness of our heavenly Father and our acceptance of His master plan for His Kingdom. The needs for the day are requested as well as forgiveness of sins (which offend our Father). Then we declare our own willingness to forgive others who sin against us. It culminates with a request to avoid temptation to sin. This prayer covers forgiveness of past sin, provision of present needs, and deliverance from future temptation. Before all our personal requests, we must first praise God and give Him the glory and honor.[70]

Jesus tells a parable about a man who came knocking on the door of his friend's home at midnight. Eastern custom dictated travelers were provided food and shelter. The man who was knocking had received a guest but had no food prepared. So he sought assistance from his friend. Instead, his friend told him to go away. Only after much persistence did the friend get up and give him some food. To understand the parable, we must realize that eastern custom also dictated you were welcome when the door was open. When it was closed, you did not disturb the household. Once everyone was up and ready for the day, the door would be opened until bedtime. The many family members slept close together on floor mats. If one got up, all were disturbed. But the knocker was persistent and the homeowner relented. All the needs of the knocker were met. Those who persistently bombard God with prayer for their needs will find those needs are met in full. "Ask and it will be given to you; seek and you will find; **knock and the door will be opened to you**."[1] (Luke 11:9) If earthly fathers who are of an evil nature know how to give their children good gifts, how much more will our heavenly Father give us?

During the Hanukkah festival Jesus was walking in Solomon's Colonnade, which was a porch on the east side of the Temple. Some Jews gathered and asked Him to tell them plainly if He was the Christ. Jesus reminded them of the miracles He had done in God's name; that should be evidence enough. He continues by saying that those who know Him (as their Savior) will never perish because He has given them eternal life. Then Jesus plainly states, "I and the Father are one."[1] (John 10:30) The Jews pick up rocks to stone Jesus for blasphemy. (Wonder where they got all those rocks inside the Temple complex?) Jesus refers to Psalm 82 where royalty are referred to as gods, but those who are wicked will die like mere men. If these men can be called gods, why do they want to stone Jesus for saying He is God's Son? All who saw His miracles should know who sent Him. Again Jesus escaped those who wished to kill Him.

Jesus crossed to the east side of the Jordan into Perea. Many heard His teaching and believed in Him.

Food for Thought: Throughout this lesson, as well as throughout the New Testament, the phrase "The Jews" refers to the enemies of Jesus. There are many Jews, both then and now, who are believers. How special it must be to be a Jew AND a believer!

November 7
Bible Readings: Luke 13:22-35; 14:1-35; 15:1-32; 16:1-31; 17:20-35,37; 18:1-14; Matt. 20:1-16

The Jews had gotten so arrogant about their ancestry as the chosen people that they now argued whether certain sects would go to Heaven whereas others would be excluded. A sect is a group bound by the same religious beliefs, e.g., Pharisees, Sadducees. Jesus replies that the entrance to Heaven is narrow (repentance of sin and belief in Jesus as the Son of God and your Savior). When God closes the door (at the time of death), it will not open again. There will be great torment in hell at the sight of the patriarchs in Heaven at the LORD's banquet where nonbelievers will never get to go. Personally, I believe part of the great torment of hell will be the condemned seeing Heaven but knowing they can never get there. God's people will be drawn from all nations of the earth.

Just as Herod feared John the Baptist, he may have feared Jesus. Possibly Herod sent the Pharisees to tell Jesus to 'run for His life.' Jesus had won many believers in Perea. Herod did not want to be caught executing (or attempting to kill) another popular prophet. Jesus' reference to driving out demons and healing today and tomorrow is another way of saying 'daily.' Jesus goes one step further and says He'll still be doing it on the third day or in the future.[73]

Both Matthew (23:37-39) and Luke (13:34-35) record a sorrowful lament spoken over the inhabitants (non-believing Jews) of Jerusalem. One is left with the implication that Jesus is the weeper. We cannot verify this, though, as the Bible records Jesus was only in Jerusalem a few times. Of course, we only have highlights of Jesus' life, not a day-by-day account. Jesus may have been longing to go in and gather the people to Him but was prevented from doing so by their hardened hearts. I believe Jesus spoke these words for several reasons: (1) it is the lament of a grieving father over his lost children, (2) it quotes Psalm 118:26, (3) Jesus and His disciples were always in perilous danger in Jerusalem making it difficult to teach at all, and (4) Herod, the so called 'King of the Jews,' lived in Jerusalem and would attempt to stop Jesus' ministry to the point of widespread murder of believers.

In a new analogy, Jesus uses guest etiquette as examples. First, invite those less fortunate and you will be blessed. Your reward will come in Heaven for showing kindness to those who could not be expected to return the kindness. Anyone can extend courtesy and honor to those who are like themselves, but true Christian love comes from assisting people who have a lowly place in life. Second, when you arrive at the banquet, choose a place of lower honor than you think you deserve. If your opinion of yourself is correct, the host will honor you in front of all other guests by moving you to a place of greater honor. (If you are wrong, you haven't embarrassed yourself by having to move down.) When Jesus is our host at the banquet of the bridegroom of the church, we want to be humble before Him and hope to be deserving of a place of honor. Be careful not to think more highly of your righteous deeds than they warrant. Third, when God calls, don't make up excuses for not responding. The Jews had lots of excuses for not doing the Will of God. Most of these were detailed legalities dictated by religious leaders. Thus, God found others who were anxious to be invited. Those who were first became last; those who were last became first. All those who accept the Lord's invitation to eternal life will be at the feast of the bridegroom. I expect to see all of you there.

Jesus gave us three good parables about the joy of just one soul being saved. (Just think of the celebration a thousand souls would evoke!) The parable of the lost sheep tells of the effort the Good Shepherd makes to seek and to save the one lost. The 99 who are counted safe are left so that the Shepherd can find the one lost soul. (Likewise, Jesus left the host of believers in Heaven to come to earth to find and save the lost soul.) Even 1 out of 100 is very important. Then there is the woman who searches her entire house looking for one lost coin out of 10. Finally, we come to the prodigal son. He asked for his inheritance and proceeded to squander it on earthly pleasures. When it was gone, he was reduced to lusting after locust pods (carob bean pods) the hogs were eating. He had been reduced to the level of the despised pig. When he reached the bottom of the pit of life, he looked to his father for help. Because he deserved nothing, he sought only to be a hired hand in his father's house. When we find ourselves face down in the mud of our pit, we look to our heavenly Father. Ashamed, we seek only the lowest position. Hired hands were even lower than slaves. Slaves were attached to a family. The daily sustenance of the slave varied according to the income of the family; everyone ate or nobody ate. But the hired hand was only guaranteed work for the day. Each day he had to take the tools of his trade and solicit work in the market place. This was the early form of unemployment advertising. If he wasn't hired, he and his family went hungry that day.[70] Just as the prodigal son's father threw a great celebration over his joy that his son had returned, our heavenly Father also celebrates the return of wayward children. Jesus told us, "This is the will of him who sent me, that I shall lose none of all that he has given me."[1] (John 6:39) God's intention is that all people be saved.

The greatest contrast in the prodigal son parable is the attitude of the humbled son when compared to the attitude of the arrogant elder son. We find the older son is envious and resentful. He seems to regret he didn't get to be irresponsible and party. Of interest is the elder son's projection of his own desires onto the younger son's adventure. The older son assumes the younger has been cavorting with prostitutes. There is no indication in this parable that this occurred. Also, the elder son reveals his belief he has had to "slave" for his father. The attitude of the elder son represents the Pharisees and Jews who have had to slave under the burden of the law. The younger son represents the Gentile believers who are humbled and grateful to be accepted into the Kingdom of God.

In the parable of the dishonest manager, we find the owner has demanded an audit of the accounts. Frantic to improve his standing in the community, the manager hurriedly calls in the debtors and generously discounted their debt. The first account was reduced by 50% and the next by 20%. Most likely these debtors owed rent for land. Generally, the rent on farmland was a portion of the crop produced. Not only does the dishonest accountant ingratiate the debtors to himself, he also involves the debtors in a conspiracy to defraud the owner, who appears to be an absentee landlord.[70] We have no reason as to why the differences in percentage of discount. Possibly this reflects the bargaining abilities of the debtors or maybe the greater potential of one debtor to 'reward' the accountant later. The real shock is that the owner praised the accountant's ingenuity! (I certainly wouldn't feel that way!) There are four morals given for this parable. (1) Christians should be as ingenious at winning souls to Jesus as worldly people are at making money and acquiring possessions. (2) Worldly possessions should be used to help others while here on earth so that your many beneficiaries in Heaven welcome you. (3) One must be honest even with little things to be entrusted with great things. If you can't be trusted with earthly things, why would you expect to be trusted with heavenly things? (4) You cannot serve both God and Money. The first commandment requires that there be no other gods before the God. Your devotion must be to the One or the other. As the wealthy class, the Pharisees hooted at this idea! But "God knows your hearts."

Jesus tells a story about the rich man and Lazarus. While the rich man lived in luxury and wealth, poor Lazarus laid begging at his gate. The description of the scene is vividly detailed. The purple and linen clothes of the rich man were the kind worn by the High Priests and were very expensive. Additionally, we are told the rich man's extravagant living was daily, not occasionally. Older manuscripts use the same word for 'glutton' as used for 'feasting' which is used in the Barclay translation or 'fared sumptuously' which is used in the King James translation. Food was eaten entirely with the hands. Wealthy people would use hunks of bread to wipe their hands. This bread was then thrown away. Lazarus patiently waited among the wild dogs, hoping for some of the wasted bread. Lazarus means "God is my help." His condition was so poor that the dogs licked his open sores. Notice that the rich man doesn't "Do" anything to Lazarus. So his sin is not in harming Lazarus but rather it is because he did not have compassion for Lazarus. The rich man had become hardened to the sight of the poor. He no longer noticed them.[70] When they died, Lazarus went to Heaven and the rich man went to hell. When the rich man saw Lazarus with Abraham, he begged for a drop of cool water to appease his agony. We are told that is impossible for a great chasm or gulf separates Heaven and hell. (Notice the first of this earth is the last in eternity. The rich man is now the beggar.) The rich man's next request is that someone be sent back from the dead to warn his 5 brothers. Abraham's reply was that they had the laws of Moses and the prophecies and teachings of the prophets. But the rich man sadly states that they won't listen to Moses and the prophets (Old Testament). Abraham responds that they won't listen even if someone arises from the dead. Of course, we know Jesus arose from the dead and millions still don't listen.

A well-known saying of Jesus' day was "Where there is a dead body, there the vultures will gather."[1] (Luke 17:37) In other words, when the situation is right or the condition is fulfilled then the promised result will happen. When God's master plan is fulfilled at the end of time, Jesus will come again. On that day, there will be friends and relatives raptured to Heaven who will be leaving friends and relatives behind. The point of this statement is to impress on the listeners that their friendship or kinship will not save others. Each person must humble himself before Jesus, repent of his sins, and accept Jesus as Lord and Savior. No one else can do it for you.

In another parable, a widow constantly petitioned a judge to give her relief from her enemy. This would have been a judge appointed by Herod or the Romans. (The Jews took their cases before the elders, not to court.) These judges were famous for taking bribes to settle cases. A poor widow would not have the money for a bribe. Without any assets, this poor woman had no hope of justice. But she was persistent. The word translated as "so that she won't eventually wear me out" also means "so that she won't give me a black eye!" The widow's persistent pleading paid off; she got justice. If a worldly judge can give justice out of exhaustion, how much greater justice will be given by a loving heavenly Father?[70]

Two men went to the Temple to pray. One was a Pharisee who stood where he could be seen while he prayed aloud about how great he was -- not like the hated tax collector. The tax collector bowed his head, standing at the back of the Court of the Jews (men). He beat his chest and begged for mercy. The humbled will be rewarded, but those exalted on earth will be humbled. The tax collector went home forgiven.

A vineyard owner went to the market place to hire men to harvest grapes. As recounted earlier, this was a rather frantic time for vineyard owners because the harvest window of opportunity was very narrow. Therefore, the owner made repeated trips to the labor market throughout the day, hiring men each time. The Jewish 'day' was from 6 a.m. to 6 p.m. So the owner hired workers at 6 a.m., 9 a.m., noon, 3 p.m., and 5 p.m. At the end of the day, all workers were paid in reverse order of hire but each received the same pay! Those who worked many hours complained because those who worked only one hour got the same pay. Put another way, all were paid equally even though some did most of the work! The owner's response was that he had the right to pay the way he wanted. God is the owner of Heaven and He has chosen to let all who are saved have eternal life. He who is saved for one minute gets into Heaven just like he who is saved 100 years or more. We serve God out of privilege and joy, not for rewards. The owner of the vineyard knew the man who worked an hour had just as much need for food as the one who worked all day. God is generous. His gift of eternal life is free. His door of opportunity is always open until closed by death.

Food for Thought: In some passages the emphasis is on being humble in the Presence of God and realizing your unworthiness to come before God at all. Other passages talk about the rewards given in Heaven to anyone even giving a glass of water to one of God's children. We must contemplate the true meaning of the parable about taking the place of honor at the banquet. First, a believer has had to humble himself to repentance before he can even get in the door to the banquet house (Heaven). Second, once he is in then the rewards of honor will be bestowed in front of all who are present. So we will be both humbled and rewarded in the Presence of God.

November 8
Bible Readings: John 11:1-54

Our entire lesson is devoted to Lazarus (not the same man as the beggar in yesterday's lesson) and his two sisters, Mary and Martha. These three people were counted among Jesus' dearest friends. They all lived in Bethany that was less than two miles from Jerusalem. Lazarus became very ill and his sisters sent for Jesus. When Jesus received the message, He knew Lazarus would die for it was God's Will. The miracle of bringing Lazarus back from the dead would be a foretelling of the resurrection of Jesus. Although, Lazarus would be brought back to life only to die again at a later time, but Jesus would be resurrected to eternal life. This part of God's master plan was meant to bring glory to His Son even though Jesus Himself only sought to bring glory to His Father.

John 11:5 says, "Jesus loved . . . . Yet . . . . he stayed . . . two more days."[1] Jesus made sure there was no doubt by all mourners that Lazarus was really dead. In the other two cases where Jesus brought people back to life, each death was so recent people could believe they had not really died but were only in comas. (We know that often happened from evidence in the tombs.) Both had also been young people (Jairus' daughter - Matt. 9:18-26, Mark 5:21-43, Luke 8:40-56) (the widow's son - Luke 7:11-16). The miracle of bringing Lazarus back to life could not be misconstrued as 'good fortune.' John tells us this event will be the ignition of a plot by the Sanhedrin (the religious ruling body composed of Pharisees and Sadducees) to kill Jesus. For this to be such a key point in John, it is interesting to note that none of the other gospels mentions this miracle at all. In fact, the other three gospels place the cleansing of the Temple as the pivotal event to Jesus' death. The Temple cleansing is placed as occurring after Jesus' final entry into Jerusalem on what we now call Palm Sunday. The magnificent response Jesus received on His triumphal last entry to Jerusalem would indicate He had developed a huge, enthusiastic crowd of followers there. This is quite a different scene than ever before when Jesus went to Jerusalem. Why the difference? Obviously, a well-known man, Lazarus, living close to Jerusalem and being raised from the dead would be such a major miracle so as to create an impromptu gathering of hundreds of thousands of people lining the street hoping to see Jesus and be blessed. These Jews would have been in Jerusalem for the Passover, possibly as many as 250,000 to 2 million people may have crowded beside the street on that famous Palm Sunday. If we view the Temple cleansing as the turning point, we can't account for the crowd celebrating Jesus' entry into Jerusalem.[79]

Returning to our story, we see that Jesus announces to His Apostles that Lazarus is dead and they must go to him. The Apostles have already voiced their concern about going to Judea. Jesus' life would be in grave danger. Now the one Apostle who displays amazing courage is the one who will later be known forever as 'the doubter,' Thomas. "Then Thomas (called Didymus) said to the rest of the disciples, 'Let us also go, that we may die with him.'"[1] (John 11:16) It is a characteristic of the evil in this world that a good, courageous Christian man is forever labeled a doubter because of one falter during a time of overwhelming grief. A doubting Thomas is a title used now as mockery. (For the story of his doubt, see John 20:24-29.) In Hebrew, Thomas means Twin; in Greek, Didymus means Twin. We do not know who Thomas' twin was.[70] At least one scholar believes it was Matthew because their names are mentioned together throughout the Gospels' listings of Apostles.[77] Also, notice that we do not see the eager spokesman Peter taking the lead here. In fact, Peter is not mentioned in chapters 5, 7-12 of John. Bible students generally believe Peter was not present at this particular event, possibly on another mission. As we learned in the introduction to the Gospels, Mark took his knowledge of Jesus' ministry from the accounts of Peter's teaching. Thus, Mark would not have included this miracle if Peter didn't teach it. At this stage of Jesus' life, Matthew draws most of his details from Mark. The problem encountered is that all Jews would have known of such a great miracle within a couple of days. The Apostles themselves would have excitedly discussed the event. How could all three of the other Gospel writers fail to include the story? This stumbling point has led many scholars to conclude that the raising of Lazarus was a story or parable used to relate the foretelling of Jesus' burial and resurrection. If this was the case, no other 'parable' contains so many details about the people and the event. Also, we know from Luke that Mary and Martha are real friends of Jesus. Luke, curiously, has a gap from 18:31-22:8 where Peter is not mentioned; thus, another indicator that Peter did not witness this miracle and, therefore, did not teach it because he taught what he saw and knew firsthand. The disappearance of Peter is evident in Matthew 20-25.[70] Personally, I believe this miracle of Lazarus' return from the dead definitely occurred.

We see Martha displaying her strong faith as she runs out to meet Jesus stating soundly that Lazarus would not have died if Jesus had been there. She goes further to say that even now God would give Jesus anything He asked. Martha acknowledges that her brother will rise in the great resurrection at the last day (orthodox Jewish belief). "Jesus said to her, 'I am the resurrection and the life. He who believes in me will live, even though he dies; and whoever lives and believes in me will never die. Do you believe this?'"[1] (John 11:25-26) Martha states her faith that Jesus is the Christ, the Son of God. Have you stated your faith in Jesus?

Martha returns to tell Mary Jesus is outside of town. Mary jumps up and goes to meet Jesus. She falls at His feet and makes the same statement as Martha, stopping short of declaring His power to resurrect. In the Luke account of Mary and Martha, we are left believing Mary had the stronger faith. In John, Martha's faith is more evident in the Lazarus story. We are told that Jesus was "deeply moved in spirit and troubles." He wept. But even now some in the crowd were questioning His power.

Lazarus would have received a typical Jewish burial: no embalming, body coated with aloe and myrrh ointment, white simple linen dress, hands and feet wrapped in linen wrappings, head wrapped with a separate linen cloth, spices to mask the odor. The Jewish belief was that the spirit of the body hung around the tomb for 3-4 days seeking to reenter the body. (Of course, this belief developed as a result of some coming out of comas in the tomb.) After 4 days, it left because the body was decomposed beyond recognition.[79] Jesus had the stone over the entrance to the tomb removed and called Lazarus to come out. What a sight this must have been! Can you imagine how fast the news of this traveled throughout the land? The chief priests and Pharisees were mortified for they risked losing their jobs, power, prestige, and livelihood to Jesus. No one would listen to them anymore. The other prominent sect was the Sadducees who didn't believe in resurrection at all! So the Sanhedrin now had a common enemy -- Jesus. They would unite to plot His death. Caiaphas, the High Priest that year, made a profound prophecy. "You know nothing at all! You do not realize that it is better for you that one man die for the people than that the whole nation perish."[1] (John 11:49-50) Jesus would die for the children of God.

Now Jesus was a wanted man. He withdrew to the town of Ephraim on the edge of the desert, 14 miles northeast of Jerusalem.[5]

Food for Thought: Don't you wish that Lazarus' story about the whole event could have been told? He must have had some amazing comments on his experience! Think about what it will be like to wake up "some glad morning when this life is o'er" to see Jesus calling and waiting for you!

November 9
Bible Readings: Matt. 19:3-30; 20:17-34; 26:6-13, Mark 10:2-52; 14:3-9,
Luke 18:15-43; 19:1-28, John 11:55-57; 12:1-11

Some Pharisees approached Jesus about a topic of hot debate among rabbis -- divorce. Two schools of rabbi training prevailed. You could say one was very liberal and one was very conservative. The school of Shammai allowed divorce only on the charge of adultery. In contrast, the school of Hillel allowed divorce for any charge including just not liking the wife anymore. To say the least, the school of Hillel prevailed because the Jewish men wanted to do as they pleased with their possessions and that included wives. Jewish law provided for compulsory divorce on either of two grounds: adultery or sterility. The latter required a ten-year marriage before it was enacted. The rampant divorce rate and violent disagreement among rabbis on grounds for divorce would be a good topic to present to Jesus.[78] The Pharisees thought at last they could trap Jesus into making a statement that would alienate many Jews. But the words of Jesus became part of the marriage ceremony. "Haven't you read that at the beginning the Creator made them male and female, for this reason a man will leave his father and mother and be united to his wife, and the two will become one flesh? So they are no longer two, but one. Therefore what God has joined together, let man not separate."[1] (Matt. 19:4-6) The Pharisees responded that Moses permitted certificates of divorce. Jesus comments that Moses conceded to divorce because the people were determined to do so, but divorce was only recognized in cases of adultery. Jesus further states that anyone who can accept remaining unmarried to serve Him should do so.

A rich young man approached Jesus wanting to know what he must do to have eternal life. He had kept the commandments all his life. Jesus found one thing lacking in him. The young man had too much devotion to his wealth and too little compassion for the poor. Jesus told him to sell everything and give all to the poor. Then, follow him. The scene ends by telling us the young man went away sad because he could not bring himself to give away all his wealth. How many of us would have left sad, too?

Jesus told his disciples that it was easier for a camel to go through the eye of a needle than for a rich man to enter Heaven. There are 3 common interpretations. (1) Walled cities often had a huge main gate with a tiny narrow gate beside it. The narrow gate was barely big enough for a man to squeeze through. At night the main gate was closed and barred, but the little gate would be left open if there was no immediate danger. This gate was purposefully small to prevent easy access by invaders. This gate was called "The Needle's Eye." The camel was the largest animal living in Palestine. If a man could barely get through the eye, then certainly a camel couldn't.[78] (2) The Greek word kamelos means camel and kamilos means ship's hawser or towing cable. The words sound almost identical when pronounced. Jesus may have said it was easier to thread a ship's cable in a sewing needle than for a rich man to enter Heaven.[78] (3) Jesus could simply have used a common idiom of His day. It is an easy picture to envision -- a camel trying to squeeze through a needle's eye.[78]

Quick to remind Jesus, Peter tells that he has left everything behind to follow Jesus. Jesus says the Apostles will have 12 thrones in Heaven and will serve as judges of the 12 tribes of Israel. Judas Iscariot becomes the betrayer. After the resurrection, he is replaced by Matthias (Acts 1:26). Paul seems to include Jesus' brother James when speaking of the Apostles. Paul himself is referred to as an Apostle. We will have to wait and see who the 12th judge really is. Those who have given up earthly family or possessions for Jesus' sake will receive 100 times as much plus eternal life.

Jesus is on the move now, making his final trip across the mountains toward Jerusalem. Again, He tells His disciples He will be accused, arrested, and condemned by the Jews. Then the Gentile Romans will mock, spit, flog, and kill Him. On the third day, Jesus will rise. Still the Apostles could not comprehend it all.

The mother of James and John requests they get to sit on either side of Jesus in eternity. Jesus said they didn't have any idea what they were requesting. Could they endure what Jesus had ahead of Him? They insisted they could. In fact, **James** will be the first martyr and the only one whose death is recorded in the New Testament. Herod Agrippa I beheaded James about 42-44 A.D.[5] **John** will be banished to the isle of Patmos for several years. We have little other than church tradition to rely on for deaths of the Apostles with the exception of James. Early church tradition says John became a martyr while later tradition says he died in Ephesus of natural causes. As for the other Apostles, **Bartholomew**, per tradition, was flayed alive and crucified upside down. To flay a man, their hands and feet were tied spread eagle between poles and a cat-of-nine-tails with hooks on each cord was used to whip him or a knife was used to skin him alive. The flesh would have been stripped from his body, the unknown Apostle who was true to the end. Tradition has it that **Andrew** was whipped and crucified on an X-shaped cross at Patrae, Achaia (Greece).[5] **Peter** was crucified like Andrew but upside down in Rome about 66 A.D. Church tradition states **Matthew** was beaten and crucified or slain or beheaded in the India-Asia area. **Philip** was whipped, stoned, imprisoned, and then crucified in Turkey. Oral tradition is that **Thomas** was run through with a lance in the India-Asia area, too. The other **James** was beaten and stoned by the Jews. **Simon** the Zealot was crucified but the location is uncertain as to Britain or Ethiopia or Mesopotamia. (Talking about a huge difference in distance!) **Judas** the son of James is also known as Thaddaeus. According to tradition, he was crucified in Edessa or Egypt or Persia. Of course, **Judas Iscariot** betrayed Jesus to the Pharisees and later hung himself.[80]

In Jericho, a crowd comes out to meet Jesus. The tax collector, Zacchaeus, was too short to see Him. So he ran ahead and climbed up a sycamore tree, which could grow 40-50 feet high.[5] Jesus called for him to come down because Jesus would be his houseguest that night. The people were astonished that Jesus would be the guest of such a sinner! Immediately Zacchaeus comes down and accepts salvation from Jesus. Zacchaeus volunteers to pay back four times the amount he has cheated from anyone and sell half of what he owns and give to the poor. Jewish law required that 20% of ill gotten gain be returned in addition to the amount taken as restitution for the sin (Lev. 6:1-5). Zacchaeus gave 50% to the poor probably because there was little way to determine who had been cheated or the amount taken over the years. Those who are viewed as the greatest sinners are often the ones who make the biggest sacrifices to follow Jesus.

On His departure from the city, Jesus hears the call of a blind man by the roadside. Bartimaeus shows his faith by calling out, "Jesus, Son of David, have mercy on me!"[1] (Matt. 20:30) Jesus told him that faith had brought healing.

Luke 19:11-27 is a unique parable Jesus told about a king. It is unique in that the story is based on a real historical event. Jesus is now near Jerusalem. Under Roman rule, the kings that ruled the land were allowed to name their successor. In the case of Herod the Great who died in 4 B.C., his will divided his kingdom among his three sons: Herod Antipas, Herod Philip, and Archelaus. This inherited position had to be approved by the Roman emperor. Archelaus waited (because of the hatred of the people for his father) to make the trip to Rome to seek approval to be king of his territory of Judea, Idumea, and Samaria. In the meantime, the Jews sent an embassy of

50 men to Rome to register their dislike of Archelaus.[70] His incompetent handling of a riot during Passover resulted in 3,000 Jews being killed.[3] To compromise, Emperor Augustus named Archelaus to a lesser position of ethnarch (governor),[5] promising to make him king if he proved to be worthy.[3] We know Joseph was warned in a dream to avoid Judea on his return out of Egypt with Mary and Jesus. Archelaus was given as the reason. He was cruel to both Jews and Samaritans. In 6 A.D., a delegation of Jews and Samaritans traveled to Rome to complain about their treatment under Archelaus. He was removed from office and banished to Vienne, France.[3,5] Now let's go to our parable.

In the parable of the minas, a nobleman has given each of ten servants a pound of money called a mina. Their charge was to 'put this money to work.' Then the nobleman left to go to a far country to be made king. Even though a group of his subjects had gone to object to his appointment, the nobleman was made king anyway. Upon his return, he sent for the servants to determine their success in increasing the money. The first one had earned 10 more pounds of money. He was given 10 cities to rule. The second one had earned 5 more pounds. He was given 5 cities to rule. We do not know the outcome for 7 of the servants but assume it is positive. The last servant gives the king his one pound of money back saying that he was too afraid of the king's harshness should he lose it, so he just stowed it away. The king was very angry, stating he should at least have put it on deposit for interest. The king took the pound of money and gave it to the servant who had earned 10 pounds. On objections, the king said, "to everyone who has, more will be given, but as for one who has nothing, even what he has will be taken away."[1] (Luke 19:26) It is also noted that the king decides to kill the men who had objected to his kingship.

This parable has several lessons for us. (1) The king trusted his servants. His wealth and the future wealth of his empire were entrusted to them. They had full control of how they invested. Jesus puts His trust in us, His servants. We are given full control over how we invest His wealth, the gifts of God. (2) The king expected to return and find his servants actively growing his wealth (kingdom). Jesus expects us to be growing the Kingdom of God. We must be investing the gifts we have been given to grow His church -- the believers. We will be held accountable for the gifts we have been given. We are being tested. (3) The servant who was most capable was rewarded with even more gifts (and responsibility) which also brought more honor. We should strive to be so honored by the Lord. (4) The servants who worked hard to increase the money ultimately had more gifts to administer. The servant who was lazy and hid the money (gift) ultimately lost all. If we work hard to walk in the ways of Jesus and try to resist temptation, we can look forward to developing a mind like Christ. There is no standing still. Either we are growing in our faith and trust in God or we are sliding backwards. The 'use it or lose it' theory is true. Jesus instructed us to use our gifts or lose them.[70]

Jesus is now ascending the mountain to Jerusalem. He knows He will soon be arrested. There are only six days until Passover. Jesus stops at Bethany to visit with His friends one last time. They eat in the home of Simon the Leper. Lazarus eats, Martha serves, and Mary is at Jesus' feet. Mary takes a pint of expensive perfume and pours it on Jesus' feet then she wipes His feet with her hair. Judas Iscariot objects, thinking it should have been sold and the money given to the poor. Notice he points out it cost a year's wages. Apparently, Judas was gifted in accounting because Jesus entrusted him with the moneybag. We are told Judas has been embezzling. His greed is evident now. He was not happy with what he had but wanted what others had, too. (He may even have been thinking that if the perfume had been sold, Mary would give Jesus the money to distribute to the poor. Then Judas could steal part of it, too!) Greed would lure him to betray Jesus. Greed would cause him to not only lose that which he had been entrusted but also his very soul. You cannot serve both God and Money. Jesus replies that Mary has saved this perfume for the time of His death. She would always be remembered for this selfless act. Then Jesus says the poor will always be with us. We can help them on any day. Jesus would soon be gone. So many people were flocking to see and hear Lazarus' miraculous new life story that the chief priests now made plans to kill him, too. Jesus was winning over too many of their followers.

This part of our lesson is very controversial. If you have been an astute reader, you have already been given a hint. (Oct. 27 - Food for Thought) The previous account of Mary anointing Jesus' body for burial is found in Matthew, Mark, and John. Luke is the only one to record the anointing by the prostitute. On comparison of the anointing by Mary to the one of the prostitute anointing Jesus' feet (Luke 7:36-50), we find several similarities.

- Simon is the host. Luke calls him Simon the Pharisee; Mark and Matthew call him Simon the Leper.
- Both involved women anointing Jesus' feet with expensive perfume. The quantity of perfume is less in the Luke account.
- Both women wipe Jesus' feet with their hair, an act of intimacy that was forbidden outside the marriage relationship.

Only John tells us the woman is Mary. Matthew and Mark do not name the woman. On the other hand, John does not mention who the host is. You are left with the impression that the meal takes place in Mary, Martha, and Lazarus' home. Barclay makes the following comment on the two stories.

The greatest difficulty in identifying the stories of Luke and of the other three gospel writers is that in Luke's story the woman was a notorious sinner; and there is no indication that that was true of Mary of Bethany. And yet the very intensity with which Mary loved Jesus may well have been the result of the depths from which he had rescued her.[78] (p. 329)

Whether or not you believe that the two stories are the same only remembered (or recorded from others' memories) differently is your decision. The Apostle Paul tells us to "continue to work out your salvation with fear and trembling."[1] (Phil. 2:12) We all have to study and pray for God's guidance in interpreting His word.

Food for Thought: Washington Gladden wrote this song in 1879. A newspaperman who joined the clergy, he was diligent to fight social injustice battles from New York City politics to the national arena.

"O Master, let me walk with Thee
In lowly paths of service free;
Tell me Thy secret; help me bear
The strain of toil, the fret of care."

November 10
<u>Bible Readings: John 12:12-36, Matt. 21:1-19, Mark 11:1-19, Luke 19:29-48</u>

It is now Sunday morning. The Passover crowd is anxiously awaiting Jesus. They have palm branches to wave and lay before Him. As they walk towards Bethany, they shout, "Hosanna! Blessed is he who comes in the name of the Lord! Blessed is the King of Israel!"[1] (John 12:13) Hosanna means 'Save now!'[78] The people are convinced their king has come to save them and to bless them. They may have been seeking deliverance from their Roman and religious oppressors more than an eternal salvation. Jesus sent two disciples to retrieve a donkey's colt that had never been ridden. Several commentators believe Jesus had prearranged for this colt to be ready and the passcode was "The Lord needs it."[75,78] The disciples placed their cloaks over the colt and took it to Jesus. Jesus got on and began to ride toward Jerusalem. This was done to fulfill the prophecy of Zech. 9:9 that the Jewish king would come not as a warrior king but rather as a gentle man riding a small donkey. Judges of the time rode donkeys from town to town. Others used donkeys to carry goods. Jesus, the King, Savior, and Judge, was headed to the holy city.

As Jesus began to descend the Mount of Olives, the crowd of millions of people becomes visible. The sound of their shouting was music to His ears. Finally, He was being welcomed into Jerusalem. But His archenemies were there, too. The Pharisees wanted Jesus to quiet the crowd. Jesus told them that the very stones would cry out if the people didn't. This was the typical reception for a popular warrior king. Jehu had received a similar welcome (2

Kings 9:13) as well as Simon Maccabaeus (1 Maccabees 13:51). "Blessed is he who comes in the name of the Lord!" was the greeting everyone spoke as they entered Jerusalem at festival time.[78] People began to lay their palm branches and their cloaks on the road in front of Jesus. As the little donkey got closer to Jerusalem, Jesus caught sight of the city He had longed to love and comfort. He began to cry. The future for Jerusalem is bleak. Their enemies will mount a siege and overrun them. Many will be killed. Every stone in the city will be knocked off the other; not two stones will be left stacked from any building. (If you review the Oct. 17 lesson, you'll realize what a feat this will be.) In 70 A.D. the Romans will completely destroy the city. Why did such a thing have to happen? Jesus tells us it is their judgment for not recognizing that the Messiah was among them.

In Jerusalem, those who didn't know Jesus inquired of others. "The crowds answered, 'This is Jesus, the prophet from Nazareth in Galilee.'"[1] (Matt. 21:11) The miracle of raising Lazarus is told throughout the throngs of people. Jesus went to the Temple. Afterwards, He and the Apostles went back to Bethany for the night. He may have spent the night in Lazarus' home, but most likely He stayed in the open to keep the crowds away from His friends.

Upon leaving Bethany the next day, Jesus sees a fig tree leafed out. He is hungry and it appears to promise fruit. When Jesus reached the tree, there was no fruit. Actually, fruit should not have been expected until June, except for some inedible early fruit that falls off.[71] Then He states that no fruit will ever be eaten from the tree again. On face value, it would seem that Jesus was upset because the tree had no fruit so He cursed the tree. But we are talking about the selfless Son of God who never invoked His power or authority for Himself. Remember His wilderness experience? Forty days without food is certainly more likely to prompt Him to react than this one breakfast fruit disappointment. (Here we have another reason to believe Jesus had not spent the night at Lazarus' home. Martha would have prepared food for Him.) So what is the point of this fig story? It is to demonstrate to the disciples the fulfillment of Jer. 8:13 where God judges Israel.[81] Like the nation of Israel, the leafy tree was inviting, promising fruit to delight and satisfy. Israel had all the blessings to be very fruitful and satisfying but, like the fig tree, it was a disappointment. The promise of the chosen people had not come to fruition. Matt. 7:19-20 states, "Every tree that does not bear good fruit is cut down and thrown into the fire."[1] God's judgment will come upon a nation who professed to worship the one and only God but did not even recognize Him among them.[71] The rest of the fig story is in tomorrow's lesson.

As I have noted in a previous lesson, Matthew, Mark, and Luke give the cleansing of the Temple after Jesus' triumphal entry into Jerusalem. Possibly, Jesus drove out moneychangers and merchants more than once. He quotes Isa. 56:7 in referring to His house as being a house of prayer, rather than a den of robbers (Jer. 7:11). Annas, a previous high priest, owned these businesses.[71]

Some Greeks approach Philip and Andrew asking to see Jesus. They probably went to these two disciples because of their Greek names. They were from the Hellenized city of Bethsaida. These Greeks are representative of the entire Gentile population that is now curious to see what Jesus offers.[73]

Jesus likens Himself to a kernel of wheat that must be sacrificed in order to produce many kernels of wheat. One man would die to bring Christianity to the whole world. Christians make up the body of Christ -- His church. God is manifested in the heart of each believer in the form of the Holy Spirit. God the Father honors those who follow Jesus.

We have heard a voice from Heaven confirm approval of Jesus at His baptism and again at the transfiguration. Now a voice states that God's name has been glorified and will be glorified again (at the death and resurrection of His Son). Judgment had come upon the evil. Righteousness would prevail. Jesus tells the disciples that He will be "lifted up" and all men will be "drawn" unto Him. Indeed Jesus will be lifted up on a cross. All mankind will be invited to accept the free gift of salvation. The crowd did not understand for they had interpreted the Torah (Old Testament) to mean the Christ would live forever to reign over them 'on earth.' They were not expecting an eternal spiritual king living and reigning over them. Those who trust in Jesus will always walk in the Light.

Food for Thought: As Thanksgiving approaches, take time to count your blessings. Don't forget to include freedom to worship and a life on the New Testament side of the Cross. Thank Him for His gift to us.

November 11
<u>Bible Readings:</u> Matt. 21:20-46; 22:1-46; 23:1-39; Mark 11:20-33; 12:1-44; Luke 20:1-47; 21:1-4

The next morning as they travel from Bethany back to Jerusalem, the disciples see the fig tree withered from its roots, indicating it is totally destroyed. The next verses (Mark 11:22-26) have similar parallel verses found scattered throughout the Gospels. There is no way to determine which one of the events is the actual one to provoke their utterance. Maybe they were all repetitious of Jesus' emphasis on faith, e.g., Matt. 17:20, Luke 17:6. Jesus testifies that faith without doubt is capable of throwing this mountain (Mount of Olives) into the sea (Dead Sea is visible from the Mount of Olives).[81]

When they arrive at the Temple the scribes and chief priests ask Jesus who gave Him the authority to perform such great miracles. Knowing it was another trap, Jesus replied with a question of His own. First, they must tell Him if John's baptism was from Heaven or men. The trap had sprung all right, but with the scribes and chief priests as its victims! Regardless of which answer they chose, many of the Jews would turn against them. They feared the crowd. Remember there are millions of people at the festival. Passover has had riots before with devastating results. So they wimped-out by saying they didn't know. The truth of the matter is they really didn't know because they knew not God. They had no idea what baptism by Heaven involved. So Jesus has a way to get out of answering their question about who has given Him authority to perform miracles. Because it was not yet time for Him to be arrested, He did not answer. Declaring that God gave Him the power and authority to do the things He had done would have certainly resulted in a premature arrest for blasphemy.

Jesus tells a series of parables to teach the people crowded around. First, there was a vineyard owner with two sons. The father told the one son to go work in the vineyard. He refused, but later he went. Later the father told the second son to go work in the vineyard. He agreed but then did not go. Which one did what was right? The crowd responded, "The first one!" Then Jesus tells them that their most despised sinners (tax collectors and prostitutes) would get into Heaven before they would! (Amazingly that didn't start a stoning!) The point of the parable is that the vilest of sinners (also representative of the Gentiles) would at first refuse God's invitation to eternal life but later would repent and accept His gift. Whereas the pious ones (represented by the Jewish scribes and Pharisees) would see God's gift but refuse it.

The second parable was about a man who developed a vineyard for rental property purposes. He built all the necessary structures for an excellent grape crop: wall, winepress, and watchtower. Successfully renting the property, the owner left to attend other businesses. (There were many absentee landowners in Palestine at this time.) When the crops came in, the landlord sent a servant to collect the portion of the crop that was payment for the rent. The servant was beaten and thrown out. Many other servants were sent. Some were persecuted; others were killed. Finally, he sent his son thinking the tenants would surely respect him. But the tenants realizing this was the only heir killed the son so the inheritance could be theirs. The owner became enraged and he determined to kill the tenants and give the vineyard to others.

This parable was steeped in Jewish interpretation of scripture. Isa. 5:7 identifies the house of Israel as God's vineyard. A wall or thick hedge was placed around a vineyard to keep out thieves and wild animals that would destroy the vineyard and eat its fruit. The fruit are God's people and the wall is the protection of God. The watchtower served as both a residence and a guard tower over the vineyard.[78] The religious leaders had been allowed to reside in the Temple complex to oversee God's people and to prevent any evil to enter the vineyard. The winepress consisted of two troughs: an upper trough where the grapes were crushed with a channel to a lower trough that collected the juice. God's chosen people had been trampled and mashed repeatedly by oppressors. By now they should have the faith of God's love and protection so that their fruit produced only the finest and purest juice. When God sent His servants, the prophets, to collect His portion of the harvest (praise and fruit of their faith), they were shamefully treated, persecuted, and killed. Finally, God sent His only Son. The tenants of the vineyard (religious leaders) saw a chance to kill God's heir to His kingdom and seize the inheritance (Kingdom of God) for themselves. (Under certain circumstances, the people who resided on the property could claim squatters' rights to the property if the owner did not claim within a given period of time.[81]) This so angered God that He determines to come and kill the tenants (religious leaders) and give the vineyards (Kingdom of God) to others (the Gentiles).

The third parable was about a king who prepared a wedding banquet for his son. (Of course you recognize the king as God, the Son and Groom as Jesus, and the church as the bride.) The king sent his servants (the prophets) to tell the invited guests (Jews) to come. The guests refused. More servants (prophets) were sent with messages urging the guests' attendance as all had been prepared and was awaiting their arrival. But the invited guests only offered excuses. Many were too busy with the ordinary responsibilities of their earthly lives to attend a wedding feast. The others mistreated and killed the servants (prophets). The king was furious. He sent His army out to kill and destroy (Judgment) their great city (Jerusalem). Those invited guests (Jews) did not deserve to come to the banquet. So people were gathered from all walks of life and all nations (Gentiles) to fill the banquet hall. When the king arrived, he spotted one guest without the proper wedding clothes. The king ordered the guest (devil) bound and thrown outside into utter darkness where there is constant fear and danger (hell). Isa. 64:6 tells us that in our evil state our very best deeds are like filthy rags. When we are saved, we are washed in the blood of Jesus and cleansed of our sin. In Rev. 19:7-9 we have the beautiful picture of the wedding of Jesus and His bride, the church. They wear the finest wedding clothes -- bright, clean, and white. An angel will deliver the invitation to the wedding supper to those of us who are washed in the blood of the Lamb. Do you have your wedding clothes on?

Again the Pharisees plot to trap Jesus. But this time they team up with a different enemy -- the Herodians. Herodians were a political party that supported Herod who owed his continued appointment to Roman officials. The taxes were imposed by Romans and collected by Herod's tax collectors. The Pharisees resented the Romans' taxes because they held that God was the only king over the Jews and, therefore, tribute shouldn't be paid to another king or god. In actuality, each party was greedy and wanted what the other was collecting. As usual, it was the people who suffered. Now it was the Herodians' turn to ask an entrapment question. "Is it right for us to pay taxes to Caesar or not?"[1] (Luke 20:25) Each and every king minted his own currency. In fact, almost every victorious battle had a coin struck commemorating the event. The king always sought to promote himself on coins, often in the form of a god. Likewise, the Temple minted its own coins. Commerce, though, depended on Roman currency. The Jews couldn't participate in only those parts of the system from which they benefited without also having to endure the parts that were detrimental. The particular tax the Herodians had questioned was the poll tax, which was applied to every living person from puberty to age 65.[70] As you would expect, there was a great deal of contention from the people over having to pay for being alive! (Now this was birth control at its finest hour!) The Jews already paid income tax (1%) and land tax (10% of grain produced and 20% of oil and wine produced).[78] Now a Jew had to pay the Romans a poll tax, a tax on storable food production, and a tax on any earned income from employment. Additionally, a Temple tax was collected. Jesus replied, "Give to Caesar what is Caesar's, and to God what is God's."[1] The Herodians had failed in their quest to trap Jesus.

Now it was the Sadducees' turn. Moses had instituted Levirate law concerning propagation of the tribes of Israel. If a man died childless, his wife was to be given to the next son. If he died childless, too, then the woman would be given to the third son. (Review the story of Judah's sons in the January 17th lesson on Genesis 38.) The Pharisees' hypothetical situation continues until 7 sons have wedded the woman and all die childless. The question: "At the resurrection, whose wife will she be?" The answer: "None of the above." The reason: the church will be the bride of the Lamb. On earth, marriage is provided by God to provide the 'helpmate' or companion for whom

Adam had longed and to provide a family unit for procreation and survival. In Heaven, there will be no emptiness, loneliness, hunger, tears, sickness, death, or struggles. Even though we as earthbound humans don't like to think about it, there will be no marriages in Heaven except in our commitment to Jesus. We will know our loved ones, but the intense longing to be with them will no longer exist. Our joy will be to praise God forever. Jesus takes the opportunity to correct the orthodox Jews' belief concerning the "resurrection of the dead." Our God is God of the Living, not the dead. The dead in spirit go to hell and those alive with the Holy Spirit go to Heaven. Let the dead bury the dead, but let the living serve God (Matt. 8:22). (Stop and read John 5:24.)

Now one of the scribes posed a theological question, "Which commandment is the most important?" Jesus replied that we must first love God with all our heart, soul, mind, and body. Then second, we must love our neighbors as ourselves. The scribe replied that Jesus was right because loving God with your total being and your neighbor as yourself was more important than all burnt offerings and sacrifices. Jesus remarked that he was not far from the Kingdom of God. If you think about the scribe and realize the legalistic religious environment in which he lived and worked, you realize how remarkable his insight really is! After all, Jews were still bringing sacrifices daily to the Temple. (See Deut. 6:4-5 that are part of the Shema.)

Jesus launches into a condemnation of those who believe themselves so pious and righteous. They can be identified easily.

- They make laws but don't keep them. (This is very evident at Jesus' trial.)
- They seek the admiration and envy of others. (Their religious trappings must be greater and more elegant than anyone else's.)
- They must always have the seats of greatest honor.
- They want to be recognized by all and greeted.
- They demand the greatest title and respect.

Jesus taught that all believers are equal. There is only one Master -- one Father of Faith -- and that is God.

Several specifically Jewish religious practices are mentioned in this passage. The first one is phylacteries, which are little leather boxes on leather cords. One is worn around the forehead with the box between the eyes. Another is worn around the left hand and wrist. They are worn during Morning Prayer except on holy days. Phylacteries trace their origin to Deut. 6:8 where the Israelites are told to bind the scripture on their hand and as frontlets between the eyes. Orthodox Jews still incorporate this practice in their worship. What do the boxes contain? They hold small strips of scripture from the Pentateuch (Genesis - Deuteronomy).[5] Apparently, the scribes and Pharisees had taken to wearing oversized phylacteries all day. They wanted to be seen as more righteous than others. Second, the cloaks of Jewish men had tassels on the four corners in accordance with Deut. 22:12. These were worn to remind them of their commitment to do God's Will and keep His commandments. Again the scribes and Pharisees wanted to be recognized as more pious than other Jews so their tassels were longer. Third, the seat of honor was given to those with the greatest respect in the community. The closer one sat to the host, the greater the honor. In the synagogue, the places of honor were on the speakers' platform in the center of the room. Those honored would face the audience so all could see their great attention and devotion to that which was taught. Finally, the title Rabbi was given only to those who demonstrated exceptional knowledge and interpretation of the scripture, in other words a Master Teacher.

As Jesus sat watching the worshippers drop their offerings in the Temple treasury box, many rich people donated large sums. A poor woman dropped in two copper coins worth less than a penny. Jesus was so emotionally moved that He called His disciples together to point out the richest worshipper in the Temple for she had given everything she had to God. The rich had given only a fraction of their abundance; she had given 100%. As children of the King, we owe Him nothing less than 100%. All that we have and all that we are belong to God.

Food for Thought:

"Have you been to Jesus for the cleansing power?
Are you washed in the blood of the Lamb?
Are you fully trusting in His grace this hour?
Are you washed in the blood of the Lamb?
Are you washed in the blood?
In the soul-cleansing blood of the Lamb?
Are your garments spotless? Are they white as snow?
Are you washed in the blood of the Lamb?"[44]

Elisha A. Hoffman - 1878

Verses of the Week: **John 13:34-35** "A new command I give you: Love one another. As I have loved you, so you must love one another. By this all men will know that you are my disciples, if you love one another."

November 12
Bible Readings: Matt. 24:1-51; 25:1-46, Mark 13:1-37, Luke 21:5-36

On leaving the Temple, Jesus' disciples are awed by the magnificence of the Temple complex. Jesus and His disciples were probably exiting through the western gate on the bridge that spanned the Tyropoeon Valley.[78] They would have a spectacular view of the Temple complex as they sat on the side of the Mount of Olives. The foundation stones weighed several tons each (See Oct. 17 lesson). Jesus responds that every one will be dislodged and the Temple destroyed. (The Romans will fulfill in 70 A.D.) Jesus' first called Apostles (Peter, Andrew, James, and John) are curious as to what signs will mark the end of time and His return.[81] First Jesus starts with a warning: Do not be deceived by false prophets. There will be wars, famines, and earthquakes throughout the world. These are only signs that the end times are beginning (referred to as "the beginning of birth pains" in Matt. 24:8). The Jews viewed this as the feared "Day of the LORD" so often mentioned in prophecy (Isa. 13:9-13). It was the terrible painful years of giving birth to the Messianic Age. (See Rev. 12:1-6.) When we see these signs, we will know the end times have started and the problems will increase until He comes again.

Those who believe in Jesus will be persecuted. Even family members will betray believers to the authorities for execution. The Apostles would suffer in the same ways Jesus would suffer. As we saw last week, only John is spared a violent death. As the evil in life increases, the love (charity) declines. Christians, as well as Apostles, are to be firm in their beliefs and true to God's Will for them even in the face of persecution. The end of time will not come until the gospel has been preached throughout the world.

The disciples should look for the desecration and destruction of the Temple again. When armies surround Jerusalem, the people must flee to the mountains in order to escape alive. Like Lot's family, they are not to go back or look back for any reason. Unfortunately, the people of Judea will not flee when the Roman armies led by Titus, siege Jerusalem. The Romans had sent forces into Judea to stop the riots that occurred in 66 A.D. The riots were primarily due to the Roman government's decision to revoke citizenship of the Jews. By 68 A.D. Judea and Perea had been conquered again. Only Jerusalem remained. Titus engaged in a five-month siege against the city.[7] Seeking to protect themselves, the people of the countryside had thronged into Jerusalem rather than flee to the mountains as Jesus warned. The Romans built a second wall around the city to ensure its captives starved to death. There were so many dead that they could not even be buried. Those who tried to bury the dead often died themselves because they were too weak for the task. Family members and neighbors turned on each other, plundering and attacking based on hope of finding food. The evil in the people emerged in full force. No mercy, charity, or love was found.

Houses were robbed while the inhabitants lay dying. In desperation to stop the stench of death, bodies were pushed over the wall into the valleys below. Josephus reports that even Titus was grieved over the way the Jews had desecrated the dead: "When Titus, in going his rounds along those valleys, saw them full of dead bodies, and the thick putrefaction running about them, he gave a groan; and spreading out his hands to heaven, called God to witness that this was not his doing: and such was the sad case of the city itself."[3] (Wars.5.12.4 - p. 724) According to Josephus, the number of Jews who died was 1,100,000 and the number taken captive was 97,000. Those captive males above 17 years of age were primarily sent into slavery in the Egyptian mines. A few were sent to Roman provinces to be killed for sport in their coliseums, this fulfills the prophecy of Hosea 8:13, 9:3, 11:3-5. Those captives under 17 were sold as slaves but not before 11,000 died of starvation.[3]

Luke 21:24 states that Jerusalem will be trodden down by the Gentiles until the time designated in God's master plan. Many believe that the return of the Jews to Jerusalem will be the primary sign that Jesus' second coming is near. Jesus said that no one knows the time of His return except the Father (Matt. 24:36). The whole event will be faster than lightning. The heavenly bodies will be dark. "The harvest is the end of the age and the harvesters are angels."[1] (Matt. 13:39) The lights will be turned out on the evil age of man.

A verse that has caused much disagreement as to interpretation is Matt. 24:34, "I tell you the truth, this generation will certainly not pass away until all these things have happened."[1] Barclay believes verses 32-34 refer to the siege and destruction of Jerusalem rather than the end of time. This would certainly have been a true prophecy as Jerusalem fell about 40 years later.[78] The Broadman Commentary adds that the phrase in verse 33 that "he is near" has two meanings in the Greek: He is near or It is near. One refers to the Son of Man being near and the other to the end of time being near. The Son of Man is viewed as One who brings judgment. Judgment definitely came to the Jews in 70 A.D.[75] If verse 34 is compared to similar verses (Matt. 16:28 and 23:36, Mark 9:1), we find that three events may be identified. Matt. 16:28 refers to Jesus' death and resurrection coming in just a few days. Matt. 23:36 refers to the Judgment on Jerusalem coming in 70 A.D. But Mark 9:1 refers to (1) the transfiguration of Jesus with Moses and Elijah where the inner circle of disciples were allowed to see Jesus in His glory[81] or (2) the lifting up of Jesus on the cross with the resurrection on the third day and His ascension into Heaven showing power and authority. So we have 3 choices for interpretation: (1) transfiguration, (2) resurrection, or (3) ascension. In all three cases, a portion of the generation of Jesus' day was present. Many believe the true underlying meaning of the verse refers to the Great Commission in Matt. 28:18-20. The Gospel must be carried throughout the world before the end of the age of man. Therefore, this generation or time of the church will not pass away until this is completed at which time Jesus marks as the end of the age (Matt. 24:14).[78] Regardless of when the end time comes, believers must be ready. Our work for the Lord must be completed, our sins repented, and our hearts humbled. We must be vigilant and keep watch.

On Judgment Day, Jesus will be the sitting Judge. All people will be gathered around and He will separate the believers (sheep) from the non-believers (goats). The sheep on Jesus' right will inherit the Kingdom of Heaven, but the goats on His left will be cast into hell. The sheep are characterized as having compassion and love for the poor, lonely, sick, and downcast. The goats lack compassion and love for those less fortunate.

Food for Thought: Is one a Christian if (s)he only "feels" sorry for others but never gives selflessly to help mankind? According to the Bible, Christians are known by the fruit they produce. If you are known as stingy, greedy, selfish, then you'll find yourself surrounded by goats. Jesus told us to love our neighbors as ourselves. Seems to me there are a lot of folks who hate themselves!

November 13
<u>Bible Readings: Matt. 26:1-5, 14-19 Mark 14:1-2, 10-16 Luke 22:1-13; 21:37-38 John 12:37-50</u>
With Passover only two days away, the chief priests and the Jewish elders met at Caiaphas' palace to figure

out how to kill Jesus. (Just imagine, religious leaders coming together to plan a murder! Scenes like this happen continually in today's world.) Judas' greed has finally overwhelmed him. He approaches the chief priests and officers of the Temple guards about selling Jesus (seemingly as a slave) to them. The price agreed upon was the average slave price (Ex. 21:32) - 30 pieces of silver. For the love of money, God's Son was sold to His enemies. This fulfilled the prophecy of Zech. 11:12. Go back to the Oct. 2 lesson from Zech. 9-14 and review. Let the prophecy of the Old Testament fully impress upon you the solemn, holy event that was about to take place. How could the learned religious teachers not have recognized that Jesus fulfilled all prophecy? They had no excuse. They were guilty. Jesus said, "If I had not come and spoken to them, they would not be guilty of sin. Now, however, they have no excuse for their sin. . . . But this is to fulfill what is written in their Law: 'They hated me without reason.'"[1] (John 15:22,25) The chief priests had kept the law all their lives, but now they fell headlong into sin. Let this be a warning to all. None of us is above committing the vilest of sins.

Jesus returns to the Mount of Olives each night after teaching in the Temple each day. The people apparently find His teachings interesting, but they don't believe in Him. This fulfills the prophecy of Isa. 53:1. The reason for their unbelief is stated in Isa. 6:9-10. (It was the commission of Isaiah to preach God's word to God's people. Isaiah is warned that the more he preaches God's word, the more the people will reject God. They simply could not turn from doing their will to doing God's Will. Rejection of God is like all other sin; it is hardest to do the first time but gets easier each time thereafter.) The hearts of God's chosen people would become hardened to His Will and His word. But even their disbelief can be used in God's master plan. Acts 13:46-48 reveals that God sent His Word first to the Jews, but when they rejected it, His Word was carried to the rest of the world. God used rejection by some to bring salvation to all. God's Will was that none would be lost. But His gift was too simple, too easy -- repent of your sins and give yourself to Him. The concepts ancient people had of gods were as stern masters, not loving fathers. God would have to send His only Son to prove His unlimited love.

We are told that some of the Jews and even some of the leaders believed in Jesus but were too afraid of the Pharisees' power to permanently ban them from the synagogue. The synagogue was the center of religious teaching and community activity. Being cut off from the synagogue was being cut off from all social functions. These believers were like the parable where the seeds were sown on rocky soil. The seeds took root but soon withered; though the outside was receptive, the inside was hardened (Matt. 13:18-23). In Mark 8:38, Jesus said, "If anyone is ashamed of me and my words in this adulterous and sinful generation, the Son of Man will be ashamed of him when he comes in his Father's glory with the holy angels."[1]

Jesus now sends the Apostles into town to make preparations for Passover. They are told to look for a man carrying a jug of water. Keep in mind that there are more than 2.5 million people crowded into Jerusalem. How would they pick out the right person? Hauling water from the well was woman's work. The Apostles could easily spot a man doing this in the crowd, especially since the jugs were carried on the head or shoulders. The Apostles were to follow the man and ask the owner of the house for space to eat the Passover. Without a doubt, Jesus had made arrangements with one of His disciples to use the banquet room or upper room of his house for this special meal.[70] It is believed to have been the house of Mark's family. Mark was a young man at the time, hardly more than a boy.[82] The day before the Passover, a search was made in every house for any leaven. All bread was made using 'starter dough' or dough that was used to grow and maintain yeast. A bit of it was pinched off and worked into the new bread mix. This process demonstrated Paul's comment in 1 Cor. 5:6-8, "Don't you know that a little yeast works through the whole batch of dough? Get rid of the old yeast that you may be a new batch without yeast -- as you really are. For Christ our Passover Lamb has been sacrificed. Therefore let us keep the Festival, not with the old yeast, the yeast of malice and wickedness, but with bread without yeast, the bread of sincerity and truth."[1] Yeast was a symbol of corruption and wickedness -- a little went a long way. Every little bit of bread dough was searched out and scraped off, swept out, or washed away from all Jewish homes before Passover began.

Food for Thought: How different would our lives be today if the people of Jesus' day had acknowledged Him as the Son of God? Would He still have been crucified? Alas, the answer is "Yes." In His parables, Jesus told us that the salvation of even one lost person (sheep) was worth giving His own life. He died so that we could live -- eternally in His kingdom.

November 14

Bible Readings: Luke 22:14-39 Matt. 26:20-35 Mark 14:17-31 John 13:1-38; 14:1-31; 16:25-33

As the Apostles recline on the couches or mats around the low table, they partake of the last supper with Jesus. We know that tradition held for the diners to have their feet pointed away from the table. They leaned on their left arms and ate with their right. At one point during the meal, John leans on Jesus' chest, so we can assume John is at the right hand of Jesus (John 13:23-25). The couches would be arranged in a horseshoe shape around 2/3 of the table. One-third of the table was left sticking out where dishes of food were placed for passing around. Those sitting at each end of the horseshoe had to serve the others. Judas seems to have been invited to the place of honor on Jesus' left. We derive that because Jesus comments that the one who sops bread with Him was the traitor (Matt. 26:23). Judas would have to be on Jesus' left to do this. The left was the place of honor for intimate friends because when the host leaned back on his left arm, his head was practically on the chest of the man. Additionally, the man had to be one who could be trusted. Also, to be given bread by the host (dipping in the same bowl) was a special honor. Jesus gave Judas every possible chance to repent of his betrayal. Only a very sinful heart could betray a man who had so honored him.[79] Peter is obviously sitting at the other end of the horseshoe arranged couches because he motions to John in John 13:24, prodding him to ask Jesus who the betrayer was. Thus, we see Peter taking to heart Jesus' teaching that those wanting to be first in Heaven should seek to serve on earth. We find Peter in the lowest place of honor.[82] First, Jesus takes the cup of wine, representing His blood and gives thanks. (The wine was mixed with water before it was blessed and passed around.) After all had drunk from the cup, it was customary for the head of the group to conduct the ceremonial hand washing prior to the meal. Apparently, this is the time the Apostles chose to argue about who was the greatest. Jesus modified the ceremony to demonstrate to His Apostles that they must serve each other and the people. Jesus removed His outer garment and got His foot washing supplies ready. Sitting on the end, Peter was the first one approached.[82] Peter was stunned that the Rabbi and Savior would perform the lowly duty of a slave for a sinner such as himself. When Jesus told Peter, "Unless I wash you, you have no part with me," Peter hurriedly tells Jesus to wash his head and hands as well! Peter wanted to be completely immersed in the cleansing love of the Savior. Yet, in only hours, Peter would deny he even knew Jesus. [Note: Many do not agree with the statement that Peter was the first apostle to be approached by Jesus to wash his feet based on John 13:5. When you read it several times, you can see that 13:5 appears to be out of sequence, fitting better **after** Peter's response rather than before it. It seems unlikely that the outspoken Peter would not have made a statement prior to this time if the other apostles' feet were being washed. The major hint is the phrase "after that." There is no reason for this phrase if the natural sequence of preparation had occurred. Obviously something had happened that caused an "after that" comment. Try placing verse 5 after verse 11 and you will understand my reasoning.]

An important part of the ceremony would involve the singing of praises to God known as the Hallel. Psalms 113-118 comprise these songs, which were sung at different times during the meal. The hymn sung at the end of the meal was the Great Hallel or Psalm 136.[78]

After the foot washing, Jesus puts on His garments and again takes His place as host. A Passover meal would entail a dipping of bitter herbs into salt water and offering a blessing. These would then be served around to the others. Next the host would break the cakes of unleavened bread. When Jesus broke the bread He told the Apostles it represented His body that would be broken for them. We are to partake of the wine and bread in remembrance of Him. After all have eaten some bread another cup of wine would be poured and blessed. Prayers would be spoken and the Hallel sung before partaking this second cup. Then came the ceremonial hand washing. This appears to be when Judas is identified as the betrayer. Only those whose hearts and souls are cleansed of sin (believers are washed in the blood of the Lamb) by repentance and by the sacrificial offering could participate. As the Lamb of God, Jesus did not need to wash, but Judas Iscariot was unclean and unrepentant. Jesus was troubled in spirit. Judas Iscariot had his last chance. Jesus comments that one among them is a traitor. All were asking, "Is it I?" Apparently, Judas whispered it, too, for Jesus replied that it was the one dipping his bread in the bowl with Him. In the place of highest honor, Judas would have done that, possibly as Jesus was saying the words. This exchange occurred privately between Jesus and Judas Iscariot because the other Apostles do not know why Judas suddenly leaves. The 'sop,' as recorded by some translations, is lamb wrapped in a piece of unleavened bread and dipped in bitter herbs. (This really doesn't sound very good to me, but I understand it is tasty - something like a sweet-and-sour fruity herbal mixture on a lamb roll.) After supper, a third cup of wine is poured and a special blessing is pronounced. (Today, Jews offer a blessing for the meat that has been eaten. The taking of any life is a time of solemn soul-searching -- even the loss of an animal's life. God gives all life. We have become too calloused about taking life. It should be done with prayer in accordance with God's Will.) A final ritual hand washing occurred at this point, as the meal was eaten with the hands. The cup is filled a fourth time, blessed, and the final songs sung.[82]

Jesus tells the Apostles that He will soon be gone and where He goes they cannot follow. Peter impetuously states he will follow Jesus even to death. You can picture Jesus just shaking His head saying, "Simon, Simon, Satan has asked to sift you as wheat. But I have prayed for you Simon that your faith may not fail. And when you have turned back, strengthen your brothers."[1] (Luke 22:31-32) Before anything happens in our lives, Jesus is interceding on our behalf so that we will have strength to withstand the trial. Now Jesus tells Peter that he will deny Him three times before the rooster crows. But Jesus follows that with "I am going there to prepare a place for you. And if I go and prepare a place for you, I will come back and take you to be with me that you also may be where I am. **You know the way to the place where I am going**."[1] (John 14:2-4) Thomas inquires into where Jesus is going; otherwise, how will they know the way? "Jesus answered, 'I am the way and the truth and the life. No one comes to the Father except through me.'"[1] (John 14:6) Now it is Philip's turn. "Lord, show us the Father and that will be enough for us."[1] (John 14:8) Jesus is disappointed. Just hours before His death and Philip doesn't realize that Jesus and the Father are one. Philip is looking at the Father! Just as we have our parents alive in us, we should expect to see God in Jesus -- but even more so! Every thing Jesus has done and said were at the direction of the Father. Those who are believers have Jesus living in them. Believers, therefore, should do as Jesus did. Jesus had love and compassion for all people. He gave selflessly to all who sought Him. He sought the Will of His Father and never failed to carry it out. Jesus tells the Apostles that they can ask for anything in His name and it will be done. We should be careful that the requests we make in the name of Jesus are those in alignment with God's Will. Altogether too many times, Jesus' name is employed ritually at the end of prayer without thought or concern about the significance. Jesus cares for us so much that He requested the Holy Spirit be sent to guide us in truth, to dwell within us, to comfort us. Those who love Jesus will experience the love of God. The Holy Spirit will reveal the interpretation of the scripture to us as we develop a mind and heart like Christ. Throughout our lives, the Holy Spirit will remind us of the teachings of Jesus. "Do not let your hearts be troubled and do not be afraid."[1] (John 14:27)

Jesus sent out His Apostles on their initial missionary journey without any possessions, explaining that their needs would be provided by those ministered unto in the towns visited. Jesus had become a popular religious figure and many would be glad to provide for the needs of His Apostles. Soon, all that would change. From now on, when they go out, they are to carry money, clothes, and a means of defense. Jesus was about to be hated by the world. He would be slain and His followers would be alone until the Holy Spirit was sent. They would need to be prepared and shrewd to stay alive. Jesus gives them directions that after His death they are to meet Him in Galilee.

Food for Thought: Passover requires four foods beside the Paschal lamb and unleavened bread: (1) salt water to represent the tears of the Israelites in Egyptian bondage and the salt water of the Red Sea through which they passed, (2) bitter herbs composed of horse-radish, chicory, endive, lettuce, hore-hound, and other herbs to represent the bitterness of slavery and the hyssop used to paint blood on the door frames, (3) Charosheth made of ground apples, dates, pomegranates, and nuts formed in a block with sticks of cinnamon to represent the mud and straw bricks made in Egypt, and (4) four cups of wine, each representing one of the promises of Exodus 6:6-7.[78] The Jews knew their Egyptian history well, but they missed the biggest event of all -- the coming of the Messiah!

November 15
Bible Readings: John 15:1-16:24; 17:1-26

The house of Israel was symbolized as God's vineyard throughout prophecy. Ezekiel tells us the vine was wild and unproductive, fit only to be burned in the fire of judgment (Ezek. 15:1-8). Now Jesus tells His Apostles that He is the **true** vine and the Father is the gardener. Just being a member of the chosen Jews will not be acceptable for eternal life. Jesus is the vine, not the Jews. Those who follow Jesus and keep His teachings will be fruitful. Their work for the kingdom of God will increase the Kingdom and bring eternal rewards. If we walk close to Jesus, He will be evident in our lives. We will be loved, protected, and guided in the path of righteousness. Jesus reiterates the importance of loving one another. If we love Jesus, His love will shine through us to others. We are commanded to love others as Jesus loved us. Then Jesus tells us that the greatest love of all is laying down one's life for his friends (which He did for us).

Jesus explained that He had to return to Heaven and send the Holy Spirit. This action was good and righteous. The believers would have a constant indwelling of Jesus' spirit known as the Holy Spirit or Counselor. It is the Holy Spirit that pricks our consciences when we sin, guides us when we are uncertain, comforts us when we grieve, and loves us when we are lonely. Now Jesus tells us just how special the gift of the Spirit is, "All that belongs to the Father is mine. That is why I said the Spirit will take from what is mine and make it known to you."[1] (John 16:15) The Holy Spirit brings us a portion of the inheritance of Jesus.

The Apostles still do not realize that Jesus' death is imminent. Jesus tells them they will weep and mourn. Their pain will be like that of childbirth (John 16:20-22), but when the Holy Spirit comes with the full realization of the joy of inheriting eternal life in the Kingdom of God, their pain will turn to rejoicing. Believers will have peace that is beyond understanding (Phil. 4:7). No one can take away the joy of a believer. Soon Jesus will no longer have to speak in symbolism and parables but will be able to speak directly and plainly to the Apostles. For now, the time is very short and when His arrest comes, the Apostles will scatter like startled birds. But Jesus will not be alone. The heavenly Father will be with Him. As long as we live in this world, we will have trouble, but the believer knows that Jesus has overcome the world! The Holy Spirit abides in us. We may lose some battles to temptation, but Jesus has won the war for us!

Jesus prays for Himself. There seem to be two types of prayer warriors: those who pray for others and those who pray for themselves. We need to strive for a 'happy median.' Without daily prayer for ourselves, we can't withstand the trials and pressures of the world. But without prayer for others, we become self-centered and lack compassion. Jesus prayed that the Father glorify Him and He, in turn, would glorify the Father. The order is important. First, we must be honored with the opportunity to be used for God's glory. Then, we must pray for God's glory to be evident in our efforts. The concept is that we are the brushes, but God is the artist. Those who see the art will appreciate the mastery of the artist. The brushes were mere tools blessed with the opportunity to be used by the greatest Creator of all! Jesus, though the Son of God, was the gift of the Creator to the world. Before Jesus, mankind was a canvas of blackness with a few representative white spots stained from the blood of the prophets. There were very few holy men of God, many of them martyred. After Jesus, the canvas is filled with splendor and beauty beyond ordinary knowledge when viewed by a believer. But when viewed by a non-believer, it

Lessons of Love

is threatening and fearful. The believer sees the promise of Heaven and the non-believer sees the judgment of hell. Jesus made all the difference.

Jesus now prays for His disciples. He makes it clear He is **not** praying for the world but only for those who believe in Him. If we want Jesus to intercede on our behalf with the Father, then we must believe in Him! Otherwise, we are on our own. God so loved people that He sent His only Son -- the gift -- that whosoever believed in Him -- the condition -- would have eternal life (John 3:16). The gift is there for all, but only those who accept it can enjoy it. Jesus does not ask that God take believers out of the evil world but rather that God protect us from evil so that we can lead others to know Him. Believers are Jesus' commissioned soldiers. We carry His banner, His message, and His gift to the enemies. Those who cross over to His side are won forever, but those who refuse Him or waver in no man's land are hopelessly lost. Jesus asks God to sanctify or set apart believers for His holy army, those soldiers who will carry the Truth to the world.

Jesus also prays for the unity of the believers. He prays believers will be as close in love and commitment as Jesus and the Father are. They share the same mission: to take the love of God and the salvation message to the world.

Food for Thought: I have a bad habit. I get so emotionally drained in praying for others I forget to spend time praying for myself. I often depend on others to pray for me because I know my weakness. I am very thankful for all prayers lifted up for me. The devil knows that I am so busy in daily life that he can sneak up on me without my awareness. When I am overwhelmed, then I wonder why I didn't remember to pray about the mounting problem. It's a case of not being able to see the forest for the trees or maybe it's really not seeing the bear in the forest. Be vigilant in prayer for yourself as well as others.

November 16
<u>Bible Readings:</u> Matt. 26:36-75; 27:1,3-10; Mark 14:32-72; 15:1; Luke 22:40-71; John 18:1-27

Jesus and the Apostles leave Jerusalem, crossing the Kidron Valley to the Mount of Olives. A small olive grove called Gethsemane was a favorite place for quiet retreat and prayer. Jesus took His inner circle of Apostles with Him to pray. Peter, James, and John were to keep watch while Jesus prayed. Jesus included His dearest friends in His time of agony. But they had eaten a big meal at the end of a hectic week. Sitting in the silent dark night, sleep crept upon them. Jesus had gone a short distance away to pray. The humanness of Jesus is clearly portrayed as He wrestles with His own fears and truncated dreams. Jesus knows the cross is ahead of Him, but at 33 He doesn't want to die and especially not in such a cruel way. Crucifixions were commonplace in Roman territory. Thousands of people were crucified. Crucifixions were performed in full view of the public, often along public highways. Everyone was familiar with the horror of the punishment. Jesus wanted the companionship of His friends and the reassurance of His Father. Jesus calls out, "Abba, Father!" which is the Jewish term used by a small child. He prayed that He be spared this cruel death if it is God's Will. (Do you feel like you are witnessing an event too personal for you to look upon?) Jesus wrestles with His human will to live and His godly will to glorify His Father. At some point in life, every person must face this same struggle. The decision made will result in a lifetime of shame in our weakness or joy in our victory over temptation. Jesus shows us the struggles and battles that we will face in the world. How do we mature in our faith so we can be strong when our own time is near? The answer comes from a lifetime of seeking God's Will and following that Will even though we don't understand it. God only wants the best for us. We must trust Him. Does that mean we will never falter? No, Jesus is the only one who never failed. But we must try to always follow the righteous Will of God. God hears our prayers for strength just as He heard Jesus' prayer. He sent an angel to strengthen His Son, as any loving father would choose to do. Jesus' anguish was so great that huge drops of sweat fell to the ground. (This is a typical response from the autonomic nervous system that is a result of *internal* causes, i.e., extreme stress, fear, pain. I recall my husband did this once in prayer. At the time, I wasn't favorably impressed, considering it was during our wedding prayer!) Jesus returns to His friends to find them asleep. His disappointment is evident. The first time He wakes them, but the next two times He seems to have exchanged His sense of urgency with one of acceptance. The Will of His Father is now all too clear. His strength and resolve have been renewed. The hour has come. He sees the torches and lanterns coming His way. For the last time, He wakes the Apostles and, with courage, walks out to meet the enemy.[78]

Judas Iscariot is leading the way. He steps forward to greet his Rabbi with a kiss -- the usual greeting between a student and his beloved teacher.[71] Forever it will be known as the 'kiss of death.' Jesus rebukes him. How could he betray Jesus with a kiss of love? Twice Jesus asks who they are looking for and twice they reply "Jesus of Nazareth." After the second time, Jesus tells them to let the Apostles go; He is the one they seek. This was done to fulfill prophecy that He lost none of those God had given Him. But impetuous Peter draws his sword and cuts off the ear of Malchus, the high priest's servant. (With aim like that, aren't you glad Peter isn't defending you in the woods on a dark night?) Jesus said to him, "Put your sword back in its place for all who draw the sword will die by the sword."[1] (Matt. 26:52) Violence will only foster more violence and more death. Jesus reminds His Apostles that if He had called, His Father would have sent 12 legions of angels to defend Him: about 36,000 to 72,000 angels.[5] Then Jesus healed the ear of His enemy. Could we have done this? To the rest of the guards, He asks if He is a rebellion leader that it takes so many with weapons to arrest Him. "But this is your hour -- when darkness reigns."[1] (Luke 22:53)

Mark tells of a young man wearing only a linen garment who was following Jesus. The guards try to seize him, but he threw off the garment and ran away naked. This boy is believed to be the young Mark. Also, many believed the last supper took place in the upper room of Mark's home. Mark may have been wrapped in a sheet because he had sneaked away from the house to follow Jesus. Or Mark may have been awakened by the clamor of guards and Judas searching the upper room for Jesus. Mark may actually have thrown the sheet around himself hurriedly to get ahead of the guards and warn Jesus. Either way, he was too late. Jesus had been arrested.[71]

Jesus is first bound and taken to Annas who had been deposed as high priest several years before. Annas still had a lot of power and was the owner of the Temple merchants and money-changing businesses. (So he also had a monetary purpose in this event.) John went into the palace courtyard with Jesus. Peter waited outside the door until John asked the servant girl to let Peter come in. All four gospels record this servant girl as the first one to identify Peter as a disciple of Jesus. Peter gives his first denial. The gospels disagree on the identity of the second and third accusers. Matthew and Mark state the accusers were two women and a group of people. Luke tells of one woman, then an unknown, followed by a man. These differences are understandable. There were many people in the courtyard; it was very dark and cold -- probably after midnight. The disciples were all confused and frightened over the events of the night. Regardless, the stories clearly show Peter denying Christ three times. Matthew states Peter called down curses on himself and swore he knew not Jesus. The rooster crowed and Jesus turned and looked at Peter. What a sad, aching, knowing look that must have been! Peter fled the palace courtyard, weeping and devastated by his own failure. Peter, of whom Jesus called the rock upon which He would build His church, was reduced to sand. His courage and leadership were gone. Soon Peter would renew his strength and his determination. He would find the mortar needed in Christ's teachings and the Holy Spirit to turn his own sand of weakness into the concrete rock churches could be built upon.

After being questioned and struck at Annas' palace, Jesus is sent to Caiaphas the son-in-law of Annas and the current high priest. Caiaphas convened the Sanhedrin, a group of 71 members of the scribes, Pharisees, Sadducees, and elders who made up the Jewish Supreme Court. They all looked for evidence to convict Jesus. The Jews are breaking several of their own laws here. First, the law stated the Sanhedrin could only convene in the daytime. Second, it was not allowed to hear a death sentence trial during Passover. Third, the Sanhedrin was bound by law to meet only in the Hall of Hewn Stone in the Temple precinct. Fourth, the job of the Sanhedrin was to present evidence of one's innocence until witnesses proved guilt. We are plainly told that the statements of many false witnesses are taken but do not agree. Therefore, another Jewish law is broken. To give false witness in a life-or-death trial meant certain death for the witness (Lev.19:16, Ex. 20:16). Jesus remained silent throughout this charade, fulfilling the prophecy of Isa. 53:7. When asked if He was the Christ, Jesus responded, "I am." At this the high priest violated Mosaic Law by tearing his robes (Lev. 21:10). The Sanhedrin sentences Jesus to death for blasphemy. In doing so, they break Jewish law again. The Sanhedrin was required to sleep over night on a guilty vote so that mercy could be contemplated. A sentence of death could only be issued the next day. The only trial that could start and end on the same day was one of 'not guilty.'[78]

In the meantime, the full realization of what his treachery had done has now hit Judas Iscariot. He returns to his 'employers' and confesses he has betrayed innocent blood. These chief priests and elders don't care, "What is that to us?" And they called themselves religious leaders! Judas threw the 30 silver coins into the Temple and left. Judas Iscariot hanged himself, forever doomed to hell. Keep in mind, the religious leaders could have taken Judas' time of confession and repentance and led him to salvation in Jesus, but they didn't. Jesus had already foretold the loss of Judas from the fold. We know that God holds religious leaders to a higher standard; these men would suffer a horrible fate. They even acknowledge that the silver is 'blood money.' They had hired a hit man. They couldn't put unclean money in the Temple treasury, so they bought the potter's field to bury foreigners. It is called the Field of Blood. This fulfilled the prophecies of Jeremiah 19 and Zechariah 11:12-13.

Food for Thought: If the three Apostles closest to Jesus were all asleep, then who recorded this scene in Gethsemane?

November 17
Bible Readings: Matt. 27:2, 11-32 Mark 15:1-22   Luke 23:1-31 John 18:28-40; 19:1-17

Jesus' last day began with Him being bound before the Roman governor (or procurator) Pilate. The trial was held outside the palace so the Jews would not be unclean from entering a Gentile dwelling. Anyone found unclean could not eat the Passover meal and was cut off from the other 'clean' Jews. This verse (John 18:28) forms the foundation for the scriptural interpretation that Jesus was crucified on Thursday rather than Friday. The Jews started their new calendar day at 6 p.m. each evening. (Our calendars start the new day right after midnight.) Passover meals could not begin until after 6 p.m. and had to be completed before daylight. Because the Jews were worried about purity for eating the Passover meal, apparently it was yet to occur. Your Bible commentator (as well as *The Broadman Bible Commentary*) presents an excellent case for Jesus being crucified on Thursday afternoon. He was buried before 6 p.m., after which the Passover meal started. Jesus paid the ultimate price; He was the sacrificial Lamb. The Paschal Lamb was sacrificed <u>before</u> the Passover meal. The meal itself was eaten on Friday by the Jewish calendar but would have been on Thursday by our calendars. A Thursday crucifixion would also have fulfilled Jesus' prophecy of being in the earth 3 days <u>and</u> 3 nights (Matt. 12:40). In order to have a Sunday morning resurrection, there would have to be a Thursday crucifixion. The argument in favor of a Friday crucifixion is based on the other three gospels, particularly Luke 22. We are told that **on the day the Passover lamb had to be sacrificed**, Jesus sent Peter and John to make preparations for the group to eat the Passover. Deut. 16:4-6 commands the lamb be sacrificed after the sun goes down (after 6 p.m.). Passover was on Nisan (earlier called Abib) 14 with the Feast of Unleavened Bread celebrated the 15th - 21st. In order to eat a lamb sacrificed in the Temple, Jesus would have eaten on Thursday night and been crucified on Friday. Most scholars holding this view strongly believe Jesus would not bypass Jewish law requiring a Temple sacrificed lamb for Passover. But Jesus did not abide by the Jewish laws that were interpreted to forbid healing on Sunday. Jesus abided by God's interpretation of the law, not man's interpretation. Jesus did not have to participate in a sacrifice of a lamb because He had no sin for which to offer sacrifice. Also, Jesus' Apostles were given bread and wine representing the real Lamb of God. To me, the better argument in favor of Friday is that Mark talks about the customary sacrifice of the Passover lamb in Mark 14. **If** the last supper were eaten in Mark's home, **then** surely he would know the day it occurred. But Mark was a young man at the time and may not have witnessed what actually happened in the upper room. Also, Mark doesn't write his gospel account for approximately 30 years after Jesus' resurrection. Did he not remember the date correctly, or did Peter, who was at the last supper, remember a different date? Why would Jesus have had so much secrecy about where He would eat

Passover? Obviously, it was because Judas Iscariot, the stool pigeon, was part of the Apostles. Jesus couldn't explain to the others about Judas' betrayal until the time was right. He couldn't let Judas' knowledge of His movements alter the events either. Was the date also different for the same reason? A Friday crucifixion would mean the members of the Sanhedrin would have had to stop during their own Passover meal to hold the mock trial of Jesus. This would not have been acceptable to the people, even if the Sanhedrin had accepted it. Was Jesus crucified on Thursday or Friday? On this issue, you can hold either opinion with many others behind you. It seems to me the actual day Jesus died pales in comparison to the main event - the resurrection! (Study all of the Gospels' accounts of the last supper and ponder the Passover and crucifixion timeline.)

Pilate wants to know what the charges are. Notice that Jesus was condemned to death for blasphemy, but the charges presented to Pilate are totally different. There are 3 charges: (1) rebelling against Rome, (2) opposing tax payment, and (3) claiming to be Christ, a king. Pilate dismisses these charges telling the Jews to deal with Jesus in their own religious system. Pilate obviously can see the charges are false. Outraged, the Jews insist they want a death penalty that only a Roman trial can decree. After questioning Him, Pilate declared there was no evidence to support the charges against Jesus. Then the false testimonies and accusations began. Jesus made no reply. He was silent before His accusers, fulfilling prophecy in Isaiah 53:7. During the testimony Pilate learned Jesus was a Galilean. Here he could get rid of this mess! Pilate could send Jesus to the Galilean governor, Herod Antipas, who was in town for the festival. Herod was anxious to meet this man who claimed to be king. After all, it was the Galilean Jewish pilgrims who had praised and worshipped Jesus as their king on Palm Sunday.[83] Herod and his soldiers ridiculed and mocked Jesus. They even took a royal robe and placed it on Jesus, possibly a robe belonging to the king. A mock crown was made from thorny vines entwined about Jesus' head. Matthew 27:29-30 tells us the soldiers put a reed (Greek translation) in Jesus' hand and pretended to worship Him mockingly. Repeatedly they hit Jesus in the head with the staff, driving the thorns into His flesh. After this horror, they sent Jesus back to Pilate.

Under Roman law, Pilate should have dismissed the charges against Jesus on his first review. Unfortunately, the Jews were a passionate people inclined to take a stand, to the point of death -- a stiff-necked people. Pilate had a procurator appointment as a result of Archelaus bungling riot control during Passover and killing thousands of the Jews. Pilate did not want any riots or political problems. Herod's insecurity as king was well known. But Herod had apparently found Jesus to be no threat to his position. Now Pilate had a real dilemma, even his wife was having disturbing dreams! She had warned him that Jesus was innocent. Pilate has a brilliant idea! Jewish Passover custom was to release a prisoner. Surely, the Jews would prefer Jesus among them rather than one of the murderers! Pilate calls in the religious leaders and the people then announces that neither he nor Herod could find Jesus guilty of the charges. Jesus did not deserve to die, but Pilate would agree to scourge Him. Many men died from scourging alone. The whip was made of plaited leather cords having bits of bone or metal woven into the strands. This did not satisfy the Jews. They were a bloodthirsty group. "Release Barabbas! Crucify Jesus!" Pilate had to use his back-up plan but not as he intended. The Jews were determined to kill Jesus. Three times Pilate asked for credible charges against Jesus; three times the crowd shouted, "Crucify!" By now Pilate must have been panic stricken trying to sort out the problems: (1) Roman law didn't allow the death penalty for innocent men, (2) The Jews were on the verge of a riot, (3) The crowd was demanding an innocent man be crucified and a notoriously guilty murderer be released. What would the emperor think? He must be sure everyone understood this man's blood was not on his hands! Pilate questions Jesus one last time. Jesus assures him the one who handed Him over was guiltier than he. Try as he might, Pilate could not dissuade the Jews. They are now accusing Pilate of being an adversary of Caesar's! Relenting, he symbolically washed his hands in front of the crowd declaring, "I am innocent of this man's blood. It is your responsibility."[1] (John 19:15) Isn't it interesting that the worthless ceremonial hand washing ritual of the Jews was being used by a Gentile to transfer the guilt of their sin back to them? Jesus taught that it was what was in a man's heart that made him unclean and sinful, not what was on the outside. The hand washing rituals didn't save the Jews and it wouldn't save Pilate. Guilt is guilt; sin is sin. A heart devoted to God should do what is right and trust in God to provide the reward. Barabbas is released and the chosen people of God condemn Jesus. Wonder if Barabbas ever realized what Jesus did for him? Did he change his life?

Crucifixions were all carried out in the same manner. The cross was a short T-shaped rough-hewn wooden instrument of death. The one convicted had to carry the crossbeam to the place of crucifixion, if he survived the scourging. The route taken was always the longest, winding route possible through the populated areas. Four soldiers accompanied the criminal at the four stations of the 'corners.' The one in front carried a wooden sign with the criminal's offense printed on it for all to see. It was meant to be a warning. Jesus was so badly beaten with His skin and muscles torn away that He could no longer hold the cross. Simon of Cyrene (father of Alexander and Rufus) was conscripted to carry the cross. Cyrene was in Africa. Jews living that far away would save most of their lives to be able to come to Jerusalem just once to celebrate Passover. Each year those not in Jerusalem would pledge, "This year here, but next year Jerusalem!" Simon must have initially felt extreme fear at being singled out by the Roman soldiers. Maybe he had shown too much compassion in his face! Then he must have also felt resentment that his lifelong dream was turning out this way, carrying a cross to Golgotha. (Why was it important that Simon be known as the "father of Alexander and Rufus?" Mark initially wrote his Gospel for the church at Rome. Could it be the Rufus mentioned in Romans 16:13 is the same one? Could the African, Simeon called Niger from Acts 13:1, be the same as Simon of Cyrene? Was Simon of Cyrene a disciple? Or did he find salvation at the cross? Maybe Simon's lifetime dream became an eternal reality.)[71]

Crucifixion involved laying the criminal on the crossbeam and nailing an arm to each end. A wooden block was between his legs or under the hips to serve as a 'saddle' to support the weight when the crossbeam was lifted into place. Otherwise, the nails would strip out of the flesh. The legs were usually tied or nailed to the shaft of the cross, after the crossbeam was dropped into the groove in the permanently installed upright shaft. The victims would hang for days before dying, sometimes as long as a week. Death came from exposure, starvation, thirst, suffocation, or hemorrhage. The garments of the criminal became the reward for the four soldiers. The victims were stripped naked as further shame and punishment. The dying man was close to the ground. His accusers could easily jeer and watch him die and even animals could attack. After death, the bodies were claimed by relatives or left on the cross to be devoured by the beasts of the field and the birds of the air. (There is that feared judgment again!)[7,71] In Jesus' case, his widowed mother was a long way from home with no available tomb. Jews did not embalm the body and, therefore, burial had to be quick. There was no way she could claim a body with nowhere to bury it.

The women who had so faithfully followed and supported Jesus are wailing loudly. Jesus tells them to weep for themselves and their children instead. Then He quotes Hosea 10:8. Stop and read from the crucifixion psalm -- Psalm 22:12-24. Pagans would have died rather than treat one of their idols this way, but the Jewish religious leaders felt no remorse at crucifying the Son of God. Our lesson ends with a question from Jesus. "For if men do these things when the tree is green, what will happen when it is dry?"[1] (Luke 23:31) In other words, if men would torture, jeer, and crucify when the Word was with them, what further degradation would happen when He had been gone thousands of years?

Food for Thought: Matthew said Jesus' robe was scarlet. Mark and John say it was purple. Luke says it was elegant. I envision it as a true wine -- a deep, rich purple of royalty that became scarlet when held up to the light. It was just like Jesus -- a royal richness of Truth that when lifted up shown scarlet, as the blood of the King brought clarity to the meaning of life.

November 18
Bible Readings: Matt. 27:33-66 Mark 15:23-47   Luke 23:32-56 John 19:18-42

Christ is crucified at Calvary (Latin for Golgotha[73]) at 9 a.m. Crucifixion was so cruel that it was only used for slaves and foreigners.[73] Jesus was sold for the price of a slave and now died as a condemned slave. As Jesus looked on His accusers, He prayed, "Father, forgive them, for they do not know what they are doing."[1] (Luke 23:34) Two criminals hung beside Him, one on the right and one on the left. Multiple crucifixions were common practice. A group of compassionate women brought wine mixed with myrrh to every crucifixion. The drugged wine helped dull the pain. Jesus refused. He would bear the full pain for our sins.

As customary, Pilate prepared a sign stating the charge against Jesus. "It read: Jesus of Nazareth, the King of the Jews."[1] (John 19:19) The sign was written in the three dominant languages of the world at that time: Aramaic, Latin, and Greek. Pilate made sure everyone knew that crucifixion was how a king would be honored among the Jews. Of course, the chief priests had loudly protested wanting Pilate to change the sign to read, "He claimed to be King of the Jews." But Pilate gets his own revenge for the Jews forcing him into a bad political situation. He at least could make sure all knew the charge was from the Sanhedrin religious leaders and not from the Roman courts. Pilate had nothing but animosity towards the Jews. They had caused him much grief and trouble in his political career. Pilate had purposefully brought the Roman army from Cesarea to Jerusalem to winter in an effort to abolish Jewish law. The Jews refused to yield or bow to any graven image in accordance with the Second Commandment. The insignia of the Romans was not a flag but rather the image of Caesar. This image was carried on the tops of standards or poles lifted above the head. Pilate brought the soldiers in at night so as to present an overwhelming show of power when the Jews discovered the images were present. On the sixth day of protest, Pilate held an open-air hearing. The soldiers stood behind him with their weapons hidden. When the Jews made their demands, Pilate signaled for the weapons to be displayed. The Jews would submit to the insignias or die. To his surprise, they immediately laid on the ground with their necks extended preferring to die than violate their law. Pilate was so deeply moved that he relented.[3] Therefore, when he heard their protests and demands at Jesus' trial, he knew they were willing to go to any length to gain their objective.

The four soldiers divided the garments of Jesus among themselves. A Jew had 5 pieces of clothing: an inner garment, an outer robe, a girdle, sandals, and a turban.[71] Jesus' inner garment was seamless and of greatest value. Rather than destroy its beauty and value by ripping it apart, the soldiers gambled for its ownership. This fulfilled the scripture Psalm 22:18. Meanwhile the hundreds of thousands of people passing by hurled insults at Jesus, mocking Him. "You who are going to destroy the temple and build it in three days, save yourself! Come down from the cross, if you are the Son of God!"[1] (Matt. 27:40) The religious leaders jeered at Him. "He saved others but he can't save himself! He's the King of Israel! Let him come down now from the cross, and we will believe in him. He trusts in God. Let God rescue him now if he wants him, for he said, 'I am the Son of God.'"[1] (Matt. 27:42-43) One of the criminals joined in the insult barrage, but the other confessed his sin before Christ and declared Jesus' innocence of any wrong. Then he asked Jesus to remember him when He came into His kingdom. Jesus responded, "I tell you the truth, today you will be with me in paradise."[1] (Luke 23:43) Different religious groups have interpreted this response in many different ways. Barclay gives the following commentary:

*The word Paradise is a Persian word meaning **a walled garden**. When a Persian king wished to do one of his subjects a very special honor he made him a companion of the garden, and he was chosen to walk in the garden with the king. It was more than immortality that Jesus promised the penitent thief. He promised him the honored place of a companion of the garden in the courts of heaven.*[70] *(pp. 299-300)*

Rev. 2:7 states, "To him who overcomes, I will give the right to eat from the tree of life, which is in the paradise of God."[1]

Jesus sees His mother, aunt, Mary the wife of Clopas, and Mary Magdalene. Mary the wife of Clopas we know nothing about. Of course, Mary Magdalene had been a long-term disciple of Jesus. As the eldest son, the care of His widowed mother had fallen to Him as a young man. Jesus appointed John to that position and told His mother that John would now care for her. Even in His final hours, Jesus' love for His mother and concern for her welfare was evident. Mary had always known that God was His Father. Their bond was both emotional and spiritual.

About noon, darkness occurred. Apparently at this hour Jesus received the full weight of the sins of the world. This was the first time in His life He experienced the consequences of sin. Jesus was separated from God. God could not look upon sin. For three hours He bore the pain and anguish of the load of sin for **all mankind** through **all the ages**! At 3 p.m. He cried out Psalm 22:1. "My God, my God, why have you forsaken me?"[1] Psalm 22 is so tightly woven throughout the crucifixion story that Jesus must have repeated it several times in His thoughts. Jesus knew all the scripture. Surely He found comfort in being victorious over the devil at each step. Then He said, "I am thirsty." His moisture on a sponge was appropriately soured wine. The pure, holy, royal wine of the blood of Jesus was in direct contrast to the sour vinegar wine of the poor. Yet Jesus was the friend of the poor and downtrodden to the end. Like a runner who has won the race, Jesus announces, "It is finished." In a loud voice so all could hear His last testimony, Jesus shouted, "Father, into your hands I commit my spirit."[1] (John 19:30) Instantly, the Temple veil was torn from the top to the bottom -- from God to mankind. The earth quaked, rocks (mountainsides) split, tombs (caves) were broken open, and many of the righteous dead were raised to life. Those raised from the dead were seen throughout the countryside. The terrified soldiers exclaimed, "Surely he was the Son of God!"[1] (Matt. 27:54) Isn't it amazing how Gentiles repeatedly recognized Jesus' deity, but the Pharisees never did?

According to your Bible, it was preparation day or Thursday. Friday was Passover and was a holy day or special Sabbath. Crucifixion was against the law on Passover. To avoid any uncleanness from dead bodies, the Jews wanted the bodies removed from the crosses in preparation for the Passover. (Besides, Passover was a very good business festival for the merchants of the Temple. The religious leaders didn't want to lose any money by possibly discouraging visitors!) The average crucifixion took 36 hours for death to come. Pilate ordered their legs be broken. Both of the thieves had their legs broken, but Jesus was already dead. They did not break His legs but instead pierced His side with a spear. The collection of bloody body fluids poured forth. This was done in accordance with the scriptures that none of Jesus' bones would be broken (Ps. 34:20, Nu. 9:12, Ex. 12:46) and they would look upon the One they had pierced. (Bones were broken so the victims could not push up their bodies to get a breath of air. The pain would also hurry along death. Often major blood vessels, which are near the bone, were severed. In those cases, hemorrhaging brought death within minutes.)

Joseph of Arimathea, a prominent member of the Sanhedrin, boldly asked Pilate for Jesus' body. It took much courage. Anyone associated with a crucified man was automatically under suspicion by the Romans. He also risked persecution, religious sanctions, or even death from his fellow council members. Joseph of Arimathea was a believer. You have to wonder what role or comments he had in the mockery of a trial Jesus was given. All we know is that Luke 23:51 says he did not consent to Jesus' conviction. Nicodemus was another believer who brought 75 pounds of myrrh and aloes to coat the body. Nicodemus was a Pharisee and also a member of the Sanhedrin.[5] Here we have two of the Sanhedrin who are believers. Why didn't they speak up at the trial? Or did they and were outvoted? Regardless of the reasons, we know that Jesus' crucifixion was God's Will -- His gift to all mankind. These two wealthy men provided Jesus with the burial of royalty. The men wrapped Jesus' hand and feet in strips. The aloe mixture with the linen strips effectively set up a resin cast around the body. Myrrh was aromatic and used in perfumes and anointing oils.[5] A white linen shroud was draped over the body. The folds were filled with fragrant spices. A linen cloth was placed around the face and head. Jesus was placed on a slab in Joseph's new tomb. The stone was rolled into place. The men must hurry for it was nearly 6 p.m. and the laws of the holy day, the special Sabbath, would be invoked. They must wash themselves and prepare to do no more work for two days -- the Special Sabbath and the regular Sabbath.

Meanwhile, the chief priests and Pharisees are still plotting. (Oh, what a tangled web we weave when first we choose to deceive!) Obviously the events surrounding Jesus' death shook them up. They ask Pilate to secure the tomb to be sure no one stole Jesus' body and tried to say He had risen. With so many of the walking dead in the countryside, they must really be worried now! So Pilate sealed the tomb and posted guards at the entrance. (Surely they knew it was Joseph's tomb. What must they have said to him?)

Food for Thought: The Pharisees and chief priests must have been very frightened to have gone to a Gentile Roman for assistance on Passover. This Passover was filled with contradictions of Jewish law. Yet the One without sin was killed for the sins of all. Numbers 19:11-13 tells us that anyone who touched a dead body was unclean for 7 days. They had to be purified or cleansed with water on the third and seventh days. Joseph and Nicodemus gave up their right to celebrate Passover so as to honor the real sacrificial Lamb.

The risen dead must have posed theological as well as ceremonially clean problems with all they encountered. What was their testimony? Where were the disciples?

> Verse of the Week: **Acts 4:12** "Salvation is found in no one else, for there is no other name under heaven given to men by which we must be saved."

November 19
Bible Readings: Matt. 28:1-20; Mark 16:1-20; Luke 24:1-53; John 20:1-31; 21:1-25; Acts 1:6-26

For two days, the Jews have observed holy days. Sunday sunrise (First Fruits) had finally arrived. The closest female followers of Christ had prepared spices to anoint Jesus' body. This was the third day since the crucifixion. The odor would be bad. They did not know that Joseph and Nicodemus had already anointed the body. Instead this would be the greatest day in history rather than the awful day they anticipated! Unbeknown to the women, the early morning earthquake at the tomb site had terrified the guards as the stone before the tomb was rolled away by an angel in dazzling white raiment. (Why was the stone rolled away? Jesus didn't need to be let out. It was because no one would investigate unless the stone was rolled away. People assume all is well at cemeteries unless something looks disrupted.) When the women arrived, the guards were gone and the tomb was open! They peered in to find an angel who told them to tell the disciples and Peter to meet the Lord in Galilee. Notice Peter was separately identified. We must assume that Peter is still in hiding and mourning -- deeply ashamed of his behavior. Luke tells us two angels appeared to the women telling them not to be looking for the living among the dead. Jesus has risen! Mary Magdalene runs ahead and tells Peter and John that Jesus is gone. John outran Peter and peered into the tomb. He saw the cast of linen lying there.[7] The linen napkin that had covered Christ's head was folded up. This had been an orderly event -- no explosion or burst of power -- no grave robbers or religious enemies.

After the disciples return to their homes, Mary Magdalene remained behind and became the first to see the risen Savior. As she wept outside the tomb, she must have been anxious about looking in the tomb. But in her devotion to Jesus, she finds a message of hope. The resurrected Christ stood before her. Hardly looking at Him, she believes the man to be the gardener. Where had they taken Jesus? Then she heard the old familiar voice say, "Mary." Jesus knows us all by name. When He calls our name, the sorrows of this world will be left behind. He instructs her to go tell the disciples that He is returning to His Father and to their Father. After Jesus appeared to Mary and her friend at the tomb, the women ran to give the report. Meanwhile the guards are also giving a report to the chief priests. These religious men have stooped to so many sins now that they only think in sinful ways. They bribe the guards not to tell the real story of the tomb but instead to say they fell asleep and the body was stolen. (If this had really been the case, the guards would have been executed. (See Acts 12:19.))

Two disciples (Cleopas & Peter?) of Jesus were on the road to Emmaus, only 7 miles from Jerusalem. They were discussing all the events of this most unusual Passover. Jesus joined them on the road, but they didn't recognize Him. When Jesus asked what they were discussing, they excitedly told of the events surrounding the crucifixion of Jesus of Nazareth. Then the risen Savior rebuked them for finding all this so wondrous when the prophets had foretold it. Jesus then proceeded to plainly explain to them all that had been revealed in the Scriptures about the Christ. In Emmaus, Jesus was invited to stay in their home for the night. At the evening meal, Jesus got some bread, gave thanks, and broke it. Immediately they recognized Him! At this, He disappeared. Wonder if they had participated in the feeding of the thousands by Jesus? Maybe it was the way He had taken, blessed, and broken the bread that triggered the recognition.

Next Jesus appeared unto the disciples, but Thomas was not present. We are told they were startled and frightened. Notice Jesus says, "Why are you troubled and why do doubts rise in your minds?"[1] (Luke 24:38) They all had doubts, but we want to persecute poor Thomas because he actually voiced his doubts and fears. After seeing Jesus' wounds, they are too amazed to react normally. Now Jesus asks for food. When they saw Him eat, they knew He was really alive and not just an apparition or ghost. Then Jesus breathed on them saying, "Receive the Holy Spirit. If you forgive anyone his sins, they are forgiven; if you do not forgive them, they are not forgiven."[1] (John 20:22-23) Later, Thomas arrives and the disciples joyously recount the news. Thomas now voices his doubts. Forever he would be remembered for wanting proof in order to believe. A week later, Thomas got his proof. Jesus appeared before him. Thomas immediately said, "My Lord and my God!" Jesus responded, "Because you have seen me, you have believed; blessed are those who have not seen and yet have believed."[1] (John 20:29)

Returning from an all-night fishing trip on the Sea of Galilee, the disciples see a man on the shore. He calls to them to throw their net on the right side of the boat. When they did, the net was totally filled. Suddenly Peter realizes the man is Jesus! He jumps in the water and swims to shore. When the others got to shore, Jesus invited them to eat breakfast with the Savior. Can you imagine opening your eyes after a long struggle and seeing Jesus waiting at sunrise with a breakfast feast? This was the Lord's third appearance to His disciples. After eating, Jesus approached Peter asking, "Do you truly love me more than these?" Peter confirmed his love. Jesus then asked a second time, "Do you truly love me?" Again Peter confirmed his love. For a third time, Jesus asks, "Do you love me?" Now Peter is hurt. Did Jesus not believe him? Peter responded, "Lord, you know all things; you know that I love you." Jesus' final reply was "Feed my sheep." (John 21:15-18) Three times Peter denied Jesus on the night of His trial. Three times now Jesus gave Peter the chance to confirm his love and renew their relationship. Notice Jesus' questions. First, He asks about Peter's love in comparison to the other disciples. Peter had been the first to declare his love and faithfulness at the last supper (Mark 14:29, Matt. 26:33, John 13:37). Jesus had told Peter of His prayers for Peter that his faith would not fail, and that upon his return to the group after the denials, he could strengthen the others. Now it was time for Peter to once again assume the leadership. Second, Jesus wants Peter to search his heart and mind. Does he truly, deeply, completely love Jesus? Does he love Jesus more than the fishing way of life he lived now? Many commentators believe the word Jesus uses for 'love' in His first two questions is agape or spiritual love. But Peter's reply uses the word phileo or earthly love. Therefore, the question was posed a third time to draw Peter to the realization of the commitment about to be requested. Other commentators believe the word usage was reversed with Peter declaring a greater love than Christ asked of him. Keep in mind this conversation was in Aramaic, but John records it in Greek. We do not know if John could fully capture the Aramaic meaning in the Greek translation.[77] Peter is being restored to leadership and his love for Jesus verified (to Peter, who now doubted himself, rather than to Jesus) before the commissioning of Peter to the mission field. Jesus officially calls Peter to feed His sheep. Now we see the full picture. The disciples were fishers of men. The net was the Gospel of Jesus Christ. The fish were the believers. The net was dropped on the right side of the boat just as Christ sits on the right hand of God. None of the fish was lost. Why does this passage specify the specific number of 153 fish? Some say that ancient mariners had recorded a total of 153 varieties of fish in existence and this number symbolizes **all** types of people would come to Jesus. Others try to explain it mathematically to mean completeness.[77] [b'n haElohim=The Son of The God; b=2, '=10, n=50, h=5, a=1, E=0, l=30, o=0, h=5, i=10, m=40 for a total of 153] Regardless of the explanation, this is no doubt Peter's call to full-time ministry. Jesus concludes by warning Peter that his death will be as a prisoner. Peter then shows emotion. Was it love of John or envy of John? He asks what John's fate will be. Jesus' advice is that Peter must follow God's Will for his own life and not concern himself about God's Will for the lives of other disciples. You and I must keep our eyes on Jesus and carry out God's Will for each of us.

Jesus now commissions all the Apostles to go unto all nations discipling people and "baptizing them in the name of the Father and of the Son and of the Holy Spirit."[1] (Matt. 28:19) This is known as the Great Commission. We are also to teach converts to obey God's commandments. Believers will be saved. Mark lists some examples (16:17-18) of the power believers will have. A few radical religious groups have literally incorporated these into their worship. Likewise Jesus said that a tiny bit of faith could move mountains, too! I don't know about you, but there aren't any mountains moving around to my knowledge! Do you believe there have never been any men of faith since Jesus' comment? The point is that Jesus provides us with what we need at the time we need it provided our faith and trust are in Him. Jesus tells the Apostles to stay in Jerusalem until the power of the Holy Spirit descends on them. Then Jesus led them a short way to the area of Bethany where He ascended into a cloud. Two angels dressed in white appeared to announce, "This same Jesus, who has been taken from you into heaven, will come back in the same way you have seen him go into heaven."[1] (Acts 1:11)

The disciples return to Jerusalem so overwhelmingly joyous that they are in constant prayer and worship. Jesus' family is now included in the group which has swelled to about 120. Peter again takes the lead and encourages the others to determine a replacement for Judas Iscariot. This fulfilled Psalm 109:8. The criterion for selection was a man who had been with them from Jesus' baptism until His ascension. Two men were selected as possibilities: Joseph Barsabbas and Matthias. The Apostles prayed for the Lord to select the right one. Then they cast lots and Matthias was selected. At this point, the mission work of the disciples began.

Food for Thought:

> "Holy Spirit, breathe on me,
> My stubborn will subdue;
> Teach me in words of living flame
> What Christ would have me do.
> Breathe on me, breathe on me;
> Holy Spirit, breathe on me;
> Take Thou my heart,
> Cleanse every part,
> Holy Spirit, breathe on me."
>
> Edwin Hatch - as altered by B.B. McKinney - 1937

November 20
Bible Readings: Acts 1:1-5; 2:1-47

Also known as the Acts of the Apostles, the Book of Acts was written by the Gentile physician Luke. We know he was a physician by the many medical terms that are used in the original text, although translated into lay language. It is interesting to note that Acts does not address the works of all the Apostles but only a few, primarily Peter and John. James' death is mentioned in 12:2. The rest of Acts focuses on the early church and the missions of Paul. Luke was a loyal friend of Paul's and the only Gentile author in the Bible. Like the Gospel of Luke, Acts is written to Theophilus, which means lover of God. Therefore, the name may be more of a friendly greeting rather than a true given name. Based on the reference to "most excellent Theophilus," this man is presumed to be a high government official. That being the case, using his real name or title may have been dangerous as Romans were expected to recognize the emperor as god. Luke also goes out of his way to tell of kindnesses and courtesies shown to Paul by Roman officials (13:12, 18:16, 16:35, 19:31, 25:25). There are some who believe that Acts was a prepared defense of Paul when he stood trial in Rome before the emperor.[84]

The actual date Acts was written is argued by scholars to vary from 62 A.D. to 90 A.D. It was definitely written after the book of Luke as a continuum of the Gospel of Luke story. Both Luke and Acts were the length of one scroll (35 feet).[5] Originally they were considered together as Luke's writings, volumes 1 and 2. Acts abruptly ends with the imprisonment of Paul in Rome, awaiting judgment. Thus, there is sufficient evidence to conclude that Luke wrote a volume 3 that is no longer available or that he intended to write another scroll, but it never materialized.[85]

Fifty days after the Feast of First Fruits is the Feast of Weeks, also known as the Feast of Harvest and Pentecost (which means fifty). The first shafts of barley were offered at the Feast of First Fruits and now it was time to bring the firstfruits of the wheat harvest into the Temple storehouse as offerings to God. Pentecost was one of the three Jewish festivals that all male Jews in and around Jerusalem were required to attend. On this particular Pentecost, a violent wind filled the meeting place. Acts 2:46 tells us this was usually the Temple court. All of the believers were filled with the Holy Spirit. They began to speak in other tongues or languages. A crowd gathered, perplexed that such wondrous teaching was being conducted in their native languages, especially since all the Apostles were Galileans. (Have you noticed that the Galilean Jews have remained true disciples throughout the events of Christ's ministry, death, and resurrection? It is the Jerusalem Jews who plot to kill and then crucify.) Barclay comments that there would have been no need to speak in any languages other than Greek and Aramaic. Even the Jews of the Dispersion could fluently speak Greek. He proposes that Luke, a Gentile, mistook the speaking in tongues as speaking in other languages. Luke was not present at this event. We know his frequent companion Paul refers to speaking in tongues in 1 Cor. 14:23 disfavorably as it accomplishes nothing for the work of the Lord if others are not able to understand it.[84] Then as now, some people made fun of them. They accused the disciples of being drunk. I don't know if you have ever been accused of being crazy when you talked of Jesus, but I have. I have been mocked, chided, rebuked, and even verbally attacked. I've made some lasting friendships in the Lord and lost some friends to the world. Jesus didn't say the life of a believer would be easy. In fact, he warns it will be very difficult, but the reward of eternal life in Heaven will be much greater than all our sacrifices on earth

Peter begins to preach. First, he reveals it is only 9 a.m. and these men aren't drunk. Next, he quotes Joel 2:28-32 which is a prophecy about the coming of the Holy Spirit. Third, Peter plainly, unequivocally charges the Jews with killing the Son of God. He explains that this was all done by God's purpose because He had foreknowledge of their treacherous thoughts and deeds. But God freed His Son from death that could not hold Him in the grave. Peter testifies of the risen Savior. Jesus has been exalted to the right hand of God. (Do you remember the significance of God's right hand?) Jesus promised the coming of the Holy Spirit. Peter now offers an invitation to the crowd: "Repent and be baptized." And three thousand were saved. (Excavations near the steps into the Temple courts have uncovered thirty or more immersion pools. These were probably used for baptizing these new converts.[7])

Food for Thought: We see the fellowship of the believers blossom and produce fruit. Have we lost the joy and exuberance of salvation? As we anticipate the holy season approaching, let's reclaim the joy of Jesus' salvation.

November 21
Bible Readings: Acts 3:1-26; 4:1-37; 5:1-42; 6:1-7

The Apostles' work dramatically turns to healing as well as preaching. At 3 p.m., Peter and John were on their way to the Temple for prayer time. Peter healed a crippled beggar at the Beautiful Gate of the Temple. This man was over 40 years old and had been crippled from birth. His joy on being healed is contagious. In Acts 3 we find him jumping, walking, and praising God! The crowd was amazed. This thankful man held on to Peter as he preached in Solomon's Colonnade. Peter's message is essentially the same: God sent His Son; you killed Him; God resurrected His Son; believe, repent, and be saved. The healed beggar was shown as an example of healing that came as a result of faith in the name of Jesus. Those who chose not to believe will be forever cut off from God's people. All the prophets have foretold of the Messiah who would come from the Jews and bring salvation to His people.

The priests and Sadducees are very upset. They stand condemned at every turn by Jesus' disciples! Instead of dispersing and destroying this movement, Jesus' crucifixion had resulted in even greater miracles and a larger following. Besides, the Sadducees didn't believe in resurrection! They had Peter and John arrested and thrown in jail. The next day they were brought before the Sanhedrin. Members of the high priest's family were there: Annas, Caiaphas, John, Alexander, and others. They asked one question: "By what power or what name did you do this?"[1] (Acts 4:7) Peter was filled with the Holy Spirit and a sermon poured forth! Imagine preaching to the murderers of Jesus! Peter point blank tells them his authority is in the name of Jesus Christ of Nazareth whom they crucified, but God resurrected. The Sanhedrin noted these were Jesus' Apostles and the council warned them not to speak in Jesus' name again. "Both Peter and John replied, 'Judge for yourselves whether it is right in God's sight to obey you rather than God. For we cannot help speaking about what we have seen and heard.'"[1] (Acts 4:19-20) The Sanhedrin was afraid to punish Peter and John because all the people were praising God for the miracle.

After Peter and John's release, all the believers met together and praised God. They prayed for the boldness to speak God's word and the opportunities to be used by God to perform miracles in the name of Jesus. Again the meeting place shook and again they were filled with the Holy Spirit. They were all of one accord -- to fulfill the Great Commission and the Great Commandment. They loved others more than themselves. Selflessly they sold their lands or houses and brought the money to those in need.

Acts 5 tells a story of a husband and wife, Ananias and Sapphira, who promised to bring the money from the sell of some property to the church. When they sold it, greed made them lie about the selling price so they could keep part of the money for themselves. Peter catches each one independently in the lie. Each one drops dead. Their sin lay not in how much they gave to the church but rather in lying to the Holy Spirit about how much they would give. To say the least, this put great fear in the rest of the church! It should put great fear in us today. Sin, even among believers, has its consequences.

The church met together in Solomon's Colonnade. By this time, non-members were afraid to meet with them due to the guilt-by-association premise of the Sanhedrin. Peter healed many in the streets and the church's number of converts continued to grow.

Again the religious leaders try to stop the spread of the Gospel. The Apostles are arrested and thrown in jail. During the night, an angel of the Lord sets them free! They were instructed to go preach in the Temple courts. The next day when the Sanhedrin calls for the prisoners, they are gone! The jail is still locked and the guards are still there, but the Apostles were gone. Wouldn't you have enjoyed seeing the Sanhedrin members' faces when the message arrived that the Apostles were preaching in the Temple courts? This time they asked the Apostles nicely to appear before the Sanhedrin! Now they were afraid the crowd would turn on the Sanhedrin and stone them!

The Apostles are rebuked for having disobeyed their previous warning. Additionally, the high priest is upset because the Apostles are teaching the people that the religious leaders are responsible for crucifying Jesus. (Wonder if Pilate is chuckling about now?) The Apostles repeat that they must follow God's Will not man's. Then they seize the opportunity to tell the Sanhedrin members to their faces that they killed Jesus! Now you know the councilors were afraid of the crowd because they didn't kill these guys on the spot (even though they wanted to kill them)! A Pharisee named Gamaliel asked for a closed session to discuss the issue. Gamaliel was loved and respected by all and he gave some wise advice. First, he cites two different men who had developed a following from their preaching. Theudas is unknown to us, but Judas had tried to start a rebellion against taxes to Caesar because he believed all gifts should go to God. Each man was killed and each time his band of followers dispersed. Jesus, too, had many followers. Now He was gone. "Leave these men alone. Let them go! For if their purpose or activity is of human origin, it will fail. But if it is from God, you will not be able to stop these men; you will only find yourselves fighting against God."[1] (Acts 5:38-39) The Sanhedrin decided to have the Apostles flogged and order them again to cease and desist from speaking in the name of Jesus.

The church was not without its problems, though. The Grecian Jews complained against the Hebraic Jews because Grecian widows were not receiving the daily food distribution. The Apostles decided they needed to concentrate on the message of God rather than ministering to physical needs. So they chose seven men who were full of wisdom and the Holy Spirit to be the first deacons: Stephen, Philip, Procorus, Nicanor, Timon, Parmenas, and Nicolas. The Apostles prayed and laid their hands on them: the first deacon commissioning.

The last sentence of today's lesson is both revealing and noteworthy. The disciples were increasing rapidly and included a large number of priests. As we know, Gamaliel was right.

Food for Thought: We need to take the responsibility of choosing deacons seriously. We often think of this as little more than a job to minister to someone's physical needs and pray for him or her. But the first disciples show us that being a deacon is much more. It involves a lifelong commitment to doing God's work. It involves ministering and witnessing in some very dangerous places and to some very dangerous people. To maintain the proper service to God, it requires much personal prayer time. Pray for deacons you know today. Offer to do something nice for them.

November 22
Bible Readings: Acts 6:8-15; 7:1-8:1

The deacon, Stephen, is the first martyr of the disciples. We know that Stephen was full of faith, full of God's grace and power, and full of the Holy Spirit. Also, we know he was a Greek Jew who preached worldwide missions. The Jews, even the Jewish believers, were not ready to let Gentiles into the fold.[84] The Synagogue of the Freedmen was "a group of Jewish slaves who had been freed by Rome and had formed their own synagogue in Jerusalem."[15] (p. 1630) Members of the Freedmen, as well as some Grecian Jews, argued with Stephen's worldwide mission beliefs. In just the same manner as the chief priests and Pharisees plotted against Jesus, these men plotted against Stephen. (Isn't it amazing how rapidly sin is learned by example?) They may not have been able to adequately debate God's word, but they were well equipped for stirring up dissension. Stephen was brought to trial before the Sanhedrin. False witnesses told their lies.

Stephen now has his turn in court. Looking as innocent and pure as an angel, Stephen recounts Jewish history. Stephen's speech before the Sanhedrin is a summary that begins with Abraham's call, follows the rise of Joseph and the enslavement of the Jews in Egypt, leaves Egypt with Moses, enters the Promised Land with Joshua, conquers pagan nations with David, and builds the Temple of Solomon. Like any layman who is dependent on learning scripture and history from oral teaching, Stephen's account is not exactly that of the present Biblical text. For one thing, it occasionally addresses details that are found in documents other than the Bible or in earlier translations of our Bible. When it comes to quotes, Stephen is like me -- he is better at paraphrasing than at direct quotes. You will find that neither the quote from Amos 5 nor the one from Isaiah 66 is exact. His speech has at least 5 other details that are not accurate by today's translation. These are mostly places and timeline problems. But Stephen's underlying theme and testimony are true. God honored His covenant with His people, but they rejected Him. Additionally, God could not be contained in a Temple made by man.[85] Stephen's details may not have been perfect, but his faith was strong and his heart was devoted to God. God took Stephen's efforts and multiplied His kingdom. God doesn't ask us to be perfect, only to be willing.

Stephen's speech ended in courage. He pointedly identifies the religious leaders as the betrayers and murderers of the Righteous One! Now they are furious. How dare he talk to them like that! (Remember, the Sanhedrin did not have the authority to condemn anyone to death. Only the Roman government could do that!) Stephen announces that he sees the glory of God and Jesus is standing at God's right hand. By now the religious leaders are acting like kids. They are yelling to obscure Stephen's words and covering their ears so they can't hear them! This is a true example of very hardened hearts! They dragged him out of the city and stoned him! In the process, they lay their cloaks at the feet of a young Pharisee named Saul. Stephen falls to his knees and asks the Lord for two things: (1) to receive his spirit and (2) to forgive his attackers. Stephen was surely a true disciple -- he followed in the footsteps of Jesus.

Food for Thought: Can you ask God to forgive those who attack you? Beyond a doubt, only those steeped in the faith could honestly and earnestly do so. Time helps heal or obliterate most wounds. But could you ask <u>during</u> the attack? Shouldn't we be able to do this? Jesus did.

November 23
Bible Readings: Acts 8:1-40; 9:1-31

After Stephen's death, many in the church were persecuted. The church, now called the Way, is scattered across Judea and Samaria. However, the Apostles remained in Jerusalem where Saul's persecution against the church grew to a vengeance. Righteous women and men alike were put in prison.

Samaria was a natural choice for refuge. The people were genetically half Jew and half Gentile. The Samaritans made a good bridge for carrying the Gospel to the Gentiles, too.[84] Deacon Philip[92] healed, preached, and drove out evil spirits. This is amazing in itself. Prior to Christ the Samaritans were hated and despised by the Jews. Now the Gospel of Jesus was being taken into the very land were Jesus Himself led the woman at the well to believe. Not only are the Samaritans receiving salvation but also it is being done in such a way as to breach the gulf between them and to heal the wounds. Philip won a magician named Simon to the Lord along with many others. Peter and John came to pray with them and lay their hands on them so they could receive the Holy Spirit. Simon made a terrible mistake. He attempted to purchase this 'laying on of hands' power from Peter. Severely rebuked, Simon asks Peter to pray for him so that the Lord would not bring upon him the judgments Peter announced. Simon's sin was twofold: (1) He wanted power and prestige that comes with the ability to heal, drive out evil spirits, and bring the Holy Spirit. Simon had enjoyed quite a following as a magician and was now trying to marry the old with the new, and (2) Simon had failed to notice that only those that were pure in heart and mind were blessed with this gift. The Apostles had given years of their lives to the teachings of Christ. Their growth in Christ was beyond the level of newer, recent converts -- even those with good hearts. Peter and John returned to Jerusalem preaching at every village along the way.

An angel of the Lord sent Philip south along the desert road toward Gaza. There he found a eunuch who was the treasurer for Candace, Queen of Ethiopia. The eunuch was reading Isaiah 53. He invites Philip to explain it to him. The man is saved. Philip baptizes him. The water of baptism symbolizes (1) the cleaning of the soul from its sin, (2) the new life of a believer, and (3) the connection believers have with Christ who was also baptized.[84] This eunuch had been to Jerusalem to worship. Many Jews had been dispersed as slaves to other lands. In so doing, many in those lands were converted to Judaism. Eunuchs, though, had no hope of ever fully participating in Jewish worship (Deut.23:1). Notice Acts 8:37 is not printed in your Biblical text but rather at the bottom of the page. This is believed to be a baptismal creed that was later inserted into this passage. At the conclusion of the baptism, we are told Philip suddenly disappeared and was taken by the spirit to Azotus, which is called Ashdod in the Hebrew. Philip preached from southern Ashdod to the northern seacoast town of Caesarea. Tradition holds that the eunuch returned to evangelize Ethiopia.[84] Meanwhile Saul is persecuting the church in every way possible. He has now asked the high priest for letters authorizing him to arrest and imprison believers in Damascus. He has obviously heard of the work of Philip and the preaching Peter and John had done on their trip through Samaria. On the road to Damascus, Jesus pays Saul a visit in the form of a bright, dazzling light. Saul fell to the ground. A voice from Heaven said, "Saul, Saul, why do you persecute me?"[1] (Acts 9:4) Jesus tells Saul to go to Damascus and wait on instructions. When Saul opened his eyes, he was blind. All his traveling companions had heard the voice, too. Saul was taken to the house of Judas on Straight Street, which is the equivalent of our Main Street. For three days he prayed. Remember Saul is a learned Pharisee. He knew a lot about God, but he didn't know God. His encounter on the Damascus road changed all that.

A disciple in Damascus named Ananias received a vision from God. Ananias was called to go to Saul and restore his sight. How could God ask him to do such a merciful miracle for such a terrible enemy of the church? This could be a suicide mission! But Ananias didn't argue; He went. God had identified Saul as His Gentile missionary. Saul's sight is restored and he is filled with the Holy Spirit. He was baptized and soon began to preach in the synagogues. All who heard him were amazed: the persecutor of the church was now preaching salvation through Jesus Christ. Some of the traditional Jews plotted to kill Saul. His followers lowered him over the wall in a basket. Saul then returned to Jerusalem to preach the Good News (Gospel). This time it's the Grecian Jews who try to kill him. The disciples accompany him to Caesarea where he sails off to Tarsus, his home. Now Saul must tell his loved ones about Jesus. Saul had watched Stephen lose his life for desiring to spread the Gospel to all lands. Saul's time had come to suffer for the Gospel of Christ. Saul would help fulfill Stephen's dream.

Food for Thought: Born in Tarsus to a family of Roman citizens, Paul was a member of the tribe of Benjamin. His Jewish heritage was very important to Paul so he had assumed the Jewish name of Saul. Paul was brought up in Jerusalem as a student of the highly respected Gamaliel of the Sanhedrin. An avid student, Paul became the 'rising star' among the Pharisees.[5] Saul had great plans for his life as a wealthy, respected, prestigious religious leader! But God had greater plans for Paul as a suffering, hunted, migrant preacher, teacher, and church builder. Paul devoted his life to God and never regretted a day of his new career. Are we devoted to God? Do we heed His plans for us? All are called, but few respond. Every believer has a work to do for God. Don't wait any longer. Pray earnestly about what God has called you to do.

November 24
Bible Readings: Acts 9:32 - 12:25

Peter continues to amaze the people by performing miracles in the name of Jesus Christ. Northwest of Jerusalem in Lydda he heals Aeneas who had been paralyzed for eight years. Later, traveling on to the seacoast town of Joppa, Peter raises a righteous woman from the dead. Dorcas had shown much charity and kindness to the poor. Obviously the clothing she made had been given to the widows of the town. The news of the events spread rapidly throughout Palestine. Many of the Jews joined the church. In the accounts of Peter's ministry, he refers to believers as saints. This early group of believers or saints saw themselves as one church - one body in Christ. Everyone's needs were met. They shared in all their earthly possessions, but they also prayed for each other. Today's many churches and denominations would do well to take some lessons from the first church.

Peter is in an area heavily populated by Gentiles and there naturally must have been many Gentiles converting to the 'Way'. Even Peter begins to show signs of a changing attitude towards the unorthodox. While in Joppa, he stays with a tanner named Simon who lives by the sea. A tanner was a profession deemed unclean by the Jews because of all the dead animals that were handled (Num. 9:11-13). An orthodox Jew would never have stayed in an unclean dwelling. Tanners were not allowed to live in towns but were forced to live separated from the 'clean' population. Simon must have been a believer that offered hospitality to Peter. The only place of privacy in the average home was on the flat roof. The roof was their version of our balcony. As Peter was praying on the roof, he fell into a trance. From Heaven, a large sheet descended with its load suspended by the four corners. Inside were animals of all types. Specifically mentioned are four-footed animals, birds, reptiles, many of which are unclean. Peter is told to kill the animals and eat the meat. He is horrified! (See Lev. 11) "Surely not, Lord! I have never eaten anything impure or unclean."[1] (Acts 10:13) Peter is told not to call anything impure that God has cleansed.

Three times this vision replayed.[84]

Unbeknown to Peter, a Roman centurion who faithfully prayed to God had also received a vision the previous day. Cornelius lived thirty miles north in the town of Caesarea. A centurion of the Italian regiment of the Roman army, Cornelius was a most unusual soldier. We are told that he is kind, compassionate, and benevolent - hardly the characteristics of a Roman officer. An angel visits Cornelius and tells him to send for Peter. Even though peace prevails for the church at this time, Cornelius sends two servants plus a trusted soldier to invite and escort Peter. Notice the group stands at Simon's gate and calls out to inquire if Peter is there. They are obviously aware that Jews do not mingle with Gentiles. The Holy Spirit told Peter to accept their invitation. The next day Peter sets out taking six of the disciples with him. The day after, they arrive at Caesarea to find an anxious Cornelius who had gathered his relatives and close friends to hear God's message. Again we see salvation's message being spoken first to loved ones and thereafter to the world. Cornelius realized the significance of the occasion. First, God had given him specific instructions in a vision. From all appearances, this is the first vision Cornelius has ever experienced. Second, Peter was extremely well known throughout the area. Would such a popular speaker come to speak to a single family? Third, a Jew in a Gentile's home was a violation of religious law. Would Peter really come? But Peter does come and delivers the story of Jesus of Nazareth, the Son of God, who became the sacrificial Lamb to bring eternal life to mankind. Peter preaches that Jesus is God's appointed Judge of the living and of the dead. In other words, the Lamb will judge both those who died prior to Jesus' resurrection and those living at the time of and after His resurrection. The miracle of the resurrection is everyone who believes in Jesus will be forgiven of their sins and have eternal life in Heaven. While Peter is speaking, the Holy Spirit comes upon these Gentiles and they begin speaking in tongues. Peter now sees the worldwide vision Christ has for His church. The Gentiles were baptized and spent the next few days hearing the teaching of Christ. This is an excellent example for today's church. New believers are most vulnerable after their mountaintop salvation experience. Most churches spend very little time and effort maximizing afterglow hunger for the Word. When one is most receptive and eager to learn is the "teachable moment." Today's churches have diminished this moment to little more than a handshake and a pat on the back. During this time the devil tries his hardest to tempt new converts back into their old sinful world. This is when we should have someone assigned to call, write, nurture, and teach these new believers daily. Churches are so caught up in saving the world that they forget to nurture the ones brought to Jesus. We all start out as babes in Christ and have to mature in the Spirit. For most of us, maturation requires a lot of teaching and guidance from other believers.

When Peter climbed the mountains back up to Jerusalem, he had a lot of explaining to do to the Jewish believers for he had broken the religious law regarding Gentiles. In Peter's explanation you will notice he specifies he took six other brothers or circumcised (Jewish) believers with him to Cornelius' house. Why so many? Was he afraid for his safety? Actually, Peter had been very shrewd in anticipating his need for witnesses. Under previous rule of the Ptolemies of Egypt, the Jews would be familiar with Egyptian law requiring seven witnesses to prove one's case in court. Peter plus six brothers made a complete set of seven witnesses to the conversion of the Gentiles.[84] The Jews were satisfied with the testimony.

Acts 11 indicates that many other believers were also taking the Gospel to both the Jews and the Gentiles throughout the Mediterranean Sea area. The church at Jerusalem sent Barnabas to Antioch to evaluate and confirm the expansion of the faith. (There were two Antiochs, one in Syria and one in Pisidia. The Antioch Barnabas visited was the one in Syria.[5]) Antioch was the third largest city in the Roman Empire. It was also the center of worship of Daphne. The temple prostitutes engaged in sexual acts with the worshippers every night in the laurel groves around the site. Additionally, Antioch had chariot races along with the gambling and corruption associated with them. Believers in Antioch would have a lot of temptation into the old way of life. Barnabas was pleased with the movement of the Holy Spirit and decided a strong leader was needed, one who could relate to the learned Greeks but also knew the Scriptures well. Saul was recruited from Tarsus.[84] For a year Barnabas and Saul taught and nurtured the new church. "The disciples were called Christians first at Antioch." (Acts 11:26)

Herod Agrippa I was the son of Aristobulus who was murdered by his own father Herod the Great. Agrippa's primary aim was to keep the Romans happy with his government. This meant keeping the Jews happy. Agrippa's mother was a descendant of the Maccabees. Thus, Agrippa was careful to keep Jewish laws, customs, and holy day observances himself. As a result, he was very politically successful. But the religious leaders of the Jews were becoming disgruntled with the rapidly spreading Christian movement. To appease the powerful leaders, Agrippa began a persecution of the church.[84] James, the brother of John, was the first one killed. Then Peter was arrested. Because it was during the Feast of Unleavened Bread, Agrippa was limited only to imprisonment. The trial was to occur after the festival.

Peter was under extra tight security. He was chained by the wrists to two soldiers with two more standing guard outside the prison cell. Every six hours, the four guards changed shifts. The church was fervently and earnestly praying for Peter. An angel of the Lord appeared in the cell and woke Peter. The chains fell off and Peter followed the angel past the guards to the gate that opened from the prison onto the city streets. Shortly the angel disappeared and Peter instinctively went to Mark's home. We find the persecuted church in prayer there. Peter had only one message for them. They were to tell James, Jesus' brother, and the other brothers about his escape. Even though Jesus' brothers had mocked and teased Him themselves during His Galilean ministry, apparently they had become believers upon His death and resurrection. James appears to be the minister for the first church at Jerusalem. He is obviously in much danger, too.

When Herod sends for Peter, the soldiers discover Peter is gone. Under Roman law, if a prisoner escapes then the guards receive the punishment. Peter's guards are executed.

Agrippa I now leaves Jerusalem to meet the ambassadors from Tyre and Sidon at a point between -- Caesarea. Tyre and Sidon had been quarreling with Agrippa over unknown causes. These towns were dependent on Agrippa for food and much of their commerce. A peaceful solution was necessary for their survival. On the day of their appointed meeting, Herod Agrippa I ascended his throne in his royal robes. According to Josephus, Agrippa's garment was made completely of silver. When he entered the theater, the reflection of the sun's rays off the silver was so brilliant the people were horrified. They were certain he was a god and cried out their adoration.[3] The king basked in the ego trip resulting in an angel of the Lord striking him with a violent illness. The Biblical passage is often interpreted as he died immediately in contrast to Josephus who states it took five days of lingering pain before he died.[3] Acts 12:23 says he was eaten by worms and died which to me indicates a massive parasitic worm infestation that likely resulted in a lingering painful death.

Food for Thought: Do believers have visions today? I think so. It is very hard to sort out what is a vision from God and what is a vision from the imitator, the devil. The devil likes to give you doubts and worries in his visions. God brings peace and comfort. Through continued prayer God will speak to you and you will soon know what to do to verify or carry out your vision. Visions are aligned with God's word. Again we need to be familiar with God's commandments and pray daily to understand God's Voice when it comes.

November 25
Bible Readings: Acts 13:1 - 15:35

Paul and Barnabas are commissioned as the first missionaries sent from the Antioch church. John Mark, Barnabas' relative, accompanies them. Their travels are outlined in the table that follows.

A conference of the Jerusalem believers was held due to a problem that arose concerning circumcision. Some of the group had taken it upon themselves to admonish the Gentiles for not being circumcised. Peter addressed the group reminding them that the Holy Spirit had been given to the Jews and Gentiles alike. Why would the Jewish believers now want to place the burden of the old Jewish laws on the Gentiles? James then offered a motion expressing his belief that only four restrictions should be requested of these Gentile believers: (1) abstaining from food offered to idols, (2) abstaining from sexual immorality, (3) abstaining from eating meat of strangled animals (for the blood was still in the animal), and (4) abstaining from ingesting blood. The motion was approved and Judas, Barnabas, Paul and Silas dispatched the letter to the church at Antioch. (Silas would be Paul's companion on his second missionary journey. He is sometimes called Silvanus.[5]) Circumcision was used as a representation of all Mosaic laws that had been replaced by the resurrection of Jesus.

Place	*Characteristics/Events*
Salamis, Cyprus	Barnabas' home/Famous for copper mines, flax, wine, fruit, honey(5)/They preached in the synagogue.
Paphos, Cyprus	Famous for its worship of Venus the love goddess(84)/Governor Sergius Paulus invited them to speak/Elymas the magician opposed them and Paul blinded him/Governor became believer
Perga, Pamphylia	Mark leaves the group to return home, possibly because Paul has supplanted Barnabas as leader
Antioch, Pisidia	Prominent commercial trade center(5)/Paul's first recorded sermon preached in the synagogue to Jews and Gentiles/Many become believers/Religious leaders persecute missionaries and expel them
Iconium, Lycaonia	Large number of Jews and Gentiles convert to Christianity/Jewish religious leaders plot to kill Paul and Barnabas
Lystra, Lycaonia	Center of Zeus worship/home of Timothy/Healed man born lame/Paul and Barnabas misinterpreted to be gods/Problems arise in trying to prevent people from worshipping the missionaries instead of God/Paul is stoned and left for dead
Derbe, Lycaonia	Many disciples won/home of Gaius (Acts 20:4)
Special Note:	Paul and Barnabas returned by way of Lystra, Iconium, Antioch of Pisidia, Attalia, Seleucia, to Antioch of Syria.

Food for Thought: Paul's first missionary journey encountered many of his old enemies. When we embark on a mission or task for God, we will encounter our old enemies whether they are persons, situations, temptations, laziness, boredom, resentment, etc. God does not call us to do the things the world calls 'fun.' God calls us to do His Will and tells us up front we will be abused for following Him, but the rewards will be great. Only in being in His perfect Will, do we find peace and joy in poverty or nonstop work or hardship. God provides our needs. He also will not call us to do that which He is not willing to support. If God calls, you can count on His provision, even if you don't see how it will come. Pray for God's assurance in your life. Pray for our missionaries today. Ask God to provide their needs.

Verses of the Week: **1 Cor. 3:16-17** "Don't you know that you yourselves are God's temple and that God's Spirit lives in you? If anyone destroys God's temple, God will destroy him; for God's temple is sacred, and you are that temple."

November 26
Bible Readings: Galatians

<u>Paul's Letter to the Churches in Galatia</u>

Circular letters such as these were to be read and circulated among all the churches of the area. This letter has three natural subdivisions, each two chapters long. First, Paul defends his right to be called an apostle. Second, Paul presents a detailed argument that the law cannot save. Salvation is only through faith in Jesus Christ. Third, Paul outlines the consequences of following Christ. The letter ends with a brief summary, admonition, and blessing.[5]

The letter to the Galatians is filled with strong outrage from Paul who sees himself as the parent of this group of young churches. Indeed, Paul had led these people to Christ. Now before they could get their beliefs well established in the Scripture, religious activists called Judaizers were leading them astray. Paul has heard his new converts are suddenly incorporating Jewish legalism into their faith. He writes a letter that is severe in its scolding of the believers. Paul warns them <u>never</u> to believe anything that does not agree with salvation through faith in Jesus Christ -- not even if an angel teaches it! This is so important that Paul says it twice.

Paul now launches into a personal testimony about his own persecution of the church and his subsequent conversion through faith in Jesus Christ. Paul clearly shows his separation from the original Apostles who were stationed in Jerusalem. Why is this important? Paul wanted the disciples to definitely understand that he did not represent the Apostles, the Jerusalem church, or the Pharisees. Paul's only goal in life was to share the gospel of the Lord Jesus Christ. He had attended the Jerusalem Conference in fear that the legalists would prevail and Paul's efforts to preach salvation only through faith in Jesus would be in vain. God knows men's hearts; external appearance makes no difference on Judgment Day. Paul shows his disappointment that so many have embraced the religious rituals, even his co-missionary Barnabas had been swayed! This is a warning to us that we must continuously be alert to false teachings, not to mention human errors in teachings. Question everything; accept nothing that is not in alignment with the gospel of Jesus Christ. Paul writes that he even had to admonish Peter for withdrawing from interacting with the Gentiles when his Jewish friends were present! Our Christian behavior should not change based on who sees us. If we follow the commands of our Lord to love our neighbors as ourselves then we have nothing of which to be ashamed!

Galatians 2:15-5:1 is often referred to as the "Magna Carta of Christian Liberty."[5] Paul provides several arguments for salvation by faith and faith alone. First, he uses logic. If we as Christians sin, does that mean Christ advocates sin? NO! Our sinful lives were crucified with Jesus and our forgiven new lives are acquired through the sacrifice Jesus paid for us. If we could have saved ourselves by keeping the law, then there would have been no reason for Jesus to die! We would have been judged 'guilty' or 'not guilty' based on our observance of the law. But we are all sinners and without the sacrificial blood of the Lamb, we are all condemned. Eternal life in Heaven comes only through faith in Jesus as Lord and Savior -- there are no extra requirements! Second, Paul paraphrases a variety of Old Testament scripture that the learned Jews, i.e., Barnabas, leading the church would understand. Jesus took on the curse of sin so we could be saved. Paul specifically mentions a prophecy from Habakkuk 2:4 that we know today as "The Just live by Faith." Christ redeemed us to be His own, set aside as His bride. He paid the price of our sins so that we could receive the promise of the Holy Spirit. All who believe in Jesus as Lord have freedom from the curse of being a religious lawbreaker, a new life in Christ, indwelling of the Holy Spirit, birth into the family of Abraham, and are heirs to the Kingdom of God! Third, Paul compares the Jews and Gentiles to being sons and adopted sons into the kingdom. The Jews had been chosen by birth while the Gentiles had been chosen by adoption. All believers are the chosen heirs of God; all have the same inheritance; all call God, "Father." (Abba is better translated for us as 'Daddy.') Verses 8-11 of chapter 4 are definitely a verbal lashing of those guilty of being led astray. Stop and read them to fully comprehend the frustration and anger Paul feels. Fourth, Paul reminds them of their loving care for him during an illness that interrupted travel plans and resulted in the gospel being preached in Galatia. There are several suppositions as to what Paul's illness was.

One suggestion is malaria. Paul had just come from the infested coastlands and in 2 Corinthians 12:4 he talks of a continuing problem. Recurrences of malaria could explain this statement. Another possibility is epilepsy. Paul had been severely stoned and left for dead. Quite possibly he was unconscious due to the hits in the head. A very likely illness, though, could be an eyesight problem. Not being able to see would also require a great deal of assistance from others. Paul refers to the Galatians as being willing to give him their own eyes. In Acts 23:1-5, Paul is tried before the Sanhedrin but fails to recognize Ananias the High Priest under whose leadership he had trained as a Pharisee! Paul did not even recognize the raiment of the High Priest! You recall that Paul's conversion on the Damascus Road consisted of being struck blind by the Lord for three days. Satan is the great imitator -- the magician -- the antichrist. Satan tries to distort the people, circumstances, and events of God to testify of Satan's power or God's lack of power! Second Corinthians 12:4 refers to Paul's illness or problem as being from Satan. Eye problems occurring after Paul's conversion to Christianity could easily be interpreted by the world to be a punishment from God or a lack of power to heal rather than an illness from Satan. Another comment that may indicate eye problems is Gal. 6:11. Back to our discussion of Paul's arguments to the Galatians, fifth is an allegory statement that talks about Abraham's two sons, one by Hagar the slave and the other by Sarah the free woman or wife. We are told Hagar represents the orthodox Jews out of Jerusalem who are enslaved to the Mosaic laws. On the other hand, Sarah represents the promise of the children of Light, the mother of all believers regardless of nationality.

Paul makes a wonderful statement in 5:6, "The only thing that counts is faith expressing itself through love." "The fruit of the spirit is love, joy, peace, patience, kindness, goodness, faithfulness, gentleness, and self-control."[1] (Gal. 5:22) Notice that the word fruit is singular, not plural. If you have the Holy Spirit within you, then you <u>have all</u> the characteristics of <u>the fruit</u>. Think of the fruit of the Spirit as a single apple. It has many parts: leaves, stem, peeling, pulp, and seeds. All the parts make up one fruit. The Holy Spirit produces the fruit in us. We let evil influences mold and control some of our characteristics part or all of the time. With prayer and effort we can put the Spirit back in charge. We need to realize that Satan, the imitator, also produces evidence of his presence. "The acts of the sinful nature are obvious: sexual immorality, impurity, and debauchery; idolatry and witchcraft; hatred, discord, jealousy, fits of rage, selfish ambition, dissensions, factions and envy; drunkenness, orgies, and the like."[1] (Gal. 5:19-21) Paul concludes his letter with a word of warning and another of encouragement. "Do not be deceived: God cannot be mocked. A man reaps what he sows. The one who sows to please his sinful nature, from that nature will reap destruction; the one who sows to please the Spirit, from the Spirit will reap eternal life. Let us not become weary in doing good, for at the proper time we will reap a harvest if we do not give up."[1] (Gal. 6:7-9)

Food for Thought: My Daddy and I are a lot alike. We are both getting older and more forgetful. My Lessons have worried Daddy because he couldn't remember it all (neither can I). Paul's letter to Galatia reassures us both that all that is required for salvation is faith in Jesus Christ as Lord and Savior. That faith is expressed in our love for others. Daddy is the kindest, sweetest, gentlest, most loving man I know. My view of the Holy Father is modeled after my Daddy.

November 27
Bible Readings: Acts 15:36 - 18:11

Paul has been called to take the message of salvation to the Gentiles. His missionary companion from the church in Jerusalem is Barnabas. Barnabas has been assigned the leadership of the first missionary journey, but Paul soon took charge. Why? Paul was a well-trained religious leader who was assertive and polished in his presentations. Barnabas was a humble man of faith who was glad to be about God's work regardless of the position he held. I'm sure he recognized Paul's eager, natural talent and the Hand of God upon him. Mark is believed by some Bible students to be Barnabas's nephew. There is no indication that Mark's father is still alive. Barnabas may well have been responsible for his brother's family. For some unknown reason, Mark left the group early during the first journey. He may have been too immature or homesick for such a long journey from home. Perhaps he did not care for Paul's abrupt demands or judgmental comments. Nevertheless, Barnabas wants to take Mark along on the second missionary journey with Paul. When Paul adamantly refuses based on Mark's previous fickle commitment, Paul and Barnabas have a falling out and parting of the ways. We think this type of situation never happened to the great men of God. This example is proof that we all are human and fall short of the perfection of Jesus. Church members have disagreements and times when they 'fall out of fellowship' with each other. Paul misjudged Mark. This young man would become the very first Gospel writer. The teachings of Jesus are preserved for us today because of Mark's dedication and faith to take the message of salvation to the entire world. We all have different talents, abilities, and callings. Regardless of what they are, God will use our obedience to further His kingdom. Barnabas would take Mark on a second missionary journey to Cyprus. Paul chose Silas to go on a second missionary journey with him to Syria and Cilicia. Paul's mission was to strengthen the churches established earlier. We generally think of mission work as 'winning lost souls.' But mission work also includes the strengthening, teaching, and encouraging of the body of Christ -- His church.

Paul and Silas set out to visit churches in Derbe and then on to Lystra, Lycaonia where they add Timothy to their group. Timothy had a Jewish mother, Eunice, and a Greek father. Paul circumcises Timothy before leaving Lystra. Why? After all, Paul has been a very outspoken opponent to circumcising Gentiles as an outward show of abiding by Mosaic Law. Was that not the topic of the Jerusalem Conference? Titus, a Greek, had also attended the conference with Paul and had not been circumcised (Gal. 2:3). What was the difference? Neither the Jews nor the Greeks accepted Timothy. His mother had violated Jewish law to marry a Greek but had reared her son in the Jewish faith. His father had obviously not accepted Judaism and had not had his son circumcised. Many people of today are 'outcasts,' not accepted by any of the religious, racial, or ethnic groups. At times, we all feel like outcasts. Timothy had a need to belong. In the Christian church, that need had been fulfilled. Paul's opposition was to Gentiles being forced to abide by Jewish laws in order to be a member of the church. Timothy was half Jew by race and a practicing Jew by religion and a believer by faith. Paul did not advocate that practicing Jews stray from the rituals of their worship but rather they must not force others to conform in order to worship with Jesus' church. This is a lesson to our own numerous church denominations. We have one Lord and Savior. Our faith in Him is the foundation of all believers' worship, regardless of the religious rituals employed. Paul who becomes Timothy's surrogate father, his father in the faith, circumcised Timothy.

Paul, Silas, and Timothy travel throughout Phrygia and Galatia, which encompasses most of the western half of modern-day Turkey.[4] A passage in Acts 16 states the Holy Spirit prevented Paul from preaching in Asia and Bithynia (Bithnia). (This Asia would be Asia Minor.) These are two areas or provinces in the extreme northwest of Turkey. Instead Paul goes to Troas, which was a seaport town. During the night, Paul receives his Macedonian call to carry the Gospel to the other side of the Aegean Sea -- to Greece. Now we know why the Spirit would not let Paul go to Bithnia. God had a different plan for Paul's journey.

Paul sails from Troas to Samothrace, Neapolis, and then to Philippi. A prominent wealthy businesswoman named Lydia becomes a believer. In that town was a young slave girl who told fortunes through an evil spirit. She made a lot of money for her owner. For days, she follows Paul's group announcing to all that these men serve the Most High God and could tell them how to be saved. After several days, she got on Paul's nerves and he cast out the evil spirit in her. Her owner was furious because his source of income was now gone! The love of money is the root of all evil. This man loved money more than anything else. Paul and Silas were dragged before the judges. (Probably Timothy was considered too young or insignificant to be liable or he wasn't present at this confrontation.) They were stripped, beaten, and imprisoned in the inner cell in stocks. At midnight we find Paul and Silas praying and singing hymns. A violent earthquake throws open the prison doors and the chains come out of the walls. The jailer wakes up during this catastrophic event and assumes the prisoners have escaped. You recall the fate of the guards when Peter escaped? This guard is about to commit suicide when Paul stops him. No one has fled! All prisoners are present. This Greek jailer who worked for the Roman government now begs to hear the plan of salvation! He washed the wounds of Paul and Silas then took them home to be fed. Probably the jailer lived above or adjacent to the jail. Taking the prisoners to his home may have been as simple as taking them up a locked inside passageway. The jailer and his entire family were saved and baptized. All classes of people are represented among the Philippian converts: slaves, middle-class jailers, and wealthy business owners.[84]

The next morning, the judges send word to release Paul and Silas. Paul is feeling feisty and demands the judges come personally to request they leave quietly. After all, Paul and Silas are Roman citizens! It was against the law to scourge a Roman citizen! Why had Paul not spoken up <u>before</u> the flogging? (I certainly don't think I would have been timid about that important detail!) To say the least, the judges are quick to comply with Paul's request. Paul and Silas stop at Lydia's house on the way out of town, presumably to pick up Timothy. Time has come to move on to Thessalonica.

For three weeks they taught in the Jewish synagogue at Thessalonica. Three different types of people became believers: Jews, God-fearing Greeks, and prominent women. So many people were being won to Christ that the Jews were outraged with jealousy! They even start a riot! The Jews charge Paul and Silas are proclaiming another king other than Caesar. These charges sound familiar -- the same as those of Jesus. When the group escapes to Berea 60 miles away, the Jews find out and send a riot group out to get them, but not before many were won to Christ. The disciples send Paul to the coast to escape harm. Apparently the rioters were primarily after the ringleader -- Paul. Silas and Timothy were left behind to nurture the eager new converts who were searching the Scriptures daily. Undoubtedly, they were in hiding and met with the believers secretly.

Paul believes in grabbing a goat by the horns and that is exactly what he does now! He heads to Athens, the capital of modern Greece! In ancient Greece, it was the state capital of Attica and the center of worship to Aphrodite, the love goddess. Athens was the center of Greek culture, philosophy, architecture, politics, and art. Both Socrates and Plato had called it home centuries earlier. Athens was a very busy seaport. Its population was riveted to the quest for beauty and knowledge. Home of the Acropolis and the Parthenon, Athens drew visitors and residents from all over the world and all walks of life. It also drew all sorts of pagan religions. Athens prided itself on its open-mindedness. It embraced all religious philosophies.[5] (Am I talking about Greece or Europe or the United States? These characteristics could describe them all!) The learned philosophers of the Epicurean and Stoic groups engaged Paul in debate! You know Paul, ever since he arrived he had been preaching in the synagogue and marketplace. Now he was formally invited to present his arguments in the Areopagus (Mars' Hill). This was a huge solid rock that had carved seats and steps going up its side.[5] Stoics were rather boring people who didn't believe in emotion or passion.[5] Every task and situation was encountered matter-of-factly as 'no big deal.' Stoics remind me of the hippies of the 1960s -- "Peace, Man. Be cool." Epicureans sought only pleasure and happiness.[5] Their theme was "If it feels good, do it!" I think you can see a mixture of the two philosophies in the hippie movement.

Paul had been very concerned with the huge number of idols in Athens. He starts his sermon to the learned men by recognizing they are very religious, even having an idol entitled "To An Unknown God" just in case they missed one! Then Paul unfolds the story of the One and only God, the Creator of the Universe who cannot be bound by the temples of mankind or bought with money. This God was obviously unknown to the people of Athens! This God had appointed Jesus Christ as Judge of the world. The risen Savior will judge with righteousness and justice on the day appointed. Some of the group accepted Jesus as Savior that day, among them were Dionysius and Damaris. We know nothing else about them other than tradition says Dionysius was martyred.[5]

Paul travels next to Corinth where he meets Aquila and Priscilla. Claudius, the Roman emperor, had expelled the Jews from Rome. Being Jews and tentmakers, Aquila and Paul become fast friends and work together. Paul taught in the synagogue on the Sabbaths. When Silas and Timothy finally arrived, Paul quit tent making and devoted himself to full-time preaching. Before long the Jews opposed him and the group had to leave the synagogue. Paul declares he will only take the message of the Gospel to the Gentiles from this point forward. Titius Justus, a Greek, welcomed Paul to his home. For a year and a half, Paul preached in Corinth. Many Corinthians believed, including Crispus, the synagogue ruler!

Food for Thought: Paul is said to be a very unattractive man by the world's standards. He was horribly scarred by the beatings and probably had poor eyesight. His hands were callused from tent making and his skin tanned like leather. A man of conviction, Paul was an able debater. Monetary wealth was not his desire. But he was rich in faith, energy, and zeal for the Lord's work. The scars of the world became a testimony for God. What scars do you bear for Christ?

November 28
Bible Readings: 1 Thessalonians

First Thessalonians was one of the first New Testament books to be written. The facts as to how Christianity came to Thessalonica are recorded in Acts 17. The church there was made up of a few Jews and a large number of Greeks among whom were some of the chief women of the city. These Greeks had previously been attached to the Jewish synagogue; doubtlessly drawn to the Jewish faith by its lofty morality which stood in striking contrast to the low morality of Greek society. Thessalonica was the capital city of Macedonia and a major seaport.

This Jewish community did not take kindly to the loss of these Greeks to Christianity and created so many problems for Paul that he had to leave the city. Paul's group went on to Berea where a church was established. Once again the Jews caused problems and Paul left for Athens. While there, he gave his famous Mars' Hill sermon (probably Paul's most famous address) but gained very few converts. Silas and Timothy caught up with Paul as he began his work with the Corinthians (around 50 A.D.). They likely brought with them a letter from Thessalonica or at least an oral report about some of the questions the church had.

The fact that Paul appears to be responding to an actual inquiry is suggested by: (1) Paul's use of "now about" (4:9,13; 5:1) which is how he introduces answers to points in a letter the Corinthians sent him (1 Cor. 7:1, 25; 8:1), (2) Other phrases also suggest that Paul was responding to what the church had written: "we also" 2:13 and "you know" (1:5; 2:1, 5-11; 3:3-4) which are taken as meaning "you said," and (3) Paul introduces some topics in such a way as to indicate that he really doesn't want to deal with them but felt obligated because of the Thessalonians' request to mention them (4:9; 5:1).[86]

In looking at the book itself, we see that it falls into two subdivisions. The first three chapters concern Paul and his associates' relationship with the church. The Apostle probably found the necessity of revisiting the past because of the campaign of slander the Jews in Thessalonica had conducted against Paul. Perhaps they claimed that his conduct was dishonorable and his motive was to make a profit out of them. In chapters one and two, Paul appears to be defending himself from these types of accusations.

Chapters four and five are exhortations to Christian living. Three topics largely concern the apostle. First, he stresses the need to live sexually pure lives. (Remember Greece was known for its immorality. Those who idolize men like Socrates and Plato should realize that these philosophers accepted the most degrading passions as normal behavior.) Second, he insists that Christians should lead quiet lives, mind their own business, and support themselves so as to be a good example for others. Third, Paul goes to some length in addressing the Thessalonians' questions regarding the Second Coming of Christ. The most memorable and often quoted passage from Thessalonians concerns the rapture (4:16-17).

Paul's advice is that we should live our lives in the expectation of Christ's coming. We should be prepared to go either through death or in the final trumpet blast at the end of time. As to the actual date of the rapture, no man or heavenly being other than God has that information. Even Jesus said he did not know (Matt. 24:36). Any mere man who claims more should be avoided.

Food for Thought: In the New Testament, hope is synonymous with Jesus Christ. Our hope for eternal life rests in our salvation through the sacrificial blood of the Lamb. Where have you placed your hope for the future?

November 29
Bible Readings: 2 Thessalonians and Acts 18:12- 19:22

The book of 2 Thessalonians was written not long after 1 Thessalonians, likely during the time Paul was preaching in Corinth. Possibly the letter was sent to correct some false impressions that had been created by a letter to the Thessalonian church by Paul's enemies (the Jews). The writer of this other letter apparently claimed to be Paul and had declared some erroneous ideas concerning the Second Coming (See 2:1-2). To assure against future imposters, Paul states how they can tell a true letter from a fake one (3:17).

Many of the topics addressed in 1 Thessalonians are also discussed in 2 Thessalonians. Most students of Thessalonians focus on chapter two and its remarks concerning the Second Coming.

In chapter two, Paul declares that Christ's coming will be preceded by a rebellion. This rebellion should be thought of as a definite act. The rebellion will be against God and His law. Those involved in it will most likely believe either that God does not exist (therefore, His moral law has no value), or that God has no claim to their obedience. We must be aware of individuals and organizations that profess and propagate these principles. This future rebellion will be led by a definite leader, identified here as the man of sin. Paul says the rebellion has not yet taken place because "he who now restrains it will do so until he is out of the way" (2:7). There has been much speculation as to whom the "he" refers in verse 7. Some have suggested that "he" is the civil government of the Roman Empire.[87] Others have claimed that "he" is an angelic being or perhaps the preaching of the gospel.[86] Or "he" could represent governments guided by reason. Consider the fact that most things that are sinful are against the law. That situation was particularly true in the early part of the 20th Century. Men of reason, even those who claim to have no faith, see the inherent value of protecting human lives and property. Even the greediest tycoon can see the value in companies presenting truth in advertising as well as truth in company business reports. The honest fact is that New Testament morals are good for business and for preserving a well-ordered and productive society. At some time in the future men of reason will be convinced that good is bad and bad is good. How this will come about is beyond our comprehension, but we can see examples of it occurring even today. This delusion will lead to a state of anarchy that will allow this man of sin to take control. We will learn more about this in Revelation.

Paul left Corinth and sailed to Asia with Priscilla and Aquila. When they reached Ephesus, Paul left his companions to travel on to Caesarea and back to Antioch. Soon Paul prepares for a third missionary journey to Galatia and Phrygia. While Paul is gone, Apollos comes to Ephesus. A learned man, he only knew of John's baptism. Priscilla and Aquila quickly bring him into the Light of Jesus' word. Apollos sets out to teach in Corinth. On arrival, he began to boldly speak in the synagogue and to debate the Jews in public. Shortly thereafter, Paul arrives in Ephesus and baptizes the new converts who receive the Holy Spirit. Paul taught in the synagogue for 3 months before giving up on the Jews who have bad-mouthed him continually. Paul now teaches in the Greek lecture hall for the next two years. He became so well known that articles of clothing that had touched Paul were believed to hold great healing power. The Jewish chief priest Sceva had 7 sons who tried to also heal and drive out evil spirits using the same words Paul used. One day an evil spirit hollered out "Jesus I know, and I know about Paul, but who are you?"[1] (Acts 19:15) Next, the evil spirit used the man in whom he dwelled to beat up the false prophets. After this, sorcery and magic were abandoned for fear of the evil spirits. Scrolls valued at more than 160 years of work wages (working 6 days/week) were burned. Paul sent Timothy and Erastus to Macedonia while he stayed a while longer in Asia.

Food for Thought: Second Thessalonians 3:10 states, "If a man will not work, he shall not eat."[1] How does this fit with Jesus' teachings on feeding, clothing, and aiding the poor? First, the poor included those who were <u>unable</u> to work or <u>unable</u> to earn enough to provide the survival basics of life. The Bible teaches the poor include those who are disabled or handicapped, widows, and orphans. Today, we have to include people who are abandoned. Unfortunately, that encompasses many elderly, children, and battered women. God never intended for the world to treat His creation in this way. Second, all able-bodied people are expected to work. Idleness is the devil's workshop. Paul tells us not to associate with those who will not work but to continue to love and pray for them.

November 30
Bible Readings: 1 Corinthians 1 - 4

Even though we refer to today's lesson as being 1 Corinthians, this is actually Paul's second letter to the church at Corinth. The first one has been lost. Paul has obviously received a response letter from the Corinth church with a number of theological questions. Meanwhile, Paul has also learned of quarreling among church members that threatens to divide the church! This being an overriding concern, Paul first addresses the issue of preacher charisma.

The Corinthian believers had allowed themselves to take pride in which Apostle baptized them or which one preached the best. Even worse, the Apostles were being held in the same regard as Christ! Paul admonishes them that Christ is not divided or parceled out! There is One and only One Lord! The Apostles were merely messengers of the mighty work of Jesus Christ so that all mankind might have salvation if they believed in Him. As Christians we must be united in one faith - the gift of salvation through Jesus Christ. For those who are lost to evil, the message of John 3:16 seems foolish. But for believers, it's the foundation of eternal life in Christ. The Apostles were weak, but God is strong.

God has revealed his own mind to us through the Holy Spirit. Only the Spirit knows the thoughts of God and He has given us the Spirit! John 14:20 tells us that Christ is in God and that we are in Christ. When we receive the gift of the Holy Spirit, we have the mind of Christ. We must continually pray for the obedience and humbleness of heart to stay true to His Will. Paul rephrases Isa. 64:4 to remind us that we are incapable of even imagining the magnificence of the place that God has prepared for us in Heaven.

Paul calls the new believers infants in Christ. It takes years of trials, study, and prayer to mature in Christ. Praise God <u>all</u> people who know Jesus as Lord and Savior have eternal life with Him - newborn to elders in Christ!

Paul reminds us that the believers' foundation is in faith in Jesus as Lord and Savior. Our elders, teachers, parents, and others along our paths build on that foundation. If what is built is not sure and true - plumb with the word - it will not last. All false teachings will be destroyed with the fire of Jesus' judgment. If a believer, the one who teaches falsely will be saved but will be scorched by the flames of judgment, escaping only with his salvation. The believer who builds with the teachings of Truth will be rewarded. The building will stand the tests of the faith.

Paul also warns that some believers will plant the seeds of faith among the lost and other believers will water those seeds. But ultimately, only God can make the seeds grow. Paul states, "My conscience is clear, but that does not make me innocent. It is the Lord who judges me."(1 Cor. 4:4) If you feel you have nothing to confess before God, then you need to pray to God to reveal your sin to you. None of us is free of sin (Rom 3:23). God knows our hearts!

Food for Thought: Father, I lift myself up to you. Make me a slave unto Your Will. "Take my life and let it be, consecrated Lord to Thee. Take my hands and let them move, at the impulse of Thy love."[44] (Frances R. Havergal, Feb. 4, 1874) Amen and Amen!

December 1
Bible Readings: 1 Corinthians 5 - 11:16

Paul now sets about answering the Corinthians' question regarding daily living. The young church is specifically asking about Jesus' commands in the areas outlined in the table on the next page. Paul makes his statements clear that they are his opinions and not any command from God.

In conclusion, Paul teaches that everything we do, see, eat, wear, hear, or speak should be within the Will of God and sensitive to the weaknesses or concerns of others. We should give up our freedom from man's religious laws in deference to the weaker consciences of those who are immature in their beliefs or are lost. We do not want to be a stumbling block to anyone. So how do we know others are offended? First, many will tell us. Second, we must be sensitive to hints, embarrassment, squirming, or refusal by others to participate. Third, we should pray that God reveals any stumbling blocks we place before others so that we may change.

Food for Thought: Have you ever been on a special diet (diabetic, weight loss, allergies, etc.) and some well-meaning person(s) kept bringing you food? Even though you tried to refuse, they acted as though they were personally offended if you didn't eat it. For the majority of Americans, "Just Say No" is a slogan they can live by provided they see examples of others living by it. As a Christian, you are held to a higher standard. You must find the strength to just say "NO!" to being a stumbling block to others. Be an example. Be aware of the weaknesses and needs of those around you. Be an encourager, not a discourager.

MEMORY TOOL

Paul's Missionary Journeys:

P – **P**aul ran the race and set the pace

A – **A**ntioch of Pisidia – 1st mission trip (~1400 miles)

C – **C**orinth area – 2nd mission trip (~2800 miles)

E – **E**phesus area – 3rd mission trip (~2700 miles)

R – **R**ome – under arrest (~2250 miles)

Issue	Paul's Responses
Sexual Immorality	Should not happen under any circumstances. The body is the temple of the Holy Spirit - the mind of Christ. Christ's temple should not be defiled.
Lawsuits Among Believers	Learned men of the church appointed to that job should settle disagreements among believers. Do not sue other church members before the pagan world and set a bad example.
Wicked will not inherit the Kingdom of God	Those who have been washed in the blood of the Lamb are free of all wickedness and must not return to it, i.e. the sexually immoral, adulterers, homosexuals, drunkards, thieves, greedy, swindlers, and slanderers.
Marriage Duty	Each man and woman must fulfill the duties of marriage to prevent the partner from being sexually tempted outside the marriage relationship.
Unmarried	Single people and widows should stay unmarried unless their sexual passion is beyond their control; then they should marry.
Marriage Separation	Separation and divorce should not happen. If married to an unbelieving spouse, the believer may eventually bring the spouse to know the Lord. In the meantime, the children will receive the training and nurturance of a believing parent. If the unbelieving spouse leaves, then the believer is free of the marriage commitment.
Circumcision	Should not be done just as outward religious ritual that is not part of your regular worship practice.
Virgins	It is good to stay unmarried if you can dedicate your thoughts and desires to God. Be concerned only for the things of God.
Widows	Free to remarry when her husband dies. As long as her husband lives she is bound to him by marriage.
Food Sacrificed to Idols	Food that is purchased in the marketplace or a restaurant should not be considered unclean. But if you know the food was sacrificed to an idol, then you should not eat it for an immature believer can be led astray by his doubts and guilt over eating idol sacrifices.
Self-Discipline	We should control our bodies through strict training so that we are worthy to serve God.
Pagan Worship	Do not participate in demon worship of any kind.
Eating and Drinking	Do not eat or drink anything that might lead a weaker believer astray.
Head Coverings	A man should not have long hair for it is a disgrace. Long hair is the glory of a woman. Paul says, "Judge for yourselves."

December 2
Bible Readings: 1 Cor. 11:17-14:40

Paul spares no words. His attack on the problems at Corinth is direct and wounding.
- Their meetings do more harm than good because of the divisions in the church.
- Instead of reverently participating in the church's Love Feast (fellowship meal) and Lord's Supper, they have made it into a gluttony party for the rich while the poor are left hungry.

Paul clarifies that the Lord's Supper is a memorial service in which its participants are to remember the body that Jesus sacrificed for believers and then drink of the wine to remember the new covenant of grace for all believers as a result of being washed in His blood. The Lord's Supper should remind us of the great love Jesus had for us to take all our sins upon Himself and to pour out His own blood so that believers could inherit the Kingdom of God right along with Jesus. Jesus told us in John 15:12-14, "My command is this: Love each other as I have loved you. Greater love has no one than this: that one lay down his life for his friends. You are my friends if you do what I command."[1] Jesus was so selfless that He wanted us to share equally in His inheritance -- Heaven! The Corinthians were making a mockery of this sacred ordinance. They had made it into a time of selfish gluttony and greed. The loving Son of God was not remembered in their partying. Paul sternly reminds the Corinthians that believers were to examine themselves before they took of the bread and wine. If they are unworthy to partake, they will be guilty of having sinned against the church and against the covenant they have with Jesus. It is a serious mistake indeed to violate the covenant of grace. Grace simply means we will receive that which we do not deserve -- eternal life in Heaven. How? By having our sins washed away in the sacrificial blood of Jesus. As we whine about our illnesses and problems we need to remember the Lord's answer to Paul, "My grace is sufficient for you, for my power is made perfect in weakness."[1] (2 Cor. 12:9) The grace of God is all we need for a powerful walk in the Lord. Empowered by God's grace, we can overcome all obstacles, but when we sin against that covenant of grace, our guilt condemns us and brings judgment on us.

Paul now jumps to answering questions the church has sent in their letter. The first response addresses spiritual gifts. All believers have the same Holy Spirit dwelling within them. This Spirit provides believers with various gifts or talents. These gifts are dispersed in such a way as to provide all with complementary talents in the Lord's work. The talent of each person is needed for the collective work of the church for God's kingdom. According to Jesus' parable in Matt. 25:29, "For everyone who has will be given more, and he will have an abundance. Whoever does not have, even what he has will be taken from him."[1] We can choose to use our talent for God, or lose it forever. There are 9 spiritual gifts listed: (1) Wisdom, (2) Knowledge, (3) Faith, (4) Healing, (5) Miracles, (6) Prophecy, (7) Discerning of spirits, (8) Speaking in tongues, and (9) Interpretation of tongues. Peter taught, "Each one should use whatever gift he has received to serve others, faithfully administering God's grace in its various forms."[1] (1 Peter 4:10) (Gifts of the Spirit are also listed in Eph. 4:11-13 and Romans 12:6-8. No list of spiritual gifts is complete. Because God's Grace is endless, so are His spiritual gifts to us. He provides as we have need when we are obedient to His Will.) Just as we all have the fruit of the Spirit, we all have the gifts of the Spirit. We choose our gifts through our own willingness to use them. Those gifts we use successfully, we nurture and they grow into our primary gifts. Those we use with discomfort and anxiety, we avoid so they wane and become obscure. This is in accordance with God's Will so that all believers will have a place of service in His kingdom.

In 1 Cor. 12:27-31, we have a list of church services to be filled by the believers: apostles, prophets, teachers, miracle workers, healers, ministers, administrators, and speaking in different tongues. Apostles are those who walk with the Lord and carry the gospel to the lost world. Prophets are those who hear God's message and communicate it to the people. Teachers share their knowledge of the Scripture and the mind of Christ with the people. Miracle workers are the prayer warriors of the church. Miracles occur through the prayers of the faithful. Healers are those who are capable of caring for the ill. Ministers care for the needs of the body and soul so that believers are comforted and encouraged. Administrators are talented in organizing, overseeing, and problem solving the projects and functions of the church. Lastly, the ability to speak and interpret foreign languages provides a valuable avenue for the growth of the church throughout the world.

The qualities of love are all encompassing: patient, kind, not envious, not boastful, not proud, not rude, not self-seeking, not easily angered, no record of wrongs, not delighted in evil, truthful, always protects, always trusts, always hopes, always perseveres. "Love never fails."[1] Whew! That is a tall order! How can we love like this? Only through the love of Jesus Christ shining through us can we come close to fulfilling our mission of 'love thy neighbor.' Now we can only see God's master plan as a dim reflection in a mirror, but when we get to Heaven we will fully understand God's plan and the part we played in it. When we are no longer on this earth and memories of us have faded, "these three remain: faith, hope, and love [charity]. But the greatest of these is love."[1] (1 Cor. 13:13)

Paul reminds us that the things we do to nurture and enrich our faith through the Spirit are for personal growth and should not be done to gain recognition from men. But the spiritual gifts of believers should be used to build and grow the Lord's church. Our worship services should be orderly, reverent, and purposeful.

God's design for His church was for men to be heads of the families and leaders of their worship. We see this design from Adam to Abraham to the Temple worship. But the Israelites thwarted God's design when they strayed into pagan worship. Pagan worship almost always involved priestesses or temple prostitutes. Paul's seemingly harsh restrictions on women were an effort to prevent the early church from incorporating paganistic rituals. Women were to be veiled, silent, modest, and obedient listeners. These female believers were seen in direct opposition to the women of the pagan temples who were brash, aggressive, alluring, and nearly naked. As I look at the girls and women in today's churches, I wonder if we aren't rapidly heading back to paganistic worship. Many seem to have no modesty at all. I see less skin and body parts revealed by patients in the hospital than what I see sitting on the pews of God's house. Truly God's house is the place for sinners to come and repent, but a repentant female or male covers nakedness and shame before the Lord. Christians have the added responsibility of being God's ambassadors to a lost and dying world. Public nakedness or near nakedness is always sinful. It is only done as a means of attracting the attention of others. God's house should be a House of Prayer. All eyes and thoughts should be on Him. Parents who allow their children to dress immodestly, especially in God's House, have failed in their spiritual training. The rewards for conforming to the world's standards will be given by the devil.

Food for Thought: My Daddy was in the Third Division of the Marine Corp on Iwo Jima and Guam in WWII. While running to protection between airstrips 1 and 2, one of his friends was gravely wounded. Daddy asked the Sergeant if he could go get him. Just as you would expect from the world, the answer was "If you do, it is at your own risk. We'll not cover you." Daddy and another friend ran out onto the battlefield. Each grabbed their wounded friend under an arm and dragged him back to the embankment. The Japanese shot the wounded man in the head just as they reached the edge of the embankment. Why did he shoot the wounded man rather than the two healthy soldiers? It is because evil always tries to demoralize God's people. God was protecting the two soldiers, but Daddy's friend's future on this earth was not to be. The devil used his only shot to demoralize his enemies as much as possible. To the world, this act of heroism was in vain - a worthless, dangerous risk. But Jesus said no greater love hath any man than to lay down his life for his friends. What did Jesus do?

Verse of the Week: **1 Corinthians 15:33** "Do not be misled: 'Bad company corrupts good character.'"

December 3
Bible Readings: 1 Cor. 15-16, Acts 19:23-20:1

Paul refers to himself as the least of the apostles because he has been a persecutor of the church. But he reminds the Corinthians that the gospel he preached was the death, burial, and resurrection of Jesus Christ. No one can be saved without believing that Jesus Christ died for the sins of all and rose again to reign as Lord. If we don't believe in the resurrection of Christ, then we don't believe in our own eternity. Our futile lives would end in death that comes from the sin Adam brought into the world. Jesus was the first to have a resurrected body - a glorified body. When believers die their spirits go to live with Christ. When Jesus comes the second time (end of time), the bodies of all those who died will rise glorified to be reunited with their spirits. The world as we know it will be gone and the New Jerusalem will descend on the leveled ground of the old Jerusalem. Glorified people will inhabit the New Jerusalem. Now many ask, "What about those believers who are burned to death or blown to pieces or lost to the elements of the sea?" Remember Ezekiel's valley of dry bones (Ezek. 37)? Better yet, remember the creation of man (Gen. 1:27)? God doesn't need a forensic scientist and DNA residue to resurrect the glorified bodies of His believers! What God promises, He will do! He doesn't need our measly preservations. Just as the seed must be devoured before the new plant comes into its glory, so will be our resurrection with Christ. When God tells Jesus it is the end of time and Jesus tells an angel to sound the trumpet, the dead in Christ (believers) shall rise first (their glorified bodies). Then those still alive will be automatically transformed into glorified bodies without ever experiencing death! Death is the consequence of sin in the world. Resurrection is the consequence of believing in Jesus Christ as Lord. It is the victory over sin. Come, Sweet Jesus!

"Be on your guard; stand firm in the faith; be men of courage; be strong. Do everything in love." (1 Cor. 16:13-14)

Paul is writing the Corinthian believers from Ephesus. He has won so many people to the Lord that the silver idol makers are having an economic decline! The silversmiths manage to stir up dissension among the pagan Ephesians toward Paul and his companions, Gaius and Aristarchus. Soon there was a public assembly in the city theater. The city clerk fears a riot is about to ensue, something the Romans did not tolerate. The Jews pushed Alexander to the speaker's stage, but the Artemis worshippers shouted him down with their cheers for Artemis. Artemis is the same pagan god the Romans called Diana. She was the goddess of virginity, the moon, and wild animals.[5] Paul wanted to defend the Christian faith, but his friends begged him to avoid the theater. Gaius and Aristarchus had already been seized and drug into the theater. The city clerk responds to the assembly, appealing to their sense of pride in being the guardians of Artemis' temple. The city clerk brings order to the group by reminding them that the courts were open for lawsuits to be brought by Demetrius and any other craftsman who had a grievance. After the crowd dispersed, Paul decided it was time for him to move on. He had served nearly three years in local ministry. Paul's parting words to the Corinthians can easily be viewed as the same to the Ephesians and to us. "Therefore, my dear brothers, stand firm. Let nothing move you. Always give yourselves fully to the work of the Lord, because you know that your labor in the Lord is not in vain."[1] (1 Cor. 15:58)

Food for Thought: "I heard an old, old story, how a Savior came from glory, How He gave His life on Calvary, to save a wretch like me; I heard about His groaning, of His precious blood's atoning, Then I repented of my sins and won the victory. Oh victory in Jesus, my Savior, forever! He sought me and bought me with His redeeming blood; He loved me ere I knew Him, and all my love is due Him - He plunged me to victory beneath the cleansing flood." (Hymn written by Eugene Monroe Bartlett)

December 4
Bible Readings: 2 Cor. 1-9

Paul travels to Troas and then on to Macedonia where Titus meets him. Titus brings an update on the Corinthian church. Paul writes again to the Corinthians. The time is about 56 A.D. and we know this letter as 2 Corinthians. This book has three major divisions: chapters 1-7, 8-9, 10-13. About 18 months have elapsed between the writing of 1 Corinthians and now 2 Corinthians. [87] Apparently the old enemies of Paul have once again come forward questioning his apostleship. You recall in 1 Corinthians that Paul urged the withdrawal of Christian fellowship with a church member who was living in sin. These instructions possibly prompted Paul's enemies to speculate on his authority to make such demands.

Paul starts by telling of his narrow escape in Ephesus. Then Paul offers special insight for believers experiencing troubles. Through the comfort God gives us, we are able to comfort others experiencing difficulties. We should share our comfort with others as well as sharing their burdens.

Paul assures the Corinthians that he has continued to conduct himself as a devout Christian. He also tells that the reason he had not visited them on a previous return visit from Macedonia was because his visit on the way to Macedonia had been a painful one. Like a spiritual father, Paul had chastised this early church for their falling away from the Scripture. Paul had lived as a good example for his 'babes in Christ' and he was hurt that they had strayed. He was even more hurt that they had been hostile towards his change in plans. In his earlier letter (1 Cor. 16:5), Paul planned a single visit. Then his plans evolved into a double visit, both going to and coming from Macedonia. Ultimately, though, with a heavy heart after his first visit, Paul did not return. As a result, his enemies had murmured against Paul regarding the honor of his word. Paul felt the need to defend his honor to his 'children,' a sad predicament for any parent. His deep love, equaled only by his deep pain, is evident in every sentence. But he doesn't fail to witness again to his loved ones (2 Cor. 1:21-22). [87]

Freshly feeling the pain of his own ostracism from the Corinthians, Paul urges the group to forgive a wayward church member and accept him back into the fellowship of the church. His punishment has been sufficient.

Paul resumes his defense. He has not preached for profit or fleeced the congregation. The believers he has won to Christ stand as his testimony. His confidence to witness has come from Christ. The gospel he has preached condemned the lost but brought life to the saved. The word of God was plainly and honestly presented, but its truth is veiled to those who do not have humbled, receptive hearts. Paul explains that the truths of the laws of Moses (concerning the nature of God) were still veiled to the people of his time. That is even more apparent in the 21st Century. Few even read the Old Testament, much less seek to understand the covenant, laws, and prophecies from God. Jesus Christ came to remove the veil from the hearts and minds of believers. The veil of Moses was lifted so believers could receive and understand God's Word; the veil in the Temple was torn into so that the people could commune directly with God, and the dividing wall of hostility between the Jews and Gentiles was forever abolished (Eph. 2:14-15).

The treasure of the glory of God manifested in the Holy Spirit is entrusted to our earthly bodies made from the dust -- jars or vessels of clay. God gave His most precious gift, Jesus, to us -- unworthy, sinful vessels of mud. Jesus, in turn, sent the Holy Spirit to dwell in all believers. Jesus said, "I am in my Father, and you are in me, and I am in you."[1] (John 14:20) In other words, the holy Trinity of God the Father, Jesus the Son, and the Holy Spirit dwell inside our fragile earthly temples. God chose to live in the mud huts of believers rather than the gold temples of pagans!

Paul proceeds to state his philosophy on the problems of the world. "We are hard pressed on every side, but not crushed; perplexed, but not in despair; persecuted, but not abandoned; struck down, but not destroyed."[1] (2 Cor. 4:8-9) Even as the body wastes away to death, faith sustains the spirit. Our hope (Jesus) is in our future with Him in Heaven. In death or the rapture, the burdens of this life will be gone, replaced by eternal joy and happiness. There will be no more pain or sorrow or hunger or disappointment. To be home in the body is to be away from the Lord. Conversely, to be away from the body is to be home with the Lord!

The Corinthians had never known persecution. Their dangers came from the pagan influences all around them. [87] Therefore, they cannot relate to Paul's experiences of torture. As believers, they do know that they are made into new people through the blood of Christ, symbolized in baptism. Paul urges that the message of reconciliation to God by the washing away of sin through the sacrifice of Christ be preached to all people. Believers are the ambassadors of Christ. The time for salvation is now. Tomorrow may be too late!

As representatives of the Christ, we should not be attached to unbelievers -- in marriage or friendship. Righteousness and wickedness are exact opposites. They have nothing in common. As Paul warned earlier, "Do not be misled: 'Bad company corrupts good character.'"[1] (1 Cor. 15:33) We are the sons and daughters of the living God Almighty, co-heirs to the Kingdom. As royalty, why would we want to wallow in filth with the pigs? Put off all that contaminates and purify your hearts, minds, and bodies, making you holy and consecrated to the Lord.

Paul now tells the Corinthians about his great joy over Titus' message of their repentance. Much like the story of the prodigal son, Paul experiences the joy that only a parent can know when a wayward child returns to the fold. Our Father in Heaven has many wayward children and even more of His created souls that are lost. How complete His joy would be to have them all come to Him!

When Paul received Peter's blessing to take the gospel to the Gentiles, it came with an exhortation to remember the poor (Gal. 2:7-10) 'The poor' specifically referred to the thousands of poor Jewish families in Jerusalem who were believers. Converting from Judaism to Christianity carried a high cost. The Orthodox Jews no longer accepted the Jewish Christians. Those who were Levites could no longer receive a portion of the Temple sacrifices. Widows and orphans simply shared in an already impoverished Christian community. The Jews would not even trade with Christian businesses. The attitude was "If we can't run them out, we'll starve them out!" Paul, too, was very unpopular because he was preaching to Gentiles. Orthodox Jews still maintain their exclusivity in being the chosen of God. During Paul's rift with the Corinthian church, taking a collection for the Jerusalem poor had been pushed aside for a year. Now Paul was calling for the Gentile Christians to show their love for their Jewish brothers by sending money for the poor in Jerusalem. [87]

Paul begins his appeal by recounting the outflow of love shown by the persecuted Macedonian churches (Thessalonica, Berea, Philippi). The believers had given sacrificially, grateful for having received the gospel from the Jews. Paul reminds the Corinthians that as the Son of God, Jesus was very rich, but He became a poor Jew in order to bring salvation to those who believed. Notice that Paul never uses the word 'money' in his solicitation. He refers to the donation as grace, gift, plenty, offering, love, and rich generosity. Money is nothing more than a conveyance method for all these contributions Paul discusses. Food, medicine, clothes could have been sent but would have been much more difficult to transport. The Macedonian Christians had experienced extreme persecution ranging from destruction of property to loss of life. For them to give anything was a great sacrifice, but Paul says they gave generously. Considering the way the Jews had traditionally treated Gentiles, it must have been very humbling to receive this gift out of their grace. Paul then tells of his plan to have several trustworthy Christian men take the Corinthians' offering to Jerusalem and administer its distribution to the poor. Corinth was one of the wealthiest cities in the world at that time. The Macedonians' gift resembled the widow's mite (Mark 12:44). The Corinthians could afford to give generously out of their wealth. Remember this: "Whoever sows sparingly will also reap sparingly, and whoever sows generously will also reap generously. Each man should give what he has decided in his heart to give, not reluctantly or under compulsion, for God loves a cheerful giver. And God is able to make all grace abound to you, so that in all things at all times, having all that you need, you will abound in every good work. . . . Now he who supplies seed to the sower and bread for food will also supply and increase your store of seed and will enlarge the harvest of your righteousness."[1] (2 Cor. 9:6-8,10) "This service that you perform is not only supplying the needs of God's people but is also overflowing in many expressions of thanks to God. . . . Thanks be to God for his indescribable gift!"[1] (2 Cor. 9:12,15)

Food for Thought: Death is but a doorway. Believers leave behind a problem-ridden life to enter a heavenly one. Christian parents spend decades of their lives praying their children will make it through the maze of life to find the treasured doorway at the end. As with every maze, there comes a point where you know you have taken the right path. For Christian parents, the greatest blessing in this life is seeing their children find the path to God.

December 5
Bible Readings: 2 Cor. 10-13, Acts 20:2-3

"The weapons we fight with are not the weapons of the world. On the contrary, they have divine power to demolish strongholds."[1] (2 Cor. 10:4) With this statement, Paul begins his defense as an Apostle. But to what weapons is he referring? First is the name of Jesus (John 14:13). The One who lives in us is greater than the one who lives in the world (1 John 4:4). We are His ambassadors. Therefore, we have the legal authority to attack the devil. The second weapon is the blood of Jesus. In Rev. 12:11 we are told that the blood of the Lamb overcame the devil. The blood of Jesus makes believers victorious over the devil. That victory can extend to every aspect of our lives if we can only humble ourselves and be obedient to God's Will. Third is the testimony Christians have of the power of God in their lives (1 John 4:11-12). Fourth is the total commitment in the believers of Christ (Prov. 16:3). Last, we have the "sword of the spirit" (Eph. 6:17), which is sharp on both sides and has a sharp point. With this we can attack to the left, the right, and in a forward charge![88] The battleground we fight upon is in our prayer life. When we pray, we should invoke the weapons God has given us. The Bible is filled with God's promises. We need only to claim them! The prize the devil seeks is our minds. If he can create doubts or plant evil thoughts, then he has robbed us of the joy of our salvation and has damaged our witness to the lost. He may have lost the war for believers' souls, but he's on a mission for damage control to his own followers. Witnessing Christians are his greatest enemies. Jesus has already defeated him. The battle now is over the number of lost souls he can retain. Paul says we should, "take captive every thought to make it obedient to Christ."[1] (2 Cor. 10:5) He fears that the Corinthians will be led astray. They have been betrothed to Christ. Now they must maintain their purity in heart and purpose. Paul attacks the "super-apostles" who have showed up claiming a different faith than the one that Paul has preached. These super-apostles are false prophets who, through their skill in public speaking, were leading the believers into false ideas about salvation. Paul declares that his speaking ability may be inferior, but his knowledge of the gospel wasn't. Apparently the Corinthians had been supporting these false prophets. Paul now takes the attitude that they have devalued his preaching because it was "free," yet he chose not to burden them. One of the sad things that I have learned teaching Bible study is that people place little value on "free gifts." But if they have to pay for it, they want their full money's worth and more! This is the lesson of Jesus. The world places more value on getting their worthless 'money's worth' than they do on enjoying the eternal benefits of the free gift of salvation.

Paul warns the Corinthians that the devil's attack often comes from within the church membership from false apostles, deceitful leaders, and infidels. Why? Christians view their church body as a respite, a haven where they can let their guards down; as a result they are vulnerable within the church body. Where best for the devil to make a sneak attack? "Satan himself masquerades as an angel of light."[1] (2 Cor. 11:14) Jesus testified, "I saw Satan fall like lightening from heaven."[1] (Luke 10:18) In actuality, Satan is a beast (Rev. 19:19), but he is also the great imitator, the deceiver, and the deluder. He wants to pull the veil over the eyes of your understanding of the Scriptures so he can lead you away from your walk with Christ. Satan is a thief. He steals your joy.

Paul lists the many persecutions he has experienced in the last third of 2 Cor. 11. His boasting is not over earthly acquisitions but is based on Jer. 9:24, the understanding and knowledge of God. Apparently the Corinthians were questioning Paul's apostleship because he had no visions as Peter has recounted or the prophets of old. In chapter 12 Paul, rather timidly, tells that he (a man of Christ) had a vision fourteen years ago. It obviously made a lasting impression on him. He was caught up to the third heaven or paradise. Paradise is also mentioned in Luke 23:43 and Rev. 2:7 and is a name often given to the Garden of Eden. Our discussion of the Luke passage described the ancient usage of the word. Paul had seen the paradise of Jesus. A vision so powerful he had not even tried to put it into words. Besides Paul did not want anything to detract from the gift of salvation from Jesus. His preaching focused on Jesus, not on himself.

In the closing chapters of his letter, Paul tells of his great love for the Corinthians. It is the love of a parent who provides for his children to the point of being spent or used up himself. He fears on his third visit to them that he will find some who have not repented of their earlier sins and others who have backslidden into sin. He challenges them to examine their lives, test their faith. If they can't pass the test, then Jesus is not living in them. Paul sends this letter with Titus and an unknown brother to Corinth. Meanwhile Paul goes to Greece where he stays for three months.

Food for Thought: All of us have strongholds in our life - footholds for the devil. For some it is the need to accumulate money, for some it is the love of food, others seek the spotlight, and the list continues. We need to use the weapons God has given us to demolish the strongholds Satan has gotten in our lives. Anything that vies for Christ as number one in our lives is a stronghold. Paul tells you to examine your life, test yourself. Ask God to reveal to you your strongholds.

December 6
Bible Readings: Rom. 1-3:20

Paul writes a letter to the church at Rome (presumably from Corinth) expressing his long-term desire to visit them. We do not know how long Christianity was established in Rome. We do know from Acts 2:10-11 that Roman Jews and Jewish converts were among those who attended Pentecost when Peter preached and three thousand people came to know Jesus as Savior. The assumption is generally made that at least a few of those saved were Roman Jews and Gentile converts. The Jewish community in Rome dates back to the second century B.C. The Jews were expelled from Rome in 19 A.D. and again in 49 A.D. Documents from the latter period indicate the expulsion was due to rioting over Chrestus - most likely Christianity. Now in 57 A.D., Rome obviously has an established Christian community. In the last chapter, Paul lists a number of the Roman believers by name. (Many of the names are Gentile in origin.) Of course, we recognize that Priscilla and Aquila have returned to Rome. The Rufus mentioned (16:13) may be the son of Simon of Cyrene who carried Jesus' cross. In just three years from the writing of this letter, Paul will be a prisoner in Rome. In Romans 15:31, Paul indicates his concern over going to Jerusalem. Obviously well founded concerns since he is arrested there. In seven years, Rome will be largely destroyed by fire. As a result, the suspicion will be focused on the unpopular Christians. After which, the persecution of Christians escalated.[89]

There have been volumes of books and whole religious denominations founded upon the teachings of Romans. Without doubt, a few lessons over the entire book will be less than even an adequate summary. The Book of Romans begins by quoting Hab. 2:4, "The righteous will live by faith."[1] This is Paul's theme. It is quoted in three books of the New Testament, all attributed to Paul (Galatians, Romans, and Hebrews). The famous Roman Road to salvation is established in chapters 3-8. Many scholars believe at least a portion of Romans should be read daily.

Paul starts by making it clear that man is without excuse for his paganism. God has clearly established His own character, immortality, and nature in the world around us. One only has to look at the fine-tuned, synchronized composition of time, seasons, and life itself to know God. Instead of worshipping the Creator, mankind chose to worship the created. As a result of their rejection, God allowed man to fully experience the extent of his sins and depravation. The old adage of "Give them enough rope and they'll hang themselves" is applicable. Mankind simply ignored the miracles and signs of their Creator. Romans 1:26-27 is a blatant condemnation of homosexuality. There can be no misinterpretation. Homosexuality is perversion. Tolerating and placating homosexual behavior in a Christian community is passive acceptance of sin and evil. As Christians we should admonish the sin and present the plan of salvation to the wayward. Never should we embrace homosexuals' sinful perversion nor give credence to their lifestyles or values. Romans 1:29-31 has a list of wickedness that chills the mind. These are the sins to which man has stooped. But Paul warns that we are not to pass judgment on others if we are committing the same sins. The righteous judgment of Jesus as Lord will bring wrath against those with unrepentant hearts. Those who believe in Jesus as Lord will have Heaven as their reward, but those who reject God's Son will inherit eternal damnation. The sheep will be separated from the goats. As believers, we are not hearers of the word but doers of the word. When God calls, we must obey; otherwise is to sin.

The Jewish religious leaders who were so proud of their Mosaic Laws and thousands of minute detail interpretations were the greatest breakers of the law. They murdered innocent people through their courts and oppressed their own people with their legalistic burden. They rejected God and led God's chosen people astray. The Jews were outwardly circumcised, but God knows the heart. And the hearts of His people were filthy with sin. God had to turn away. He cannot abide sin. Circumcision of the heart is performed by the Holy Spirit. Our commitment to God is evident in our hearts. Regardless of our heritage, the future is the same: believers in Jesus as Lord will go to Heaven and non-believers will go to hell. God has no favorites; you are either a sheep or a goat (Matt. 25:31-46). Only through the cleansing of our hearts by the shed blood of Jesus Christ can we be saved. "For all have sinned and fall short of the glory of God, and are justified truly by his grace through the redemption that came by Christ Jesus."[1] (Rom 3:23) Only through our awareness that we are breaking God's laws do we come to the realization of our need for salvation. Only through the grace of God do we find it.

Food for Thought: As we scurry about making and buying gifts for our loved ones, let's not forget that God gave the greatest gift of all - an eternal gift - His only Son.

December 7
Bible Readings: Rom. 3:21-8:39

God's only Son was given as an atonement sacrifice for our sins. Only once per year was the high priest of the Israelites allowed to enter the Holy of Holies to atone for the sins of the nation by sprinkling blood on the atonement cover or mercy seat of God. Even this he couldn't do without first atoning for his own sins. But Jesus allowed Himself to be sacrificed once for all who would believe in Him. He became the blood on God's mercy seat. Jesus became our High Priest. Believers have continuous access to God because their filthy rags of sin have become the white linen garments of priests. By faith in Jesus as our Lord and Savior we are justified and made righteous. Believers observe God's laws but we do not depend on that observance for salvation. The law does not save us. On the contrary, it condemns us, for we are not capable of keeping God's laws in both thought and deed. (God's laws are in the Torah, but primarily in Deuteronomy and Leviticus.) Only the blood of God's Lamb saves us through faith.

Paul reminds us that Abraham had faith in God's promise to make him a great nation. As a result of his faith in God, Abraham was circumcised as a symbol of the covenant or promise between he and God (Gen. 17:11). If works could save us, we could earn our way to Heaven. But all the good works under the sun cannot bleach away a single dirty spot of sin. By faith, not by works, Abraham became the father of all believers. Abraham believed what he could not understand.

After having just read in 2 Corinthians the long list of persecutions Paul has endured, Paul rejoicing in those ordeals is hard to imagine. In Romans 5:3-5, Paul states that believers "rejoice in our sufferings, because we know that suffering produces perseverance; perseverance, character; and character, hope. And hope does not disappoint us, because God has poured out his love into our hearts by the Holy Spirit, whom he has given us."[1] Christ is our hope. At the perfect time in God's master plan, Jesus died for us while we were still rebellious sinners. Reconciled to God through Jesus His Son, we are forever dead to the power of sin and forever alive in the power of Christ.[90]

God's creation was pure and perfect until Adam and Eve succumbed to temptation and sinned. The earthly man Adam brought death and darkness into the world through his sin. Adam's sin was counted against him because he disobeyed a direct command from God. Without the Holy Spirit to convict the conscience, man did not always recognize sin. Therefore, God gave the law through Moses. Only laws or commands can be transgressed and a law cannot be transgressed until it first exists! Sin, on the other hand, includes both breaking of the law and failure to follow God's requirements. Man plainly had God's commands and laws. All could recognize transgressions of the law. Adam in his sin represented all mankind. All have sinned, but transgressions could only be counted against those who broke God's commands and laws -- Adam and those living after the giving of the law to Moses. When we rebel against God, we sin, whether in thought or deed or word, even if we aren't breaking a specific law.[5] Without the law, there would be no transgressions (law breaking), but sin (evil) would still exist. The law condemns us because of our transgressions. The attitudes of our heart condemn us because of our sin. Abraham's faith was counted as righteousness. Thus, Abraham became the father of all who live by faith. And through the promise given to Abraham, we receive Jesus -- the gift of grace from God. Jesus is the second Adam, the spiritual man, representing all that is life and light. From the earthly Adam, we inherited death and hell, but from the spiritual 'Adam,' we inherit eternal life in Heaven. God's grace is unlimited. No sinner is beyond God's ability to forgive. But forgiveness requires true repentance; true repentance requires humbleness of heart and the desire to turn from sin. Just as surely as Jesus died and was resurrected, believers also will die to the sinful world and be resurrected into the heavenly realm. Jesus paid the price of the lawlessness and sin of those who believe in Him. We belong to Him. Our will must be subordinate to His Will. We must yield to the Master and willingly be His servants -- His slaves. As such, we have a sole purpose in life: to bear fruit for God, or put another way, to grow His kingdom by winning lost souls and ministering to the needs of God's people. We are no longer in bondage to the law. Our penalty was paid. Freed from the law, we live under grace.

Romans 7:7 begins a passage of personal confession and testimony for Paul. Using personal experience as his example, Paul confesses that those things forbidden by the law became enticing to him -- the idea that forbidden fruit is more desirable. In Romans 7:15-19, Paul says, "I don't understand myself at all, for I really want to do what is right, but I can't. . . . I know perfectly well that what I am doing is wrong, ... But I can't help myself, ... It is sin inside me that is stronger than I am that makes me do these evil things. I know I am rotten through and through . . . . No matter which way I turn I can't make myself do right. I want to, but I can't. When I want to do good, I don't; and when I try not to do wrong, I do it anyway."[15] Can you relate to Paul's despair and frustration? He continues talking of the spiritual warfare of the Holy Spirit in our hearts and minds against the carnal desires of our bodies. In Ephesians 6:10-20, Paul detailed the preparation believers must undergo in order to withstand the forces of evil. Make no mistake -- spiritual warfare is fierce and continual. Believers who aren't prepared will be wounded by evil, but their souls are protected in the hand of Jesus (John 10:28). Don't just stand there letting the devil wage war on you -- ATTACK! The only offensive weapon listed by Paul is the Scripture -- God's promises. Study them, learn them, claim them as your own, and invoke them against all evil! Paul assumes believers have already activated their other weapons: your Christian testimony, the name of Jesus, the blood of Jesus, and your commitment to Christ.

Jesus died as the sin offering for believers. When He was resurrected, He sent His Spirit to live within us. If Jesus lives within us, then believers are guaranteed a resurrection. Jesus' dead body wasn't left behind in the tomb. It was transformed into a glorified body. That is our promise, too, for we are also children of God, brothers and sisters of Jesus. Our hope for eternity is in Jesus. If He was a finite entity, we could measure, compare, analyze, explain, and predict the future. But Jesus is infinite. He has no beginning or end. John 1:1 tells us Jesus existed before the world was created and His resurrection assures He lives forever. As our Intercessor with the Father, the Holy Spirit prays for us. Jesus and the Father and the Holy Spirit are One. All problems and joys, encounters and isolations are woven into God's master plan to accomplish good in the lives of believers. If God is for us, who can stand against us? "For I am convinced that neither death nor life, neither angels nor demons, neither the present nor the future, nor any powers, neither height nor depth, nor anything else in all creation, will be able to separate us from the love of God that is in Christ Jesus our Lord"[1] (Rom. 8:38-39)

Food for Thought: Heavenly Savior, make me a slave unto Your Will. Mold me and use me as a tool in Your Right Hand. Grow Your Kingdom with my service. Amen

December 8
Bible Readings: Rom. 9-11

Paul comments that not all who descended from Israel (Jacob) are Israelites (chosen ones). Sarah gave the promise from God to Abraham's son. Abraham had other sons by Hagar and Keturah, but they did not carry the spiritual promise, descendants of the same father but not destined to be Israelites. God's chosen people were not based on birthright but on God's promise. Only descendants of the promise became Israelites. (To me, this explains the hatred between the Arabs and the Jews.) Even Isaac's twin sons did not both carry the promise - only Jacob, and God revealed that to Rebekah before he was even born! We now enter the much-misunderstood doctrines of election and predestination. Simply put, predestination is God's master plan for the universe and election is God's omniscient knowledge of those who have a heart for Him (the elect) and, thus, He calls them to salvation through His grace.[5] God not only calls the elect to accept Jesus as Savior but He also expects them to serve. Each Christian has the freedom to choose to actively serve God or passively absorb the outcomes of the service of others. Those who do not serve will not change God's predestined master plan but they will lose rewards in the eternal kingdom. God's master plan is greater than you or I or any group of people. Not even rejection by the Jews could stop God's plan.

God gave His Son so that mankind could be reconciled to God - redeemed by the blood of the Lamb. Many cannot accept such an enormous free gift. After all, acceptance would make them 'beholding to God.' So instead, this gift becomes a stumbling block. Pride has kept many people from accepting Jesus as Savior. They can't get beyond confessing their own sin. The plan of salvation is summed up in Romans 10:9. To be saved, we must simply Confess our sins, Believe Jesus is the risen Son of God, and Accept Him as Savior and Lord. Belonging to a certain race or tribe or family cannot save you. Only a personal relationship with Jesus Christ will save you. Most of God's original chosen people (Israelites) were not saved, only those who accepted Jesus as the Christ (Messiah). Believers are elected; the elected are called to be believers. We should worship God out of a heart of love rather than obey out of fear. God's gift of salvation cannot be revoked (Rom. 11:29). It is guaranteed to all who believe.

Food for Thought: In Southeast Texas, there is a scrubby, spindly, bush-type tree called Tallow Tree. The residents primarily think of it as a worthless nuisance. On any hot summer day, it would take six or eight Tallow Trees to shade one man. But even this tree has a place in God's master plan. Every fall, Tallow Trees put on a color show that rivals maples and other hardwoods. And not just one color, but a whole palette of colors! Seemingly worthless to man but God sees potential. Faithfully, the Tallow Tree answers its call to serve. Have you answered God's call?

December 9
Bible Readings: Rom. 12-16

Believers are to offer their "bodies as living sacrifices, holy and pleasing to God." (Rom. 12:1) Paul warns us to mold our bodies into the image and mind of Christ - not of the world. Only when spiritually renewed will we be able to understand God's Will for our lives. Do not let yourselves become proud or conceited over your grace from God. Instead, humble yourself before God and serve others. Regardless of what spiritual gift you have been given, use it to glorify God. Hate evil and cling to righteousness. "Be joyful in hope, patient in affliction, faithful in prayer."[1] (Rom. 12:12) Use your gift to minister unto the needs of other Christians. Live peacefully, sharing both the joys and burdens of your neighbors. Do not be conceited and puffed up for the same God who gave you talent, attractiveness, skills, and position can take it all away. Even then we are to rejoice and praise God! God's predestined plan must continue. Our call to service may put us in a position of authority or one of subservience. In either place we are to serve God joyfully and to the best of our ability knowing that He has promised to provide all our needs. In all we do, we must be careful to live as holy, sanctified people who represent a Holy God. We must be righteously different from the world. Let others see Jesus in you.

Duties of Believers	**Reactions of Believers**
1. Love sincerely	1. Bless those who persecute you
2. Hate evil	2. Bless instead of curse
3. Cling to good	3. Rejoice with the joyful
4. Love one another	4. Mourn with those who are sad
5. Honor others above yourself	5. Live peacefully
6. Be zealous in spiritual endeavors	6. Be humble
7. Rejoice in your hope	7. Treat others righteously
8. Be patient in troubles	8. Avoid evil
9. Pray faithfully	9. Submit to government authorities
10. Share with the needy	10. Pay indebtedness
11. Be hospitable	11. Love others
12. Honor and respect those due it	
13. Clothe your heart with the spirit	
14. Judge not others	

The phrase "I am not my brother's keeper" is commonly heard but untrue. As believers, we are responsible for the welfare of others. We are to take the gospel to all, share in our material blessings, minister unto the sick and needy, and sacrifice our own desires to aid those who are weaker. We must not exercise our freedom under grace if by doing so our actions offend others. For example, many groups of people still abide by certain dietary laws. If our own freedom to eat all foods offends their sensitivities or beliefs, then we should abstain from eating the offensive food. Giving respect to those who are lost may allow you the opportunity to bring them to Jesus Christ.

Paul's letter becomes personal. He writes of a planned visit to Spain, at which time he will stop to visit the Romans. He boasts of how the Gentile church has shared their material blessings with the poor Jews in Jerusalem. Paul sees this as only right because the Jews have shared their spiritual blessings from God with the Gentiles. Paul asks for prayer in his travel to Jerusalem. He is very aware of the dangers from the religious leaders.

Food for Thought: It is certainly not too early to start thinking and praying about what God would have you do in the coming new year. Be a well-rounded Christian. Set goals in giving, studying, witnessing, leading, and praying. God blesses and multiplies all efforts in His glorification and worship. Decide that you will be a better church member and disciple next year than you have been this year. There is always room for improvement. We must strive to be like Jesus. Seek to have the heart and mind of Christ.

> Verses of the Week: **Eph. 4:22-24** "You were taught, with regard to your former way of life, to put off your old self, which is being corrupted by its deceitful desires; to be made new in the attitude of your minds; and to put on the new self, created to be like God in true righteousness and holiness."

December 10
Bible Readings: Acts 20:3-21:16

Paul spent the three winter months in Greece in 56-57 A.D. He stayed with Gaius in Corinth. Apparently he planned to take a Jewish pilgrim ship to one of the Jewish ports. These pilgrim ships transported Jews to the festival. Paul's ship was arriving in Syria in time for Passover. Discovering the Jews on board planned to eliminate him (possibly by throwing him overboard at sea), Paul altered his plans, going instead to Macedonia. This is probably when he visited Illyricum in the extreme north of the province. He traveled west on Egnatian Road. (Paul has eight trusted disciples assisting him.) At Philippi, Paul celebrated the Feast of Unleavened Bread (April 14) and then set sail for Troas where his disciples had gone earlier. Paul's enthusiasm to preach God's word is evident in Troas. After sundown, the believers pack into a disciples' upper room, having worked all day. At midnight, church continued, but a young man named Eutychus fell asleep and fell out the window to the courtyard below. Luke, the physician and author of Acts, says the man was dead. Paul revived the young man and then continued to preach until dawn.

Sailing from Troas, the ship stops at several ports before reaching Miletus. Paul sent for the leaders of the Ephesian church and presented his farewell speech. They beg him not to go to Jerusalem, but Paul feels compelled by the Spirit to continue on the journey, knowing persecution awaited him. "However, I consider my life worth nothing to me, if only I may finish the race and complete the task the Lord Jesus has given me - the task of testifying to the gospel of God's grace." (Acts 20:24) Paul warns that they must be on guard for the savage wolves that will come to destroy the flock - even from among their own members. Paul's speech is reminiscent of Jesus' in Matt. 10:16-18.

Paul prays with the Ephesians before continuing on his voyage. After several stops, he finally arrives in Tyre where he spends seven days with the disciples there. From Tyre he sails to Caesarea and stayed with one of the seven named Philip. A few days later Agabus, a prophet, prophesies that Paul will be arrested, bound and handed over to the Gentiles (Roman Government) in Jerusalem. This resembles the words of Jesus as He told of being handed over to the Jews by the Roman government (Mark 10:33). The disciples were grieved and begged Paul not to continue. The parting comment was, "The Lord's Will be done."

Food for Thought: God has richly blessed me, but I must not take too long to feel good about my blessings because the devil is always on reconnaissance, looking for a soul at ease to attack. Give God the glory but be ever wary of the world! Pray that you win the Medal of Honor at the last troops' review.

December 11
Bible Readings: Acts 21:17-23:35

Paul, Luke, and their companions arrive in Jerusalem and give a complete report to James, the pastor, and the elders of the Jerusalem church. Although the leaders rejoiced at Paul's report, they feared for his life. The Gentiles obviously held no ill will toward the Jews. Several of the Gentile churches' representatives were with Paul with their generous donation to the Jewish poor. Unfortunately, many of the Jewish faith had been told that Paul was advocating Jews spurn the laws of Moses. Of course, this wasn't true. Paul had only taught that Gentiles did not have to become Jews to be saved. The Jewish religious leaders were outraged as well as many of the Jewish Christians. (This is good evidence on how easy it is to be led astray.)

We do not know how many leaders are with James. We do know they represented thousands of Jews. Possibly, there were seventy or so leaders making up a Christian version of the Sanhedrin with James in charge. Their recommendation to Paul is that he should participate in the purification rites of four men who had taken temporary Nazirite vows but now needed to be purified due to some defilement[91] (possibly contact with Paul's Gentile travelers). Also, Paul was to pay for their required sacrifices. Paul's generosity in assisting with this Jewish religious rite, as well as his public participation, was to be a witness to all Jews that Paul had not abandoned his ancestral heritage. The Nazirite vow was taken as a show of gratitude to God for some special blessing they had received. The vow lasted thirty days, during which time their hair grew and they did not eat meat or drink wine. Apparently, the vows of these four men included spending the last seven days in the Temple courts. The price Paul had to pay would be steep. The offering consisted of a year-old male lamb, a ram, a basket of unleavened bread, wafers spread with oil, a year-old ewe lamb, and a drink offering.[84] (Num. 6:14-15) Now this was expensive for one person, but Paul was to pay for four men! (Paul seems to be constantly defending himself before some group or the other. I'm glad he thought we were worth it!) The elders confirm their endorsement of the Jerusalem conference and the letter they had dispatched to the Gentiles (Acts 15:19-20). Paul agreed to their recommendation.

The next day, Paul and the four men purified themselves. Paul notified the priest as to when the offering would be made. Before the seven days of purification were up, some Jews from the province of Asia saw Paul and incited a riot, claiming Paul had brought Gentiles into the Court of the Jews. Now this is proof of how far evil men will go for the love of money. Remember Demetrius and the silversmiths in Ephesus? Remember how they persecuted Paul? Paul's enemies from his Ephesus (Asia) ministry are in town for Pentecost. Even on this religious holiday, they are bent on hatred. Quickly, the whole city was engulfed in the protest. Paul was being beaten furiously when the Roman troops arrived. Not being able to discern the charge against Paul, the Roman Commander bound Paul in chains and moved him to the fortress of Antonia in the northwest corner of the Temple complex area. This fortress housed Roman troops specifically for the purpose of maintaining order in the Temple of the passionate and explosive Jews! How could they give their sacrifices one minute and try to kill a fellow worshipper the next? (A centurion commanded one hundred men and since the word is plural, we assume at least two hundred soldiers are present.[91]) Taking a Gentile into the Court of Israel (Jews) was punishable by death under religious laws. At this point in time, the Romans yielded to religious law for this particular offense because of the mass riots that would occur otherwise. But in Paul's case no one could testify to seeing him do that with which he was charged. The mob became so violent Paul had to be carried by the soldiers who formed a wall around him. All the time, the crowd was shouting for Paul's demise. Paul asks (apparently in Greek) the guards to allow him to speak to the crowd. Because of the angry mob and Paul's command of the Greek language, the soldiers assumed that Paul must be the Egyptian false prophet who had led an attack on Jerusalem from the Mount of Olives in 54 A.D.[85] Josephus says the false prophet had thirty thousand men, but Luke records four thousand. Felix, the procurator at the time, had successfully defended the city, killing four hundred and capturing two hundred, but the Egyptian escaped.[85] Paul quickly declared he was a Jew from Tarsus, Cilicia. Paul is allowed to speak to the crowd. He speaks in Aramaic, making it clear he is one of them. His presentation is an autobiography summation from his birth to his salvation experience to his call to carry the message to the Gentiles. Again the Jewish hatred of the Gentiles flared. They wanted Paul dead. No one was going to tell them that God had chosen people other than themselves! (Isn't it strange how grown men can throw such tantrums when they get mad? We are told they shouted, threw off their coats, and threw dirt in the air! It sounds like a bunch of charging bulls!) Paul's offense is still a mystery to the Romans. To get a confession or at least more information, Commander Claudius Lysias orders Paul scourged. Just as the soldiers have him spread-eagle, Paul announces he is a Roman citizen! Now, don't you wonder why he didn't do this in Philippi (Nov. 27 lesson)? My only answer is that in Philippi he was only whipped as punishment. Now he was to be scourged like Jesus had been. Few men survived scourging and the ones that did were crippled for life.[91] A Roman citizen had to be tried and found guilty before he could be bound and scourged. The centurion informed Claudius at once. Claudius is shaken. He had to pay a great price to buy his citizenship. Paul, though, was born a Roman citizen. Paul was released and Claudius demanded the Sanhedrin assemble the next day. It is in this assembly that Paul speaks harshly to the high priest, apparently because he cannot see him. Paul now changes his tactics. He declares his Pharisaical views of the resurrection. Knowing the internal fighting between the Pharisee and Sadducee members of the Sanhedrin, Paul has cunningly opened the wound for them to devour each other! Soon the assembly is in an uproar and Claudius fears Paul will be torn to pieces! Paul is taken into custody for his own protection.

The next day more than forty Jews bind themselves to a vow not to eat or drink until they have killed Paul! Murder and evil are rampant in their hearts. To top it all off, they tell the chief priest and elders of the Temple and are assisted in their plot! And these people claim to know God? Paul's nephew quickly informs Claudius who orders two hundred soldiers, seventy cavalry, and two hundred spearmen to escort Paul at 9 p.m. to Caesarea. Claudius wants this Roman citizen safely in the hands of the governor, Felix. Claudius later orders Paul's accusers to present their case to the governor. By the next day, Paul is in Herod's palace in Caesarea, waiting to present his defense.

Food for Thought: Paul lives several years after this riot. Wonder if the forty would-be murderers lived that long? Wonder if they broke their vow and ate and drank?

December 12
Bible Readings: Acts 24:1-26:32

Five days after Paul arrives in Caesarea, he faces his accusers: Ananias the high priest, some Jewish elders, and their lawyer Tertullus. The prosecution started by flattering the judge and then moved to the charges: troublemaker, desecrator of the Temple, and a leader of the Nazarenes whose teachings often caused riots. Paul defends himself. He had been purified, had come to Jerusalem to bring gifts to the poor and to offer sacrifices in the Temple, and he was minding his own business when falsely accused by some Asian Jews. Paul declares the real reason he is on trial is because he believes in the resurrection of the dead.

Felix ordered Paul kept under guard but with the freedom to have guests. For two years, Felix talked with Paul several times, hoping Paul would try to bribe him. This was the custom of the day. Those who had money and were willing to make the bribe escaped punishment. Felix had no morals or scruples. He had three wives, one of whom was Drusilla. Felix had stooped to enticing Drusilla away from her first husband Azizus, King of Emesen, by promising to make her very happy. Drusilla violated her Jewish laws and left her husband for Felix. Felix was also a murderer. He had many of those who opposed him killed including Jonathan, the high priest. The men Felix used for his 'hit men' soon came to be known as the Sicarii. Because of their hold over Felix (their knowledge of his crimes), they confidently ran amuck throughout Judea plundering, burning, and killing, knowing Felix was in no position to stop them.[3] These assassins finally caused Felix to be toppled and replaced by Festus. Felix left Paul in prison. Festus's charge from the Romans was to stop the unrest and bring civil order back to Judea. One of his first actions was to go to Jerusalem and meet with the high priest to determine what the Jewish unrest was about. Of course, the blame was placed on Paul. About ten days later, Festus is back in Caesarea holding court for Paul. Festus requests Paul go to Jerusalem to stand trial. (This would put Festus in favor with the Jews - a good political move.) Paul knows going back to Jerusalem means instant death, so he plays his trump card. He appeals to Caesar -- the right of all Roman citizens.

A few days later, King Agrippa II and his sister Bernice arrive to visit Festus and Drusilla. Drusilla is Agrippa and Bernice's sister.[3] During the course of that visit, Festus and Agrippa discuss Paul. Agrippa requests to hear the case himself. The next day, Paul again has the opportunity to give his Christian testimony. Festus accuses Paul of being insane. Agrippa II was well known among the Jews as knowledgeable of Jewish law and custom. Agrippa II had maintained Jewish support by participating in the Jewish festivals as his father Agrippa I had done. Paul states that he preaches the words of the prophets and Moses and those words have come true in Jesus the Messiah. Paul puts Agrippa on the spot by asking if he believed the prophets. If Agrippa said "No" he would have the ire of the Jews. If he said "Yes" he would appear to be in agreement with Paul's statements. So Agrippa takes an alternate approach by responding with a question of his own: "Do you think that in such a short time you can persuade me to be a Christian?"[1] (Acts 26:28) Paul expresses his desire that all should become Christians. Agrippa finds no fault with Paul either. Soon he will go to Rome to be reviewed by Caesar.

Food for Thought: Bernice and Drusilla were daughters of Agrippa I. Bernice had three husbands before moving in with Agrippa II. Later she would become mistress to both a father and his son (Vespasian and Titus). These were two of the most despicable women among the Jews. They had total disregard for all Jewish laws. The Jews are in a real mess. Their religious leaders are murderers and their government leaders are immoral and corrupt. As you look at today's world, are we moving in that direction ourselves? Pray for a true return of God.

December 13
Bible Readings: Acts 27:1-28:31

Paul sets sail for Rome, Italy under the guard of Julius, a centurion from the Imperial regiment from Caesarea; they followed the coastline sailing between the island of Cyprus and the coast. Both Luke and Aristarchus are on board sharing in Paul's travels. At Myra, Lycia, Paul and his company have to change ships for the next leg of the journey. They board an Egyptian corn ship and set sail between the islands of the southeastern Aegean Sea. Blown off course they port at Lasea, Crete. It is past the Day of Atonement (Oct. 5, 59 A.D.) and winter is upon them. The worst leg of the journey is yet to come. Now they must cross the open sea. The greatest danger this time of year was the northeastern winter storms that would blow the ships south until they were destroyed on the rocks and beaches of the Syrtis Sands of North Africa. This site had become the dreaded graveyard for many ships that were foolishly caught at sea during a gale.[84] The ship's captain is unhappy with the Fair Havens port as a winter dock. Against Paul's admonishment of the ensuing danger, the centurion agrees for the ship to sail sixty miles to a better port at Phoenix. But what a difference that decision will make! An Egyptian corn ship was a massive structure (140 feet deep) that was the same width and shape at the bow as at the stern, except for a gooseneck curl on the top of the stern. It had no rudder but used two stern paddles to provide some maneuverability. It had one mast with one large square sail. It was a workhorse ship designed to slowly carry large cargos to their destination. In the northeasterly gale the group encounters, the sailors are forced to 'frap' the ship. They do so by running hawsers under the ship's hull and tightening them on both sides of the ship with winches to literally hold the ship together.[84] (This would certainly not give me a sense of security!) They lowered the anchor into the sea to provide additional drag in an effort to avoid being blown towards Africa. The next day they throw the cargo overboard and the day after they throw the tackle overboard. The storm is fierce. The sailors fight for their lives. Paul is visited during the night by an angel who assures Paul he will make it to Rome and all on board the ship will live. Paul assures the others of his message.

Two weeks later, the sailors can tell the water is growing shallow. They fear they are near North Africa and decide to escape on the lifeboat. Paul assures the centurion that if everyone stays with the ship they will be saved. We see the great respect and trust the centurion has in Paul. He orders the lifeboat be cut loose. There are no more earthly rescues available; faith must get them through the storm. Paul commands they eat as much as they can hold to sustain them through the survival events to come. When they finish, the rest of the food is thrown overboard. (Don't you know the fish loved the feast!) When the ship struck a sand bar, some swam and others floated on debris to the island.

There is much we can learn from this story concerning the storms of life. First, Paul had friends he could rely on because Paul knew how to be a friend. Paul was honorable, loyal, and dependable -- three primary characteristics of a real friend. Paul had Luke and Aristarchus as old friends and the centurion as a new friend. Second, Paul used good common sense. His experiences in his travels had taught him that caution and prudence were required to survive the sea this time of year. We know Paul had been shipwrecked three other times prior (2 Cor. 11:25). God expects us to use our experiences to grow in the faith, comfort others, and make wiser decisions. Third, Paul called heavily upon his faith. We know Paul is a praying man and God provides a message. Paul shows his faith by boldly declaring this message to the entire crew. All 276 on board would live. Paul's strong faith gives courage to those with him. Fourth is a return to the basics. When life gets complicated, we need to cut our ties to the frivolous, the weighty, the trappings, and the unnecessary. Get back to the basics of prayer, Bible study, and simple faith in God. The "we must have" and "we must do" of life drags us like an anchor on the open sea of storm. The only thing we must have is belief in Jesus Christ as our Savior. The only thing we must do in life is serve Him. Finally, we must be good stewards of our time, energy, and health. Otherwise, we cannot serve Him to the best of our ability. Many of us must learn to say "No!"; others must learn to say, "Yes!" Serving God requires periods of renewal, as well as periods of sacrifice.[92]

On Malta, the men are welcomed with a warm fire. While gathering brush for the fire, Paul is bitten by a poisonous snake. The islanders think he must truly be a condemned man. When he does not die or even get sick they believe he is a god. Paul, Luke, and Aristarchus are sheltered in the house of Publius, the highest official on the island. After three months of healing the sick, spring comes and it is time to go to Rome. Paul must have wondered how he would be received. Many Roman believers who had walked the Appian Way highway from Rome were present at the forum of Appius (forty-three miles from Rome) to greet Paul! Many more waited at The Three Taverns rest stop (thirty-three miles from Rome).[91] Three years ago Paul had written his letter to the Romans, but his great faith continued to be well known. The storm was over and Paul thanks God for the encouragement he has been sent.

Paul was treated kindly in Rome. He had a private dwelling where he could receive friends and visitors. (You know this must have irked the Jews back in Jerusalem!) A single guard was assigned to Paul per shift. Three days after his arrival, Paul calls a meeting of the Jewish leaders. He defends his honor and his teachings. But the response of the leaders is that no one has reported any charges against Paul to them! Paul must be shocked when the Jews actually ask to hear Paul preach! Can you imagine how he prayed in preparation for that sermon? Finally, the day came and Paul preached a twelve-hour sermon! Some found salvation, but others did not. Paul seems frustrated when he quotes Isa. 6:9-10. The Jews would hear the word but not receive it. Thus, God's salvation was sent to those who would listen - the Gentiles!

Acts reports Paul was in custody for two years, then it abruptly ends. Scholars are reasonably certain Paul was freed for 2-3 years, later sentenced to death in Rome as a leader of the Christians, and finally he was beheaded at the seaport town of Ostria around 63 A.D.[89]

Food for Thought: In many ways, Paul's life parallels Jesus' life. They are both heavily persecuted by the Jews, arrested in Jerusalem, falsely charged with religious offenses, found innocent, but sentenced to die anyway. Like Jesus' parable in Matt. 18, he who requires much forgiveness must show much mercy. Paul had much to be forgiven, but his life was spent showing much mercy. Are you merciful to those who persecute you?

December 14
Bible Readings: Colossians and Philemon

During Paul's stay in Rome, he wrote four letters that have become known as his Prison Epistles. The first is to the church at Colosse where Epaphras has been preaching. Epaphras enjoys a fellowship with Paul in their common effort to preach the gospel of Christ. Epaphras has communicated the success of Christianity in the Colosse area, but he has also related the paganism of the non-believing community. Paul begins his letter to the Colossian saints (believers) with a prayerful, thankful heart for their faith. Paul's prayer for them is that they bear fruit, grow in their endurance and patience, and give thanks in all situations for they have been redeemed and have inherited the kingdom of God. Paul's purpose in writing this letter is to combat the teachings of the Gnostics of the area. The Gnostics believed that knowledge of God led to salvation. Paul reiterates his words to the Corinthians. Christians are characterized by faith, hope, and love (charity), not knowledge.[15]

Paul describes who Christ is based on his Supremacy. Christ is the image of the invisible God. Gen. 9:6 tells us man was made in God's image and Luke tells us Jesus came to earth in the form of man. Proverbs 8:22-23 tells us Divine Wisdom personified has reigned with God from the beginning of time. Jesus is the Son of God (John 3:16). God is in Him and He is in the Father (John 14:20). Psalm 89:27 states He is the firstborn of God and the firstborn of the resurrected. Through the cleansing of sins and the changing of hearts, believers are transformed into the image of Christ (Rom. 8:29). The blood of Jesus was shed for believers (Isa. 53:5-6). We are reconciled to God. Through the blood of the Holy Lamb, we find salvation and peace. The sign of a true believer is one who holds steadfastly to his faith in Jesus and his hope in Jesus as the author and finisher of his salvation. Psalm 39:7 tells us the Lord is the Originator of all hope. Christ is our hope of glory, the mystery that was hidden in the prophecies of old.

The Colossians were located in the midst of the Asian Jews. The intense hatred and persecution Paul received from these Jews made it perilous for those who had converted to Christianity. Paul assures these believers that he is with them in spirit and praying for their faithfulness. He also prays that the treasures of the Wisdom and Knowledge of God will be revealed to them as they acquire the mind and heart of Christ. Paul warns them against false teaching. Jesus came to forever forgive the sins of believers and cancel the penalties of the laws and regulations. Our sin was nailed to His cross. Through Him, we have put off the old sinful self and put on the new purified self. On Judgment Day, Jesus will be our Judge and there will be only one criterion: Is your name in the Lamb's Book of Life? Paul warns against worshipping angels or men who claim spiritual supremacy. The Gnostics believed that knowledge freed the spiritual man to ascend to the heavenly realm leaving the earthly man to determine his own walk in life. The Gnostics also thought God created the universe, but lesser gods created everything else. Some Gnostics tried to separate themselves from all evil while others felt liberated to indulge in all evil.[5] But Paul taught that believers had put off the old sinful nature and put on a new life, which was the image of Christ. The evil emotions of the evil self are replaced by the emotions of the Christian - faith, hope, love, forgiveness, kindness, humility, gentleness, and patience. Lastly, Paul gives the following advice.

- Wives - submit to your husbands
- Husbands - love your wives
- Children - obey your parents
- Fathers - don't abuse your children
- Slaves - obey your masters
- Masters - be just and fair

In closing, Paul asks for their prayers that he preach the gospel boldly; he is sending this letter by Tychicus and Onesimus. Epaphras, Demas, Justus, Mark, Aristarchus, and Luke send their greetings. (Several scholars identify Mark as a nephew, as a cousin of Barnabas in the NIV, and as a relative in *The Living Bible*.) Paul includes a personal note of encouragement to a fellow preacher named Archippus. The Colossian converts are instructed to exchange letters with the Laodiceans (eleven miles away) so that each can benefit from Paul's teachings (without long, repetitious writing for Paul). The letter to the Laodiceans has been lost.

Paul now writes a second letter. This one is to Philemon, the owner of Onesimus, assumed to be a runaway slave. Apparently, Philemon was one of Paul's converts who now served as a church leader. Onesimus, too, was a convert of Paul's but a more recent one. Paul says that Onesimus was previously useless to Philemon (possibly a rebellious slave), but now he would be useful (the meaning of his name). Paul obviously favors Onesimus and expresses the desire for his services. Onesimus, though, was the property of Philemon and must return. Paul asks that Philemon accept Onesimus as a brother in Christ, freeing him from slavery. Additionally, Paul offers to accept the costs of any financial damage Philemon assesses Onesimus. In the same breath, Paul reminds Philemon that he owes his own gift of eternal life to Paul who brought the gospel message to the Gentiles. In other words, Paul had sacrificed for Philemon, now he was asking Philemon to sacrifice for Onesimus. Paul closes with a hopeful note. He asks for a guest room to be prepared in anticipation of Paul's release -- in answer to their prayers. Four fellow Christians are with Paul at the writing of this letter: Mark, Aristarchus, Demas, and Luke.

Both the letter to the Colossians and the letter to Philemon mention Mark favorably. Apparently Paul and Mark are now reconciled since their falling out on Paul's first missionary journey. Reconciliation is an important part of life. Even the Apostle Paul required many years for this process to be completed. Trust is a fragile bridge between two people. It is hard to establish, easily broken, and exceptionally difficult to reestablish. A Christian lifestyle fosters trust.

Food for Thought: This is the perfect time for us to reflect on the Ten Commandments (Ex. 20).

December 15
Bible Readings: Ephesians

Ephesus was a wealthy, booming commercial seaport. It was home to one of the seven wonders of the ancient world, the Temple of Artemis. Ephesus also boasted the largest open-air theater,[93] seating twenty-five thousand people.[5] Paul traveled through Ephesus several times but actually lived there for three years during his third missionary journey.[93]

Written as a letter to circulate among the churches in the area, Paul starts by giving a summary of his faith in God. Verses 3-14 of Chapter 1 may actually be Paul's hymn of praise. Paul lists the blessings God has bestowed on believers: (1) We have been given the Holy Spirit as an extension of Christ to live in us, (2) God's master plan included a holy sacrifice to purify and consecrate believers, (3) God's master plan also included adopting believers as His sons and daughters, (4) We have been given abundant wisdom and understanding of God's love and grace, (5) Our sins have been washed away and we have been redeemed through the blood of Jesus, and (6) Believers are sealed with the Holy Spirit as a guarantee that we belong to God and have eternal inheritance in His Kingdom. The plan of salvation is the "mystery of His Will" that the prophecies of old foretold. The Old Testament showed people the means whereby God would bring salvation to the world (as predicted by the prophets), but it was a mystery. They anxiously awaited the Messiah who was promised, but they failed to understand He would come as a suffering servant. Isn't it wonderful that Christian believers have a binding, infinite contract with God who gave His Son Jesus to pay the price for our sins and then gave us the Holy Spirit as both a deposit and guarantee of our inheritance? Just think of that! God's promise comes with a guarantee![94]

Paul's prayer for the saints (believers) is that (1) the eyes of their hearts be enlightened (their hearts will be receptive to God), (2) they will know the hope He has called them to (they will know Jesus as Savior), (3) they will experience the incomparable power believers have through God, and (4) they will recognize and comprehend the extreme wealth they have received from their Holy Father. Believers have inherited the kingdom of the King! Jesus has been resurrected to be the ruler of all creation, the Shepherd of the Church. Our sins had condemned us to defeat by death and hell, but Jesus was victorious over death. He fought the battle for us, on the cross, defeating Satan. He continues to empower us through the Holy Spirit so that we can keep Satan at bay in our day-to-day lives. Regardless of how much sin baggage we drag to the cross, God's mercy and forgiveness are even greater!

There is no sin God cannot forgive, but there is one He will not forgive - rejection of His salvation. The Bible calls it "blaspheming the Holy Spirit." By God's mercy on us as condemned slaves, we are saved from hell. By God's grace and love, we are made sons and daughters of the Kingdom. We cannot earn salvation. It is God's free gift to all who believe in Jesus Christ as Lord and Savior. Without Christ, all men are equally condemned. With Christ, all men are equally redeemed!

Paul reminds the Gentiles of the great blessing they have received by being included in His covenant or promise originally offered only to the Israelites. Now all men had access to God and could become God's chosen people. The dividing wall between the circumcised and uncircumcised was washed away by the extension of the covenant promise to all people. You will recall that the dividing wall between the Temple courtyards was only 4.5 feet tall, allowing the Gentiles to see the holy sacrifices offered for God's forgiveness of sins and the riches of God's promise. But the wall also carried the hostile warning of death to any Gentile who crossed the barrier.[7] Jesus broke down the wall so that all believers had access to God. Better yet, Jesus Himself presents us to God as His holy property and represents us as an Intercessor in our prayers. In other words, Jesus personally presents our prayers and requests before God our Father. What a Brother! He not only suffered and died for us, but He also pleads for our needs. He is the cornerstone of our salvation, the foundation of our faith. The church (believers) of God is built on Jesus Christ.

Notice the long dash after 3:1. This represents a complete interruption of Paul's original thought process. After expressing in verse 1 that he was in prison for the sake of the Gentiles (for teaching salvation was for Gentiles, too), Paul suddenly realizes that many of the audience hearing his words may not know who he is or by what authority he speaks. So verses 2-13 are given as an impromptu introduction of Paul. He explains that the mystery of the Old Testament prophecies of a Messiah was revealed to him to be Jesus. The salvation that comes through Jesus has also been given to the Gentiles, allowing them to be co-heirs with Christ. It is this one salvation gift that unites all believers as brothers and sisters in Christ, regardless of race, height, weight, intelligence, appearance, gender, age, or ability. Our commitment to Jesus draws us together as a single-minded church on a mission - to take the message of the gospel, the plan of salvation, to the world. As God's children, we can approach Him without fear. (Remember the fear of death Esther faced when she decided to go before the king without a summons to appear?) We can go to the King, our Daddy, our Holy Father anytime we want. We must fear His power if we are rebellious but bask in His love when we are obedient. Paul's prayer is that the saints, through their great love in Christ, fully comprehend the unlimited expanse of God's love for them. Additionally, Paul prays they will be filled to the brim with the peace and love of God. Our earthly barriers and false parameters limit God's power in our lives. God is greater than we are capable of imagining!

Paul issues a charge to the church: be humble, be worthy, be gentle, be patient, be forbearing, be peaceful, and be unified. As believers we have "one Lord, one faith, one baptism; one God and Father of all"[1] (3:6)

Eph. 4:8-9 is very controversial in its interpretation. Paul apparently quotes a version of Psalm 68:18 that more closely follows the Syriac text than the Hebrew. Thus the interpretation is more open to question than the extensive Hebrew written records would allow. The four interpretations I have found are all plausible, depending on one's understanding of Scripture. First, it may represent Christ's descent from Heaven in the form of man (birth) to re-ascend after His resurrection. Second, it may refer to Christ descending into the depths of hell after His death to battle Satan and ascend or be resurrected victorious. Third, this reference may be to the ascension of Christ in the lives of believers by the receipt of spiritual gifts.[87] Fourth, it may simply represent His burial in the earth (descent) and resurrection into Heaven (ascent).[5] To ancient people, there were various layers of existence. For example, there was the underworld, the earthly life, the heavens (where the heavenly bodies were suspended), the universe, and Heaven. Paul states that Jesus "descended to the lower, earthly regions" which would be the region of man. He ascended to a place higher than the heavens or The Heaven, in order to fill the entire universe with His Presence. The psalmist David told us that Jesus would make His enemies His footstool (Psalm 110:1).

Isaiah says Heaven is Jesus' throne and earth is His footstool. (Isa. 66:1) Psalm 68 refers to God coming from earthly Sinai to dwell in His eternal sanctuary. When He ascended to His throne, He led captives in His train. Some believe this refers to legions of angels captured from Satan, most believe it refers to souls won from mankind secured forever in Heaven. The psalmist continues to say that the LORD received gifts from both believers and non-believers to prove His supremacy over all creation. The gifts from men are praise and worship. Rom. 14:11 teaches that every face shall bow and every tongue shall confess that Jesus is Lord, even the tongues of the rebellious. Paul's interpretation sees the gifts as spiritual gifts man receives from God. In fact, he lists many types of them: apostles, prophets, evangelists, pastors, teachers, and service. As one body, the church works in unity toward a common goal: to tell others about salvation through Jesus.

Paul admonishes the saints to put on their new attitude of righteousness: to be truthful; to put aside anger; to be honest; to do useful work; to use only wholesome talk; to eliminate bitterness, fighting, slander, hatred; to be kind and compassionate; to forgive each other. We are to imitate Christ who loved us so much that He voluntarily took our place for the death penalty. Christians are to keep themselves morally pure, free of greed, and pure in heart. Coarse, crude, and obscene language is not acceptable. God's anger is poured on those who are disobedient. Believers are children of Light (Jesus) therefore we should act accordingly. We are to be filled with the Holy Spirit until songs of praise pour from our hearts.

Again Paul provides a list of rules to live by:

- Christians submit to each other.
- Wives submit to your husbands.
- Husbands love your wives as much as you love yourself and live as one flesh serving Christ together.
- Children obey your parents.
- Fathers do not anger your children to the point their anger cannot find peace.
- Slaves (employees) obey your masters.
- Masters (employers) be good to your slaves.

Chapter 6 of Ephesians is by far the best known. Paul instructs believers to put on the whole armor of God so they can stand firm in their faith and ward off evil. As a soldier in God's army, we should wear:

- The Belt of Truth (Jesus) that girds around us holding all our weapons for ready use.
- The Breastplate of Righteousness, which protects our hearts from attacks by evil.
- The Shoes (cleats) that allow us to dig into the foundation of our faith and stand firm.
- The Shield of Faith which is God's Holy Word that is capable of extinguishing the enemy attacks through deliverance of its thirty thousand promises to help us and protect us
- The Sword of the Spirit is the Word of God that cuts through all evil and pierces the hearts of the enemy

Paul concludes with a warning to be alert to evil and lift up God's army in prayer. Tychicus will be the bearer of Paul's letter.

Food for Thought: Would you go to work without all your clothes? Without the tools for your job? Would you work in dangerous situations without any safety devices? Why then do we march out to face the battle of our lives (against evil) without being prepared? We can only fight evil effectively when we know God's word, we have salvation secured, we are filled with the Holy Spirit, and our weapons are ready to be used. Our battleground is in the spiritual world. Prayer is our chariot. It has the power and speed to plow through evil's pulls on our hearts and minds and reach the throne of God. Our "Abba, Father" is always waiting to talk with us. Is your chariot rusty? Are your weapons rusty? Is your armor tattered and incomplete?

December 16
Bible Readings: Philippians

When we become believers, God begins molding us to have the mind, attitude, and heart of Jesus. His work will continue in His children until Jesus comes again. This truth applies to all believers, but Paul is particularly writing to the church at Philippi, located in modern Greece. Previously in Philippi, Paul converted Lydia, a businesswoman dealing in purple cloth. Also in Philippi, Paul and Silas were arrested and flogged for casting out evil spirits. The church at Philippi was young and small. It was vulnerable to attack and persecution. Paul's letter goes with prayer for their increase in righteousness, love, and understanding of God's Word.

Paul writes that his bondage has set an example for others who otherwise would have been timid in their proclamation of Jesus Christ as Savior and Lord. Paul surely surprised his readers by saying one's motives for preaching God's word did not have to be pure! God can still use their efforts to grow His Kingdom.

Paul's selfless sacrifice is summed up in his statement, "For to me, to live is Christ and to die is gain."[1] (Phil. 1:21) He longs for Heaven but has resigned himself to remaining on earth to carry out the ministry of Christ. The Philippians are part of Paul's family. He instructs them to conduct themselves worthy to be counted among Christ's followers regardless of what happens to him. As any parent would, Paul requests they stay unified in purpose and spirit, humbly serving one another. When reading Philippians, you have the sense that Paul knows his time on earth is growing short. His writing has taken on a lot of "if" and "when" clauses as if he is preparing his children for living without him. He admonishes them not to be selfish but rather take on the loving, suffering, servant attitude of Christ. Verse 6 of chapter 2 begins a glorious hymn of praise to Jesus who is exalted to the highest position in Heaven to be Judge over all creation. "At the name of Jesus every knee should bow, in heaven and on earth and under the earth, and every tongue confess that Jesus Christ is Lord, to the glory of God the Father."[1] (Phil. 2:6-11) Make no mistake; everyone will bow before Christ - even pagans. On Judgment Day, ALL will submit to Him. How much better our lives will be if we humble ourselves before Him now and do His Will rather than be forced to our knees in rebellion!

These young, immature believers are encouraged to "continue to work out your salvation with fear and trembling."[1] (Phil. 2:12) God will cause His work to be achieved through the efforts of His church. Our challenge is to keep our eyes and hearts on Jesus. Do not be distracted. Keep on course. Do everything in humbleness and unity without bickering and complaining.

Timothy has become more than a convert to Paul. Timothy has become Paul's son in Christ. The younger man has worked alongside the apostle. He has served faithfully and remained loyal to Paul. Phil. 2:24 finally gives an indication that Paul's spirit is more hopeful about his future. Letters were generally written over days. Thus, one's outlook could change several times. Paul generally dictated his letters, probably because of poor eyesight. Most likely Timothy served as secretary for this letter.

Epaphroditus has brought donations to Paul from the Philippians. Without an outside income, Paul could not have provided food, clothing, and shelter for himself for years except for the generosity of believers. Now Paul is sending Epaphroditus back to Philippi. We learn he has been gravely ill, but upon recuperation, he was homesick. Apparently, his mission to serve Paul's needs was not completed. But Paul is compassionate and touched by Epaphroditus' willingness to risk death in order to minister in the name of Jesus. Paul tells the congregation to welcome back Epaphroditus and honor him for his sacrifice to the work.

Warnings are stated in chapter 3 against the Jews. Paul calls them the most despicable of names: dogs, evildoers, and mutilators. Those circumcised of the heart by the Holy Spirit are the true chosen children of God --

not those who have only physical circumcision. Paul lists his own pedigree as an example. He was as Jewish as they come, but only the Holy Spirit had truly changed his heart and transformed his life. The Holy Spirit only comes to live in those who believe in Jesus as Savior. All earthly treasure and inheritance is worthless without the salvation of one's soul. "Forgetting what is behind and straining toward what is ahead, I push on toward the goal to win the prize for which God has called me heavenward in Christ Jesus."[1] (Phil. 3:13-14) Those who are enemies of Jesus, and the meaning of his sacrifice for our sins, will be destroyed. When your focus is on earthly pleasures and treasures then your eternity will be in torment.

Chapter 4 begins a personal appeal to Euodia and Syntyche, two women of the church who are bickering. They should rejoice in the Lord always. Paul gives some advice we would all do well to heed. "Do not be anxious about anything, but in everything, by prayer and petition, with thanksgiving, present your requests to God, and the peace of God which transcends all understanding will guard your hearts and your minds in Christ Jesus."[1] (Phil. 4:6-7) When we earnestly turn our worries and our fears over to God in prayer, we can have peace in our problems. We must also discipline our minds so that we can develop the mind of Christ. Paul tells us to think about "whatever is true, whatever is noble, whatever is right, whatever is pure, whatever is lovely, whatever is admirable, anything that is excellent or praiseworthy."[1] (Phil. 4:8) Training our minds is a difficult on-going task. What we allow to enter our minds changes our hearts and our lives. We make choices daily between good and evil. The goal of the movie/TV/computer industry is to control our minds. Once they control our minds, then they control us. Take Paul's advice. Refuse to allow unwholesome thoughts to enter your mind. Stop watching or hearing anything that would bring shame to Jesus and debase the body of Christ. The church is composed of many bodies but a single, unified mind - the mind of Christ. If any member does not think on the things of God, then the unified mind of Christ has a weakness where the devil can attack the church.

Paul looks back on his life and can say without reservation that he was content in all circumstances whether hungry or well fed, poor or rich because he knew the secret to a happy life: he could do anything through Christ who gave him strength. This same Jesus wants to give us the strength to be happy in all situations. Complete faith and trust in Him is the answer. Claiming His promises in prayer is the source of our strength.

The rest of chapter 4 is dedicated to Paul's expressed appreciation to the Philippians for their faithful support of his needs. The church at Philippi has the distinction of having supported Paul throughout his Macedonian ministry - Paul compares their gifts to a fragrant sacrifice, acceptable and pleasing to God. The altar of incense offers the prayers of God's people as a sweet smelling fragrance. Our gifts from the heart to God's Work are always a sweet aroma to God - His people cheerfully doing His work. God will meet all of our needs with rewards and gifts and blessings that are in accordance with the splendor of His Kingdom.

Food for Thought: I pray that I will have the mind of Christ. Fortify my resolve to discipline my mind. Seal my mind with the power of the Holy Spirit. Strengthen me with the power of Jesus to resist temptation of the mind as well as the body. And make me joyful always in all situations. Amen.

Verse of the Week: **James 4:7** "Submit yourselves, then, to God. Resist the devil, and he will flee from you."

December 17
Bible Readings: 1 Timothy

The Pastoral Epistles include 1 Timothy, 2 Timothy, and Titus. Even though the books are attributed to Paul, many of the statements are much harsher than what Paul has traditionally espoused. For example, good deeds are stressed as important for church leaders rather then Paul's usually strong stance of faith by justification through Christ and nothing else. Many of those who believe salvation requires faith plus works derive their ideas from the Pastoral Epistles. Additionally the historical facts of Paul leaving Timothy in Ephesus and Titus in Crete are not mentioned in Acts where Paul's travels are detailed. Even the wording is not consistent with Paul's other letters.[5] Some Bible students have conjectured that a secretary to Paul wrote these letters using the general thoughts and ideas of Paul's preaching. Others believe these letters are different primarily because they offer practical advice from an older preacher to a young pastor. The advice of identifying those of good reputations and good deeds for church leadership positions may simply be a method to aid the inexperienced young pastor in choosing leaders wisely.

Paul had taken Timothy under his tutelage, molding and maturing his faith. Now Paul was encouraging a young minister who was facing the heretical teachings of the Gnostics and the persecutions of the pagans. In addition, the Jews still held fast to teaching that their Jewish lineage guaranteed their chosen status with God. The first letter to Timothy notes that Paul is in Macedonia, leaving Timothy to minister to the Ephesians. The church is instructed to take a stand against false teachers of the law. Laws are made for the ungodly for the righteous do what is good and right. Two men are named as being given over to Satan because of their blasphemy: Hymenaeus and Alexander. Hymenaeus claimed the resurrection of the dead was past. In other words, the resurrection of the glorified bodies at the Second Coming wouldn't happen.[5] There is some evidence to connect this Alexander with the one in 2 Tim. 4:14 but not enough to connect with Acts 19:33. Both men were part of the church at Ephesus. They were now put out of the fellowship of the church. This was done to protect the young, immature church and to remove the speaking theater currently abused by these two men. Their false teachings had disrupted the church and brought doubts and questions.

Paul urges the church to pray for rulers and officials that they may lead wisely and peacefully. The women of the church should dress modestly and be known for their good Christian deeds. Paul's admonishment that women should be quiet and submissive is best interpreted as humble. Jesus came to free all people from the bondage of the religious laws, including women. Paul warns that their new freedom of religion should not be used to overpower, grandstand, or undermine the leadership of the men. You recall that the women had been relegated to a segregated courtyard in the Jewish Temple. Generally, when freedom suddenly comes to those in bondage, there is an overzealous impulse to push that freedom to the limit. Paul warns women not to abuse their newfound freedom.[95] Paul now states that it was Eve who was deceived not Adam. This statement is rather strangely worded but simply means that Eve was tricked into being led astray, but Adam sinned with full knowledge and awareness of his wrong. Women will suffer the consequences of Eve's sin through the pain of bearing God's creation. Their future direction was to teach God's word to the next generation. Through their witnessing efforts with children, women would find favor with God.

Paul outlines the qualifications for church leaders:

Church Official	**Deacon**
Above reproach	Respected
Only one wife	Sincere
Even-tempered	Honest
Self-controlled	Clings to the faith
Respectable	Church must evaluate
Teacher	No drunkenness
No drunkenness	
Not Violent	**Deacon's Wife**
Not Quarrelsome	Not gossiper
Not greedy	Even-tempered
Good manager	Trustworthy
Respected by children	Respected
Mature Believer	
Good Reputation	
Hospitable	

First Timothy 3:16 is a hymn that is a succinct summary of Jesus' earthly role in God's master plan. The Greek version sounds more poetic than the English translation.[95] Paul warns Timothy that some will leave the faith to follow deceiving spirits. This has already been revealed through Judas Iscariot leaving the Apostles and Jesus to pursue the deceiving spirits of the Jewish leaders. So, can believers really fall from grace? No! The Bible teaches that many followers will know about Christ and will believe there is a God. The difference between them and true believers is a personal relationship with God. True believers feel God in their hearts, are shamed by their sins, seek to have the mind of Christ, and know God as "Abba, Father."

The Christian nurturer in Paul shows itself in the instructions he gives Timothy. He should live a godly life and put his hope in the one, true, living God. Also, he must be confident in his faith, set an example for others, treat church members as he would family members, and train himself in God's word. Timothy had received the blessings of the church leaders when he was ordained to preach. Paul reminds him not to neglect his Christian growth and ministerial duties.

In Mosaic Law, orphans and widows were always to be provided for and protected (Ex. 22:22; Deut. 10:18). God, Himself, was their guardian. As ambassadors of Christ, the church represented God in this function, but even by Paul's day the generosity of the church was being abused. Paul outlines the characteristics of widows who should be and should not be sustained by the church.

1) Children and grandchildren should care for any widowed family members.
2) The widow must be over sixty years old or basically unable to work enough to sustain her life.
3) The widow must have been faithful to her husband and known for her good deeds.
4) Younger widows should remarry to avoid idleness and gossiping.

Paul warns Timothy about the false teachers whose doctrine is faulty, whose lives are examples of ungodliness, and whose goal is financial increase. "For we brought nothing into the world, and we take nothing out of it. . . . people who want to get rich fall into temptation. . . . for the love of money is a root of all kinds of evil."[1] (1 Tim. 6:7-10) Flee from all ungodliness and maintain the faith. In verses 15-16, Paul launches into a short prayer or hymn of praise.

Food for Thought: Dear God, bring peace to our brothers and sisters in Christ. Give us unity of Spirit and fill our hearts with love for each other. Be our constant companion and seal us in your care. Amen.

December 18
Bible Readings: Titus

Titus was obviously a special son in the faith to Paul, also. Titus and Timothy are the only two men honored by a theological letter written solely to them. (Philemon was simply a letter of request.) Unlike Timothy who was on the mainland, Titus was on the island of Crete. A circular letter would not have reached Titus for many months due to the dangerous winter weather. So Paul writes Titus a letter similar to Timothy's, addressing most of the same pastor-congregation issues. Titus had been with Paul at the Jerusalem Conference. He had been the example of an uncircumcised Gentile who had received the Holy Spirit. Titus had already had a revival with the troubled church at Corinth after divisions had formed over what apostle they followed. With Paul's written admonishment and teaching, Titus had managed to reorganize the church and set it on the right path again. Now Titus was at another church in trouble. This time the problem lay with false teaching and immortality. You might say Titus assesses the situation, institutes damage control, reorganizes, and reunites churches.

Paul starts by telling Titus to choose church leaders with the following qualifications: blameless, only one wife, Christian children, not wild, not disobedient, not overbearing, even-tempered, no drunkenness, not violent, honest, hospitable, lover of goodness, self-controlled, upright, holy, disciplined, and sound doctrine. If you are like me, you wonder if anyone could measure up to all these qualities! We all have weaknesses, faults, and sins that violate several of these ideals, depending on the season of our lives. The point Paul is really making is that those who are working daily to follow in the footsteps of Jesus, are sound in their beliefs, and are striving to do God's Will in their lives will be producing the fruit of the Holy Spirit. "By their fruit you will recognize them."[1] (Matt. 7:16) Jesus said, "I chose you to go and bear fruit - fruit that will last."[1] (John 15:16)

Paul now reaches the main point of his letter: warning against false teachers -- deceivers -- and rebellious filibusters. The instruction is blunt: they must be silenced. We are told these men are preaching for profit and apparently teaching what the earthly man desires to hear rather than the word of God. Paul quotes a philosopher from about 600 B.C. who was a Greek poet named Epimenides of Knossos.[5] Both Aristotle and Cicero called him a prophet and he is ultimately revered. His quote demonstrates the moral decay in the lives of the Cretans. Paul declares their hearts, minds, and consciences are corrupt.

Instructions are given as to the values that must be taught to the church members.

Older men	Older Women	Younger Men	Younger Women
Temperance	Reverent	Self-controlled	Love their husbands
Respectable	Not gossips	Integrity	Love their children
Self-controlled	No drunkenness	Serious speech	Self-controlled
Strong faith	Teach good morals	Sound doctrine	Pure
Love of Christ			Subject to their husbands
Perseverance			Busy homemakers
			Kind

The grace of God "teaches us to say 'No' to ungodliness and worldly passions, and to live self-controlled, upright and godly lives in this present age, while we wait for the blessed hope - the glorious appearing of our great God and Savior, Jesus Christ, who gave himself for us to redeem us from all wickedness and to purify for himself a people that are his own, eager to do what is good."[1] (Titus 2:12-14)

Paul warns against bickering and quarreling that serve only to divide, not unify God's people. He tells Titus to warn the divisive person twice and, if he chooses to continue, then ostracize him. This rogue is like cancer and will spread throughout the congregation without radical means of excising the evil. Titus is to expect a replacement so that he can spend the winter months with Paul in Nicopolis, Greece (western seaport city in Greece).

Food for Thought: Evaluate your life against Paul's list of qualifications. Where do you need to improve? Make 'New Life' resolutions today and change.

December 19
Bible Readings: 2 Timothy

Have you ever written a Last Will and Testament letter about your spiritual beliefs? It's very difficult. First, you must get past the emotional aspect of realizing that these are the last words of instruction you will ever communicate to your loved ones. Second, you must really analyze your beliefs and know what truths you want to leave for others. Third, you must write in such a way as to be clearly and unequivocally understood. As you read 2 Timothy, you realize Paul is recording the basics of his own beliefs, as well as the testimony of his life, for those he loves.

Paul starts by saying he has a clear conscience. Then he talks of the love he has for Timothy, his vigilant prayers for Timothy, and his confidence in Timothy's faith. Paul charges Timothy to always testify about his salvation through Jesus without shame or timidity. He is not to be ashamed of Paul, the prisoner, either. Paul's sufferings have been for the gospel as a messenger to the Gentiles. "Yet I am not ashamed, because I know whom I have believed, and am convinced that he is able to guard what I have entrusted to him for that day." (2 Tim. 1:12) Our soul is not our possession. It was created by God and given to us to feed and grow. At some point in life, we face the decisions of choice given to us by God. We call this the age of accountability. It is the point when we are aware of the spiritual world - good and evil - and must choose which path we will follow. This is the point where all the 'others' significant to our lives become real, living testimonies. Once we choose the path to either good or evil, then we still have another decision to make: to whom will we deposit our soul for safekeeping? Regardless of the path we have taken in life, both Jesus and Satan await our final decision. If we choose to believe and trust in Jesus, then our souls are locked up so tight in His powerful Hand that no evil can ever wrench it loose. But if we choose the worldly Satan, our souls are used, abused, hardened, cynical, bitter, angry, frightened, and without hope. Every evil, every demon has access to our very core or presence of life. Jesus can rescue us regardless of the path we have taken but not without a battle with Satan every step of the way - Satan wants to kidnap our eternity. You must decide.

Multiple times in 2 Timothy, Paul refers to people who assisted, abandoned, or persecuted him.

Good Disciples	*Deeds*
Onesiphorus	Ministered unto the needs of Paul, the freeman and the prisoner.
Priscilla and Aquila	Long-term followers of Christ who became friends with Paul in Corinth while on his second missionary journey. They later moved to Rome and continued to serve Christ.
Tychicus	A loyal supporter of Paul who often served as messenger and worker. He carried letters to the Ephesians and Colossians. Later he was sent to Crete and Ephesus.
Crescens	Went to Galatia for reasons unknown, presumably as a missionary.
Titus	Served as church revivalist and reorganizer. Also sent as a missionary to Dalmatia in modern day Croatia.
Mark and Luke	Faithful disciples, each wrote one of the gospels.

Evil Men	*Deeds*
Demus	Sought worldly pleasures.
Alexander	A metalworker in Ephesus who strongly opposed Paul's preaching due to the negative impact it had on his idol business.
Hymenaeus	A church member who went astray and began teaching false doctrine that the resurrection of the dead (into glorified bodies) had already taken place.
Philetus	Also a false teacher from the early church who apparently advocated Gnostic beliefs that only the spirit could be saved and the body was lost forever to evil.
Phygelus and Hermogenes	Christians in Asia who deserted Paul.

Timothy is instructed to guard the precious Holy Spirit that has been given him. He is to keep his heart, mind, and body free of all evil so that he may be found blameless before God and man. Quarrels are to be avoided in favor of peace, love, and righteousness. All God-fearing Christians who walk in the footsteps of Jesus can expect persecution. Our maturity in our faith allows us to handle persecution with prayer, drawing strength from the Holy Spirit. We need to be prayed-up and ready because persecution seldom gives advanced warning. Paul gives some descriptions of people living in the terrible last days: selfish, ungrateful, brutal, greedy, unholy, out-of-control, boastful, no compassion, treacherous, proud, unforgiving, rash, abusive, slanderous, conceited, disobedient, no self-control, and pleasure seekers. Christians are to have nothing to do with these evil people.

Arguably the most important verse in 2 Timothy is 3:16. Paul confidently assumes that God inspires all Scripture through His prophets and apostles. It is used for training in daily living, teaching of doctrine, rebuking evil, and correcting believers to lead godly lives. The Scripture is God's written word, whereas Jesus is God's living Word.[5]

Paul is in prison in Rome and may well have been executed before Timothy arrived, but he made sure Timothy knew his heart: he had fought evil well, he had finished his mission for Christ, and he had kept the faith. Paul was

Lessons of Love

looking forward to his crown of righteousness. Timothy is challenged to stay the course and be prepared to present the gospel. His pastoral duties included correcting, rebuking, and encouraging the flock. Paul tells him to stay in control of his emotions, endure the hardships, and faithfully perform his work for the Lord.

Food for Thought: Write a letter today to your loved ones. Imagine this is your last chance to tell them about your faith -- your last witness to all who will come after you. When you are finished, prayerfully read and edit it. Then send copies to all your loved ones. It will change your life and theirs forever.

December 20
Bible Readings: James and Jude

The author of James is assumed to be Jesus' brother (sometimes referred to as Jesus' half-brother because their fathers were different - God versus Joseph). Although there were two apostles named James, Jesus' brother James was head of the Jerusalem church and most likely to have written a letter destined to be called the "manual for discipleship." This letter is written specifically to the Israelites dispersed throughout the world, but generally to all Christians. We can make this assumption based on Gal. 3:29 that all who believe become children of Abraham. Our author does not boast of his personal family tie to Jesus but rather assumes the role of a servant of God and Jesus.

The Gnostics have deeply penetrated the Christian ranks and their false doctrines can be found in every city. James writes to these dispersed Christians to face their trials with joyful hearts knowing that perseverance and spiritual growth develop as a result. Proverb 9:10 tells us the fear of the LORD is the beginning of wisdom and Proverb 3:13 says the man who finds wisdom is happy or joyful. First we must realize that as sinners we should be terrified of the power and judgment of the LORD. Thus, fear opens our hearts to see our sins and repent. Then the wisdom of salvation through the shed blood of Jesus Christ is revealed to the penitent (humble). Through salvation, believers find wisdom and happiness in the mind of Christ given to us by the Holy Spirit. James 3:17 tells us, "Wisdom that comes from heaven is first of all pure; then peace-loving, considerate, submissive, full of mercy and good fruit, impartial, and sincere."[1] Doubt is of the devil. Just as peace and turmoil cannot reign together, neither can belief and doubt reign together. Doubt diminishes the power of the Spirit (Matt. 14:31). Perseverance in the faith brings the crown of eternal life in Heaven.

God is all righteousness and holiness. He does not tempt us. Temptation comes from the devil, who plants evil and doubt in our minds just as he did to Adam and Eve. Our punishment comes from being separated from the love of God by our sin. When Jesus cried out on the cross, "My God, My God, why have you forsaken me?"[1] (Matt. 27:46), God had turned away from Him because Jesus bore the sins of the world. God cannot look upon or associate with sin. Judgment is not punishment but rather condemnation. Earthly punishment is the consequence of sin. Spiritual condemnation is the consequence of rejecting (blaspheming) the salvation of Jesus Christ and His gift to believers of the Holy Spirit. Although punishment is generally measured in earthly terms, condemnation is eternal. Though we strive to be like Jesus, believers know that they are not always successful. Thus, we suffer punishment when we sin, but we do not have to worry about condemnation. Those who are lost to sin suffer both punishment and condemnation. Believers are the firstfruits of creation, those who are consecrated - set aside - for God. (Newer versions of the Bible often translate the Hebrew word for destroy as punishment which is not accurate.)

James gives Christians some practical guidelines for living righteously.

1. Be quick to listen and slow to speak.
2. Be slow to become angry.
3. Eliminate moral filth from your life.
4. Do what the Bible teaches.

5. Discipline your tongue.
6. Avoid evil.
7. Help those in need.
8. Don't discriminate or judge.
9. Be merciful.
10. Do good deeds for others out of love.
11. Be obedient.
12. Be particularly careful to accurately teach God's word.
13. Do not curse or swear.
14. Do not be envious or selfish.
15. Seek spiritual wisdom.
16. Avoid quarreling.
17. Seek God's Will.
18. Be humble.
19. Be patient and persevere.
20. Be fair and just.
21. Repent of your sin.
22. Pray continually.
23. Witness to others.

No one would disagree that these practices would build one's righteousness. Yet, James has come under attack as being opposed to Paul's teaching that salvation is through faith only; works cannot get anyone into Heaven. This opposition is particularly founded on 2:14-20. To understand James' intent, we must remember this letter is written to believers - they already had received salvation. James wanted to teach believers (the church) how to be ambassadors for Christ during an age where so-called 'religious leaders' were corrupt. Put yourself in James' place. From your town, how would you teach, through written words, believers throughout the world to live righteously when many of their own 'leaders' did not? What would you have put into a single, succinct letter to be read to people of all races, ethnic backgrounds, and political situations? Some of these people would be persecuted, imprisoned, elderly, abandoned, poor, or sick. Others would be free, rich, healthy, loved, or powerful. James took on an awesome responsibility. His premise was that the love of Jesus would be evident in the lives of believers. If we believe, then Jesus lives in us in the form of the Holy Spirit who gives us the mind of Christ. Jesus Christ loves all men and gave totally of Himself to all mankind. We cannot claim to be believers without His love being evident in our lives. Knowledge of the Scripture is not evidence of faith. Even demons know the Scripture. (See Jesus' temptation in the wilderness when the devil quotes Scripture - Matt. 4.) The Jewish religious leaders knew the Torah (law) and the Gnostics knew the Scripture, but neither group had faith in Jesus Christ as their Savior. Jesus empowered us to be living witnesses to the world that He has brought salvation to all who would believe as a free gift out of the Grace and Mercy of God.

Jude identifies himself as a brother of James. Therefore, he is also a brother to Jesus. Jude's audience is believers. The message of the letter is a warning against the false teachers who have infiltrated the congregations. These false teachers are a fulfillment of Christ's words in Matt. 7:15. Matt. 7:16, though, provides us a way to identify them. We will know them by the fruits they bear. These men have denied the deity of Jesus and encouraged believers to use their freedom from the religious laws in vile ways. These Gnostics taught that the body and spirit were separate, allowing the body to do any type of immoral act without affecting the spirit. Many believers were led astray because their flesh was willing. Jude reminds all believers that God is greater than evil and judgment will come to the ungodly.

As an interesting note, much of Jude's message is also found in 2 Peter. The verb tense gives a clue as to their relationship. Jude uses past tense in referring to the warning about heresy, but 2 Peter uses future tense. Thus, 2 Peter was written first warning believers that false teachers will invade their groups and Jude was written after they had already spread their false doctrines to the churches.[96] Given this scenario, Jude and 2 Peter should actually be swapped in the chronological positions assigned in your Bible.

Jude 5-6 states that even angels are judged and those who are unworthy are condemned to eternal darkness. Jude's reference to fallen angels is undoubtedly concerning a passage from the pseudepigrapha book of 1 Enoch. This account states 200 angels conspired to leave Heaven and enter into sexual union with earthly women on Mt. Hermon.[96] (Gen. 6:2 may refer to 1 Enoch, also, which is a story of folklore.) The pseudepigrapha consists of a collection of various Jewish folktales and literacy works that were written to encourage Jews to live according to Mosaic Law. The books were named after well-known righteous men but were not necessarily authored by them.[5] According to 1 Enoch, God sent archangels Raphael and Gabriel down to earth to bind up the rebellious angels and throw them into darkness to await judgment.[96]

Jude gives three examples of God's condemnation of the ungodly: death in the wilderness for those who disobeyed God's command to go into the Promised Land, judgment of wicked angels, and condemnation of Sodom and Gomorrah. When referring to the destruction of Sodom and Gomorrah, some Biblical versions refer to it as punishment rather than a better translation as judgment or condemnation. Judgment is always depicted as fire. Those who survive the fire of judgment are the righteous. (Remember, Daniel's friends Shadrach, Meshach, and Abednego escaped the fiery furnace unsinged in Daniel 3.)

False teachers still encourage others to do what feels good rather than to do what is righteous. Jude makes reference to another pseudepigrapha book The Assumption of Moses. The story of Moses' death on Mt. Nebo is reported as a dispute between the archangel Michael and the devil over the body of Moses. (Deut. 34:6 tells us Moses was buried in a valley of Moab.) Jude points out that even God's main archangel would not attack the vilest of fallen angels (devil) but instead declared the Lord would judge him. Jude warns against false teachers who slander angels, grumble and boast, and flatter others for selfish reasons. Jude also challenges believers to be merciful to those of weaker faith, snatch those who have fallen away from the faith to save them from judgment, and teach believers to be in reverential awe of God.[96]

Jude ends with one of the greatest doxologies ever written. Read Jude 24-25 and ponder each phrase. Amen (I agree).

Food for Thought: My Sunday School teacher has a rule to live by that I love, "Trust God's heart even when you don't understand His commands." God only wants the best for us so we must trust Him to always lead us in the right path - even when we don't understand.

December 21
Bible Readings: 1 Peter

Peter was the apostle sent to the Jews with the salvation message. His church-planting career included Mark who has become a valuable companion and fellow worker to Barnabas, Peter, and Paul. Even though Peter's work is widespread, we have very little that was written by Peter. In fact Silas may actually have written the two letters attributed to Peter or another scribe based on principles and teachings of Peter. Scribes were generally given much leeway in communication, as they were educated in the nuances of formal grammar and phraseology. Some arguments in favor of this include the fact that (1) nothing is mentioned about the life of Jesus even though Peter was an enthusiastic observer, (2) nothing refers to the Mosaic Law, but Peter was dedicated to ministering to the Jews, (3) quotes are from the Greek rather than the Hebrew Old Testament, and (4) Peter was not believed to be an educated man (Acts 4:13), probably was deficient in Greek (Mark was his interpreter), and thus could not have written the excellent Greek of 1 Peter. These letters do, though, resemble the writing style of 1 and 2 Thessalonians authored by Paul during Silas' sojourn with him.[96]

Peter's letters are addressed to Christians in the Greco-Roman Empire. Commentaries disagree on who the recipients were. Some say they were Jews of the dispersion, some say they were Gentile Christians, and others believe Peter was writing to all Christians.[97] Verse 2:10 indicates it was written to Gentile Christians. Geographical regions listed east to west identify those receiving this letter: Pontus, Galatia, Cappadocia, Asia, and Bithynia.[96] This would be the natural order in which a single messenger traveling across the trade route read the letter to the congregations. Tradition is that Peter resided in Rome during the 60s A.D. If so, these letters were likely written during that period.[96]

First Peter is a letter of hope and encouragement written to persecuted Christians. Under Nero, Domitian, and Trajan, the Romans persecuted the Christians during their three terms of power: (1) 62-64 A.D., (2) 90-97 A.D., and (3) 111 A.D. For those who do not believe Peter was involved in writing this letter, the circumstances of the last time frame suit best. Pliny was the governor of the province of Bithynia and, as such, he wrote a letter to Emperor Trajan asking for clarification as to just whom the Christians were he was to persecute. The same wording from his letter is found in 1 Peter 2:12 and similar wording is in 4: 12-16.[96] There is also the possibility of a fourth persecution not approved by the Romans: persecution by pagans. In this light, 1 Peter 2:12 may actually be the charge brought by the pagans before the Roman government in an effort to get approval for Christian persecution. Paul's experience at Ephesus would certainly indicate the pagans were ruthless and persistent. Based on the source of persecution, Peter could have written the letter in the early 60s. Possibly Paul had been released from his first Roman imprisonment and was actually away in Spain as he had planned. If so, Peter would have felt the need to shepherd Paul's churches in Galatia and Asia.

Peter starts by reminding Christians of their salvation through Jesus who is their hope for eternal life in Heaven. Jesus is their cornerstone, the foundation of their faith, and the stumbling block of the lost. Christians "are a chosen people, a royal priesthood, a holy nation, a people belonging to God . . .." (1 Peter 2:9) The second major section of this letter begins in verse 11 of chapter 2. Peter provides some guidelines for living.

1. Prepare your minds to act for Christ.
2. Be self-controlled.
3. Stand firm in Christ.
4. Do not give in to evil desires.
5. Be holy in everything you do.
6. Rid yourselves of all malice, deceit, hypocrisy, envy, and slander.
7. Submit yourselves to authorities.
8. Be servants of God to others.
9. Be considerate and respectful of others.
10. Live in peace and harmony.
11. Love each other as brothers and sisters in Christ.
12. Do not avenge wrongs.
13. Be hospitable.
14. Be humble.
15. Do not be greedy.
16. Do not be proud.
17. Do not fear the persecution of the world.
18. Be committed to God.
19. Do not be ashamed of being a Christian.

Peter reminds Christians that pagans view their deeds as an example of their faith. This teaching is consistent with that of James. Wives are exhorted to be submissive, gentle and quiet in spirit, pure and reverent, and beautiful in their inner selves. Husbands are exhorted to be considerate and respectful, treating their wives as equal heirs to Heaven - their sisters in Christ.

The third major section of this letter starts in 3:13. This section provides instructions for living in the trials and persecutions of the world. Christians are to keep clear consciences and be prepared to defend their beliefs. Verses 18-20 of chapter 3 are the focal point of many extensive debates. Interpretations exceed 30 different ones. In fact, this passage even garnered an entire book dedicated to its interpretation in the early 20th Century![96] (See Bo Reicke, *The Disobedient Spirits and Christian Baptism*, 1946.) Major religious groups have treatises on this topic. Many view this passage as proof that Jesus had to descend into hell as a part of His suffering for our sins before He was resurrected to reign forever as the Judge of all creation. But, why would He preach only to those before the flood of Noah and not to all lost people prior to Jesus' own death? The Greek word translated "preached" in the NIV is better translated "proclaimed." Josephus states that the Hebrews believed the "sons of God" in the flood story (Gen. 6:1-8) were fallen angels.[3] One idea is that the vile, wicked people who lived prior to the flood were half human and half fallen angel causing God to drown their bodies and put their spirits in the Abyss. (Also, read Genesis19 to see interactions between angels and humans.) Thus, Jesus proclaimed His victory over death to these demon spirits in the Abyss. Another idea is that Jesus showed Himself to those who had rejected Him as proof of his deity.[96]

Baptism is clearly described as a symbol of dying to the old life of sin and being reborn into the new life of the Spirit. More specifically, the baptismal water is the actual symbol with the act of baptism occurring at the spiritual level. Verses 7-11 of chapter 4 refer to the end times. Peter reminds Christians that efforts made out of love are rewarded even when things do not go as intended. Commit yourselves to the work of the Lord. "Cast all your anxiety on him because he cares for you."[1] (1 Peter 5:7)

Food for Thought: "Be self-controlled and alert. Your enemy the devil prowls around like a roaring lion looking for someone to devour."[1] (1 Peter 5:8) Peter warns us we should have our minds ready and our weapons prepared. In doing so we can stand firm in the face of adversity. Are you ready to defend your beliefs?

December 22
Bible Readings: 2 Peter

A review of our lesson of Jude reminds us that 2 Peter was written to warn Christians against false teachers. They are to hold fast to the teachings of the Old Testament and those of Jesus. As with Jude, 2 Peter specifically attacks the heresy of the Gnostics.

The flawless Greek grammar of 1 Peter is definitely not seen in 2 Peter. The letters were written by two different men or, at the very least, two different scribes. The Greek of 2 Peter is very poor causing some to believe Peter actually wrote the letter himself rather then using a scribe.

Peter states that only knowledge of Jesus as our personal Savior can bring salvation. This was in direct contrast to the Gnostics who believed that knowledge merely released one's spirit to begin the journey to reunite with God. Then more knowledge allowed that spirit to penetrate each of the heavenly layers until the world of light was reached.[5] We see Paul's influence in 2 Peter 1:5-7. At verse 13, Peter announces his life is growing short and by verse 15, he indicates this letter is an effort to leave the believers with a lasting memory or reminder of his teachings. Here we have another reason to believe Peter may have written this letter himself instead of using a scribe. As Paul had done in 2 Timothy 3, Peter emphasizes that all Scripture originated with God with prophecy being specifically mentioned. Second Peter carries the same warnings and message as Jude. God condemns the wicked and exalts (or lifts up) the righteous. False teachers can be identified by their evil desires and deeds: slaves of depravity.

Chapter 3 addresses the Second Coming of Christ. Jesus taught (Matt. 24) that false prophets and antichrists would appear in the end times. Great signs and miracles would be performed in an effort to deceive the elect or those called to serve Christ. Ever since the ascension of Jesus (Luke 24), Christians had been expecting His return. Many had sold all they owned and donated the money to the spread of the Gospel (Acts 4:32-37). Paul reiterated the need for Christians to be watchful for Christ's return (1 Thess. 5:1-11). In 2 Thess. 2, Paul describes events that will occur prior to the Second Coming. Just as we do now, Christians in the First Century attempted to assign various leaders and circumstances to the events indicating the end times. Peter was writing 30 years after Jesus' resurrection. Christians were wondering if He really would come again. Outside evil influences were making inroads into the minds of Christians. Peter explained that the Lord would return on His timetable not ours. (Psalm 90:4 is paraphrased here.) After all, He delayed only so that all people would have a chance to hear the Gospel and be saved. Faith in Jesus as Lord and Savior comes from hearing the message of salvation (Rom. 10:17).

The description of the Second Coming is both awesome and frightening. A mighty roar will announce the end of the heavens and the earth, which will be destroyed by fire. (See Rev. 8:5.) Believers will be taken out of this world before the judgment comes. Until that Day, we must live holy, godly lives and be ever watching for Christ's return.

Food for Thought: The best gift believers can give to Jesus is our obedience. He told us to "feed His sheep." This holiday season give the greatest gift of all; tell someone about salvation through Jesus Christ.

December 23
Bible Readings: Hebrews 1 - 6:12

Hebrews and 1 John are the only letters included in the Bible that do not have an opening salutation to identify the author and recipients.[5] In the past, Paul has been given credit for writing Hebrews, but there is a great amount of evidence that discredits this assumption. Others proposed as the writer include Luke, Barnabas, Apollos, and Silas.[98] The recipients are Messianic Jews apparently of the Dispersion. Thus, it is called the letter to the Hebrews (Abraham's descendants). The magnificent Temple in Jerusalem was destroyed in 70 A.D. Due to this severe blow to the Jews, all writings after 70 A.D. refer to the Temple destruction. Because it is not mentioned in this letter, we assume it was written prior to that date.

The letter begins by reviewing prophecy that pointed to the majestic deity of Christ. Jesus came as the Son of God. He is in the Father and the Father is in Him. Jesus brought glory to the Father through His obedience. John 1:3 tells us all creation was made through Jesus. Because Jesus loved us, He willingly took on all our sins, purifying and consecrating all who believed in Him. Believers share in Jesus' inheritance -- the magnificent Kingdom of God. Jesus was elevated to the powerful right Hand of God. He is the judge of all creation. He had been made a little lower than the angels in order to be born a man, but in His resurrection He became Ruler of all creation, including celestial beings. By believing in Jesus Christ as our Lord and Savior, we are exalted above the angels for 1 Cor. 6:3 tells us believers (saints) will judge the angels! The heavens and earth will pass away at the Second Coming, but God in the forms of Father, Son, and Holy Spirit will never end.

The writer warns against falling away from the faith (Heb 2:1). Many religions believe this is not possible based on a 'once saved, always saved' foundation traced primarily to John 10:28. Luther rejected Hebrews, because of this falling away from grace teaching.[96] Others explain this passage based on a Judas Iscariot example of those who know about Jesus, see the miracles of Jesus, and follow His teachings but never truly accept Him as Lord and Savior of their lives. Still others view this as a doctrine of apostasy, a falling away of believers. Examples of apostasy are given as King Saul (1 Sam. 15:11), Hymenaeus and Alexander (1 Tim. 1:19-20), and Demas (2 Tim. 4-10).[5] The New American Standard Bible states apostasy will be the forerunner of the Second Coming (2 Thess. 2:3). The NEB describes apostasy as the final rebellion of wickedness against God (2 Thess. 2:3). Apostasy is defined "as the determined, willful rejection of Christ and His teachings by a Christian believer."[5] (p. 78) Which one is correct? A doctrine of apostasy? Each person must study the Scripture with prayer and work out his own salvation and beliefs (Phil. 2:12-13). Paul warned the Ephesians that when He was gone wolves would come in among the sheep and the flock would not be spared (Acts 20:29). Jesus told the disciples He was sending them out to spread the Gospel like sheep among wolves (Matt. 10:16). Matt. 7:15 tells us whom the wolves are -- false prophets disguised as Christians. Believers are not to blindly follow leaders, teachers, or religious denominations but rather they are to question everything by measuring it against God's Holy Word. There are many people who belong to churches but do not know Jesus as Lord and Savior. When persecution begins, these will 'fall away from the faith' or will leave the espoused beliefs of their faith behind. I received an e-mail this week about a story of two armed terrorists who entered a church demanding those who were willing to take a bullet for Jesus stand still. The story goes that most of the leaders, teachers, choir, and congregation fled. Out of 2,000 members, only 20 were left standing up for the Lord. I believe this is what our Hebrews writer is saying: many claim to be believers, but they will flee when persecution comes. Put yourself in that same situation. Would you stand or run? Like Judas Iscariot, apostates believe in God (even demons believe this - James 2:29) but do not make Him Lord and Savior of their lives. Jesus told us that if we disowned Him before men, He would disown us before the heavenly host (Luke 12:9). Before the Second Coming, there will be persecution of the church and a 'falling away' of many who profess to be believers. But Jesus tells true believers, "If you hold to my teachings, you are really my disciples. Then you will know the truth, and the truth will set you free."[1] (John 8:31). Those who truly believe will be set free from the bondage of sin.

Heb. 4:2 states that both believers and non-believers in the church have heard the word of God preached, but the difference is that believers combined the Good News with their faith in God to become new creations looking forward to their rest with God for eternity. The thoughts and deeds of all mankind will be laid bare before God. What you do in secret and hide to the world will be exposed in full on Judgment Day. Believers will be given mercy for they have been purified in the blood of Christ -- God's grace. Jesus was the One and only sacrifice to forever wash away sins. Tempted as a man, Jesus shows compassion on us. He resisted temptation through His submissive obedience before God, but He knows the difficulties we face and is merciful. We can approach His throne of grace with confidence that He knows us, forgives us, and loves us. All He asks is a repentant heart that is humbled before Him and obedient to His Will.

Food for Thought: "Are we, in the modern church, spending so much time trying to add members to our religious institutions and train them in the first principles of the faith that we have no energy left to cultivate the maturity which has a dynamic magnetism about it, which would draw people to the Savior more than all of our organized activities can hope to do?"[96] (p.44)

Verse of the Week: **Rev. 3:20** "Here I am! I stand at the door and knock. If anyone hears my voice and opens the door, I will come in and eat with him, and he with me."

December 24
Bible Readings: Hebrews 6:13 - 10:18

The Hebrews writer paints a glorious picture of our Lord in chapters 6-10, describing Him as follows.

1. A high priest like Melchizedek (Gen. 14:18-20) who had no beginning and no end.
2. An anchor for our faith, holding securely.
3. The guarantee of God's promise to believers.
4. A permanent High Priest who sacrificed only once for our sins.
5. The Interceder with God on our behalf.
6. Holy, blameless, pure, consecrated.

7. Seated at the right Hand of God the Father.
8. Mediator of God's covenant with His people.
9. The Ransom that set us free from sin.
10. Provider of eternal redemption.
11. Bearer of salvation to the righteous.
12. Author and Perfecter of our faith (12:2).
13. Finisher of God's plan of salvation (4:3).
14. Ruler and Judge over all creation.

Obviously, none who has ever lived is greater than Jesus. He deserves our trust, faith, and obedience.

Much explanation is given to the need for God to pledge His promise with an oath. God's oath was not to hold Him accountable for His promise but rather to bind mankind accountable for our actions. One of the tools of counseling is the written contract. All people know that verbal promises are easily made and soon forgotten. God provided Abraham with a contract ceremony that would be hard to forget (Gen. 15). He commanded that the people of that first covenant bear upon their bodies a constant reminder of the covenant (circumcision). Even then, they turned from God and repeatedly broke the covenant. So God decided to make a better covenant - the ultimate covenant - with all who believe. He would send His only Son. God is the God of second chances. Sinners everywhere have been given a second chance at having eternal salvation. But those who reject this covenant will be lost forever. This covenant was sealed with the blood of God's only Son. There will be no third covenant.

Chapter 7 is devoted to a discussion of Melchizedek who was both the high priest and king of Salem which was renamed Jerusalem. Melchizedek brought bread and wine out to Abraham (symbolizing the body and blood of Jesus). Abraham recognized Melchizedek's spiritual superiority and gave a tenth of his plunder to Melchizedek as an offering. Centuries later, Abraham's great grandson Levi's lineage is singled out by God as the priestly lineage. The Levites collected tithes and offerings from the people. But their great-grandfather Abraham had given offerings to Melchizedek before they were even born! In this sense, the Levites (priests) were giving an offering to one superior to themselves through Abraham. Melchizedek represented the coming Messiah. God promised a second covenant before mankind had even broken the first! Alas, He knew our hearts even before our births.

The Hebrews writer reminds us that the early tabernacle was a foreshadowing of God's covenant with His people. The courtyard was surrounded with the white linen walls representing God's wall of holiness around His people. (Review the Jan. 29 lesson.) The bronze sacrificial altar represents the feet of Jesus (Rev. 1:15) where we are to lay our sins that are cleansed by the blood of the sacrifice (Jesus). The tabernacle tent contained two rooms: the Holy Place and the Most Holy Place. The reference in Hebrews to the golden incense altar being in the Most Holy Place has been a disputed one. Exodus 30:6 clearly states the incense altar stood in front of the veil separating the Most Holy Place. One explanation seems to be that when the veil was pulled back once a year to allow entrance of the high priest into the Most Holy Place (Holy of Holies), the golden incense altar could then be seen from the Holy of Holies.[98] Regardless, this certainly seems to eliminate Paul, a trained Pharisee, from authorship of Hebrews. The earthly tabernacle with its ministering high priest was but a copy or shadow of the real High Priest in Heaven who judges from His Throne of Mercy. All of Heaven is His sanctuary. Believers are His worshipers washed pure by the blood of His sacrifice. The copy or shadow of earth's tabernacle faded and disappeared with time, but our heavenly King preserves our real treasures forever.

Food for Thought: "Jesus Christ is the same yesterday and today and forever."[1] (Heb. 13:8) He is the gift that never disappoints, never fades, never wears out, never dies, and never leaves us. Do you seek a constant presence of strength, a true friend who gives perfect guidance, an eternal peace, a purpose in life, or an unending joy? Jesus provides all these and more. If you have moved away from Christ, come back now. If you don't know Him, confess, repent, and believe now. Jesus is waiting to hear from you. Won't you come to Him?

Lessons of Love

December 25
Bible Readings: Hebrews 10:19 - 13:25

The Hebrews writer reminds us that our Savior is a living Savior. He arose from the grave victorious over death! We can confidently enter God's Presence without fear of death! Believers' hearts have been cleansed from the guilt of sin and our bodies have been washed and purified from our contamination. Do not become discouraged! Cling to your faith and hold fast to your hope in Jesus Christ. Encourage each other and continue to meet together, fellowshipping one with another. Realize that believers who purposefully choose to continue in their sin face the wrath of God. When we have been washed in the very blood of our holy sacrifice, we trample that purity with our sin-stained feet when we continue to live like the devil. True believers cannot sin without the pain of their guilt overwhelming them. Believers struggle continually with temptation and sometimes lose the battle. But we repent and strive to do better and live in righteousness. Jesus knows our hearts. Facing the judgment of God is a fearful moment indeed. Ask God to reveal your sins so that you may repent and be forgiven. Persevere in the faith and God will reward beyond expectation.

Hebrews 11 is known as God's Hall of Fame. The Hebrews writer is addressing persecuted Christians. He seeks to encourage by reminding them of their great faith predecessors. The definition of faith is "being sure of what we hope for and certain of what we do not see."[1] (Heb. 11:1) The same God we believe and trust to save us and keep us in His eternal care breathed all creation into existence. With faith in God all things are possible; without faith in God, there is no hope. The great faithful ones listed are Abel, Enoch, Noah, Abraham, Isaac, Jacob, Joseph, and Moses followed by the faith of the Israelites when they crossed the Red Sea and a host of judges, kings, and prophets. All of these people died while watching, waiting, and hoping for the promises of God to be fulfilled. Those living after the resurrection of Jesus have a greater blessing than those who came before. For it is only through the blood of Jesus and our belief in Him that we receive the gift of the Holy Spirit. For those who believed God prior to Jesus did so with blind faith - believing in a promise. But those living after the resurrection have been given spiritual sight. We have the ability to understand the mystery of God's word. We can understand the mystery of the prophecy - the gift of salvation through the suffering servant Jesus. These great people of faith form a great cloud of witnesses who testify to us who live under the blessing of the Holy Spirit. Clouds symbolize God's Presence and, too, His coming with a heavenly army of witnesses and warriors. Mark 13:26 tells us Jesus will return in clouds with power and glory. Jesus' mighty army of the faithful will come to take us home.

In the interim, we are called to serve God, resist temptation, and persevere in our faith, keeping our eyes on Jesus, the One who endured such great persecutions to bring salvation to those He loved. When we remember the trials and pain Jesus suffered for us, we are encouraged to continue firm in our faith. Heb. 12:5-6 is a loose quote of Prov. 3:11-12. The most notable difference is that the Proverb does not contain the word 'punishes.' In fact, the tone is a positive one that states discipline comes from a loving Father who delights in His sons. Trials and tribulations discipline believers to trust and depend on God's guidance, bringing spiritual maturity to their faith. The proverbs are replete with wisdom sayings on discipline. Heb. 12:11 tells us, "No discipline seems pleasant at the time, but painful."[1] The results of growth and knowledge produced through discipline are righteousness and peace. Believers do not have to fear the death judgment of the law but can instead approach a loving God who has forgiven their sins. We must present ourselves as a holy, undefiled people who worship the One and only God of the universe.

Surely the Hebrews writer had Genesis 18 in mind when he advised, "Do not forget to entertain strangers, for by so doing some people have entertained angels without knowing it."[1] (Heb. 13:2) As with Paul and Peter, warnings and advice are given for practicing holy living.

1. Love others and empathize with their pain and suffering.
2. Be hospitable.

3. Be true to your marriage.
4. Do not be greedy.
5. Be content in all situations.
6. Live as examples to others.
7. Do not be led astray from the faith.
8. Submit to authority.
9. Do good works and share with others.
10. Obey those who serve as true church leaders.

The author closes with a request for prayer and amusingly refers to having written only a short letter! Our only clues to the writer's identity are that he is a fellow worker with Timothy who has been released from prison and he is writing from Italy.

Food for Thought: The birth of a little baby in an animal stable over 2,000 years ago made all the difference to a dark and dying world. Let the Light of Jesus shine through you. Tell someone today about the gift of life.

December 26
Bible Readings: 1 John, 2 John, 3 John

The Apostle John undoubtedly wrote the Johanine Epistles in the latter part of the First Century. Both Irenaeus and Tertullian, church fathers of the Second Century, attribute the letters to John.[106] There is also a close connection between 1 John and the gospel of John that would suggest they share a common author. For example, each book has "the same love of opposites set in stark contrast to one another, light and darkness, life and death, love and hate, truth and falsehood."[105]

The author also speaks with great authority. He is sure of his facts. Once my mother testified to one of her relatives shortly before his death. His reply was, "It all sounds great if only we could be sure it is true." For John there is no doubt. What he knows of Christ was verified by his hearing, sight, and touch. His emphasis upon the humanity of Christ was likely inspired by an early heresy that John is rebuking. Docetism doctrine stated that matter was evil and spirit was good. They attempted to distinguish between the man Jesus and the heavenly Christ, claiming the spiritual Christ descended on Jesus in the form of a dove after He was baptized but left Him before His death.[106] John refutes these claims of those who deny that, "Jesus Christ has come in the flesh."

The first chapter of 1 John is memorable in that it explains the plan of salvation in the simplest terms. First, John argues that all men have sinned (1:8). Sin literally means "to miss the mark" as when a spear is thrown at a target. It can also be used for missing a road, for failure in one's plan or hope or purpose.[107] The New Testament teaches that *hamartia* (sin) can have man in its grasp (Gal. 3:22, Rom. 3:9) and make man its slave (John 8:34, Rom. 6:17). When most men's sins are brought up, they want to compare their sins with something much worse. God compares us to Jesus Christ the only One who didn't miss the mark. Rather than defend ourselves, we need to acknowledge our own failures.

Secondly, John tells us that if we confess our sins, God will forgive us and cleanse us (1 John 1:9). The Greek word for confess is *homolegeo* that means, "to acknowledge," but the idea is that we are to lay them before God and to seek forgiveness. The most common word in the New Testament for forgiveness is *aphiesthai*, which has a wide variety of meanings, such as being used for releasing a man from some sentence that has already been passed, for remitting a charge that has justly been made, or for releasing a man from a duty that he could have been compelled to carry out.[107] God provides cleansing, *katharos*. This word also has many shades of meaning. Some of those include water that has been purified, grain that has been winnowed, metals that are without alloy, and feelings that are unmixed or sincere. It is used in the sense of being free of debt, free from guilt, or as a saying whose authenticity cannot be doubted. Life's greatest folly would be to reject this forgiveness and cleansing. The rest of 1 John largely concerns how Christians are to treat each other.

The 2 John and 3 John letters are very consistent with the conventional letterform of the First Century Roman world. The second letter is concerned with the same issues addressed in the first letter: those deceivers who do not confess that Jesus Christ has come in the flesh (7) and the need for Christians to love one another.

The third letter is sent to a single individual, Gaius, who has shown hospitality to certain messengers sent by John. These messengers had not been received by Gaius' church because of the objection of a prominent member named Diotrephes.

Food for Thought: Don't be a Diotrephes. Be absolutely sure you do not stand in the way of the messengers of God's word. On the other hand, you must also be sure you compare all messages to the word of God for authenticity. Too many false teachers are present in our world. Be discriminating about what you hear and believe and be discerning about who is teaching in the Spirit. Do this through Bible study and prayer.

December 27
Bible Readings: Revelation 1:1 - 3:22

The Revelation is from Jesus Christ to John the Apostle almost certainly in 95 A.D.[96] John was exiled on the Isle of Patmos that is located 28 miles[99] off the southwest coast of modern Turkey, called Asia Minor at the writing of the Revelation. The island was roughly 10 miles long and 6 miles wide. It was barren and was used as a type of forced labor camp where prisoners worked in mines and quarries. We must assume John suffered the same harsh punishment that any other prisoner endured.[5] The historian Eusebius recorded His length of stay as 18 months. John had been banished to the volcanic island because of his testimony and preaching about salvation through Jesus Christ.[99] Even though John's vision occurred on Patmos, he apparently recorded it after he was released (1:9). Prisoners in concentration-type camps would not have had writing materials available.[100] There was a change in emperors in 96 A.D. that Eusebius attributed to John's return to freedom.[99]

Like the Book of Daniel, Revelation is classified as apocalyptic writing. There are many apocalyptic books that were excluded from the canonized biblical books, e.g., 1 Enoch, 4 Ezra, 2 Baruch. Also, certain passages of the Bible are considered apocalyptic outside the two books previously named, i.e., Isa. 24-27, Mark 13, 2 Thess. 2:1-12.[96] The Revelation refers to Daniel 7 thirty-one times as well as referring to Zech. 12:10.[99] As with most apocalyptic writing, the Revelation had both a current meaning for Christians of the time and a futuristic interpretation of events to come.[96] Thus, it becomes easier to understand when viewed in both respects. The imagery was common to such writings; it often involved animals, demons, angels, visions, and numerology. Numbers in Revelation may be literal as well as symbolic. For example, seven letters were sent to seven churches literally, but seven also means the completion or fullness of God's word was sent to all churches everywhere, whereas the seven churches identified represent God's universal church of believers.

CITY	COMMENDATIONS	REPRIMANDS WARNING	PROMISE
Ephesus	Good deeds, hard work, perseverance, no tolerance of evil, tested teachings, endured hardships, not grown weary, hate false teachers	Forsaken first love - their love of Jesus through whom their brotherly love had poured out	The right to eat of the tree of life in the paradise of God.
Smyrna	Physical and material sacrifices, endured slander, rich in spirit	Some will be imprisoned and persecuted for 10 days (No reprimands)	Crown of life - eternal life
Pergamum	True to Christ though living in the center of evil, faithful during persecution	Some have fallen to false teachings	Bread of life - a white (not guilty) stone with a new name, one that is in the Lamb's Book of Life
Thyatira	Good deeds, love and faith, service and perseverance, increased efforts for the faith	Too tolerant of a false teacher leading some into sexual immorality	Ruling power over the nations and the resurrection of Christ
Sardis	Past reputation of living for God, some are still worthy (No current commendations)	Repent and turn back to God or die spiritually	Clothed in purity, assurance of salvation, Jesus will acknowledge before God and the angels
Philadelphia	Kept God's word, patiently endured, faithful despite weakness, doorway to Christ	Hold fast to what you have! (No reprimands)	Become a pillar of God's Temple, receive registration as the property of God
Laodicea	(NONE)	Lukewarm faith, wretched souls, pitiful, poor, blind, naked	Invited to the banquet table of Jesus

The Revelation to John of Jesus' role in God's master plan is grouped into units that are complete (groups of 7): 7 churches, 7 seals, 7 trumpets, and 7 bowls. There are even 7 beatitudes woven into the tapestry of the drama: 1:3, 14:13, 16:15, 19:9, 20:6, 22:7, 22:14.[96]

First let's set the stage for this drama by examining the historical events occurring at the time of John's revelation. Emperor Domitian ruled the Roman Empire from 81-96 A.D. Domitian was devoted to the gods of Rome and built temples throughout the kingdom to these pagan gods. He further commanded all people to worship these Roman gods that included statues of the emperor. Caligula, an earlier emperor, had ordered his statue be worshipped only to find himself in an uproar from the Jews. As a result, Jews were exempted, but new religions like Christianity were banned. This exemption of the Jews continued into Domitian's rule but now carried a hefty tax, too. Domitian had Christians executed as atheists because they didn't worship the Roman gods. Emperor worship reached its finest in the province of Asia with various cities competing for the bragging rights of being a temple-keeper. Temples were erected to Julius Caesar in Ephesus and Nicea; to the Roman gods in Smyrna, Ephesus, and Nicea; and to Augustus in Pergamum.[96] Emperor worship was rapidly increasing with the blessings and encouragement of the community. With this in mind, John fears the persecutions of the believers in Asia Minor will be severe. John is worshipping God on the Lord's Day. (This is the only place in the New Testament where the day of worship is called the Lord's Day. Most scholars interpret this to be the first day of the week -- Sunday -- honoring the resurrection of Jesus. This practice seems to have been practiced in the early days of the church as evidenced in 1 Cor. 16:2 and Acts 20:7.) An angel appears to John bringing the message from Jesus. (Compare Rev. 1:4 to Heb. 13:8.) The angel's salutation is from God the Father, the Holy Spirit, and Jesus Christ. (Seven spirits is simply a designation for the fullness of the Spirit.) Jesus is identified as a faithful witness, the firstborn (set aside for God) of the resurrection, and the Ruler of the earth. Believers are described as being loved, freed from sin, priests, and the people of God's kingdom. A paraphrase of Dan. 7:13 and Zech. 12:10 reminds the readers that Jesus will return with His clouds of witnesses, or soldiers of the cross, and all people will know He is the Son of God. God is called the Alpha and Omega (in Greek) or A to Z (in English), the infinite Almighty, the great I AM. (Compare to Ex. 3:13-14 and to Rev. 22:13.) Many of the early concepts in Revelation are reiterated in the last chapter. John hears a loud voice like a trumpet. (See Zech. 9:14, Isa. 27:13, 1 Cor. 15:52.) Like in the days of Moses, the Lord's trumpet announces the call to worshipers to assemble. John sees Jesus standing among 7 golden lampstands with 7 stars in His mighty right hand. The lampstands represent the churches of believers protected in Jesus' right hand. The 7 stars are the 7 angels of the churches. This latter point is less understood. Some scholars believe that 7 angels served as messengers or carriers of the letters to the churches. But each letter gives a different portion of Christ's description. Only when read together would the churches 'see' the image of Christ. Because the letters are addressed to the angel of each church, other scholars believe the stars are the elders or leaders or the churches' shepherds (pastor or bishop).[96] Jesus is dressed in a long, white robe of purity with a golden sash of royalty across His chest. His head and hair are white symbolizing wisdom. (See Dan. 7:9.) His eyes are like the blazing fire of judgment, all-seeing and all-knowing. His feet are strong bronze, represented in the altar of sacrifice in the tabernacle. His voice was as the sound of rushing waters, so powerful that nothing can stand in its way. From His mouth came His only weapon, the sharp double-edged sword of the Spirit -- the word of God. (See Eph. 6:17 and Heb. 4:12 and Rev. 19:15.) The brilliance of His face was like the sun. (See Ex. 34:29-35. Jesus removed the veil between God and us.) John falls at Jesus' feet to worship Him. Notice in Rev. 22:8-9 John falls at the feet of an angel to worship and is immediately rebuked. Angels are servants of God just as believers are. We are to worship God and God alone (as Father, Son, and Spirit). Jesus tells John who He is -- the First, the Last, the Living One, the One who died for our sins, and the One who was resurrected forevermore. He is victorious over death and hell, holding the prison keys of both. Jesus is making it clear He has the power and authority to bind up both forever.

John is instructed to write letters to the 7 churches identified in a clockwise pattern around the circular highway of the province of Asia. The churches are identified as follows:

1. Ephesus - Loveless Church
2. Smyrna - Persecuted Church
3. Pergamum - Tolerant Church
4. Thyatira - Corrupt Church

5. Sardis - Dead Church
6. Philadelphia - Faithful Church
7. Laodicea - Lukewarm Church

In general, the letters use the same format: (1) salutation, (2) identification of Christ by using different qualities each time from the chapter 1 list, (3) commendation of good points, (4) corrective reprimand for bad points, (5) warning, (6) challenge to do better, (7) promise for believers who stand firm in their faith. All of the descriptions or qualities of Christ used in the letters must be combined to form the unified body of Christ given in chapter 1. Thus, all believers of the churches form the universal body of Christ. All of the promises of the letters are combined in the last chapters of Revelation to form the whole picture of eternal life in Heaven. The promises are only given to those who overcome evil that can only be defeated by the blood of the Lamb.

Two churches received no commendations: Sardis and Laodicea. Two others received no reprimands: Smyrna and Philadelphia. Laodicea received the strongest warning of all.

Food for Thought: What response would you have for your flock if Jesus sent you a letter like Laodicea's? Like Philadelphia's? Would a letter from God change your church? Your community? You?

December 28
Bible Readings: Revelation 4:1 - 8:6

Now John is given a chance to see into Heaven and view God's throne. First, he sees a door into Heaven standing open. The clear trumpet voice of Jesus commands John to come see the future. As always, Jesus is the gateway, the only way, into Heaven. Instantly, John was transformed into the spirit state. There upon the throne was God who had the appearance of jasper and carnelian. (These stones cannot be definitely identified because the Hebrews assigned gem names based on color and hardness.) Both the jasper and carnelian were red stones. The carnelian is also translated ruby, sardin, and sardius.[5] A dark green emerald that circled around the throne contrasts with this ruby red. (Rainbow can be translated as arch or circle.) Surrounding God's throne were the 24 thrones of the 24 elders. The 24 elders are commonly believed to be the 12 patriarchs (sons of Israel) representing the church of the Old Testament and the 12 apostles representing the church of the New Testament.[100] These elders have distinct characteristics. They are seated, indicating their work is completed, and they are wearing white robes of purity and gold crowns of royalty. From the throne of God came lightning, rumblings, and thunder. (See also Ex. 19:16, Ezek. 1:13, Ps 18:13-15.) Before the throne are 7 torches or lamps representing the complete fullness of the Holy Spirit who has carried out His work on earth to completion. Stretched out in front of this scene is a vast 'sea' of crystal. There are several points to note. Many scholars believe the immense sea to be a chasm or barrier between God and man or good and evil. This interpretation is supported by the fact the New Jerusalem does not have a sea (Rev. 21:1) because there is no more evil. The redeemed believers must cross the sea (gulf) likened unto the Israelites crossing the Red Sea.[100] Also note, the sea is crystal clear, not tainted with the dirt and filth of sin. Any element touching God's throne would have to be free of contamination and precious in value. Kings generally had a pavement of precious stone leading to their thrones. By comparison, God's pavement was enormous symbolizing His superiority. (Also, see Ex. 24:10 and Rev. 15:2-3.)

Surrounding God's throne are 4 guardians. They are very similar to the four living creatures described in Ezekiel 1 (See Aug. 15 lesson). Rev. 4:8 (Isa. 6:2) tells us each creature had 6 wings. The creatures were totally covered with eyes. As guardians of the throne, they were ever alert and all seeing. They worshipped God day and night and were responsible for calling forth the judgments (Rev. 6:1,3,5,7). Every time the creatures praised God (Isa. 6:3), the 24 elders laid their crowns before the throne and praised His glory, honor, and power as the Creator of the universe. The creatures praise God's innate qualities while the elders praise God's glory in creation.[96]

John now sees a scroll in the mighty right Hand of God. It is written on front and back and is a book in roll form. For an idea of size, scrolls were usually 8-10 inches high and 10-35 feet long! The Revelation would require a scroll 15 feet long whereas Luke would need 32 feet. The writing was done in narrow columns about 3 inches wide. The fact that both sides were used indicates the quantity of the contents.[101] Seven seals were used to protect the secrecy and authority of the documents. By Roman law, 7 witnesses were needed to validate a will. Each witness affixed his personal seal on the closed document.[96] In the case of God's scroll, an angel calls out to all of Heaven, hell, and earth for one who is worthy to open and read from the scroll of God. Described as the Lion of the tribe of Judah (Gen. 49:9), the Root of David (Isa. 11:1, 10), and victor over death, Jesus is able to open the seals of God. Jesus is seen as a slain Lamb, standing in the center of the throne. (Remember He is in the Father and the Father is in Him.) He has 7 horns (complete power), 7 eyes (perfect all-seeing justice), and the fullness of the Holy Spirit. When He takes the scroll, all knees throughout the universe bow (Isa. 45:23; Rom. 14:11; Phil. 2:10) and all tongues confess that Jesus is worthy to reign forever.

The Lamb opens the first seal and the white horse of the Conqueror comes forth. (Review Sept. 27 lesson.) He is crowned as victor and rides forth in conquest. The second seal is broken and a red horse rides out. Its rider carries a large sword and is endowed with the power to bring about world war. Death will come by the sword. The third seal is broken and a black horse appears. The scales for measuring food are in his hand. A voice announces a prophecy concerning famine. In 92 A.D. Domitian ordered that half of the vineyards in Italy be destroyed and no new ones could be planted. The vacated ground was to be planted in grain. Bread, oil, and wine were the primary food staples. The announcement is that a man could only make enough money in one day to buy food for himself. How would he provide for his family? The famine would be severe, but survival was possible as some food would be available.[96] The latter part of the statement seems to be a warning against further destruction of the vineyards and any damage to the olive groves. The fourth seal is broken and a pale horse of Death appears with Hades following behind. We have a picture of the grim reaper bringing death by sword, famine, plagues, or wild beasts to be visited upon one-fourth of the world's population. Hades or hell follows closely to glean all the souls it can get. When the fifth seal is opened, John sees all the souls of the martyred saints under the altar. They pray to be avenged. This appears to be the altar of incense where their prayers are mingled with the incense offered before God. The martyred souls are given white robes of purity and told to be patient a little longer until others destined to be martyrs for the faith join them. God's response includes a reward, rest, and reason for the delay.[96] The indication here is that believers will see their persecutors judged and condemned. The sixth seal is broken and a great earthquake occurs. The sun turns black (no light can penetrate the atmospheric particle content). Stars fall from the sky. The heavens appear to be rolled away from our sight (Heb. 1:10-12). Mountains and islands are moved out-of-place. Christians are raptured. Every person on earth seeks refuge in any available crevice or behind any barrier. They beg to die rather than endure the Judgment. Then John sees 4 angels holding back the 4 winds (Isa. 11:12; Ezek. 7:2) of destruction awaiting the command to release. Another angel comes forth out of the east and declares that he must first seal the 144,000 from the tribes of Israel. His seal is placed on the foreheads of 12,000 from each tribe except Dan. To Messianic Jews, this is further evidence that the primary antichrist will come from the tribe of Dan. Then a great multitude of those saved during the Great Tribulation appear before Jesus. Their robes have been washed in the blood of the Lamb represented by their pure white color. The palm branches they carry symbolize the peace that comes from their victory over persecution. Every nation, tribe, people, and language is represented among this group. All of Heaven falls down before God to worship Him in hymns. The promises of Jesus are being fulfilled. (See Isa. 49:10; John 6:51; John 4:13; Rev. 2:17.) Finally, the seventh seal is opened. It marks completion of the seal judgments and total silence occurs for half an hour in anticipation of the judgments to come. The 7 archangels stand before God and are given 7 trumpets, ready to begin the trumpet judgments. An angel brings incense and mixes it with the prayers of the saints presenting it on the incense altar before God. The angel takes fire from the altar and hurls it at earth. When He does, thunder, rumblings, and lightning once again are judgment's trademark. Another earthquake occurs.

Food for Thought: Angels are given much power. Just think, we are going to be their judges!

December 29
<u>Bible Readings: Revelation 8:7 - 13:18</u>

The 7 angels prepare to sound the trumpet judgments.

Trumpet	Judgment
1	Hail and fire mixed with blood hurled to earth - 1/3 earth burned, 1/3 trees burned, all grass burned
2	Huge blazing mountain-like object thrown into sea - 1/3 sea turned to blood, 1/3 sea creatures die, 1/3 ships destroyed
3	Blazing meteor falls from sky - 1/3 of fresh water turned bitter causing many people to die
4	1/3 of sun gone, 1/3 of moon gone, 1/3 of stars gone, 1/3 day gone, 1/3 night gone - blackness
5	Devil opens the Abyss and smoke boils out blocking all natural light - Locusts poured out with poison scorpion tails. Their mission is only to torture people who are not sealed by the Lamb. This lasts 5 months. These locusts have gold coloring on top of their heads, faces that resemble humans, hairy-looking antennae, insatiable appetites (96), extremely hard precipices, wings that beat so rapidly that loud sounds come from their flapping, and tails like scorpions that sting. Their king is the devil (also known as Satan, Abaddon, and Apollyon).
6	Voice from the horns of the incense altar saying, "Release the angels of destruction from the Euphrates." 1/3 of mankind killed by the three plagues of fire, smoke, and sulfur from the 200,000,000 cavalry troops. Troops wear vibrant red, blue, and yellow breastplates and ride horses having heads like lions with fire, smoke, and sulfur coming from their mouths. Their tails are like snakes but their mouths are deadly.
7	Loud heavenly voices announce Judgment Day has arrived. All elders in Heaven fall down and worship God. God's Temple in Heaven is opened and the Ark of the Covenant is revealed. Again there is lightning, rumblings, thunder, earthquake, and now a great hailstorm.

The first trumpet judgment is an unusual mix of ice and fire made even more unusual by blood. Blood may be symbolic for a red substance such as the red Sahara Desert sands. Rains have been recorded as late as 1901 in Italy as being very red from this sand contamination. Refer to Zech. 13:8-9 concerning the one-third prophesy. With so much vegetation gone, famine is certain. This is similar to the 7th plague of the Egyptians prior to the exodus.[96]

The second trumpet judgment sounds very much like a severe volcanic eruption. In the state of Washington, Mount St. Helens lost its entire north wall from what was actually a moderate volcanic eruption. When Vesuvius erupted in 79 A.D., it destroyed the cities of Herculaneum and Pompeii and much of the coast. Islands are made from volcanic eruptions beneath the sea. The heat and molten rock destroy life for miles around. The first Egyptian plague involved turning the Nile into blood.[96]

The third trumpet judgment appears to be a continuation of the above plague. Both salt water (2nd trumpet) and fresh water are now affected. The fourth trumpet judgment corresponds to the ninth plague of darkness. The fifth trumpet judgment is a much more horrifying form of Egypt's eight plague. When the sixth trumpet sounds, people lose their lives similar to the tenth plague of Egypt when the death angel struck down their firstborn. The seventh trumpet announces a complete condemnation on evil much like the scene at the Red Sea when Egypt's army was consumed.

Imagine having survived the first 4 trumpet judgments only to hear the scream of an eagle (whose eyesight can spot the tiniest victim below) that three worse woes were yet to come! But Revelation states the people still do not repent even after the 6th trumpet! A warning is shouted throughout the world by another archangel. The seven thunders represent the completion of all warnings. The antichrist is about to be loosed on the earth.[102] John is instructed to take the little scroll from the angel and eat it, just as Ezekiel did in Eze. 2:9-3:3 and as Jeremiah prophesied in Jer. 15:16-17. In the Old Testament cases, the little scroll represented God's word. In Revelation, we must assume the scroll contains God's pronouncement or historical account of the terrible judgment about to come. It is sweet to believers but bitter to those condemned. John is being commissioned or called to take God's revelation to the world.[100]

John is given a measuring stick to measure the Temple sanctuary in Jerusalem along with the altar. He is also told to count the number of worshipers. This is done so all can be protected, sealed against the final judgment. For 3.5 years (42 months) the Gentiles will dominate Jerusalem. Some interpret 3.5 years as a standard for a period of distress.[102] Others interpret it literally.[96] The problem with interpreting this passage is that the Romans destroyed the Jerusalem Temple more than 25 years prior to the Revelation and it was never rebuilt. So what Temple is being measured? Could it refer to some future Temple such as Ezekiel's? Currently, the Jews are working laboriously on researching and collecting materials needed for a new Temple. They have discovered the exact components of the holy incense. Many of the needed building materials have already been stockpiled[103] awaiting the time the Jews regain control of the Temple Mount.

God will raise two witnesses, believed by most scholars to be Moses and Elijah, to testify to the world. Other suggestions include Peter and Paul or the Law and the Prophets. But compare Rev. 11:6 with 1 Kings 17:1 and Ex. 7:20. Their sackcloth clearly depicts their prophet status and mourning over the evil in the people. Deut. 19:15 and 17:6 state Jewish law requires at least two witnesses before a man can be condemned. The witnesses will stand as the olive trees of Zech. 4 continually proclaiming Jesus Christ as the Light of the world for 3.5 years.[96] During that time, they have the power to use their mouths as flamethrowers to consume anyone trying to harm them. Then the devil will rise up and kill them. For 3.5 days the people will celebrate. At the end of that time, God will bring them back to life! They ascend into Heaven on a cloud just like Jesus did -- and the earth begins to quake. One-tenth of the city is destroyed and 7,000 people die.

Notice the three woes or last three judgments have scenes or mini-dramas between them. God gives mankind every possible chance to turn to Him. He doesn't charge an already weakened enemy but instead chooses to send His message of love. With the seventh trumpet judgment, Jesus presents the Kingdom of God and the feared Judgment Day is at hand.[96] Notice also, that each stage of the Revelation is announced by powerful natural phenomena used almost as a giant fireworks display from nature. At the beginning of John's vision there were lightning, thunder, and rumblings (Rev. 4:5). Between the seal judgments and the trumpet judgments, there were lightning, thunder, rumblings, and earthquake (Rev. 8:5). After the trumpet judgments, all of the previous occur plus a great hailstorm.

The next scene in the drama is best understood if we first know who is assigned to each part.[102] (This is one of many interpretations.)

1. Woman - Israel
2. Child - Jesus Christ
3. Dragon - Satan (leviathan, devil)
4. Michael - archangel and commander of God's army
5. Beast from the sea - Roman Empire[100] - antichrist
6. Beast from the land - administrators of emperor worship (includes false prophet, pagan priests, government officials)
7. Saints - believers[102]

The Israelites are shown in their most glorious moment giving birth to the Messiah. Satan appears as the complete ruler (7 heads) who is extremely mighty (10 horns)(Dan. 7:24). (Recall Marduk? This chief pagan god of Babylon was depicted as a red sea dragon on the raised carvings of his temple.) Archangel Michael and God's army kick Satan out of Heaven (a fallen angel) along with Satan's followers, one-third of the angels. The blood of Jesus, God's Lamb, defeats Satan. He tries to kill the Messiah but fails. The Messiah will live victoriously and be resurrected to eternal life with the Father. Israelites will flee from persecution for 3.5 years by going into the wilderness of Asia Minor. Israelites escape on the arms (wings) of God. The devil (sea dragon) tries to drown the Israelites (See Ex. 19:4 and Ps. 124.), but the unusual natural phenomenon (from God) rescues it. While under God's protection, the Israelites spread throughout the world only to become the target of Satan's attacks. The Roman Empire rose up with a mighty power. (Compare Rev. 13:1-4 to Daniel 7.) It blasphemed God through its emperor worship. But one of its many emperors is mortally wounded and then healed (Nero). This miraculous recovery results in a huge following of the emperor. He turned into a vicious beast, practicing every type of vile immorality and violence. Those followers of the beast are condemned. For 3.5 years, he persecuted Christians. But Israel patiently and faithfully endured.

Then a second beast arose as the imperial priesthood. This group of collective individuals represents false teachers and appears as a false lamb or antichrist. The beast was able to perform sorcery and magic of all kinds resulting in miraculous signs. He has the power to revive the empire of the first beast. All people are commanded to receive a mark (666) on their right hand or forehead to show they belong to the empire. (No one is allowed to buy or sell any products without the mark. Six is the number of man who was created on the sixth day in Gen. 1.) [A Hebrew letter that resembles a 'W' is a 'sin' (pronounced sheen)(also can be spelled shin). It is put on the outside of the prayer phylacteries and the leather strap around the wrist that hold the phylactery is tied through the fingers to form a 'W.' 'W' is the first letter of the Hebrew word Shaddai or Almighty God.[103] If you write 666 with a 45-degree slant to the left, draw a line between the tops of the numbers, and then turn it upside-down, you have a close resemblance to a 'sin.' Also, the Hebrew letter for 6 is 'waw' or the symbol '1'. Three of those together written with a left slant form a false 'W.' The antichrist even tries to copy the symbol of Almighty God.[103]] This second beast becomes known as the false prophet.[100] He is an agent of the devil who seeks to lead mankind away from the true God. Those without the mark of the beast will have difficulty surviving. They will become scavengers for food and goods.

Food for Thought: I don't know about you, but I will be gone to live forever with my Lord before this lesson's events occur! Praise God! Praise God, I'm a child of the King!

December 30
<u>Bible Readings: Revelation 14:1 - 19:5</u>

The Lamb of God now appears on Mt. Zion with His 144,000 sealed Israelite followers. (Many scholars believe this is a symbolic number for the church rather than a literal number.) The Messianic Jews believe the 144,000 will be very young men possibly young teenagers, who will be found pure in body and mind. God's children are singing a new song of worship to the sound of harps. Only believers can learn this special worship song.

Three angels appear. The first one proclaims the gospel to all the earth, calling for repentance. The second announces the fall of Babylon, which is generally considered to be Rome. Some scholars have further interpreted it to be the Roman Catholic Church with the Pope as the antichrist. Roman Catholicism is the only vestige left of ancient Rome. (In the 1800s, this interpretation was the foundation of the Ku Klux Klan in America. That is why they persecuted Italians initially.) Other scholars see the antichrist as Hitler, John Knox, Martin Luther, Napoleon, and many more.[102] The third angel throws the followers of the beast into the Lake of Fire. (Remember the picture of the burning Dead Sea and the burning trash heap of Jerusalem in the Hinnom Valley?)

John sees Jesus seated (indicating His work is completed) on a cloud. An angel (messenger from the Father) (Mark 13:32) calls out to Jesus that the time has come for harvest of the earth (Joel 3:13). The followers of the beast are to be trodden down, pressed, and squeezed of their life's blood outside of Jerusalem just as Christ was crucified outside the city. The picture of the blood running in the streets is interpreted to be a complete judgment of Palestine (vertically 180 miles long). The blood will be 4 feet deep over the country. Zech. 14:1-4 and Joel 3:12-16 depict heathen nations attempting a last attack on Jerusalem but are defeated.[102] (Review Oct. 2 lesson.)

God's wrath is completed in the form of 7 bowls -- each containing a different plague. Those believers reaped from the Great Tribulation are standing beside God's crystal sea singing the song of Moses and the song of the Lamb as they watch the judgment of their persecutors. The House of God is opened and 7 angels come forth. One of the living creatures (throne guardian) gives each angel a bowl of wrath with instructions to pour it out on the earth.

1. Ugly, painful sores on the followers of the beast.
2. Sea turns to blood and all sea life dies.
3. Fresh water sources turn to blood.
4. Sun blazes and scorches people.
5. Darkness covers the earth.
6. The Euphrates River dries up and kings invade from the east. (This is a reflection of Cyrus blocking the Euphrates and capturing Babylon. Also, the antichrist (Nero) was believed to be returning from the eastern country of Iran.[102]) The dragon, beast, and false prophet all spew out frogs (unclean spirits) over the land. (See Ex. 8:5-11; Ps. 105:30; Ps. 78:45.)[102] The demons gather their forces for the great battle at Armageddon believed to take place between Mt. Carmel and Jezreel near the ancient site of Meggiddo.[5] (Zech. 12:11)
7. Just as Jesus said in John 19:30, "It is finished," God now says, "It is done."[1] Again there are lightning, rumblings, thunder, severe earthquake, and hailstones. But this time the hailstones weigh 100 pounds each! Islands disappear and mountains are leveled. Rome splits into three parts and the capitals of her 10 supporting countries are destroyed.[102] (Notice we are told after the 4th and 5th plagues that the people would not repent. By the 6th plague the forces of good and evil are in full battle on earth. With the 7th plague, it is too late to repent.)

In Rev. 17, one of the angels of the bowls reveals Rome's punishment. Depicted as a great prostitute because of the evil she engaged in with other nations, Rome is described as sitting on many waters (describing ancient Babylon in Jer. 51:13[100]). The Bible has several cases where men meet God in the wilderness: Moses, Elijah, and John the Baptist. This woman appears in the desert or wilderness riding on Satan who is covered with the names of her pagan gods (his property). The woman is dressed in all the luxury Rome enjoyed. In her hand is a golden cup

(See Jer. 51:7) filled with her sins. Her name is on her forehead just as the Roman prostitutes wore nametags tied to their heads. She was drunk with the blood of martyred saints.[102]

Rome is further identified as the city of 7 hills. This was a well-known fact about the city. We are told there are also 7 kings and 5 have fallen (Augustus, Tiberius, Caligula, Claudius, Nero). The one at the time of Revelation is Vespasian. Titus, who only reigned two years, followed him. The eighth emperor is identified with the beast and is Domitian. The ten kings to come to power are presumed to come from the eastern countries where the antichrist is expected to arise. (Many scholars have now decided the antichrist will come from the U.S.A.) They will come to power for a very short time (by God's measurement) allying with the antichrist to war against Jesus Christ. Rome comes to ruins as a result of their concerted attack.[102]

An angel heralds the fall of Rome quoting prophecy from Isa. 21:9. (From this point to the end of today's lesson, proponents for the U.S.A. producing the antichrist establish their case.[103]) Some of the characteristics identified are a nation that (1) is home to all types of evil, (2) has compromised her standards to form allies with many nations, (3) has businessmen who have become rich in selling luxuries to excess, (4) has sins piled up to the heavens, (5) is rich in jewels and gold, and (6) is dressed in the finest textiles. The warning in 18:8 is assumed by most scholars to be multiple bombs over a short period of time. 'Babylon' is mourned by all nations of the earth who have come to economic ruin because of the loss. Kings, businessmen, and mariners see the smoke of her burning and mourn their resultant poverty. The destruction is so great that all life is gone. And the multitude of souls in Heaven shouted, "Amen, Hallelujah!"

Food for Thought: Regardless of who you believe the antichrist is or will be, and regardless of what city or nation you believe Babylon is or will be, one point is certain -- Jesus Christ will be coming again to take believers to Heaven and reign victorious forevermore! Are you prepared to meet God? The gift of salvation is free. To receive the gift, confess your sins, believe Jesus died and rose again for your sins, and accept Him as Lord and Savior of your life.

December 31
<u>Bible Readings: Revelation 19:6 - 22:21</u>

Today's lesson is one of endless joy. It describes the rewards waiting for God's faithful believers. To begin, believers are invited by an angel from God to a great wedding banquet of Jesus and His bride, the church. The church has prepared itself for this holy event. Her robes have been washed in the blood of the Lamb. Now they are dressed in the finest white linen. The gates of Heaven are open. Jesus, the bridegroom, is riding a white horse. He is beside us ready to judge our persecutors and conquer our enemies. (Roman generals always rode on a white horse to celebrate their triumphs.[102]) As King of all nations, Jesus wears many crowns and rules with strength and power. Many names are given Him: Faithful and True, Word of God, King of Kings, Lord of Lords. (Note these latter two names are on His robe and His thigh, for all to see. A horseman would have one on the lower part of his dress robes at eye level for all to identify him.[102]) One of his names is written on Him and is unknown to everyone else. Phil. 2:9-11 refers to the name above all others: kurios or Lord. Possibly this is the name given to Him by the Father that is too precious to even reveal to His bride. As the bride walks with her groom and King to the great wedding feast, birds are called in to await the flesh of the evil ones about to meet their fate (Ezek. 39:17-19).[102]

The forces of evil, made up of the ten kings with their nations who had supported the antichrist, gather their forces for the great Battle of Armageddon, but it is already over. The beast and the false prophet are captured and thrown into the lake of fire and burning sulfur.[100] The Word of God struck down the army having the mark of Satan. The dragon (Satan) is chained up and thrown into the bottomless pit that is locked and sealed for a thousand years.

Those martyred for the sake of Christ are resurrected to their glorified bodies and reign with Christ for a thousand years. (This is the only passage in the Bible that teaches the resurrection of martyrs before all others to reign with Christ for a thousand years before loosing the devil to reign a thousand years.[102]) This is called the first resurrection after which Satan begins a thousand year stint for gathering more recruits for a new army. We are told he will scour the earth looking for followers. (See Ezek. 38-39 in the Sept. 2 lesson.) Gog is the ruler of Magog, believed to be Asia, part of Europe, and part of Africa. (If you consider the U.S.A. to be Babylon, then that would explain elimination from this group because it was destroyed earlier. Also keep in mind, John's world was limited to Asia, Europe, and Africa. Generally considered to be flat, the earth had four corners. In referring to the "four corners of the earth," we are to interpret it to mean the whole world.) This new army of evildoers marches on Jerusalem and surrounds the Holy City. God devoured Satan's army in a fireball from Heaven. Satan was thrown into the lake of fire to live in eternal torment with his old pals the beast and false prophet.

Judgment Day is here. All the dead stand before the great white throne and the books are opened. (Notice 'books" is plural.) <u>Another</u> book called the book of life is opened. Some students of the Bible believe there are multiple books of the lost loosely based on those who adamantly rejected the Holy Spirit as compared to those just too apathetic to care.[103] I believe the number of lost souls will be so great that multiple books are needed to record all their names. Nevertheless, anyone NOT in the book of life is condemned to the second death -- spiritual death -- and the sentence is to live eternally in the lake of fire.

John sees the <u>new</u> Heaven and <u>new</u> earth descend from God. The previous Heaven and earth contained Temples and seas that are no longer. New Jerusalem is where God and men dwell together and there is no pain, tears, sorrow, or death. All who have overcome evil to believe in the Son of God and make Him Lord of their lives will inherit God's kingdom. It is brilliant, clean, and pure, illuminated only by the glory of God. (Remember the brilliance of Moses' face when he was in the Presence of God?) One of the angels who had previously poured out a bowl of wrath now measures the Holy City with a gold measuring stick. The city is cube shaped, being 1,400 miles on every side. There is a high wall around the city with 12 gates, three on each side. Each gate was named for a tribe of Israel. Each gate was made from a single pearl, a very significant choice. The world placed pain or grit in our flesh, but through the love of Jesus Christ, we had a 'covering' for our ugly agony. We could have become infected and died, but Jesus covered and protected us. The painful experience from our sins left a pearl of great worth. When the body is gone, the pearl remains.[104] (Matt. 13:46) The wall had 12 foundations, each one a gemstone, each foundation named after an apostle. (After Judas Iscariot died, the other 11 apostles elected a replacement. Paul also declared he was an apostle. We don't know whose name God will choose as the twelfth apostle.) Imagine the beautiful colors! Now imagine a city of pure gold but transparent so we can always see God! God is its light and He shines through His Son Jesus. There are a lot of 'No's' in New Jerusalem: no night, no sun, no moon, no Temple, no evil, no tears, no pain, no sorrow, no death, no impurity, no sea, no altar of burnt offering, no segregation. A river containing the water of life flows from the throne of God right through the heart of the city. A tree of life is growing on each side. Unlike Adam and Eve who were barred from eating of it because of their sin, the saints will eat from these trees forever. The trees will bear a new crop of fruit every month -- producing true fruit of the Spirit (Gal. 5:22). (See Ezek. 47:12.) Their leaves will be used to heal the hard feelings, animosity, and dislike breaches among the many different ethnic peoples. Love for all mankind will abound. The throne of God and Jesus will be within the city, the gates will always be open, and they will reign forever.[102]

Most of Rev. 22:6-21 is contained in Rev. 1. Thus, Revelation ends as it began -- with the verification that it is a message from the One and only Christ -- the Alpha and Omega, First and Last, Beginning and End, Root and Offspring of David (Isa. 11:1), bright Morning Star (Num. 24:17). Those who have been washed in the blood of the Lamb will enter God's Kingdom, eat of the tree of life, and drink from the water of life. Amen! Come, Lord Jesus!

Food for Thought: Rev. 22:18-19 serves as a warning to anyone who adds or takes away from Revelation. I do not profess to have any special insight into any book of the Bible, but God has revealed much to me personally through this study. Read, study, question, and pray for God's Word to be revealed both to you and through you. Live for Jesus, testify about Jesus, die in Jesus, and live with Jesus forever. I'll see you in the New Jerusalem!

FINAL NOTE: This is your last lesson. I hope you have developed a love of God's word during this year. Additionally, I hope that you have completed reading the Bible from Genesis to maps. God's word warms your heart and provides peace in troubled times. Only when the Word is hidden in our hearts can we be prepared to face the evil world on a daily basis. We are living in the last days. The time is short. Tell others about the saving power of Jesus Christ!

TEMPLE FACTS

Solomon's Temple:
90 feet long, 30 feet wide, 45 feet high
blocks of dressed stone
Destroyed by the Babylonians on the ninth day of the month Av in 586 BC. (Existed 410 years from 960 to 586 BC.)

Zerubbabel's Temple
90 feet high, 90 feet wide
3 courses of large stones
1 course of timber
Later, this temple was remodeled and enlarged by Herod. (Existed 446 years from 516 BC to 50 BC.)

Herod's Temple
15 stories tall (main building) [~twice the height of Zerubbabel's Temple]
Marble and gold
Destroyed by the Romans on the ninth day of the month Av in 70 AD. (Lasted six years from 64 AD to 70 AD.)

Ezekiel's Temple
~175 feet long, 105 feet wide
Never been built (see p. 267)
Believed to be Millennial Temple.

REFERENCES

1. *The Thompson Chain-Reference Bible*, New International Version (NIV), Frank Charles Thompson (Editor), Zondervan Bible Publishers, Grand Rapids, MI, 1983.

2. *Discovering Genesis 1-24: The Guideposts Bible Study Program*, Floyd W. Thatcher (General Editor), Guideposts, Carmel, NY, 1987.

3. *The Works of Josephus*, New Updated Edition, William Whiston (Translator), Hendrickson Publishers, Peabody, MA, 1999.

4. *Bible Map Insert*, Son Light Publishers, Fort Smith, AR, 1998.

5. *Nelson's Illustrated Bible Dictionary*, Herbert Lockyer, Sr. (General Editor), Guideposts, Carmel, NY, 1986.

6. *Old Testament History*, John H. Sailhamer, Zondervan Publishing House, Grand Rapids, MI, 1998.

7. *New Illustrated Bible Manners & Customs: How the People of the Bible Really Lived*, Howard E. Vos, Thomas Nelson Publishers, Nashville, TN, 1999.

8. *The American Heritage Dictionary of the English Language*, William Morris, Editor, American Heritage Publishing Co. & Houghton Mifflin Company, New York, NY, 1970.

9. *Eerdmans' Family Encyclopedia of the Bible*, Pat Alexander, Organizing Editor, Guideposts, Carmel, NY, 1978.

10. *Discovering Genesis 25-50: The Guideposts Bible Study Program*, Floyd W. Thatcher, General Editor, Guideposts, Carmel, NY, 1987.

11. *Commentary on the Old Testament: The Pentateuch*, C.F. Keil and F. Delitzsch, William B. Eerdmans Publishing Company, Grand Rapids, MI, 1976.

12. *Discovering Exodus: The Guideposts Bible Study Program*, Floyd W. Thatcher, General Editor, Guideposts, Carmel, NY, 1988.

13. *Exodus: An Introduction and Commentary*, R. Alan Cole, Inter-Varsity Press, Downers Grove, IL, 1973.

14. *The New International Commentary on the Old Testament: The Book of Leviticus*, G. J. Wenham, William B. Eerdmans Publishing Company, Grand Rapids, MI, 1979.

15. *Life Application Bible: The Living Bible*, Tyndale House Publishers, Wheaton, IL, 1971.

16. *Bible Study Commentary: Numbers*, F. B. Huey, Jr., Zondervan Publishing House, Grand Rapids, MI, 1981.

17. *Discovering Leviticus, Numbers, Deuteronomy: The Guideposts Home Bible Study Program*, Floyd W. Thatcher, General Editor, Carmel, NY, 1988.

18. *The Book of Deuteronomy: A Study Manual*, Clyde T. Francisco, Baker Book House Company, Ann Arbor, MI, 1964.

19. *Deuteronomy: An Introduction and Commentary*, J. A. Thompson, Inter-Varsity Press, Leicester, England, 1974.

20. *The Interlinear Bible: Hebrew-Greek-English*, Jay P. Green, Sr., General Editor and Translator, Hendrickson Publishers, Peabody, MA, 1985.

21. *The Gospel of Matthew*, Revised Edition, Volume 2, William Barclay, Translator, The Westminster Press, Philadelphia, PA, 1975.

22. *The Merck Manual Home Edition*, Merck Sharp & Dohme Research Laboratories, Merck & Co., Inc., Whitehouse Station, NJ, 1995-2001.

23. *Commentary on the Old Testament: Joshua, Judges, Ruth, I & II Samuel*, C.F. Keil and F. Delitzsch, William B. Eerdmans Publishing Company, Grand Rapids, MI, 1976.

24. *Handfuls on Purpose: For Christian Workers and Bible Students*, James Smith and Robert Lee, William B. Eerdmans Publishing Company, Grand Rapids, MI, 1971.

25. *Commentary on the Old Testament: I & II Kings, I & II Chronicles, Ezra, Nehemiah*, C.F. Keil and F. Delitzsch, William B. Eerdmans Publishing Company, Grand Rapids, MI, 1976.

26. *Cambridge Bible for Schools and Colleges: The Book of Psalms I-XLI*, A.F. Kirkpatrick, At the University Press, Cambridge, 1900.

27. *Psalms 1-72: An Introduction and Commentary*, Derek Kidner, Inter-Varsity Press, Downers Grove, IL, 1973.

28. *Psalms 73-150: A Commentary on Books III-V of the Psalms*, Derek Kidner, Inter-Varsity Press, Downers Grove, IL, 1973.

29. *New American Standard Bible, The Open Bible Edition*, The Lockman Foundation, Thomas Nelson Publishers, Nashville, TN, 1979

30. *Discovering Kings & Chronicles: The Guideposts Bible Study Program*, Floyd W. Thatcher, General Editor, Carmel, NY, 1989.

31. *Commentary on the Old Testament: Proverbs, Ecclesiastes, Song of Solomon*, C. F. Keil and F. Delitzsch, William B. Eerdmans Publishing Company, Grand Rapids, MI, 1976.

32. *The New Scofield Reference Bible: Authorized King James Version*, C.I. Scofield, Editor, Oxford University Press, New York, NY, 1969.

33. *Eerdmans' Handbook to the Bible*, David Alexander and Pat Alexander, Editors, William B. Eerdmans Publishing Company, Grand Rapids, MI, 1973.

34. *The Broadman Bible Commentary: Proverbs - Isaiah*, Vol. 5, Clifton J. Allen, General Editor, Broadman Press, Nashville, TN, 1971.

35. *Discovering Proverbs, Ecclesiastes, Song of Songs*, Floyd W. Thatcher, General Editor, Guideposts, Carmel, NY, 1989.

36. *Easton's Bible Dictionary*, 3rd Edition, M. G. Easton, Thomas Nelson, Nashville, TN, 1897.

37. *The Broadman Bible Commentary: Hosea - Malachi*, Vol. 7, Clifton J. Allen, General Editor, Broadman Press, Nashville, TN, 1972.

38. *Tyndale Old Testament Commentary: The Book of Hosea*, David Allan Hubbard, Inter-Varsity Press, Downers Grove, IL, 1989.

39. *Discovering Isaiah*, Floyd W. Thatcher, General Editor, Guideposts, Carmel, NY, 1989.

40. *Discovering the Minor Prophets: Micah through Malachi*, Floyd W. Thatcher, General Editor, Guideposts, Carmel, NY, 1990.

41. *The One Year Book of Hymns*, Robert K. Brown and Mark R. Norton, Tyndale House Publishers, Wheaton, IL, 1995.

42. *Commentary on the Old Testament: Isaiah*, C.F. Keil and F. Delitzsch, William B. Eerdmans Publishing Company, Grand Rapids, MI, 1976.

43. *The Book of Isaiah*, Vol. 1-3, Edward J. Young, William B. Eerdmans Publishing Company, Grand Rapids, MI, 1969.

44. *Baptist Hymnal*, Convention Press, Nashville, TN, 1975.

45. *The New International Commentary on the Old Testament: The Books of Nahum, Habakkuk, and Zephaniah*, O. Palmer Robertson, William B. Eerdmans Publishing Company, Grand Rapids, MI, 1990.

46. *Commentary on the Old Testament: Jeremiah, Lamentations*, C.F. Keil and F. Delitzsch, William B. Eerdmans Publishing Company, Grand Rapids, MI, 1977.

47. *Discovering Jeremiah & Lamentations*, Floyd W. Thatcher, General Editor, Guideposts, Carmel, NY, 1990.

48. *Atlas of the Bible Lands*, C.S. Hammond & Co., New York, NY, 1959.

49. *The New International Commentary on the Old Testament: The Book of Jeremiah*, J. A. Thompson, William B. Eerdmans Publishing Company, Grand Rapids, MI, 1980.

50. *Discovering Ezekiel and Daniel*, Floyd W. Thatcher, General Editor, Guideposts, Carmel, NY, 1990.

51. *Commentary on the Old Testament: Ezekiel, Daniel*, C.F. Keil and F. Delitzsch, William B. Eerdmans Publishing Company, Grand Rapids, MI, 1976.

52. *The Broadman Bible Commentary: Jeremiah - Daniel*, Clifton J. Allen, General Editor, Broadman Press, Nashville, TN, 1971.

53. *Introduction to the Old Testament*, Roland K. Harrison, William B. Eerdmans Publishing Company, Grand Rapids, MI, 1969.

54. *The Revelation of John*, Vol. 1, William Barclay, John Knox Press, Louisville, KY, 1976.

55. *Cambridge Bible for Schools and Colleges: The Book of The Prophet Jeremiah together with the Lamentations*, A.W. Streane, At the University Press, Cambridge, 1888.

56. *The Broadman Bible Commentary: Esther-Psalms*, Clifton J. Allen, General Editor, Broadman Press, Nashville, TN, 1971.

57. *Biblical Numerology: A Basic Study of the Use of Numbers in the Bible*, John J. Davis, Baker Book House, Grand Rapids, MI, 1968.

58. *Job: A Study Guide*, D. David Garland, Zondervan Publishing House, Grand Rapids, MI, 1971.

59. *Commentary on the Old Testament: Psalms*, C.F. Keil and F. Delitzsch, William B. Eerdmans Publishing Company, Grand Rapids, MI, 1976.

60. *An In-Depth Look at the Prophecies of the Seventy Weeks of Daniel: Prophecies of the First Sixty-Nine Weeks Fulfilled*, www.bibleinsight.com.

61. *The Seventy Weeks of Daniel 9*, www.gobedo.com.

62. *Second Temple Times*, Lambert Dolphin, www.templemount.org.

63. *Discovering Ezra, Nehemiah, & Esther*, Floyd W. Thatcher, General Editor, Guideposts, Carmel, NY, 1989.

64. *The Bible as History*, 2nd Revised Edition, Werner Keller, William Morrow and Company, New York, NY, 1981.

65. *Commentary on the Old Testament: Minor Prophets*, C.F. Keil and F. Delitzsch, William B. Eerdmans Publishing Company, Grand Rapids, MI, 1977.

66. *Discovering the Minor Prophets*, Floyd W. Thatcher, General Editor, Guideposts, Carmel, NY, 1990.

67. *Esther: Character Under Pressure*, Patty Pell, InterVarsity Press, Downers Grove, IL, 1995.

68. *In the Footsteps of the Messiah*, "Purim: And then came Mordecai," "Purim: For Such a Time as This," Joseph Good, TBN videotape, 1990.

69. *The Broadman Bible Commentary: 1 Samuel - Nehemiah*, Clifton J. Allen, General Editor, Broadman Press, Nashville, TN, 1970.

70. *The Gospel of Luke*, William Barclay, The Westminster Press, Philadelphia, PA, 1956.

71. *The Gospel of Mark*, Revised Edition, William Barclay, The Westminster Press, Philadelphia, PA, 1975.

72. *The Gospel of John*, Revised Edition, Vol. 1, William Barclay, The Westminster Press, Philadelphia, PA, 1975.

73. *The Broadman Bible Commentary: Luke-John*, Clifton J. Allen, General Editor, Broadman Press, Nashville, TN, 1970.

74. *The Gospel of Matthew*, Revised Edition, Vol. 1, William Barclay, The Westminster Press, Philadelphia, PA, 1975.

75. *The Broadman Bible Commentary: Matthew-Mark*, Clifton J. Allen, General Editor, Broadman Press, Nashville, TN, 1970.

76. *The Revelation*, Joseph Good, audiotapes, Hatikva Ministries, Nederland, TX.

77. *The New International Commentary on the New Testament: The Gospel According to John*, Leon Morris, Wm B. Eerdmans Publishing Co., Grand Rapids, MI, 1971.

78. *The Gospel of Matthew*, Revised Edition, Vol. 2, William Barclay, The Westminister Press, Philadelphia, PA, 1975.

79. *The Gospel of John*, Revised Edition, Vol. 2, William Barclay, The Westminister Press, Philadelphia, PA, 1975.

80. *Everything Made Simple* @ www.whyprophets.com.

81. *The New International Commentary on the New Testament: The Gospel According to Mark*, William Lane, Wm B. Eerdmans Publishing Co., Grand Rapids, MI, 1974.

82. *The Life and Times of Jesus the Messiah*, Alfred Edershem, William B. Eerdmans' Publishing Co., Grand Rapids, MI, 1972.

83. *The New International Commentary on the New Testament: The Gospel According to Luke*, William Lane, Wm B. Eerdmans Publishing Co., Grand Rapids, MI, 1977.

84. *The Acts of the Apostles*, Rev. Edition, William Barclay, Westminister John Knox Press, Louisville, KY, 1976.

85. *The Broadman Bible Commentary: Acts - 1 Corinthians*, Clifton J. Allen, General Editor, Broadman Press, Nashville, TN, 1970.

86. *The Tyndale New Testament Commentaries: 1 and 2 Thessalonians*, Rev. Edition, Leon Morris, William B. Eerdmans Publishing Co., Grand Rapids, MI, 1989.

87. *The Broadman Bible Commentary: 2 Corinthians - Philemon*, Clifton J. Allen, General Editor, Broadman Press, Nashville, TN, 1971.

88. *Everyday Victory for Everyday People*, First Place Bible Study Series, Gospel Light, U.S.A., 2001.

89. *The Epistle of Paul to the Romans*, F.F. Bruce, Wm. B. Eerdmans Publishing Company, Grand Rapids, MI, 1963.

90. *A Study Guide Commentary: Romans*, Bruce Corley and Curtis Vaughan, Zondervan Publishing House, Grand Rapids, MI, 1976.

91. *The New International Commentary on the New Testament: The Book of Acts*, F.F. Bruce, Wm B. Eerdmans Publishing Co., Grand Rapids, MI, 1976.

92. *Discovering Acts: The Guideposts Study Program*, Floyd W. Thatcher, General Editor, Guideposts, Carmel, NY, 1985.

93. *The New International Commentary on the New Testament: Ephesians and Colossians*, E. K. Simpson and F.F. Bruce, Wm B. Eerdmans Publishing Co., Grand Rapids, MI, 1975.

94. *Discovering Ephesians: The Guideposts Study Program*, Floyd W. Thatcher, General Editor, Guideposts, Carmel, NY, 1986.

95. *The Tyndale New Testament Commentaries: The Pastoral Epistles*, Donald Guthrie, Wm B. Eerdmans Publishing Company, Grand Rapids, MI, 1974.

96. *The Broadman Bible Commentary: Hebrews - Revelation*, Clifton J. Allen, General Editor, Broadman Press, Nashville, TN, 1972.

97. *Discovering James, Peter, John, & Jude: The Guideposts Study Program*, Floyd W. Thatcher, General Editor, Guideposts, Carmel, NY, 1987.

98. *The Tyndale New Testament Commentaries: The Epistle to the Hebrews*, Thomas Hewitt, Wm B. Eerdmans Publishing Company, Grand Rapids, MI, 1976.

99. *Discovering Revelation: The Guideposts Study Program*, Floyd W. Thatcher, General Editor, Guideposts, Carmel, NY, 1987.

100. *A Commentary on the Revelation of John*, George Eldon Ladd, William B. Eerdmans Publishing Company, Grand Rapids, MI, 1972.

101. *The Revelation of John*, Rev. Ed., Vol. 1, William Barclay, Westminster John Knox Press, Louisville, KY, 1976.

102. *The Revelation of John*, Rev. Ed., Vol. 2, William Barclay, Westminster John Knox Press, Louisville, KY, 1976.

103. *Revelation*, (audiotapes), Joseph Good, Hatikva Ministries, Nederland, TX.

104. *Pearl School*, (audiotape), Jerry Smith, Companion message to The Secret, 1997.

105. *The Tyndale New Testament Commentaries: The Epistles of John*, John R. W. Stott, William B. Eerdmans Publishing Company, Grand Rapids, MI, 1978.

106. *The Epistles of John*, F.F. Bruce, William B. Eerdmans Publishing Company, Grand Rapids, MI, 1970.

107. *New Testament Words*, William Barclay, The Westminister Press, Philadelphia, PN, 1974.

108. *Nelson's Complete Book of Bible Maps & Charts*, Thomas Nelson Publishers, Atlanta, GA, 1996.

109. *God's Amazing Creation—Human Cells*, Dr. Dick Couey, First Place Motivational Audiocassettes, Audiocassette 2, Gospel Light, Ventura, CA, 2001.

110. *Ezekiel*, Ralph H. Alexander, Moody Press, Chicago, IL, 1976. Note: All graphics for Ezekiel's temple in the September 5th lesson are from this source.

111. *Ryrie Study Bible, Expanded Edition*, New American Standard Version (NAS), Charles Caldwell Ryrie, Moody Press, Chicago, IL, 1995.

112. *Kingdom of Priests: A History of Old Testament Israel*, Eugene H. Merrill, Baker Academic, Grand Rapids, MI, 2006.

SCRIPTURE INDEX

Old Testament		19:15-29	17	34:5-31	31	2:11-25	39
		19:30-38	17	35:1-10	31	3:1-6	39
GENESIS	page	20:1-13	18	35:11-29	31	3:7-22	39
1:1-8	9	20:14-18	18	36:1-19	32	4:1-23	39
1:9-30	9	21:1-7	18	36:20-39	32	4:24-31	39
1:31	9	21:8-19	18	36:40-43	32	5:1-14	41
2:1-4a	9	21:20-21	18	37:1-11	33	5:15-23	41
2:4b-22	9	21:22-34	18	37:12-35	33	6:1-13	41
2:23-25	9	22:1-14	20	37:36	33	6:14-27	39
3:1-15	9	22:15-24	20	38:1-19	33	6:28-30	41
3:16-24	9	23:1-18	20	38:20-30	33	7:1-24	41
4:1-16	11	23:19-20	20	39:1-18	35	7:25	41
4:17-26	11	24:1-9	22	39:19-23	35	8:1-24	41
5:1-2	11	24:10-32	22	40:1-19	35	8:25-32	41
5:3-32	11	24:33-61	22	40:20-23	35	9:1-26	43
6:1-8	12	24:62-67	22	41:1-24	35	9:27-35	43
6:9-21	12	25:1-6	23	41:25-46a	35	10:1-2	43
6:22	12	25:7-10	23	41:46b-57	35	10:3-23	43
7:1-23	12	25:11	23	42:1-12	35,36	10:24-29	43
7:24	12	25:12-18	23	42:13-34	36	11:1-10	43
8:1-22	12	25:19-28	23	42:35-38	36	12:1-20	43
9:1-17	12	25:29-34	23	43:1-15	36	12:21-36	43
9:18-29	12	26:1-22	23	43:16-34	36	12:37-42	43
10:1-31	13	26:23-35	23,24	44:1-5	36	12:43-50	43
10:32	13	27:1-4	24	44:6-34	36	12:51	43
11:1-9	13	27:5-29	24	45:1-20	36,38	13:1-22	43,44
11:10-17	13	27:30-41	24	45:21-28	38	14:1-18	44
11:18-26	13	27:42-46	24	46:1-27	38	14:19-31	44
11:27-32	13	28:1-17	24	46:28-34	38	15:1-18	44
12:1-9	14	28:18-22	24	47:1-19	38	15:19-25a	44,45
12:10-20	14	29:1-8	27	47:20-31	38	15:25b-27	45
13:1-18	14	29:9-30	27	48:1-7	38	16:1-21	45
14:1-7	14	29:31-35	27	48:8-20	38	16:22-36	45
14:8-24	14	30:1-21	27	48:21-22	38	17:1-7	45
15:1-6	16	30:22-36	27	49:1-12	38	17:8-16	45
15:7-21	16	30:37-43	27	49:13-26	38	18:1-12	45
16:1-12	16	31:1-13	28	49:27-33	38	18:13-27	45
16:13-16	16	31:14-35	28	50:1-9	38	19:1-25	46
17:1-22	16	31:36-55	28	50:10-26	38	20:1-20	46
17:23-27	16	32:1-21	28			20:21-26	46
18:1-8	17	32:22-32	28	EXODUS	page	21:1-11	77
18:9-15	17	33:1-11	28	1:1-7	39	21:12-14	76
18:16-33	17	33:12-20	28	1:8-22	39	21:15	76
19:1-14	17	34:1-4	31	2:1-10	39	21:16	76

SCRIPTURE INDEX

Ref	Page	Ref	Page	Ref	Page	Ref	Page
21:17	84	29:35-46	49	4:22-35	72	18:23-30	78
21:18-21	76	30:1-16	49	5:1-13	72	19:1-2	75
21:22-27	76,77	30:17-38	49	5:14-19	73	19:3a	84
21:28-36	77	31:1-11	49	6:1-7	73	19:3b	69
22:1	77	31:12-17	69	6:8-13	71	19:4	68
22:2-3a	76	31:18	49	6:14-23	71	19:5-8	72
22:3b	77	32:1-6	50	6:24-30	72	19:9-10	84
22:4	77	32:7-20	50	7:1-10	73	19:11	77
22:5-6	77	32:21-35	50	7:11-21	72	19:12	77
22:7-17	77	33:1-6	50	7:22-27	82	19:13	77
22:18	69	33:7-23	50	7:28-36	72	19:14	84
22:19	78	34:1-7	50	7:37-38	73	19:15	76
22:20	68	34:8-16	50	8:1-21	53	19:16-18	84
22:21-24	84	34:17	68	8:22-36	53	19:19a	75
22:25-27	77	34:18	70	9:1-7	53	19:19b	75
22:28a	69	34:19-20	69	9:8-24	53	19:19c	75
22:28b	76	34:21	69	10:1-3	53	19:20-22	78
22:29-30	69	34:22	70	10:4-20	53	19:23-25	69
22:31	82	34:23	70	11:1-23	82	19:26a	69
23:1-2	76	34:24	70	11:24-40	82	19:26b	82
23:3	76	34:25	73	11:41-47	82	19:27-28	68
23:4-5	84	34:26a	69	12:1-8	74	19:29	78
23:6	76	34:26b	82	13:1-8	80	19:30	69
23:7	76	34:27-35	50	13:9-28	80	19:31	69
23:8	76	35:1-2	69	13:29-59	80	19:32-34	84
23:9	84	35:3	69	14:1-9	74	19:35-37	77
23:10-11	73	35:4-29	51	14:10-32	74	20:1-5	68
23:12	69	35:30-35	51	14:33-47	80	20:6-8	69
23:13	68	36:1-19	51	14:48-57	80	20:9	84
23:14-17	70	36:20-38	51	15:1-12	80	20:10	78
23:18	73	37:1-9	51	15:13-15	74	20:11	78
23:19a	69	37:10-29	51	15:16-18	80	20:12-14	78
23:19b	82	38:1-7	51	15:19-27	80	20:15-16	78
23:20-22	46	38:8-31	51	15:28-30	74	20:17	78
23:23-33	46	39:1-26	51,52	15:31-33	80	20:18-21	78
24:1-11	46	39:27-43	52	16:1-14	70	20:22-24	78
24:12-18	46	40:1-11	52	16:15-34	70	20:25-26	82
25:1-9	47	40:12-35	52	17:1-7	72	20:27	69
25:10-40	47	40:36-38	57	17:8-9	71	21:1-9	73
26:1-30	47			17:10-16	82	21:10-24	73
26:31-37	47	LEVITICUS	page	18:1-5	78	22:1-9	73
27:1-19	47	1:1-9	71	18:6-11	78	22:10-16	73
27:20-21	47	1:10-17	71	18:12-19	78	22:16-30	73
28:1-43	47	2:1-16	71	18:20	78	22:31-33	85
29:1-9	49	3:1-17	72	18:21	68	23:1-3	69
29:10-34	49	4:1-21	72	18:22	78	23:4-14	70

SCRIPTURE INDEX

23:15-21	70	5:5-10	77	21:1-18a	60	DEUTERONOMY	pg.
23:22	84	5:11-31	78	21:18b-35	60	1:1-18	66
23:23-25	70	6:1-5	75	22:1-20	61	1:19-40	66
23:26-36	70	6:6-21	75	22:21-41	61	1:41-46	66
23:37-38	70	6:22-27	73	23:1-16	61	2:1-15	66
23:39-41	70	7:1-5	54	23:17-30	61	2:16-37	66
23:42-43	70	7:6-35	54	24:1-9	61	3:1-11	66
23:44	70	7:36-59	54	24:10-25	61	3:12-22	66
24:1-4	73	7:60-88	54	25:1-18	62	3:23-29	66
24:5-9	73	7:89	54	26:1-11	63	4:1-24	66
24:10-16	69	8:1-4	54	26:12-27	63	4:25-40	66
24:17	76	8:5-13	54	26:28-43	63	4:41-43	64
24:18	77	8:14-15	54	26:44-62	63	4:44-49	66
24:19-20	76	8:16-18	54	26:63-65	63	5:1-5a	66
24:21a	76	8:19-26	54	27:1-4	77	5:5b-10	68
24:21b	77	9:1-12	55	27:5-11	77	5:11	69
24:22	84	9:13	70	27:12-14	86	5:12-15	69
24:23	69	9:14	70	27:15-23	64	5:16	84
25:1-10	73	9:15-23	57	28:1-8	71	5:17	76
25:11-34	73	10:1-20	57	28:9-15	73	5:18	78
25:35-38	84	10:21-36	57	28:16-25	70	5:19	77
25:39-43	73	11:1-15	57	28:26-31	70	5:20	76
25:44-46	77	11:16-35	57	29:1-6	70	5:21	84
25:47-55	73	12:1-16	58	29:7-11	70	5:22-33	66
26:1	68	13:1-16	58	29:12-38	70	6:1-15	66
26:2	69	13:17-33	58	29:39-40	70	6:16-25	66
26:3-17	85	14:1-10a	58	30:1-5	77	7:1-11	66
26:18-42	85	14:10b-35	58	30:6-16	77	7:12-26	66
26:43-46	85	14:36-45	58	31:1-6	62	8:1-5	66
27:1-25	75	15:1-16	71	31:7-54	62	8:6-20	66
27:26-34	75	15:17-21	71	32:1-27	64	9:1-5	67
		15:22-26	72	32:28-42	64	9:6-29	67
NUMBERS	page	15:27-28	72	33:1-37	60	10:1-22	67
1:1-19	55	15:29-31	72	33:38-49	60	11:1	67
1:20-39	55	15:32-36	69	33:50-56	64	11:2-25	67
1:40-54	55	15:37-41	85	34:1-12	64	11:26-32	67
2:1-16	55	16:1-26	59	34:13-29	64	12:1-15	68
2:17-34	55	16:27-50	59	35:1-8	64	12:16	82
3:1-13	54	17:1-13	59	35:9-15	76	12:17-22	68
3:14-20	56	18:1-7	59	35:16-21	76	12:23-25	82
3:21-39	56	18:8-32	59	35:22-28	76	12:26-28	68
3:40-51	56	19:1-10	74	35:29-31	76	12:29-31	68
4:1-15	56	19:11-19	74	35:32	76	12:32	85
4:16-28	56	19:20-22	74	35:33-34	76	13:1-5	69
4:29-49	56	20:1-9	60	36:1-13	77	13:6-18	68
5:1-4	80	20:10-29	60			14:1-2	68

461

SCRIPTURE INDEX

Ref	Page	Ref	Page	Ref	Page	Ref	Page
14:3-20	82	23:17-18	78	33:1-6	86	17:7-10	90
14:21a	82	23:19-20	77	33:7-17	86	17:11-13	94
14:21b	82	23:21-23	75	33:18-29	86	17:14-18	90
14:22-29	69	23:24-25	84	34:1-12	86	18:1-10	90
15:1-11	77	24:1-4	78			18:11-28	90
15:12-18	77	24:5	78,84	**JOSHUA**	**page**	19:1-9	90
15:19-23	69	24:6	77	1:1-9	87	19:10-39	90
16:1-7	70	24:7	76	1:10-18	87	19:40-51	90
16:8-12	70	24:8-9	80	2:1-21	87	20:1-9	90
16:13-15	70	24:10-11	77	2:22-24	87	21:1-7	90
16:16-17	70	24:12-13	77	3:1	87	21:8-33	90
16:18-20	76	24:14-15	77	3:2-13	87	21:34-45	90
16:21-22	68	24:16	76	3:14-17	87	22:1-20	93
17:1	73	24:17-18	76,77	4:1-13	87	22:21-34	93
17:2-7	68	24:19-22	84	4:14	87	23:1-16	93
17:8-13	76	25:1-3	76	4:15-18	87	24:1-13	93
17:14-20	76	25:4	84	4:19-24	87	24:14-27	93
18:1-5	69	25:5-10	77	5:1-9	87	24:28-30	93,94
18:6-8	69	25:11-12	77	5:10-15	87	24:31	95
18:9-14	69	25:13-16	77	6:1-11	88	24:32-33	94
18:15-22	69	25:17-19	64	6:12-27	88		
19:1-10	76	26:1-11	69	7:1-15	88	**JUDGES**	**page**
19:11-13	76	26:12-15	69	7:16-26	88	1:1-10	94
19:14	77	26:16-19	85	8:1-9	88	1:11-15	94
19:15-21	76	27:1-8	85	8:10-33	88	1:16-19	94
20:1-18	84	27:9-26	85	8:34-35	88	1:20a	90
20:19-20	84	28:1-14	85	9:1-15	89	1:20b	94
21:1-9	73	28:15-35	85	9:16-27	89	1:21	94
21:10-14	78,84	28:36-57	85	10:1-21	89	1:22-29	94
21:15-17	77	28:58-68	85	10:22-43	89	1:30-36	94
21:18-21	84	29:1	85	11:1-23	89	2:1-5	94
21:22-23	76	29:2-9	85	12:1-24	89	2:6	93
22:1-4	84	29:10-29	85	13:1-7	90	2:7	95
22:5	78	30:1-10	85	13:8-12	90	2:8-9	94
22:6-7	84	30:11-20	85	13:13	94	2:10-23	95
22:8	77	31:1-8	86	13:14-31	90	3:1-4	95
22:9	75	31:9-13	85	13:32-33	90	3:5-25	95
22:10-11	75	31:14-15	86	14:1-15a	90	3:26-31	95
22:12	85	31:16-22	86	14:15b	89	4:1-3	96
22:13-21	78	31:23	86	15:1-12	90	4:4-22	96
22:22-24	78	31:24-30	86	15:13-19	94	4:23-24	96
22:25-29	76	32:1-6	86	15:20-62	90	5:1-18	96
22:30	78	32:7-14	86	15:63	94	5:19-27	96
23:1-8	75	32:15-33	86	16:1-9	90	5:28-31	96
23:9-14	84	32:34-43	86	16:10	94	6:1-6	96
23:15-16	77	32:44-52	86	17:1-6	90	6:7-27	96

SCRIPTURE INDEX

Ref	Page	Ref	Page	Ref	Page	Ref	Page
6:28-40	96	1 SAMUEL	page	21:13-15	108	8:9-14	114
7:1-8	96	1:1-8	104	22:1-2	108	8:15-18	113
7:9-25	96	1:9-28	104	22:3-5	108	9:1-13	113
8:1-21	96,98	2:1-11	104	22:6-23	109	10:1-19	113
8:22-35	98	2:12-17	104	23:1-12	109	11:1-5	113
9:1-6	98	2:18-36	104	23:13-18	109	11:6-27	113
9:7-29	98	3:1-21	104	23:19-29	109	12:1-13a	113
9:30-54	98	4:1-22	104	24:1-22	109	12:13b-23	113,114
9:55-57	98	5:1-12	104	25:1-8	109	12:24-25	115
10:1-9	99	6:1-12	104	25:9-31	109	12:26-31	114
10:10-18	99	6:13-21	104	25:32-44	109	13:1-14	115
11:1-13	99	7:1	104	26:1-20	109	13:15-29	115
11:14-40	99	7:2-17	104	26:21-25	109	13:30-39	115
12:1-15	99	8:1-22	105	27:1-12	109	14:1-11	115
13:1-23	101	9:1-5	105	28:1-2	109	14:12-24	115
13:24-25	101	9:6-27	105	28:3-25	110	14:25-33	116
14:1-14	101	10:1-13	105	29:1-11	109	15:1-12	116
14:15-20	101	10:14-27	105	30:1-8	109	15:13-37	116
15:1-8	101	11:1-11	105	30:9-31	109	16:1-14	116
15:9-20	101	11:12-15	105	31:1-13	110	16:15-23	116
16:1-5	101	12:1-15	105			17:1-4	116
16:6-22	101	12:16-25	105	2 SAMUEL	page	17:5-22	116
16:23-31	101	13:1	106	1:1-27	110	17:23-29	116
17:1-6	102	13:2-15	106	2:1-4a	111	18:1-18	116
17:7-13	102	13:16-22	106	2:4b-10	111	18:19-28	116
18:1-10	102	14:1-13	106	2:11	111	18:29-33	116
18:11-29	102	14:14-30	106	2:12-29	111	19:1-10	116,117
18:30-31	102	14:31-48	106	2:30-32	111	19:11-40	117
19:1-9	103	14:49-51	106	3:1-13	111	19:41-43	117
19:10-30	103	14:52	106	3:14-39	111	20:1-13	117
20:1-23	103	15:1-21	106	4:1-3	111	20:14-22	117
20:24-46	103	15:22-33	106	4:4	110	20:23-26	117
20:47-48	103	15:34-35	106	4:5-12	111	21:1-9	118
21:1-15	103	16:1-5	107	5:1-3	111	21:10-14	118
21:16-25	103	16:6-23	107	5:4-8	111,112	21:15-22	113
		17:1-31	107	5:9-12	112	22:1-51	112
RUTH	page	17:32-47	107	5:13-16	115	23:1-7	135
1:1-14	100	17:48-58	107	5:17-25	112	23:8-17	114
1:15-22	100	18:1-11	107	6:1-11	112	23:18-39	114
2:1-16	100	18:12-30	107	6:12a	112	24:1-9	118
2:17-23	100	19:1-7	107	6:12b-19	112	24:10-25	118
3:1-13	100	19:8-18	107	6:20-23	113		
3:14-18	100	19:19-24	107	7:1-17	113	1 KINGS	page
4:1-12	100	20:1-23	107	7:18-29	113	1:1-27	135
4:13-22	100	20:24-42	107	8:1	113	1:28-48	135
		21:1-12	108	8:2-8	114	1:49-53	135

SCRIPTURE INDEX

Ref	Page	Ref	Page	Ref	Page	Ref	Page
2:1-9	135	10:26	139	21:1-16	161	8:23-27	170
2:10	135	10:27	139	21:17-24	161	8:28-29	170
2:11	111	10:28-29	139	21:25-26	158	9:1-13	170
2:12	135	11:1-8	151	21:27-29	161	9:14a	170
2:13-27	136	11:9-40	151	22:1	161	9:14b-15a	170
2:28-46	136	11:41-43	151,155	22:2-4	161	9:15b-26	170
3:1-14	136	12:1-11	155	22:5-28	161	9:27	170
3:15-28	136	12:12-24	155	22:29-40a	162	9:28	170
4:1-21	139	12:25-33	155	22:40b	162	9:29	170
4:22-23	139	13:1-3	155	22:41-43	158	9:30-37	170
4:24-26	139	13:4-24	155	22:44	158	10:1-11	170
4:27-28	139	13:25-34	155,157	22:45	165	10:12-17	170
4:29-34	139	14:1-16	157,158	22:46-47	158	10:18-28	171
5:1-9	137	14:17-18	157	22:48-49	162	10:29-31	171
5:10-18	137	14:19-20	158	22:50	165	10:32-36	173
6:1	137	14:21	157	22:51	158	11:1-3	171
6:2-8	137	14:22-24	157	22:52-53	162	11:4-12	171
6:9a	137	14:25-31	157			11:13-21	171
6:9b-13	137	15:1-2	157	2 KINGS	page	12:1-3	171
6:14-15	137	15:3-5	157	1:1	162	12:4-5	173
6:16-22	137	15:6	157	1:2-8	162	12:6-16	173
6:23-35	137	15:7a	157	1:9-18	162	12:17-18	173
6:36	137	15:7b	157	2:1-11	163	12:19-21	173,174
6:37-38	137	15:8-11	157,158	2:12-25	163	13:1-2	173
7:1-12	139	15:12-21	158	3:1-3	162	13:3	173
7:13-22	137	15:22	158	3:4-5	162	13:4	173
7:23-37	137	15:23-24	158	3:6-9	165	13:5-6	175
7:38-39a	137	15:25-31	158	3:10-27	165	13:7-11	173
7:39b	137	15:32	158	4:1-7	163	13:12-13	174
7:40-50	137	15:33-34	158	4:8-44	163	13:14-19	173
7:51	137	16:1-10	158	5:1-14	167	13:20a	173
8:1-11	139	16:11-13	158	5:15-19a	167	13:20b-25	174
8:12-30	139	16:14	158	5:19b-27	167	14:1-6	174
8:31-43	139	16:15-28a	158	6:1-7	163	14:7	174
8:44-61	139	16:28b-30	158	6:8-12	167	14:8-16	174
8:62-66	139	16:31a	158	6:13-23	167	14:17-21	178
9:1-9	139	16:31b-34	158	6:24-33	167	14:22	178
9:10-15	139	17:1-24	158	7:1-2	167	14:23	174
9:16	136	18:1-21	158	7:3-16	167	14:24	174
9:17-24	139	18:22-39	158	7:17-20	167	14:25-27	175
9:25	139	18:40-46	158	8:1-2	163	14:28-29	181
9:26-28	139	19:1-12	158	8:3-6	167	15:1-2	178
10:1-13	139	19:13-21	158	8:7-13	170	15:3-4	178
10:14-21	139	20:1-22	161	8:14-15	170	15:5	181
10:22	139	20:23-34	161	8:16-17	165	15:6-7	184
10:23-25	139	20:35-43	161	8:18-22	165	15:8-15	181

SCRIPTURE INDEX

Ref	Page	Ref	Page	Ref	Page	Ref	Page
15:16-18	181	24:8-9	235	11:20-47	114	29:28-30	135
15:19-28	184	24:10-20a	235	12:1-7	109		
15:29	187	24:20b	247	12:8-18	108	2 CHRONICLES	page
15:30-31	187	25:1	247	12:19-22	109	1:1	135
15:32-34	184	25:2-10	256	12:23-40	111	1:2-12	136
15:35a	184	25:11-21	256	13:1-14	112	1:13	136
15:35b	184	25:22	256	14:1-2	112	1:14	139
15:36-38	187	25:23-24	258	14:3-7	115	1:15	139
16:1-4	187	25:25	258	14:8-17	112	1:16-17	139
16:5-6	188	25:26	258	15:1-10	112	2:1	137
16:7-16	191	25:27-30	272	15:11-24	112	2:2	137
16:17-20	191			15:25-29	112	2:3-16	137
17:1-2	187	1 CHRONICLES	pg.	16:1-36	112	2:17-18	137
17:3-14	197	1:1-16	320	16:37-43	113	3:1-2	137
17:15-41	197	1:17-37	320	17:1-15	113	3:3-7a	137
18:1-7a	191	1:38-54	320	17:16-27	113	3:7b	137
18:7b-8	197	2:1-24	320	18:1	113	3:8-9	137
18:9-12	197	2:25-55	320	18:2-8	114	3:10-17	137
18:13-16	200	3:1-4a	111	18:9-13	114	4:1-5	137
18:17-25	200	3:4b	111	18:14-17	113	4:6a-6b	137
18:26-37	200	3:4c-9	115	19:1-19	113	4:6c	137
19:1-4	200	3:10-16	320	20:1a	113	4:7-9	137
19:5-34	200	3:17-24	320	20:1b-3	114	4:10	137
19:35-36	200	4:1-23	320	20:4-8	113	4:11-22	137
19:37	211	4:24-43	321	21:1-6	118	5:1-14	137,139
20:1-11	200	5:1-9	321	21:7-30	118	6:1-21	139
20:12-19	200	5:10	106	22:1-16	118	6:22-33	139
20:20-21	200,201	5:11-17	321	22:17-19	118	6:34-42	139
21:1-9	201	5:18-22	106	23:1a	119	7:1-10	139
21:10-16	201	5:23-26	187	23:1b	119	7:11-22	139
21:17-26	212	6:1-19a	321	23:2-11	119	8:1-11	139
22:1-2	212	6:19b-47	321	23:12-32	119	8:12-16	137
22:3-7	224	6:48-81	321	24:1-19	119	8:17-18	139
22:8-20	224	7:1-5	321	24:20-31	119	9:1-12	139
23:1-2	224	7:6-12	321	25:1-31	119	9:13-20	139
23:3-14	224	7:13-19	321	26:1-11	119	9:21	139
23:15-23	224	7:20-40	321	26:12-28	120	9:22-24	139
23:24	224	8:1-40	321	26:29-32	120	9:25-26	139
23:25	212	9:1-32	321	27:1-15	120	9:27	139
23:26-27	212	9:33-34	321	27:16-34	120	9:28	139
23:28	224	9:35-44	106	28:1-19	120	9:29-31	155
23:29-37	226	10:1-14	110	28:20-21	120	10:1-11	155
24:1a	230	11:1-3	111	29:1-20	120	10:12-19	155
24:1b-4	233	11:4-5	112	29:21-22	120	11:1-4	155
24:5-6	233,235	11:6-9	112	29:23-25	135	11:5-12	157
24:7	230	11:10-19	114	29:26-27	111	11:13-17	155

SCRIPTURE INDEX

11:18-23	157	24:6-14	173	34:1-2	212	10:1-44	312
12:1	157	24:15-22	173	34:3-7	213		
12:2-13	157	24:23-24	173	34:8-13	224	NEHEMIAH	page
12:14	157	24:25-27	173,174	34:14-30	224	1:1-11a	313
12:15-16	157	25:1-4	174	34:31-33	224	1:11b	313
13:1-2a	157	25:5-12	174	35:1-19	224	2:1-16	313
13:2b-20a	157	25:13-24	174	35:20-25	226	2:17-20	313
13:20b	157	25:25-28	178	35:26-27	224	3:1-32	315
13:21	157	26:1	178	36:1-5	226	4:1-3	315
13:22	157	26:2	178	36:6-7	230	4:4-23	315
14:1-8	157,158	26:3	178	36:8-9	233,235	5:1-16	315
14:9-15	157	26:4-15	178	36:10-11	235	5:17-19	315
15:1-19	158	26:16-21	181	36:12	235	6:1-13	315
16:1-5	158	26:22-23	184	36:13a	235	6:14-19	315
16:6-10	158	27:1-2a	184	36:13b-16	235	7:1-73	317
16:11-14	158	27:2b	184	36:17	256	8:1-18	318
17:1-6	158	27:3-6	184	36:18	256	9:1-25	318
17:7-19	158	27:7	187	36:19	256	9:26-38	318
18:1	158	27:8	184	36:20-21	256	10:1-27	318
18:2-3	161	27:9	187	36:22-23	293	10:28-39	318
18:4-27	161	28:1-4	187			11:1-19	317
18:28-34	162	28:5-15	188	EZRA	page	11:20-36	317
19:1-3	162	28:16-21	188	1:1-4	293	12:1-9	317
19:4-11	162	28:22-27	191	1:5-11	293	12:10-26	317
20:1-12	162	29:1-2	191	2:1-35	293	12:27-42	319
20:13-24	162	29:3-19	193	2:36-63	293	12:43-47	319
20:25-30	162	29:20-36	193	2:64-70	293	13:1-3	319
20:31-33	158	30:1-22	193	3:1-6	293	13:4-11	319
20:34	165	30:23-27	193	3:7-13	293	13:12-14	319
20:35-37	162	31:1-8	193	4:1-3	293	13:15-22	319
21:1	165	31:9-21	193	4:4-5	293	13:23-31	319
21:2-5	165	32:1-8	200	4:6-16	297		
21:6-17	165	32:9-15	200	4:17-24	297	ESTHER	page
21:18	167	32:16	200	5:1-2	297	1:1-22	307
21:19	170	32:17	200	5:3-17	297	2:1-23	307
21:20a	165	32:18-19	200	6:1-13	297	3:1-15	307
21:20b	170	32:20	200	6:14-22	301	4:1-17	307
22:1-4	170	32:21a-21b	200	7:1-7	311	5:1-14	309
22:5-6	170	32:21c	211	7:8-10	311	6:1-14	309
22:7	170	32:22-23	200	7:11-26	311	7:1-10	309
22:8-9	170	32:24	200	7:27-28	311	8:1-17	309
22:10-12	171	32:25-31	200	8:1-14	311	9:1-17	309
23:1-11	171	32:32-33	200,201	8:15-20	311	9:18-32	309
23:12-21	171	33:1-9	201	8:21-32	311	10:1-3	309
24:1-2	171	33:10-17	211	8:33-36	311		
24:3-5	173	33:18-25	212	9:1-15	312		

SCRIPTURE INDEX

JOB	page	25:1-6	280	11	120	57	109
1:1-12	273	26:1-14	280	12	131	58	132
1:13-22	273	27:1-12	280	13	121	59	107
2:1-9	273	27:13-23	280	14	124	60	113
2:10-13	273	28:1-19	280	15	124	61	122
3:1-26	273	28:20-28	280	16	126	62	122
4:1-11	275	29:1-6	280	17	121	63	109
4:12-21	275	29:7-25	280	18	112	64	122
5:1-16	275	30:1-19	280	19	126	65	126
5:17-27	275	30:20-31	280	20	131	66	126
6:1-7	275	31:1-8	280	21	126	67	126
6:8-27	275	31:9-28	280	22	133	68	126
6:28-30	275	31:29-40	280	23	121	69	122
7:1-16	275	32:1-5	281	24	126	70	123
7:17-21	275	32:6-22	281	25	131	71	123
8:1-19	276	33:1-7	281	26	121	72:1-19	139
8:20-22	276	33:8-28	281	27	133	72:20	134
9:1-13	276	33:29-33	281	28	121	73	125
9:14-35	276	34:1-9	281	29	126	74	285
10:1-17	276	34:10-30	281	30	118	75	126
10:18-22	276	34:31-37	281	31	121	76	125
11:1-20	277	35:1-16	281	32	131	77	123
12:1-12	277	36:1-15	281	33	126	78	301
12:13-25	277	36:16-33	281	34	108	79	285
13:1-12	277	37:1-13	281	35	122	80	285
13:13-28	277	37:14-24	281	36	124	81	132
14:1-6	277	38:1-21	284	37	124	82	125
14:7-22	277	38:22-38	284	38	131	83	123
15:1-35	278	38:39-41	284	39	124	84	125
16:1-6	278	39:1-30	284	40	125	85	285
16:7-22	278	40:1-14	284	41	122	86	123
17:1-9	278	40:15-24	284	42	132	87	134
17:10-16	278	41:1-34	284	43	122	88	123
18:1-21	278	42:1-17	284	44	285	89	285
19:1-12	278			45	134	90	125
19:13-29	278	PSALMS	page	46	122	91	123
20:1-29	278	1	124	47	134	92	125
21:1-18	278	2	133	48	134	93	126
21:19-33	278	3	116	49	125	94	126
21:34	278	4	131	50	125	95	123
22:1-20	280	5	120	51	113	96	112
22:21-30	280	6	120	52	109	97	126
23:1-12	280	7	120	53	132	98	126
23:13-17	280	8	126	54	109	99	126
24:1-17	280	9	126	55	122	100	126
24:18-25	280	10	120	56	108	101	132

SCRIPTURE INDEX

102	287	148	130	10:13-14	142	12:21	142
103	127	149	303	10:15	147	12:22	145
104	127	150	130	10:16	142	12:23	145
105	112			10:17	142	12:24	147
106	287	PROVERBS	page	10:18	145	12:25	144
107	302	1:1-7	142	10:19-21	145	12:26	148
108	123	1:8-9	148	10:22	142	12:27	147
109	123	1:10-19	146	10:23	142	12:28	142
110	134	1:20-33	141	10:24-25	142	13:1	142
111	133	2:1-22	141	10:26	147	13:2	145
112	125	3:1-2	142	10:27	142	13:3	145
113	127	3:3-4	144	10:28-30	142	13:4	147
114	127	3:5-8	142	10:31-32	145	13:5	146
115	125	3:9-10	147	11:1	146	13:6	142
116	302	3:11-12	142	11:2	144	13:7	144
117	127	3:13-24	141	11:3	144	13:8	147
118	302	3:25-26	148	11:4	147	13:9	142
119	128	3:27-28	147	11:5-10	142	13:10	144
120	124	3:29-30	146	11:11	145	13:11	146
121	124	3:31-32	146	11:12-13	145	13:12	148
122	129	3:33-35	142	11:14	142	13:13	142
123	287	4:1-27	141	11:15	147	13:14	142
124	129	5:1-20	144	11:16-17	144	13:15-16	142
125	302	5:21-23	144	11:18-20	142	13:17	148
126	303	6:1-5	147	11:21	142	13:18	142
127	149	6:6-11	147	11:22	148	13:19	148
128	303	6:12-15	144	11:23	142	13:20	148
129	303	6:16-19	146	11:24-26	147	13:21	142
130	133	6:20-35	144	11:27	142	13:22	147
131	133	7:1-23	144	11:28	147	13:23	147
132	303	7:24-27	144	11:29	148	13:24	142
133	129	8:1-31	141	11:30-31	142	13:25	142
134	129	8:32-36	141	12:1	142	14:1	148
135	129	9:1-6	141	12:2-3	142	14:2	142
136	129	9:7-9	142	12:4	148	14:3	145
137	287	9:10-12	142	12:5-8	142	14:4	147
138	129	9:13-18	141	12:9-10	144	14:5	146
139	130	10:1	148	12:11	147	14:6	142
140	124	10:2	146	12:12	142	14:7	148
141	133	10:3	142	12:13-14	145	14:8	142
142	108	10:4-5	147	12:15	142	14:9	142
143	124	10:6-7	142	12:16	144	14:10	148
144	124	10:8	142	12:17	146	14:11	142
145	130	10:9	142	12:18	145	14:12	142
146	133	10:10-11	144	12:19	145	14:13	148
147	303	10:12	144	12:20	146	14:14	142

SCRIPTURE INDEX

Verse	Page	Verse	Page	Verse	Page	Verse	Page
14:15	142	15:28	145	17:13	142	19:13-14	148
14:16-17	144	15:29	144	17:14	145	19:15	147
14:18	142	15:30	148	17:15	146	19:16	142
14:19	142	15:31	142	17:16	147	19:17	147
14:20	147	15:32	142	17:17	148	19:18	142
14:21	147	15:33	142	17:18	147	19:19	144
14:22	142	16:1	142	17:19-20	145	19:20	142
14:23	147	16:2	144	17:21	148	19:21	142
14:24	142	16:3-4	142	17:22	148	19:22	145
14:25	146	16:5	144	17:23	146	19:23	142
14:26-27	142	16:6	144	17:24	142	19:24	147
14:28	148	16:7	142	17:25	148	19:25	142
14:29	144	16:8	147	17:26	146	19:26	148
14:30	144	16:9	142	17:27-28	145	19:27	142
14:31	147	16:10	148	18:1	144	19:28	146
14:32	148	16:11	146	18:2	142	19:29	142
14:33	142	16:12-15	148	18:3	142	20:1	144
14:34	142	16:16	142	18:4	142	20:2	148
14:35	148	16:17	148	18:5	146	20:3	145
15:1	145	16:18-19	144	18:6-7	145	20:4	147
15:2	145	16:20	142	18:8	145	20:5	142
15:3	142	16:21	145	18:9	147	20:6	144
15:4	145	16:22	142	18:10	142	20:7	142
15:5	142	16:23	145	18:11	147	20:8	148
15:6	142	16:24	145	18:12	144	20:9	144
15:7	145	16:25	142	18:13	145	20:10	146
15:8	144	16:26	147	18:14	148	20:11	144
15:9	142	16:27	145	18:15	142	20:12	142
15:10	142	16:28	145	18:16	147	20:13	147
15:11	144	16:29	146	18:17	146	20:14	144
15:12	142	16:30	144	18:18-19	146	20:15	142
15:13	148	16:31	148	18:20-21	145	20:16	147
15:14	142	16:32	144	18:22	148	20:17	146
15:15	147	16:33	142	18:23	147	20:18	142
15:16	147	17:1	146	18:24	148	20:19	145
15:17	144	17:2	148	19:1	145	20:20	148
15:18	144	17:3	144	19:2	142	20:21	146
15:19	147	17:4	145	19:3	142	20:22	146
15:20	148	17:5	144	19:4	147	20:23	146
15:21	142	17:6	148	19:5	145	20:24	142
15:22	142	17:7	148	19:6-7	147	20:25	144
15:23	145	17:8	146	19:8	142	20:26	148
15:24	142	17:9	145	19:9	146	20:27	144
15:25	144	17:10	142	19:10	144	20:28	148
15:26	142	17:11	148	19:11	144	20:29	148
15:27	146	17:12	142	19:12	148	20:30	142

SCRIPTURE INDEX

21:1	148	22:24-25	144	25:20	148	28:6	147
21:2-3	144	22:26-27	147	25:21-22	144	28:7	142
21:4	144	22:28	146	25:23	145	28:8	147
21:5	144	22:29	147	25:24	148	28:9	142
21:6	145	23:1-3	148	25:25	148	28:10	146
21:7	146	23:4-5	147	25:26	146	28:11	147
21:8	142	23:6-8	144	25:27-28	144	28:12	142
21:9	148	23:9	142	26:1	142	28:13	142
21:10	144	23:10-11	146	26:2	145	28:14	142
21:11	142	23:12	142	26:3	142	28:15-16	148
21:12	142	23:13-14	142	26:4-11	142	28:17	146
21:13	147	23:15-16	145	26:12	142	28:18	142
21:14	146	23:17-18	148	26:13	148	28:19	147
21:15	146	23:19-21	144	26:14	147	28:20-22	147
21:16	142	23:22-25	148	26:15	147	28:23	145
21:17	147	23:26-28	145	26:16	144	28:24	148
21:18	142	23:29-35	144	26:17-19	146	28:25	144
21:19	148	24:1-2	148	26:20	145	28:26	142
21:20	147	24:3-4	142	26:21	145	28:27	147
21:21	142	24:5-6	142	26:22	145	28:28	142
21:22	142	24:7	142	26:23-26	144	29:1	142
21:23	145	24:8-9	142	26:27	142	29:2	142
21:24	144	24:10	148	26:28	145	29:3	144
21:25-26	147	24:11-12	146	27:1	142	29:4	148
21:27	144	24:13-14	142	27:2	144	29:5	145
21:28	146	24:15-16	142	27:3	146	29:6	148
21:29	146	24:17-18	144	27:4	144	29:7	147
21:30-31	142	24:19-20	144	27:5-6	142	29:8	144
22:1	148	24:21-22	148	27:7	147	29:9	142
22:2	147	24:23-25	146	27:8-10	148	29:10	142
22:3	148	24:26	146	27:11	148	29:11	144
22:4	144	24:27	147	27:12	148	29:12	148
22:5	148	24:28-29	146	27:13	147	29:13	147
22:6	142	24:30-34	147	27:14	145	29:14	142
22:7	147	25:1	142	27:15-16	148	29:15	142
22:8	142	25:2-7	148	27:17	142	29:16	142
22:9	147	25:8	144	27:18	147	29:17-19	142
22:10	145	25:9-10	148	27:19	144	29:20	144
22:11	148	25:11	145	27:20	148	29:21	142
22:12	142	25:12	142	27:21	144	29:22	144
22:13	148	25:13	148	27:22	142	29:23	144
22:14	144	25:14	147	27:23-27	147	29:24	148
22:15	142	25:15	145	28:1	148	29:25	142
22:16	147	25:16-17	144	28:2-3	148	29:26	146
22:17-21	142	25:18	146	28:4	142	29:27	142
22:22-23	147	25:19	144	28:5	148	30:1-4	148

SCRIPTURE INDEX

Reference	Page	Reference	Page	Reference	Page	Reference	Page
30:5-19	148	4:16	149	16:1-14	190	37:38	211
30:20-33	148	5:1-8	149	17:1-14	190	38:1-8	200
31:1-7	148	5:9-16	149	18:1-7	198	38:9-20	200
31:8-31	148	6:1-12	149	19:1-15	198	38:21-22	200
		6:13	149	19:16-22	198	39:1-8	200
ECCLESIASTES pg.		7:1-13	149	19:23-25	198	40:1-5	201
1:1-3	152	8:1-4	149	20:1-6	198	40:6-14	201
1:4-11	152	8:5-9	149	21:1-10	192	40:15-31	201
1:12-18	153	8:10-14	149	21:11-12	191	41:1-10	201
2:1-11	153			21:13-17	191	41:11-20	202
2:12-16	152	**ISAIAH**	page	22:1-14	195	41:21-29	202
2:17-26	153	1:1-9	182	22:15-25	196	42:1-4	202
3:1-17	155	1:10-17	182	23:1-18	191	42:5-17	202
3:18-22	152	1:18-20	182,184	24:1-23	194	42:18-25	202
4:1-16	153	1:21-26	182	25:1-12	194	43:1-7	202
5:1-20	153	1:27-31	184	26:1-7	194	43:8-15	204
6:1-9	153	2:1-5	184	26:8-18	194	43:16-28	204
6:10-12	152	2:6-18	182	26:19-21	194	44:1-20	204
7:1-6	154	2:19-22	184	27:1	194	44:21-23	204
7:7-12	154	3:1-7	184	27:2-13	196	44:24-28	204
7:13-14	153	3:8-26	182	28:1-15	195	45:1-7	204
7:15-18	154	4:1	182	28:16-22	195	45:8-13	204
7:19-26	154	4:2-6	184	28:23-29	195	45:14-25	204
7:27-29	154	5:1-7	182	29:1-4	195	46:1-7	204
8:1	154	5:8-14	182	29:5-12	195	46:8-13	204
8:2-15	153	5:15-23	182	29:13	195	47:1-11	204
8:16-17	152	5:24-30	184	29:14-24	195,196	47:12-15	204
9:1-10	152	6:1-13	184	30:1-7	198	48:1-15	204
9:11-12	152	7:1-9	187	30:8-18	198	48:16-22	206
9:13-18	153	7:10-25	187	30:19-33	198	49:1-4	206
10:1-20	154	8:1-10	187	31:1-9	198	49:5-13	206
11:1-6	154	8:11-22	187	32:1-8	194	49:14-23	206
11:7-10	155	9:1-21	187	32:9-11	182	49:24-26	206
12:1-8	155	10:1-4	188	32:12-20	196	50:1-9	206
12:9-10	154	10:5-19	188	33:1	195	50:10-11	206
12:11-12	154	10:20-34	188	33:2-16	196	51:1-8	207
12:13-14	155	11:1-9	188	33:17-24	196	51:9-16	207
		11:10-16	188	34:1-4	190	51:17-23	207
SONG OF SONGS p.		12:1-6	188	34:5-17	191	52:1-2	207
1:1-7	149	13:1-8	192	35:1-10	194	52:3-12	207
1:8-17	149	13:9-22	192	36:1	200	52:13-15	207
2:1	149	14:1-11	192	36:2-10	200	53:1-9	207
2:2-15	149	14:12-23	192	36:11-22	200	53:10-12	207
2:16-17	149	14:24-27	190	37:1-4	200	54:1-3	207
3:1-11	149	14:28-32	192	37:5-35	200	54:4-17	208
4:1-15	149	15:1-9	190	37:36-37	200	55:1-13	208

SCRIPTURE INDEX

56:1-8	208	8:1-3	217	26:7-24	226	43:1-13	258
56:9-12	208	8:4-12	217	27:1-11	235	44:1-14	258
57:1-13	208	8:13-22	217	27:12-22	235	44:15-19	258
57:14-21	208	9:1-2	217	28:1-9	235	44:20-30	258
58:1-12	208	9:3-9	217	28:10-17	235	45:1-5	231
58:13-14	208	9:10-22	217	29:1-23	235	46:1-11	228
59:1-15	208	9:23-26	217	29:24-32	235	46:12-26	228
59:16-20	208	10:1-10	218	30:1-15	250	46:27-28	228
59:21	208	10:11-22	218	30:16-24	250	47:1-7	228
60:1-14	209	10:23-25	218	31:1-14	250	48:1-13	233
60:15-22	209	11:1-13	218	31:15-25	250	48:14-28	233
61:1-9	209	11:14-23	218	31:26	250	48:29-39	233
61:10-11	209	12:1-17	218	31:27-34	251	48:40-47	233
62:1-5	209	13:1-11	219	31:35-40	251	49:1-6	233
62:6-12	209	13:12-21	219	32:1-5	249	49:7-22	233
63:1-6	209	13:22-27	219	32:6-25	249	49:23-33	233
63:7-14	209	14:1-6	219	32:26-44	249	49:34-39	238
63:15-19	209	14:7-18	219	33:1-13	249,250	50:1-3	237
64:1-12	209	14:19-22	219	33:14-22	251	50:4-13	237
65:1-10	211	15:1-9	219	33:23-26	251	50:14-20	237
65:11-25	211	15:10-21	221	34:1-7	249	50:21-32	237
66:1-6	211	16:1-21	221	34:8-16	238	50:33-46	237,238
66:7-14	211	17:1-4	221	34:17-22	238	51:1-10	238
66:15-24	211	17:5-18	221	35:1-12	230	51:11-16	238
		17:19-27	222	35:13-19	230	51:17-33	238
JEREMIAH	page	18:1-17	222	36:1-3	231	51:34-44	238
1:1-16	214	18:18-23	222	36:4-15	231	51:45-50	238
1:17-19	214	19:1-9	222	36:16-32	231	51:51-58	238
2:1-9	214	19:10-15	222	37:1	235	51:59	237
2:10-19	214	20:1-6	222	37:2	235	51:60-64a	238
2:20-29	214	20:7-18	222	37:3-16	255	51:64b	238
2:30-37	214	21:1-7	249	37:17-21	255	52:1	235
3:1-22a	214,215	21:8-14	249	38:1-13	255	52:2-3a	235
3:22b-25	215	22:1-9	249	38:14-28	255	52:3b-4	247
4:1-9	215	22:10-17	226	39:1	247	52:5-14	256
4:10-21	215	22:18-23	233	39:2-8	256	52:15-30	256
4:22-31	215	22:24-30	235	39:9-10	256	52:31-34	272
5:1-11	215	23:1-8	251	39:11-18	256		
5:12-25	215,216	23:9-14	236	40:1-5	256	LAMENTATIONS	pg
5:26-31	216	23:15-32	236	40:6	256	1:1-6	257
6:1-8	216	23:33-40	236	40:7-10	258	1:7-11	257
6:9-14	216	24:1-10	235	40:11-16	258	1:12-22	257
6:15-26	216	25:1-11	230	41:1-15	258	2:1-10	257
6:27-30	216	25:12-32	230	41:16-18	258	2:11-17	257
7:1-15	217	25:33-38	230	42:1-18	258	2:18-22	257
7:16-34	217	26:1-6	226	42:19-22	258	3:1-21	257

SCRIPTURE INDEX

Reference	Page	Reference	Page	Reference	Page	Reference	Page
3:22-54	257	23:46-49	247	44:1-3	265	11:21-35	295
3:55-66	257	24:1-14	248	44:4-23	270	11:36-45	295
4:1-10	257	24:15-24	248	44:24a	270	12:1-13	295
4:11-22	257	24:25-27	248	44:24b-27	270		
5:1-18	257	25:1-17	252	44:28-30	270	HOSEA	page
5:19-22	257	26:1-14	253	44:31	270	1:1-11	176
		26:15-21	253	45:1-12	270	2:1	176
EZEKIEL	page	27:1-11	253	45:13-25	270	2:2-13	176
1:1-24	240	27:12-36	253	46:1-8	270	2:14-23	176
1:25-28	240	28:1-10	253	46:9-20	270	3:1-3	176
2:1-10	240	28:11-19	253	46:21-24	270	3:4-5	176
3:1-11	240	28:20-26	253	47:1-14	270	4:1-9	177
3:12-27	240	29:1-16	252	47:15-23	270	4:10-19	177
4:1-17	240	29:17-21	272	48:1-14	270	5:1-15	177
5:1-17	240	30:1-19	252	48:15-29	270	6:1-11	177
6:1-14	240	30:20-26	252	48:30-35	270	7:1-7	177
7:1-27	240	31:1-18	252			7:8-16	177
8:1-4	241	32:1-10	263	DANIEL	page	8:1-14	177
8:5-18	241	32:11-16	263	1:1-2	235	9:1-17	177
9:1-11	241	32:17-32	263	1:3-20	232	10:1-15	178
10:1-22	241	33:1-16	263	1:21	292	11:1-11	178
11:1-21	241	33:17-20	263	2:1-11	232	11:12	178
11:22-25	241	33:21-26	260	2:12-30	232	12:1-14	178
12:1-16	242	33:27-33	260	2:31-49	232	13:1-3	178
12:17-28	242	34:1-10	260	3:1-7	264	13:4-16	178
13:1-23	242	34:11-31	260	3:8-27	264	14:1-9	178
14:1-11	242	35:1-15	260	3:28-30	264		
14:12-23	242	36:1-7	260	4:1-3	272	JOEL	page
15:1-8	243	36:8-32	260	4:4-27	272	1:1-12	172
16:1-22	243	36:33-38	260	4:28-37	273	1:13-20	172
16:23-43	243	37:1-14	262	5:1-9	291	2:1-11	172
16:44-63	243	37:15-28	262	5:10-28	291	2:12-27	172
17:1-18	243	38:1-16	262	5:29-31	291	2:28-32	172
17:19-24	243	38:17-23	262	6:1-15	292	3:1-17	172
18:1-20	243	39:1-16	262	6:16-27	292	3:18-21	172
18:21-32	243	39:17-29	262	6:28	292		
19:1-9	245	40:1-4	265	7:1-14	288	AMOS	page
19:10-14	245	40:5-23	265	7:15-28	288	1:1-10	179
20:1-12	245	40:24-43	265	8:1-26	288	1:11-15	179
20:13-38	245	40:44-49	265	8:27	288	2:1-5	179
20:39-49	245	41:1-12	265	9:1-2	291	2:6-16	179
21:1-17	245	41:13-26	265	9:3-19	291	3:1-10	179
21:18-32	245	42:1-14	265	9:20-27	291	3:11-15	179
22:1-31	245	42:15-20	265	10:1-6	295	4:1-11	179
23:1-13	247	43:1-9	265	10:7-21	295	4:12-13	179
23:14-45	247	43:10-27	265	11:1-20	295	5:1-15	180

SCRIPTURE INDEX

Reference	Page	Reference	Page	Reference	Page	Reference	Page
5:16-20	180	3:1-11	211	14:1-19	305	11:2-15	340
5:21-27	180	3:12-19	211	14:20-21	305	11:16-19	340
6:1-7	180					11:20-24	356
6:8-14	180	**HABAKKUK**	page	**MALACHI**	page	11:25-30	356
7:1-9	180	1:1-17	229	1:1	311	12:1-14	337
7:10-13	181	2:1	229	1:2-14	311	12:15-21	337
7:14-17	181	2:2-17	229	2:1-9	311	12:22-42	340
8:1-14	180	2:18-20	229	2:10-17	311	12:43-50	340
9:1-10	180	3:1-19	229	3:1-4	311	13:1-9	344
9:11-15	180			3:5-18	311	13:10-30	344
		ZEPHANIAH	page	4:1-4	311	13:31-33	344
OBADIAH	page	1:1-13	213	4:5-6	311	13:34-35	344
1-4	166	1:14-18	213			13:36-44	344
5-18	166	2:1-7	213	**New Testament**		13:45-52	344
19-21	166	2:8-15	213			13:53-58	345
		3:1-7	213	**MATTHEW**	page	14:1-12a	347
JONAH	page	3:8-13	213	1:1-17	328	14:12b-13	347
1:1-16	175	3:14-20	213	1:18-25a	329	14:14-33	348
1:17	175			1:25b	329	14:34-36	348
2:1-9	175	**HAGGAI**	page	2:1-8	331	15:1-20	348
2:10	175	1:1-11	298	2:9-18	331	15:21-31	349
3:1-10	175	1:12-15	298	2:19-23	331	15:32-39	349
4:1-11	175	2:1-9	298	3:1-3	332	16:1-12	349
		2:10-19	298	3:4-17	332	16:13-28	350
MICAH	page	2:20-23	298	4:1-11	332	17:1-8	350
1:1	185			4:12-17	336	17:9-21	350
1:2-16	185	**ZECHARIAH**	page	4:18-25	336	17:22-27	350
2:1-5	185	1:1-6	298	5:1-12	339	18:1-6	350
2:6-13	185	1:7-17	299	5:13-32	339	18:7-9	350
3:1-4	185	1:18-21	299	5:33-48	339	18:10-14	350
3:5-12	185	2:1-13	299	6:1-15	339	18:15-35	350
4:1-5	185	3:1-10	299	6:16-34	339	19:1-2	356
4:6-13	185	4:1-14	299	7:1-23	339	19:3-15	363
5:1-9	185	5:1-11	299	7:24-29	339	19:16-30	363
5:10-15	185	6:1-15	299	8:1-4	336	20:1-16	358
6:1-5	186	7:1-14	301	8:5-13	340	20:17-23	363
6:6-16	186	8:1-23	301	8:14-17	336	20:24-34	363
7:1-7	186	9:1-13	305	8:18-22	345	21:1-11	366
7:8-13	186	9:14-17	305	8:23-34	345	21:12-16	366
7:14-20	186	10:1-3	305	9:1-8	336	21:17	366
		10:4-12	305	9:9-17	337	21:18-19	366
NAHUM	page	11:1-3	305	9:18-31	345	21:20-32	368
1:1-8	211	11:4-17	305	9:32-38	345,347	21:33-46	368
1:9-15	211	12:1-9	305	10:1-33	347	22:1-14	368
2:1-2	211	12:10-14	305	10:34-42	347	22:15-40	368
2:3-13	211	13:1-9	305	11:1	347	22:41-46	368

SCRIPTURE INDEX

Reference	Page	Reference	Page	Reference	Page	Reference	Page
23:1-22	368	2:13-22	337	14:10-11	372	5:1-10a	336
23:23-39	368	2:23-28	337	14:12-16	372	5:10b-11	336
24:1-35	371	3:1-6	337	14:17-21	374	5:12-26	336
24:36-51	371	3:7-19	337	14:22-25	374	5:27-39	337
25:1-13	371	3:20-30	340	14:26-31	374	6:1-11	337
25:14-30	371	3:31-35	340	14:32-34	377	6:12-19	337
25:31-46	371	4:1-9	344	14:35-47	377	6:20-26	339
26:1-5	372	4:10-20	344	14:48-52	377	6:27-36	339
26:6-13	363	4:21-32	344	14:53-64	377	6:37-45	339
26:14-16	372	4:33-34	344	14:65	377	6:46-49	339
26:17-19	372	4:35-41	345	14:66-70a	377	7:1-10	340
26:20-25	374	5:1-20	345	14:70b-72	377	7:11-30	340
26:26-29	374	5:21-43	345	15:1a	377	7:31-50	340
26:30-35	374	6:1-6	345	15:1b-5	379	8:1-3	340
26:36-38	377	6:7-11	347	15:6-10	379	8:4-8	344
26:39-54	377	6:12-29	347	15:11-14	379	8:9-15	344
26:55-56	377	6:30-33	347	15:15	379	8:16-18	344
26:57-66	377	6:34-52	348	15:16-19	379	8:19-21	340
26:67-68	377	6:53-56	348	15:20-22	379	8:22-39	345
26:69-72	377	7:1-23	348	15:23-32	381	8:40-56	345
26:73-75	377	7:24-37	349	15:33-41	381	9:1-5	347
27:1	377	8:1-21	349	15:42-47	381	9:6-9	347
27:2	379	8:22-26	349	16:1-9	384	9:10-11a	347
27:3-10	377	8:27-38	350	16:10-12	384	9:11b-17	348
27:11-14	379	9:1-8	350	16:13-14	384	9:18-36a	350
27:15-19	379	9:9-29	350	16:15-18	384	9:36b-43a	350
27:20-23	379	9:30-37	350	16:19	384	9:43b-48	350
27:24-26	379	9:38-41	350	16:20	384	9:49-50	350
27:27-30	379	9:42	350			9:51-56	356
27:31-32	379	9:43-50	350	LUKE	page	9:57-62	345
27:33-44	381	10:1	356	1:1-4	327	10:1-16	356
27:45-56	381	10:2-16	363	1:5-25	329	10:17-37	356
27:57-66	381	10:17-40	363	1:26-56	329	10:38-42	356
28:1-7	384	10:41-52	363	1:57-80	329	11:1-13	356
28:8-15	384	11:1-11	366	2:1-14	329	11:14-23	340
28:16-20	384	11:12-18	366	2:15-38	329	11:24-28	340
		11:19	366	2:39-52	331	11:29-32	340
MARK	page	11:20-33	368	3:1-6	332	11:33-44	340,342
1:1	327	12:1-12	368	3:7-18	332	11:45-54	342
1:2-4	332	12:13-34	368	3:19-20	334	12:1-21	342
1:5-11	332	12:35-40	368	3:21-23a	332	12:22-40	342
1:12-13	332	12:41-44	368	3:23b-38	328	12:41-59	342
1:14-15	336	13:1-31	371	4:1-13	332	13:1-9	342
1:16-39	336	13:32-37	371	4:14-15	336	13:10-17	342
1:40-45	336	14:1-2	372	4:16-30	336	13:18-21	344
2:1-12	336	14:3-9	363	4:31-44	336	13:22-35	358

SCRIPTURE INDEX

14:1-33	358	23:50-56	381	13:36-38	374	6:1-15	387,389
14:34-35	358	24:1-8	384	14:1-21	374	7:1-38	389
15:1-32	358	24:9-11	384	14:22-31	374	7:39-53	389
16:1-13	358	24:12	384	15:1-17	376	7:54-60	389
16:14-31	358	24:13-27	384	15:18-27	376	8:1a	389
17:1	350	24:28-44	384	16:1-24	376	8:1b-24	390
17:2-3a	350	24:45-53	384	16:25-33	374	8:25-40	390
17:3b-4	350			17:1-19	376	9:1-16	390
17:5-6	350	JOHN	page	17:20-26	376	9:17-31	390
17:7-10	350	1:1-18	327	18:1	377	9:32-43	391
17:11-19	356	1:19-34	332	18:2-11	377	10:1-29	391
17:20-37	358	1:35-51	334	18:12-17	377	10:30-48	391
18:1-14	358	2:1-25	334	18:18-25	377	11:1-18	391
18:15-17	363	3:1-21	334	18:26-27	377	11:19-30	391
18:18-34	363	3:22-36	334	18:28-38	379	12:1-17	391
18:35-43	363	4:1-26	334	18:39	379	12:18-25	391
19:1-10	363	4:27-54	334	18:40	379	13:1-25	393
19:11-28	363	5:1-29	337	19:1-15	379	13:26-41	393
19:29-44	366	5:30-47	337	19:16-17	379	13:42-52	393
19:45-48	366	6:1	347	19:18-24	381	14:1-18	393
20:1-8	368	6:2-21	348	19:25-37	381	14:19-28	393
20:9-19	368	6:22-40	348	19:38-42	381	15:1-21	393
20:20-40	368	6:41-71	348	20:1-17	384	15:22-35	393
20:41-47	368	7:1	348	20:18	384	15:36-41	396
21:1-4	368	7:2-31	353	20:19-23	384	16:1-15	396
21:5-33	371	7:32-52	353	20:24-29	384	16:16-40	396
21:34-36	371	7:53	353	20:30-31	384	17:1-31	396
21:37-38	372	8:1-30	353,355	21:1-17	384	17:32-34	396
22:1-6	372	8:31-59	355	21:18-24	384	18:1-11	396
22:7-13	372	9:1-23	355	21:25	384	18:12-17	400
22:14-21	374	9:24-41	355			18:18-28	400
22:22	374	10:1-6	355	ACTS	page	19:1-7	400
22:23-30	374	10:7-21	355	1:1-5	386	19:8-22	400
22:31-34	374	10:22-42	356	1:6-22	384	19:23-41	406
22:35-39	374	11:1-4	361	1:23-26	384	20:1	406
22:40	377	11:5-37	361	2:1-36	386	20:2-3a	409
22:41-51	377	11:38-54	361	2:37-41	386	20:3b-35	415
22:52-53	377	11:55-57	363	2:42-47	386	20:36-38	415
22:54-58	377	12:1-8	363	3:1-10	387	21:1-14	415
22:59-71	377	12:9-13	363,366	3:11-26	387	21:15-26	415
23:1-4	379	12:14-19	366	4:1-12	387	21:27-40	415
23:5-17	379	12:20-26	366	4:13-31	387	22:1-21	415
23:18-23	379	12:27-36	366	4:32-37	387	22:22-29	415
23:24-31	379	12:37-50	372	5:1-16	387	22:30	415
23:32-43	381	13:1-11	374	5:17-39	387	23:1-22	415
23:44-49	381	13:12-35	374	5:40-42	387	23:23-35	415

SCRIPTURE INDEX

Reference	Page	Reference	Page	Reference	Page	Reference	Page
24:1-21	417	1 CORINTHIANS	pg.	10:1-6	409	1:15-29	419
24:22-27	417	1:1-25	401	10:7-18	409	2:1-5	419
25:1-12	417	1:26-31	401	11:1-11	409	2:6-23	419
25:13-27	417	2:1-16	401	11:12-33	409	3:1-11	419
26:1-23	417	3:1-23	401	12:1-6	409	3:12-25	419
26:24-32	417	4:1-5	401	12:7-21	409	4:1-6	419
27:1-12	418	4:6-21	401	13:1-10	409	4:7-18	419
27:13-38	418	5:1-5	401	13:11-14	409		
27:39-44	418	5:6-13	401			1 THESSALONIANS	
28:1-15	418	6:1-20	401	GALATIANS	page	1:1-10	399
28:16-29	418	7:1-24	401	1:1-12	395	2:1-12	399
28:30-31	418	7:25-40	401	1:13-24	395	2:13-20	399
		8:1-3	401	2:1-14	395	3:1-10	399
ROMANS	page	8:4-13	401	2:15-21	395	3:11-13	399
1:1-23	410	9:1-14	401	3:1-18	395	4:1-18	399
1:24-32	410	9:15-27	401	3:19-29	395	5:1-11	399
2:1-16	410	10:1-13	401	4:1-20	395	5:12-28	399
2:17-29	410	10:14-33	401	4:21	395		
3:1-18	410	11:1-10	401	5:1-12	395	2 THESSALONIANS	
3:19-31	410,411	11:11-34	401,404	5:13-26	395	1:1-4	400
4:1-5	411	12:1-26	404	6:1-16	395	1:5-12	400
4:6-25	411	12:27-31	404	6:17-18	395	2:1-17	400
5:1-21	411	13:1-13	404			3:1-18	400
6:1-23	411	14:1-12	404	EPHESIANS	page		
7:1-3	411	14:13-33a	404	1:1-23	421	1 TIMOTHY	page
7:4-25	411	14:33b-40	404	2:1-22	421	1:17	425
8:1-25	411	15:1-19	406	3:1-6	421	1:18-20	425
8:26-39	411	15:20-50	406	3:7-21	421	2:1-15	425
9:1-13	413	15:51-58	406	4:1-13	421	3:1-13	425
9:14-29	413	16:1-14	406	4:14-32	421	3:14-16	425
9:30-33	413	16:15-24	406	5:1-6	421	4:1-16	425
10:1-17	413			5:7-33	421	5:1-2	425
10:18-21	413	2 CORINTHIANS	pg.	6:1-4	421	5:3-23	425
11:1-16	413	1:1-11	406	6:5-24	421	5:24-25	425
11:17-36	413	1:12-24	406			6:1-19	425
12:1-21	414	2:1-11	406	PHILIPPIANS	page	6:20-21	425
13:1-7	414	2:12-17	406	1:1-11	424		
13:8-14	414	3:1-18	406	1:12-30	424	2 TIMOTHY	page
14:1-12	414	4:1-18	406	2:1-11	424	1:1-7	429
14:13-23	414	5:1-10	406	2:12-30	424	1:8-18	429
15:1-13	414	5:11-21	406	3:1-21	424	2:1-13	429
15:14-33	414	6:1-18	406	4:1-3	424	2:14-26	429
16:1-2	414	7:1	406	4:4-23	424	3:1-17	429
16:3-24	414	7:2-16	406			4:1-22	429
16:25-27	414	8:1-24	406	COLOSSIANS	page		
		9:1-15	406	1:1-14	419		

SCRIPTURE INDEX

TITUS	page	1 PETER	page	2:18-29	441
1:1-16	428	1:1-7	433	3:1-6	441
2:1	428	1:8-25	433	3:7-22	441
2:2-15	428	2:1-3	433	4:1-6	444
3:1-8	428	2:4-25	433	4:7-11	444
3:9-15	428	3:1-17	433	5:1-10	444
		3:18-22	433	5:11-14	444
PHILEMON	page	4:1-19	433	6:1-6	444
1-7	419	5:1-14	433	6:7-17	444
8-25	419			7:1-8	444
		2 PETER	page	7:9-17	444
HEBREWS	page	1:1-15	435	8:1-6	444
1:1-14	436	1:16-21	435	8:7-13	446
2:1-13	436	2:1-16	435	9:1-12	446
2:14-18	436	2:17-22	435	9:13-21	446
3:1-19	436	3:1-13	435	10:1-11	446
4:1-16	436	3:14-18	435	11:1-15	446
5:1-14	436			11:16-19	446
6:1-12	436	1 JOHN	page	12:1-12	446
6:13-20	437	1:1-7	440	12:13-17	446
7:1-19	437	1:8-10	440	13:1-10	446
7:20-28	437	2:1-17	440	13:11-18	446
8:1-7	437	2:18-29	440	14:1-7	448
8:8-13	437	3:1-10	440	14:8-13	448
9:1-10	437	3:11-24	440	14:14-20	448
9:11-28	437	4:1-6	440	15:1-4	448
10:1-4	437	4:7-21	440	15:5-8	448
10:5-31	437,439	5:1-12	440	16:1-11	448
10:32-39	439	5:13-21	440	16:12-21	448
11:1-7	439			17:1-6	448
11:8-28	439	2 JOHN	page	17:7-18	448
11:29-40	439	1-6	440	18:1-8	448
12:1-11	439	7-13	440	18:9-20	448
12:12-29	439			18:21-24	448
13:1-3	439	3 JOHN	page	19:1-5	448
13:4-25	439	1-10	440	19:6-21	450
		11-14	440	20:1-15	450
JAMES	page			21:1-5	450
1:1	431	JUDE	page	21:6-21	450
1:2-27	431	1-4	431	21:22-27	450
2:1-26	431	5-25	431	22:1-16	450
3:1-18	431			22:17-21	450
4:1-4	431	REVELATION	page		
4:5-17	431	1:1-16	441		
5:1-11	431	1:17-20	441		
5:12-20	431	2:1-17	441		

Also available from Dr. Shirley Loges:

Rolling out the Plan of Salvation

The Book of Leviticus teaches God's people how to become a holy nation of priests who can come before a holy God without fear. Maybe the most exciting outcome is the increased understanding of the many passages in both the Old and New Testaments that mention the various offerings. Suddenly, those passages have added meaning and become more endeared to the reader.

Rolling out the Plan of Salvation is the only in-depth individual or small group study guide available on Leviticus. The participant learns to understand not only the different sacrifices but also the order in which each had to be presented and why the order was crucial.

If the leader chooses to use the suggested guide in the back of the book, the participants will get a sensory challenge to better understand "an aroma pleasing to the LORD." Participants have five short daily lessons to complete each week. Answers to the questions are located in the back of the book to ensure the teachable moment is not missed during the time of study.

Shirley Ann Baker Loges, Ph.D.

Shirley Loges is available for speaking engagements and personal appearances. For more information contact:

Dr. Shirley Loges
C/O Advantage Books
1475 Rodeo Road #230
Santa Fe, NM 87505

To order additional copies of this book or to see a complete list of all **ADVANTAGE BOOKS™** visit our online bookstore at: www.advbookstore.com

Orlando, Florida, USA

"we bring dreams to life"™
www.advbooks.com